The American People

A History

Pauline Maier is Professor of History at Massachusetts Institute of Technology, Cambridge, Massachusetts. She graduated from Radcliffe College and received her Ph.D. from Harvard University. Her publications include *From Resistance to Revolution: Colonial Radicals and the Development of American Opposition to Britain, 1765-1776* and *The Old Revolutionaries: Political Lives in the Age of Samuel Adams.*

Student Activities were prepared by *Timothy Dove*, American history teacher, Worthingway Middle School, Worthington, Ohio.

Improve Your Reading pages were written by *Richard P. Santeusanio*, Director of Reading and Special Services, Danvers Public Schools, Danvers, Massachusetts.

Chapter 11, How the Government Works, was written by *Henry Billings*. He taught American government for 16 years in the Boston, Massachusetts, area.

The **Highlighting People** features were written by *Linda Scher*, a curriculum developer and writer from Raleigh, North Carolina.

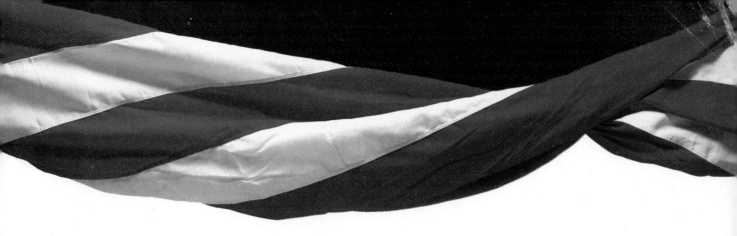

The
American
People

A History

Pauline Maier

D. C. Heath and Company
Lexington, Massachusetts   Toronto

The cover painting is by James G. Evans. It shows the celebration of George Washington's birthday aboard the USS *Constitution* in 1837.

Acknowledgments

Design: Robert Botsford **Art Edit and Layout:** Ann Barnard, Julie Fair, Mary Keefe **Photo Research:** Pembroke Herbert/Picture Research Consultants **Maps:** Dick and John Sanderson **Maps 762-765:** R.R. Donnelley Cartographic **Charts:** David R. Hannum/graphic ideas, inc.

Cover: "Celebration, 1837 of Washington's Birthday at Malta On Board the USS Constitution" by J.C. Evans. Courtesy United States Naval Academy Museum.

Photo Credits Unit One: 1: Robert Harding Picture Library Ltd. **2:** Robert Frerck (Odyssey Productions). **7:** Lee Boltin. **8:** Robert Frerck (Odyssey Productions). **10,11:** Museum of the American Indian, Heye Foundation. **14:** Lee Boltin. **15:l&r** Codex Florentino, Biblioteca Laurenzina, Florence. **16:** Lee Boltin. **20:** Detail from "Vallard Atlas" chart #9(HM29)1547. The Huntington Library, San Marino, California. **22:** Trustees of The British Museum. Derek Bayes/Aspect Picture Library Ltd. **26:** "Isabella Praying" by Felipe Vigarny. Granada Cathedral, photo Oronoz. **27:** "Columbus" by Ridolgo Ghirlandaio. Scala/Art Resource. **31:** "Cortez and Montezuma, #1412. Library Services Department, American Museum of Natural History. **36:** "Orbis Habitabilis" by Carolus Allard, Amsterdam, ca.1690. Rare Book and Manuscript Division, New York Public Library. Astor, Lenox and Tilden Foundations. **38:** The Bettmann Archive.

Unit Two: 42-43: "Map of North America" (The Virginia Company Chart) 1608. I.N. Phelps Stokes Collection, Prints Division, New York Public Library, Astor, Lenox and Tilden Foundations. **44:** "Jamestown about 1614" Painting by Sidney King, National Park Service, Jamestown. **46:** Colonial Williamsburg Photograph. **47:** Rare Books and Manuscript Division, New York Public Library. Astor, Lenox and Tilden Foundations. **50:** "Virginia" by John Smith (detail) Princeton University Library. **51:** Virginia State Library. **52:** "Theatrum Imperii Magnae Britanniae" by Speed, 1676, Map Room, New York Public Library. Astor, Lenox and Tilden Foundations. **53:** Arents Collection, New York Public Library. **55:** Virginia State Library. **57:** "Pocahontas" by unidentified artist after Simon van de Passe, National Portrait Gallery, Smithsonian Institution. Transfer from the National Gallery of Art; gift of Andrew W. Mellon. **62:** Cary Wolinsky (Stock, Boston). **64:** "James I listening to a Sermon in the Churchyard of St. Paul's Cathedral" 1620. Society of Antiquaries, London. **66:** "A Quay at Leyden" by Jan van der Heyden. Private Collection. **67:** "Massasoit" by Cyrus E. Dallin. Photo by The Dicksons, Plymouth. **69:** American Antiquarian Society. **70:** King's Collection, Trustees of the British Museum. **71:** "Poems" by Anne Bradstreet. Massachusetts Historical Society. **75:** "Anne Hutchinson". Photo by Robert Frerck (Odyssey Productions). **79:** "The Mason Children" Private Collection. **82:** The Maryland Historical Society. **85:** "Cecil Calvert, Second Lord Baltimore" by Gerard Soest. Enoch Pratt Free Library. **88:** "Henrietta Johnston" by Ann Broughton. Yale University Art Gallery. John Hill Morgan

(Continued on p. 785)

Published simultaneously in Canada.

Printed in the United States of America.

International Standard Book Number: 0-669-04883-6

6 7 8 9 0

Contents

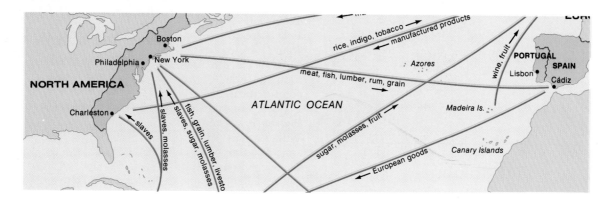

Labels visible on map: rice, indigo, tobacco — manufactured products — wine, fruit — PORTUGAL — SPAIN — Boston — Philadelphia — New York — Azores — Lisbon — Cádiz — NORTH AMERICA — meat, fish, lumber, rum, grain — ATLANTIC OCEAN — Madeira Is. — Charleston — slaves — slaves, molasses — fish, grain, lumber, livesto — slaves, sugar, molasses — sugar, molasses, fruit — Canary Islands — European goods

Maps

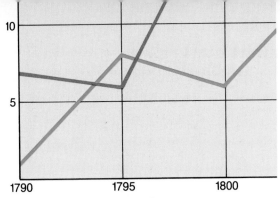

Charts and Graphs

Highlighting People

In Their Own Words

UNIT ONE

The First Americans

Machu Picchu was a mountaintop city built by the Inca along a ridge in the Andes Mountains. The Inca set up a great empire in South America. They were conquered by the Spanish in the 1500's. Although the Spanish destroyed much of Inca culture, they never reached Machu Picchu. The city remained unknown until 1911, when Hiram Bingham found its ruins.

Chapter 1

The Peoples of Ancient America

These cliff drawings were made by an early American artist. They are one of the attractions at Dinosaur National Park located near Vernal, Utah.

At first, there were no people in the Americas. The land existed, but for hundreds of thousands of years no human beings lived upon it. Human life first appeared on other parts of Earth. As a result, the Americas had to be discovered before they could be settled. All those who made the Americas their home were immigrants, people who came there from somewhere else, or the descendants of immigrants. This chapter is about the very first people to settle North and South America. They were the people who later became known as Indians, and they created many different ways of life. The chapter describes a few of the groups of people who lived in the Americas before Europeans arrived. It also tells about the earliest known Europeans to visit the Americas.

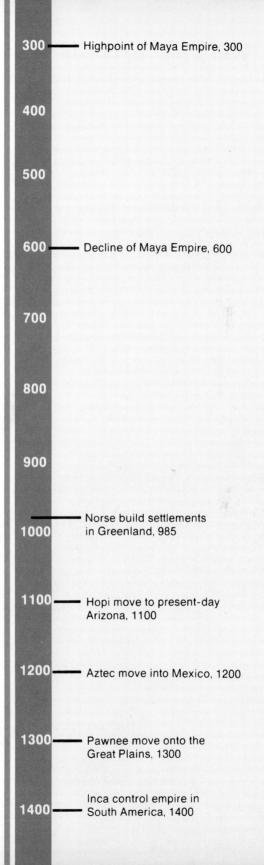

300 — Highpoint of Maya Empire, 300

400

500

600 — Decline of Maya Empire, 600

700

800

900

— Norse build settlements
1000   in Greenland, 985

1100 — Hopi move to present-day
       Arizona, 1100

1200 — Aztec move into Mexico, 1200

1300 — Pawnee move onto the
       Great Plains, 1300

       Inca control empire in
1400 — South America, 1400

I. The First Arrivals

The first people to discover the Americas came on foot, looking for food. Other people like them followed the same route over many thousands of years. They slowly moved across vast stretches of land. As they settled down, they created many different ways of life.

When and How They Came

Most experts agree that the Americas were discovered some 30,000 or 40,000 years ago by hunters from Asia. They crossed to Alaska from Siberia in the far northeastern part of Asia. Their trip was probably not difficult. They crossed at the Bering Strait, where only 56 miles separate Asia from North America.

When people first crossed from Asia, the Bering Strait was dry land. At that time, huge **glaciers** (glā′shərz), large masses of moving ice, covered much of North America. The glaciers held so much water that the level of the ocean sank, exposing a bridge of land between Asia and North America.

When the glaciers melted about 8,000 to 10,000 years ago, the sea rose again. Then it was possible to walk from Asia to North America only when the Bering Strait froze over.

Different groups of newcomers slowly spread across North America and into South America. They found many animals that have long since disappeared. For example, they

Map Study *Follow the route of the first Americans. From what continent did they travel to reach North America? What other continent did they settle?*

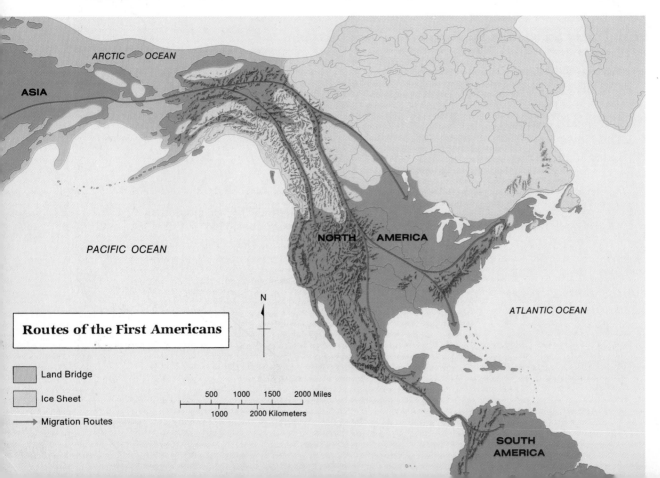

Routes of the First Americans

- Land Bridge
- Ice Sheet
- → Migration Routes

500   1000   1500   2000 Miles
1000   2000 Kilometers

ARCTIC OCEAN
ASIA
PACIFIC OCEAN
NORTH AMERICA
ATLANTIC OCEAN
N
SOUTH AMERICA

found mammoths, which were elephants with long, thick hair and curled-up tusks. They found camels, antelopes with four horns, and an ancient kind of buffalo. By around 11,000 years ago, people had reached the tip of South America.

▶**1.** How did the first people reach the Americas?

How We Know about Them

The first Americans left no written records of their lives and times. However, they did leave **artifacts,** or objects such as spear points, pottery, and sculptures. They also left the remains of homes and buildings.

Archaeologists (är′kē ol′ə jists) are scientists who study these kinds of clues to learn about the lives of people who lived long ago. Ar-chaeologists have learned many things about the people who lived in the Americas before Europeans arrived. It is clear that the peoples of ancient America were not all alike. They had many different **cultures,** or ways of life.

▶**2.** What do archaeologists study?

Reviewing Section I

Identify Alaska, Siberia, Bering Strait, glaciers, artifacts, archaeologists, cultures

Questions to Answer
1. Where do scientists think the first Americans came from?
2. Why did the first Americans come?

A Question to Think About What can archaeology teach us?

IMPROVE YOUR SKILLS
The Purpose of History

Who are you? Who *are* you? How you answer this question depends in part on who's asking. If a student from another school asks, you may say, "I'm from Washington School." If a teacher from your school asks you who you are, you may say, "I'm from room 210."

If you are in a foreign country and a native asks "Who are you?" the most likely answer is, "I am from the United States." What if someone asks, "What is the United States?" How would you answer?

Your course in the history of the United States is designed to help you answer that question. What is so important about knowing history? President John F. Kennedy answered that question very well. "History," he said, "is the memory of the nation."

"A country's history," Kennedy said, is also "a statement of its values and hopes." It helps a nation decide if it is doing the right thing. He also said this:

Our past judges our present . . . This history of our nation tells us that every action taken *against* the freedoms of conscience and expression, *against* equality before the law and equality of opportunity, *against* the ordinary men and women of the country is an action taken *against* the American tradition.

"The nation's history," Kennedy said, "is shared by all its people—those who have been here for centuries as well as recent immigrants." Even though citizens of the United States come from many different backgrounds and places, history helps tie them together.

The more you learn about history, the more you can profit from it. The more you know about using the tools of history, such as maps, graphs, charts, and sources, the easier your task will become. In every chapter of this text is an Improve Your Skills page designed to help you build and practice the skills used by historians.

Early Peoples of North America

Culture Areas
- Arctic
- Subarctic
- Northwest Coast
- Plateau
- Great Basin
- California
- Southwest
- Plains
- Eastern Woodlands
- Southeast
- Mexico and Central America
- Caribbean

INUIT
TANAINA
INGALIK
KUTCHIN
DOGRIB
YELLOW KNIFE
INUIT
KASKA
SLAVE
CHIPPEWYAN
INUIT
TLINGIT
BEAVER
TSIMSHIAN
HAIDA
CREE
MONTAGNAIS-NASKAPI
SARSI
BEOTHUK
KWAKIUTL
NOOTKA
SHUSWAP
BLACKFOOT
MICMAC
SALISH
THOMPSON
SANPOIL
OJIBWA
CHINOOK
GROS VENTRE
ASSINIBOIN
OTTAWA
ABNAKI
YAKIMA
NEZ PERCE
FLATHEAD
HURON
IROQUOIS
MOHAWK
ONEIDA
ONONDAGA
CAYUGA
SENECA
ALGONQUIAN
YUROK
CROW
MANDAN
MENOMINI
SHOSHONE
ARIKARA
SAUK
FOX
WINNEBAGO
POTAWATOMI
ERIE
SUSQUEHANNA
DELAWARE
CHEYENNE
DAKOTA (SIOUX)
POMO
WASHO
GOSIUTE
PAWNEE
MIAMI
YOKUTS
ARAPAHO
ILLINOIS
POWHATAN
CHUMASH
LUISENA
PAIUTE
UTE
OSAGE
SHAWNEE
TUTELO
WALAPAI
HOPI
MOHAVE
NAVAJO
YUMA
PIMA
ZUÑI
KIOWA
CHEROKEE
CHICKASAW
CREEK
PAPAGO
APACHE
WICHITA
CADDO
CHOCTAW
COMANCHE
NATCHEZ
MOBILE
TIMUCUA
CALUSA
LUCAYO
COAHUILTEC
TAMAULIPEC
CIBONEY
SUBTAINO
TAINO
CARIB
OTOMI
TARASCAN
TOTONAC
TOLTEC
MAYA
AZTEC
OLMEC
MIXTEC
ZAPOTEC
ZOQUE
LENCA
MOSQUITO

0   300   600 Miles
0   300   600 Kilometers

II. Early Peoples of North America

As people spread across North America, their ways of life changed greatly. Some experts think that about ten million people lived in North America by A.D. 1500. Those people were broken up into hundreds of groups with different languages and customs.

Scientists have grouped the early peoples of North America into **culture areas** according to their ways of obtaining food and building shelters and their rules for living together. There are, of course, many differences among groups living in the same culture area. So for greater precision, scientists divide each large culture area into even smaller culture areas. The next sections examine the way one group lived in each of four different culture areas. The four culture areas examined are the Pacific Northwest, the Southwest, the Plains, and the Eastern Woodlands.

The Pacific Northwest

Along the Pacific Coast, the climate is generally mild and rainy. The tallest trees in North America grow there. A chain of mountains separates the narrow coastal area from the rest of the continent. Many rivers flow from the mountains into the ocean.

The Haida (hī'dah) were one of the groups of people living on the narrow bits of land along the Pacific Coast. They could find food easily. There were many kinds of fish in the rivers and the ocean, including halibut, trout, and herring as well as a variety of shellfish. The Haida also gathered edible seaweed.

The mainstay of the Haida diet was salmon. Once a year the rivers of the Pacific Coast became clogged as thousands of salmon swam upstream to spawn, or lay their eggs. The Haida built traps across the rivers to catch the salmon. They dried much of the salmon

This Haida "seabear" mask was made of copper and trimmed with sea otter fur and shells.

catch to provide food for the rest of the year or to trade with other groups.

The Haida could collect a year's worth of food in the summer months. In the winter, they occasionally hunted animals that came down from the mountains, but the winter was basically free for resting, woodworking, basketmaking, and other activities.

▶**1.** What sorts of food were available on the Pacific Coast?

Social Structure People only become concerned with wealth when they have plenty of food. The Haida, who had an abundance of food, built a complicated society based on rank and wealth. Rank was partly inherited, but it was also possible to rise in rank by becoming rich. A person could become rich by trading up and down the Pacific Coast.

◀**Map Study** *Use the map to locate the major cultural areas of the earliest Americans. Find the Iroquois on the map. In which cultural area did they live?*

7

A person who accumulated extra food or made goods such as the prized Haida canoe could trade for other valuable goods. Another way to become rich was to take goods and slaves in wars with other groups.

Rank affected almost every part of Haida life. Men and women tried to marry someone very close to their own rank. Even so, one member of the couple claimed superiority. At the bottom of Haida society were slaves—people who were captured or conquered in wars.

▶2. How could the Haida improve their rank in society?

Housing The Haida used the tall cedar trees of the coast to build their houses. These houses were large enough for many families. In the center of the wood floor of a house was a fire pit. A smoke hole in the roof could be covered in bad weather. The outside of a house was covered with overlapping planks to keep it watertight. Each family had its own sleeping area along the walls of the house. The areas were arranged by the ranks of the families. Slaves slept beside the door, while the highest ranking family had its quarters opposite the door. The most important family might enclose its area with decorated wooden partitions. Less important families hung skins for privacy. Outside the house was a large carved pole decorated with symbols and emblems important to the most important family of the house.

▶3. What sort of houses did the Haida build?

The Desert Southwest

The Hopi (hō′pē) lived in a dry land that was very different from that of the Haida. The Hopi lived in the northeastern part of today's Arizona. The Hopi came there sometime after A.D. 1100, when drought drove them from their homes farther east.

The Hopi once lived in these cliff pueblos in the northeastern part of Arizona. They had one of the most complex societies in North America.

The land the Hopi found is a land of contrasts. The days are very hot, but the nights are very cool. It is a land of mountains with pine forests at their tops, with deep canyons, and with dry, rocky plains. There is little rain anywhere except in the mountains. When it does rain, there is often flooding.

The Hopi built their houses on high ground that could easily be defended. Farmers sometimes had to walk as far as ten miles to their fields on the flatlands. The houses, built of stone and covered with mud, look much like present-day apartment buildings. Most houses, however, had no doors or windows. The entrance was through a roof that was reached by ladders. The Spanish later called these houses **pueblos** (pweb′lōz), or towns.

The houses all faced a central plaza. The plaza was the heart of the village, and here many religious and other community events took place. The **kiva** (kē′və), an underground room used in some ceremonies, was located under the plaza.

▶**4.** What does *pueblo* mean?

Food The Hopi men were farmers. They grew corn, squash, tobacco, and beans. Water for the crops was always a problem. The Hopi farmed on the flatlands where springs and water runoffs from higher ground watered the crops. They learned to plant their crops very deep so the roots could collect moisture. They also planted each crop in several fields so that they could be sure that one would grow.

▶**5.** How did the Hopi grow crops in a dry climate?

Social Structure In the Hopi society, men and women worked at different tasks. Men farmed and did some hunting. However, they hunted more for animal skins for leggings than for food. Men wove most of their families' clothes from cotton. Older men who did not farm could weave all year round.

Men were also responsible for projects that involved the whole village, such as religious and ceremonial events. These were very important. The Hopi felt that their rituals helped them to live in balance with the rest of nature. To make a mistake in a ceremony might result in disaster.

Hopi women owned the houses and made the house rules. Women also owned the seeds for planting and the harvest. They ground the grain and cooked the food. Women also made pottery and baskets.

A man belonged to his mother's clan. He had more responsibility for his sister's children, who belonged to his clan, than for his own children. When a couple married, the man moved into his wife's house.

The entire village was headed by a senior leader. He presided over a council of the village leaders, generally representing the different clans of the village.

▶**6.** What were the tasks of men and of women in Hopi society?

The Plains

Sloping away from the Rockies to the Mississippi River are the flat, open grasslands called the Plains. The Plains, like the Southwest, are full of contrasts. The winters are cold with much snow, and the summers are hot and dry. Along the many rivers that cut through the Plains are woods teeming with game. Huge herds of buffalo once roamed these grasslands.

The Pawnee (pô′nē) drifted onto the Plains from east Texas around A.D. 1300. They settled along the Platte River and the smaller rivers that flow into the Platte.

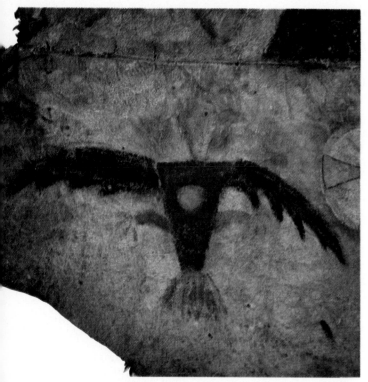

The picture above shows a detail from a Pawnee buffalo battle robe decorated with colorful drawings.

The Pawnee were both farmers and hunters. In the spring, families planted corn, squash, and beans. They worked hard to see that the plots were well weeded and watered. Once the plants were strong, the entire Pawnee village packed up for the spring buffalo hunt. The Pawnee had tame dogs that they used to carry their belongings. Men, women, and children hunted in small groups. There was other game in the grasslands and along the rivers, which the Pawnee hunted. However, the huge herds of buffalo that roamed the Plains were their most important prey. When the villagers returned to their homes after the hunt, their crops were ready for harvesting. The Pawnee hunted buffalo again in the fall.

▶**7.** What were the foods grown and hunted by the Pawnee?

Social Structure The Pawnee lived in villages. Each village was independent and had several leaders and priests. A leader always had a sacred bundle—a group of objects that the Pawnee believed came from a star. Most leaders inherited their bundles—and their position as leaders—from their fathers. However, a man could rise to a position of leadership by the consent of the village. He could then buy a sacred bundle. Outstanding warriors had as high a place in the village society as the official leaders.

The villages had a deep tradition of unity and worked together in all seasons. Men and women worked together to plant and cultivate crops. Women and children helped in the buffalo hunt, although the men were responsible for tracking and killing the animals. Women harvested the crops, prepared the buffalo skins for use as clothing and bedding, and did most of the building of dwellings.

▶**8.** By what two ways did men become leaders of the Pawnee?

Housing The Pawnee lived in lodges built of logs that were covered with layers of dirt and grass. After about ten years, the houses would collapse. By that time, timber would be scarce, and the group would move upstream.

On the hunt, the Pawnee lived in portable houses made of buffalo skins called **tepees.** The women cleaned the skins and sewed the skins together to make the tepees.

▶**9.** What kinds of houses did the Pawnee build?

The Eastern Woodlands

The Eastern Woodlands extended north and south all along the Atlantic Coast. They reached as far west as the Mississippi River. Except for lakes and rivers, that whole area was dense forest in 1500. It is said that a squirrel could have traveled from Tennessee through the Eastern Woodlands to New York without ever touching the ground.

People who spoke the Iroquois (ir'ə kwoi) language lived in the Eastern Woodlands near the eastern Great Lakes in upstate New York. The most important of the Iroquois-speaking groups belonged to five separate nations: the Mohawk, Oneida (ō nī'də), Onondaga (on'ən dô'gə), Cayuga (kā ü'gə), and Seneca (sen'ə kə).

▶**10.** Name the five Iroquois nations.

Food The Iroquois lived in a rich country where the men hunted deer, beavers, and turkeys and fished in nearby lakes and streams. Ducks and geese were plentiful in the marshes along the rivers. The Iroquois learned to tap maple trees for their sweet syrup. Other trees provided nuts and fruits. Farming was not difficult in the low river bottoms and valleys between the mountains. The Iroquois women grew squash as well as around 15 different kinds of corn and 60 types of beans.

▶**11.** What sorts of food did the Iroquois hunt, gather, and grow?

Housing The Iroquois built their villages along riverbanks. They surrounded the villages with fences of strong wooden posts. The Iroquois moved their villages upstream or downstream as the soil in their fields became less fertile after many plantings. Many families lived together in **longhouses** that were perhaps 50 to 150 feet long. The sides and slanted roofs were made of poles covered with elm bark. Inside there were fire pits every 15 feet or so down the middle. Slits in the roofs let smoke out. Along the sides of houses were double-deck bunks, about 12 feet long and 6 feet wide. There individual families slept, ate, and kept their clothes and other

Iroquois women used deer hide to make many things. Below is a blanket made from dyed deer hide, decorated with a quill work design.

11

possessions. Around 50 or 60 people lived in each longhouse, and there might be 40 longhouses in a village.

All the people who lived in a longhouse were related through their mothers. Males went to live in their wives' longhouses. All the property of a family belonged to its women. The oldest woman in the longhouse ruled the dwelling.

▶**12.** What connected the people who lived in the same longhouse?

Iroquois League Until the 1300's, the Iroquois nations were small tribes that constantly fought each other. Then, in the 1300's, they made peace. To end their many wars and to help each other against their enemies, the five large Iroquois nations formed a **league,** an association, and an alliance, with each other. Boundaries for each nation were decided. Each nation had control of a large lake or river. Each nation governed itself in councils.

The great questions of war and peace, however, were decided through the league. Each nation sent representatives to the council meetings of the league. Representatives were selected by the nation's leading women. The women could also dismiss a member of the council who they felt was not doing a good job. The decisions of the councillors had to be unanimous. The unity of the Iroquois in the league made them very powerful.

▶**13.** What sorts of decisions were made by the Iroquois league?

What the Early Peoples Shared

It is not surprising that the early peoples of North America developed quite different ways of living. It is surprising, however, how much the groups had in common.

North American peoples lived in families and groups of related families called **clans.** Each group had rules for organizing its people. Most groups grew at least part of their food and lived in settled villages.

Respect for nature was part of the religions of all groups. All North American peoples believed in a creator. The land and all things on the land, such as plants, animals, lakes, and rivers, were gifts from the creator. People had to use those gifts wisely.

Early people did use the land for farming and hunting and gathering. In some groups, families had their own farm plots and passed them on to their children. People protected their hunting areas from other groups. However, American families did not believe in owning land in the way Europeans did or in the way we do now. If a group moved to new lands, the land they left behind was open for others to use. The idea of buying and selling land was not a part of any native American culture.

▶**14.** What was the Indian feeling about owning land?

Reviewing Section II

Identify culture areas, Haida, Hopi, pueblos, kiva, Pawnee, teepees, Iroquois, longhouses, league, clans

Questions to Answer

1. What were some of the things that all North American early groups had in common?

2. What were the main differences between the way the Haida lived and the way the Iroquois lived?

A Question to Think About Why do you think the attitude of early people toward the land will be an important concept as you study American history?

The Hopi people believed that the balance of nature depended on their careful observance of many ceremonies, or rituals. The ceremonies began at birth. When a baby was born, the father's mother washed the child's head and took charge of planning a naming ceremony and feast.

The ceremony took place 20 days after the baby's birth. At dawn, the baby's father sprinkled cornmeal on a path leading to the end of a small plateau where the ground dropped off steeply. The cornmeal represented the road of life and the parents' wish that their child begin life properly. The parents presented their child to the rising sun and gave it a name.

As Hopi children grew older, they were introduced to the mysteries of the kachinas. The Hopi believed that the kachinas were supernatural beings. Without the blessings of these spirits, Hopi fields would dry up. For part of the year, from June to December, the kachinas lived as spirits in a mythical land. Then in December, when the winter solstice brings the shortest day, the kachinas left their homes to spend six months among the Hopi. There they lived in the bodies of kachina impersonators—Hopi men who wore kachina masks and costumes.

Hopi children learned early about the kachinas. As small infants, they received prized kachina dolls. These were not playthings. Rather they helped the children identify the many kachinas and learn to respect them.

When they were three or four, the children were first introduced to kachina impersonators. Some were beautiful to look at. They gave the children presents. Others were terrifying. They frightened the children and threatened them if they had been bad.

When Hopi boys were about 8 or 9, they learned the truth about the kachinas. In a dramatic and terrifying ceremony, the kachina impersonators unmasked and showed the children their human forms. Once the children knew the holy secret, they were not allowed to reveal the truth to those younger than themselves.

There was also a special ceremony for Hopi girls. Sometime between the ages of 16 and 20, they spent four days grinding corn in a darkened room. At the conclusion of those four days, the girls assumed the dress and hairstyle of women ready to marry.

Hopi marriage ceremonies were complicated. During one part of the ceremony, the couple prayed to the sun. The woman's hair was arranged in braids, a style that would not change for the rest of her life. After the ceremony, the couple lived with the groom's parents until he finished weaving a marriage costume for his bride. Then the couple moved to the house of the mother of the bride, where they lived permanently.

The ceremony of death was among the simplest of the Hopi people. The body was dressed and carried to the edge of the mesa. There it was buried. The household of the dead person mourned for four days and then resumed their normal tasks.

The Hopi year was also marked by many special ceremonies. In late August, for example, the Hopi held a snake dance that was meant to bring the rain needed for a good harvest. The ceremony lasted for nine full days and involved both poisonous and nonpoisonous snakes that Hopi men captured in the desert. At the ceremony's dramatic conclusion, the snakes were released to go back into the desert.

III. Complex Societies of the Americas

North America was very lightly populated compared to Central and South America. Estimates of how many people lived in the Americas in the late 1400's vary greatly. One expert puts the total at 13 million, while another gives a total of between 90 and 100 million people. Experts agree, however, that most people lived in Mexico, Central and South America. Some of the people there, especially the Maya (mī'ə), Aztec (az'tek), and Inca (ing'kə), developed **complex societies** quite different from any in North America.

These complex societies were based on a **division of labor.** That means that some people were full-time farmers. The farmers grew enough food so that some other people were free to work full-time at other tasks. Artisans, for example, made things such as pottery or cloth. Many artisans lived in large cities. They exchanged the things they made for food the farmers brought to the cities.

The Maya, the Aztec, and the Inca each had a formal, structured government that controlled the whole society and also, to some extent, the lives of individuals. The concept

Map Study *Use the map to locate the lands that once belonged to the Maya, Aztec, and Inca. Which group lived in the Andes Mountains?*

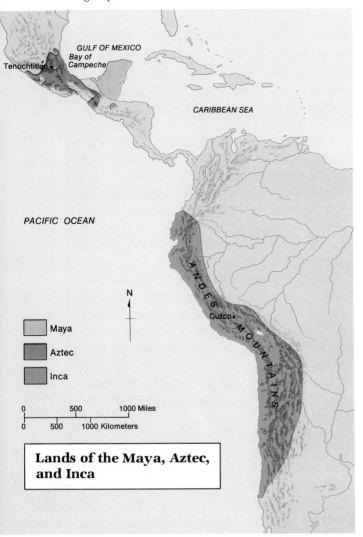

GULF OF MEXICO
Bay of Campeche
Tenochtitlán
CARIBBEAN SEA
PACIFIC OCEAN
ANDES MOUNTAINS
Cuzco
N

■ Maya
■ Aztec
■ Inca

0   500   1000 Miles
0   500   1000 Kilometers

Lands of the Maya, Aztec, and Inca

This Maya figure, made of clay, was found on the island of Jaina in Compeche, Mexico.

On the left is an Aztec drawing showing a farmer storing grain in case of famine.
On the right is an Aztec artisan working with gold.

of time, with the ideas of past, present, and future, was very important to each of these societies. These peoples put great effort into developing calendars. The Maya, the Aztec, and the Inca also had ways of writing.

The Maya

The Maya were perhaps the most learned people of the ancient Americas. They lived in the southern parts of Central America, where the land is covered with dense tropical forests. Maya centers were located in the Yucatán Peninsula of present-day Mexico and in Guatemala. Maya also lived in present-day Belize (be lēz′), El Salvador, and Honduras. (See map, page 14.)

The Maya invented a numbering system and had an advanced form of mathematics. They used that knowledge to design a very accurate calendar. Unfortunately, very few examples of Maya writing have survived.

The Maya were peaceful people who were governed by their priests instead of by warriors. In that way, they were very different from many of their neighbors. Most of the Maya lived in small farming villages of 20 to 40 families. However, they built great cities with huge pyramids covered with carving. These cities were probably religious centers that the villagers visited only for special occasions.

The Maya were at their greatest strength from around A.D. 300 to A.D. 900. Starting around A.D. 900, they abandoned their cities. The reasons for the decline of the Maya are still unknown.

▶1. What happened to the cities of the Maya?

15

This Inca figurine, made of gold, was found covered with a robe of woven Peruvian cloth.

The Aztec

The Aztec moved into Mexico from the north and conquered the area in the 1400's. The Aztec made their home in the Valley of Mexico, a high flatland surrounded by mountains. There they set up their capital city, Tenochtitlán (ta nôch'tə tlän'), where Mexico City now stands.

The Aztec built their city on an island in a large lake. That made it easy to defend. As the Aztec grew in power, the city grew in size. By 1500, it probably included about 300,000 people, which made it far larger than the cities of Europe at that time.

Tenochtitlán was a beautiful city. The Pyramid of the Sun stood in the center of the city. Around it, the Aztec built streets, bridges, plazas, causeways, and theaters. The Aztec grew some crops on rafts they built and anchored in the lake.

The Aztec conquered most of the surrounding peoples. They ruled these peoples from Tenochtitlán. The Aztec, in other words,

created an **empire.** The conquered people had to work for the Aztec. They also had to pay taxes, or **tributes,** to the Aztec.

▶**2.** What was special about the way Tenochtitlán was built?

The Inca

The Inca lived on the west coast of South America high in the Andes Mountains of today's Peru and Bolivia. They, too, had a powerful empire.

The leader of these people was called the Inca. He was considered a god. Relatives of the Inca helped him rule his empire.

High in the mountains, the Inca people built huge temples and other public buildings. They had a system of roads that connected faraway places with their capital, Cuzco (kü'skō). They even had a postal system.

The Inca people learned to work with metals such as gold, silver, and sometimes bronze. They taught that skill to other peoples in South and Central America. The Inca used metal only for decoration, however. They made their tools out of stone.

▶**3.** What were some of the achievements of the Inca?

Reviewing Section III

Identify complex societies, division of labor, Maya, Yucatán Peninsula, Belize, El Salvador, Honduras, Aztec, Tenochtitlán, empire, tributes, Inca, Cuzco

Questions to Answer

1. In what way was the government of the Maya different from that of the Aztec and the Inca?
2. What did the Aztec and the Inca have in common?

A Question to Think About Why is a division of labor important in a complex society?

IV. Europeans Arrive

For thousands of years, the first Americans, the descendants of hunters from Asia, had the Americas to themselves. Then another group of people "discovered" the Americas. They came from Europe, across the Atlantic Ocean.

The Norse

The first Europeans to push westward were people from Scandinavia—present-day Norway, Denmark, and Sweden. They were called the **Norse**. Much of our knowledge about Norse explorers comes from long stories called **sagas.** The sagas were recited and passed from one generation to the next. They were not written down until 200 years after the events they described. Naturally, by that time many of the details in the sagas were distorted by retelling. But the work of archaeologists can confirm some of the basic stories.

▶ **1.** Where do we get much of our knowledge about the Norse explorers?

The Family of Eric the Red Eric the Red, according to the sagas, led a group of settlers from Iceland to Greenland, an island in the North Atlantic, in A.D. 985 or 986. The stories say that he had killed a man in Iceland and was fleeing for his life. Eric's sons, Leif (lāv) and Thorstein, and his daughter, Freydis, visited the eastern coast of Canada sometime early in the next century. They also set up a settlement on the coast of Newfoundland at a site archaeologists discovered and studied in the 1960's.

The Norse did not stay long. Their visits stopped around A.D. 1010. The reason is not known. Perhaps the people living on Newfoundland, whom the Norse called Skraelings (skrā'lingz), drove them away by their fierce attacks. During one such attack, Freydis, who was called the Fearless, grabbed a sword and led the men against the Skraelings.

The Norse did not have much contact with the rest of Europe. So stories of the lands Eric and Freydis had discovered remained buried in the sagas until much later—in fact, until long after other Europeans had settled in the Americas.

▶ **2.** Why did no other Europeans follow the Norse to North America?

Later Visitors

In the 1400's, Portuguese sailors ventured over the Atlantic. At the same time, English fishermen from the city of Bristol edged close to present-day Newfoundland in their search for new fishing grounds. It is likely that some of these sailors may have landed on the coast of North America. If so, their landings had little effect. The many groups of Indians continued their ways of life undisturbed.

▶ **3.** What groups were edging toward the Americas from Europe in the 1400's?

Reviewing Section IV

Identify Norse, sagas, Eric the Red, Greenland, Leif, Thorstein, Freydis

Questions to Answer
1. When did the Norse visit Newfoundland? How do we know about their visits?
2. Why is it possible that Portuguese sailors or fishermen from Bristol may have landed in the Americas?

A Question to Think About What would the Norse have needed to make a permanent settlement in Newfoundland?

★★The United States and the World ★★★★★★★★★★★★★★★
Who Discovered America?

When archaeologists found evidence to "prove" that the Norse had been to Newfoundland before Columbus "sailed the ocean blue in 1492," the news made headlines.

There are other theories and claims that people from all over the world discovered the Americas. Evidence to prove these theories has not been found, but scientists are still looking.

Various scholars claim that people from Ireland, Japan, China, the Mediterranean, Africa, and the South Pacific had visited or settled in the Americas before Columbus arrived.

Perhaps enough evidence will be found to prove or disprove these claims. However, Columbus's arrival remains the one that changed life for the first Americans and for all who followed.

IMPROVE YOUR READING
Comparison/Contrast

Parts of this chapter *compare* and *contrast* information about people living in early America. That is, the people's similarities and differences are highlighted. To help you understand and remember some of this information, make a chart like the one below, using Chapter One to help you. When you have filled in the information on the chart correctly, you will have a handy summary and study guide that *compares* and *contrasts* information about some of the early Americans.

Some spaces on the chart have already been filled in for you. You may refer to Chapter 1 to complete the chart.

Name of Group	Where Group Lived	Major Sources of Food	Leader of Group	Type of Home
Haida	Pacific Northwest			
Hopi		Corn, squash, beans		
Pawnee			Inherited leadership from father or gained by village vote	
Iroquois				Longhouses made of poles covered with elm bark

CHAPTER 1 REVIEW

Vocabulary Check

On a separate sheet of paper, write the letter of the definition for each of the numbered terms below.

1. Culture area
2. Empire
3. Complex society
4. Clan
5. League

a. A group that has developed a division of labor and cities
b. Division of early American peoples into groups with similar ways of living
c. An association and alliance of different groups
d. A group of people that has control of surrounding lands and people
e. Groups of related families

Time Check

For each pair of events, write the letter of the event that happened first. Be sure to write your answers on a separate sheet of paper.

1. a. Glaciers melt and the seas rise.
   b. Asian hunters first discover the Americas.
2. a. The Norse land on Newfoundland.
   b. Maya cities collapse.
3. a. The Aztec build their capital at Tenochtitlán.
   b. Maya civilization is at its height.
4. a. Pawnee move onto the Plains.
   b. The Norse leave Newfoundland.
5. a. Hopi move into northeastern Arizona.
   b. The Iroquois league is founded.

Fact Check

Write the name of the Indian group you have studied that matches each statement below.

1. This group had a plentiful supply of food from the sea and rivers.
2. This group relied on farming for most of its food.
3. This group formed a league to stop wars among its nations.
4. This group conquered the peoples of Mexico in the 1400's.
5. This group built cities for religious purposes.

Think and Write

1. What sorts of rules did early Americans make for living together?
2. Why does a society need a division of labor for life in cities?
3. What did the way that the Haida, the Hopi, and the Iroquois built their houses show about their way of life?
4. Explain this statement: The Hopi and the Haida used the available resources.
5. Explain why the Norse settlement in Newfoundland did not change the lives of Indian groups in North America.

Chapter 2

The New Age of Discovery

This early map of the east coast of North America was printed in 1546. The drawings give the artist's impression of the landing of Jacques Cartier.

The visits of the Norse and of fishermen from Portugal and England had little effect on the lives of those people who first settled the Americas, the Indians. In the late 1400's and 1500's, other Europeans came to the Americas. Their arrival caused major changes in the lives of the Indians and of people in Europe and Africa as well.

This chapter describes some of the reasons Europeans began exploring parts of the world new to them. Portugal took the lead in exploring, but Spain was the first European nation to create an American empire. France and England started colonies in the Americas long after Spain.

1450

Dias sails around Africa, 1487

Columbus's first voyage to the Americas, 1492

Cabot explores North America, 1497

da Gama reaches India, 1498

1500

Balboa sights the Pacific, 1513
Ponce de Leon explores Florida, 1513

Cortés begins conquest of Mexico, 1519

Magellan's crew circles the globe, 1522

Verrazano explores North America, 1524

Pizarro begins conquest of Peru, 1531

Cartier sails up the St. Lawrence, 1535

Coronado explores southwestern part of present-day U.S., 1540

de Soto sights the Mississippi, 1541

1550

English defeat the Spanish Armada, 1588

1600

I. The Beginnings of Exploration

In the 1400's, many Europeans were eager to sail the oceans in search of lands new to them and in search of new routes to places they already knew. It was the great age of European exploration. Why were Europeans interested in exploring? Simple curiosity for one thing. Europeans at that time wanted to know more about the world they lived in.

Europeans were also eager to trade with Asians. Asia had many kinds of goods in short supply in Europe. None were more sought after than spices.

Spices—pepper, cinnamon, ginger, cloves—helped preserve and flavor food. That was important in the days before refrigeration.

The ivory saltcellar was carved by an African artisan from Benin in the early 1500's.

Asian spices were shipped to Europe overland, and many people were involved in the trade. So spices were expensive.

Western Europeans wanted to find an all-water route to Asia. Then they could get spices and other things from Asia faster and cheaper.
▶**1.** Why did Europeans want to find an all-water route to Asia?

Portugal Leads the Way

The countries of Europe did not all begin exploring the outside world at the same time. Portugal was the first country to begin serious exploring. Then other nations joined in.

The Portuguese began exploring in the 1400's because of the efforts of Prince Henry, son of King John I. Prince Henry was curious about "things which were hidden from other men, and secret." He was also interested in finding new lands and riches for Portugal.

Starting in 1420, Prince Henry sent out sailors who discovered and conquered several islands in the Atlantic—the Canaries, Madeira, and the Azores. Then he began to send out crews to explore the western coast of Africa.
▶**2.** Why was Prince Henry so willing to support exploration?

Sagres Henry never went exploring himself, but he sponsored many voyages. He also set up a center where sailing and **navigation** were studied at the town of Sagres (sä′grēsh) in southwest Portugal. Navigation is the science of finding the positions of ships and planning their routes.

At Sagres, Henry gathered sailors, shipbuilders, and mapmakers. They built better ships and sailing tools. One of the most important new developments at Sagres was the **caravel** (kăr′əvel), a fast sailing ship with a long, narrow body. It became the favorite ship for explorers in the fifteenth and sixteenth centuries. Many other useful instruments were also developed at Sagres.

Henry became known as Prince Henry the Navigator because of his support of exploring. When he died in 1460, Portugal stopped exploring for a time. Prince Henry's grand nephew King John II started it again in 1481. He dreamed of sending ships all the way around Africa and on to India.

▶**3.** Why was Prince Henry called the Navigator?

Marco Polo's Book King John's strong desire to reach Asia was shared by many Europeans at the time. Their dreams were inspired in part by a book. The idea of setting up direct trade between Europe and Asia went back at least to the thirteenth century. At that time, two merchants from Venice, Maffeo and Nicolo Polo, made two trips overland to China. They took Nicolo's teenage son Marco on their second trip. Later Marco wrote the story of his trip. He described the great riches of China, where spices were sold for almost nothing.

At first, only a few people who could buy the expensive, hand-copied book read his story. Then, in the 1450's, the printing press was invented. Marco Polo's story of his trip to China was printed in 1477, which meant that many more people could read the book. It became one of the most popular books printed on the new presses. It excited its readers and strengthened the desire for a sea route to Asia.

▶**4.** What was the effect of the printing of Marco Polo's book?

Portugal's Route to India

The most likely country to find a route to Asia was, of course, Portugal. Portugal had

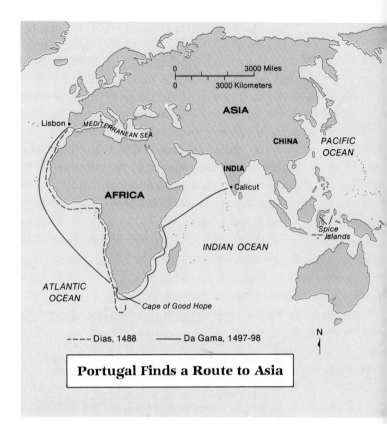

Portugal Finds a Route to Asia

Map Study Whose voyages are shown on the map? Who sailed to the Cape of Good Hope? What city in India is labeled on the map?

already started the work of exploring. It also had ships and navigation tools.

King John told his ship captains to sail south around the tip of Africa and then northeast. He urged his captains to go even farther along the coast of Africa. He told them to build high pillars at the farthest point they reached. Then he urged the next set of explorers to travel beyond those pillars.

Sailors needed urging and promises of great rewards to overcome their fear of sailing into unknown waters. Such voyages were hard not only because of the terror of the unknown but also because food and water quickly spoiled. Sailors had to eat and drink what was available until they got new supplies.

In 1488, a bold captain named Bartholomeu Dias (dē'äs) pushed past the southernmost part of Africa. Dias became the first European to sail around Africa from the west coast to the east coast. Dias continued to sail some 400 miles into the Indian Ocean. Then his terrified crew forced him to turn back.

Dias called the newly discovered tip of Africa the Tempestuous Cape because of its stormy weather. King John named it instead the Cape of Good Hope because it showed the way to Asia.

▶5. Who was the first European explorer to sail around the tip of Africa?

Reviewing Section I————————

Identify Portugal, Prince Henry, navigation, Sagres, caravel, King John II, Marco Polo, Dias, Cape of Good Hope

Questions to Answer
1. How did Marco Polo's book encourage exploration?
2. What was the Portuguese route to Asia?

A Question to Think About What connection might there be between Portugal's location and its role as a leader in exploring?

II. Columbus Sails for Spain

With Dias's voyage, Portugal had a clear path to Asia. Vasco da Gama finally reached India and returned to Portugal in 1498. In the meantime, Portugal's neighbor, Spain, explored another route to Asia.

Columbus's Dream

The good news Dias brought back was bad news for a sailor who dreamed of reaching Asia by a different route. Christopher Columbus was born in Genoa, Italy, in about 1451. By the 1480's, Columbus was a master mariner. He had learned much from the Portuguese, the most skillful sailors in Europe. In 1476, Columbus was on a ship that sank off the coast of Portugal. He made his way to shore and found work for a time in a map-making office. Then he went back to sea, sailing from Portugal. After a while, he was ready to use his knowledge on a voyage to Asia. He believed Asia could best be reached by sailing west across the Atlantic.

▶1. How did Columbus think he could reach Asia?

Columbus's Theory A ship could reach Asia by sailing west, Columbus argued, because the world was round. No one disagreed with him there. The ancient Greek geographer Ptolemy (tol'ə mē) had taught that the world was round, and his writings were well known in Columbus's day.

Columbus thought, however, that the distance between Europe and Asia was much smaller than it is. In fact, the east coast of China is three times farther from Spain than Columbus thought. Also the Americas blocked the way, making the voyage to Asia far more complicated than Columbus had ever dreamed.

▶2. How was Columbus's estimate of the distance between Asia and Europe incorrect?

Finding a Sponsor How could Columbus test his theory? By sailing west. But to do so, he needed money. He first turned to Portugal's King John for help. King John did not find Columbus very convincing. Besides once Dias sailed around the Cape of Good Hope, Portugal had a good route to Asia.

IMPROVE YOUR SKILLS
Map Reading: Title and Legend

People have used maps for centuries to define and explain their knowledge of the world. There are many different kinds of maps. Different sorts of maps are used to show landforms, the location of minerals, political boundaries, ocean currents, and population. Most of the maps you will use as you study American history are historical maps. Their purpose is to help you locate where events occurred. Reading maps properly can help you understand history.

The title of a map is very important. It tells you what you are looking at. The title of a map can also tell you what kind of map you are seeing. The legend, or key, is another important part of a map. The legend is usually located below the title. The legend explains what the special symbols or colors used on the map represent.

Use the title and legend of the map below to answer the following questions.

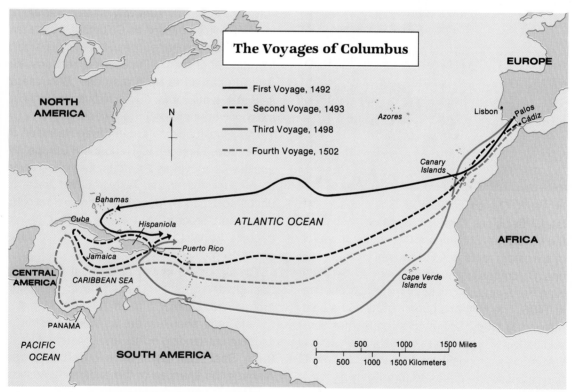

1. What is the title of this map?
2. How many items are shown in the legend?
3. What color is the line for the first voyage?
4. What color is the line for the fourth voyage?
5. On which voyages did Columbus sail past the Cape Verde Islands?

Highlighting People
Queen Isabella

In 1492, Queen Isabella of Spain made two fateful decisions. The first decision, to finance the voyage of Christopher Columbus in search of a western route to Asia, had not been a hasty one. Columbus first came to Queen Isabella and King Ferdinand, her husband, six years before, in 1486. The king and queen appointed a commission to study Columbus's request for ships and sailors. The commission members debated Columbus's proposal for four years. In 1490, they advised the queen to turn it down.

During these years, war had been occupying Isabella's time far more than Columbus's schemes. The war that her armies fought was not a new one. In fact, it had begun hundreds of years before when Muslims invaded Spain.

The Muslims had first entered Spain in the 700's. Many Christians in Spain did not want to live under Muslim rule. The fight had begun in northern Spain in the 1000's. Slowly Christian armies had moved south.

By the 1400's, the Spanish Muslims, or Moors as they were called, held only Granada in southeastern Spain. Then in 1469, Princess Isabella of the Kingdom of Castille married Prince Ferdinand of the Kingdom of Aragon. The two rulers combined their powerful armies and marched against Granada. In 1492, they were successful. In that same year, Queen Isabella decided to grant Columbus his request.

No one knows for sure why Isabella was willing to risk Spain's treasury on Columbus's uncertain project. Perhaps her success against the Moors had made her bold. Whatever her reasons, the decision proved to be a wise one. Because of it, Spain would one day become the richest, most powerful nation in the world.

The other decision Queen Isabella made in 1492 proved less wise. Throughout Europe, Isabella was known as an ardent Catholic. Driven by her devotion to her faith and her desire to unite the Spanish people under one religion, the queen ordered that all Jews must either become Christians or leave Spain. Most Jews chose to go.

The departure of the Jews from Spain hurt the country greatly. Spanish Jews had been among the country's most talented bankers, traders, and shopkeepers as well as some of its most outstanding artists and thinkers. Without them, Spain had fewer experienced people to manage the finances of the expanding empire.

When Queen Isabella died in 1502, she believed she had made her country stronger by pushing out the Jews. She had not. She also believed that Columbus's voyage had been a failure. It had not. No one had yet dreamed of the riches that would pour into Spain from the lands that Columbus had found.

Columbus tried to convince the rulers of Spain, England, and France to help him. But he had no luck. Finally, in 1492, the Spanish queen, Isabella of Castile, agreed to sponsor him. She hoped that Columbus's voyage would bring wealth to Spain. She also hoped it would lead to the spread of Christianity. She gave Columbus permission to "discover and acquire certain islands and mainland in the ocean." She also gave him the money he needed.

▶ **3.** Why did Columbus sail for Spain instead of Portugal?

Columbus's First Voyage

So it was that on August 3, 1492, Columbus and a crew of about 90 men set out from Spain in 3 small ships, the *Niña*, the *Pinta*, and the *Santa Maria*. The fleet first visited the Canary Islands. Then, on September 6, it turned bravely west.

The journey took far longer than Columbus had expected. He had never heard of people sailing more than three weeks out of sight of land. Yet five weeks passed before the *Pinta*'s lookout sighted a tiny island in the Bahamas on October 12. Columbus named it San Salvador, or Holy Savior.

When the Spaniards landed on the island, they were greeted by a group of Arawak (ä'rä wäk) people. The gentle Arawak had wooden spears, but they did not attack the Spaniards. Instead, they brought gifts. The Spanish noticed with interest that some of the Arawak wore small gold pendants in their noses. The Arawak only had a small amount of gold, but the Spanish were eager to find its source.

▶ **4.** Describe Columbus's voyage to San Salvador.

Starting a Settlement Columbus only spent a few days on San Salvador. He explored the

This portrait of Columbus is believed to be the most accurate likeness of the explorer.

Bahamas and the northeastern coast of Cuba, which he thought was part of the mainland of Asia.

On Christmas Day, the *Santa Maria* was wrecked on a coral reef of an island Columbus had named Hispaniola (his'pa nyo'lə), or Spanish Island. Columbus took the loss to be a sign from God that he should found a colony on this island. He used wood from the lost ship to build a fort at what he called Villa de la Navidad, or Christmas Town. Some of the crew of the *Santa Maria* stayed there. On January 4, 1493, the *Niña* and the *Pinta* set sail for Spain.

▶ **5.** Where did Columbus start a settlement?

What Had Columbus Found? At each island he visited, Columbus searched for proof that he had reached Asia. He also searched for gold. In the report he sent to Queen Isabella and her husband, King Ferdinand of Aragon, Columbus claimed he had found both. He made the new lands sound like the China Marco Polo had described. Columbus praised the people of the islands, whom he called Indians. He said that the land was rich and that it had good harbors. Besides gold, it held spices, cotton plants, wood, and "a thousand other things of value."

Map Study Which of the lines of demarcation drawn by the Pope cuts through South America?

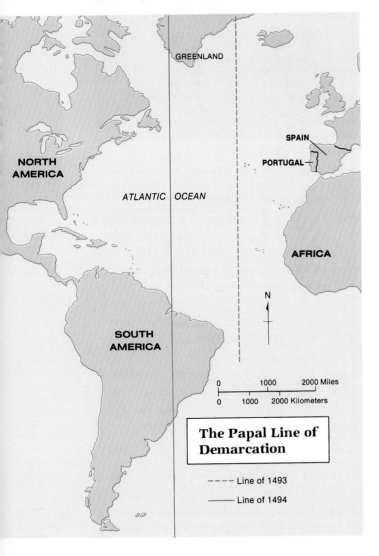

The Papal Line of Demarcation

- - - - - Line of 1493

———— Line of 1494

Actually Columbus did not find much gold except some gold jewelry worn by the Indians. He did see other things that would in time be valuable to Europeans, however. In Cuba, for example, he saw men smoking cigars. That was the first time a European had seen tobacco. Columbus also described new foods such as sweet potatoes, corn, and other vegetables Europeans had never heard of before.

▶**6.** How did Columbus describe the lands he had found?

Dividing Columbus's Finds

News of Columbus's discoveries caused great excitement in Europe except in Portugal. King John II believed that Columbus had found only a few new islands in the Atlantic. And those, John said, were really part of the Azores and belonged to Portugal.

▶**7.** What did King John of Portugal think of Columbus's discoveries?

The Pope Divides the New Lands Spain asked the Pope to decide who owned the new lands. So in 1493 Pope Alexander VI drew a line on a map about 300 miles west of the Azores. He said that west of that line all newly discovered lands would belong to Spain. Those east of the line would belong to Portugal.

King John was fairly content with this solution. Still he wanted the line moved farther west so it would be about halfway between the Azores and the lands Columbus visited. Spain agreed. In 1494, the **Papal Line of Demarcation** (dē'mär kā'shən) was accepted by both countries.

King John was wiser than he knew. The second line cut from the mainland of South America a bulge of land that would later become Brazil.

▶**8.** How did Portugal gain control of Brazil?

Further Explorations

As soon as Queen Isabella heard of Columbus's discoveries, she gave permission for a second voyage. In September 1493, Columbus once again set sail. This time he had an impressive fleet of 17 ships with about 1,200 men aboard. Still looking for the Asian mainland, he explored several islands in the West Indies, including Puerto Rico and Jamaica.

When Columbus returned to Hispaniola, he discovered that Indians had killed the sailors he had left there. So he started a new settlement that he called Isabella on the same island. It was the first permanent Spanish settlement in the New World.

Columbus made two other voyages before his death in 1506. He decided that he had discovered a "very great continent . . . hitherto unknown." However, Columbus thought that this new continent was part of Asia. He never had any idea of the shape of the Americas or of the size of the Pacific Ocean.

▶**9.** Did Columbus ever realize the full extent of his discoveries?

Amerigo Vespucci Amerigo Vespucci (ä mėr'ə go ve spü'chē), an Italian navigator, suspected that Columbus was wrong in thinking that he had reached Asia. In the late 1490's, Vespucci explored the coast of South America. He suggested that what he had seen "may be called a New World, since our ancestors had no knowledge of it."

A German mapmaker was convinced by Vespucci. On a map that he published in 1507, he named the new lands America, for Amerigo. The name gave more honor to Vespucci than he deserved and was hardly fair to Columbus. Still, America became the accepted name for the continents of North and South America.

▶**10.** How did America get its name?

Balboa Meanwhile others continued the work of discovery, and the vastness of the new lands soon became clear. In 1513, Vasco Núñez de Balboa (nü'nyās dā bal bō'ə) hacked his way across the Isthmus of Panama and sighted the Pacific Ocean. He was the first European to see that vast body of water from American shores.

▶**11.** Who was the first European to see the Pacific Ocean?

Magellan Ferdinand Magellan (mə jel'ən) explored the Pacific Ocean and also gave it its name. Magellan started from Spain in 1519 with 5 ships and 237 men. He sailed around South America through the strait that is now named for him. Then he entered an ocean that he named Pacific, or peaceful, because the water was so calm. Magellan sailed across the Pacific and reached the Philippines, where he was killed in a battle.

In 1522, one of his ships returned to Spain after sailing all the way around the world. Only 18 crew members had survived. Magellan's voyage was important because it gave people a clear idea of the size of the world and the location of the Americas.

▶**12.** Why was Magellan's voyage important?

Reviewing Section II

Identify DaGama, Columbus, Genoa, Isabella of Castile, San Salvador, Arawak, Hispaniola, Papal Line of Demarcation, Vespucci, Balboa, Magellan

Questions to Answer
1. What did Columbus find in the Americas?
2. What did the discoveries of Balboa and Magellan prove about Columbus's voyage?

A Question to Think About Why did people like Dias, Columbus, and Magellan risk their lives to explore?

The Renaissance

Christopher Columbus lived during an era called the **Renaissance.** This exciting period in Europe's history lasted from about 1300 to 1600. The Renaissance was inspired in part by the Crusades. The Crusades were expeditions to the Middle East to win back control of the places sacred to Christians from their Muslim conquerors. The Crusades were not successful in military terms. However, during these expeditions to the Middle East, Europeans came in contact with the riches of the East. Desire for more trade was a direct result of the Crusades.

In the Middle East the Crusaders met Muslim scholars. They learned about Muslim advances in geography, medicine, and science. Muslims had also preserved much writing from ancient Greece. These writings had been lost in Europe.

In Europe, the rebirth of interest in ancient Greece and Rome became known as the Renaissance. There was also a rebirth of curiosity about many subjects. Columbus's curiosity about the way to Asia was typical of the Renaissance desire to learn about the world.

III. Conquering and Ruling the Land

With the voyage of Magellan, the Spanish knew for certain that the Americas were not Asia. By then they had already begun to seize the rich, new lands. First **conquistadores** (kon kwis'tə dorz), or conquerors, took control of several islands in the West Indies. Then, in 1513, Juan Ponce de Leon (pons'də lē'ən) set out from Puerto Rico. He discovered and explored the land he called Florida, or land of flowers. Since he had found no gold in Florida, other explorers did not retrace his route. Instead, they looked elsewhere for new lands to conquer.

The Valley of Mexico

Around 1518, the Spanish heard about the great wealth of the powerful Aztec people in the Valley of Mexico on the mainland of North America. In 1519, Hernando Cortés set out with a small army to take over the Aztec.

Along the way, the shrewd Cortés made alliances with groups of Indians who had been conquered by the Aztec. These groups were happy to help Cortés defeat their Aztec enemy. They gave him supplies and thousands of soldiers.

Cortés also was helped by an Indian woman whom the Spanish named Doña Marina (dō'nya mə rē'nə). She served as translator for Cortés. She also helped him deal with Indian groups.

▶**1.** Why were some Indians willing to help Cortés?

Tenochtitlán　When the Spaniards first saw the Aztec capital, Tenochtitlán, they were amazed. The city was one of the largest in the world. Their wonder grew as the soldiers entered the capital. The Spaniards were, of course, horrified by the "heathen" Aztec temples. The marketplace was more to their liking. Every day between 60,000 and 80,000 people met there to buy and sell. They sold, the Spaniards reported, "every imaginable kind of merchandise."

▶**2.** Describe the Spanish reaction to Tenochtitlán.

Montezuma Cortés and his men were most amazed by the huge palaces and gardens of the Aztec emperor Montezuma (mon′tə zü′mə). Clearly that leader had great power and wealth.

Montezuma at first welcomed the Spanish. They returned his welcome by making him their prisoner. They ruled through him for a time. Meanwhile, they carried off as much gold and silver as they could. Montezuma was killed during a great uprising in 1520, when the Aztec drove the Spanish from their city. In 1521, however, the Spanish returned, crushed the Aztec, and began to rule the Valley of Mexico by themselves.

▶**3.** What happened when the Aztec drove the Spanish from Tenochtitlán in 1520?

Other Conquests

Once the Spanish had a hold in Mexico, other conquistadores searched for new empires. Among them was Francisco Pizarro (pi zär′ō). He led a band of soldiers south along the west coast of South America to the highlands of present-day Peru. There he defeated the Inca. The Inca had even greater stores of precious metals than the Aztec. The Spanish melted down jewelry and sculptures and sent them to Spain. Peru became a base for further Spanish conquests in South America.

Conquistadores who headed north from Mexico found little treasure. Still they claimed vast amounts of land for Spain. Francisco de Coronado explored parts of the present

Doña Marina is shown acting as an interpreter between Cortés and the Aztec.

states of Arizona, New Mexico, Colorado, Oklahoma, and Kansas between 1540 and 1542. Hernando de Soto (di sō′tō) discovered the Mississippi River in 1541. Juan Rodriguez Cabrillo (kä brē′yō) sailed up the California coast and claimed that country for Spain in 1542.

▶**4.** Give two reasons why Peru was important to the Spanish.

The Fate of the Indians

Spain rewarded the conquistadores and early officials in the Americas by giving them control over a group of Indian families. This was called the **encomienda** (en cō mē yen′da) system. The men who received such privileges were called **encomenderos** (en cō men der′ōs). The Indians had to work for the encomenderos and pay them tributes, or taxes. In return, the encomenderos had to give military service to Spain and convert the Indians to Christianity.

The encomenderos put the Indians to work growing sugar cane and tobacco on the islands. In Mexico and Peru, Indians were forced to work in gold and silver mines. The encomenderos treated the Indians like slaves. This poor treatment of the Indians angered the Spanish rulers. They also feared the growing power of the encomenderos. As a result, the rulers stopped giving encomiendas and tried to take back those they had already granted.

▶**5.** What was the encomienda system?

Disease The encomienda system eventually died out, in part because the Indian population began to decline as soon as the Spanish arrived in the Americas. Great numbers of Indians died because the Spanish brought to the Americas the germs of diseases common in Europe. Europeans themselves were often **immune** (i myün′) to these diseases. That is, their bodies resisted them. People are born with some immunities, or they become immune to a disease after having a form of it. The Indians, however, had no immunity to European diseases. As a result, those diseases had devasting effects on the Indians.

▶**6.** Why were Indians so likely to catch European diseases?

Smallpox Smallpox was the worst disease the Europeans brought. The disease broke out in the West Indies very soon after the Europeans first arrived in the 1490's. By 1519, it had killed most of the Indians on Hispaniola. It quickly spread to the other islands and then traveled with the Spaniards to the mainland. Cortés's soldiers brought smallpox to Mexico, where it soon killed half the people of Tenochtitlán. Indeed, the disease weakened the Aztec and made it easier for Cortés to defeat them. Much the same was true in Peru. Smallpox spread ahead of the Spaniards, killing many Inca—including the emperor—even before Pizarro arrived.

Indians who did not die of smallpox still had to face other terrible diseases brought to the Americas by Europeans. Measles, typhoid fever, influenza, and bubonic (byù bon′ik) plague—one epidemic followed another throughout the 1500's.

▶**7.** What role did smallpox play in the Spanish conquest of the Aztec and the Inca?

The Effects The results were terrible. In some places, especially the islands first visited by the Spanish, the Indian population was completely wiped out. There were as many as 25 million people in Mexico when Cortés arrived in 1519—but only 1 million in 1605. About 1620, the Indian population of the mainland began to grow again but at a very slow rate.

▶**8.** What were the effects of European diseases on the islands and on the mainland?

Slavery of Blacks

As the Indians died, the Spanish found themselves short of workers, especially for the sugar plantations of the islands. So they brought new people from Africa to take the Indians' places. Since Africans had long been in contact with Europeans, they were less likely than Indians to die from European diseases.

The Spanish rulers did not take the Africans under their protection as they had the Indians. So the colonists were able to make slaves of Africans.

▶**9.** How did the Spanish replace their Indian work force?

Ruling the Spanish Colonies

Spain very quickly set up an efficient and orderly system of government for all the new territory it claimed. The Spanish colonies in

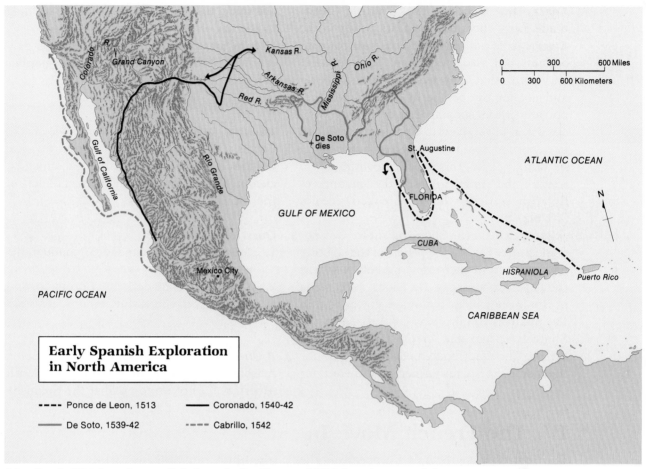

Map Study *Which explorer sailed along the Pacific coast? Which explorer traveled from Cuba to North America? From Puerto Rico to North America?*

the Americas belonged not to the people of Spain, but to the Spanish **Crown.** (Crown means the king or queen.)

Soon after Columbus returned to Spain, Queen Isabella appointed advisors to help her govern her American lands. In 1524, those advisors became the **Council of the Indies.** They stayed in Spain but controlled the colonies in the name of the Crown. The council had great power. Its members helped the Crown fill all offices in the Americas. They also supervised the officials after they were appointed. The members of the council

drafted laws and even acted as a court of appeals for cases that began in the Americas.

Soon after lands in the Americas were conquered, the council set up governments known as **viceroyalties** to rule them. It founded the viceroyalty of New Spain, which included Mexico, in 1534. The viceroyalty of New Castile, which governed Peru, was begun in 1542. The men in charge of the viceroyalties were called viceroys. They were the most important Spanish officials in the Americas.

▶**10.** Who were the most important officials in Spanish America?

33

Centralized Control The Spanish Crown made every effort to protect its power in the Americas. It not only appointed all colonial officials but also paid them. That made it very clear that they worked for the Crown and not for the people in the colonies. Important offices such as that of viceroy were almost always given to Spaniards who had been born in Spain and hoped to return there. As years passed, this practice continued, to irritate the American-born descendants of Spanish settlers who were called Creoles (krē′ōlz).

Power within the Spanish Empire was not democratic. That is, the people of the colonies had no part in their government. Nor was the government local. Decisions were made in Spain, not in the colonies. Power within the Spanish Empire was centralized in the Spanish Crown and in the Council of the Indies. That fact had important results for the history of Spanish America. It meant, for one thing, that the colonists had little training in the art of self-government.

▶**11.** What is meant by saying that the government of the Spanish colonies was neither democratic nor local?

Reviewing Section III

Identify conquistadores, Ponce de Leon, Cortés, Doña Marina, Montezuma, Pizarro, Coronado, De Soto, Cabrillo, encomienda, encomenderos, immune, Crown, Council of the Indies, viceroyalties

Questions to Answer
1. How did Cortés manage to conquer the Aztec so easily?
2. Why were Ponce de Leon, Coronado, and De Soto both successful and unsuccessful?

A Question to Think About What are some reasons the Indians of Central and South America did not unite against the Spanish?

IV. The French Move In

The Spanish were the only Europeans in the Americas for a brief time. Then, in 1500, the Portuguese explorer Pedro Alvarez Cabral discovered Brazil. By the 1530's, the Portuguese had started settlements. The French and the English were not far behind in claiming parts of the Americas. Their efforts were, however, very weak at first.

The Beginnings of New France

The French king Francis I sponsored a voyage by Giovanni da Verrazano (var′rä tsa′nō′) in 1524 to look for a route through the Americas to the Pacific and Asia. Verrazano explored the coast of North America from the Carolinas to Nova Scotia, visiting Manhattan Island (the future site of New York City) along the way. He called the lands he visited New France and claimed them all for France.

Francis I also sent the explorer Jacques Cartier (kär tyā′) to North America. Cartier was to look for a passage to Asia and to find new lands for France. In 1535, Cartier sailed up the river he named the St. Lawrence. He went as far as today's Montreal. His voyage was very important. It was the basis for France's claim to the St. Lawrence River and the land along it, which provided a route to the Great Lakes.

Like Verrazano, Cartier never found a route to Asia. During the 1540's the French tried to start a settlement in the land Cartier discovered. The settlement failed. Through the rest of the 1500's, the French more or less ignored North America. They did not, however, give up their claims to New France.

▶1. Who were the first explorers to claim land in North America for France?

Reasons for Delay Why did France ignore the Americas? Because through most of the late 1500's the French were too busy fighting wars in Europe. Also Cartier's description of the St. Lawrence River Valley, with its long and cold winters, was not very appealing. He brought home no gold and silver. He found no trade routes to Asia. Therefore, French explorers lost interest in North America.

So, for many years, the French claims in North America were left to French fishermen. With other fishermen from England, Spain, and Portugal, they came to fish the waters off Newfoundland. They lived in shacks for the summer. When winter came, they sailed home.

▶2. Why did the French delay building a settlement in North America?

The Growth of the Fur Trade

While on shore, the French fishermen traded with nearby Indians. As a result of that trade, they found something more valuable than fish to take home—furs. Fur coats had always been prized in Europe, but the fur trade really boomed when hats made from beaver skins became popular.

King Henry IV decided that France needed to secure its control of the fur trade. So he brought together a group of merchants who agreed to start a colony in New France. In return, they were given the right to all the trade in furs between their American lands and France.

▶3. What made North America valuable to France?

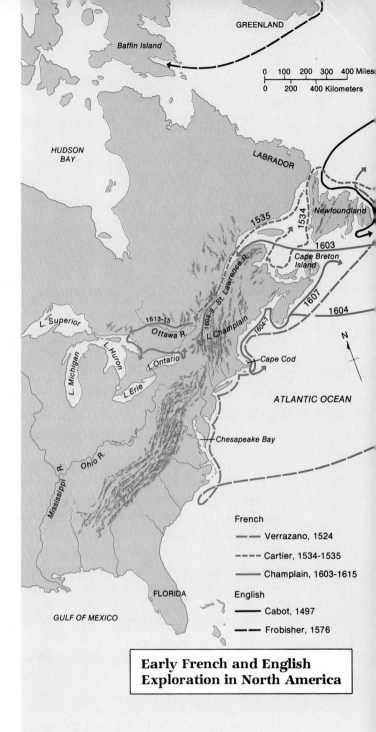

Early French and English Exploration in North America

Map Study *Name the explorer who sailed past Chesapeake Bay. What river did Champlain explore?*

The early French explorers returned to France with descriptions of North America as a land rich in fur-bearing animals and waters teeming with fish.

Champlain Those merchants sent Samuel de Champlain (sham plān') to build their colony. He became known as the Father of New France. In 1608, he built a trading post at Quebec. It became the first permanent settlement in New France. Others, such as Montreal, followed. But for many years, those settlements were only bleak trading posts for the fur trade.

Altogether Champlain made 11 exploring and trading trips in New France. In 1609, he ventured as far as Lake Champlain. It is, of course, named for him. Later he went as far west as Lake Huron.

In the course of his exploring, Champlain became friendly with the Huron Indians, for whom the lake is named. In fact, he helped the Huron in a battle with their traditional enemies, the Iroquois. While he won the friendship of the Huron for the French, Champlain made enemies of the Iroquois.

▶**4.** How did Champlain make friends of the Huron and enemies of the Iroquois?

Reviewing Section IV

Identify Verrazano, Cartier, Montreal, St. Lawrence River, Champlain, Quebec, Lake Champlain

Questions to Answer
1. Why did the French delay in settling North America?
2. Why did the Iroquois become enemies of the French?

A Question to Think About How is the story of early New France different from the story of early New Spain?

V. English Explorations

England's story was much like that of France. The English made some promising beginnings in North America. Then, for a long time, they did almost nothing.

England's King Henry VII sponsored a voyage by John Cabot in 1497. Cabot was looking for a water route to Asia. He did not find one, but he did explore Newfoundland, Labrador, and Nova Scotia. He claimed those lands for England. Cabot died in 1498.

His son, Sebastian, continued the work. He explored Hudson Bay in 1508 and 1509 while again searching for a water route to Asia. However, young Cabot received so little encouragement in England that he went to work for Spain. The only contact England had with North America in the early 1500's was through English fishermen who fished each summer off the coast of Newfoundland.

The Reasons for Delay

The reasons why the English showed so little interest in the Americas were partly economic. During the early 1500's, while the Spanish were conquering Mexico and Peru, the English were content to stay home. England's main product at the time was wool. Merchants traded the wool for foreign goods at the great port of Antwerp in present-day Belgium. That trade grew slowly and brought steady profits to London merchants.

The wool trade was also convenient. Most of England's trade with Antwerp came and went in foreign ships. So the wool merchants of London saw little reason to get into more risky ventures. However, without ships, the English could do very little outside their homeland.

There was another important reason for England's hesitation to expand into the Americas. In the early 1500's, England was a friend of Spain, which claimed most of the Americas. France's King Francis I made clear that he did not feel bound by that claim. However, France was an enemy of Spain. England could not explore and found colonies in the Americas while it was tied to Spain.

▶**1.** Why did England hesitate to start settlements in the Americas?

England's Situation Changes

England's alliance with Spain came to a sudden end in the 1530's, when England's King Henry VIII divorced his first wife, Catherine of Aragon, a Spaniard. The Pope did not approve. So Henry took his country out of the Catholic Church and made himself head of the Church of England. Suddenly England became a **Protestant** country. It was one of several countries that broke from the Catholic Church. Spain, however, remained a Catholic country.

Then, in the 1550's, the trade with Antwerp collapsed. England had to start trade with other parts of the world. English merchants needed to get their own ships to do that.

▶**2.** How did England's trade and alliance situation change in the 1500's?

England's Great Queen

When Henry VIII died, his Protestant daughter, Elizabeth, became queen. The reign of Elizabeth I saw a complete change in England's place in the world.

Elizabeth ruled England for nearly 50 years from 1558 to 1603. At the beginning of her reign, Spain worked to undermine her power and to restore England to the Catholic Church. However, at the end of her reign, England was firmly Protestant and stronger than ever.

▶**3.** Why did Spain work to undermine Queen Elizabeth I?

During the reign of Queen Elizabeth I, England entered a "Golden Age."

Sea Dogs Early in her reign, Elizabeth tried to avoid war with Spain, which was the richest and most powerful country in Europe. Instead, she fought in other ways. Daring sailors called sea dogs set out with her knowledge—and sometimes with her secret support—to raid Spanish ships.

One of the most famous sea dogs was Francis Drake, who sailed around the world looting Spanish ships. In 1580, Drake returned to England with his ship loaded with gold and silver. Queen Elizabeth knighted him on the deck of his ship. Naturally the Spanish were not pleased. They prepared for war. Elizabeth did the same. She hired John Hawkins, another sea dog, to build up the country's navy. He turned it into an effective fighting force.
▶**4.** Who were the sea dogs?

The Armada In 1588, Spain sent a massive fleet of ships, its Armada (är mä′də), to invade England. The Armada was destroyed by the English in one of the great naval battles in history. Clearly England had become something more than an enemy of Spain. It had, as if overnight, become a great naval power.

Elizabeth supported England's seafarers, much as Henry the Navigator did in Portugal over a century earlier. Her reign was the golden age of English exploration.
▶**5.** What was the Armada?

A Slow Start Many people in England still wanted to find a way to Asia through the northern parts of the Americas. For that purpose, a group of London merchants sent Martin Frobisher on three expeditions in the 1570's. He failed, of course, but he did learn a great deal about Hudson Bay. Others added more knowledge.

Gradually, more and more was learned about North America. However, England did not start a permanent settlement in the Americas during Elizabeth's reign. England got a lasting foothold in North America only in 1607, about the time that France was founding Quebec. By then, the Spanish had held colonies in the Americas for over 100 years.

What difference did the delay make for England and France? It meant that the French and the English were left parts of the Americas that Spain did not want. Their lands were less rich in gold and silver than those the Spanish claimed. So they had to find other ways to make their American lands pay.

▶ **6.** What difference did their delay in starting settlements make for England and France?

Reviewing Section V

Identify John Cabot, Newfoundland, Labrador, Nova Scotia, Hudson Bay, Protestant, Elizabeth I, sea dogs, Armada, Frobisher

Questions to Answer
1. How was the wool trade connected with English colonies in North America?
2. Why was England's defeat of the Spanish Armada important?

A Question to Think About Why was England more likely to begin colonies in the Americas after it became a Protestant country?

IMPROVE YOUR READING
Cause and Effect

Most events that occur have a *cause*. A cause is the reason something happens. For example, you were jogging. Then you tripped and fell over your untied sneaker laces. What caused you to trip and fall was your flapping shoe laces. So untied sneaker laces are the *cause* and tripping and falling are the *effects*.

In this chapter, several cause-and-effect relationships are presented. Sometimes signal words point out a cause-and-effect relationship. The following are some examples of signal words: *because*, *consequently*, *since*, *so*, *as a result*, and *therefore*. Here is a sentence from Chapter 2 with a signal word pointing to a cause-and-effect relationship: "Great numbers of Indians died because the Spanish brought to the Americas the germs of diseases common in Europe." In this sentence the signal word *because* helps you to understand that the death of many Indians was *caused* by germs of diseases brought by the Spanish from Europe.

In some cases, two sentences are used to explain a cause-and-effect relationship—for example: "Asian spices were shipped to Europe overland, and many people were involved in the trade. So spices were expensive." The signal word here is *so*. It points out that the high price of spices was *caused* by overland shipping that involved many people.

Each of the following sentences or groups of sentences from Chapter 2 describes a cause-and-effect relationship. On your paper, write the signal word in each sentence that points out the cause-and-effect relationship.

1. Dias called the newly-discovered tip of Africa the Tempestuous Cape because of its stormy weather. (p. 24)
2. Henry became known as Prince Henry the Navigator because of his support of exploring. (p. 23)
3. Spain asked the Pope to decide who owned the new lands. So in 1493 Pope Alexander VI drew a line on a map some 300 miles west of the Azores. (p. 28)
4. When Columbus returned to Hispaniola, he discovered that Indians had killed the sailors he had left there. So he started a new settlement that he called Isabella on the same island. (p. 29)
5. Since Africans had long been in contact with Europeans, they were less likely than Indians to die from European diseases. (p. 32)

CHAPTER 2 REVIEW

Vocabulary Check

Write the letter for the definition of each numbered item.

1. Papal Line of Demarcation
2. Council of the Indies
3. Crown
4. Viceroyalties
5. Encomenderos

a. Governments set up by the Council of the Indies in the Americas
b. Spaniards with control over Indian families
c. King or queen
d. Advisors to the Spanish Crown on the Americas
e. Pope's division of land between Spain and Portugal

Fact Check

Write the name of the explorer described in each of the phrases below.

1. The Father of New France
2. Portuguese explorer who first sailed around Africa
3. Spaniard who explored Florida
4. Explorer whose crew sailed around the world
5. Spaniard who discovered the Mississippi River
6. First European to see the Pacific Ocean
7. Conquistador who claimed Mexico for Spain
8. French explorer who sailed up the St. Lawrence River
9. Conquistador who defeated the Inca
10. Explorer who visited the southwestern part of the present-day United States

Skills Check

Use the map on page 35 to answer the following questions.

1. The explorations of what two nations are shown on this map?
2. What part of the world is shown on this map?
3. Which explorer made a voyage in 1524?
4. Which explorer sailed the farthest south along the coast?
5. For what country did Frobisher sail?

Time Check

On your paper, write the number of the following events in proper chronological order.

1. The Americas are named.
2. Bartholomeu Dias sails around Africa.
3. English sea dogs destroy Spanish ships.
4. Elizabeth becomes queen of England.
5. Columbus lands in the West Indies.

Think and Write

1. Why did Spain take the lead in exploring the Americas?
2. Why did the defeat of the Spanish Armada affect England's role in the Americas?
3. How did the Spanish Crown maintain tight control over its colonies?
4. What effect did the "discovery" of the Americas by Europeans have on the Indians?
5. What role did religion play in the early exploration of the Americas?

REVIEWING UNIT 1

Reviewing the Facts I.

The sentences below are not correct. Write the number of each incorrect sentence on your paper. Then write the sentence, changing what is needed to make it correct.

1. Most scholars agree that the first people came to the Americas from Africa.
2. At one time, the Bering Strait was much deeper than it is today.
3. The Hopi Indians were a powerful group in the Eastern Woodlands.
4. Women had no voice in the government of the Iroquois.
5. There is no archaeological proof for the story of the Norse visits to Newfoundland.
6. England was quick to start settlements in the Americas.
7. Marco Polo's book described his travels in the Americas.
8. Portugal's route to Asia was around South America.
9. The Spanish bought land from the Indians in Mexico and Peru.
10. Cortés conquered Mexico after Pizarro conquered Peru.
11. The Spanish were most interested in their claims to lands in the present-day United States.
12. The Spanish Crown forbade the use of Africans as slaves in the Americas.
13. Spain encouraged its colonists in the Americas to participate in their government.
14. France considered the major wealth of North America to be in its fish.
15. Queen Elizabeth discouraged exploration in the Americas.

Reviewing the Facts II.

Each of the statements below describes one or more of the following countries: Portugal, Spain, France, England. Write the name of the proper country or countries for each item.

1. The Papal Line of Demarcation gave these two countries claims in the Americas.
2. This country claimed the St. Lawrence River.
3. Champlain came from this country.
4. A prince of this country set up a center for the study of navigation.
5. Giovanni da Verrazano sailed for this country.
6. The defeat of the Armada showed that this country was a naval power.
7. An Italian navigator, funded by the rulers of this country, was the first European explorer to visit the Americas.
8. Magellan sailed for this country.
9. Merchants from this country had a very successful wool trade until the 1550's.
10. This country claimed Brazil.

Reviewing Ideas

1. Why did people first come to the Americas?
2. Why do we divide the Indians of North America into culture areas?
3. In what ways did the Haida Indians differ from the Hopi?
4. Why did the first Spanish come to the Americas?
5. What countries had claimed land in the Americas by 1607?

UNIT TWO

The First English Colonies

This map of the east coast of North America was issued by the London Company of England in 1608. It shows colonies started by France (Nova Francia), Spain (Florida), and England (Virginia). During the 1600's, the English worked hard to settle the coast between the French and the Spanish colonies.

Chapter 3

Settling Virginia

This artist's view of Jamestown shows what England's first permanent colony in North America probably looked like around 1625.

The English had a much harder time than the Spanish winning a foothold in the Americas. Their first attempts to found a colony on Roanoke Island were miserable failures. This chapter tells about Roanoke and also about the more successful colony at Jamestown in Virginia.

The Virginia Colony was a miserable place, full of death and disappointment. Still the colony survived and became the first permanent English settlement in North America. It also became a place unlike anywhere else English people lived.

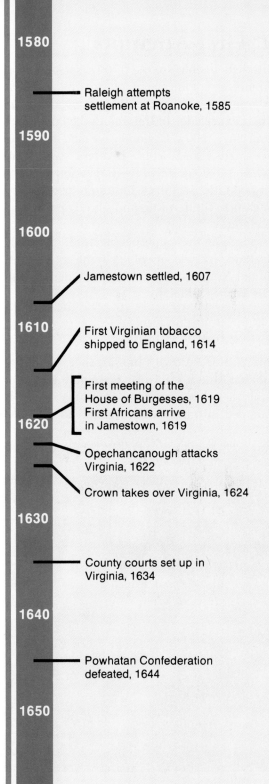

1580

Raleigh attempts
settlement at Roanoke, 1585

1590

1600

Jamestown settled, 1607

1610

First Virginian tobacco
shipped to England, 1614

First meeting of the
House of Burgesses, 1619
First Africans arrive
in Jamestown, 1619

1620

Opechancanough attacks
Virginia, 1622

Crown takes over Virginia, 1624

1630

County courts set up in
Virginia, 1634

1640

Powhatan Confederation
defeated, 1644

1650

I. First Attempts

English people in the 1700's spoke not of founding colonies, but of starting overseas plantations. The word *plantation* came from their experience in Ireland. In the late 1500's and early 1600's, England gave land in Ireland to English and Scots "planters" who were willing to go and live there. The settlements, or plantations, of those Protestant people were meant to tighten England's hold on Catholic Ireland.

Some of the same people who "planted" Ireland were also involved in the early planting of North America. One such person was Sir Walter Raleigh.

Raleigh and Roanoke

Sir Walter Raleigh's half-brother, Sir Humphrey Gilbert, had drowned while trying to start a colony in North America. Raleigh stepped into his half-brother's shoes.

Sir Walter Raleigh failed in two attempts to establish a colony in North America.

Raleigh was one of Queen Elizabeth's favorites at court. In 1584, she gave him a **royal charter,** that is, a written, legal grant of privileges. Raleigh's charter allowed him to discover and take over lands in North America. Raleigh quickly sent ships to explore the American coast south of Chesapeake Bay. The crews returned with promising reports on the climate, soil, minerals, and Indians of the region. Raleigh then asked the unmarried Queen Elizabeth for permission to name the new land Virginia after her, his virgin queen. She agreed.

▶**1.** What is a royal charter?

The First Attempt   In 1585, Raleigh sent out an expedition with about 100 men. They founded a settlement on Roanoke (rō′ ə nōk) Island, off the coast of present-day North Carolina. (See map, page 49.) But supplies were scarce. By the end of a year, the colonists were desperate enough to eat dogs. When an English ship visited the new colony in June 1586, the settlers decided to return home.

▶**2.** Why did the first Roanoke settlers return to England?

The Second Attempt   Raleigh tried again in 1587. This time he convinced 117 people, including 17 women and 9 children, to make another "planting." The group settled on Roanoke Island in July.

A month later its governor, John White, returned to England for supplies. He left behind his daughter, his son-in-law, and their newborn baby, Virginia Dare, the first English child born in the Americas.

White could not return to Roanoke until 1590 because England was at war with Spain. When he landed, the island was empty. The word *CROATOAN*, the name of another island, was carved in a doorpost, but the settlers were not there. There were no other clues to what happened to them. Their fate is still a great mystery.

▶**3.** What is the mystery of Roanoke Island?

The Lessons Learned

It was some time before the English tried to start another settlement in North America. The failures of Roanoke had shown how difficult it was to build a colony. For one thing, North America had a way of swallowing up settlers. Also a great deal of money was needed to start a colony. The amounts needed were far beyond the wealth of any person, family, or group of friends.

Some greater source of funds had to be found. But where? Not from the Crown. Elizabeth refused to give the needed funds. So did the rulers who came after her. The Crown was willing to help people start colonies by giving them charters and other privileges. However, the money would have to come from some other source.

▶**4.** Why did colonizers need a source of funds?

One Solution: The Joint-Stock

In the late sixteenth century, English trading companies had developed a new way of raising money. People put money in a common fund (the **joint-stock**). Each received a share of the profits. How much a person received depended on how much he or she **invested,** that is, put into the joint-stock.

Investors could buy one or many shares in a company. They could also buy shares in several companies. In that way, they spread out their risks and also their chances to make profits. The joint-stock method would provide money for starting the next English colonies.

▶**5.** Why would a person invest in a joint-stock company?

NOVA BRITANNIA.
OFFERING MOST
Excellent fruites by Planting in
VIRGINIA.

Exciting all such as be well affected
to further the same.

LONDON
Printed for SAMVEL MACHAM, and are to be sold at
his Shop in Pauls Church-yard, at the
Signe of the Bul-head.
1609.

The London Company published this pamphlet hoping to attract settlers to Virginia.

Reviewing Section I

Identify plantations, Sir Walter Raleigh, royal charter, Chesapeake Bay, Roanoke Island, John White, Virginia Dare, Croatoan, joint-stock, invested

Questions to Answer
1. What happened to Sir Walter Raleigh's two plantations?
2. To what problem was the joint-stock the solution?

A Question to Think About How did the joint-stock idea give many people chances to make money?

II. The Virginia Company

The next major effort to settle America was made by the Virginia Company, which was modeled on earlier trading companies. It included two different groups of investors. One group was based in London. The other group was in Plymouth, a smaller port on England's southern coast.

In 1606, the company won a charter from the Crown that gave it the right to settle Virginia. Virginia then included all the North American coast from present-day Maine to North Carolina. The Plymouth investors were told to make their first settlement in the northern part of Virginia. The London investors were to go farther south.

The Virginia Company of Plymouth founded a colony at Sagadahoc (sag' əd ə häk'), by the mouth of the Kennebec River in Maine. The colony lasted only a year. As a result, the honor of establishing the first English colony in North America went to the Virginia Company of London.

Jamestown

In December 1606, the Virginia Company of London sent 144 men to sea on 3 ships, the *Susan Constant, Goodspeed,* and *Discovery.* They reached the coast of Virginia in April and then spent a month looking for a place to settle. The company in London wanted to avoid the mistakes of Roanoke. It gave the settlers many directions about the colony's location. It should be on easily defended land that was far enough inland to avoid attacks by sea. It should be on a wide river so settlers could easily trade with Indians farther upriver. Colonists were also supposed to avoid swamps, a direction they unfortunately ignored.

The colonists built a plantation, called **Jamestown,** in 1607 on a swampy peninsula 30 miles up a river they named the James after King James I. In the area were several groups of Algonquian-speaking Indians. The Indians never entirely trusted the newcomers, but they did help them by supplying corn the settlers needed to survive.

▶**1.** Describe the location of Jamestown.

Trouble At first, Jamestown's future did not look very bright. The colonists no more than set foot on land before they began quarreling with each other. That delayed the important work of building a fort and houses and of planting crops.

Some people refused to work on company projects. They tried to make their own fortunes by trading privately with the Indians. Some settlers traded tools and other goods stolen from the company's storehouse. Many others went off to search for gold.

▶**2.** Why did Jamestown's future not look bright?

Captain John Smith That the colony survived at all was due to Captain John Smith, a 27-year-old adventurer. He had already seen much of the world before joining the Virginia expedition of 1606. The company had appointed Smith to a seat on a council of seven settlers that was to govern in Virginia. At its first meeting, however, the council expelled Smith from office because he supposedly had taken part in a mutiny at sea.

So Smith set off on his own to explore the land and learn about its people. In the summer of 1608, he investigated Chesapeake Bay. On his return to Jamestown, he found the colony with "no talk, no hope, nor worke but dig gold, wash gold, refine gold, and load gold." There was, however, no gold in Virginia.

IMPROVE YOUR SKILLS
Reading Maps: Scale

Some maps show the entire world. Other maps show only a few blocks of a city. In all cases, however, a map itself is always smaller than the places it represents. You can find out how large an area really is by using the map's *scale*. The scale tells you how to translate distances on the map into the real distances. In the map below, the scale shows how many miles each inch on the map stands for and how many kilometers each inch on the map represents.

To answer the following questions, you need to measure the scale. Use a ruler or a piece of string on which you make marks for the beginning and the end of the scale.

1. How many miles does an inch stand for?
2. Measure the distance between Williamsburg and Jamestown? How many miles does that represent?
3. How far is Roanoke Island from Jamestown?
4. What is the distance between Old Point Comfort and Jamestown by the shortest route?
5. How long is the trip between Old Point Comfort and Jamestown if one travels only on the James River?

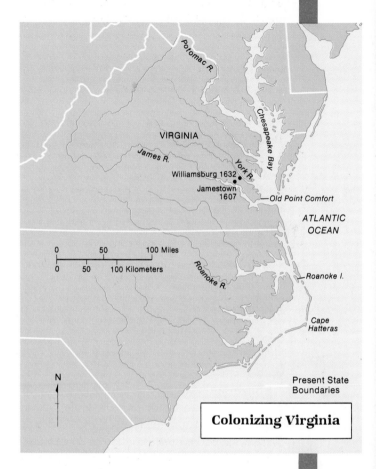

Colonizing Virginia

Worse yet, in their fever for gold, the settlers did not store food for the winter. Unless someone acted quickly, they would starve during the cold months. So Smith went out again and got supplies from the Indians. A few days later, in September 1608, he was elected president of the governing council.

▶3. Why did the Jamestown settlers not store food for the first winter?

Smith's Rule Smith governed with an iron hand. He made a rule that those who did not work at what he told them to do would not eat. Soon the colonists began building houses and a fort and planting crops. Smith even managed to send a shipload of cedarwood to England for the company's profit.

Smith also improved relations with many neighboring Indians. He won the respect of

This artist's view of the Indian leader Powhatan was drawn on John Smith's map of Virginia.

Powhatan (pou′ə tan′), the leader of several neighboring Indian groups. This was not an easy thing to do. According to Smith's story, he and Powhatan did not start out on very good terms.

Smith said that he was captured by members of Powhatan's tribe in 1608 while looking for food. Powhatan ordered Smith's death. He was saved because Pocahontas (po kə hon′ təs), Powhatan's daughter, pleaded for Smith's life. Whether or not this story is true, Powhatan did come to trust Smith's word.

In the summer of 1609, Smith was burned in a gunpowder explosion. He was forced to return to England. By then, it looked as if the colony might survive even without him.
▶**4.** What did Smith accomplish while he governed Virginia?

The Company's Rule The Virginia Company had learned from Smith's example that the colony needed strong leaders. So it decided in 1609 that Virginia would be ruled by a governor and a council. The governor would appoint the members of the council and his decisions would be final.

Between 1610 and 1618 a series of strong and severe governors ruled the colony. They ordered that the settlers march to work each morning to the beat of a drum. Those who refused or lagged behind faced harsh punishments. People could be executed for stealing from the company store, trading with the Indians without permission, selling goods produced in Virginia for their own profit, or taking food from gardens. Colonists could also be punished for many other crimes, including criticizing the company in London. The colony managed to survive under those severe laws. Survival was in itself quite an achievement.
▶**5.** What sorts of rules did the Virginia settlers have to obey between 1610 and 1618?

Hard Times in Virginia

Although the Virginia settlement survived, it did not thrive. The company's investors spent a lot of money on the new settlement, and its officers did everything they could to make Virginia grow and prosper. However, the harder the company tried, the more the colony seemed to fail.

The death rate of its settlers was the biggest threat to the colony. Of the 144 persons who sailed for Virginia in December 1606, only 38 were still alive 13 months later. Only about a dozen settlers died during the winter of 1608 and 1609, when John Smith was in control. After he left, however, the death rate shot back up.

The company kept sending over new settlers who rarely lived to tell their stories. Worst of all was the winter of 1609 and 1610 known as Virginia's starving time. Of 500 colonists alive in the fall, only 60 remained the next spring. To survive, the settlers ate anything they could find.

John Smith is best known for his leadership of the Jamestown colony. Yet even before he reached the Americas, Smith had had more adventures than most other people have in a lifetime.

John Smith was born in Willoughby, England, around 1580. The son of a fairly successful farmer, he spent his early years working on his father's farm and going to school. At the age of 15, he left the farm and became apprenticed to a well-to-do merchant. But the work turned out to be too demanding and boring for the adventurous youth. So, at 16, he ran away to seek his fortune.

Smith's first adventure was as a soldier in the Dutch army that was battling the Spanish for control of the Netherlands. Next he joined the fight of Hungary and several other East European countries against invasion by the Turks. During this time, he so impressed his commander that he was granted the rank of captain and a sum of money to boost his fortune.

Shortly after this great success, Smith's good luck came to an end. He was wounded by the Tartars, allies of the Turks, and was given as a slave to a Turkish noblewoman living in far-off Constantinople.

The Turkish noblewoman treated Smith kindly. To protect him from others in her country, she sent him to live with her brother who ruled a neighboring kingdom.

The brother turned out to be a cruel master. Smith killed him and journeyed over 1,000 miles back to Hungary. He then wandered over the continent before returning to England in 1604. Two years later, in 1606, he joined the Virginia Company of London and sailed for the first time to the Americas.

Smith's leadership of Jamestown from 1606 to 1609 made him famous. Yet the contributions that he made in later years to the founding of New England are equally important. Those contributions began in 1614, when he sailed for a second time to the Americas. This time his mission was to seek out gold and whales for London merchants.

During this second trip, Smith found neither whales nor gold. He did, however, explore the northern coast of the Virginia territory, make maps of the area, and name the region New England. The books he wrote in later years about this and previous adventures earned him a place in history not only as a colonist, an explorer, and an adventurer but also as a mapmaker, a writer, and a historian.

Those who had lived through that winter had had enough. They decided to abandon Virginia. The settlers packed up, piled on board some ships, and started down the James River. There they met a fleet of ships. On the ships were the colony's new governor, Lord De La Warr, several hundred more colonists, and a great store of food and supplies. The settlers turned back, and the colony continued.

▶6. What was the biggest threat to the Jamestown colony?

Disease Why did the colonists die in such numbers? Some were killed or executed by other colonists. A few were killed by Indians. Most died of natural causes. They had arrived in Virginia weakened by their long sea voyage and poor food. Thirty-eight people who had

People from all walks of life settled Jamestown. Many had to learn new skills to survive.

A NOBLE-MAN   A GENTLEMAN   A COUNTRYMAN

A LADY   A GENTLE WOMAN   A COUNTRY WOMAN

sailed with the first fleet in 1606 died before ever setting foot on American soil.

Those who made it to Virginia had to live their first months in the colony on supplies they had brought with them. There were of course "fish in the sea, fowls in the air, and beasts in the woods," as John Smith observed. However, the colonists, Smith reported, were too "weak and ignorant" to fish and hunt.

The new arrivals also had to adjust to a much warmer climate than that of England. Mosquitoes bred in the swamps surrounding Jamestown and carried the disease malaria. In the summer, germs bred in the water at Jamestown and the water became extremely dangerous to drink.

In hot weather, the Indians moved to healthier places. The English settlers needed time to learn how to live in this strange place—time to learn, that is, what the Indians already knew.

▶7. Why did so many settlers die in Virginia?

Mistakes of the Company Unfortunately the company could not give them that time. It wanted each voyage to pay for itself and return a profit to its investors. At least the colonists should send some promise of future profits. During those first, critical years in Virginia, the company ordered the settlers to send back gold or news of a route to China. If the settlers could find neither gold nor a route to China, at least they ought to provide things such as glass, tar, and cut timber that England usually had to buy from other countries.

The company also sent over many new colonists before the settlement was ready for them. The people it sent were not suited to the needs of Virginia. Many were gentlemen, and *gentlemen* by definition meant people who did not work with their hands. Some were workers with skills that were all but useless in the wilderness. One set of early arrivals included, for example, a jeweler, two goldsmiths, and a perfumer. What Virginia needed was farmers and laborers.

▶**8.** What mistakes did the Virginia Company make in running its colony?

Work Habits

The death rate of new settlers was only one of the colony's problems. Another was the settlers' refusal to work hard, even when their lives depended upon it. Only force could get them to work, and then they rarely stuck to their jobs very long. When Governor Thomas Dale first arrived in May 1611, he found the settlers at "their daily and usual workes, bowling in the streets."

Why were they so lazy? People in England at that time did not work very hard. The English labor system was designed to give everybody a little to do. The colonists expected to work even less than people in England. Early reports from Virginia suggested life there would be easy. The first accounts Raleigh had of Virginia, for example, said that "the earth bringeth forth all things in abundance . . . without toil or labor."

▶**9.** Why were the settlers not willing to work?

The Discovery of Tobacco

Fortunately, in 1614, the Virginians at last found a product that they could sell for a great profit: tobacco. Europeans had learned about tobacco from the Indians. Columbus was the first to see Indians smoking tobacco. Soon the Spanish were shipping tobacco from the West Indies and South America to Europe. Many Europeans quickly became addicted.

The Indians in Virginia smoked a type of tobacco that Europeans found unpleasant. So, in 1612, a colonist, John Rolfe, tried

This drawing of a tobacco plant is from a sixteenth-century European book.

growing a milder variety of the plant that he had imported from the West Indies. Two years later he sold four barrels of his tobacco in England. His success gave Virginians a **cash crop,** one that could be sold in quantity in Europe.

▶**10.** What was Virginia's cash crop?

Reviewing Section II

Identify Virginia Company, Jamestown, John Smith, Powhatan, Pocahontas, John Rolfe, cash crop

Questions to Answer
1. Why did the Virginia Company start appointing governors for its colony in 1609?
2. Why was John Rolfe's mild tobacco plant important?

A Question to Think About What did the Company and its settlers have to learn about Virginia?

The Colony Built on Smoke

King Charles I said that Virginia was built on smoke. Indeed, the English demand for tobacco helped the colony survive.

The Spanish had introduced tobacco to Europe. At first, it was used as medicine. Later people began to smoke for pleasure. We know now, of course, that the use of tobacco is habit-forming, so people had a strong desire for tobacco.

Trendsetters like Sir Walter Raleigh showed the fashionable world in England how to smoke.

Some people opposed the use of tobacco. One of them was King James I. He called tobacco a "vile and stinking weed" and said that it would cause lung and brain damage to those who used it.

Most people ignored the warnings of the king, and tobacco continued as Virginia's cash crop. Settlers grew tobacco in the streets of Jamestown. Until the twentieth century, rents and doctor's bills were paid in tobacco in some parts of Virginia.

III. Changes and Reforms

While the Virginia settlers were struggling to stay alive, some important changes were taking place in the way the colony was governed.

New Charters

The English Crown gave the Virginia Company of London new charters in 1609 and 1612. Those charters expanded the land controlled by the company. They made it easier for the company to raise money, and they also gave the company more power. The new charters were important because the company later gave some of that power to the settlers themselves. That marked the beginning of self-government in the English colonies.
▶1. Why were the charters of 1609 and 1612 important?

The Charter of 1609 The charter of 1609 gave the company control over an area 200 miles north and 200 miles south of Old Point Comfort and "from sea to sea, west and northwest." Obviously the English had no idea how far it was from the Atlantic to the Pacific Ocean.

The Charter of 1609 also made the Virginia Company of London a joint-stock company, able to sell shares in the company to the public. In addition, it placed "full power and authority" over the colony in a council that met in England and reported to the Crown.
▶2. What were the main changes made by the Charter of 1609?

The Charter of 1612 The company won still more privileges from the Crown in the Charter of 1612. The new charter changed the way the Virginia Company was managed. Instead of a council, the company's shareholders now had power over the colony. They were to make decisions about the colony in four annual meetings, or great courts.

That change was very important for American history. In the Spanish Empire the Crown held all power. However, in 1612, the English king gave real power over his country's first American colony to a group of private investors. In turn, those investors chose to share their power with the colonists themselves. Thus the division of power in the English Empire became very different from that in the Spanish Empire.

▶**3.** How did the Charter of 1612 make the sharing of power in the English Empire different from that in the Spanish Empire?

The Reforms of 1618

In 1618, the Virginia Company adopted a set of reforms meant to attract more people to Virginia and to make the settlers work harder. It also tried to cut the company's costs.

First of all, the company gave land to the settlers. Those who had come to Virginia before 1616 received at least 100 acres. Those who had come later were given 50 acres. Tradespeople were promised a house and 4 acres of land in Virginia as long as they continued to practice their trades.

It cost the company almost nothing to give land away. In Europe, however, land was difficult to come by. Only people in the highest social classes owned large tracts of land. Many people were eager to come to Virginia in order to become landowners.

▶**4.** Why did the company promise to give land to settlers?

Bringing People to the Colony There were, of course, people who wanted to come to Virginia but could not pay for the trip. So the company offered to pay their way if they would work for the company for 7 years. When the 7 years were over, they would get 50 acres of their own.

The company also hit upon another way to bring more people to Virginia. It promised to give people 50 acres for every person they brought to Virginia. That scheme came to be known as the **headright system.**

The company hoped that Virginians would work harder when they were working for themselves on their own land. The more tobacco Virginians grew, the more money the company would make, since it alone controlled the colony's trade.

▶**5.** What was the headright system?

The General Assembly Finally the company changed the form of Virginia's government. English people were proud of their liberty. They were hesitant to make homes where they would be less free than they had been in England. So the company gave settlers a share in their own government.

The company told the governor to set up a **general assembly.** The assembly would have two parts. One part was the Governor's Council, whose members were appointed by the company. The second part was the **House of Burgesses** (bėr′jis es). Its members (the burgesses) would be elected by the people of the colony. The General Assembly would meet at least once a year to pass laws for the colony. The laws could, however, be **vetoed,** or struck down, by the governor and by the company

The House of Burgesses was the first elected law-making body in the English colonies.

in London. The company could also pass laws for the colony. However, those laws would not go into effect until the General Assembly agreed to them.

The first meeting of Virginia's General Assembly was held on July 30, 1619. The date is important. It marked the beginning in North America of government by the people through representatives they had chosen.

The company's reforms did attract new settlers. In three years, twice as many people went to Virginia as had gone in the colony's past.

▶6. What was the House of Burgesses?

Reviewing Section III

Identify Charter of 1609, Charter of 1612, headright system, general assembly, House of Burgesses, vetoed

Questions to Answer
1. Why was land so attractive to people in Europe?
2. Why did the Virginia Company give its settlers a share in their government?

A Question to Think About What would the government of Virginia have been like if it had been part of the Spanish Empire?

IV. New Troubles for the Company

The success of the Virginia colony in growing tobacco and attracting new settlers created some new problems. The settlers needed more land to grow tobacco. However, as they took up more land, they came into conflict with the Indians. Another problem was caused by greedy tobacco planters who overworked and underfed their workers, causing many to die.

Indian Conflict

By 1618, there were enough English people in Virginia so that some settlers began to move outside Jamestown. People started farms on both sides of the James River and along other rivers that ran throughout the **Tidewater,** the flatlands along the Atlantic coast.

The Tidewater was home to dozens of groups of Algonquian-speaking Indians. They belonged to a **confederation,** an association or league, led by Powhatan. The Algonquians lived in ways much like other Indians of the Eastern Woodlands. The men hunted and fished, while the women tended the fields.
▶1. Who lived in the Tidewater before the Jamestown settlers started to spread out?

Uneasy Peace In the early days of Jamestown, the Indians were more powerful than the English settlers. For one thing, the Indians knew how to live in Virginia. Also, the settlers needed the Indians to survive. The Indians traded their extra corn for iron pots, knives, and other products from Europe. Without that corn, the settlers would have died.

Relations between the settlers and Indians were uneasy from the beginning. Still, the colonists were not at first a real threat to Powhatan's people. Tensions increased as it became clear to the Indians that the colonists were going to stay.

Then, in 1613, the situation suddenly changed. That year a settler kidnapped Powhatan's daughter, Pocahontas. She was held hostage because Powhatan's people had captured some colonists. During her stay in Jamestown, Pocahontas became a Christian. The next year she married John Rolfe, the tobacco planter. As a result of his daughter's marriage, Powhatan made peace with the colony.
▶2. Why did tension increase between the settlers and the Indians?

Opechancanough Virginia had several years of peace. However, just as the colony began to grow, Powhatan died. He was succeeded by Opechancanough (ō pē′ chan kā′ nō). He planned to end once and for all the gradual takeover of his people's lands by the English. On March 22, 1622, the Indians killed 347 colonists and drove the others back from their scattered farms to Jamestown.

For the Indians, that victory was the beginning of the end. The English moved against them with no holds barred, destroying Indian villages and crops. Still the Indians held on.

In 1644, the aged Opechancanough took the offensive again. His warriors killed about 500 colonists in 2 days. In the battle that followed, Opechancanough was killed. The power of the Powhatan confederation was broken. A few Indians remained in Virginia, but most of the survivors moved, many to the Eastern Shore of Chesapeake Bay.

▶**3.** What happened to most of the Virginia Indians after Opechancanough was killed?

A New Starving Time

In the years after 1618, settlers died almost as quickly as the company sent them to Virginia. The settlers were dying of hunger. However, the colony was growing enough food for its settlers. Why were they starving? Because of the greed of a few men.

Newcomers often fell into the hands of powerful men who made them work long hours and fed them little. A planter with enough workers could make a great fortune in tobacco in the 1620's when tobacco prices were high. Those who could forced people to work for them. Those big planters controlled the colony's food supply, and they let others go hungry.

▶**4.** Why were people starving in Virginia in the 1620's?

This painting of Pocahontas shows her as she looked when she visited England in 1616.

Workers for Virginia

There were a few black slaves in Virginia. The first of them arrived in 1619. However, slavery did not grow rapidly in Virginia at that time. Planters who needed workers could hire **indentured** (in den′ chər d) **servants.** Those were Europeans who agreed to work for a master for a term of seven or sometimes four years. In return, the master paid their way to Virginia and gave them food, shelter, and clothing during their years of indenture. An **indenture** was the agreement between master and servant.

Planters saw one big advantage in purchasing slaves. Slaves worked for a lifetime, not a few years. However, slaves cost far more than servants. Also slaves might die before working long enough to make back their purchase price.

After 1700, slavery grew on the North American mainland. Through most of the 1600's, however, the English colonists usually used the labor of other Europeans.

▶**5.** Why did planters prefer indentured servants to slaves in the 1600's?

The End of the Virginia Company

The news arriving in England from Virginia during the early 1620's was not good. The death figures were staggering. Also, though the colony's leaders may have been making money, the company was making none. Since the planters often traded illegally, the company did not profit from the growth in the tobacco trade.

Investigators for the Crown decided that the company was poorly managed. As a result,

in 1624, the Virginia Company lost its charter, and the Crown took over the colony.

▶**6.** Why did the Virginia Company lose its charter?

Reviewing Section IV————————

Identify Tidewater, confederation, Opechancanough, indentured servants, indenture

Questions to Answer
1. Why did the Indians have little to fear from the settlers at first?
2. What did the high price of tobacco have to do with suffering and death in Virginia?

A Question to Think About What might have happened if the Indians had refused to help or trade with the Virginia settlers?

V. A New Kind of Place

By the time the Virginia Company had its last charter, there was a new kind of community in Virginia. Although populated by English people, Virginia was not like England. Virginians built new kinds of houses and grew new crops. Even their family structure was often unlike that in England.

Housing

One of the most obvious ways Virginia differed from England was in its houses. In England, a house was a solid thing made of stone or brick. English houses were built to last many years.

In Virginia of the 1620's, houses were built of wood. They were, in fact, more like shacks thrown together. Their owners expected to be in the grave or back in England after a few years. Houses became sturdier in the

1630's. The great plantation homes of the South remained, however, a long way off. Most of them were built after 1700.

▶**1.** How were Virginia houses different from houses in England?

Agriculture

In England, people earned their living in many different ways, and farmers grew many crops. Those varied ways of earning a living gave England what is called a **diversified economy.**

Virginians grew tobacco. They did very little else. The Virginia Company had tried to give its colony a more diversified economy. After 1618, it had urged glassmakers, ironmasters, winegrowers, and other skilled people to settle in Virginia. Few of the artisans practiced their trades in the colony, however.

Many died. The others gave up their trades for the quick profits of tobacco. By 1620, nearly everyone was growing tobacco.

Virginians did grow some corn. After four years or so, a piece of land would no longer grow tobacco, but it could grow corn for a few more years. Then the plot was abandoned and a new one was started.

The Virginians learned this easygoing style of farming from the Indians. It made sense in Virginia, where land was plentiful and workers were scarce. It was certainly not an English system. In England, fields were carefully groomed and tended.

The price of tobacco fell in the 1630's, and so some Virginians began to raise cattle and hogs. They used another easygoing method called **pasture farming.** In pasture farming, cattle or hogs are turned loose. They find their own food and generally take care of themselves.

Some of the first colonists in Virginia had tried pasture farming. However, Indians took some of the cattle and hogs, and wolves ate the rest. By the 1630's, however, the Virginians had pushed the Indians farther west. The settlers built a great fence to keep wolves from entering the settled area. Then they turned their animals loose. The animals multiplied far faster than Virginia's human population.

There were some pasture farmers in England. But pasture farming in the Virginia style needed acres of open land. Virginia had far more open land than England.

▶**2.** What is a diversified economy?

Family Life

What made Virginia most unlike England? Perhaps its lack of women. In 1625, there were four adult men in Virginia for every adult woman.

In its earliest years, Virginia was in part a military outpost. As the colony became more of a community, women arrived in greater numbers. In 1619, for example, the company sent over a shipload of women.

However, the spread of tobacco farming helped keep down the number of women in Virginia. English women did not work in the fields. So people seeking indentured servants preferred men. In the 1650's, there were still about three men to every woman in the colony. Without women, family life suffered, and few children were born.

Virginians died at a younger age than people in England. A woman born in Virginia in the 1600's could expect to die in her late 30's. A man could expect to live 9 years longer.

When adults died young, their children, if they had any, became orphans. A third of the children in one section of Virginia were orphans by age eighteen.

Widows and widowers often remarried. If their second spouse died, they married a third time. The resulting families became very complicated. Sometimes they included children with no surviving natural parent. Children had to grow up fast. They had to protect any property they had inherited.

▶**3.** In what ways did family life in Virginia differ from that in England?

Patterns of Power

As the colonists of Virginia spread out from Jamestown, local government became very important and powerful. In 1634, the Virginia General Assembly took the important step of setting up **county courts** as local governments. They included justices of the peace, sheriffs, and some other officials.

Gradually the county courts took on more and more work that had once been done by the governor and the General Assembly. They heard minor legal cases, settled estates, even saw to it that bridges and ferries were repaired. In short, a good part of the day-to-day concerns of the people of Virginia were handled by the county courts. It became a custom in Virginia that young men of important families learned the ropes of government in the county courts. Some then went on to serve in the House of Burgesses.

Those leaders were very different from the gentlemen who first ruled Virginia. The new leaders were tough, self-made men. They not only survived the harsh life in early Virginia but also succeeded there.

Those leaders showed that something important had happened in Virginia. Power had settled at a different place in English America than in Spanish America. Power in Virginia was local, in the General Assembly and in the county courts.

▶**4.** Why is it important that power in Virginia was local power?

Reviewing Section V

Identify diversified economy, pasture farming, county courts

Questions to Answer
1. Why was the Virginia Company unable to give its colony a diversified economy?
2. In what ways was life in Virginia different from life in England?

A Question to Think About How were the leaders of early Virginia different from leaders in the Spanish Empire?

IMPROVE YOUR READING
Problem/Solution

All of us at various stages of our lives are faced with *problems*. Our natural action is to try to *solve* our problems.

Chapter 3 describes many problems involved in the settling of Virginia. Various attempts were made to solve those problems. The activity that follows is designed to help you understand the problems and solutions that were discussed in this chapter.

The column at the upper right lists problems and the column below it lists some solutions. Your task is to match the appropriate solution to each of the problems. Number your paper from 1 to 5. Next to each number, write the letter of the statement that represents the solution to the problem. For example, solution e is the solution used to solve problem 1. If necessary, reread sections of Chapter 3 to complete this exercise.

Problems

1. The settlers had little they could sell for profit.
2. There were insufficient funds to start a colony.
3. The Virginia Company was poorly managed.
4. The first settlers refused to work hard.
5. Conflict existed between Powhatan and the settlers.

Solutions

a. Captain John Smith made the settlers work to eat.
b. The Virginia Company of London was funded by investors.
c. The marriage of Pocahontas to John Smith helped solve this problem.
d. The Crown took control of the colony.
e. John Rolfe learned to grow mild tobacco in Virginia.

CHAPTER 3 REVIEW

Vocabulary Check

Write the letter for the definition of each numbered item.

1. Indenture
2. Royal charter
3. House of Burgesses
4. Joint-stock
5. Cash crop

a. Agreement between a servant and a master
b. Written legal grant of privileges
c. The part of the Virginia General Assembly elected by the colonists
d. Enabled the colony to make money
e. Common fund invested by a trading company

Fact Check

Write the name of the person described in each of the phrases below.

1. Sponsored a settlement on Roanoke Island
2. Took command of Jamestown
3. Grew mild tobacco in Virginia
4. Daughter of Powhatan
5. Led Indians against the English

Skills Check

Use the map on page 49 to answer the following questions.

1. Which rivers are labeled on the map?
2. What boundaries are shown?
3. Would you describe the mouths of the James and York rivers as large or small?
4. How many miles long is Chesapeake Bay?
5. What year was Williamsburg founded?

Time Check

On your paper, write the numbers of the following events in proper chronological order.

1. The Charter of 1612 gives power over the colony to the Virginia Company's shareholders.
2. Jamestown is founded.
3. Opechancanough attacks the settlements for the last time.
4. The Virginia Company wins a charter to settle Virginia.
5. The first settlement at Roanoke Island is started.

Think and Write

1. How was life in Virginia different from the colonists' expectations?
2. What did the Virginia Company learn from John Smith's rule?
3. What incentives to work did the Virginia Company give colonists after 1618?
4. Why did power become local in Virginia?
5. Why was the high price of tobacco both good and bad for colonists in Virginia?

Chapter 4

Settling New England

This reconstruction of Plymouth shows some of the buildings as they probably appeared about seven years after the colony was founded.

Only harsh laws could make Virginians work together. That was not the case in the next colonies the English settled, those of New England. The people who founded the New England colonies were Puritans. Their religious beliefs made life in their settlements very different from life in Virginia. Yet the patterns of power in Virginia and New England were remarkably alike.

The first group of Puritans who came to North America founded Plymouth Colony. Another group settled the Massachusetts Bay Colony. The Puritans also built the new colonies of Rhode Island, Connecticut, and New Haven. Some people moved to those colonies by choice. Others were banished by the Puritan leaders of the older colonies. This chapter tells the stories of those colonies. It explains how the Puritans' religious beliefs helped to make their colonies thriving places. It also describes the ways of life and forms of government they created.

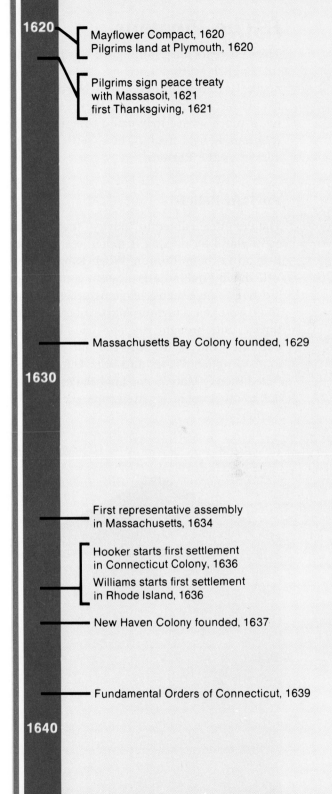

1620

Mayflower Compact, 1620
Pilgrims land at Plymouth, 1620

Pilgrims sign peace treaty with Massasoit, 1621
first Thanksgiving, 1621

Massachusetts Bay Colony founded, 1629

1630

First representative assembly in Massachusetts, 1634

Hooker starts first settlement in Connecticut Colony, 1636
Williams starts first settlement in Rhode Island, 1636

New Haven Colony founded, 1637

Fundamental Orders of Connecticut, 1639

1640

I. The Puritans

Thirteen years after Jamestown was founded, the English started a second colony farther north. Its founders did not go to North America in search of gold. Instead, they were seeking a place where they could practice their religious beliefs freely. Those settlers were known as the **Puritans.**

Puritan Beliefs

The Puritans wanted to "purify" the Church of England by making it much less like the Roman Catholic Church. When King Henry VIII made England a Protestant country, he did not change many religious practices. In 1553, his older daughter, Mary, inherited the throne. She brought England back into the Catholic Church. Because she put to death many English Protestants, the Queen was called Bloody Mary. Some English Protestants fled to other countries in Europe, such as the Netherlands.

The Pilgrims were opposed to the elaborate church services such as the one shown here.

When Mary died in 1558, her Protestant half-sister, Elizabeth, came to the throne. Then the Protestants who had fled England were able to return. Many of them wanted to make the English church like the Protestant churches of the Netherlands. The most extreme of those reformers were given the name Puritan by their enemies.

The Puritan reformers wanted a far simpler church than that of the Catholics. They wanted to do away with many levels of church authority, such as bishops. They wanted plain church services in buildings without statues or paintings. They thought believers should spend time reflecting on God and the Bible.
▶**1.** What reforms did the Puritans seek?

The Covenant

For Puritans, the church was a community of believers, not a building. They had a very definite idea of what made up that community. God, they believed, had divided all humans into the saved and the damned. Those who were saved were God's "saints."

On Earth, the saints formed a church by coming together and agreeing to live in a Christian community. Its members promised to help each other fulfill God's will. They called that agreement a **covenant.** When a new church was formed, its members wrote a new covenant. The damned had no place in such a church. So the Puritans did not welcome everyone into their churches.
▶**2.** What was the Puritan covenant?

Separatists

The Puritan notion of a church was very different from the Church of England. Anyone born in England was presumed to be a member of the Church of England. No one was excluded, not even terrible sinners. Many English Puritans felt they could not remain within the Church of England. To live according to their beliefs, those Puritans—known as **Separatists**—thought that they had to break away from the Church of England. They wanted to found their own, separate churches. Other Puritans thought it was still possible to remain within the Church of England. They were nonseparatists.

▶**3.** Why did separatists feel they had to break with the Church of England?

Reviewing Section I

Identify Puritans, covenant, Separatists

Questions to Answer
1. What were some of the main beliefs of the Puritans?
2. Why was the covenant an important Puritan idea?

A Question to Think About How do you think the Puritans got along with the other English people?

II. Plymouth

The separatists wanted to live where they could worship God according to their beliefs. For that reason, some went to the Netherlands first. Later they founded Plymouth Colony in what is now Massachusetts. Those separatists became known as **Pilgrims**, or people who make a long journey to do God's will.

Starting for Virginia

In the Netherlands, the Pilgrims lived as a community under a covenant. They stayed first in the city of Amsterdam and then in Leyden (līd′ n). The Dutch mostly left them alone, which was all the Pilgrims asked.

As time went on, however, some Pilgrims feared that their children were becoming too much like the Dutch. They were forgetting the English language, forgetting even that their parents were English. Their children were also failing to honor the Sabbath and committing other sins.

What could be done? The church members fasted and prayed for God's guidance. In the end, many of the English separatists at Leyden decided to solve the problem by making a new life in North America.

Because they had little money and few influential friends, the Pilgrims did not have complete control over their journey. They reached an agreement with a group of London merchants who promised the Pilgrims the support they needed to found a settlement in Virginia. The merchants also promised the Pilgrims that they could govern themselves without interference from England.

The Pilgrims sailed for Virginia in September 1620 aboard the small ship *Mayflower*. However, many of the 101 passengers on the *Mayflower* were not Puritans. Those men and women had been hired by the merchants. Some were not even people of very good character. The Pilgrims worried that they would not be able to make their colony an orderly Christian community.

▶**1.** How did the Pilgrims obtain funds for their colony in North America?

The Mayflower Compact

The Pilgrims worried more about the non-Puritan settlers when it became clear that the *Mayflower* would not land in Virginia at all. The ship was off course, and it would

Several groups of Pilgrims moved to the city of Leyden in the Netherlands. There they were free to worship as they pleased.

land farther north in the area John Smith had named New England. Some of the passengers declared that no one had power over them outside Virginia and that on shore they would act as they chose.

Then the Pilgrim leaders used their experience with making covenants. They drafted a solemn agreement called the **Mayflower Compact.** It was signed in the ship's cabin by 41 adults. It set up a government and proclaimed the loyalty of the new colony to the king.

Over half the signers came from Leyden. They managed to have one of their number, John Carver, chosen as governor. When Carver died the next spring, the new governor, William Bradford, was also a separatist. Bradford was elected governor of Plymouth Colony for 30 of the next 35 years.

▶ **2.** What was the Mayflower Compact?

In Their Own Words

The Mayflower Compact, 1620

In the name of God, Amen. We whose names are [written below] . . . having undertaken . . . a voyage to plant the first colony in the Northern parts of Virginia, do . . . solemnly and mutually in the presence of God, and of one another, convenant and combine ourselves together into a civil body politic; for our better ordering and preservation . . . [and under that covenant shall make] such just and equal laws . . . as shall be thought most [fitting and convenient] for the general good of the colony, unto which we promise all due submission and obedience.

The First Winter

The *Mayflower* reached Cape Cod in November 1620. The Pilgrims sent out parties to explore the shore. They finally selected Plymouth harbor for their settlement. They started building a town there in late December.

The winter of 1620 and 1621 was warmer than most. Still, about 50 of the settlers died. Some suffered from scurvy—a sickness caused by a lack of fresh fruit and vegetables. Others died of diseases brought on by their long days at sea, poor diet, and lack of good shelter on land.

▶**3.** Why did many Pilgrims die during the first winter in New England?

Chief Massasoit and Squanto The few Indians of the area helped the Pilgrims survive. The Indian population was small because many Indians of the Plymouth area had died in a smallpox epidemic between 1617 and 1619 before the Pilgrims arrived.

In the spring of 1621, the Pilgrims made a peace treaty with Massasoit (mas′ ə soit), leader of the Wampanoag (wäm pə nō′ ag), the strongest group of the nearby Indians. The agreement was honored by both sides for more than a half a century.

When Massasoit first visited Plymouth, he brought with him an Indian named Squanto (skwön′ tō). Squanto had been captured by an English sea captain in 1614 but managed to escape before he could be sold into slavery. Squanto spoke English and served as the Pilgrims' interpreter. He showed the Pilgrims how to plant corn and where to fish. He was so helpful to the Pilgrims that Governor Bradford described him as ''a special instrument sent of God.''

▶**4.** Who were Chief Massasoit and Squanto?

The First Thanksgiving The Pilgrims had only one winter of starving time. After that,

This statue of Massasoit stands on a Pilgrim burial ground in Plymouth, Massachusetts.

they did much better. By the late fall of 1621, after their harvest was in, the Pilgrims had a great feast to give thanks—the first Thanksgiving. They were joined in the feast by Massasoit and some 90 Indian men, who presented the governor with 5 deer they had killed for the feast.

▶**5.** When was the first Thanksgiving?

Reviewing Section II

Identify Plymouth Colony, Pilgrims, Leyden, *Mayflower*, Mayflower Compact, Massasoit, Wampanoag, Squanto

Questions to Answer
1. What made the Pilgrims different from the Virginia settlers?
2. What was the importance of the Mayflower Compact?

A Question to Think About Why did Chief Massasoit and Squanto help the Pilgrims?

67

III. Massachusetts Bay

In 1630, another group of Puritans started a new settlement in New England called the Massachusetts Bay Colony. The people who settled the Massachusetts Bay Colony were very different from the simple country folk who went to Plymouth. They were better educated, including among them men who had studied at England's Cambridge University. They were, on the whole, wealthier as well. Most important yet, they had friends in high places within the English government.

Map Study *What does the map show? What town is closest to the Merrimack River? How far is Attleboro from Boston?*

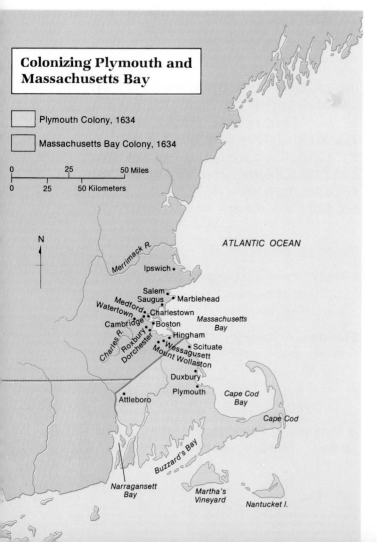

Colonizing Plymouth and Massachusetts Bay

Plymouth Colony, 1634

Massachusetts Bay Colony, 1634

0   25   50 Miles
0 25   50 Kilometers

N

ATLANTIC OCEAN

Merrimack R.
Ipswich
Salem
Saugus   Marblehead
Medford
Watertown   Charlestown
Cambridge   Boston   Massachusetts Bay
Charles R.   Roxbury
Dorchester   Hingham
Wessagusett
Mount Wollaston   Scituate
Duxbury
Attleboro   Plymouth   Cape Cod Bay
Cape Cod
Buzzard's Bay
Narragansett Bay   Martha's Vineyard
Nantucket I.

Why They Came

The Massachusetts Bay colonists were Puritans just as the Pilgrims were. They were not, however, separatists. They had found ways to follow their beliefs within the Church of England. By the late 1620's, however, that was becoming harder to do. King Charles I, who came to the throne in 1625, did all he could to harass the Puritans. Some Puritans feared that before long they would not be able to practice their beliefs in England.

The Puritans who went to Massachusetts Bay in 1630 did not, however, do so only to be able to follow their beliefs. They wanted to build a model community to show how much better the world would be if people lived by Puritan beliefs. They wanted their colony to be a first step toward changing the world, or at least the English world.

"We shall be as a City upon a Hill," the first governor of Massachusetts Bay said of the colony. "The eyes of all people are upon us." He meant that people would watch the way the colonists acted. Their colony would be an example to others.

▶**1.** Why did the Puritans want to start a model colony?

The Massachusetts Bay Company

Because the Puritans had money and support in high places, they were able to control their journey and their colony. In that way, they differed from the Pilgrims.

The Puritans formed their own company, the **Massachusetts Bay Company,** for which they managed to get a royal charter in March 1629. That charter gave them a right to the lands they wanted to settle. It also gave the company the right to govern any colony it established.

The charter alone did not give the Puritans much confidence in their independence. After all, the Crown had taken back the Virginia Company's charter only five years earlier.

Sometime in the summer or fall of 1629, a group of Puritan leaders decided to take the charter with them to North America, some 3,000 miles from the king. Then there would be no company in England for the Puritans' enemies to take over. In fact, the company and the colony became the same thing.

The Massachusetts Bay Company left a small office in London to handle its financial affairs and to keep the king from figuring out what it had done. Not until 1634 did the Crown learn that the company and charter were no longer in England. Then it started proceedings to take back the charter. It took the Crown 50 years, however, to revoke the charter.

▶**2.** Why did the Puritans take the charter with them to their new colony?

A Good Beginning

Unlike the Pilgrims, the Massachusetts Bay Puritans were well equipped and well prepared for their voyage to New England. They left England in March 1630 in a fleet of 11 ships—7 to carry some 700 passengers and the others to carry their supplies. Clearly that was not a penny-pinching operation. The Puritans sailed in March so they could arrive in New England while there was still time to plant a crop for harvesting in the fall. They brought with them a supply of limes so they would not suffer from scurvy.

▶**3.** What showed that the voyage to Massachusetts Bay was well planned?

The Puritans' Vision

All the immigrants of 1630 were Puritans. They went where they had planned to go, to

John Winthrop was governor of the Massachusetts Bay Colony for many years.

the territory for which they had legal title. They carried with them a charter that was the basis for the colony's government. The Puritans even selected a governor before they sailed. They chose John Winthrop, a gentleman trained in the law and with some experience in government.

Winthrop had a very clear idea of what the Puritan colony should be. He outlined his ideas in a sermon he gave on board the ship on which he sailed to Massachusetts. The people of the colony would not be equal, he said. Instead, some people would be more important than others. That was how God wanted things, Winthrop thought.

Winthrop told the colonists that they were to be "knit together" by a "bond of love" as were the early Christians. They must always think of the community, not of themselves. If the poor needed help, the rich were to give that help. That was part of their sacred covenant with God. If they broke their covenant

This map shows some of the early towns New Englanders had started along the Piscataqua River in New Hampshire and Maine by about 1670.

and looked only to their own interests, then "the Lord will surely break out in wrath against us," Winthrop said.

▶**4.** What did Winthrop feel was the Puritan covenant with God?

The Founding of Towns

Winthrop and the other Massachusetts Bay leaders expected that the new colony's people would live together in one place called Boston. The Reverend John Cotton of Boston, England, had preached to the Puritans before they sailed. He so pleased them that they decided to name their new town in his honor. However, they had no idea where the town would be. So their first task in America was to find a place to build Boston.

▶**5.** Why did the Puritans decide to name their new town Boston?

Where Was Boston? The fleet's first ships arrived in June 1630 at Salem. Five days later the search began for a permanent site for the colony.

The leaders could not agree where to settle, and so they decided to set up a temporary camp on a narrow peninsula of land between the Charles and Mystic rivers. It later became Charlestown. Then disease broke out in the camp. Soon after, there were rumors that the French were about to attack the settlement. So the leaders gave orders to leave.

From late July to September, small groups of colonists left the camp at Charlestown, each with one or two important Puritan leaders. They spread out, founding what became seven towns along the Massachusetts Bay and the rivers that emptied into it. The settlement on the Shawmut peninsula became Boston.

Anne Bradstreet, America's first poet, was born Anne Dudley in Northhampton, England, in 1612. At seven, her family moved to Sempringham, Lincolnshire, where her father, Thomas Dudley, managed the vast estates of the young Earl of Lincoln. Her father's high position influenced Anne greatly. So did his Puritan beliefs. As a young girl, Anne claimed to have suffered for her "vanity and the follies of her youth."

Thomas Dudley carefully supervised his daughter's education which took place at home. She recalled the busy pace of her schooling many years later, noting that "When I was about seven . . . I had at one time eight tutors . . . in language, music, dancing." As she grew older, Anne also turned for an education to the hundreds of books in the earl's library.

At 16, Anne Dudley married Simon Bradstreet. As a young man, Simon had been taken into the family of the earl. He had then studied at Cambridge University before becoming the earl's steward, or manager. Like the Dudleys, Simon Bradstreet was also a Puritan.

In 1630, two years after her marriage, Anne Bradstreet, her husband, and her parents sailed for New England with other Puritan families. On board the ship, her father was named deputy governor of the Massachusetts Bay Company. Her husband was already an official.

The Bradstreets settled for a while in Cambridge and then Ipswich before moving to North Andover. Anne Bradstreet accepted her new life in the true spirit of a pioneer woman, although at first she found "new manners, at which my heart rose."

It was at her home in North Andover that Anne Bradstreet wrote many of the poems that made her famous in later years. It was never her intention to publish those poems. However, her brother-in-law John Woodridge liked her poetry so well that he took the manuscript with

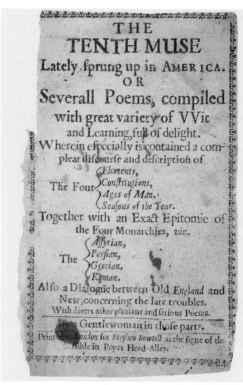

him to London. There, in 1650, without her knowledge, he had it published under the title *The Tenth Muse Lately Sprung Up in America.*

Anne Bradstreet's first collection of poetry tells little of her New England experiences. It is in a later collection, published after her death, that she paints a picture of the New England landscape and her life as a Puritan woman, wife, and devoted mother. Adrienne Rich, a present-day poet, has this to say about Anne Bradstreet's work: "To have written these, the first good poems in America, while rearing eight children, lying frequently sick, and keeping house at the edge of a wilderness, was to have managed a poet's range and extensions within confines as severe as [those within which] any other American poet wrote."

Anne Bradstreet died in North Andover in the fall of 1672. She was 60 years old.

Once the colonists left, there was no bringing them back. Boston became the capital because it was easy for people who lived in other towns nearby to get there by water.

▶**6.** Why did Boston become the capital of the Massachusetts Bay Colony?

More New Towns As the persecution of Puritans in England grew worse, other Puritans fled to Massachusetts. About 20,000 arrived between 1630 and 1643. They could not all find homes and adequate farmland in Boston. So some moved to other towns or founded new ones.

The colony's leaders tried to limit the scattering of its people. They wanted to keep all the Puritans close to one another so they could be "knit together." However, the Massachusetts Bay colonists continued to move.

Meanwhile Plymouth Plantation was having much the same problem. As Plymouth prospered, its people also spread out in search of more and better lands. In the 70 years that Plymouth remained an independent colony, its people founded 21 towns. In 1691, Plymouth became part of Massachusetts Bay Colony.

▶**7.** Why did some Puritans want to start new towns?

Town Covenants

The people moving away from Boston and Plymouth did not just scatter, however. In Virginia, settlers founded individual farms or plantations along the rivers that emptied into Chesapeake Bay. In New England, settlers moved in groups and founded towns. Each of those towns was a closely knit community in its early years.

Settlers often formally bound themselves together under **town covenants** that were much like the covenants that church members made.

Those town covenants might say how many families the town would accept, how its lands would be divided, or how disputes would be settled. They always made clear that the settlers had come together to perform God's will and that they intended the towns to be made up of Christians living in peace with one another.

The founders of New England did not intend their towns to be short-term affairs. They did not expect, like the first Virginians, to make a quick fortune in North America and then return to England. The Puritans were building for the future.

▶**8.** What were town covenants?

Government for a Colony of Towns

The colony's charter defined its first government. At its head was the governor and a set of officials who served as his advisers. They were called the **Court of Assistants.** The governor and assistants ruled the colony alone for its first year.

The charter also provided for a **general court,** a meeting of all the company's shareholders with the governor and Court of Assistants. As the colony grew and as people spread out in towns across Massachusetts, the colony's government had to change.

▶**9.** What sort of government did the colony's charter set up?

Representative Government In 1631, the General Court made some important decisions. It ruled that only members of covenanted churches could become **freemen** of Massachusetts, that is, voting members of its government. However, not all the freemen could meet together in the General Court. There were just too many of them.

So, in 1634, the General Court was changed again. Instead of all the freemen meeting together, the freemen elected two representatives, or deputies, for each town in Massachusetts. In that way, the General Court became a **representative assembly**, similar to the House of Burgesses in Virginia. Today the legislature of Massachusetts is still called the General Court.

▶**10.** Why did the General Court become a representative assembly?

A Two-House Legislature In the 1630's, about 20 deputies from the towns met in the General Court with the assistants and the governor. Then, in 1644, the assistants and deputies got into a heated battle over who owned a pig that had been wandering through Boston. The assistants sided with a rich and unpopular merchant. The deputies sided with a woman who owned a boarding house where many deputies stayed while attending the General Court. The argument would not have been important except that this battle had lasting effects.

The deputies became so upset over the issue that from 1644 on they met apart from the Court of Assistants. The General Court became a **bicameral** (bī kam′ ər al) **legislature;** that is, it included two separate groups, or houses. Although the deputies and the assistants met separately, both houses had to agree before any law was passed by the General Court. Thus the power of the deputies became equal to that of the assistants.

Later other colonies went through much the same process, and bicameral legislatures became common. A growing sense of importance on the part of the representatives was always the cause of that development. In early Massachusetts, the deputies' sense of importance came from the growing importance of the towns they represented.

▶**11.** How did the General Court become a bicameral legislature?

Town Governments The governor and assistants gave the towns many responsibilities. They found the towns very helpful in governing the people.

When the General Court began meeting regularly, it too gave more powers to the towns. Some of the tasks given to the towns were small. Town governments inspected fencing, for example, and decided how many pigs a family could keep. Towns were also responsible for larger tasks such as collecting taxes and defending themselves and the colony. More important, the colony granted land to the towns and said the towns could decide how to divide that land among their people.

The towns exercised those rights and responsibilities through **town meetings**, in which all or most of the town's adult males voted. The decisions made in town meetings were carried out by a smaller group of elected officials, the **selectmen.**

▶**12.** What was the role of the town meeting?

Reviewing Section III

Identify Massachusetts Bay Company, John Winthrop, Boston, Salem, Charlestown, town covenants, Court of Assistants, General Court, freemen, representative assembly, bicameral legislature, town meetings, selectmen

Questions to Answer
1. Why did the Puritan leaders want the settlers to stay close together?
2. Describe the government of the Massachusetts Bay Colony.

A Question to Think About Why did the Massachusetts Bay Company decide to take its charter to New England?

IV. Three More Colonies

Three new colonies quickly grew from Massachusetts. They were founded for different reasons. The colony of Rhode Island was begun by people banished from Massachusetts Bay. Puritans who felt cramped in Massachusetts Bay started one colony in Connecticut. Others who wanted a stricter form of Puritan rule began a colony at New Haven.

Rhode Island

The Puritans of early Massachusetts had come to America to found a colony of like-minded people. They did not believe that they had to welcome everyone to their colony. They did not have to keep people who disagreed with them on important matters. If people did, they could leave. If they refused, the colony's government might force them out.

▶**1.** What happened to people who disagreed with the Puritans?

Map Study *Name four English colonies shown on the map. Name five settlements that were started along the Connecticut River.*

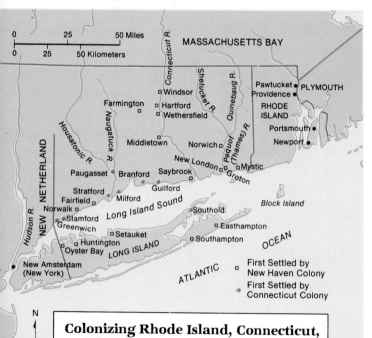

Colonizing Rhode Island, Connecticut, and New Haven

Roger Williams Roger Williams disagreed with the Puritans. He was an educated man who had studied at Cambridge University in England. He also held many ideas that were unacceptable to the Puritans of Massachusetts.

Williams first aired his views in Plymouth. There he argued that the land still belonged to the Indians. The Plymouth people did not want to hear that. Williams was asked to leave Plymouth.

Next Williams went to Boston. There he took up another cause. No government, he said, should interfere with the practice of religion. All who lived in the Bay Colony were required to attend Puritan services. Williams did not think that was right.

The Puritan leaders considered Williams's views dangerous. Despite their warnings, Williams refused to be quiet. So the leaders decided that he would have to leave.

Officials intended to send him back to England, but Williams slipped away to Narragansett Bay. There, with his family and followers, he founded the town of Providence in what became Rhode Island Colony in 1636. It was the only New England colony where all religions, including Judaism, were allowed to exist side by side.

▶**2.** Which was the only New England colony to allow freedom of religion?

Anne Hutchinson Anne Hutchinson was another difficult Puritan. She claimed that God spoke to his saints directly. The Puritan leaders taught that God spoke to people through the Bible, their ministers, and their public officials. The idea that God spoke to individuals directly was not only wrong but also dangerous, since such people would obey what they said God told them, not the laws of church and state.

Hutchinson first expressed her ideas before small groups of women. Then men started attending her meetings. For all practical purposes, Hutchinson was acting like a minister. Women were not supposed to lead meetings. For a woman to step out of her place in the social order and to act like a man was thought shocking and dangerous.

In November 1637, the General Court banished Anne Hutchinson from the colony. She was allowed to stay through the winter because she was expecting a child. Hutchinson and her family made their way to Rhode Island the next spring. There she helped found the town of Portsmouth.

▶ **3.** Why were the teachings and behavior of Anne Hutchinson not acceptable to the Puritan leaders?

The New Colony Even though the Rhode Islanders were tolerant of different religions, they had trouble getting along with each other. So groups broke away and founded new towns. By about 1645, there were four towns: Providence, Portsmouth, Newport, and Warwick. Together they included no more than 200 families.

In 1644, Roger Williams secured permission from England for the towns to form a union and rule themselves. But power in Rhode Island, even more than in the Massachusetts Bay Colony, stayed in the towns. Only the towns had the right to propose laws. The towns also had to approve every new law before it went into effect.

▶ **4.** How powerful were town governments in Rhode Island?

Connecticut and New Haven

While some members of the Bay Colony went south to Rhode Island, others left for the rich lands of the Connecticut River Valley.

Anne Hutchinson was forced to leave Massachusetts Bay because of her religious beliefs.

One of the first groups to settle in Connecticut Colony moved from Massachusetts Bay in 1636 with their minister, Thomas Hooker. Many other groups followed.

▶ **5.** Who was Thomas Hooker?

The Connecticut Colony At first, the Connecticut settlements were governed as part of Massachusetts Bay. In 1639, three towns— Hartford, Windsor, and Wethersfield—agreed to the **Fundamental Orders of Connecticut,** a covenant that set up a central government for the infant colony. Again, power remained first and foremost in the people of the towns.

▶ **6.** What were the Fundamental Orders of Connecticut?

The New Haven Colony The Fundamental Orders did not cover all the settlements that would eventually be part of Connecticut Colony. Farther south was New Haven, a community founded in 1637 by a group of very strict English Puritans. They thought Massachusetts Bay was too permissive.

Before long, New Haven also gave birth to a series of new towns—Milford, Guilford, Stamford, Fairfield, Medford, Greenwich, Branford. In 1643, they came together to form New Haven Colony.

▶7. Who started New Haven Colony?

Reviewing Section IV

Identify Roger Williams, Narragansett Bay, Providence, Anne Hutchinson, Thomas Hooker, the Fundamental Orders of Connecticut, New Haven Colony

Questions to Answer
1. Why did the Puritan leaders consider Roger Williams's ideas dangerous?
2. For what reason was Providence founded? Connecticut Colony? New Haven?

A Question to Think About Why did the Puritan leaders believe they should banish those who disagreed with them?

V. The Place Called New England

By the middle of the seventeenth century, there were five colonies in New England—Plymouth, Massachusetts Bay, Rhode Island, Connecticut, and New Haven. Each had its unique traits, but all had much in common. They had all been founded by Puritans of one sort or another. Puritanism was not just a religion. It was a way of life.

How the New Englanders Lived

The way of life in Puritan New England was in many ways very different from that in Virginia. The Puritans' way of life helped them survive and then to prosper.

First of all, the Puritan settlers moved in groups and built towns as the Virginians did not. The Puritans stayed together not by force of military rule but by force of the covenants they made with God and with each other.

Building towns helped the New Englanders. Towns were easier to defend than the lonely farms and plantations started by the Virginians. The Puritans could work together to build houses and clear land. They were able to help each other in times of trouble.

New Englanders shared more than work. They shared their material wealth, too. God made people wealthy, the Puritans taught, and so they could do good for others.

The Puritans even had laws enforcing just prices, that is, prices that allowed people to buy what they needed without giving the seller too much profit. They had laws against charging high interest on loans because they did not think a lender should profit from a neighbor's need. Such laws became harder to enforce as time went on. In the beginning, however, they encouraged people to help one another much more than was done in Virginia. That helped New England survive its first, most difficult days.

▶1. How did Puritan rules help the colony survive?

Farming, Fishing, and Trading

New England quickly began to thrive. There was no labor problem in New England like that in Virginia. Puritans were eager to work. They believed God wanted them to work at the callings God gave them.

IMPROVE YOUR SKILLS
Map Reading: Direction

If you know one direction on a map, you can figure out all the others. A direction finder near the keys of the maps in this text points to the North Pole. South, of course, is opposite to north. When you face a map directly with north at the top, east is to your right. That leaves west, which is to your left. North, south, east, and west are the four cardinal directions.

Other directions are a combination of the four cardinal directions. The direction halfway between north and east is northeast. Northeast is an intermediate direction. The other intermediate directions are southeast, northwest, and southwest.

Use the map below to answer the following questions.

1. What country is directly east of Philadelphia?
2. Spain is in what direction from England?
3. What direction is the Ivory Coast of Africa from New York?
4. What direction is England from Guadeloupe?
5. What direction is Charleston from Boston?

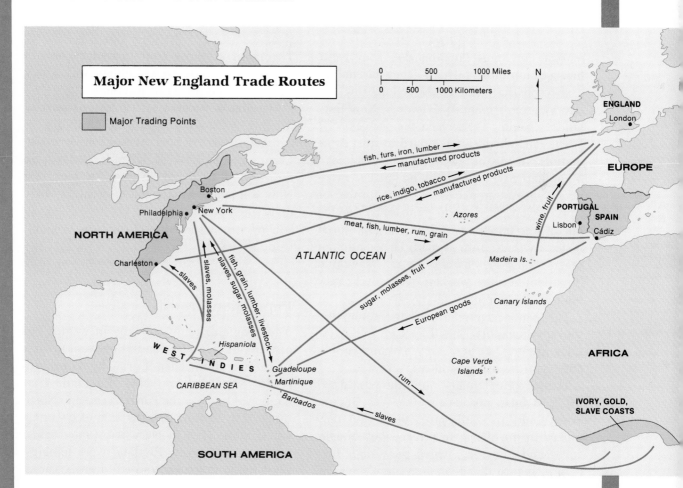

Major New England Trade Routes

The Triangular Trade

For many years, historians called the major trade routes of New England merchants the Triangular Trade. They meant that the pattern the trade routes made on a map looked like a triangle. One side of the triangle was a line showing rum going from New England to Africa. The second side of the triangle showed slaves going from Africa to the West Indies. The triangle was completed by a line showing molasses and sugar going from the West Indies to New England.

Today historians say that New England trade routes looked more like the map on page 77.

Ships sailed back and forth among the islands of the West Indies, trading fish, fruit, lumber, spices, and slaves. A ship's captain tried never to sail anywhere without a cargo that could be sold at a profit. Sometimes the traders went to England. Sometimes they brought slaves from Africa directly to South Carolina or the Chesapeake area. Where New England traders sailed depended on many things, such as the weather, how much credit they had, or where they saw a chance to make a quick profit.

What did most Puritans do? They were, first and foremost, farmers. They had no one cash crop that they could sell in England like Virginia's tobacco. However, New Englanders could at least feed themselves.

The Puritans also tried hard to start some **manufacturing** but without much success. Manufacturing means making finished products from raw materials, such as lumber or iron. It generally made more sense for the Puritans to **import** manufactured goods, that is, to buy them from abroad. They could not make such goods as cheaply as they could buy them because workers' wages were very high in the colonies.

The New Englanders needed something they could **export,** or sell abroad, to pay for their imports. At first, they had furs to sell, and then the fishing industry grew.

The New Englanders found they could sell fish and farm produce in the West Indies. They could also sell slaves there that they picked up in Africa. In return, they bought sugar and molasses, which they made into rum either to drink or to trade elsewhere.

The point of those complicated exchanges was to allow the New Englanders to buy manufactured goods in England.

Merchants became an important part of life in New England, and Boston rapidly became the largest port in English America. **Commerce,** or large-scale trade, thrived. So did agriculture and fishing. In fact, the New Englanders managed to create a fairly diversified economy.

▶**2.** What was the point of the New England trade system?

Population Growth

New England grew not only in wealth but also in numbers. Its population went up first by immigration. Then it grew by natural increase—by births in New England. That happened because the Puritans came to North America in communities that included women and children. Two of every five of the original immigrants to New England were females. That made marriage and children possible.

Early New England women married young and often lived through their childbearing years. As a result, New England families were large. Families often had six or eight children. By 1643, around 20,000 immigrants had come to New England. By 1700, its population had grown to 90,000. By contrast, during the 1600's about 60,000 immigrants went to Virginia. Yet in 1700 its population was still about 60,000.

New England was a healthy place. In the 1600's, New Englanders often lived into their 60's and even into their 70's. That was about 10 years longer than people lived in England and 20 years longer than in Virginia. People lived so long, in fact, that New England can be said to have invented grandparents. No where else in the English world were children so likely to know their parents' parents.

New England's quick growth caused some problems. People settled first around town centers. Then they divided up land farther out. In time, some New England towns grew so large that many families had a long way to come for church services or town meetings. As a result, many towns split up. Each had its own town center and church. Some new towns were built when groups of young people moved to land on the **frontier,** land along the edge of a settled area.

▶**3.** Why did the population of New England grow?

Patterns of Power

The Crown did not have much power in early New England or much to say about the colonies' day-to-day affairs. Both the Virginia and New England colonies had central governments with representative assemblies. In both places, however, real power was at the local level, in the county courts of Virginia and the towns of New England. By the 1650's

This portrait of three New England children — David, Joanna, and Abigail Mason — was painted by an unknown Boston artist around 1670.

local government was becoming an American way of government.

▶**4.** What form of government was becoming the American way of government by the middle of the seventeenth century?

Reviewing Section V

Identify manufacturing, import, export, commerce, frontier

Questions to Answer
1. What did the New England colonies import? What did they export?
2. In what ways was the government of the Puritan colonies similar to that of Virginia?

A Question to Think About How do you think the system of local power in the colonies might lead to trouble?

IMPROVE YOUR READING
Main Idea and Details

As you read the first chapters of this book, you probably noticed that each chapter is organized in a similar way. Each chapter contains section headings, main headings, and subheadings. At the beginning of each chapter, the section headings are outlined for you.

Those various kinds of headings can help you to understand the chapter. By studying them, you quickly learn the chapter's *topics. Topic* means "subject matter."

Once you identify a topic, you should ask yourself, What, in general, does the author tell me about this topic? The answer to that question tells you the *main idea* of the section. In other words, a main idea is a general statement about a topic. Very specific statements about a topic are *details.*

For example, on page 65, the main heading is "The Mayflower Compact." That is a topic. In general, the author says that the Mayflower Compact was a solemn agreement that established a government and declared the new colony's loyalty to the king.

This section also tells *who* signed the compact (41 adults), *why* it was needed (to set up a government for the new colony), and *where* it was signed (in the *Mayflower's* cabin). Those are specific statements about the topic. So those statements are details.

In the following exercise, write the letter of the main idea for each group of statements. The topic and the page on which the topic begins are given.

1. "A Good Beginning" (p. 69)
   a. The Massachusetts Bay Puritans were well equipped and well prepared for their voyage to New England.
   b. The Puritans sailed in March so that they could arrive in New England while there was still time to plant a crop for harvesting in the fall.
   c. The Puritans brought with them a supply of limes so they would not suffer from scurvy.
2. "Roger Williams" (p. 74)
   a. Most people in Massachusetts expected residents to have similar ideas on religion.
   b. Puritan leaders considered Roger Williams's ideas dangerous.
   c. Roger Williams founded Providence in what became Rhode Island, where a variety of religious views were tolerated.
3. "Anne Hutchinson" (p. 74)
   a. Because she acted like a minister and said God talked directly to his saints, Anne Hutchinson was considered dangerous.
   b. Anne Hutchinson was banished from Massachusetts Bay Colony.
   c. Anne Hutchinson held meetings attended by men and women.
4. "Farming, Fishing, and Trading" (p. 76)
   a. Puritans were not successful at manufacturing.
   b. Puritans fed themselves well and imported manufactured goods.
   c. Puritans were eager to work.
5. "Population Growth" (p. 78)
   a. New England's population increased.
   b. Its population went up first by immigration.
   c. New England families were large.

CHAPTER 4 REVIEW

Vocabulary Check

On your paper, write the correct term to fill in the blank or blanks in each of the following sentences.

1. The written agreement between members of a Puritan church is a ____.
2. Puritan ____ felt they had to break away from the Church of England.
3. The assembly of Massachusetts is called the ____.
4. A legislature with two houses is called a ____ legislature.
5. The Puritans ____ manufactured goods from abroad and ____ fish and farm produce.

Fact Check

Match the name of the proper colony with each of the statements below.

Massachusetts Bay Colony
Plymouth Colony
Rhode Island Colony
Connecticut Colony
New Haven Colony

1. It was the first colony to offer freedom of religion.
2. Its founders wrote a compact setting up a government for their colony before landing in New England.
3. It was founded by a group of fairly wealthy Puritans who had connections with the English government.
4. The founders of this colony thought Massachusetts Bay Colony was not strict enough.
5. It was founded by a group of Puritans and their minister, Thomas Hooker.

Time Check

On a separate sheet of paper, write the letters of the following events in proper chronological order.

1. Providence is founded in Rhode Island.
2. Queen Mary begins her rule of England.
3. The first Thanksgiving is celebrated in New England.
4. The Massachusetts Bay Company receives a royal charter.
5. Hartford, Windsor, and Wethersfield adopt the Fundamental Orders of Connecticut.

Skills Check

Use the map on page 74 to answer the following questions.

1. What does the map show?
2. Which is the most northern colony shown on the map?
3. Find Southampton on Long Island. What town is northeast of Southampton? What body of water is south of it?
4. People from which colony first settled Middletown?
5. How far is Newport, Rhode Island, from Norwich, Connecticut?

Think and Write

1. Why did the Puritans live in towns?
2. Why was the development of towns important in shaping New England?
3. Describe the government of the Massachusetts Bay Colony in the 1640's.
4. How did the way of life created in the Massachusetts Bay Colony differ from that of early Virginia?
5. Describe how Rhode Island Colony came to be founded.

Chapter 5

Filling in the Coast

Baltimore was founded in 1729 as a trading center for nearby tobacco growers. This painting shows how the city had grown by 1752.

Both the Virginia and the Massachusetts Bay colonies were founded by trading companies. However, investors learned that founding colonies was not a good way to make money. By the time the next English colonies were founded, few investors were still willing to invest in such companies. Instead, the new colonies were begun by one person or a small group of people, the **proprietor** or proprietors.

The proprietors thought they could make money from their colonies. They could get other people to bring settlers to America by offering land in return. Then the proprietors could charge annual fees on that land, called quitrents. As the populations of the colonies grew, so would the proprietors' profits.

In this chapter you will read about five new proprietary colonies started between 1634 and 1681.

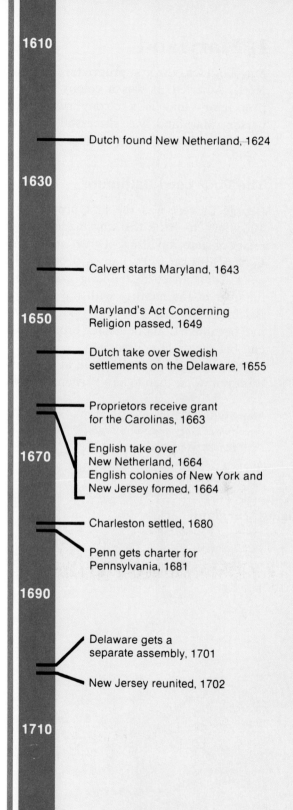

1610

Dutch found New Netherland, 1624

1630

Calvert starts Maryland, 1643

1650
Maryland's Act Concerning Religion passed, 1649

Dutch take over Swedish settlements on the Delaware, 1655

Proprietors receive grant for the Carolinas, 1663

1670
English take over New Netherland, 1664
English colonies of New York and New Jersey formed, 1664

Charleston settled, 1680

Penn gets charter for Pennsylvania, 1681

1690

Delaware gets a separate assembly, 1701

New Jersey reunited, 1702

1710

I. Maryland

Maryland was the first **proprietary colony** in North America. It was a colony run by a proprietor—that is a colony run by one person. Maryland was successful from the first.

The First Lord Baltimore

George Calvert was the first proprietor of Maryland. In 1619, the king made him secretary of state, a position of great importance. Calvert also sat in Parliament from 1609 to 1624. Then, in 1625, the king made him a member of the nobility with the title Lord Baltimore. By then, however, George Calvert had become a Catholic, which brought to an end his career in government.

To be a Catholic in England at that time was even worse than to be a Puritan. Catholics

Map Study *Which colony is farthest south? What direction is Maryland from Virginia? Name the bay that divides Maryland.*

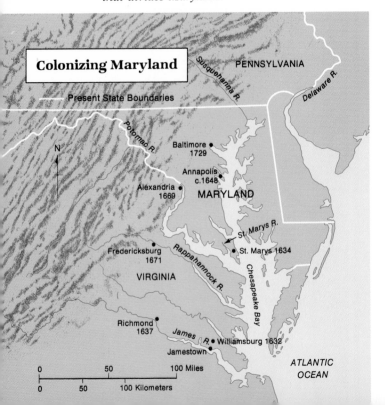

were suspected of disloyalty to the Crown. By law, English Catholics could not be lawyers or teachers or doctors. They could not hold public office. They could be punished severely for not attending the services of the Church of England.

Most Catholics were loyal to the English Crown. Kings James I and Charles I did not enforce the laws against them strictly. However, Catholics in England were hardly secure or comfortable.

When he left the king's service, Baltimore began to think about starting a settlement in North America. He wanted to set up a colony where Catholics could find peace and security. He also wanted to have a great estate in North America like those of the wealthiest nobles in England.

In 1628, Baltimore went to Newfoundland to start a settlement. However, the colony was threatened by the French, who also claimed Newfoundland. In addition, Baltimore found the winter too harsh. He decided to start again, farther south, in a warmer climate. He visited Virginia, but the Virginians made clear that they did not welcome Catholics. So Baltimore returned to England, determined to get a grant to unclaimed lands near Virginia.

▶ **1.** Why did Baltimore want to start a settlement in North America?

Maryland's Charter

Baltimore asked King Charles I to grant him lands in North America. In 1632, the king gave him a charter for 10 million acres north of Virginia. The new colony was named Maryland for the queen, Henrietta Maria.

Baltimore's charter gave him great power over the colony. He appointed all the officials of the colony. He, not the king, issued all legal orders. Baltimore could pardon criminals, impose taxes, and set up towns. He could even give noble titles to Marylanders he wanted to honor.

The charter did say that the colony's freemen, adult males who were not indentured servants, had to give their advice and consent to new laws. But only the proprietor could propose new laws.

Why did Baltimore receive such enormous powers? For one thing, he had a big hand in writing the charter. With years of experience in English government, he knew how to get the most rights with the fewest obligations in return. Second, the new colony was on the frontier of the English settlement. To its north was a Dutch colony. It was long understood in England that such outposts needed power so they could defend themselves. Finally, the king was generous because he knew and trusted Lord Baltimore.

▶2. Who had the power to make laws in Maryland under its charter?

The Second Lord Baltimore

By the time the Maryland charter was officially granted, Lord Baltimore had died. Therefore the charter was issued to his 26-year-old son, Cecilius Calvert, the second Lord Baltimore. Cecilius Calvert shared his father's ambitions and his Catholic religion.

Young Baltimore also seemed to know quite a bit about starting a settlement. He gave the first settlers especially large grants of land, with a bonus for those settlers who brought five or more people with them.

Young Baltimore told the colonists to plant food crops before starting any other projects so they could feed themselves. He wanted no starving time in Maryland. In that regard, he was successful, partly because the local

Cecilius Calvert, the second Lord Baltimore, founded Maryland in 1634.

Indians helped the first colonists by selling them corn.

Young Baltimore expected to sail with the first colonists who reached Maryland in 1634. However, he could not do so. He had to stay in England to defend his charter. Though he lived another 40 years, until 1675, he was never able to join the colonists. Baltimore had many enemies, and he was kept busy in England.

▶3. How did young Baltimore attract settlers?

The Proprietor's Troubles

The Virginians were among Baltimore's enemies. They fought against him and his charter because the territory of Maryland had once been part of the Virginia Company's lands.

The Maryland settlers also caused problems for Baltimore. Most of them were Protestants. They were not happy with the great powers of the proprietor or with the colony's other Catholic leaders. They used the advice-and-consent clause in the charter to insist on their right to have an assembly.

The assembly first met with the governor and his council in 1638. Right away it began questioning the proprietor's rights. Four years later the assembly tried to separate from the governor and the council. Maryland's assembly finally became bicameral in 1650.

▶4. What clause in the charter did Marylanders use to insist on an assembly?

Religious Conflicts Baltimore thought that Catholics and Protestants could live together in peace. He was disappointed. Catholics and Protestants became more and more hostile to each other.

To protect the colony's Catholic minority, Baltimore wrote Maryland's famous **Act Concerning Religion** of 1649. It promised that most Christians could practice their religion freely. The law did not apply to non-Christians, and even some Christians did not fit under its terms. The assembly, with a Protestant majority, approved the law after adding some amendments spelling out harsh punishments for offenses such as cursing or calling people heretics.

▶5. What were the provisions of the Act concerning Religion?

Civil War in England Maryland Protestants remained unhappy with Baltimore's power over the colony. Soon events in England made them think that they could overthrow the proprietor.

Charles I was not a popular king. He persecuted Puritans. He tried to govern without Parliament. In the 1640's, civil war broke out, that is a war between groups of English people. Puritans and the supporters of Parliament fought together against the forces of the king. The king was defeated, and in 1649 he was beheaded.

During the 1650's, the Puritans Oliver and Richard Cromwell ruled England. The Protestant Marylanders had good reason to think they could get English support to bring down Lord Baltimore. However, Maryland operated under its original charter for almost 40 years.

▶6. Who ruled England after the revolt against Charles I?

A Place like Virginia

In some ways, Maryland developed much as Virginia did. There, too, the settlers became avid tobacco farmers. There, too, the colonists tended to live in isolated farms spread along the rivers rather than to gather together in towns. Power in Maryland, as in Virginia, tended to settle in county courts.

The two colonies were so much alike that they formed, along with the northern parts of Carolina, a single social and economic section of the American colonies. It was known as the **Chesapeake.**

▶7. In what ways was Maryland similar to Virginia?

Reviewing Section I

Identify proprietary colony, George Calvert, Cecilius Calvert, Act Concerning Religion, King Charles I, Oliver and Richard Cromwell, Chesapeake

Questions to Answer
1. Why did Lord Baltimore have enemies?
2. Why were the Maryland settlers unhappy with Baltimore's charter?

A Question to Think About Did the Act Concerning Religion grow out of religious tolerance or intolerance?

II. The Carolinas

Thirty years passed before England began another great effort to settle the coast of North America. In the 1660's, the English people called Charles I's son to the throne. He became King Charles II. The country returned to peace and stability. Soon new proprietary grants were made.

The Carolina Proprietors

The first of the new king's land grants was the Carolina grant of 1663. Carolina had been named earlier by King Charles I to honor himself. King Charles II gave it to eight proprietors, all of whom had helped him to regain the throne. The eight men had also been active in setting England's colonial policy. They believed they could make the colony work.

There was no need, they thought, to send settlers from England to Carolina. Instead, they hoped to attract land-poor people from older colonies, especially from those in the West Indies, where small planters were being pushed out by the owners of large sugar plantations. The proprietors also thought that settlers from the West Indies might be immune to the fevers that struck down other Europeans in Carolina.

▶1. Why did the Carolina proprietors hope to attract settlers from colonies in the West Indies?

The Carolina Charter

The charter the proprietors received in 1663 was generous. It gave them rights over all the land from the southern border of Virginia to Florida (including what is today North Carolina, South Carolina, and Georgia) and from sea to sea, that is, from the Atlantic all the way to the Pacific.

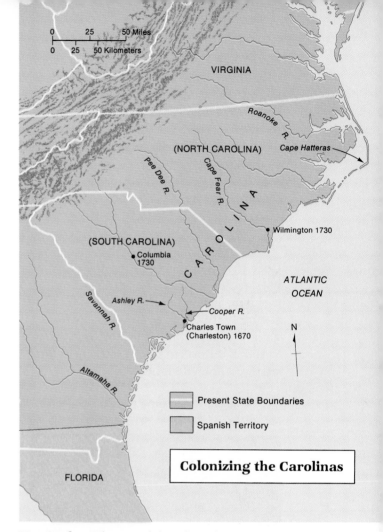

Colonizing the Carolinas

Map Study *Who owned the colony that was south of South Carolina? Approximately how far is Columbia from Charleston?*

The king gave the proprietors power to govern the colony much like that given to Lord Baltimore. The king also gave Carolina settlers the right to worship as they chose, a privilege he was unwilling to give his subjects in England. That right, the king hoped, would help attract more settlers to Carolina.

Why did the Carolina proprietors receive so generous a charter? For the same reasons Lord Baltimore did. The proprietors were experienced in government. They could shape their charter pretty much as they chose. Their lands, like Baltimore's, were on a frontier. Carolina would be the English settlement nearest the Spanish in Florida. The proprietors needed power to control the colony and its defense. The proprietors also received such a generous charter because they were friends of the king.

▶ **2.** What were the main provisions of the Carolina charter?

"Planting" a Settlement

Once they had their charter, the proprietors tried to get settlers. They promised religious freedom, generous grants of land, even an assembly. But only a few colonists from Virginia straggled into the northern parts of Carolina. Efforts to start a settlement farther south completely failed.

An English artist, Henrietta Johnson, made this portrait of a Charleston lady in 1720.

Finally one of the proprietors, Anthony Ashley Cooper, Earl of Shaftesbury, recruited settlers who arrived in the Carolinas in 1670. They planted their settlement about 25 miles up the Ashley River, where they thought the Spanish would have difficulty attacking them. Shaftesbury's "planting" took root. Ten years later the settlement moved to a point on the coast where the Ashley and Cooper rivers joined and ran into the sea. It became the town of Charleston, which was known as Charles Town in colonial days.

▶ **3.** What was the name of the successful settlement in the southern part of Carolina?

The Two Carolinas

Neither the settlements in the southern parts of Carolina nor those nearer Virginia grew very rapidly. By 1700, there were only about 3,000 people in the north and another 5,000 in the south. The two sections never had very much in common, but they did not become the separate colonies of North and South Carolina until 1729. What became North Carolina remained similar to Virginia. Its people grew tobacco. They also sold wood and **naval stores** from their rich pine forests. Naval stores are products such as pitch, tar, and turpentine that are used to build or repair wooden ships.

What became South Carolina was very different from the northern part of the colony. Many of its settlers came from the West Indies, from the island of Barbados (bär bā′doz). The Barbadians (bär bā′dē ənz) did not come to Carolina alone. They brought with them their slaves, for slavery was already well established on that island.

In other parts of North America, too, the number of African slaves began to grow during the final years of the seventeenth century, but South Carolina never had any other labor

England developed colonies in other parts of the Americas besides the mainland of North America. Although Spain claimed all of the Caribbean, England quietly took over several islands in the West Indies before Spain even noticed.

In 1623, an Englishman named Thomas Warner explored St. Christopher Island while sailing back to England from South America. He deposited a few people there, continued to England, and then returned with a royal charter for a colony. That settlement on St. Kitts, as the English called the island, was the first English settlement in the Caribbean. By the 1640's, there were English settlements on Barbados, Nevis, Montserrat, Antigua, the Bahamas, and other islands of the chain called the Lesser Antilles. In 1655, an English force led by Admiral Penn tried to take the island of Hispaniola from Spain. Although the original plan failed, Penn's fleet took Jamaica instead.

Other nations settled islands in the Spanish Main, as the Caribbean was called. By 1650, the Dutch had taken Saba, Curaçao, St. Martin, and St. Eustatius. The French settled in Guadeloupe and Martinique and some smaller islands.

Originally the English grew tobacco on their Caribbean islands. By the 1630's, however, the price of tobacco had fallen. West Indies settlers turned to sugar as their cash crop. Sugar quickly became the only major source of wealth on the islands. A few rich planters took over large amounts of land. Smaller planters were forced out, and some made their way to the mainland English colonies.

Besides sugar, there was one other way of making a fortune in the West Indies—by raiding Spanish ships and settlements. For many years, men from many countries lived a free-and-easy life on the more secluded islands. Those men were called buccaneers, from the Indian word *boucan*, which referred to the wooden platform the men used to broil meat.

Buccaneers did not need to work hard. There was always plenty of fish and fruit. The islands teemed with wild cattle and hogs descended from animals brought by the Spanish. Some buccaneers sold animal hides and provisions to French, English, and Dutch sailors. However, when life grew dull, the buccaneers grouped together for a raid on a ship or town.

force. As many as a third of all its first settlers were black slaves. Their numbers multiplied. By 1708, slaves were a majority.

▶**4.** How were northern and southern Carolina different?

South Carolina's Black Majority

Why were so many slaves brought to South Carolina? For one thing, many Africans were immune to diseases such as yellow fever and malaria. So they lived longer than servants brought from Europe. For another, many slaves had skills from Africa that were helpful in Carolina. African slaves taught their owners a kind of open-field cattle herding that was very important in the early days of Carolina. In fact, meat and hides were the colony's most important products. Slaves also taught their owners how to build and use African canoes and fishing tools in Carolina rivers.

In the 1690's, South Carolina developed its own cash crop—rice. English people did not know about growing rice, but many

The wool quilt shown above gets it bright blue color from a dye that was made from the indigo plant. Right: Workers on an indigo plantation are shown harvesting and preparing the plant for sale.

Africans did. African slaves probably taught their owners how to grow and process rice. With the discovery of rice growing, the number of African slaves brought to the southern part of Carolina mushroomed.

In the 1740's, a 17-year-old girl helped South Carolina develop another cash crop, indigo (in′də gō). While her father was away on business, Eliza Lucas managed the family plantations. She decided to grow indigo. Indigo plants produce a blue dye that was much in demand in England. Helped by some slaves who had grown the plant in the West Indies, she finally found a way to grow indigo in South Carolina.

Indigo made a good second cash crop for rice growers. Indigo plants grow on higher ground than rice, and it uses workers at a time when they are not needed to plant or harvest the rice crop.

▶**5.** Why were so many slaves brought to South Carolina?

Reviewing Section II

Identify King Charles II, Carolina, Anthony Ashley Cooper, Charleston, naval stores, Barbados, indigo, Eliza Lucas

Questions to Answer
1. How did slaves first come to South Carolina?
2. What products did slaves help develop in South Carolina?

A Question to Think About Why do you suppose the king was willing to grant freedom of religion in Carolina but not in England?

Eliza Lucas Pinckney was born around 1722 on Antigua in the West Indies. She was the oldest of four children of George Lucas, a lieutenant colonel in the British army. In 1738, when Eliza was about 16 years old, her father moved the family to one of several plantations he had inherited in South Carolina. Here he hoped his sick wife would grow stronger.

Just a year after the move, the colonel was forced to return to his military post on Antigua. The job of managing his three plantations fell to Eliza.

At the age of 16, Eliza was already an accomplished young woman. She was a gifted musician who could "tumble over one little tune" on the flute. She also spoke French and read many of the great classics that she found in her father's library. Her lively, interesting letters make up one of the largest surviving collections of letters of a colonial woman.

Among Eliza's many interests was the cultivation of new plants. Charles Lucas encouraged his daughter by sending her West Indian seeds with which to experiment. This she did eagerly. After a year of trial with these seeds, she noted in her journal, "Wrote to my father . . . On the pains I have taken to bring the Indigo, Ginger, Cotton . . . to perfection and had greater hopes from the Indigo than any of the other things I had tried."

Eliza worked for three years before she was able to grow indigo successfully. Through a process of trial and error, she then learned how to make blue dye from the stems and leaves of the plant. In 1744, Eliza Lucas sold her first shipment of indigo dye to England. By 1747, Carolina planters were shipping over 100,000 pounds of dye to England. Money from this valuable export poured into the colony.

Indigo was not Eliza Lucas's only agricultural success. Shortly after her marriage in 1744 to Charles Pinckney, she began experimenting with other crops. At her husband's plantation near Charleston, she tried growing flax, hemp, and silk. She was successful enough with silk to establish "a private silk manufacture."

In 1753, Eliza Pinckney moved with her husband and four children to England. In 1758, after war broke out between England and France, she and her husband returned home. That same year Charles Pinckney contracted malaria and died.

After her husband's death, Eliza Pinckney once again turned her energies to directing a large plantation (see above). The care and education of her four children also kept her very busy. Her two sons, Charles and Thomas, grew up to play important roles in the founding of the American nation.

Eliza Lucas Pinckney died in 1793. She was 71 years old at the time of her death. President George Washington honored her by serving as a pallbearer at her funeral.

III. New York and New Jersey

The area directly south of New England was first claimed by the Dutch. The Dutch were conquered by the English early in the 1660's. Soon the former Dutch lands were added to the growing list of England's proprietary colonies. They became the colonies of New York and New Jersey.

The Dutch Colony

The Dutch West India Company founded the colony of New Netherland in 1624. It set up a series of trading posts, the most important of which were along the Hudson River. On Manhattan Island, where the Hudson ran into the Atlantic Ocean, was the Dutch settlement known as New Amsterdam. It later became New York City. Farther north, near where the Hudson joined the Mohawk River, was Fort Orange, which later became the city of Albany. A Dutch director-general, who lived in New Amsterdam, governed the spread-out settlements of New Netherland.

▶ **1.** Where were the most important Dutch settlements?

Effect on the Indians

The arrival of Dutch and other European traders greatly changed the lives of North American Indians. The traders brought diseases new to North America. As a result, many Indians died. Traders also indirectly and sometimes directly encouraged wars between Indian groups.

The Indians wanted European goods such as metal knives, guns, and wool blankets. The more furs the Indians collected, the more such goods they could get. As a result, great struggles broke out between different groups of Indians for control of the fur trade.

When the Dutch began trading along the upper parts of the Hudson River, the most powerful group of nearby Indians, the Iroquois, decided to take control of that trade. So they drove the Indians who lived near Fort Orange to the eastern side of the Hudson. Then the Iroquois attacked the Huron, their main rivals for the fur trade. The Huron lived farther west. By the 1650's, the Iroquois had almost totally destroyed the Huron.

The Iroquois then controlled not just the route from the west to Fort Orange but also all the territory from the Hudson to the Great Lakes. By increasing their own power, the Iroquois also increased the profits of the Dutch with all the furs they brought to trade.

▶ **2.** Why did wars begin between the Huron and Iroquois?

Finding Settlers

The Dutch West India Company was not so interested in its North American settlements as it was in other ventures in Africa and South America. Nor were Dutch people eager to come to America. Even the promise of large land grants, or **patroonships** (pə trün′ ships), for persons who would bring 50 settlers to America was not enough to pull the Dutch out of the Netherlands. Only one such large holding, Rensselaerswyck (rent′ sə liərs′ wick), in the upper reaches of the Hudson Valley, was set up under the Dutch.

So the Dutch West India Company turned to other places to find settlers. From the earliest years of the New Netherland Colony, a good part of its people were French Protestants, or **Huguenots** (hyü′ gə nots). They suffered for their beliefs in Catholic France.

The Dutch colony included Germans and some Scandinavians, since in 1655 the Dutch

This view of New Amsterdam was painted in the early 1600's. Located at the mouth of the Hudson River, it became an important trading center.

took over several Swedish settlements on the Delaware River. A group of Puritan New Englanders also came into Dutch territory. They settled on the eastern end of Long Island.

The Dutch imported slaves for labor. By the 1660's, about one of every five people in New Amsterdam was black—a higher proportion than in the tobacco plantations of the Chesapeake at that time.

The settlement, nevertheless, grew very slowly. In the 1660's all of New Netherland had only about 5,000 people. That was about a tenth of the population of New England.

▶ **3.** What groups of people settled the Dutch colony?

The English Take Over

In March 1664, totally ignoring the Dutch colony, Charles II gave all of the land between the Connecticut and Delaware rivers to his brother James, Duke of York. That included the present states of New York and New Jersey as well as a good chunk of Connecticut. The duke easily settled the problems his grant caused with Connecticut. It seemed unlikely

Map Study *Along what river were most of the settlements in New Netherland located? Along what bay were settlements in New Sweden started?* ▶

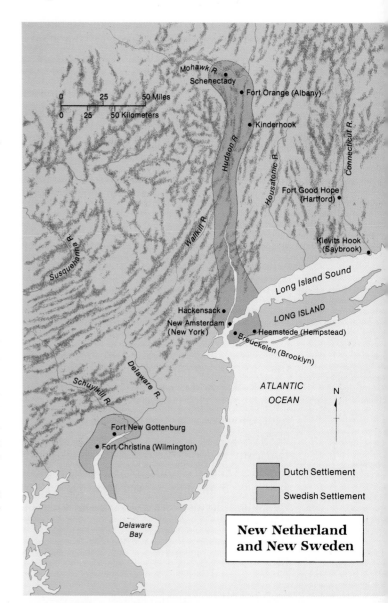

New Netherland and New Sweden

IMPROVE YOUR SKILLS
The Vocabulary of Time

Understanding time relationships is very important in studying history. There are many words which describe divisions of time. Some of these words are vague. When we say something happened "in the past," we could mean that it happened 5 minutes ago or 500 years ago.

There are other divisions of time that are more precise. A *decade,* for example, means 10 years. A *century* means 100 years.

People in Europe and the United States count years forward and backward from the birth of Jesus. That year is the year A.D. 1. The abbreviation A.D. stands for the Latin words meaning "in the year of our Lord." Dates for events that happened before the year A.D. 1 are signaled by the abbreviation B.C. which stands for "before Christ."

The hundred years from A.D. 1 to A.D. 100 make up the first century. On January 1, A.D. 100, the second century began. When Columbus discovered America in 1492, it was the fifteenth century.

The relationship between a date and its century is similar to the relationship between your birth date and your age. When you were born, you were starting your first year of life. On your first birthday, when you became one year old, you started your second year of life.

Test your understanding of the vocabulary of time by answering the following questions.

1. In which century did each of the following events occur? (a) Columbus makes his first voyage to the Americas. (b) Elizabeth becomes queen of England. (c) Jamestown is founded. (d) The first settlers reach Maryland. (e) Carolina splits into two colonies.
2. How many decades passed between 1607 and 1687?
3. How many centuries have passed since 1600?
4. If an event happened in the middle of the seventeenth century, around what year did it happen?
5. If an event happened in the early part of the seventeenth century, around which years did it happen?
6. If something happened in the late seventeenth century, around which years did it happen?

that he could do that so peacefully with the Dutch. So James sent a fleet to take New Netherland. The English were prepared to fight. However, in August 1664, the Dutch director-general, Peter Stuyvesant (stī′ və sənt), surrendered the colony without firing a shot. Then the Duke of York gave New Netherland another name—New York.

▶ 4. Which lands were given to the Duke of York?

The Duke of York's Rule

The duke's charter gave him all the usual rights of proprietors and a few more. He did not have to share his power with a representative assembly as other proprietors did. On the other hand, New Yorkers had to swear allegiance to the king, not to the duke. That did not make a difference for long. When Charles II died in 1685, the duke became

King James II. His proprietary colony then became a royal colony.

The duke was generous with the Dutch colonists. He confirmed their titles to their lands and promised them religious freedom. The Dutch were not upset over not having an assembly, since they did not have one before the English takeover.

The New Englanders living on Long Island were harder to please. They complained about not having an assembly. Their complaints may have kept other settlers away. By the end of the century, the population of New York was only about 18,000.

Without more settlers, the colony could not make money for the duke. So, in 1683, he quieted the New Englanders by allowing an assembly. It did not last long. Once he became king, James abolished the new assembly. After that, some people who might have settled in New York chose to go to New Jersey instead.

▶**5.** Why did James briefly give New Yorkers an assembly?

New Jersey

Shortly after he received his grant, James gave the land between the Hudson and Delaware rivers—New Jersey—to two of his friends. They were Lord John Berkeley, and Sir George Carteret (kar tər′ et). Both men were also proprietors of Carolina.

The two worked hard at encouraging people to settle in New Jersey. They offered religious freedom, large land grants, and a representative assembly. Those benefits attracted many settlers.

Unfortunately, James had not told his governor in North America that he was giving New Jersey to two friends. As a result, the governor gave much of the land in New Jersey to Puritans from New England before he

learned that those lands belonged to Berkeley and Carteret. The New Englanders lost no time in settling in New Jersey.

To add to the confusion, Berkeley and Carteret divided New Jersey in 1674. Berkeley took the western half, and Carteret took the eastern part. Before long, both halves of New Jersey were sold.

The confusion continued until the Jerseys were reunited under one royal government in 1702. Conflicts over land titles continued for a long time after that, however.

Map Study *In what century was the town of Burlington founded? What body of water separates West Jersey from Delaware?*

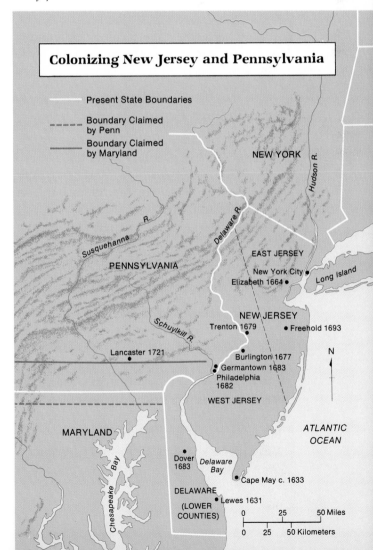

▶**6.** Why was there confusion about land claims in New Jersey?

Reviewing Section III

Identify New Netherland, New Amsterdam, Albany, the Iroquois, the Huron, patroonships, Huguenots, Duke of York, New York, New Jersey, Peter Stuyvesant

Questions to Answer
1. Why did the coming of the Dutch result in wars between Indian groups?
2. What did it mean for New Yorkers when the Duke of York became king?

A Question to Think About Why were the New Englanders living in New York harder to please than the Dutch settlers?

IV. Pennsylvania and Delaware

The last of the seventeenth-century proprietary colonies—Pennsylvania, which included Delaware—was not founded until the 1680's. It was different from all the other colonies, in part because of the ideas of its founder, William Penn. He was the son of a man who was also named William Penn.

The William Penns

Old William Penn was a self-made man. He started out as an ordinary sailor and worked his way up to the rank of admiral. For a time, he served England's Puritan rulers, but later he supported Charles II.

When Charles was crowned in 1660, Admiral Penn was present with his 16-year-old son, William. The admiral went on to work in the king's navy office. Young Penn went on to break his father's heart.

At first, young Penn seemed much like other gentlemen's sons. He went to Oxford—and was expelled after two years. So his father sent him off on a great tour through Europe, a standard part of a gentleman's education. He was a dashing young man, skilled with a sword, good humored, and well liked by both Charles II and his brother James, the Duke of York. Young Penn studied law for a time. Then, soon after a great fire in London

in 1666, he went off to manage his father's Irish properties.

In Ireland, he did something that was unusual among young gentlemen. Penn joined the Society of Friends, a religious group whose members were called Quakers by their enemies.

▶**1.** What unusual thing did young William Penn do in Ireland?

This portrait of William Penn is believed to be the most authentic likeness of him in existence.

The Quakers

The Quakers had some things in common with the Puritans. They too believed in a simple religious service. Like the Puritans, Quakers thought that the most important thing in life was God's grace. The Quakers called that grace their inner light. Unlike the Puritans, however, the Quakers said that every person had an inner light and needed only to live by it to be saved.

Since every person had an inner light, the Quakers thought all people were equal—men and women, rulers and ordinary people. So they refused to honor one person over another. They considered titles meaningless.

Quakers wore the plainest of clothes. They refused to take oaths, including oaths of loyalty to the king. They also refused to go to war, even to defend themselves or their country. They believed that no person had the right to take another's life.

For the Quakers, the church was not a community affair. They believed that each person with God's grace was a complete church. Believers came together in meeting houses with no minister in charge. The assembled Friends sat in silence until someone—man or woman—was moved to speak. They had no Sabbath, since all days were God's and all days were meant for worship.

Clearly the Friends were different from other Christians. Many thought the Quakers were a danger to England's safety and its way of life.

▶**2.** What were some of the beliefs of Quakers that were different from Puritan beliefs?

A Colony for Quakers

The reign of Charles II was not a good time to be a Quaker. It was even difficult for a man like young Penn, who was on good terms with the king.

In 1668, Penn was thrown in jail with some other Quakers and kept there nine months. His father "had intended to make William a great man," Penn's mother commented, "but the boy would not hearken." Father and son made their peace by the time of the admiral's death in 1670. The boy would become a great man as his father dreamed, but in his own way.

Young Penn wanted King Charles to grant him land in North America. There he and his fellow Quakers could live in peace. King Charles liked Penn but found it awkward to give a proprietary grant to a Quaker.

Penn found an excuse for the king. He asked Charles to pay back a loan from Admiral Penn of £16,000—a considerable sum of money. Young Penn suggested that the debt could be settled by a grant of land in North America. In 1681, the king granted Penn's request. Perhaps he was even happy to see so many troublesome people going to North America.

▶**3.** How did Penn make it easier for King Charles II to give him a proprietary colony?

Penn's Charter

The king gave Penn a huge area of land. It lay west of the Jerseys, between New York and Maryland. The king called the new colony Pennsylvania for Admiral Penn. The following year Penn also bought what is today the state of Delaware from the Duke of York.

The charter the king gave Penn made him owner of all the land in his colony. He could suggest laws and enforce them but only with the advice and consent of the colony's freemen. He could also appoint judges and pardon all crimes except treason and murder.

Penn's charter limited his power in several ways. For one thing, his lands did not extend to the Pacific. They went only 300 miles west from their eastern boundary.

Penn also had to honor all of England's commercial laws and to allow the king's agents to collect taxes on trade. So there would be officials within Pennsylvania who worked for the Crown, not for the proprietor.

The charter said that Pennsylvania could have a **militia,** an armed force of its own citizens to defend the colony against attack. In no other way, however, could the colony carry on war.

The Crown also kept some say about the legislative and judicial government of Pennsylvania. Every five years Penn had to send copies of all the colony's laws to the king, who could, if he chose, refuse to allow some or all of them to remain in force. Appeals from court cases could be carried beyond the proprietor to the king.

▶ **4.** In what ways were Penn's powers limited?

Pennsylvania Grows

Penn planned his new settlement carefully. He wanted it to be a center for trade as well as an agricultural colony. Pennsylvania's main port, Penn decided, would be a great city. He called it Philadelphia, which means "brotherly love."

For the colony to grow, it would need more people than it could draw from English Quakers alone. Penn tried to attract people from various parts of England, Scotland, and Ireland. He sent recruiters to many parts of Europe to find settlers. He wrote pamphlets describing the colony. They were translated into French, German, and Dutch. Penn promised settlers land, low taxes, a representative assembly, and religious freedom for all—including non-Christians.

Penn's campaign for settlers was very successful. Many German people came to Pennsylvania. (The Germans came to be called Dutch because their word for German,

Deutsch, sounds like the word *Dutch.*) Just 5 years after its charter was issued, Pennsylvania had about 12,000 people—as many as it took Virginia 30 years to collect.

Philadelphia grew too. Merchants and artisans settled there. Within a few years, it had 2,000 people, and it was becoming a trading center. Wheat grown in Pennsylvania was shipped to other colonies, the West Indies, or England from Philadelphia.

During Penn's life, his colony had peaceful relations with the local Delaware Indians. The Quakers respected the Indians, and Penn carefully bought land from the Delaware before giving it out to settlers. Penn even learned the Delaware language.

▶ **5.** How did Penn attract settlers?

Government

Penn gave much thought to the new colony's form of government. He wrote a Frame of Government in 1682. It said that the colony would be headed by the proprietor or by a governor appointed by the proprietor. It would have a council elected by the voters. The council could propose laws, appoint officers, and was to watch over the colony. Voters would elect an assembly. It would have more members than the council, but its powers would be limited. Penn thought it would only be able to approve or disapprove proposals that came before it.

The members of the assembly had other ideas. They complained endlessly about the powers of the council. They insisted on the right to propose laws themselves. They joined with members of the council in criticizing Penn's governors.

Finally, Penn let the settlers draw up their own plan of government. When they did so in 1701, they cut back the powers of the governor still more and got rid of the council.

Pennsylvania then became the only colony with a one-house, or **unicameral**, legislature.

In 1701, the Delaware settlers won the right to have their own assembly, separate from that of Pennsylvania. Delaware and Pennsylvania continued to be ruled by the same governor, however.

▶**6.** How did Pennsylvania come to have a unicameral legislature?

Penn's Worries

Except for one brief trip to Pennsylvania between 1699 and 1701, Penn spent the rest of his life in England. He had many troubles that kept him there—troubles with Lord Baltimore and others over his charter rights and troubles with people to whom he owed money. He was imprisoned several times. Still, when Penn died in 1718, he had fulfilled his father's dream by becoming a great man. He started one of the fastest-growing and most prosperous colonies in British North America. In addition, only there and in Rhode Island were persons of all religions allowed to exist freely under the law.

▶**7.** Why did Penn stay in England?

Reviewing Section IV

Identify Admiral William Penn, William Penn, the Society of Friends, Pennsylvania, militia, Philadelphia, unicameral

Questions to Answer
1. How was Penn's charter limited?
2. Where did Pennsylvania find its settlers?

A Question to Think About Why was Pennsylvania more peaceful and prosperous than any other colony you have studied?

IMPROVE YOUR READING
Comparison and Contrast

You have learned that ideas and events can be *compared* and *contrasted*. This means that events have similarities (comparisons) and differences (contrasts). Authors frequently describe a new item in terms of its similarities to or differences from items you have already read about. In that way, authors build on your previous knowledge.

The following exercise is designed to help you understand some of the people, places, and events that the author of this text has compared and contrasted in this chapter.

Each statement contains in parentheses the words *similar* and *different*. On your paper, write which of these two words makes the statement correct. Then write a brief explanation of your choice.

For example, look at the following sentence: "The growth of slavery was (different/similar) in the northern part of Carolina and the southern part." The word that makes an accurate sentence is *different*. The text explains that the southern part of Carolina, unlike any of the other colonies, never had another labor force besides slaves.

1. Virginia and Maryland developed in a (similar/different) manner.
2. Admiral William Penn and his son had (similar/different) ideas on religion.
3. Pennsylvania had a unicameral legislature. That was (similar to/different from) the other colonies.
4. The powers given to the proprietors of Carolina were (similar to/different from) the powers given to Lord Baltimore.
5. Quakers were (similar to/different from) Puritans in their belief that God's grace was the most important thing in life.

CHAPTER 5 REVIEW

Vocabulary Check
Write a short definition for each of the following words.

1. Proprietary colony
2. Huguenots
3. Militia
4. Naval stores
5. Patroonships

Fact Check
Write the word to fill in the blanks below.

1. _____ was the first proprietor of Maryland.
2. South Carolina's first successful cash crop was _____.
3. _____ founded a colony where Quakers could practice their religion.
4. The _____ gained control of the fur trade from the Hudson River to the Great Lakes.
5. The colony of New York was first settled by the _____.
6. Delaware became a part of _____ Colony.
7. Great confusion over land claims existed in _____ Colony.
8. The Protestant majority in Maryland was unhappy because most of the colony's leaders were followers of the _____ religion.
9. Maryland, Virginia, and the northern parts of Carolina made up a region known as the _____.
10. _____ surrendered New Netherland to the English.

Skills Check
Use the map on page 95 to help you answer the following questions.

1. Name the town shown on the map that was not first settled in the seventeenth century.
2. In which century was that town settled?
3. About how far is Philadelphia from New York City?
4. What settlement was made a decade after Germantown and Dover?
5. What river is the boundary between New Jersey and Pennsylvania?

Think and Write
1. What reasons did people have for wishing to start colonies in North America?
2. What did proprietors promise in order to attract settlers to their colonies?
3. Why was the Crown willing to give great powers to colonial proprietors?
4. Why did Carolina eventually split into two colonies?
5. How did Penn's charter differ from the charter given to Lord Baltimore?

REVIEWING UNIT 2

Reviewing the Facts I.

The sentences below are not correct. Write the number of each sentence on your paper. Then rewrite the sentence changing what is needed to make it correct.

1. Pennsylvania was founded as a haven for Catholics.
2. Roger Williams founded Providence because he was looking for better farmland.
3. The Dutch in New York took over a colony started by the Germans.
4. William Penn was given more power in his charter than the other proprietors of colonies.
5. The House of Burgesses was the assembly in Massachusetts.
6. Virginia was started by a proprietor.
7. Connecticut Colony was founded by Puritans wanting a stricter way of life than that in Massachusetts.
8. A distinctive feature of the Chesapeake colonies was the growth of towns.
9. Power in Virginia and the New England colonies was centralized.
10. Slavery grew the fastest in New Jersey.

Reviewing the Facts II.

Write the name of the proper colony for each statement below.

1. Its cash crop was tobacco.
2. Its people lived in towns.
3. It was the colony closest to the Spanish in the late 1600's.
4. Its proprietor maintained good relations with the Indians.
5. Its founders took their charter with them.
6. Its founders wrote the Mayflower Compact.
7. Its founder was banished from Massachusetts Bay Colony.
8. This colony split into two parts.
9. This colony had an assembly for a very brief time.
10. Because this colony had an assembly, some settlers who might have gone to New York settled there.

Reviewing Ideas

1. Why did the Virginia Colony go through harder times than the other colonies?
2. What was the importance of the covenant in the Puritan colonies?
3. Describe freedom of religion in the colonies around 1685.
4. Describe the growth of slavery in the colonies until 1685.
5. Why was Pennsylvania able to grow so much faster than the other colonies?

UNIT THREE

Growth and Revolution

In the 1760's, Britain took a stronger role in governing its North American colonies. The colonists were not pleased with the new British policies. In New York, colonists showed their anger by pulling down a statue of King George III. The growing discontent caused the colonists to seek independence from Britain.

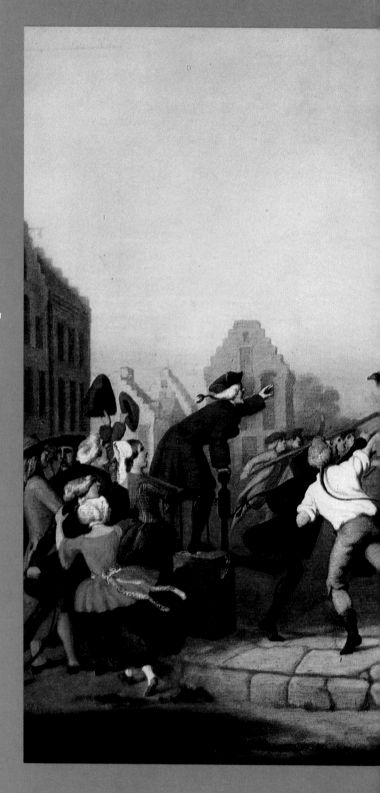

Chapter 6

North America and the British Empire

John Smibert's view of the Boston of 1738 is one of the earliest-known paintings of the city. The painting shows Boston from a hill overlooking the harbor.

Earlier chapters told about the first English colonists in North America. Life was harder for them than it was for later settlers. By the late 1600's, the colonies were growing and prospering. But their troubles were not over.

This chapter tells of the difficulties the colonies faced in the late seventeenth century. They were torn by war and rebellion. Changes in the government and the laws of Britain also caused confusion and unrest in North America. By 1700, colonial life had become more settled. The British government, however, held more power over the colonies than it had before the time of troubles began.

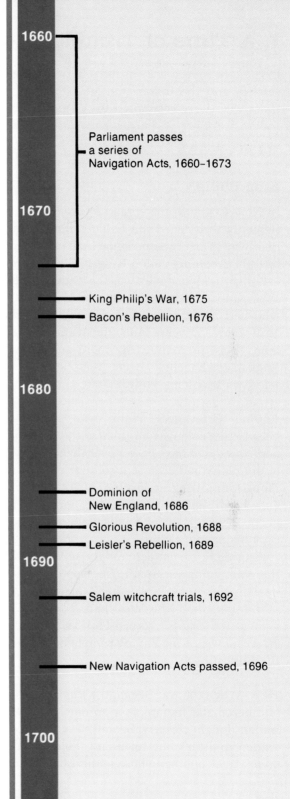

1660

Parliament passes
a series of
Navigation Acts, 1660–1673

1670

King Philip's War, 1675
Bacon's Rebellion, 1676

1680

Dominion of
New England, 1686

Glorious Revolution, 1688
Leisler's Rebellion, 1689

1690

Salem witchcraft trials, 1692

New Navigation Acts passed, 1696

1700

I. A Time of Troubles

In the late 1600's, wars erupted between the settlers and the Indians. In New England, those wars were very costly. In Virginia, the Indian wars set off battles between groups of colonists.

King Philip's War

In New England, the spread of English settlements threatened the Indians' lands and their way of life. Eventually the Indians fought back in a conflict called **King Philip's War.**

Philip, or Metacomet, was the leader of the Wampanoag. He was the son of Massasoit, who had made peace with the Pilgrims in 1621. Now, 50 years later, the Wampanoag lands were surrounded by more and more English settlements.
▶**1.** Who was King Philip?

Philip's Grievances Philip was unhappy because the colonists humiliated the Indians and claimed to have power over them. Plymouth Colony had even sent soldiers to arrest Philip for plotting against the colony in 1671. As a result, he had to pay a fine, admit that his people came under English law, and turn over his people's guns.

Fighting broke out between the settlers and the Wampanoag in June 1675. Soon the Nipmuck (nip'muk) and the Narragansett (nar'ə gan'sit), who also had grievances against the English, joined Philip's people.
▶**2.** What were King Philip's complaints about the English?

War When the war began, the English outnumbered the Indians four to one, but the Indians fought cleverly. Sometimes they pretended to attack one town and then darted off to attack another whose soldiers had gone

to help their neighbors. At other times, they attacked while the settlers were at Sunday services. The Indians destroyed 13 western Massachusetts towns. The war ended in 1676, when the Indians ran out of supplies, Philip was killed, and the Indian alliance fell apart.

King Philip's War was very costly to both sides. About 5,000 Indians were killed. Many others were captured and sold as slaves in the West Indies. The colonists too paid a heavy price. About one tenth of the men of military age in New England were killed.
▶**3.** What were the results of King Philip's War?

Trouble in Virginia

At about the same time as King Philip's War, there were also clashes between settlers and Indians in Virginia. However, the clashes that occurred in Virginia were very different from King Philip's War. In Virginia, battles with the Indians sparked battles between groups of colonists. A civil war, a war between opposing groups of the same nation, began.
▶**4.** What sort of trouble took place in Virginia in the late 1600's?

Governor Berkeley and Friends Tension between two groups of Virginians had existed for some time. On one side were Governor William Berkeley and his friends, wealthy planters who owned large amounts of land. Berkeley and his friends controlled the government of the colony. Because the members of the House of Burgesses generally did as he wished, Berkeley had not called for a new election of burgesses in 14 years.

In 1670, Berkeley's friends on the Council and in the House of Burgesses tightened their control of the colony. They passed a law that limited the right to vote to owners of large plantations. Plantation owners were likely to support Berkeley.

▶**5.** How did Governor Berkeley and his friends tighten their control in Virginia?

Berkeley's Opposition Opposing Berkeley and his friends were farmers who lived on the edge of the settled area, or the frontier. Since these settlers lived closer to the Indians, they had reason to fear Indian attacks. However, Berkeley and his friends were making money from the Indian trade, which depended on good relations with the Indians. As a result, settlers on the frontier claimed that the governor was not willing to protect them from the Indians.

Others opposed to Berkeley were former indentured servants who found it hard to buy any land at all. There had been a time in Virginia when newly-freed servants were able to get land of their own. By 1660, however, most of the land in the Virginia Tidewater was already owned. At the same time, Berkeley did not allow colonists to settle too far west. That, he thought, might anger the Indians.

Because they could not get land, many former servants wandered through the Chesapeake colonies. They lived by hunting, by farming for other people, or by stealing. Most were young and unmarried. They had guns because that was part of life on the Virginia frontier. They were dangerous men, especially when Indians and rich planters crossed their paths.

▶**6.** Who opposed Berkeley?

Trouble Starts Those Virginians opposed to Berkeley were especially concerned over Indian policy. In 1675, a few Indians from Maryland crossed into Virginia, murdered some settlers, and then returned home. The

William Berkeley posed for this portrait during his second term as governor of Virginia.

Virginians responded by punishing not just the Indians involved but also the neighboring Susquehanna (sus'kwə han'ə). The Susquehanna, in turn, attacked several settlements in northern Virginia.

Governor Berkeley tried to stop the Indian attacks by sending the militia to forts in the west. However, the angry Indians simply slipped past the forts. By March 1676, over 300 English settlers had been killed.

▶**7.** Why did the Susquehanna attack in northern Virginia?

Nathaniel Bacon Many colonists were ready to take affairs into their own hands. Nathaniel Bacon, a tobacco planter, became their leader.

Bacon's background was similar to that of Governor Berkeley's supporters. Bacon came from a wealthy English family. However, he had a genius for getting into trouble. After he was expelled from Cambridge University in England, his father decided to send him to Virginia for a fresh start in life.

In 1674, Bacon arrived in Virginia with enough money to buy a fine piece of land along the James River. Berkeley welcomed Bacon to the colony and gave him a place on the governor's Council. Soon, however, the two men quarreled, perhaps because the governor turned down Bacon's request to buy control of the Indian trade.

▶**8.** Who was Nathaniel Bacon?

Bacon's Rebellion

Bacon's overseer, the man in charge of his plantation, was killed in an Indian raid. So, in April 1676, Bacon, without the governor's permission, set off with a small army of volunteers to stop the Indian attacks. Many of the members of Bacon's army were former indentured servants. They killed 150 Indians before returning home. Many people, including some wealthy landowners, hailed Bacon and his men as heroes. The governor did not agree. He called Bacon and his followers rebels, or criminals.

Governor Berkeley tried to win more support for himself by calling a new election of burgesses—the first in 14 years. Despite the law of 1670, he let all freemen vote, not only the rich. The newly-elected members of the House of Burgesses turned against the governor. They passed laws to reduce his power and made the qualifications for the voting the same as they were before 1670.

Berkeley could see how much support Bacon had among the burgesses. So he gave Bacon permission to raise another army to fight the Indians. However, as soon as the meeting of the House of Burgesses ended in late June, Berkeley again declared Bacon and his followers to be rebels.

▶**9.** What happened as a result of the new election for members to the House of Burgesses?

True Rebels At that point, Bacon and his army did become rebels. They forced Berkeley to flee from Virginia. Bacon took over the government. The minute Bacon marched after the Indians again, however, Berkeley returned to Jamestown. So Bacon turned around, seized Jamestown, and burned it so Berkeley could not occupy it again.

When news of the rebellion reached England, Charles II sent out a fleet of eleven ships with a thousand soldiers on board to help Berkeley. Clearly the Crown was taking much more interest in its colonies than it had in the past. Bacon became very ill before the troops arrived and died in October 1676. Soon after, the rebellion collapsed, and Berkeley was back in power. Berkeley himself died in 1677.

▶**10.** How did Bacon's rebellion end?

The Results What difference did Bacon's rebellion make for Virginia? The laws passed by the House of Burgesses in 1676 were all repealed after the rebellion collapsed. The rebellion did, however, lead to a new Indian policy. After the rebellion, the colonists attacked the Indians more fiercely. Soon the colonists had pushed the Indians beyond the mountains. Then settlers began moving onto the **Piedmont** (pēd'mont), the area of rolling hills and forests between the Tidewater and the mountains.

The footloose, armed men who fought under Bacon still threatened order in Virginia. As a result, the planters did not want to bring more indentured servants to Virginia. New servants would eventually add to the number of wandering free whites. Soon the planters began buying slaves instead. Slaves never became free, and they could be prevented by law from carrying guns.

▶11. What were the major results of Bacon's rebellion?

Reviewing Section I

Identify King Philip's War, William Berkeley, Nathaniel Bacon, Piedmont

Questions to Answer
1. Why were Bacon and his followers dissatisfied with Berkeley's government?
2. What changes took place as a result of Bacon's rebellion?

A Question to Think About Why did Berkeley and his friends want to control the government of Virginia?

II. England Changes Its Policies

The next troubles for the colonies came from the government in England where Charles II had been "restored" to the throne after the rule of the Cromwells. At first, Charles did not change English colonial policy very much. He gave the new proprietors of Carolina the power to control their colony. He was, of course, grateful to them, for they had supported his return to the throne. He was also grateful to his colonists in Virginia who had shown their loyalty to the Crown.

New Charters for New England

The king was also generous to the New England colonies that had supported his enemies. He gave charters to Connecticut and Rhode Island in 1662 and 1663. New Haven Colony was joined with other Connecticut towns under the Connecticut charter. That did not please New Haven. Otherwise, there was little in the new charters to cause discontent. Connecticut and Rhode Island were given governments like that of Massachusetts. All officials were chosen by the colonists. The charters did say that laws had to be issued in the king's name and be like those of England. However, since there was no one in England watching what the colonists did during the 1660's, that rule meant very little.

King Charles II was even generous with Massachusetts Bay, the most difficult of his colonies. Although it had been slow to proclaim its loyalty to him, the king offered to renew the Massachusetts charter.

The king did make a few demands. He wanted the colony's people to take an oath of allegiance to him. He wanted the assembly to repeal any laws that interfered with his authority. More important, he said members of the Church of England should be allowed to worship freely and to vote. For the Puritan leaders of Massachusetts, that was too much to ask. So they ignored the king's demand.

▶1. What demand of the king did the leaders of Massachusetts ignore?

The Navigation Acts

At first, King Charles II and his advisors had no desire to interfere with the colonies' self-government. They did, however, want to regulate the colonies' trade with other countries. When they had trouble doing that, the royal policy changed dramatically.

King Charles II and his advisors were determined to make the colonies help England. They especially wanted the colonies to help the growing English shipping industry. For that reason, Parliament passed, with the king's consent, a set of trade laws known as the **Navigation Acts** in 1660 and 1663.

▶**2.** What was the purpose of the Navigation Acts?

Provisions of the Acts The Navigation Acts said all goods shipped to and from the colonies had to be carried by ships that had been built in England or in English colonies and whose officers and crews were English. The acts also said that certain products from the colonies—known as **enumerated commodities** (i nü′mə rāt′əd kə mod′ə tēz)—could be sent only to England or to English colonies. Some of the most profitable colonial products, such as tobacco, were enumerated commodities. The laws also said most goods from other parts of Europe had to be brought to England before being shipped to the Americas. Spanish or French products, for example, had to be brought to England and be unloaded. There shippers had to pay a **duty**, a tax on goods brought into the country from foreign places. Then the products were reloaded on English ships and taken to the colonies.

Some colonists continued to ship enumerated commodities directly to Europe despite the Navigation Acts. So, in 1673, Parliament passed another Navigation Act. It said the duties on goods had to be collected in the Americas before the goods were shipped out. Shippers also had to put up money to ensure that the goods they carried went to an English port. They lost that money if they took the goods anywhere else.

▶**3.** What were the major provisions of the Navigation Acts?

Effects of the Acts The Navigation Acts brought great changes to the colonies. The law of 1673 said the king must have his own customs officer in each of the colonies to collect duties. For the first time, the king had his own agents in all the colonies.

IMPROVE YOUR SKILLS
Reading Charts

Charts are often used in newspapers, books, and magazines to help the reader summarize or compare information quickly. Charts always have titles. The title tells you in general what the chart is about. Both the vertical columns and the horizontal columns of charts have headings. The column headings tell you the specific information the chart contains.

Charts are read column by column, from left to right. However, very often you need not read an entire chart. By using the column headings, you can locate just the pieces of information you need.

Use the chart on page 111 to answer the following questions.

1. (a) What is the general topic of the chart? (b) Where did you look to find the answer?
2. (a) What are the headings for the vertical column? (b) What three pieces of information does the chart tell you about each of the colonies? (c) What period of time does the chart cover?
3. What type of government did Virginia have in 1607? In 1763?
4. (a) In what year was the last English colony founded? (b) What type of government did it have at that time?
5. In 1763, what type of government did most of the colonies have?

The laws had important economic effects. For example, all of Virginia's tobacco was shipped to England even though the English could not use it all. So, tobacco prices fell sharply. The laws cut off most direct colonial trade with Europe. New England merchants found ways around the laws.

▶**4.** How did the Navigation Acts affect the colonies?

Colonial Responses In their fight against the Navigation Acts, the leaders of Massachusetts denied that Parliament had the right to pass *any* laws for their colony. The Massachusetts charter of 1629, they said, gave the colony the right to govern itself. What the colony's leaders feared was not the Navigation Acts themselves but the idea of Parliament telling Massachusetts what it could

Types of Colonies

The Colonies	Date Founded as English Colony	Type of Government at Founding	Type of Government in 1763
New England Colonies			
Massachusetts Bay	1629	Corporate	Corporate / Royal
New Hampshire	1622	Proprietary	Royal
Connecticut			
Hartford	1636	Corporate ⎱	Corporate
New Haven	1637	Corporate ⎰	
Rhode Island	1636	Corporate	Corporate
Middle Colonies			
New York	1664	Proprietary	Royal
Delaware	1664	Proprietary	Proprietary
New Jersey	1664	Proprietary	Royal
Pennsylvania	1682	Proprietary	Proprietary
Southern Colonies			
Virginia	1607	Corporate	Royal
Maryland	1634	Proprietary	Proprietary
The Carolinas			
North Carolina	1663	Proprietary	Royal
South Carolina	1663	Proprietary	Royal
Georgia	1732	Proprietary	Royal

◀*Lumber, produced at sawmills such as the one shown here, was a major colonial export.*

and could not do. If Parliament could tell the colony how to carry on its trade, it could also change the colony's laws on religion.
▶**5.** Why were people in Massachusetts so opposed to the Navigation Acts?

The Lords of Trade

Soon Massachusetts had even more reason to fear for its rights. In 1675, the king set up a group to advise him on colonial matters. Known as the Lords of Trade, the group had far less power than Spain's Council of the Indies. The lords could only make suggestions to the king and his closest advisors. They could not put policies into effect. Still the

★★ The United States and the World ★★★★★★★★★★★★★★
Mercantilism

There were many reasons why England first adopted the Navigation Acts. England wanted to build its own commercial strength over that of its rival, the Netherlands. The Crown also hoped the new laws would bring in more revenue, and make jobs for poor people in England. Later, after the Glorious Revolution, English writers developed an economic theory known as *mercantilism.* It encouraged the passage of new navigation laws.

Many mercantilists thought that a nation's wealth was measured in gold and silver. To accumulate gold and silver, a country should always export goods worth more than those it imported.

Mercantilist countries tried to develop manufactures so that they could export more and import less. They also made sure that their exports were carried on their country's ships.

Mercantilists assumed that there was only a limited amount of trade possible in the world. If one nation's trade grew, other countries lost out. As a result, mercantilism encouraged fierce rivalries between countries.

Mercantilists also thought that colonies existed mainly to buy their home country's manufactures and to supply it with raw materials. Colonists did not always agree. As a result, mercantilism caused tension between colonists and the home countries.

Lords of Trade took charge of the English colonies in America more effectively than any group before them had done.

The Lords of Trade received many disturbing reports from Massachusetts. The people of that colony, it seemed, were doing all they could to block enforcement of the Navigation Acts. Clearly something had to be done. To start with, the Lords of Trade, with the king's approval, had New Hampshire taken from Massachusetts. In 1679, New Hampshire became a royal colony—the first in North America since the Crown took control of Virginia over 50 years before.

Then, in 1683, the lords announced there would be no new proprietary charters. For the Navigation Acts to be respected in America, the Lords decided, the Crown would have to govern its colonies directly.

In 1684, the Crown finally managed to have the Massachusetts charter revoked. Soon the charters of Rhode Island and Connecticut were also taken away. The Crown then began proceedings against proprietary titles to other colonies.

▶ **6.** How did royal power over the New England colonies increase?

This is a painting of Moses Marcy, a colonial merchant who worked in Massachusetts.

Questions to Answer
1. Why did the Lords of Trade recommend that the king govern his colonies directly?
2. Why was New Hampshire taken from Massachusetts?

A Question to Think About Could Massachusetts have avoided the loss of its charter?

Reviewing Section II——————

Identify Charles II, Navigation Acts, enumerated commodities, duty, Lords of Trade

III. Dominion and Revolution

Charles II died in 1685, and his brother, the Duke of York, became King James II. As soon as he became king, James ended the assembly in the colony of New York. He did not believe a king should share power with the people.

The Dominion of New England

James hoped to create in English America great blocks of colonies under royal power, much like the viceroyalties of Spain.

James started his new system with New England. In 1686, he combined what had been the separate colonies of New Hampshire, Massachusetts, Plymouth, Connecticut, and Rhode Island in a single government known as the **Dominion of New England.** He added New York and New Jersey to the dominion two years later. He abolished the assemblies of all those colonies. The dominion was to be ruled by a governor and a council, both appointed by the king. James appointed Sir Edmund Andros, who worked out of Boston, as governor.

▶**1.** What was the Dominion of New England?

Effects on New England

Most New Englanders disliked the dominion from the beginning. They resented the loss of their assemblies. Like people in England, the colonists believed that they could not be

Sir Edmund Andros, governor of the Dominion of New England, was a harsh, demanding ruler.

taxed without the consent of their representatives. So when Governor Andros tried to impose taxes without an assembly, some towns refused to pay. The governor sent the leaders of the resistance to jail and decided that towns could hold meetings only once each year.

▶**2.** Why did some towns refuse to pay taxes imposed by Andros?

Rents and Commons Soon the colonists had more grievances. Governor Andros told them they had to request new titles to their lands, which would be issued in the king's name. Landowners would have to pay a fee for the new title. Then they would have to pay fees known as quitrents for their land. People who could not prove they had owned their land to Andros's satisfaction lost the land.

To make matters worse, Andros announced that the Crown now owned all town lands not yet divided up, including the town commons. The towns needed their commons for pastures. They also needed their undivided lands to provide farms for their children.

Andros could do as he pleased with all the land he seized. He made large grants to his friends. New Englanders thought it unjust that the land for which they and their parents had worked and suffered should go to such greedy newcomers.

▶**3.** What did Andros do that New Englanders resented?

The Dominion and the Puritans Governor Andros and his officials also began tearing down the religious foundations of Massachusetts. The Dominion of New England allowed people of all religions to worship freely. This pleased Rhode Islanders but not the Puritans of Massachusetts.

The dominion broke the connection between the Puritan church and the Puritan government. It refused even to let town governments raise money to pay their ministers. Those changes undermined much of what had been Puritan New England.

▶4. How did the dominion try to break the Puritan hold on New England?

Glorious Revolutions in England and North America

Events in England gave the New Englanders a chance to fight against the new rules. King James II ruled England in much the same way he ruled the colonies. There too he attacked the charters that gave certain places such as the city of London special rights and powers. There too he tried to rule without Parliament. To make matters worse, James was a Catholic and openly gave public offices to Catholics, which was against English law.

In 1688, the English people forced James II from the throne. Parliament invited his oldest Protestant daughter, Mary, and her husband, William of Orange, a Dutch prince, to come to England and be the new queen and king. The English also made clear, once and for all, that their country could not and would not be ruled without Parliament. They called those events the **Glorious Revolution.**

▶5. What was the Glorious Revolution?

Massachusetts New England began its own glorious revolution on April 18, 1689. Gangs of armed men gathered in the streets of Boston. They seized a dozen of Andros's officials. About noon, the town's Puritan leaders met and issued a declaration justifying the revolt. They were removing James II's officials in New England out of loyalty to the new king and queen, the leaders said.

Governor Andros and his royal officials were arrested and put in jail. There they remained until February 1690.

▶6. What actions did the leaders of Massachusetts take in their glorious revolution?

Leisler's Rebellion New York soon followed Boston's example. That colony was also ruled by Governor Andros. Because it was so far from Boston, actual day-to-day control had been given to a lieutenant governor and a group of councillors who lived in or near New York City.

At the time of the Boston uprising, New York had been part of the Dominion for only about a year. New Yorkers had lost their assembly, but other things bothered them more. They were upset by the number of Catholics in office there. They were also unhappy about high taxes.

When news of the events in Boston arrived, uprisings broke out in the counties outside New York City. Gradually they spread to Manhattan. There, on May 30, 1689, people seized the fort on the southern tip of the island. When the lieutenant governor left for England, captains of the militia took control. One of them, Jacob Leisler (līs'lėr), gradually emerged as their leader and ruled the colony. The glorious revolution in New York is called **Leisler's Rebellion.**

When the British Crown appointed a governor for New York in 1691, Leisler questioned his authority. The new governor made Leisler pay heavily for his caution. He was tried for treason and executed.

▶7. Why is the glorious revolution in New York called Leisler's Rebellion?

Maryland and Pennsylvania Marylanders soon followed the Bostonians and New Yorkers. Maryland was not part of the Dominion of New England. However, Protestants there, who by 1688 made up 95 percent of the population, had tried for years to overthrow the Catholic proprietor, Lord Baltimore.

Jacob Leisler's house, located on Whitehall Street, was one of the largest and most attractive homes in New York City.

When Marylanders heard about the Glorious Revolution in England and about the events at Boston and New York, they wondered why Lord Baltimore had not ordered the colony to honor the new king and queen. Could it be that he remained loyal to his fellow Catholic, King James II? Did he intend to hand the colony over to Catholic France? On the strength of such rumors, a Protestant association took over the colony by force. On September 10, 1689, it proclaimed allegiance to the new king and queen. The next spring it set up a new government for Maryland. As a result of those events, Lord Baltimore finally lost his charter.

Because William Penn was a friend of James II and because Quakers of his colony refused to fight in any war, William and Mary revoked the Pennsylvania charter. Royal rule lasted

only two years, however. Then Penn got the charter back.

▶**8.** How did the Glorious Revolution affect Maryland? Pennsylvania?

Salem Witchcraft

After the Glorious Revolutions of 1689 but before new governments were defined for the colonies, uncertainty and fear were widespread in the colonies. In one town, fear took a very destructive form. In 1692, some young girls in Salem Village (now Danvers, Massachusetts) started accusing older people, mostly women, of being witches.

In the seventeenth century, most educated people believed in witches. At the time, people were executed for witchcraft in many parts of the world, including England.

In 1689, Massachusetts colonists seized and put into prison Governor Edmund Andros and several other British officials. Among those officials was an English agent named Edward Randolph. No one was surprised that Randolph was among those arrested. There had been hard feelings between Randolph and the colonists ever since his arrival in Massachusetts over 10 years before.

Edward Randolph had first arrived in Massachusetts in 1676. He had been sent there by Charles II to investigate complaints against the Massachusetts Bay Colony. One of those complaints involved a claim that the colony had taken over land in New Hampshire to which it had no right. There was also evidence that the colonists were not observing the Navigation Acts.

Randolph was told to look around and report back on what he learned. What he learned both shocked and amazed him. At the Boston docks, he saw tobacco, sugar, cotton, and other goods being loaded aboard ships bound for Europe. He also saw Spanish and French goods being unloaded in the harbor. Both acts were direct violations of the Navigation Acts, which had been passed three years earlier.

Randolph grew even angrier as he traveled to other parts of New England and saw the same resistance to the king's laws. He vowed to return to London and convince officials there that something had to be done about the stubborn colonists.

When Randolph arrived in London, it quickly became apparent to him that he cared about the colonists' defiance more than the English officials did. But Randolph was an ambitious, determined young man, and he pushed the authorities to defend the king's power over the hard-headed Puritan leaders. He hoped that in time his efforts would be rewarded by a position in the king's service, one that would bring him wealth and power.

In 1679, Randolph got his reward. King Charles appointed him the King's Collector of Customs in New England. Randolph returned to New England to take up his new responsibilities.

From the beginning, there was trouble. Few colonists cooperated with his efforts to enforce the Navigation Acts. Most openly disobeyed him. Randolph spent hours writing letters to English officials, urging them to take away the company's charter. He also made several trips back home to England to try to enforce his views.

In 1684, Randolph won his fight. The English Crown took away the charter. It also began a campaign to regain the powers it had lost. That campaign was the start of a major change in English colonial policy in the 1670's and 1680's. In time, its impact would reach far beyond New England.

In 1686, Randolph returned once again to New England. His new position was that of advisor to Governor Edmund Andros. It was during this stay that the colonists rebelled against the harsh policies of Andros and his officials. The colonists rose up and imprisoned the men who governed them.

Randolph remained in prison a year before returning to England. For the last 13 years of his life, he moved back and forth between the colonies and England, trying to enforce British policies in North America. Then, as in the past, his actions did little to improve relations between England and its colonies. Rather, Randolph was one of many British officials who planted the seeds that would one day grow into revolution.

The Salem crisis spread wildly. By the end of the hysteria, 165 people had been accused of witchcraft, and 20 accused witches had been executed.

Most of the accused witches came from Salem Town, a rich and thriving port. The accusers came from inland Salem Village, where most people were farmers. The village was governed by Salem Town.

Salem Town was part of the world of trade. Its people were shopkeepers, sea captains, and merchants. They had wealth and power that the villagers both envied and feared. Too easily Salem Town came to stand for all the modern ways that threatened the villagers' older way of life. The witchcraft episode may have been a last effort to strike out against the forces of change.

The hysteria came to an end when the girls accused the wife of the new royal governor. That claim was too much. Leading ministers of Massachusetts began to question the kind of evidence used in the trials. With their support, Governor Phipps stopped all new arrests for witchcraft in October 1692. In 1693, he released all remaining prisoners and issued a general pardon.

▶ **9.** How did the Salem witchcraft crisis begin and end?

Reviewing Section III

Identify King James II, Dominion of New England, Sir Edmund Andros, Glorious Revolution, Leisler's Rebellion, Salem witch trials

Questions to Answer
1. What were the effects of the Dominion of New England?
2. What form did the glorious revolutions take in Boston, New York, and Maryland?

A Question to Think About Why did the colonists not revolt before the Glorious Revolution?

IV. The Settlement

What form of government for the colonies emerged from all this confusion? William and Mary abandoned James II's experiment with the Dominion of New England. They did not, however, abandon the effort to exercise more control over England's colonies.

Governing the Empire

William and Mary kept the Navigation Acts in effect. In fact, a new navigation act in 1696 tightened enforcement of the old laws. It provided for **vice-admiralty courts** in the colonies to try cases involving the Navigation Acts. The advantage of vice-admiralty courts, from the Crown's point of view, was that they did not have juries. Too often local jury members had sympathized with smugglers and had found them not guilty.

In 1696, the new rulers also reorganized the Lords of Trade. From the change came the **Board of Trade.** It was made up of eight well-paid officials of the king charged with keeping track of the American colonies.

The new Board of Trade had much the same powers as the Lords of Trade. The board could still only make suggestions which, if accepted, were to be put into effect by other parts of the English government.

The Crown decided to govern the colonies individually rather than grouping them. However, Plymouth remained part of Massachusetts Bay, and New Haven stayed a part of Connecticut.

▶1. How did William and Mary try to enforce the Navigation Acts?

The Proprietary Colonies The proprietary colonies were supervised by the Crown more closely than was true in the past. After a time, both Penn and Baltimore were given back their charters. However, both men had to pay a price. In the future, the king would review their choices for governor, and the king's officials would review all the colonies' laws.

The government of most proprietary colonies included an elected assembly. The proprietor appointed a governor and a council. After 1701, Pennsylvania allowed Delaware to have its own assembly, which made it more like a separate colony. It remained, however, under the governor of Pennsylvania.

▶2. What changes were made in the government of proprietary colonies?

Corporate Colonies Rhode Island, Connecticut, and Massachusetts tried to get their charters back or to get new ones. Eventually they succeeded. They were **corporate colonies** because their charters were granted not to a proprietor but to the colonists themselves, bound together in a legal body called a corporation. Their governments consisted of governors, councils, and assemblies.

In Rhode Island and Connecticut, the settlers chose their own governors and other officials. With Massachusetts, the great troublemaker of the past, the Crown took more care. It gave the Bay Colony a new charter in 1691. However, the king appointed the colony's governor. Its councillors were elected by the lower house of the assembly. However, all laws passed in the colony had to be sent to England for review. In addition, the vote was given to all men who owned a certain amount of property, as was the case

in other colonies. Membership in a Puritan church no longer brought the vote. The charter also gave freedom of worship to all Christians except Catholics.

After 1691, the Puritans had to share power with others—with royal officials, with other Christians. And their province, once so fiercely independent, was brought under the wing of the Crown.

▶3. How did the government of Massachusetts Bay colony change after 1691?

Royal Colonies A growth in the number of royal colonies was another sign of the times. Slowly the Crown took over one colony and then another. By 1730, half of all the British North American colonies—6 of 12—were governed directly by the Crown.

A royal colony was governed by a governor and councillors appointed by the king. After

The Glorious Revolution brought William and Mary to the English throne.

the Glorious Revolution, all royal colonies also had elected assemblies. The Glorious Revolution firmly defined the role of Parliament in England, and it settled the future of assemblies in America. From then on, the importance of the assemblies grew.

▶**4.** How was a royal colony governed?

Unanswered Questions

The changes in the way England ruled its colonies were compromises between the Crown's desire for power and the colonists' desire for a voice in their government. The new systems left some issues unsettled. Who owned the colonies? The king, as in Spain? Or the people of England? If the colonies belonged to the king, he alone could rule them. If they belonged to the people of England, who were represented in Parliament, then Parliament also had power over the colonies.

Most people were more than happy to leave the issue unsettled. They had had enough conflict for one lifetime. In time, however, the issue would arise again. It would not be easy to settle.

▶**5.** What question did the settlements after the Glorious Revolution leave unanswered?

Reviewing Section IV

Identify vice-admiralty courts, Board of Trade, corporate colonies

Questions to Answer
1. How did the king tighten control on the proprietary colonies?
2. What was a corporate colony?

A Question to Think About Why was the issue of who owned the colonies likely to emerge again?

IMPROVE YOUR READING
Using Categories

Reporters for newspapers and television generally explain *who* is involved in a story, *what* happened in the story, *when* and *where* it happened, and *why* it happened in their first few sentences. These five *w*'s—*who, what, when, where,* and *why*—contain the most essential information about an event.

Chapter 6 describes several conflicts that troubled the colonies in the mid and late 1660's. You will be able to understand and remember these conflicts better by categorizing them according to the five *w*'s.

The lists below will help you to do this. The people involved in each conflict are identified (the *who* column). Your task is to complete each list on a separate sheet of paper. Fill in the proper information to explain what, where, when, and why. Notice that some information has already been provided.

Who: Indians versus the colonists	
What:	
Where: New England	
When:	
Why:	

Who: Bacon versus Governor Berkeley	
What:	
Where:	
When: 1676	
Why:	

CHAPTER 6 REVIEW

Vocabulary Check

On a sheet of paper, write the correct term or terms to complete each of the following sentences.

1. The conflict between the colonists and Indians in New England was called _____.
2. The land between the Tidewater and the mountains is the _____.
3. Under the Navigation Acts, goods called _____ had to be shipped directly to England or to English colonies.
4. James II's single government for the New England colonies, New York, and New Jersey was called the _____.
5. Legal actions growing out of the Navigation Acts could be tried in _____ courts.

Fact Check

Write the name of the person or group described in each of the phrases below.

1. Leader of Wampanoag who attacked Plymouth colony in 1675
2. Governor of Virginia in 1670 who, with his friends, had control of the government
3. Rebel who led his followers against the governor of Virginia
4. Governor of the Dominion of New England
5. Rulers of England as a result of the Glorious Revolution

Time Check

On a separate sheet of paper, write the number of the following events in proper chronological order.

1. Fighting breaks out between New Englanders and the Wampanoag.
2. Nathaniel Bacon dies and his rebellion collapses.
3. Governor Andros allows people of all religions to worship freely.
4. James II is removed as king in the Glorious Revolution.
5. New Englanders remove Andros and his officials from office.
6. The Salem witch crisis begins.

Skills Check

Use the chart on page 111 to answer the following questions.

1. (a) What was the first colony founded in New England? (b) When was it founded?
2. (a) Name the Middle Colonies. (b) Which two had a change in government in 1763?
3. Name a Southern Colony that was founded in the eighteenth century.
4. Name two colonies that had a corporate government in 1763.
5. (a) What type of government did most of the colonies have at the time they were founded? (b) How had this changed by 1763?

Think and Write

1. Why did a war between the Indians and the colonists in New England break out in the late 1600's?
2. How did trouble between the Indians and the colonists in Virginia lead to a civil war?
3. (a) Why did Charles II and his advisors ask Parliament to pass a series of Navigation Acts? (b) How did Massachusetts react to the Navigation Acts?
4. How did James II plan to rule his North American colonies?
5. How did the Glorious Revolution affect England's North American colonies?

Chapter 7

The Struggle for North America

This painting shows British troops, led by General Wolfe, scaling the steep cliff near Quebec in preparation for an attack on the French.

Throughout all the disorder and confusion of the late 1600's, the English colonies in North America continued to grow. The nearby colonies of Spain and France also grew. England, Spain, and France were in a struggle for control of North America.

Starting in the 1680's, those three countries fought a series of wars both in North America and in Europe. The last of the wars, which the English colonists called the French and Indian War, ended with a great victory for England. As a result, England won control over huge stretches of land in North America.

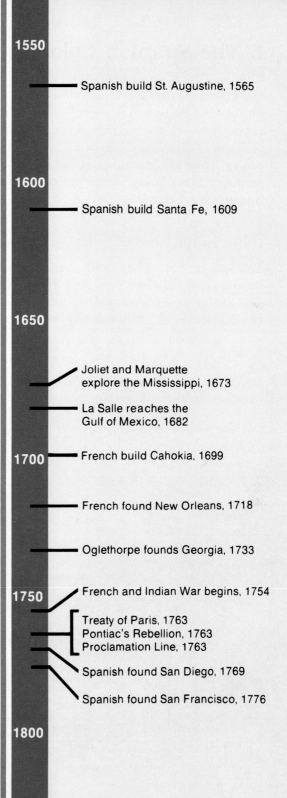

1550

Spanish build St. Augustine, 1565

1600

Spanish build Santa Fe, 1609

1650

Joliet and Marquette
explore the Mississippi, 1673

La Salle reaches the
Gulf of Mexico, 1682

1700 — French build Cahokia, 1699

French found New Orleans, 1718

Oglethorpe founds Georgia, 1733

1750 — French and Indian War begins, 1754

Treaty of Paris, 1763
Pontiac's Rebellion, 1763
Proclamation Line, 1763

Spanish found San Diego, 1769

Spanish found San Francisco, 1776

1800

I. The Spanish Colonies of North America

Although the Spanish had a huge empire in the Americas, they were more interested in Mexico and Peru than in their lands farther north. However, the Spanish did explore and claim much land in the present-day United States. They also set up some small settlements in these lands, which are called the **Spanish borderlands.**

Bases in the Borderlands

The Spanish built a base at St. Augustine on the east coast of Florida in 1565. It was the first European settlement in the present-day United States. Then, in the late 1600's, the Spanish set up several other bases in Florida, including a fort at Pensacola on the Gulf of Mexico. Pensacola was started in 1698.

The Spanish built a base at Santa Fe, in present-day New Mexico, in 1609. Although Santa Fe was a center for Spanish activities throughout the Southwest, the Spanish were slow to build other settlements in New Mexico or other parts of the borderlands. They did not begin to settle the coast of California until about 200 years after they first explored the area. San Diego was founded in 1769, and San Francisco was begun in 1776.

▶**1.** When did the Spanish build settlements in Florida? New Mexico? California?

Map Study *Find the Sacramento River. It is in the present-day state of California. Name seven settlements built by the Spanish in California.*

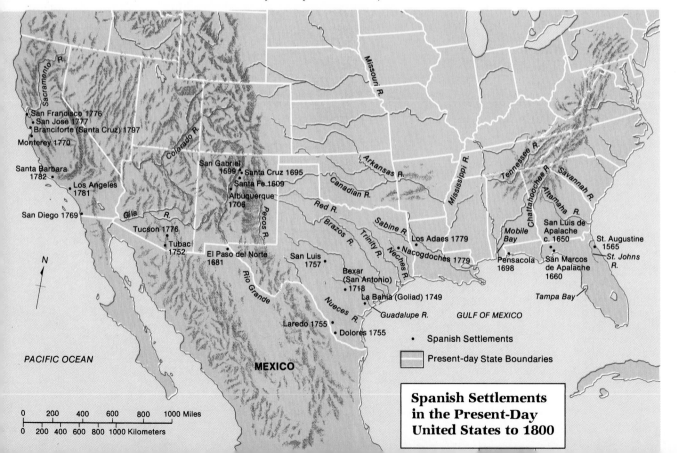

Spanish Settlements
in the Present-Day
United States to 1800

This drawing of the fort at St. Augustine was done in 1593. The Spanish placed guns around the fort to protect treasure ships on their way to Spain.

Forts and Missions Spanish settlements in the borderlands generally consisted of a **presidio** (pri sid'ē ō), or fort, and a Catholic mission. Sometimes the two were in the same building. The settlements had three main purposes. They were meant to protect Spain's claim to the borderlands. They also served as bases for trade with the Indians and centers for Spanish missionaries, who worked to convert the Indians to Catholicism.

The Spanish thought converting the Indians meant more than just changing their religious beliefs. The Spanish wanted the Indians to live like Europeans. As a result, in Florida and California, the Spanish got the Indians to live at the missions. There the missionaries could supervise the Indians' activities. Life in the missions had some sad effects. Though the missionaries' intentions were good, many of the Indians died of diseases Europeans unknowingly introduced.

▶**2.** Why did the process of converting the Indians sometimes have harmful effects?

Popé's Rebellion In the Southwest, the Spanish built their missions at the outskirts of the large villages of the Pueblo people. Then in the 1680's, about the time of the Indian wars in New England and Virginia, the Pueblo rebelled. They destroyed Spanish churches and killed Spanish priests. That uprising was known as **Popé's** (pō pāz') **Rebellion** after its Pueblo leader. By late 1680's, the Indians had driven the Spanish all the way back to El Paso on the Rio Grande. After Popé died in 1692, however, the Spanish returned.

▶**3.** What was Popé's Rebellion?

The Spanish and the English

There were fewer than 4,000 Spaniards in the area from Florida to California by 1700. Still the English worried about Spain's power in North America. The Spanish claimed the land along the east coast of North America up almost to Charleston in South Carolina.

125

They worked hard to keep good relations with the Creek and Cherokee of the Southeast. The Spanish encouraged bad feelings between their Indian allies and the English and the French.

The Spanish angered the English further by promising freedom to slaves who reached Florida. Many slaves made the dangerous journey, and before long a community of freed slaves grew up north of St. Augustine. English slave owners resented the loss of what they considered their property.

▶ **4.** Why did the Spanish bases in Florida worry the English?

Reviewing Section I

Identify Spanish borderlands, St. Augustine, Pensacola, Santa Fe, San Diego, San Francisco, presidio, Pope's Rebellion

Questions to Answer
1. For what purposes did the Spanish use their bases in the borderlands?
2. How did the few Spanish settlers in Florida threaten the English?

A Question to Think About How might the history of the borderlands have been different if the Spanish had found gold or silver there?

II. New France

The Spanish threatened the English colonies from the south. To the north of the English colonies lay another threat, New France. As the French began to move onto lands west of the English colonies, that threat increased.

Canada

The center of New France lay in the settlements along the St. Lawrence River, which were known together as **Canada.** The Company of New France, which was first set up in 1627, had charge of Canada. It tried to attract settlers by offering them large grants of land. All settlers, however, had to be French and Catholic. French Protestants, or Huguenots, were not welcome in Canada. Some Huguenots went to English or Dutch colonies.

There were only 356 French people in Canada by 1640. Ten years later the French population had grown to 2,000, but Canada was still very small.

▶ **1.** What people were allowed to settle in Canada?

Fur Traders and Missionaries

Even with a small population, New France produced profits for the company. Fishing brought in some money, but most of the wealth of New France came from the fur trade. Montreal and Quebec were centers for the fur trade and also for missionary efforts with the Indians.

The French fur traders, often accompanied by missionaries, worked closely with the Huron who lived near the lake that is now named Lake Huron. They also collected furs from Indians who lived along the Ottawa River.

▶ **2.** What made New France profitable?

Relations with the Indians The French, unlike the English, maintained good relations with the Indians. There were only a few French settlers, and not all of them were farmers or planters. So the French did not intrude on Indian lands as much as the English settlers did. In addition, the French fur traders and missionaries needed cooperation from the Indians. So their attitude toward the Indians was much more peaceful and respectful than that of the English or the Spanish settlers.

In the early days of New France, when there were few French women in Canada, French men often married Indian women. Also the French priests did not try to change the Indian way of life as much as English or Spanish missionaries did.

▶**3.** Why did the French maintain good relations with the Indians?

Iroquois Attacks However, the French had never had good relations with one group of Indians, the Iroquois. Those people, who traded with the Dutch, began fighting the Huron in the 1640's for control of the fur trade. The Iroquois attacked the French as trading partners of the Huron.

The Indian wars drained strength from New France. They also ended the fur trade for a time. The Huron were badly beaten by the Iroquois. Those Huron who had not been killed or captured were pushed far to the west. They could no longer collect furs for the French. Eventually the French made contact with other Indian groups, chiefly the Ottawa, who had been driven west of Lake Michigan into the Wisconsin Territory. Soon the fur trade prospered again with their help.

▶**4.** What happened as a result of the Iroquois attacks on the Huron?

A Government for New France

In the 1660's, King Louis XIV of France and his skillful minister, Jean Baptiste Colbert (kol bär'), decided to increase their power over New France. They wanted to build up the colony.

Map Study *Who controlled the land south of the English colonies? What names did the French give to their North American colonies?* ▶

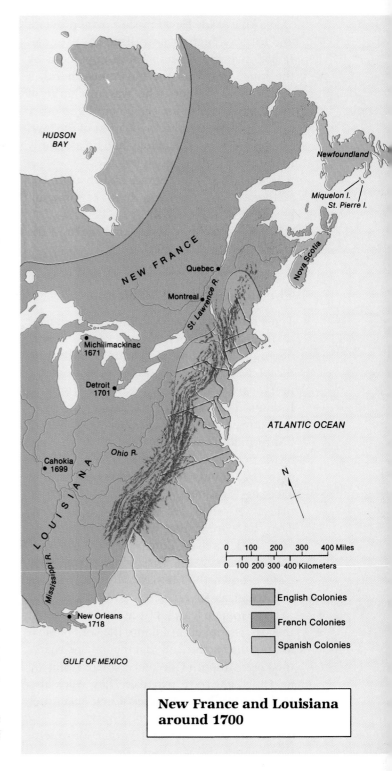

New France and Louisiana around 1700

127

The king made New France a royal province and set up a highly-centralized government. It had two top officials, both appointed by the king. One was the **governor-general,** a professional soldier, who was in charge of order and defense for the colony. The other official, the **intendant,** made most of the laws for New France. The colony had no assembly like those of the English colonies.

By the 1680's, New France had about 10,000 settlers. It had become a threat of some importance to the English.

▶**5.** What changes did the king make in the government of New France?

The Beginnings of Louisiana

The French became even more of a danger to the English when they began to spread down the Mississippi River and into the middle of North America. French missionaries first heard about the Mississippi from the Indians. The Indians described a great river that flowed to the "sea of Florida or that of California." That is, it went either to the Gulf of Mexico or to the Pacific.

In 1673, Louis Joliet (jō′lē et) and Father Jacques Marquette (mär ket′), a Catholic priest, set out to see where the river went. They left Green Bay on Lake Michigan in June and traveled down the Fox and Wisconsin rivers to the Mississippi River. They canoed down the Mississippi until it joined the Arkansas River.

The two men learned from the Indians that the Mississippi emptied into the Gulf of Mexico, not the Pacific, and that the Indians nearer the river's mouth (the place where it flowed into the sea) were warlike. They were also told that farther south they might encounter the Spanish. So they turned back.

▶**6.** What did Joliet and Father Marquette learn about the Mississippi?

La Salle's Dream   The reports of Joliet and Marquette inspired yet another Frenchman. René-Robert Cavelier, the Sieur de La Salle (lə sal′), wanted to claim the whole Mississippi Valley for France. He hoped to build a chain of forts around the Great Lakes region and along the Mississippi River to protect that claim. The forts would also be bases for the fur trade.

La Salle was a skilled fur trader. He had the wilderness skills important for his scheme, and he knew several Indian languages.

In 1677, La Salle went to France to win the king's support for his scheme. Colbert helped him get royal backing for his project.

La Salle returned to North America and in late 1681 started down the Mississippi. His expedition was made up of 54 people, including 31 Indians. On April 9, 1682, he arrived at the Gulf of Mexico. At a place not far from the present city of New Orleans, he claimed for France "all the nations, peoples, provinces, cities, towns, villages, mines, minerals, fisheries, streams, and rivers" that lay along the Mississippi from the mouth of the Ohio River (where it ran into the Mississippi) to the Gulf of Mexico. La Salle named the new lands **Louisiana,** after his king.

▶**7.** What lands did La Salle claim?

Louisiana   La Salle went to France to get the king's help starting a settlement at the mouth of the Mississippi. In 1684, La Salle sailed from France with 4 ships and 200 people.

He passed the Mississippi delta and landed instead on the Texas coast. La Salle thought the mouth of the Mississippi was in Texas. When he discovered his mistake, he tried to lead the expedition to the river by land. In 1687, La Salle was murdered by some of his men. Most of his followers died or were seized by the Spanish.

Years went by before France did much in Louisiana. Finally, in 1699, the French set up a fort on the Mississippi River at Cahokia, across the river from today's St. Louis. Then they built forts on the Gulf of Mexico at Biloxi and Mobile, west of the Spanish fort at Pensacola. In the north, they built forts at Michilimackinac (mish'ə lē mak'ə nak') in upper Michigan and at Detroit. Finally, in 1718, the French laid out a settlement called New Orleans at the mouth of the Mississippi. Four years later New Orleans became the center of French Louisiana.

Louisiana had trouble getting started. For one thing, the French king said furs from the northland had to be shipped to France through the St. Lawrence River, not the Mississippi. That lost Louisiana a lot of business. Indian wars and high death rates also kept settlers away. Finally, Louisiana turned to slaves for a labor force. In 1746, there were only about 4,100 French people in the province, and 800 of those were soldiers. There were also about 4,000 blacks in the colony.

▶8. Where did the French build forts in Louisiana?

Reviewing Section II

Identify Canada, Company of New France, the Huron, Louis XIV, Jean Baptiste Colbert, governor-general, intendant, Louis Joliet, Jacques Marquette, the Sieur de La Salle, Louisiana, Cahokia, Biloxi, Mobile, Michilimackinac, Detroit, New Orleans

Questions to Answer
1. What was La Salle's mistake?
2. How did the French try to protect their claim to Louisiana?

A Question to Think About Which of the English North American colonies was most like Louisiana?

III. The British Colonies

Although France's control of Louisiana was weak, its presence there worried the British. It meant that the French held the lands both to the north and to the west of the British colonies. To the south of the British colonies were the Spanish. Sooner or later competition for land and trade was bound to bring war with France or Spain—or with both.

Early Georgia

In order to hold off the Spanish, Britain's Board of Trade recommended the founding of a new colony south of the Carolinas in 1730. The new colony, Georgia, would tighten Britain's hold on the area. The board suggested that Georgia be settled by "the poor persons of London." It recruited General James Oglethorpe to choose the settlers and start the colony. Oglethorpe hated the Spanish, and he sympathized with the British poor. The challenge of setting up such a colony suited him perfectly.

In 1732, the Crown gave a royal charter to Oglethorpe and 20 other trustees of Georgia. They were granted the land between the Savannah and Altamaha (ål'tə mə hå) rivers, but only for 21 years. After that, all rights would return to the Crown, and Georgia would become a royal colony.

▶1. Why was Georgia started?

Rules for Georgia In 1733, Oglethorpe brought 32 families to a site he had chosen on a high bluff along the Savannah River. Oglethorpe chose that site for Georgia's first settlement, called Savannah, because it could be defended easily.

The trustees set rules for the new colony that made sense for a military outpost. Farms had to be kept small so they would be close together and easy to defend. Women were not allowed to inherit land because women could not be soldiers. Slavery was not allowed in the colony because slave owners did not want their slaves to have guns or be soldiers. No rum or other "strong waters" were allowed in the colony, either.

The colony was governed by a president and a common council appointed by the trustees. It had no assembly, since army posts are rarely run by their soldiers.

▶**2.** Why were the trustees' rules for Georgia so different from the laws of any other British colony?

The Rules Change The trustees selected settlers with care, sifting through England's poor for those who were virtuous and industrious. The trustees also welcomed Protestants from other European countries as settlers if they could prove they were good, hard-working folk.

Still the colony did not thrive. The population remained small. By 1740 about 3,000 people had come to Georgia, but many had already left.

So the trustees started changing their rules. First, they increased the amount of land a settler could have. Then they let women inherit land. Soon they also lifted the ban on liquor. Finally, in 1750, they allowed Georgians to own slaves.

The trustees even let the colonists have an assembly but not, it seems, to pass laws. The colonists used the assembly to air their complaints. The settlers complained so much that the trustees gave the colony back to the Crown two years before they had to.

▶**3.** Why did the trustees change their rules for Georgia?

More Colonists, More Land

Although Georgia got off to a slow start, the British colonies in North America as a whole grew dramatically from 1700 to 1775. The British colonies had about 250,000 people in 1700. In 1775, they had 10 times as many— 2,500,000. The population grew so rapidly in part because most women had families of from four to eight children. British colonists were healthy, and many lived long lives.

The population also grew because many immigrants came to the British colonies in the 1700's. By 1763, over one third of the population was **immigrants,** people who left their homelands to settle in the colonies.

▶**4.** Why did the population of the British colonies grow so rapidly in the 1700's?

The Immigrants The immigrants came from many different places in Europe. People from Scotland came to escape poverty. Many Scots settled in the western parts of North Carolina and in upstate New York. A few settled in the Chesapeake colonies, where they soon controlled the tobacco trade. French Huguenots, oppressed in Catholic France, settled throughout the British colonies. They were even welcomed in Massachusetts, which did not welcome many non-English immigrants. About 1,500 Jews came before 1775. Most of them settled in cities such as Newport and New York City.

One of the largest groups of immigrants came from what today is Germany. Some lost their homes during wars and fled to the British colonies. Protestant groups, such as the Mennonites and the Amish, came looking for religious freedom and good land.

Another large number of immigrants were called Scots-Irish by other colonists. They were Protestants from Ireland. They left Ireland for many reasons. British laws hurt them financially and also punished them for being **dissenters,** that is, Protestants who did not belong to the Church of England. Then drought ruined their crops, and their English landlords raised their rents.

Once in North America, many Scots-Irish immigrants moved more than once before finding somewhere they wanted to stay. They tended to take up empty lands whether they owned them or not. That habit made them some enemies.

▶**5.** What groups immigrated to the British colonies in North America?

Pushing Back the Frontier Many German and Scots-Irish immigrants moved to the Pennsylvania and southern frontiers. They started by settling along the Susquehanna (sus′kwə han′ə) River. Others moved farther west until they came to the less rich farming lands along the Juniata (jü′nē at′ə) River, which runs into the Susquehannah. Those rivers lead through the Appalachians toward the Ohio Country. However, the immigrants did not cross the mountains. They left the Ohio Country to the French and the Indians.

Instead, the immigrants turned south. They traveled through the Great Valley of the Appalachians toward lands even cheaper than those in Pennsylvania. They made farms in the Shenandoah Valley of Virginia and then spilled eastward through the mountains onto the Piedmont. By 1750, immigrants were moving still farther south, into the Carolinas.

The immigrants helped settle an area known as the **southern backcountry,** which includes the lands west of the Tidewater. Most families in the backcountry supported

Map Study *Along what body of water were most of the settlements built? Name four settlements that were started before 1700.* ▶

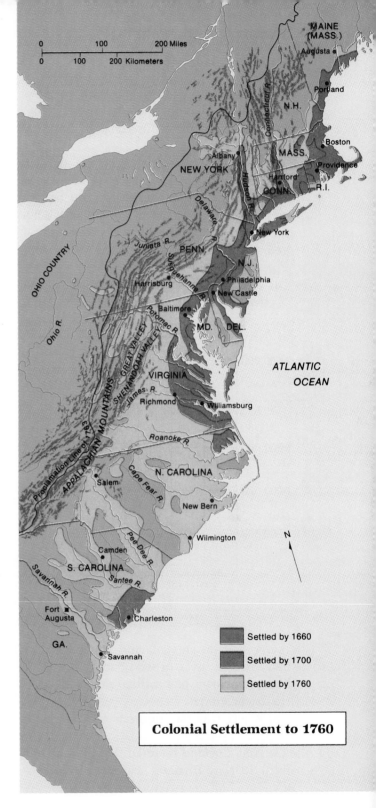

Colonial Settlement to 1760

■ Settled by 1660
■ Settled by 1700
□ Settled by 1760

IMPROVE YOUR SKILLS
Reading Line Graphs

A line graph is a good way to show trends or changes that take place over a period of time. It is also a good way to compare statistical information.

Look at the graph below. The title explains that the graph is about the growth of the colonies from 1630 to 1780. The numbers along the horizontal axis, the bottom of the graph, tell the years it covers. The numbers along the vertical axis, the side of the graph, show the number of people living in the colonies.

If you want to know the population of the colonies for a year between 1630 and 1780, look for the year on the horizontal axis. Then move up the graph along the vertical axis until you reach the line that shows the population.

Use the graph to answer the following questions. (Answers may be approximate.)

1. What information does the graph show?
2. In what year was the population the smallest?
3. What was the population in 1760?
4. Did the population increase or decrease between 1630 and 1780?
5. In what decade did the population rise above 500,000?

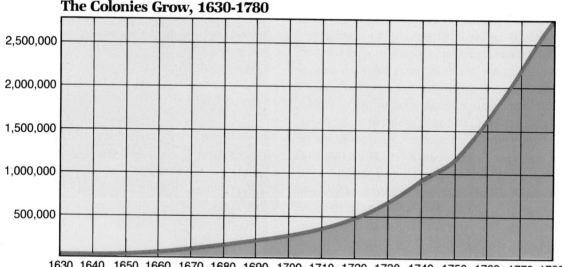

The Colonies Grow, 1630-1780

Source: Historical Statistics of the United States

themselves on small farms. However, they had little left over to sell or trade. By 1775, about a quarter of a million people lived in the backcountry.

▶6. Where was the southern backcountry?

The New England Frontier Few immigrants went to New England. However, New Englanders had many children. As a result, by the 1750's, Connecticut, Rhode Island, and almost all of Massachusetts were filled to their western borders. The children of New England townspeople moved into the part of New York that would one day become Vermont. They also started adding to the small settlements already begun in New Hampshire and along the coast of Maine.

▶7. Where was the New England frontier?

Establishment of Black Slavery

Not all the newcomers to British North America were Europeans. Many Africans were brought to the colonies as slaves.

In the late 1600's and early 1700's, the number of black slaves in the British colonies rose dramatically. Virginia, for example, had only about 300 slaves in 1649. That was about 3 percent of its population. By 1730, 40 percent of all Virginians were slaves. By the end of the colonial period, one in every five persons in British North America was black.

Although most slaves lived in the Southern Colonies, there were slaves in the North too. Persons of African descent made up as much as 20 percent of the population of New York City in the eighteenth century. Some of those people were free, but most were slaves.

The reasons colonists owned slaves varied from colony to colony. Sometimes, as in South Carolina, the slaves' skill at growing rice and their immunity to malaria and yellow fever were important. But once the death rates dropped, colonists everywhere saw advantages in buying a slave's lifetime of labor as opposed to a few years of work from an indentured servant.

▶**8.** Where did slaves live in the late 1600's and early 1700's?

Slavery and the Law In all the colonies, slavery meant being owned by someone else. What else it meant was not clear, since there was no such thing as slavery in English law. However, beginning in the late 1600's, colonial legislatures began passing laws that defined slavery in British North America.

Those laws varied a little in each colony. However, the laws of every colony made clear that slaves were the property of their owners for life. Children born of slave women were also slaves even if their fathers were free.

Slavery was defined by color. American slaves were black. There were a few Indian slaves, but most enslaved Indians were sent to the West Indies, where they could run home less easily.

The laws limited the number of things slaves could do. Slaves could not carry arms. They could not marry whites. Even marriages between slaves were not legally binding like the marriages of whites. Slaves could not practice certain skilled trades for fear they would compete with white artisans. Slaves could not travel without their owners' permission.

▶**9.** What laws did the colonies establish concerning slavery?

The Journey to the Colonies Most African-born people became slaves in one of three ways. Some became slaves after being taken prisoner in local African wars. Others were sold as slaves in punishment for crimes. Some were simply stolen by African traders who exchanged people for goods from Europe. Eventually all of the African slaves reached the west coast of Africa. There traders from Europe came to buy slaves from local African suppliers.

This watercolor was painted by Godfrey Meynall, an eyewitness to the slave trade.

Slaves were then packed into ships and sent across the Atlantic Ocean. The terrible **Middle Passage**—the months-long voyage from the African coast to the West Indies—came next. Many slaves died before ever reaching the colonies.

Over 40 percent of the Africans who survived the Middle Passage stayed in the West Indies. The rest went to mainland colonies, including those in British North America.

▶**10.** How did Africans become slaves?

Life in the Colonies Many slaves did not accept their new life in the colonies without resistance. Some fought back by poisoning their masters or setting fire to their property. There were a number of slave uprisings in the early 1700's. When the rebellions failed, slaves turned to more subtle forms of resisting. Some broke tools. Others pretended to be stupid or sick to avoid work. They sang songs that kept alive their dreams of freedom.

Despite all odds, some slaves managed to create close families and a sense of community with other slaves. In South Carolina, large numbers of slaves lived together on the rice plantations near the coast. These slaves developed their own distinctive society.

They even created a unique language, Gullah (gəl'ə), to overcome the differences in their African languages.

▶**11.** How did slaves respond to slavery?

Stronger Economies and Larger Cities

As the population of the colonies grew, the colonial economies grew stronger. Slave labor brought boom times to tobacco planters in the Chesapeake colonies. Rich planters began to build great plantation houses and to fill them with fine furniture. By increasing the amount of rice and indigo that could be grown in South Carolina, slaves helped make that colony the richest of all. The economies of the Northern Colonies improved too.

The increasing number of colonists made more products to sell and bought more things as well. In most colonies, selling and buying were carried on in cities. As a result, the cities grew, and those that grew the fastest were near some water route to the west.

Philadelphia's population went from about 13,000 to 24,000 between 1743 and 1763. It was then the largest city in British North America. Next came New York, with 18,000

Lucy Harrison, a neighbor of William Bird, painted this view of his mansion, Westover. Begun in 1690, Westover was located 30 miles from Jamestown.

people in 1763. Boston, whose rivers did not go far to the west, declined in size.

Colonial cities were much smaller than great European cities like Paris and London. However, places like Philadelphia, New York, Boston, Charleston, Newport, and Baltimore had an importance beyond their size. Legislatures met and newspapers were published in the cities. There merchants sat in coffee houses, discussing colonial affairs. The cities were the cultural and political centers of the British North American colonies. Their growth was one sign that those colonies were steadily becoming richer and stronger.

▶ 12. What was the importance of colonial cities?

Reviewing Section III

Identify Georgia, James Oglethorpe, Savannah, immigrants, Scots-Irish dissenters, southern backcountry, Middle Passage, Philadelphia

Questions to Answer
1. Name two reasons Georgia was unique among the British colonies in North America.
2. Where were the frontiers of the British colonies in North America in 1750?

A Question to Think About Why did slavery in the colonies have to be defined by law?

IV. The Great Wars for Empire

As the British colonies grew richer and stronger, it became more difficult for them to avoid war with their French and Spanish neighbors. In fact, the British colonies went to war with France and Spain several times before 1750. Those wars, however, did not begin in the colonies. They began in Europe and spilled over into North America. Then, in 1754, a decisive war began in the colonies and spread to Europe.

The First Colonial Wars

In the colonies, the first of the wars was called King William's War (1689–1697). Next came Queen Anne's War (1702–1713) and King George's War (1740–1748).

In each of those wars, battles were fought between the French and the British in the northern part of the British colonies and between the Spanish and British in the southern part. Great effort and many lives were spent in those wars for few lasting results. Little territory changed hands.

For example, over 4,000 New Englanders set out in 1745 to take the French fortress at Louisbourg (lü′ē bərg′). It was the strongest fortress in North America and a major danger to British colonists in the North. The colonists won. However, when the peace treaty was negotiated, Britain gave the fortress back to France.

Deerfield, Massachusetts, was the site of many battles during King Philip's War.

The wars made colonial life more insecure. Both French and English colonists feared that the other side would turn its Indian allies against them. In 1689, the Iroquois, allies of the English, nearly destroyed the French village of La Chine (lə shēn′) near Montreal. Then the French sent their Indian allies to attack Schenectady (skə nek′təd ē) and other English settlements.

Again, in 1703, the Indians attacked. At Deerfield, Massachusetts, they killed 38 settlers and carried another 100 off to Canada. Not even peace treaties ended such troubles. For example, in 1713, two years after the end of Queen Anne's War, the Spanish encouraged the Yamasee and Creek Indians to begin a year-long war against settlements on the South Carolina frontier.

Wars also made the seas less safe. During wartime, European countries gave permission to attack enemy shipping to certain privately owned ships known as **privateers.** Privateering could be very profitable, and so the practice was hard to stop when peace came. Some owners of privateers simply became pirates who attacked the ships of any nation, including ships belonging to their own nation.

▶**1.** What were the results of the early colonial wars?

The Ohio Country

After King George's War there was no major war for a time, but there were clashes between the French and the British. Most of the conflict was over the Ohio Country, the rich and fertile land west of the Appalachian Mountains. By the middle of the eighteenth century, there was no keeping British colonists out of the Ohio Country. Pennsylvanians started to trade with the Indians there. Virginians claimed that their charter of 1609 gave them the Ohio Country.

In 1747, a group of Virginia planters and London merchants organized the Ohio Company to settle the Ohio Valley. Two years later the British Crown gave the company 200,000 acres in the Ohio Country. The Crown promised more land if the company settled 200 families there within 7 years.

The French also claimed the Ohio Country, and they tried to keep the British colonists out. They carved the message that the Ohio Country belonged to France on lead plates and then placed them along the Allegheny and Ohio rivers. Neither the English nor the Indians were very impressed, and so the French acted more forcefully. They destroyed the major post where Indians and Pennsylvanians traded in the Ohio Country and began to build a number of forts nearby.

The Virginians decided to beat the French at their own game. They started a fort at the important location where the Allegheny River joins the Monongahela (mə non′gə hē′lə) to form the Ohio River. The city of Pittsburgh stands there now. French soldiers drove the Virginians out before they were half done. Then the French built their own Fort Duquesne (dü kān′) on the same spot.

Meanwhile, soldiers led by a 22-year-old militia officer named George Washington were on their way to protect Virginia's fort builders. Washington defeated a small party of French soldiers near Great Meadows in western Pennsylvania on May 28, 1754. Then, on July 3, he was defeated by a larger French force at a hastily-built shelter named Fort Necessity. Washington and his men surrendered, and the French allowed them to return to Virginia. However, they had done something of great importance. Without intending to, Washington and his men had begun a major war.

▶**2.** What happened to George Washington at Fort Necessity?

The French and Indian War

The war that started in 1754 at Great Meadows was the last of the eighteenth-century wars for empire. The British colonists called it the **French and Indian War** because they fought mainly against the French and France's Indian allies.

▶**3.** Why did the British colonists call the war that began in 1754 the French and Indian War?

The Albany Congress After Washington's defeat at Fort Necessity, the Board of Trade tried to prepare the colonists for war. It ordered a conference at Albany where representatives of 7 colonies met with 150 Iroquois leaders in June 1754. The representatives tried to convince the Iroquois to support the British in the war. They failed. The Iroquois had helped the British in the past, but they would not promise to take sides this time.

The colonial delegates agreed, however, on a plan of union proposed by Benjamin Franklin, an ingenious colonist from Philadelphia. Franklin's plan, known as the **Albany Plan of Union,** was based in part on the Iroquois League. Colonial assemblies would send delegates to a council that would be responsible for Indian affairs and defense. Those issues concerned people in all the colonies.

Benjamin Franklin's cartoon expressed his desire for the colonists to work together.

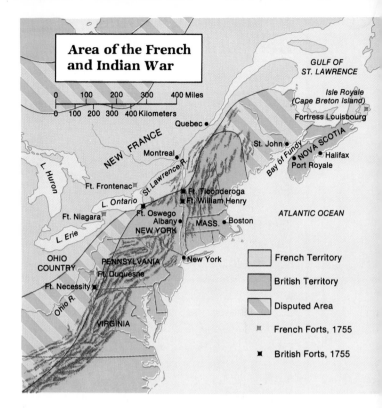

Map Study *In what present-day state is Fort Necessity located? Name two French cities located along the St. Lawrence River.*

When the delegates went home from Albany, they could not interest their colonies in Franklin's scheme, however. The Crown was not interested, either.

▶**4.** What was the Albany Plan of Union?

Braddock's Defeat The British were discouraged by early battles in the French and Indian War. General Edward Braddock dragged tons of heavy cannon through the mountains toward Fort Duquesne. Unfortunately, he did not keep a good lookout for the enemy. On July 9, 1755, the French made a surprise attack on the British soldiers who were about eight miles from Fort Duquesne. Braddock himself was among the hundreds of redcoats who died that day.

▶**5.** Why was Braddock defeated?

137

Benjamin Franklin

On January 17, 1706, the 15th child and youngest son of Josiah and Abiah Franklin was born in Boston, Massachusetts. The child, named Benjamin, would grow up to become one of the most famous Americans of all times.

From the beginning, Ben loved to learn. But his father, who worked hard to earn a living as soap and candle maker, could not afford to keep the child in school. So after only two years of public education, Ben left school and worked at home for his father.

Although no longer in school, Ben did not stop learning. Instead, he started a practice that was to last all his life. He taught himself. This trait, more than any other, was to be responsible for Benjamin Franklin's remarkable career as printer, author, inventor, scientist, and statesman.

Not long after Ben left school, his father urged him to work for Ben's brother, a printer. Young Ben soon became a skilled printer, but he did not get along with his brother. The two quarreled frequently, and Ben longed to become his own master. Finally, when he was about 17 years old, he left Boston and ran away to the largest, most exciting city in the British colonies — Philadelphia. He arrived there with one Dutch dollar and a copper shilling.

In his new home, Ben worked hard to earn a living, first for himself and later for his wife and children. He began his career as a printer. In time, he was able to open up his own shop. His newspaper, the *Pennsylvania Gazette*, soon became the most famous in the city.

Although his newspaper helped make him famous, Ben's greatest success as a printer and writer came from a small collection of interesting facts and anecdotes that he published under the title *Poor Richard's Almanac*. Even today people quote sayings from this famous work.

Throughout his life, Franklin worked hard to improve himself and everything around him. This included the city of Philadelphia, which he loved. It was he who began a project to get the muddy streets of the city paved. He also helped organize a volunteer fire company and a militia.

When he was not occupied with community activities, Franklin found time for the study of science. He proved that lightning is a form of electricity; and he also invented, among other things, the lightning rod, bifocals, and a wood-burning stove that is still used today.

No doubt Franklin's list of inventions would have been even longer if he had not given up his scientific studies to serve his country. He earned a place in American history for the part he played in writing and signing four important documents: the Declaration of Independence, the Constitution, and two peace treaties. When he died in 1790 at the age of 84, he was honored at his funeral by 20,000 Americans. They knew that the nation had lost an extraordinary leader.

Pitt Takes Charge The British faced one defeat after another until 1757. Then William Pitt became the king's minister, and Britain's situation changed. Pitt was a brilliant leader. He created a plan for crushing the French. First, he had the British take Fort Louisbourg again. That gave them control of the St. Lawrence River. British troops also took Fort Duquesne, important for holding the West. In July 1759, the British captured Fort Niagara between Lake Ontario and Lake Erie. Once the British had Fort Niagara, the French were cut off from the entire Great Lakes area.

Pitt's next target was Quebec. The British held posts to the east and to the west of Quebec. Pitt planned a twofold attack on the city. One group of soldiers would come up from New York, and another would come up the St. Lawrence.

The expedition from New York was stalled, and so the attack on Quebec was left to the British force coming up the St. Lawrence. It was led by General James Wolfe, a thin 30-year-old with a sunken chin and a nasty temper. Wolfe, however, had proved himself a better officer than many older men. That was what mattered to Pitt, who hoped Wolfe would help him beat the French.

▶**6.** What French forts did Pitt have the British take before they attacked Quebec?

★★★★★★★★★★★★★★★★★★The United States and the World★★
Taking Fortress Louisbourg

During King George's War, the New England colonists felt threatened by the powerful French fortress at Louisbourg on Cape Breton Island. Louisbourg was an imposing sight. The fortress was built on a bit of land jutting into the ocean. On one side was the Atlantic Ocean, and on the other side was a large harbor. Louisbourg guarded the entrance to the St. Lawrence River.

English leaders were unwilling to take troops from the war in Europe to fight in North America. So Governor William Shirley of Massachusetts decided that New Englanders should take Louisbourg by themselves. Volunteers from all over New England quickly put together an army of merchants and farmers.

Pepperell assembled a few small boats, and the British navy in the West Indies sent more. On March 24, 1745, the New Englanders set sail for Louisbourg.

Pepperell thought that the key to Louisbourg was the Royal Garrison, the cannon that stood a mile across the harbor from the fortress. If the New Englanders could take that garrison, they might survive to take the fort.

The French were waiting for the New Englanders. French ships sailed out to gun down the attackers. However, through a series of French mistakes and New England luck, some of Pepperell's troops landed and took the garrison.

The colonists turned the garrison's cannon around and aimed them at the fort. For days, cannon balls pounded the walls of the fortress. Finally the French surrendered on June 15, 1745. The New Englanders were pleased for they had won a great victory.

Paris and London were astonished at the news that Louisbourg had fallen. However, it was the New Englanders who were astonished at the peace treaty that was signed in 1748. England gave Louisbourg back to the French in exchange for Madras, a small foothold in India. New Englanders were outraged. England, it seemed, did not have their interests at heart.

General Wolfe led British troops against the French in Quebec during the French and Indian War.

Montcalm and Wolfe The French commander at Quebec was Louis Joseph, the Marquis de Montcalm (mon kalm′). He was not worried when Wolfe arrived in June 1759. Quebec was high on a cliff above the St. Lawrence River, which made it easy to defend. Montcalm thought there was no way for the British to reach the city without being cut down by French guns.

Wolfe, however, was a daring soldier. After several other schemes failed, he managed to sneak his men up the river at night. They climbed up an undefended path to the Plains of Abraham, a field just west of the city. Then, on September 13, Montcalm awoke to find the enemy at hand. Four days later both Montcalm and Wolfe were dead, but Quebec was a British city.

Wolfe's great victory did not end the war. Montreal fell to the British the next year, and fighting continued for another three years in Europe. Yet, for all practical purposes, the fight over North America was decided in 1759 on the Plains of Abraham. When the French lost Quebec, they lost their empire in North America.

▶**7.** Who won the battle of Quebec?

The Peace of Paris

In 1763, a peace treaty was signed at Paris. It gave Great Britain all of French North America east of the Mississippi except for the city of New Orleans. Spain, France's ally in the war, had to give Florida to Britain. France then gave its territory west of the Mississippi and the city of New Orleans to Spain for its help in the war. The Peace of Paris, in short, brought the French North American empire to an end and pushed the western boundary of British North America from the Appalachians to the Mississippi.

▶**8.** What were the major provisions of the Peace of Paris?

The Effects of the Peace The Peace of Paris changed the lives of all Americans. However, those most affected by it were the French and Spanish settlers and those Indians who suddenly found themselves under British rule.

Most French settlers decided to remain where they were. The British treated them well and allowed practice of the Catholic religion. On the other hand, most of the people in Spanish Florida fled to other Spanish colonies such as Cuba and Mexico. The first to go were former slaves who did not want to fall into the hands of their old owners in the British colonies.

The Indians who lived west of the Appalachians were also affected by the Peace of Paris. The French, they said, had no right to give their lands to the British. To win Indian cooperation during the war, the British had promised to respect Indian rights to the Ohio

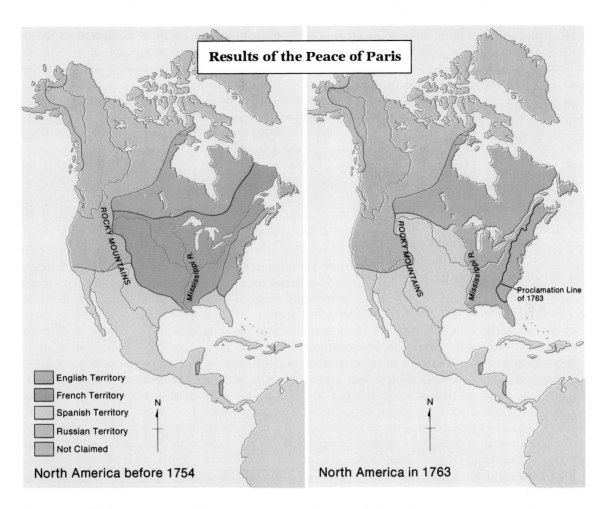

Results of the Peace of Paris

English Territory
French Territory
Spanish Territory
Russian Territory
Not Claimed

ROCKY MOUNTAINS

Mississippi R.

N

North America before 1754

ROCKY MOUNTAINS

Mississippi R.

Proclamation Line of 1763

N

North America in 1763

Map Study *Which country gained the greatest amount of territory in North America as a result of the Peace of Paris?*

Country. However, British settlers soon began moving onto lands that belonged to the Delaware and Iroquois.

The British disturbed the Indians in other ways too. They raised the price of goods sold to the Indians. They refused to pay rents for posts on Indian lands or to give the Indians ammunition for hunting as the French had done.

▶**9.** What were the responses of the French and Spanish colonists to the Peace of Paris?

Pontiac's Rebellion Because of grievances against the British, Ottawa leader Pontiac brought many Indian groups in the west—including the Ottawa, Huron, Chippewa, Seneca, Miami, and Delaware—into a great alliance. In May 1763, these allied groups began a war against the British that is known as **Pontiac's Rebellion.**

The Indians seized most of the old French forts in the West, which were now held by the British. They killed some 2,000 settlers

141

along the Virginia and Pennsylvania frontier before they were defeated by British troops.

The British government tried to stop clashes between the colonists and the Indians by its **Proclamation of 1763.** It said that the lands between the Appalachians and the Mississippi were reserved for the Indians. No settlers could enter those lands, and settlers already there were told they had to move to the eastern side of the Appalachians.

Pontiac's Rebellion was put down soon after the proclamation was issued. The Indians had tried their strength against the British and lost. Their future did not look promising.
▶**10.** What was Pontiac's Rebellion?

The British Colonists Only the British colonists of North America had reason to celebrate in 1763. Now that the French and Spanish were gone, they could hope to live at last in peace. In short, the war seemed to open a new era in the lives of the British colonists in North America. Never before had the colonists been more confident of the future or prouder of being British.
▶**11.** How did the British colonists feel after the Peace of Paris?

Reviewing Section IV———————

Identify Louisbourg, privateers, Fort Duquesne, George Washington, Fort Necessity, French and Indian War, Albany Plan of Union, Edward Braddock, William Pitt, James Wolfe, the Marquis de Montcalm, Peace of Paris, Pontiac's Rebellion, Proclamation of 1763

Questions to Answer
1. What were the immediate results of the Peace of Paris?
2. Why were the British colonists proud and happy at the conclusion of the French and Indian War?

A Question to Think About Why were the colonies not interested in Franklin's Albany Plan of Union?

IMPROVE YOUR READING
Reviewing Cause and Effect

Each of the phrases below is one half of a cause and effect statement based on information from Chapter 7. Your task is to complete each of the statements by filling in the missing cause or effect. Write your answer on a separate sheet of paper.

1. _____ so the French did not intrude on Indian lands as much as the English settlers did.
2. The fur trade in Louisiana was not very profitable partly because _____.
3. New Englanders had many children. As a result, by the 1750's, _____.
4. In Georgia, because women could not be soldiers, they _____.
5. The population of New England grew rapidly because _____.
6. Since there were no English laws to define slavery, _____.
7. In most colonies, selling and buying were carried on in cities. As a result, _____.
8. The British colonists called the war that lasted from 1754 to 1763 the French and Indian War because _____.
9. Montcalm was not worried when Wolfe reached Quebec because _____.
10. Pontiac brought many Indian groups into a great alliance because _____.

CHAPTER 7 REVIEW

Vocabulary Check

On a separate sheet of paper, write the letter of the definition that best explains each of the numbered terms.

1. Presidio
2. Canada
3. Louisiana
4. Immigrants
5. Middle Passage

a. The voyage across the Atlantic from Africa to the West Indies
b. The French settlements along the St. Lawrence River
c. The name for the fort found in Spanish settlements
d. The land claimed for France by La Salle
e. People who leave their homelands to settle in another country

Fact Check

On a separate sheet of paper, fill in the word or words that best complete each of the following sentences.

1. The ____ built several bases in Florida, the southwestern part of what is today the United States, and California.
2. James Oglethorpe founded ____ partly to protect Britain's colonies in North America.
3. The ____ were the cultural and political centers of British North America.
4. France lost its huge empire in North America as a result of the ____.
5. The ____ set aside the land between the Appalachians and the Mississippi River for the Indians.

Time Check

On a separate sheet of paper, put the following events in chronological order.

1. La Salle claims Louisiana.
2. French and Indian War begins.
3. St. Augustine is founded.
4. Oglethorpe starts Georgia.
5. Treaty of Paris is signed.

Skills Check

Use the information below to draw a line graph showing the growth of the black population of New York from 1700 to 1750. Entitle the graph "Estimated Black Population of New York from 1700 to 1750." Write the years along the horizontal axis of the graph and the number of people along the vertical axis. The numbers have been rounded off. Begin the vertical axis of the graph with the number 2,000 and end it at 11,000.

1700	2,250	1730	7,000
1710	2,800	1740	9,000
1720	5,700	1750	11,000

Think and Write

1. Why did the Spanish build forts and missions in North America?
2. Compare the French and British colonies in North America in the mid 1700's.
3. Why did the English want a colony south of the Carolinas?
4. (a) Why did Scots-Irish and Germans emigrate to North America? (b) Where did they settle?
5. (a) What caused the French and Indian War? (b) What happened to New France as a result?

Chapter 8

Toward Independence

British soldiers are shown practicing drills on the Boston Common in 1768. The large house in the background was owned by merchant John Hancock.

The colonists of the thirteen British colonies in North America were proud to be British subjects in 1763. The British had won the French and Indian War, and the colonists had helped win that great victory. They looked forward to a peaceful and prosperous future under British rule. However, only thirteen years later, the colonists' feelings about the British had changed completely. In 1776, the British colonies of North America declared their independence from Great Britain and founded a new nation, the United States of America.

What changed the loyal colonists of 1763 into the revolutionaries of 1776? A long train of events convinced the colonists that Great Britain was trying to take away their freedom. Those events began after the Peace of Paris, when the British tried to tax the colonists to pay for the French and Indian War. The colonists said Parliament had no right to do that. The British disagreed. From that point, the conflict grew. Finally the colonists decided that for their good and that of their children they had to break away from the British government and rule themselves.

I. **The Beginning of Conflict**
   Britain Needs Money
   The Colonists' Arguments
   The British Answer

II. **The Colonists Resist**
   The Stamp Act Uprisings
   Peaceful Resistance
   The Repeal of the Stamp Act
   The Townshend Crisis

III. **The Path to War**
   The Tea Crisis
   The Intolerable Acts
   The Continental Congress
   The Fighting Begins

IV. **The Break with Britain**
   The People Take Power
   Common Sense
   The Declaration of Independence

1760

Sugar Act, 1764

Stamp Act, 1765
Virginia Resolves proposed, 1765

Stamp Act repealed, 1766
Declaratory Act, 1766

Townshend Acts, 1767

1770 — Boston Massacre, 1770

Boston Tea Party, 1773

Intolerable Acts, 1774
Meeting of the
First Continental Congress, 1774

Battles of Lexington,
Concord, and Bunker Hill, 1775

Common Sense published, 1776
Declaration of Independence, 1776

1780

I. The Beginning of Conflict

Soon after the French and Indian War, conflict between the thirteen colonies and Great Britain began over Britain's attempts to tax the colonists. The colonists raised the cry "No taxation without representation." In other words, since the colonies did not have representatives in Parliament, Parliament could not pass laws taxing the colonies. Feelings ran high on both sides.

Britain Needs Money

The British paid a high price for their victory in the French and Indian War. King George III, who had inherited the throne in 1760, and his chief minister, George Grenville, faced huge debts at the end of the war.

The people of the British Isles were already heavily taxed. Grenville thought it only fair that the colonists share that burden. After all, the colonies had benefited from the war as much as or more than people in Britain. Besides, the colonies had become more expensive to maintain. Britain had to keep an army on the frontier. It also had to support its new colonies in Canada and Florida. Clearly the colonists should help pay those costs.

▶**1.** Why did Grenville think the colonists should help pay Britain's debts from the French and Indian War?

The Trade Laws Some money could be raised through Britain's trade laws, but not much. They were designed to stop the colonies from trading with other nations, not to raise money for the British treasury. In the past, the colonists had ignored some trade laws. Now the British planned to see that the laws were enforced.

▶**2.** Why could the trade laws produce only a small amount of money for Britain?

The Molasses Act The Molasses Act of 1733 was one of the trade laws the colonists ignored. Molasses is produced when sugar cane is made into sugar. The colonists used it as a sweetener. They also made it into rum, which they either drank or traded elsewhere. In Africa, the colonists traded rum for slaves.

The purpose of the Molasses Act was to encourage the colonists to buy molasses from planters in the British West Indies. The Molasses Act put a duty, or tax on imported goods, of six pence on each gallon of molasses bought from the non-British West Indies.

The British West Indies, however, did not make enough molasses to fill the colonists' needs. In addition, the British charged more for molasses than the French. So, for years, the colonists bought French molasses and smuggled it home or bribed customs agents to look the other way.

Grenville ordered the customs agents to be stricter, and he ordered the British navy to help enforce the customs laws. Then he presented some new laws to Parliament.

▶**3.** What was the purpose of the Molasses Act of 1733?

The Sugar Act The first of Grenville's laws approved by Parliament was the Revenue Act of 1764, also called the **Sugar Act.** The new law cut in half the duty on molasses from the non-British West Indies. However, unlike the Molasses Act, the Sugar Act was to be strictly enforced.

The Sugar Act also set up new rules for the trials of people accused of smuggling. They could be tried in a new admiralty court in Halifax, Nova Scotia, even if they lived

Colonists in New Hampshire showed their feelings about the Stamp Act by throwing rocks at a doll-like figure of the local stamp collector.

in faraway Georgia. The Sugar Act also said the accused would be considered guilty until they proved themselves innocent. Under British law the accused is usually considered innocent until proven guilty.

▶ **4.** What were the major provisions of the Sugar Act?

The Stamp Act Grenville wrote another bill, called the **Stamp Act,** to raise even more money. Parliament passed this law in February 1765. It taxed legal documents such as deeds and wills, newpapers and other printed matter, playing cards, and even dice. Taxable items had to carry stamps that showed that the tax had been paid. People accused of breaking the new law could be tried in vice-admiralty courts, which usually tried only cases that had to do with the high seas. Vice-admiralty courts did not have juries, and so people tried there could not have jury trials.

Grenville did not expect the Stamp Act to cause much trouble. He was wrong.

▶ **5.** What items were taxed by Grenville's Stamp Act?

The Colonists' Arguments

Colonists opposed both the Sugar Act and the Stamp Act. They argued that the Sugar Act was unwise. The duty on foreign molasses would wipe out colonial trade with the non-British West Indies. Without the income that came from that trade, the colonists could not continue to buy as many British products as they had in recent years. British business, the colonists argued, would lose more in profits than the British government would gain in duties from the Sugar Act.

The colonists did not, however, question Parliament's right to pass the Sugar Act. Parliament had, after all, regulated colonial trade for over a century. Most colonists thought that, on the whole, the trade laws helped the colonies.

▶ **6.** Why did colonists question the wisdom of the Sugar Act?

Response to the Stamp Act The colonists' arguments against the Stamp Act were entirely different. They said Parliament had no right to pass the Stamp Act because it was

In 1815, Thomas Sully painted this portrait of Patrick Henry, which hangs in the Capitol.

not a trade law but a tax law. In Britain, the people had to give their consent to a tax through their representatives in Parliament. Since the colonists had no representatives in Parliament, it could not tax them, they said.

The colonists also were angered because those accused of violating the Stamp Act were to be tried without juries. To take the right of trial by jury from the colonists was to deny them their rights as British subjects.

▶7. How did the colonists argue against the Stamp Act?

Resolves and Petitions   A number of colonial assemblies passed resolutions against the Stamp Act. The most famous of them were the **Virginia Resolves.** They were proposed to the House of Burgesses by Patrick Henry in May 1765. The brash young son of a Scottish immigrant, Henry argued that only the House of Burgesses had the right to tax Virginians.

The burgesses did not adopt all of Henry's resolutions, but those they did pass were clear enough. They said the Virginians had all the liberties and privileges that were "at any time . . . held . . . by the people of Great Britain." They also said that "the distinguishing characteristic" of British freedom was the right of the people to be taxed by representatives they chose.

The Virginia Resolves became a model for resolutions passed by other colonial legislatures. The assemblies also sent **petitions,** or formal written pleas, to Parliament against the Sugar and Stamp acts.

▶8. What argument did Patrick Henry make in the Virginia Resolves?

The Stamp Act Congress   In October 1765, representatives from nine colonies met at New York. (New Hampshire, Virginia, North Carolina, and Georgia did not send delegates.) That meeting, the **Stamp Act Congress,** was the first time the colonies sent representatives to an intercolonial congress since the Albany Congress in 1754. The Stamp Act Congress sent a petition to Parliament that said the colonists had the same rights and liberties as the king's subjects in England.

▶9. What was the Stamp Act Congress?

The British Answer

The British responded to the colonists by defending Parliament's right to tax the colonists. They agreed that Britons could be taxed only with their consent or with that of their representatives in Parliament. However, the British argued that the colonists *were* represented in Parliament. The colonists did not vote for members of Parliament, they said, but neither did nine-tenths of the people in Britain. Yet all British subjects, voters and nonvoters alike, had **virtual representation** in Parliament, they said. By this, they meant that members of Parliament defended not just the interests of those who elected them but also the interests of all British subjects. Therefore, Parliament could tax the colonists just as it could tax the people in Britain who could not vote.

The notion of virtual representation did not make much sense to the colonists. In the colonies, the people had **direct representation** rather than virtual representation. Almost all white male colonists who were heads of families could vote. (Women, children, blacks, and Indians did not vote.) Representatives elected to colonial assemblies spoke directly for the people who voted for them. The members of the colonial assemblies were also colonists. They knew what taxes the people could pay. The representatives also had to pay any taxes passed by the assembly. The members of Parliament did not know the colonists that well. Nor did they have to pay the taxes that they voted for the colonies. In fact, the more

Parliament taxed the Americans, the less people in Britain had to be taxed.

For those reasons, the colonists denied that they were virtually represented in Parliament. The colonists' interests were represented only in their own assemblies, they said. Only their assemblies could tax them.

▶**10.** What was the colonial response to the idea of virtual representation?

Reviewing Section I

Identify George III, George Grenville, Molasses Act, Sugar Act, Stamp Act, Virginia Resolves, Patrick Henry, petitions, Stamp Act Congress, virtual representation, direct representation

Questions to Answer
1. Why did Grenville feel that the colonies should be taxed?
2. Why did the colonists disagree?

A Question to Think About Why was the issue of taxes so important to the colonists?

II. The Colonists Resist

The colonists' arguments against the Stamp Act had little effect. If anything, they made the British more determined than ever to enforce the law. During the summer of 1765, the colonists faced a crisis. The Stamp Act was to go into effect on November 1, 1765. Once it went into effect, Parliament's right to tax would be established. Although most colonists opposed the Stamp Act, they could not see a way to block it. Then Boston showed the way.

The Stamp Act Uprisings

The Bostonians' scheme to oppose the Stamp Act was simple. Each colony had a stamp distributor, an official appointed by the Crown

to sell the stamps and enforce the law. If all the stamp distributors resigned, the law could not go into effect.

Bostonians forced the Massachusetts stamp man, Andrew Oliver, to resign. Early on the morning of August 14, 1765, an **effigy,** a stuffed doll-like figure, of Oliver hung from a tree in a central part of the city. That night a crowd tore down a small building Oliver had built to conduct the stamp business—or so the crowd thought—and burned the effigy. Another group attacked Oliver's home. The next day Oliver promised to give up his job as stamp man.

Other colonies followed Boston's example. Eventually the stamp men resigned everywhere but in Georgia.

In some of the colonies, demonstrations against the Stamp Act led to wider violence. On August 26, crowds in Boston destroyed the elegant house of the lieutenant governor, Thomas Hutchinson. In Newport, an orderly demonstration against the Stamp Act gave way to several days of wild rioting. Such violence made people doubt the justice of a cause that led to such actions.

▶ **1.** How did the colonists first resist the Stamp Act?

Peaceful Resistance

In late 1765, colonial resistance became more organized. Groups of people who called themselves the **Sons of Liberty** first appeared in October and November. Then, in December, those groups began to contact each other and set up links between groups in different colonies.

The Sons of Liberty were ready to fight the British army if necessary to keep the Stamp Act from going into effect. They did not, however, want all government to end. Nor did they want to encourage the kind of

This teapot was made in the colonies to convince colonists not to buy the British stamps.

violence that hurt their cause. So they worked "to maintain the Laws, and to preserve Peace and good Order."

Gradually the patriots, or supporters of the American cause, found nonviolent ways to resist the Stamp Act. For one thing, they began to punish supporters of the Act with **boycotts.** That is, they refused to do business with anyone who favored the law. Some patriots in Essex County, New Jersey, vowed that they would not even speak to Stamp Act supporters "unless it be to inform them of their Vileness." The colonists also refused to buy goods made in Britain. As a result, British businesses suffered, and many British workers lost their jobs.

▶ **2.** What peaceful ways did the colonists find to resist the Stamp Act?

The Repeal of the Stamp Act

The colonists' resistance was very effective. Only in Georgia did the Stamp Act go into effect, and there it lasted only a brief time. Finally, in March 1766, Parliament repealed the Stamp Act.

At the same time, it passed a new law, the **Declaratory Act.** This act said that Parliament had the right to "make Laws . . . to bind the Colonists and People of America . . . in all Cases whatsoever." In other words, Parliament could pass any law it wished for the colonies.

Most colonists celebrated the Stamp Act's repeal. There were, however, a handful of colonists who remained suspicious because of the Declaratory Act. One of them was Samuel Adams, a short, stocky leader of the Boston town meeting. He predicted that Parliament would find a new way to try to trick the colonists into paying taxes. Events soon showed that his suspicions were well-founded.

▶ **3.** What was the Declaratory Act?

The Townshend Crisis

By July 1766, William Pitt, now the Earl of Chatham, was once again prime minister. However, Chatham was a sick man. Charles Townshend, who headed the Exchequer, or treasury, was in many ways the actual leader of the government.

▶**4.** Who was Charles Townshend?

The Townshend Act Townshend was determined to raise money by taxing the colonists. He wrote the Revenue Act of 1767, known as the **Townshend Act.** It set new duties to be collected in the colonies on some everyday items colonists imported from Britain, including glass, lead, painter's colors, paper, and tea. The wording of the law clearly stated that it was meant to raise money. That purpose made it a tax law, the colonists said.

The law also said that the money raised was to be used to pay the salaries of royal governors and other colonial officials. In the past, the colonial assemblies paid those people. So the Townshend Act hurt the assemblies in two ways. It took away their exclusive right to tax the the colonists. It also cut back their power over governors and other royal officials.

▶**5.** In what ways did the Townshend Act hurt the colonial assemblies?

Assemblies Dissolved Three days after Parliament approved the Townshend Act, it voted to **suspend** the New York assembly, that is, to forbid it to meet for a time. Parliament took that action because the New York assembly had refused to obey another law—the **Quartering Act** of 1765. That law said colonial assemblies had to supply British troops with such items as vinegar, rum, and cider. New Yorkers refused to obey the law because, they said, it was a tax passed by

Mercy Otis Warren's house was a meeting place for the patriots during the Revolutionary War.

Parliament without their consent. Taxes could be paid in rum and cider as well as in money.

When the Massachusetts legislature heard about the Townshend taxes, it sent a letter to the other colonies. It urged the assemblies to work together to protect their rights. The British government was outraged by the letter. It told the governor of Massachusetts to insist that the assembly call its letter back. When the members refused, the governor dissolved the assembly. Throughout the colonies, people praised the Massachusetts assembly for its courage. However, praise was not enough to save colonial assemblies.

▶**6.** Why were the assemblies of New York and Massachusetts dissolved?

Royal Troops Colonists saw another danger to their liberties in the presence of British troops. The British said they needed to tax the colonists to help pay for their army in North America. Some colonists wondered why they needed an army in North America at

Highlighting People
Samuel Adams

Samuel Adams was born in Boston in 1722. Like most other Americans of his time, he spent much of his life in one colony — Massachusetts. There his family had lived since the 1600's. There too he attended Harvard College. After graduating from Harvard in 1740, he entered private business. He failed at business, however. By 1764, he was deeply in debt.

Adam's failure in business did not keep him from becoming involved in colonial affairs. He first defended colonial rights in the newspapers and at Boston town meetings. Then, in 1765, the people of Boston elected him to the Massachusetts legislature. As its clerk, he was in constant touch with other colonial leaders.

The clerkship was only one of Adams's many political interests. He was also a friend of the Boston Sons of Liberty during the Stamp Act crisis and strongly supported nonimportation in

the late 1760's. After the massacre of 1770, he spoke for his fellow Bostonians, insisting that British troops be removed from Boston. Finally, in 1772, he organized the Boston Committee of Correspondence. The committee kept people in Massachusetts informed about British activities.

Adams was above all a master politician who tried to make people work together peacefully through assemblies and committees. He was willing to justify the use of force only if all else failed. Violence, he felt, had a way of dividing people. That was why he told Bostonians in 1774, "Nothing can ruin us but our violence."

In 1774, Massachusetts sent Adams to the Continental Congress. Two years later, in 1776, he was one of many who signed the Declaration of Independence. His career, however, did not end there. He remained a hard-working member of the Continental Congress for another five years. Then he returned to Massachusetts, which he never again left. He became president of the state senate, lieutenant governor, and finally — in the 1790's — governor of Massachusetts.

To younger Americans, Adams seemed increasingly out of place in those later years. No doubt the short, stocky patriot seemed strange walking around in the three-cornered hat of revolutionary times long after it had gone out of fashion. Even after 1800, he insisted, "The Puritans of New England were the men to set an example to the world."

Actually, Adams was in many ways a good model for the young. He never used public office to make money for himself. In fact, he died a poor man. He also never lost his faith in the people and in the Revolution. In 1801, two years before his death, he wrote Thomas Jefferson of his hopes for the future. "The ideals of the American Revolution will spread," he said, "bringing peace and freedom to oppressed people everywhere."

all. France and Spain were no longer dangers. If the army was supposed to defend the colonies against Indian attacks, why had Charles Townshend shifted the troops from the West to coastal cities like New York? Colonists wondered if the army would be used against colonists who argued for their rights.

That suspicion was no sooner felt than it seemed to be confirmed. On October 1, 1768, royal troops began arriving in Boston, the center of colonial protest. By the next year, there were about 4,000 soldiers in a town of 15,000. Bostonians did not welcome the troops. They said that free people were not to be governed at the point of a gun.

▶**7.** Why were the colonists concerned by the presence of British troops in the colonies?

Petitions and Nonimportation Meanwhile some colonists sent petitions to the king and to Parliament asking for relief. When that did not work, they organized **nonimportation associations,** groups of merchants who promised not to order certain British goods. The nonimportation associations of 1768 and 1769 were very successful. They sharply cut colonial imports from Britain.

In several places, groups of women met to spin thread or weave cloth so they would not need to buy those things from Britain. Sometimes such groups of women called themselves the **Daughters of Liberty.**

▶**8.** How did the nonimportation associations hurt British merchants?

The Boston Massacre Bostonians resented the British troops in their city more and more. They thought the soldiers were rowdy and rude. Also off-duty soldiers took jobs from colonists by working for very low wages.

The soldiers, on the other hand, were angry because whenever there was trouble, they were arrested. Local judges sometimes fined them heavily even for minor offenses.

The conflict reached a crisis on March 5, 1770. During the day, angry people attacked soldiers on the streets of Boston. That evening, bells tolled through the town, calling more people into the streets. Crowds gathered on the icy streets outside the Customs House.

The artist's view of British ships blockading Boston Harbor in 1768 is shown in this Christian Remick painting.

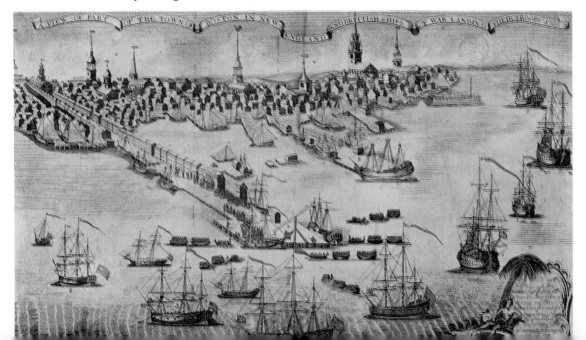

Paul Revere, a Boston silversmith, made this engraving of the Boston Massacre.

Captain Thomas Preston, the British officer in charge, sent soldiers to help the one guard on duty there. The crowd pelted the soldiers with snowballs, some packed around rocks. Then someone shouted "Fire," and the troops shot into the crowd. Samuel Gray, a rope maker, James Caldwell, a sailor, and a very tall black man named Crispus Attucks were killed right away. Two others died later of wounds. Angry colonists called those killings the **Boston Massacre.**

III. The Path to War

On the same day the Boston Massacre took place, Parliament repealed all the Townshend duties except the one on tea. Before long colonial merchants went back to buying British goods as usual.

The attitudes of the colonists toward Britain had changed during the years of protest. Few could still think of the king's ministers or of

The acting governor, Thomas Hutchinson, prevented more violence by promising that the soldiers would be tried in court for their actions. Under pressure from Samuel Adams and the Boston town meeting, Hutchinson agreed to remove all British troops from Boston. Finally peace returned to the town.

In the fall of 1770, local juries agreed that Preston and his men had acted in self defense. All but two of the soldiers were found innocent. The other two were convicted of manslaughter, a less serious crime than murder. John Adams, a patriot from Braintree, Massachusetts, and a cousin of Samuel Adams, was one of the lawyers who defended the soldiers.

▶9. Describe the Boston Massacre.

Reviewing Section II

Identify effigy, Sons of Liberty, boycotts, Declaratory Act, Samuel Adams, Townshend Act, suspend, Quartering Act of 1765, non-importation associations, Daughters of Liberty, Boston Massacre, John Adams

Questions to Answer
1. What colonial methods of resistance were most successful against the Stamp Act?
2. Why did Bostonians resent the troops in their city?

A Question to Think About What could Britain have done at this point to restore peace with the colonies?

Parliament as friends. When new trouble broke out over tea, the colonists moved more rapidly toward war and independence.

The Tea Crisis

Some colonists continued to boycott tea. Other colonists bought tea smuggled from the Netherlands. In 1773, Parliament passed the Tea Act. It was designed to help the East India Company, one of the great British trading companies. The effect of the law was to make British tea cheaper in the colonies than tea smuggled from the Netherlands. Many patriots felt the law was a clever effort to trick them into paying the tax on tea.

▶1. Why did many patriots think the Tea Act was a trick?

The Colonial Response Patriots worked to keep the taxed tea from going on sale in the colonies. In Philadelphia and New York, local committees convinced the captains of ships carrying East India tea to turn around and go back to England without unloading the tea. In Charleston, a tea ship entered the harbor, but no one claimed its tea. Finally customs officials seized the tea and locked it up in the basement of the Customs House.

▶2. What happened to the tea ships in New York, Philadelphia, and Charleston?

The Boston Tea Party Bostonians were not able to get the tea ships in their harbor to go back to England. However, no one dared unload the tea. If it was still unclaimed after 20 days, the tea would be seized by custom agents. But Bostonians did not think it would remain locked up, as in Charleston. Since the Massachusetts tea agents were the sons of the acting governor, Bostonians were sure the tea would somehow be removed and sold.

Finally, late on the night of December 16, 1773, the twentieth day since the tea ships had arrived, a group of patriots boarded the ships, opened 342 chests of tea, and threw their contents into the water. Accounts of the event say that everything was done very quietly, and that every effort was made to keep people from stealing tea or damaging property other than tea. The Boston patriots thought their **Boston Tea Party**, the name they gave to their actions on that December night, had gone very well.

▶3. What was the Boston Tea Party?

Boston patriots throwing tea into Boston Harbor is shown in this engraving by W. D. Cooper.

The Intolerable Acts

Members of Parliament were outraged when they heard about the Boston Tea Party. They quickly passed a series of laws to punish the city. The **Boston Port Act** closed the port of Boston until the town agreed to pay for the destroyed tea. Another law, the **Massachusetts Government Act,** changed the colony's charter of 1691. It gave the Crown the right to appoint members of the Massachusetts Council. Previously members were elected by the assembly. The Government Act also increased the power of the royal governor. His consent was needed for towns to meet more than once a year to elect local officials.

The king also appointed a new governor for the colony. He was General Thomas Gage, the commander of the British army in North America. In May 1774, Gage arrived in Boston with 4,000 soldiers. Boston and the rest of Massachusetts were under military rule.

Parliament also passed a new **Quartering Act** that allowed the British to house their troops in private homes. The **Justice Act** said that if royal officials were accused of committing murder in the course of their duties, they could be tried in Britain. The colonists called all these laws the **Intolerable Acts** because they seemed unbearable.

Sometimes the colonists called the **Quebec Act** of 1774 an intolerable act too. It set up a regular government for Britain's new colony of Quebec, which had been New France until 1763. The law said that a royal governor and a council appointed by the Crown would govern the colony. Quebec would have no elected assembly. The law plainly said that Parliament had the right to tax the colonists of Quebec. Catholics were given rights they did not have in Britain. The law also extended the boundaries of Quebec to include the land north of the Ohio River between the Mississippi River and the Appalachians. However, Virginia, Massachusetts, and Connecticut also had claims to those lands.

The colonists protested the Quebec Act not just because of the lands they had lost but because they felt the government of Quebec was unfree. The Quebec Act seemed to show clearly what Britain wanted to do with all its American colonies.

▶**4.** What were the Intolerable Acts and the Quebec Act?

The Continental Congress

Colonists all along the Atlantic coast rallied to support Boston. They sent food and money to the Bostonians who were put out of work when the British closed the port of Boston. Soon calls went out for a colonial congress. In September and October of 1774, all the colonies except Georgia sent delegates to a meeting at Carpenter's Hall in Philadelphia, known as the **First Continental Congress.** Many important patriots, including Samuel and John Adams, George Washington, and Patrick Henry, were delegates.

Even though the Congress did not have the authority of a government, it acted forcefully. The Congress approved the **Suffolk Resolves,** which had first been passed by the people of Suffolk County, Massachusetts. The resolves said colonists should not obey the Intolerable Acts. They also called on the people to prepare for war.

The Congress also approved the **Continental Association,** by which the colonies agreed not to import British goods and to discontinue the slave trade. The delegates agreed that as of September 1775, the colonies would no longer export their own goods to Britain. The Association was enforced by local committees, elected by those who could vote for assembly delegates.

The Congress still hoped to settle its disagreements with Britain. It sent petitions to

The line graph below shows imports from England to the colonies from 1763 to 1776. Along the vertical axis is a note that the numbers shown represent thousands of pounds sterling. The pound is the basic unit of British currency.

Use the graph and the information in the chapter to answer the following questions.

1. (a) In what year shown on the graph were imports at their highest? (b) Lowest?

2. (a) What was the approximate value of goods imported in 1774? (b) In 1775? (c) In 1776?

3. (a) What happened in the colonies in 1774 that affected imports? (b) How did it affect them?

4. (a) What was the value of imports in 1770? (b) In 1771?

5. What happened between 1770 and 1771 to account for the increase in imports?

Value of Imports from England to the Thirteen Colonies, 1763-1776

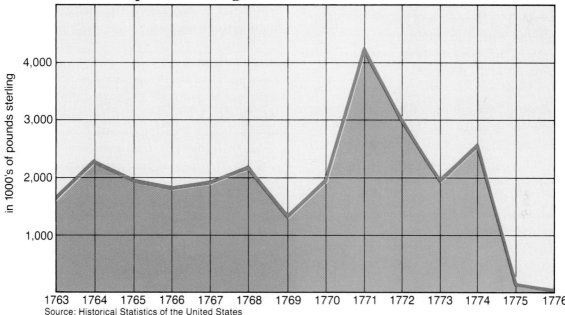

in 1000's of pounds sterling

1763 1764 1765 1766 1767 1768 1769 1770 1771 1772 1773 1774 1775 1776
Source: Historical Statistics of the United States

other British colonies and also to the people of Great Britain and the king. "Peace and love" between Britain and its American colonies could still be restored, the Congress's secretary said, "but we are on the brink of a precipice [a steep, overhanging place]."

Before the Continental Congress met again in May 1775, the colonies had moved nearer the edge of that sharp ledge. War seemed closer than ever.

▶ 5. What actions were taken by the First Continental Congress?

The Fighting Begins

The patriot leaders tried hard to avoid clashes between the royal troops (redcoats, as they were called by the colonists) and Bostonians. They were afraid a war would start before the other colonies were ready to support Massachusetts. However, on April 19, 1775, fighting began. During the previous night, General Gage had sent 700 British troops to seize guns and ammunition stored by colonists at Concord, a town about 15 miles west of Boston. On the way, the soldiers were to stop in Lexington and arrest two patriot leaders, Samuel Adams and John Hancock. Patriots in Boston sent the silversmith and engraver Paul Revere and his friend William Dawes to warn the people.

▶**6.** Why did General Gage send troops to Lexington and Concord?

Lexington   By the time the British soldiers finally got to Lexington, Adams and Hancock were gone. Instead, some 70 **minutemen** were waiting on the village green. They were members of the local militia, or citizen soldiers. They called themselves minutemen because they could be ready to fight with a minute's warning.

The British commander told the minutemen to go home. Before they could do that, someone—no one knows who—fired a shot. Suddenly the redcoats opened fire, killing 8 colonists and wounding 10. Only one British soldier was wounded. The Battle of Lexington lasted only 15 minutes.

▶**7.** Who were the minutemen?

Concord   Revere and Dawes were captured on their way to Concord. Another patriot, Samuel Prescott, carried the warning for them. When the British reached Concord, most of the town's military supplies had been carted away. The town was quiet. However, on their way out of Concord, the British found the local minutemen waiting at North Bridge. The Battle of Concord lasted five minutes. At its end, two more American patriots were dead. Three British soldiers had also died, and another nine were wounded. The British decided to return to Boston.

The trip to Boston was not easy. Americans shot at the redcoats all along the route—from windows and trees, from behind stone walls, and from both sides of the road. The angry people of Massachusetts killed 70 retreating British soldiers and wounded 165. Another 26 were missing by the day's end.

▶**8.** What happened to the British during their retreat to Boston?

An American Army   The fight was on. Three days after the battles of Lexington and Concord, the Massachusetts Provincial Congress, which the colonists elected to manage their affairs, held a meeting. It called for an army of 13,000 soldiers from all over New England.

Soon men began pouring into a camp at Cambridge, across the Charles River from Boston. They were disorganized and poorly supplied. Only the Rhode Islanders had tents. Other soldiers lived in private houses, in makeshift shacks, or at nearby Harvard College. None had uniforms. Instead, they wore work or hunting clothes, just as many American soldiers did throughout the war. Soldiers brought guns and swords if they could.

In May of 1776, the **Second Continental Congress** met. It took charge of the army and appointed as its commander a 43-year-old veteran of the French and Indian War, George Washington. A tall, dignified man, Washington was a wealthy planter from Virginia who was used to having his orders obeyed. He had the job of building a respectable American, or **Continental Army.**

This engraving, by Amos Doolittle, shows the British retreat from Concord in 1775.

Washington did not arrive in Cambridge until July 2. By then, his troops had fought the British again, this time in a battle more important than those at Lexington and Concord.

▶**9.** Who appointed Washington as commander of the Continental Army?

Bunker Hill To protect their hold on Boston, the British decided to take nearby Charlestown. The Americans got there first. On the night of June 16, 1775, they built a **redoubt,** or dug-out fort, at the top of Breed's Hill. From there, they could look down on the British in Boston.

The next day General William Howe, a British officer who had helped take Quebec in 1760, ordered his men to take the redoubt. Marching in three long lines, they slowly made their way upward.

The Americans at the top of the hill remained quiet. The legend is that their commander, a tough farmer named William Prescott, told them to hold their fire until they could see the whites of the British soldiers' eyes. Finally Prescott gave the order to shoot. The redcoats fell back.

Howe ordered his soldiers up the hill a second time. Like good soldiers, they obeyed, stepping over the bodies of the dead. Once again the attack failed.

When Howe ordered a third attack, Prescott's men ran out of ammunition. As the redcoats jumped over the sides of the fort, the colonials swung their muskets and threw stones at the attackers. Prescott pulled his men back to nearby Bunker Hill (after which, strangely, the battle is named), and then farther west to Cambridge. Howe did not chase them. He had already lost over a thousand men—226 killed and 828 wounded. The American losses were also high—140 dead, 271 wounded and 30 captured.

The British really won the battle, since they took the hill from the Americans. However, a victory won at such a high cost was hardly a victory at all. British officers could hardly believe that inexperienced Americans had held their ground against trained British troops.

▶10. Who won the Battle of Bunker Hill?

Reviewing Section III———————

Identify Boston Tea Party, Boston Port Act, Massachusetts Government Act, Quartering Act, Justice Act, Intolerable Acts, Quebec Act, First Continental Congress, Suffolk Resolves, Continental Association, Paul Revere, minutemen, Battle of Lexington, Battle of Concord, Second Continental Congress, Continental Army, redoubt, Breed's Hill, William Prescott

Questions to Answer
1. Why were the patriots so opposed to the Tea Act?
2. Why was the Battle of Bunker Hill both a loss and a victory for the patriots?

A Question to Think About What mistake did Parliament make in passing the Intolerable Acts?

IV. The Break with Britain

In spite of the early battles of 1775, most colonists still hoped to remain British. However, their hopes did not last out the year.

In August 1775, King George III declared that the colonists were carrying on an "open and avowed rebellion." Determined to end the rebellion, he hired German soldiers, called **Hessians** after their homeland in Germany, to fight the Americans. The king's actions destroyed the colonists' hopes that he would help them. The Americans still thought that the British people might come to their support. They did not. So, by 1775, the colonists felt cut off from the Crown and the British people.

The People Take Power

The governments under the Crown began to collapse in one colony after another. In 1774 and 1775, the colonists wanted to send aid to Boston, to elect delegates to the Second Continental Congress, and to raise and equip an army. They could not do those things through their assemblies. If they tried, the royal governors just dissolved the assemblies. So the colonists established **provincial conventions,** or congresses.

The conventions were representative bodies like the assemblies. In fact, they often included the same delegates who had sat in the assemblies. In Virginia, for example, when the governor dissolved the House of Burgesses, the members just went to nearby Raleigh Tavern and continued their business.

The assemblies had been part of a whole structure of British government. The conventions acted as entire governments in themselves. Their power came from the people who elected their members. The royal governors looked on helplessly as the conventions grew in power. Before long, many of the governors fled the colonies and went to Great Britain.

▶1. From whom did the provincial conventions get their authority?

Common Sense

Although British government in the colonies was in tatters, most colonists were not willing to separate from Britain. Then, in January 1776, Thomas Paine published an important pamphlet, *Common Sense*, which urged the colonists to declare their independence from Britain. Paine was a former corset maker and customs agent who had come to the colonies only two years earlier.

In his pamphlet, Paine argued that the war ended all hope that Britain and the colonies could resolve their differences. In any case, no settlement between the colonies and Britain could last. So the colonists should declare their independence. Then they could get other European countries to help them in the war with Britain.

Paine gave many reasons why he believed that the colonies would sooner or later have to part from Britain. Most important was his argument against the structure of the British government. It included a king and the House of Lords, most of whose members inherited their offices from their parents. Hereditary rule, Paine argued, was wrong and dangerous. Hereditary rulers became proud and overly powerful. They were always a danger to the people's liberty. Paine said that the only good part of the British government was the House of Commons, whose members were elected by the people.

Americans should break from Britain and start their own government, Paine argued. The Americans should start a **republic,** a government in which all power comes from the people. Then their freedom would be secure.

Paine's pamphlet was read widely from New England to Georgia. It was soon published in Britain, the Netherlands, and France as well.

▶**2.** What were Paine's main arguments for independence in *Common Sense?*

In Their Own Words

Patrick Henry speaks before the Virginia convention in 1775 in favor of arming the colony in preparation for war:

The battle, sir, is not to the strong alone; it is to the vigilant, the active, the brave. Besides, sir, we have no [choice]. If we were base enough to desire it, it is now too late to retire from the contest. There is no retreat but in submission and slavery! Our chains are forged. Their clanking may be heard on the plains of Boston! The war is inevitable—and let it come! I repeat it, sir, let it come!

The gentlemen may cry, Peace, peace! but there is no peace. The war has actually begun! The next gale that sweeps from the north will bring to our ears the clash of resounding arms! Our brethren are already in the field! Why stand we here idle? What is it that the gentlemen wish? What would they have? Is life so dear or peace so sweet as to be purchased at the price of chains and slavery? Forbid it, Almighty God. I know not what course others may take, but as for me, give me liberty or give me death!

The Declaration of Independence

Congress followed Thomas Paine's advice. On June 7, Richard Henry Lee, a member of one of Virginia's first families, introduced a resolution. It said that "these United Colonies are, and of right ought to be, free and independent States . . ." Congress debated Lee's proposal. Then it set up a committee to draft a declaration of independence.

161

Sources of the Declaration of Independence

In writing the Declaration of Independence, Thomas Jefferson used ideas that were familiar to Britons and colonists alike. Jefferson himself said, "I did not consider it as any part of my charge to invent new ideas."

Where did the ideas come from that Jefferson expressed so well? Some came from Greek and Roman writers. Some came from British legal tradition. However, Jefferson drew many ideas from a group of English writers who justified the English revolutions of the 1600's. One king was executed, and another removed from the throne during those revolutions.

John Locke was one of those writers. The words of the Declaration of Independence are in some places very close to those in his *Second Treatise of Government*, which was first published in 1690.

Jefferson also drew on essays by John Trenchard and Thomas Gordon, which were published together as *Cato's Letters* in 1721. Many colonists were more familiar with those essays than with Locke's writings.

The basic ideas of these writers were similar. They said all people have certain natural rights including the rights to life, liberty, and property. (Jefferson changed property to the pursuit of happiness.) People set up governments to protect those rights. However, people need not obey rulers who threaten their rights. In fact, the people have a right and a duty to resist such rulers.

Jefferson expressed these ideas briefly and beautifully. As a result, the American Declaration of Independence has been an inspiration to oppressed people in many parts of the world.

Thomas Jefferson, a young Virginia planter with a flair for words, was chairman of the committee. He wrote the document that congress accepted as the Declaration of Independence on July 2. Congress then spent two days editing the Declaration before sending it to the printer on July 4, 1776.

▶**3.** Who was the author of the Declaration of Independence?

Preface to the Declaration Congress wanted a written declaration to explain to all the world why the Americans were separating from Britain. The Declaration began with an eloquent statement of the right of the colonies to revolt.

All men were created equal, it said, and had "certain unalienable Rights"—rights that could not be given or taken away—including those of "Life, Liberty, and the pursuit of Happiness." People formed governments to protect those rights. Therefore, if a government threatened those rights, the people had a duty to change their government or create a new one.

Changing a government was not to be done lightly. However, if a "long train of abuses" showed that the government planned to keep the people totally under its power, then it was the people's right and duty "to throw off such Government" and to provide for their future security.

▶**4.** According to the Declaration of Independence, when did people have the duty to create a new government?

A Long Train of Abuses The Declaration then listed a long series of events to prove that the British government did indeed have a plan to keep the colonies under its total power. Those events were blamed on the king. The Declaration of Independence was the first public document to attack the king directly. That was the way to declare a revolution. The king stood for the power of the government. To say that the king had seriously abused his power was to say that the king's government no longer had rightful power.

Jefferson also added to the Declaration a section on the British people. The Americans, it said, had appealed to their "British brethren" for help. But the British ignored those appeals. Jefferson's version was long and emotional. Congress changed it so the Declaration said simply that in the future the Americans would hold the British people "as we hold the rest of mankind, Enemies in War, in Peace, Friends."

▶5. Why did the Declaration of Independence blame all Britain's abuses on the king?

Conclusion The Declaration ended by stating that the members of congress made this Declaration "in the Name, and by Authority of the good People of these Colonies," that the colonies were "Free and Independent States; ... Absolved from all Allegiance to the British Crown," with all the powers of a free state. "And for the support of this Declaration, with a firm reliance on the protection of divine Providence," it ended, "we mutually pledge to each other our Lives, our Fortunes, and our sacred Honor."

For the United States, the Declaration of Independence was only a beginning, but it was a very good beginning. Its stirring words, especially in asserting the equality of all men, had a lasting influence on the people of the new nation.

▶6. By whose authority did the Congress adopt the Declaration of Independence?

John Trumbull made this painting of the signing of the Declaration of Independence.

Reviewing Section IV

Identify Hessians, provincial conventions, Thomas Paine, *Common Sense*, republic, Richard Henry Lee, Thomas Jefferson, Declaration of Independence

Questions to Answer
1. Why did Congress want to issue a written declaration of independence?
2. What role did Thomas Paine play in the American Revolution?

A Question to Think About How did the provincial conventions continue the colonial tradition of local power?

IMPROVE YOUR READING
Reviewing Main Idea

Very often the first sentence of a paragraph gives the main idea of that paragraph. However, that is not always true. Sometimes the first sentence in a paragraph links the new paragraph to ideas that have gone before. Sometimes a paragraph describes a series of events. The sentence that explains the importance or connection of the events gives the main idea.

The following paragraphs are from Chapter 8. On a separate piece of paper, write the sentence that gives the main idea of each paragraph.

1. The Molasses Act of 1733 was also one of the trade laws the colonists ignored. Molasses is produced when sugar cane is made into sugar. The colonists used it as a sweetener. They also made it into rum, which they either drank or traded elsewhere. In Africa, the colonists traded rum for slaves.

2. The colonists' arguments against the Stamp Act were entirely different. They said Parliament had no right to pass the Stamp Act because it was not a trade law but a tax law. In Britain, the people had to give their consent to a tax through their representatives in Parliament. Since the colonists had no representatives in Parliament, it could not tax them, they said.

3. Patriots worked to keep the taxed tea from going on sale in the colonies. In Philadelphia and New York, local committees convinced the captains of ships carrying East India tea to turn around and go back to England without unloading the tea. In Charleston, a tea ship entered the harbor, but no one claimed its tea. Finally customs officials seized the tea and locked it up in the basement of the Customs House.

4. Members of Parliament were outraged when they heard about the Boston Tea Party. They quickly passed a series of laws to punish the city. The Boston Port Act closed the port of Boston until the town agreed to pay for the destroyed tea. Another law, the Massachusetts Government Act, changed the colony's charter of 1691. It gave the Crown the right to appoint members of the Massachusetts Council. Previously members were elected by the assembly. The Government Act also increased the power of the royal governor. His consent was needed for towns to meet more than once a year to elect local officials.

5. The governments under the Crown began to collapse in one colony after another. In 1774 and 1775, the colonists wanted to send aid to Boston, to elect delegates to the Second Continental Congress, and to raise and equip an army. They could not do those things through their assemblies. If they tried, the royal governors just dissolved the assemblies. So the colonists established provincial conventions, or congresses.

CHAPTER 8 REVIEW

Vocabulary Check

On a separate sheet of paper, write the letter of the definition that explains each of the terms listed below.

1. Redoubt
2. Petition
3. Boycotts
4. Suspend
5. Republic

a. Showing disapproval by refusing to buy goods or do business
b. To stop temporarily
c. A formal written request
d. A dug-out fort
e. A government in which all power comes from the people

Fact Check

On a separate sheet of paper, write the name of the person or group described in each of the phrases below.

1. King of England in 1760
2. He proposed resolutions against the Stamp Act in the House of Burgesses
3. Citizen soldiers
4. Group organized in several colonies to oppose the Stamp Act
5. He was the author of the Declaration of Independence
6. Groups of women who boycotted British-made goods
7. They were captured by the British while riding to Concord to warn the patriots of the British advance
8. Group that appointed Washington as head of the army
9. German troops hired to fight for the British
10. Author of *Common Sense*

Time Check

On a separate sheet of paper, place the following events in chronological order.

1. Battles of Lexington and Concord
2. Stamp Act
3. Boston Tea Party
4. Stamp Act Congress
5. Sugar Act
6. Declaratory Act
7. Townshend Act
8. Tea Act
9. Boston Massacre
10. Intolerable Acts

Skills Check

Make a line graph using the following data. Divide the vertical axis by thousands of pounds sterling. Numbers are rounded off.

Value of Exports from the American Colonies to England, 1765–1775
(in pounds sterling)

1767	1,100,000	1772	1,259,000
1768	1,250,000	1773	1,370,000
1769	1,060,000	1774	1,374,000
1770	1,016,000	1775	2,000,000
1771	1,340,000	1776	104,000

Think and Write

1. How did England plan to raise money after the French and Indian War?
2. Explain the difference between *virtual* representation and *direct* representation.
3. Describe three ways the colonists resisted Parliament's attempts to tax them.
4. How did the colonists try to avoid war with Great Britain?
5. Why did the colonists issue the Declaration of Independence?

Chapter 9

The War for Independence

James Peale made this painting ten years after the Battle of Princeton in which his father—Hugh Mercer, an American Officer—was killed.

From the battles of Lexington and Concord and Bunker Hill, it was just a few steps to a full-blown war between the Americans and the British. Sometimes people call that war the American Revolution. But the war and the Revolution were not the same thing. The Revolution lay in the major changes Americans made in their lives and their government. It lay, above all, in the Americans' decision to become independent and to found a republic.

Unless the Americans won their war with Great Britain, however, their revolution would fail. They would find themselves back under the rule of Britain's king. Somehow the weak, new nation had to defeat Great Britain, one of the most powerful countries of the world.

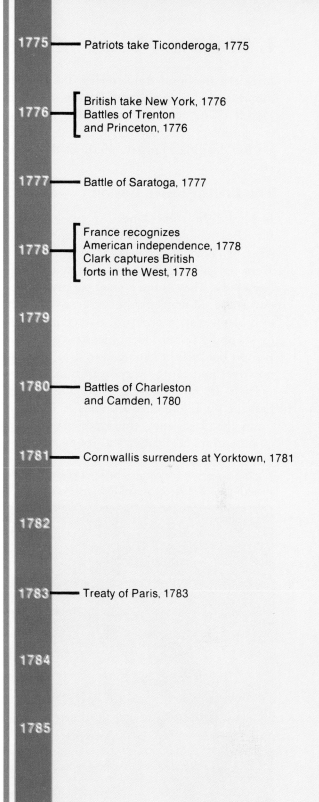

1775 — Patriots take Ticonderoga, 1775

1776 — British take New York, 1776
Battles of Trenton
and Princeton, 1776

1777 — Battle of Saratoga, 1777

1778 — France recognizes
American independence, 1778
Clark captures British
forts in the West, 1778

1779

1780 — Battles of Charleston
and Camden, 1780

1781 — Cornwallis surrenders at Yorktown, 1781

1782

1783 — Treaty of Paris, 1783

1784

1785

I. The First Years of the War

After the Battle of Bunker Hill, the British found it hard to move from Boston. Then, in March 1776, the Americans did something extraordinary. They forced the British to leave Boston, leading to a new phase of the war.

The British Leave Boston

In May 1775, some American troops under Benedict Arnold of Connecticut and Ethan Allen of Vermont had seized the British Fort Ticonderoga on Lake Champlain in northern New York. They found a good supply of cannon there. Moving the heavy guns was not easy. However, a group of determined colonists under Colonel Henry Knox, a one-time Boston bookseller, managed to drag 59 cannon overland all the way to Boston.

Then, in early March 1776, Washington had the guns pulled to Dorchester Heights. From that high spot, the American cannon could command Boston and its harbor.

Charles Wilson Peale painted this portrait of George Washington before the Revolutionary War began.

The British had to decide whether to fight the Americans or to **evacuate,** that is, to leave, the city. The British commander, General William Howe, decided it made no sense for the British to stay. They had come to Boston to put down a handful of trouble makers. Now they were at war with all the colonies. New England was not the best place for the British to fight such a war. New York, Howe thought, would be easier to take. Then the British hoped to separate New England from the South, making it harder for the colonists to help each other.

So, on March 17, 1776, the last of Howe's soldiers piled onto ships and set sail for Halifax, Nova Scotia. The next summer they arrived in New York.

▶**1.** Why did the British leave Boston?

British Strengths and Weaknesses

The British were not worried about fighting the Americans. The British felt that they had so many advantages that victory was certain.

The British had an established army with experienced officers leading trained, professional soldiers. The British also had a strong government that could tax its people to support that army. By August 1776, the British had assembled the strongest force ever seen in North America. General Howe had over 30,000 soldiers under his command. He also had the help of his older brother Richard, Lord Howe, a British admiral who was nearby with another 13,000 sailors on over 400 ships.

The British also had some weaknesses. England was some 3,000 miles from North America. Yet supplies had to come from England. The government in London was not always able to ship supplies on time. The supply ships could be blown off course or

American privateers could seize them. Once the ships arrived in North America, they were easy for the British to sail from one seaport to another. However, it was difficult for the British to move their armies and supplies in the rugged lands away from the coast.

The British had other problems as well. Their officers had trouble working with each other. Each wanted to win the war himself, in his own way. None of the officers really understood what they had to do to defeat the Americans. In Europe, an army had only to defeat its enemy's army to win a war. In America, the British faced a new situation. They not only had to defeat an army but also to defeat a people—or to win the people over to their side. It took a long time for the British to learn that.

▶**2.** What were the British strengths and weaknesses in the war?

American Weaknesses and Advantages

General Washington understood the American weaknesses and advantages very well. He was dismayed at the army he took over at Cambridge. It was full of volunteers who rushed to the camp in the opening days of the war when excitement was high. They had no training, no order, no discipline, and, of course, very few supplies.

Washington tried to make the Cambridge soldiers into a respectable army. However, the rules he set up drove some men away. Others left when the war moved farther from their homes and families. Still more would leave when the American army started to lose battles. Soldiers in the army only signed up for a year. At the end of December, most of them went home.

▶**3.** What were the problems of the American army in 1775?

The Creation of an Army What Washington needed was an army of paid, professional soldiers who would remain in the army until the war was over. Congress finally agreed. In 1776, it allowed the Continental Army to recruit soldiers by promising them a **bounty,** or cash payment, for signing up, support during the war, and 100 acres of land if they served throughout the war.

Few of the new Continental soldiers were farmers or artisans. Most were drawn from the poorest people in the the colonies. Many from the North were black slaves who were promised freedom in exchange for service in the army. Most soldiers were young—in their teens or twenties. They were not fighting to protect their families and property because they often had neither. They were fighting for the chance to acquire land and get a start in life.

▶**4.** Why did men enlist in the Continental Army?

A Weak Government Could the Congress keep its promises to the soldiers? It could not itself raise taxes to pay and supply the army. It could only ask the states for funds. The states did not always do what the Congress asked of them. Congress could print money to pay its bills. However, it printed too many Continental dollars, and the money lost value. "Not worth a continental" became a common expression for something worthless.

▶**5.** Why did the Congress have trouble supplying the Continental Army?

American Advantages The Americans did have some advantages in the war. From the beginning of the war, they received help from the French government. Before the war was over, France would increase its aid.

Wherever the Continental Army fought, it could call on local militia to help. The local

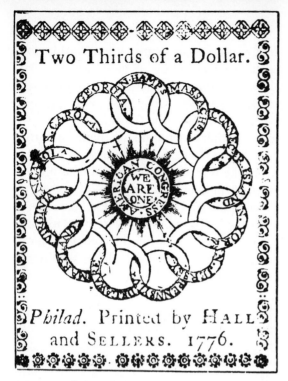

Americans believed that the money Congress issued was not worth the paper it was printed on.

militia were not trained, professional soldiers. They had a tendency to run from the battlefield when the fighting began. However, some commanders found good ways to use them anyway. The militia also knew their area well and could serve as guides or scouts.

Above all, however, the Americans had the advantage of strong leadership. While the British went from one commander to another, General Washington commanded the Americans for the entire war. He could hold the respect of his officers and make men want to fight. Washington knew the Americans did not have to keep winning battles to win the war. They had only to wear down the British army until it could afford to remain in America no longer. Time was on the Americans' side. That was perhaps their greatest advantage in the war.

▶**6.** What were the American advantages in the war?

Loyalists

Some Americans opposed independence. They were known as **Loyalists**. Throughout the war, the British expected a lot more support from such people than they ever received. In fact, only about one American in five was a Loyalist.

Some Loyalists felt a special tie to the king because they had served him as judges, councillors, or governors. Most Loyalists, however, were ordinary people of modest means. Some of them were Loyalists from ignorance. They lived far from the cities and knew nothing of the events that made other Americans into revolutionaries. Others became Loyalists because they thought the British were going to win the war and they wanted to avoid being punished as rebels. Still others were Loyalists because they thought the Crown would protect their rights better than the new republican governments. Members of the Church of England living in Puritan New England, for example, tended to be Loyalists.

▶**7.** Why did some people remain loyal to Britain?

New Roles and Opportunities

The War for Independence changed the lives of many people besides the Loyalists. Women, left alone when the men of their families went off to war, took on new responsibilities. Many slaves found in the war an opportunity to earn their freedom by fighting for the British or the Americans.

▶**8.** What other groups of people did the war affect?

The Homefront and the Battlefront Many American women spent the years of the war coping with life on the homefront—raising their children, taking care of the family farm

Abigail Adams, famous both in her own right and as wife of the second President of the United States, was born Abigail Smith on November 11, 1744. She spent her childhood in Weymouth, Massachusetts, where her father was minister of the Congregational church. Of her childhood she said, "I never was sent to any school. I was always sick." What she learned she "picked up . . . as an eager gatherer."

Abigail was indeed an eager gatherer. Her curious mind took advantage of the books, lively conversation, and interesting people that filled her home. As a young girl, she learned French and read many of the great classics.

When Abigail was 14, a young lawyer named John Adams visited her home. Adams quickly became a frequent visitor, and by 1762, he and Abigail were exchanging love letters. Two years later, in 1764, the couple was married.

From the beginning, the marriage was a good match. Abigail's calm, gentle nature and her faith in John's ability gave him the confidence he lacked. They spent the first ten years of their marriage building John's career as a lawyer and being parents to five children.

John's departure in 1774 to the Continental Congress in Philadelphia marked the first of many separations for the couple. While he was away, Abigail successfully ran the farm and managed their affairs. It was then too that Abigail developed her talent as a letter writer.

Abigail wrote to her husband about a variety of topics. In 1776, when the Continental Congress was framing the Declaration of Independence, she sent this plea: "Remember the Ladies, and be more generous and favourable to them than your ancestors. Do not put such unlimited power in the hands of their husbands . . ."

Abigail Adams felt strongly about women's rights at a time when few people gave the rights of women much thought. She frequently spoke out about the poor educational opportunities for women. She also defended the rights of blacks to have an education.

In 1788, John Adams became the first Vice President of the United States. Nine years later, in 1797, he became its second President. As his wife, Abigail Adams played an active role in public affairs. When John Adams failed to get elected to a second term, the couple returned to Massachusetts. There they expected to have a dull, cheerless retirement.

Abigail Adams's retirement from public life was anything but dull. She used this time to be with friends and to give increasing attention to the rising political career of her oldest son, John Quincy Adams. John Quincy did not disappoint his mother. In 1825, he became the sixth President of the United States.

Abigail Adams did not live to see her son become President. She died on her Massachusetts farm in 1818. She was 74 years old.

Deborah Sampson received a federal pension for her military service during the war.

Some women, often with their children, followed their husbands as they moved about with the army. These women served as nurses, tailors, cooks, clerks, and porters.

Some women even fought on the battlefields. Margaret Corbin and Mary McCauley were two such women. Corbin took over her husband's position at his cannon when he was killed during the Battle of Fort Washington. Corbin herself was badly wounded later in the battle. Mary McCauley was called Molly Pitcher because she came and went on the battlefield with a pitcher of water for the soldiers. During the Battle of Monmouth in 1778, she also took over her wounded husband's job at a cannon.

At least one woman, Deborah Sampson, is known to have disguised herself as a man and enlisted in the army. She served in the army for 20 months until she was found to be a woman. Other women served the Continentals as spies and messengers.

▶9. What different roles did American women play during the Revolution?

or business, trying to keep in touch with their husbands in the army, militia, or Congress. Those women often performed tasks that were not considered proper women's work before the war.

One such woman was Abigail Adams. Her husband, John Adams, was away from their Massachusetts home serving the Contintental Congress for most of the war years. Abigail wrote long letters to John, describing conditions at home. She gave him her opinions on issues before the Congress and kept him informed about how others felt as well. Abigail was hesitant to make decisions about the family finances and business at first. By the end of the war, however, she had become a skillful manager.

A Way to Freedom Many blacks, slave and free, fought for the American cause. Salem Poor and Peter Salem were blacks who fought at the Battle of Bunker Hill. When Washington became commander of the army, blacks were not allowed to enlist for a time. That ruling was changed after the British began using slaves to help their army.

In November 1775, Lord Dunmore, the governor of Virginia, offered freedom to all slaves and indentured servants who joined the British. About 2,000 slaves took up Dunmore's offer in 1775 and 1776. Throughout the war, large numbers of slaves in the South joined the British in exchange for freedom.

In all the states except Georgia and South Carolina, slaves were promised their freedom if they joined the American army. Most slaves who joined were from the North because few southern owners would grant their slaves permission to join the army.

▶**10.** What motivated slaves to fight in the Revolution?

Reviewing Section I————————

Identify   Benedict Arnold, Ethan Allen, Fort Ticonderoga, Henry Knox, Dorchester Heights, evacuate, William Howe, bounty, Loyalists, Abigail Adams, Margaret Corbin, Mary McCauley, Deborah Sampson, Salem Poor, Peter Salem

Questions to Answer
1. What were the American disadvantages at the beginning of the war?
2. How did the war affect women and slaves?

A Question to Think About   Why did most Loyalists stay in the colonies during the war?

Agrippa Hull, a freeborn black from Massachusetts, enlisted with the Patriots in 1777.

II. The War in the Middle Colonies

Soon after the British evacuated Boston, it became clear that they would attack the Middle Colonies next. The Congress insisted that Washington defend New York. So the general brought his army there although he knew it would have to fight under a great disadvantage. New York City is on the island of Manhattan, but the Americans had almost no navy.

The Fight for New York

The British navy, with no force to stop it, arrived in July and soon controlled the waters around Manhattan. The British could use their navy to move troops about, mount attacks, and cut off retreats.

With no navy, the patriots tried to stop the British from going up the Hudson River by sinking old ships in the river and building gun batteries along its sides. Farther north, near the town of West Point, the Americans even stretched a big chain across the river.
▶**1.** How did the lack of a navy hurt Washington in his attempt to hold New York City?

Brooklyn Heights   Brooklyn Heights, located on Long Island, overlooks New York City. The Americans knew that to lose the Heights was to lose New York City. Washington put Major General Israel Putnam in charge of the American troops there. Putnam was a veteran of the French and Indian War. He had been a leader of the Connecticut Sons

173

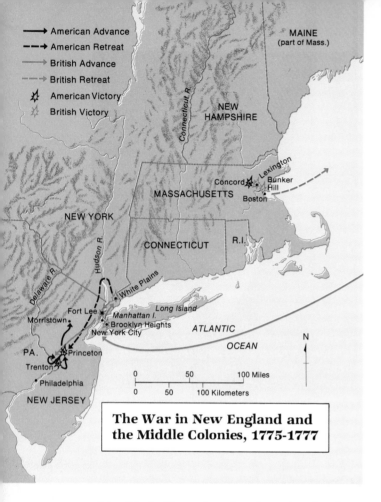

Map legend:
- → American Advance
- ⇢ American Retreat
- → British Advance
- ⇢ British Retreat
- ⚔ American Victory
- ⚔ British Victory

MAINE
(part of Mass.)

NEW HAMPSHIRE

Connecticut R.

NEW YORK

MASSACHUSETTS

Lexington
Concord
Bunker Hill
Boston

CONNECTICUT

R.I.

Hudson R.

White Plains

Fort Lee
Morristown
Delaware R.
Manhattan I.
Brooklyn Heights
New York City

Long Island

ATLANTIC

OCEAN

N

PA.
Princeton
Trenton

Philadelphia

NEW JERSEY

0   50   100 Miles
0   50   100 Kilometers

The War in New England and the Middle Colonies, 1775-1777

Map Study *Name three American victories shown on the map. Name four British victories. About how far is Trenton from Princeton?*

of Liberty during the Stamp Act crisis. At the news of Lexington and Concord, he had left his Connecticut farm and marched off to Cambridge. He had fought in the Battle of Bunker Hill. Putnam could not, however, hold Brooklyn Heights.

The British attacked the Heights from two sides on August 27. The Americans had to retreat. Washington brought more soldiers to help. Fortunately some of them were fishermen from the coastal town of Marblehead, Massachusetts. On the night of August 29, 1776, in a heavy rainstorm, the Marblehead

men rowed the American troops safely across the East River from Brooklyn to Manhattan. Even so, about 1,500 of the Americans were killed, wounded, or captured.

▶**2.** What was the outcome of the Battle of Brooklyn Heights?

The Big Retreat Manhattan was no easier to hold than Brooklyn Heights. In early September, Washington moved his troops to the northern part of Manhattan. The Americans and British fought a series of small battles there which are known together as the Battle of Harlem Heights. Then, in early October, the British forced Washington from Manhattan altogether. He led his army north into Westchester County with Howe following closely behind him.

Washington had left thousands of soldiers at Fort Washington on Manhattan and at Fort Lee across the Hudson in New Jersey. Howe knew that. So, after a brief battle with Washington at the town of White Plains in Westchester County, he doubled back toward Fort Washington. On November 16, the British took the fort along with its 3,000 American soldiers, cannon, and other supplies. That loss was a disaster for the Americans, who soon were also forced to abandon Fort Lee.

▶**3.** Why was the loss of Fort Washington a disaster?

The Crisis

Washington led what remained of his army down through New Jersey and across the Delaware River into Pennsylvania. That was the low point of the war. Even Washington said, "I think the game is pretty near up." In New Jersey, 3,000 people agreed with him. They were so certain that Washington would be defeated that they took oaths of loyalty to the king.

Thomas Paine called this bleak time *The Crisis*. He gave that title to a pamphlet in which he tried to rally support for the Americans. He wrote the following:

> These are the times that try men's souls. The summer soldier and sunshine patriot will, in this crisis, shrink from the service of his country; but he that stands *now* deserves the love and thanks of man and woman.

Washington ordered Paine's words read to his troops, and they helped to raise the soldiers' spirits.

▶ **4.** What did Paine attempt to do by writing his pamphlet *The Crisis*?

Trenton and Princeton The spirits of the Americans rose after two small victories in New Jersey. On Christmas Eve, 1776, during a blinding sleet storm, the Marblehead men ferried Washington and his men back across the Delaware River into New Jersey. The next day Washington made a surprise attack on the British at Trenton. Only two Americans were wounded in the Battle of Trenton, and none were killed. The Americans captured nearly 900 Hessians.

Then, in early January, Washington attacked the British at Princeton. Washington led his men into battle. Only 30 yards from the enemy, he gave the order to fire. Gunsmoke filled the air as shots flew from both sides. When the air cleared, there was Washington still sitting calmly on his horse. The British were running away with the Americans on their heels. "It's a fine fox chase, my boys," Washington called out. After the Battle of Princeton, Washington led his army into winter camp at Morristown, New Jersey.

In 1851, Emanuel Leutze completed this inaccurate, but well-known painting of Washington crossing the Delaware River on Christmas Eve, 1776.

The victories at Trenton and Princeton may have been the most important of the war. They stopped the British rush toward victory and gave new life to the American cause. Neither the war nor the revolution had been lost. The American army had survived to fight another day.

▶5. Why were the battles at Trenton and Princeton important?

Philadelphia In 1777, General Howe decided to take Philadelphia. That city is not very far from New York by land. It is not too far by water, either, if a traveler sails south along the Atlantic coast and then up the Delaware River. However, Howe decided to go all the

Map Study *What direction did St. Leger travel from Montreal to Oriskany? Who won the battle at Monmouth Court House?*

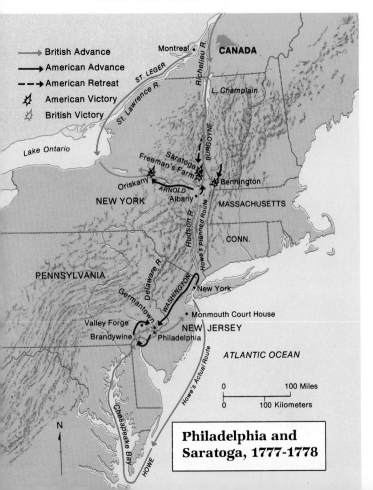

British Advance
American Advance
American Retreat
American Victory
British Victory

CANADA
Montreal
ST. LEGER
Richelieu R.
L. Champlain
St. Lawrence R.
Lake Ontario
BURGOYNE
Saratoga
Freeman's Farm
Oriskany
ARNOLD
Bennington
NEW YORK
Albany
MASSACHUSETTS
Hudson R.
Howe's planned Route
CONN.
PENNSYLVANIA
Delaware R.
WASHINGTON
New York
Germantown
Monmouth Court House
Valley Forge
NEW JERSEY
Brandywine
Philadelphia
ATLANTIC OCEAN
Howe's Actual Route
0   100 Miles
0   100 Kilometers
N
Chesapeake Bay
HOWE

Philadelphia and Saratoga, 1777-1778

way around the Chesapeake Peninsula and then up Chesapeake Bay. As a result, he spent 6 weeks sailing an extra 300 miles against winds that made the voyage more like one of 1,000 miles. Then he had to march 50 miles overland to get to Philadelphia.

Washington tried to stop Howe from reaching Philadelphia, but he failed. He was defeated by the British in a battle on September 11 at Brandywine Creek, southwest of Philadelphia. By September 26, the British held the city. One week later, Washington attacked the British at Germantown, seven miles from Philadelphia. His battle plan was, however, complicated and failed. In December, Washington led his men into winter quarters at Valley Forge, Pennsylvania.

▶6. What route did General Howe take to Philadelphia?

Turning Point at Saratoga

Meanwhile Howe's roundabout trip had some serious results for the British. Howe missed his part in a three-way attack designed to cut off New England from the rest of the colonies.

The British plans for the summer of 1777 had called for three armies to meet at Albany in New York. Howe was to move north up the Hudson River. General John Burgoyne was to march south from Canada via Lake Champlain to the Hudson River. Colonel Barry St. Leger was to move eastward from Lake Ontario through New York.

▶7. What was the British plan for the summer of 1777?

The Plan Fails St. Leger had the help of Joseph Brant, an Iroquois who led a force of Indians and Loyalists. At Oriskany, in western New York, a force of American militia stopped the British. Then the dashing, ambitious

Benedict Arnold, now a general in the army, came to help. He managed to scare off the Iroquois. Without his Indian allies, St. Leger gave up and returned to Canada in August of 1777.

"Gentleman Johnny" Burgoyne did not find his route easy either. He left the St. Lawrence River on June 1, 1777. With him were some 7,000 regular soldiers, 1,400 Indians, about 2,000 women and children, and much too much baggage. Burgoyne's personal "necessities," including silverware and champagne, filled 30 carts. His army carried all of those through the wilderness, where they had to hack their way through fallen trees, build bridges over streams, and even at one point lay a two-mile timber road. Obviously Burgoyne could not move quickly.

General Horatio Gates, a former British officer from Virginia, led the Continentals who faced Burgoyne. Gates was cautious and not very inspiring. However, he was helped by a group of soldiers called the Green Mountain Boys. Led by General John Stark, they defeated a large British raiding party near Bennington in what later became Vermont. With that victory, more militia swelled Gates's forces. Then Washington sent a regiment of sharp-shooting Continentals called Morgan's Rifles. They were named for their commander, Daniel Morgan.

Gates and his troops stopped Burgoyne's advance on September 19 when they defeated a British force at Freeman's Farm on the Hudson River. Then, on October 7, at the same place, Arnold daringly led Connecticut troops against Burgoyne, stopping only when a flash of British fire broke his leg and killed his horse beneath him. Meanwhile Morgan's Rifles did their part. Burgoyne was forced to retreat.

Even though he abandoned some 500 sick and wounded men, it took Burgoyne 3 days

Joseph Brant commanded the Iroquois forces that fought for the British during the war.

to move through pouring rain to the town of Saratoga, New York, only 7 miles away. There he stopped. As the news spread through the countryside, militia poured in until Gates commanded an army of 17,000. By then, Burgoyne's army numbered only about 5,000. The Americans surrounded him, and on October 17, 1777, Burgoyne surrendered.

▶8. Who helped Gates defeat Burgoyne?

The Result of Saratoga Burgoyne's surrender at Saratoga marked a turning point in the war. It was important because it showed the French that the Americans could win.

France was already sending supplies to the Americans as a way of striking at its enemy, Great Britain. After Saratoga, the French were willing to go even further. On February 6, 1778, they signed an alliance with the United

States. France formally recognized American independence. It also agreed that if France and Britain went to war, as they soon did, neither the United States nor France would make peace with Great Britain without the other's consent. France gave up all claims to lands in North America and agreed that any territory won in the war would go to the United States.

The French alliance gave the Americans the help of the French navy. The patriots needed that sea power for a decisive victory. Otherwise the strong British navy would continue to hold major cities along the Atlantic coast.

▶**9.** What was the result of the American victory at Saratoga?

Valley Forge With the victory at Saratoga, the fortunes of the Americans seemed to be on the rise. However, the American troops who spent the winter of 1777–1778 at Valley Forge endured some of the most severe hardships of the war. They went cold and hungry and even barefoot. In the quick moves between battles, the army had lost many supplies.

The army that emerged from Valley Forge in the spring, however, was stronger and more skilled—thanks to the work of General Baron Frederick von Steuben. In February 1778, the Prussian von Steuben arrived at Valley Forge to teach the Americans the art of warfare.

Von Steuben claimed to be a baron and a high officer in the Prussian army. He was, it seems, neither. However, he knew a lot about armies, and he developed a simple set of drills to teach the Continental soldiers. Often it was funny when he drilled the soldiers, since he knew very little English. He directed the soldiers with his hands and sometimes swore at them. However, the

★★ The United States and the World ★★★★★★★★★★★★★★★★★
Help from Abroad for the Revolution

Soldiers from many countries flocked to North America to help the patriots fight the Revolution. Without the help of France, the United States probably would not have been able to defeat Britain. French money helped to keep the army supplied, and the French fleet blockaded Cornwallis at Yorktown.

Perhaps the most famous French friend of the Revolution was the Marquis de Lafayette. The son of a wealthy family, Lafayette was only 19 years old when he arrived in North America with a group of adventurers. He offered his services to the Second Continental Congress and joined Washington's staff. Lafayette fought in many battles during the Revolution and attained the rank of major general.

At the time of the Revolution, Haiti was a French colony. So over 500 black Haitian volunteers fought with the Americans during the Revolution. Henri Christophe, who later became the first king of Haiti, was one such volunteer.

Two famous soldiers from Poland also fought with the patriots during the Revolution. Casimir Pulaski died during the Battle of Savannah. Thaddeaus Kosciusko built fortifications along the Delaware and Hudson rivers and at West Point.

troops came to love him. General Baron Frederick von Steuben was clearly devoted to the American cause.

▶10. Describe the winter of l777–1778 at Valley Forge.

George Rogers Clark Holds the West

Even as the war was being fought in New England and the Middle Colonies, pioneers continued to move across the Appalachians. The British along with their Indian allies attacked these Americans from forts they had acquired from the French after the French and Indian War.

In 1777, George Rogers Clark, a militia leader on the Virginia frontier, decided to take action. He and 175 sharpshooters started at Fort Pitt in Pennsylvania. From there, they floated down the Ohio River to the Mississippi. Then they turned northwest. On July 4, 1778, Clark and his men captured the British fort at Kaskaskia in present-day Illinois. They also captured Cahokia in Illinois and Vincennes in present-day Indiana.

In December, the British recaptured Vincennes. Clark led his men from Kaskaskia across flooded, icy swamps and rivers to take Vincennes again. The British surrendered in February 1779. Although British-inspired Indian raids continued throughout the War, Clark harrassed the British and kept the raids from becoming more serious.

▶11. What western forts did Clark take from the British?

Reviewing Section II

Identify Brooklyn Heights, Israel Putnam, *The Crisis*, Battle of Trenton, Battle of Princeton, Valley Forge, John Burgoyne, Joseph Brant, Horatio Gates, Morgan's Rifles,

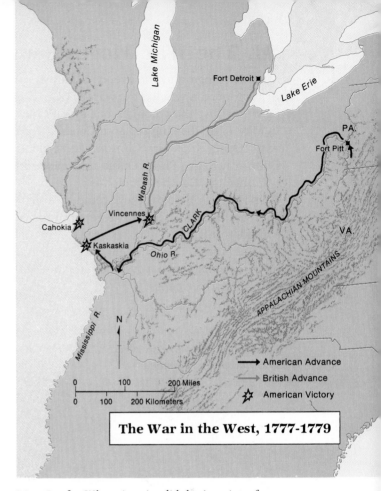

Map Study *What victories did the American forces have in the West? What river did George Rogers Clark follow to reach Kaskaskia?*

Saratoga, Baron von Stueben, George Rogers Clark, Kaskaskia, Cahokia, Vincennes

Questions to Answer
1. What period in the war was called the crisis?
2. Why did the major British campaign of 1777 fail?

A Question to Think About Which was more important, the victory at Saratoga or those at Trenton and Princeton? Give reasons for your answer.

179

III. The War Moves South

After Saratoga and the French alliance, the British faced a whole new war. They had to fight not just the colonists but also France. In May 1778, the king replaced General Howe with General Henry Clinton. He ordered Clinton to leave Philadelphia and move the war into the Southern Colonies.

The British thought they would be able to control the South because its population was spread thinly over a large area. More important, the British thought the South had many Loyalists who would help them defeat the other Americans.

Map Study *Name the bay that the French blockaded. What city did the British retreat to after the battle at Guilford Court House?*

The War in the South, 1778-1781

As Clinton marched from Philadelphia to his headquarters in New York City, Washington attacked at Monmouth, New Jersey, on June 28, 1778. After a fierce battle, neither side could claim victory. Monmouth was the last major battle in the North. Some of the British stayed in New York City. The rest followed orders to move south.

British Victories in the South

The British plan was to take strongholds along the Southern coast. Then, as the army pushed on, they planned to use Loyalists to control the local people.

With the help of the navy, General Clinton took Savannah, Georgia, in late 1778. The British then went on to take the more populated parts of Georgia. Next General Clinton turned northward toward Charleston, South Carolina.

Clinton had been in Charleston before, in 1776, when the British first tried to take the city. At that time, local patriots, led by Colonel William Moultrie, had stopped him. Moultrie had the patriots use logs from palmetto trees to build forts on the islands guarding Charleston Harbor. The spongy palmetto logs swallowed the cannon balls fired at the fort by the British. Meanwhile the colonists did so much damage to the British fleet that it was forced to sail off.

Four years later, however, Moultrie's forts were in decay. In May 1780, Clinton was able to capture Charleston and the American army there, which was led by General Benjamin Lincoln. It was a major victory for the British. The future looked so good that Clinton returned to New York. He left another general, Lord Charles Cornwallis, to finish taking the Carolinas.

Cornwallis had one big victory of his own. On the night of August 16, 1780, near Camden, South Carolina, his troops almost bumped into American troops under General Gates. The armies pulled back and prepared for battle in the morning. The British drove the Americans from the field. Gates himself fled some 65 miles that day to Charlotte, North Carolina. Then he ran on another 120 miles to Hillsboro. His reputation was in ruins. The forces General Gates commanded were in tatters too.

▶**1.** What were Clinton's successes in the South?

Arnold's Treason Threatens the North

About the same time Gates lost the battle at Camden, more sad news came from the North. West Point, the key American fort on the Hudson, was almost sold to the British by its commander, Benedict Arnold. The ambitious Arnold thought the Americans did not appreciate him enough. He had also developed expensive tastes and had many debts. In May 1779, he offered his services to the British—for a price. In 1780, he promised to turn over to the British the garrison at West Point.

Clinton sent his favorite aide, the handsome Major John André, to talk with Arnold. On his way back to Clinton, André was captured. Hidden in his stockings were papers that made Arnold's treason clear. As soon as Arnold heard of André's capture, he fled at breakneck speed to the British. West Point remained in American hands, but Arnold's treason badly shook General Washington.

The British kept their word. They made Arnold a brigadier general in the king's army and paid him handsomely for his services. André did not fare so well. Although many American officers liked and respected him, André was hanged as a spy.

▶**2.** Why did Benedict Arnold turn traitor?

The War in the Carolinas

With the defeat of Gates's troops, there was no Continental Army in the Carolinas. Still Cornwallis found it hard to hold those states. As soon as he set up Loyalist militias to control an area, out came rebels from the swamps or mountains or from beyond British-held territory. They raided Loyalist strongholds and harried the British troops. Colonists like the famous Swamp Fox, Francis Marion, proved to be very good at that kind of irregular war. As the British fought, they were drawn away from their supply bases.

Then, in October 1780, Washington ordered General Nathanael Greene to put together a new American army in the South. Greene did so with the help of Daniel Morgan. Even before Greene's Continentals were in the field, however, some tough American frontiersmen defeated an army of Loyalists at King's Mountain in South Carolina on October 7, 1780. As a result, Cornwallis pulled back into South Carolina.

In early December, Greene took command in the South. He divided his troops and ordered them to harass Cornwallis. One group under Morgan met the British at a place called Hannah's Cowpens near the Broad River in western South Carolina on January 16, 1781. Morgan led both militia and regular Continental soldiers. He put the militia in front, had them shoot two rounds, and then pull back. Behind them were the regulars. When the British soldiers chased the retreating militia, they ran right into the Continentals. By the end of the day, the British had lost almost 1,000 men. The Americans had lost only about 70 soldiers.

Greene himself commmanded the next important battle, near Guilford Court House in North Carolina on March 14. At the end of the day, however, the British held the field. The victory, though, cost them another 500 soldiers. Soon Cornwallis realized that he was in trouble and led his army to Chesapeake Bay in Virginia. There he could get new troops and supplies by sea. He set up camp at Yorktown, a small port on a peninsula between the James and the York rivers.

▶**3.** What victories did the Americans win in the Carolinas?

Yorktown

Washington saw his chance at Yorktown. He could trap Cornwallis on the peninsula. Washington had the help of a fleet of 20 French warships under Admiral de Grasse. They swung into position at the mouth of Chesapeake Bay, preventing Clinton from sending help to Cornwallis by sea. American soldiers under the Marquis de Lafayette kept Cornwallis from pulling back up the peninsula. Lafayette was a young Frenchman who first joined the American army early in the war when he was only 19 years old.

Soon Washington arrived. He had 7,000 French soldiers in addition to his Continentals and militia. Washington's troops outnumbered the British two to one. The Americans kept the British under seige for three weeks. At last, the strength of the mighty British was broken.

On October 17, 1781, exactly four years after the American victory at the Battle of Saratoga, Cornwallis surrendered. There was

John Trumbull's painting "The Surrender of Cornwallis" shows General Benjamin Lincoln (on horseback) accepting the surrender of the British at Yorktown.

Locate the major battles of the American Revolution by identifying the letters on the map.

Yorktown
Savannah
Trenton
Charleston
Bunker Hill (Boston)
Princeton
Saratoga
Cowpens
New York
Germantown

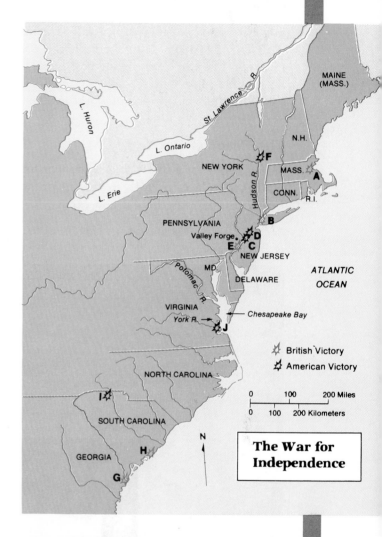

The War for Independence

an impressive ceremony to mark the event. French and American troops stood beneath their waving flags in lines that stretched a half mile. The French wore splendid uniforms. The Americans, as usual, were in hunting shirts. As the British and German soldiers turned over their guns, the band played a song entitled "The World Turned Upside Down."

The war was over, but Washington did not know it. He tried to get De Grasse to help him take Charleston or New York, both of which the British still held. However, when Lord North, the king's minister, heard the news of Yorktown, he said, "Oh, God! It is all over." He knew that Parliament would not and could not replace Cornwallis's army with its 7,241 men, 214 cannon, and 6,658 muskets. The war had already cost enough. So it came to an end.

▶**4.** Why did the war end at Yorktown?

The Peace of Paris

Negotiations for a treaty to end the war formally took place in Paris. Representing the United States was the old and experienced diplomat, Benjamin Franklin. John Adams was there too. John Jay, a New York lawyer, and a merchant and planter from South Carolina named Henry Laurens were the other peace commissioners.

The Americans found France was less friendly to their interests than they had expected. As a result, they settled with the British first and told the French about it later. In that way, they saw to it that the **Treaty of Paris,** signed on September 3, 1783, was very favorable to the United States.

The treaty recognized the independence of the United States of America. The boundaries of the new country went all the way to the

Benjamin West never finished his painting of the men who negotiated the Treaty of Paris in 1783 because the British negotiators refused to pose.

Mississippi River in the West, to the northern boundary of Florida in the South, and to the Great Lakes in the North. Britain agreed to abandon its forts in the west. In return, the Americans agreed that Congress would recommend that the states repay Loyalists for their losses. They also promised not to interfere with efforts to collect debts owed by Americans to the British.

"The harder the conflict," Paine had written, "the more glorious the triumph." Many former British colonists, now citizens of the United States of America, agreed. The thirteen original British colonies had become their own rulers in their own Republic.

▶5. What were the major provisions of the Peace of Paris?

Reviewing Section III

Identify   Henry Clinton, Monmouth, William Moultrie, Benjamin Lincoln, Lord Charles Cornwallis, West Point, Benedict Arnold, Francis Marion, Nathanael Greene, King's Mountain, Hannah's Cowpens, Guilford Court House, De Grasse, the Marquis de Lafayette, Yorktown, Treaty of Paris

Questions to Answer
1. Why did the British plan for winning the South fail?
2. Why did the war end at Yorktown?

A Question to Think About   Did the Americans win at Yorktown or did the British lose?

IMPROVE YOUR READING
Sequence

Most of us follow a routine each day. For example, the first and most obvious thing you did yesterday was to wake up. Then you probably ate breakfast, dressed, went to school, attended classes, had lunch, returned to class, went home, had dinner, finished your homework, and went to bed. Maybe the sequence was a little different for you. However, the point is that these events followed a sequence that is fairly easy for you to remember.

When we are not totally familiar with events such as historical battles, it is not so easy to recall the order in which they took place. In books, often the writer helps us by noting specific dates and by using certain signal words like *then, later, next, during, first, second, third, beginning, end, finally, soon, while,* etc.

The purpose of the exercise that follows is to help you understand the sequence of events in section III of this chapter. Review section III

(pages 180–185). Look for dates and signal words that help explain the sequence of events, that is, the order in which they occurred. Then, on a separate sheet of paper, write the letters for the events in the proper order.

a. Colonel Moultrie stops Clinton at Charleston.
b. Washington orders Greene to put together a new army in the South.
c. Washington attacks Clinton at Monmouth in the last major battle in the North.
d. Clinton captures Charleston.
e. Treaty of Paris is signed.
f. British win an expensive victory near Guilford Court House in North Carolina.
g. British take Savannah, Georgia.
h. Cornwallis wins at Camden.
i. Cornwallis surrenders at Yorktown.
j. Americans win at King's Mountain in North Carolina.

CHAPTER 9 REVIEW

Vocabulary Check
Write a short explanation for each of the following terms.

1. Bounty
2. Evacuate
3. Treaty of Paris
4. Militia
5. Loyalists

Fact Check
On a separate sheet of paper, fill in the word or words that best complete each of the following sentences.

1. At the beginning of the war, Britain's _____ and _____ were much larger than the Americans'.
2. At the start of the war, Americans lacked an _____ and a _____.
3. The _____ was a major turning point in the war.
4. The last major battle of the war took place at _____.
5. By the terms of the Treaty of Paris, Great Britain recognized the _____ of the United States of America.

Time Check
For each pair of events, write the letter of the event that happened first.

1. a. Lord Dunmore offers freedom to all slaves who join the British.
   b. Slaves are promised their freedom if they join the American army.
2. a. The British evacuate Boston.
   b. Washington builds an American army.
3. a. France formally recognizes American independence.
   b. Americans win the Battle of Saratoga.
4. a. Washington's army spends a difficult winter at Valley Forge.
   b. Washington leads his army to victory at Trenton and Princeton.
5. a. Washington orders General Greene to put together a new American army in the South.
   b. General Cornwallis leads his army to Yorktown.

Skills Check
Study the map on page 176 and answer the following questions.

1. Approximately how many miles did St. Leger travel from Montreal?
2. If St. Leger had traveled by the shortest route from Montreal to Albany, how many miles would he have traveled?
3. What river did Burgoyne travel on?
4. What is the distance between Brandywine and Germantown?
5. What is the distance between Valley Forge and Germantown?

Think and Write

1. (a) Describe two advantages of the British at the outbreak of the American Revolution. (b) Describe two disadvantages.
2. (a) Describe two advantages of the Americans when the war started. (b) Describe two disadvantages.
3. Explain how the Revolution opened opportunities for some women and black Americans.
4. Why was the Battle of Saragota the turning point of the war?
5. What were the terms of the Treaty of Paris?

REVIEWING UNIT 3

Reviewing the Facts I.

Match each phrase in Group A with the proper word or words in Group B. You will not use all the terms in Group B.

Group A

1. The fighting between colonists in New England and several local Indian groups
2. Laws passed by Parliament to control colonial trade
3. Defined the role of Parliament in England and the future of assemblies in North America
4. First Spanish settlement in Florida
5. French settlements along the St. Lawrence River
6. Forced voyage from Africa to the West Indies made by African slaves
7. War fought between England and France over land in the Ohio Valley
8. War for Independence ended here
9. British law that put a tax on all legal documents and other materials printed in the colonies
10. American victory that was the turning point of the War for Independence

Group B

a. Saratoga
b. King Philip's War
c. Glorious Revolution
d. Middle Passage
e. Stamp Act
f. Navigation Acts
g. French and Indian War
h. Yorktown
i. St. Augustine
j. Declaratory Act
k. Canada
l. Declaration of Independence

Reviewing the Facts II.

The statements below describe a person or group of people. On a sheet of paper, identify the person or group described.

1. Name given to colonists who remained loyal to England during the Revolution
2. Leader of the Continental Army
3. Author of the Declaration of Independence
4. Author of *Common Sense*
5. Indian leader who united several Indian groups and attacked settlements on the western frontier in 1763

Reviewing Ideas

1. What events caused trouble for the colonists in the late 1660's?
2. In what ways did the colonies change during the years from 1700 to 1750?
3. How did the Spanish borderlands and the French colonies in North America develop differently from the British colonies?
4. (a) What caused the French and Indian War? (b) How did claims to land in North America change when the war ended?
5. (a) Why did Parliament pass a series of trade laws? (b) What changes came about in the colonies as a result?
6. Why did the colonists feel they were justified in declaring independence?
7. Explain the difference between *direct* and *virtual* representation.
8. Why did the British expect to defeat the patriots in the American Revolution?
9. How were the Americans able to defeat Great Britain?
10. (a) List three heroes or heroines of the American Revolution. (b) Which do you think was most important to the success of the patriots? (c) Why?

UNIT FOUR

The Republic Begins

On April 30, 1789, George Washington became the first President of the United States. He is shown here on his way to New York to take the oath of office. Washington guided the new nation in its first years. The four Presidents who followed Washington faced many challenges. Each challenge helped the young nation to grow stronger.

Chapter 10

Founding the American Republic

George Washington, seated on the right, is shown presiding over the Constitutional Convention. In total, 55 delegates attended the Convention.

Winning independence was only part of the American Revolution. Even while fighting the war, Americans began designing governments for their new Republic. There were no republics in the world at that time, no governments whose rulers held office not by heredity but by the choice of the governed. Republics were considered impractical because they never lasted very long. The republics of times past had broken up into warring groups until their people turned to strong rulers or despots to end the disorder. As a result, many Europeans watched with interest the Americans' effort to found something new—a lasting republic.

First, the Americans set up republican governments for the separate states. They also created a confederation, a league or alliance of states, to serve as a central government for the nation. Later, the Americans built on their experience in the states and under the confederation to design the federal Constitution of 1787.

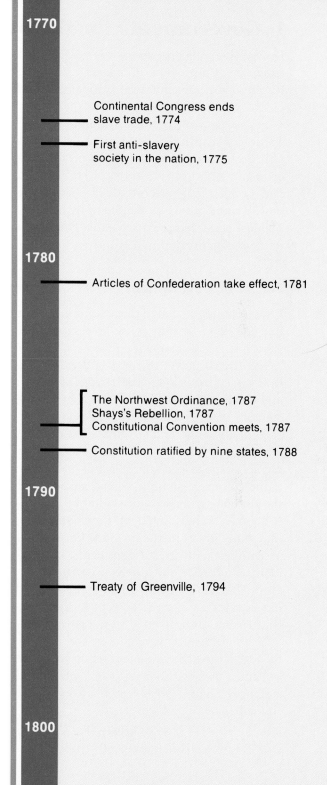

1770

Continental Congress ends slave trade, 1774

First anti-slavery society in the nation, 1775

1780

Articles of Confederation take effect, 1781

The Northwest Ordinance, 1787
Shays's Rebellion, 1787
Constitutional Convention meets, 1787

Constitution ratified by nine states, 1788

1790

Treaty of Greenville, 1794

1800

I. Governments for the States

By May 1776, independence was near. At that time, the Continental Congress asked the states to set up regular governments based on the will of the people.

Ten states wrote new **constitutions** by 1777. Those constitutions were sets of basic laws that both created and set limits on the government. Another two states, Rhode Island and Connecticut, altered their charters so power came from the people, not the king. The last state, Massachusetts, finally adopted its new constitution in 1780.

Forms of Government

It was exciting to design the new governments but not easy. To start with, how should the governments be shaped?

The British government was divided into three parts: the king, the House of Lords, and the House of Commons. On that model, colonial governments were made up of governors, councils, and assemblies. Colonists trusted the assemblies most, since their members spoke for the people, not the Crown. Some colonists thought a good government should consist only of an assembly.

Thomas Paine stated in *Common Sense,* that state governments be made up solely of assemblies with presiding officers, or presidents. Colonists did not want strong governors like those the king had appointed. So most states gave great powers to their legislators and almost none to the governors.

Often governors were chosen and paid by the legislatures. Some states had no governor. In Paine's own state, Pennsylvania, the elected assembly shared power with an executive council instead of a governor.

▶1. Which part of government had the most power under the first state constitutions?

Toward Balanced Government

Because they gave so much power to the assemblies, the first state constitutions were unbalanced. That is, they did not divide and balance power between different parts of government as the British and colonial governments had tried to do.

Some people, including John Adams and Thomas Jefferson, said assemblies with so much power were a danger to freedom. And soon the all-powerful assemblies began interfering with people's rights. They took away the property of Loyalists, for example. They also ignored the rights of creditors by letting debtors pay back old loans with paper money

Tom Paine urged the newly formed states to create strong, powerful assemblies.

192

that was now worth much less than when they had borrowed it.

▶**2.** What problems occurred because of the power of state legislatures?

The Massachusetts Constitution Adams believed that power had to be divided and balanced for a government to work well. He got a chance to apply his ideas in 1780, when he helped write the new Massachusetts constitution.

Under that constitution, the people elected a legislature with two houses—a senate and a house of representatives. However, the people also elected a governor who was not dependent on the legislature. The governor could even **veto** bills the legislature had passed. That is, the governor could prevent them from becoming law. Because the Massachusetts constitution divided power in that way, it created a balanced government.

▶**3.** How did the Massachusetts constitution create a form of government that was more balanced than earlier state constitutions?

The Work of the People The first constitutions were written and passed by assemblies. As a result, the assemblies often felt free to change the constitutions just as they changed ordinary laws. Was there any way to create a constitution that could limit the legislature?

People in Massachusetts found a way to do that. They refused to let the assembly write their constitution. Instead, the people sent representatives to a special meeting called a **constitutional convention.** The task of the convention was to write a constitution for the state.

The convention sent a draft of its constitution back to the towns. Then the people there held meetings to decide whether or not to **ratify,** or approve, the constitution. That made the Massachusetts constitution a special kind of law because it was enacted directly by the people. And in a republic, the people were **sovereign** (sov'ran). That is, they hold the highest power. Such a law could limit the legislature as well as other parts of government. Other states soon followed that example when they revised or replaced their constitutions.

▶**4.** What was the advantage of the Massachusetts method of ratifying the state constitution?

Reviewing Section I

Identify constitutions, veto, constitutional convention, ratify, sovereign

Questions to Answer
1. Why did most state constitutions give great power to the legislature?
2. What made the Massachusetts constitution different from other state laws?

A Question to Think About Why did the people who planned the new governments think it was important to limit the powers of those governments?

II. The Growth of Freedom

The American Revolution did more than change the government. The new Republic's fight for independence also increased the freedom of individuals, including blacks and women.

Freeing the Slaves
The colonists often complained that Britain was trying to reduce them to slavery. Many Americans thought that people who fought hard for their freedom should not themselves

193

Elizabeth Freeman's suit for freedom led to the outlawing of slavery in Massachusetts.

keep slaves. As a result, some important steps were taken toward freedom for slaves.

In the fall of 1774, the first Continental Congress passed an agreement to end the slave trade. In 1775, a group of Quakers started the first American antislavery society at Philadelphia. Other religious groups soon formed their own societies. The antislavery movement was becoming an important cause throughout the colonies.

After independence, state after state in the North ended slavery. Some did it through special provisions in their state constitutions. In other states, slavery was ended by law or through court decisions. **Emancipation** (i man′sǝ pā′shǝn), the freeing of slaves, was most often done gradually. That is, not all slaves were freed at one time.

Slaves themselves played an important part in winning their freedom. They brought several cases to the courts and petitioned legislatures. For example, a group of slaves from Portsmouth asked the New Hampshire legislature to abolish slavery.

Virginia, Maryland, and Delaware all passed laws that made it easier for owners to free their slaves. However, slavery was not abolished in any southern state. As a result, slavery became a southern institution.

▶**1.** What is emancipation?

Rights for Women

When Thomas Jefferson wrote in the Declaration of Independence that "all Men are created equal," he did not mean all people. He meant all males. At that time, women were not considered the equal of men. Women did not have the same rights as men either.

A married woman had no legal status except through her husband. All property she brought into the marriage became her husband's, as did any money she earned after the marriage. Children were under their father's legal control—and under his alone.

The situation of unmarried women and widows was a little better. They could run their own businesses and own property.

In 1776, Abigail Adams urged her husband, John, to "remember the ladies" in writing laws for the new republic. She wanted the power of husbands over their wives to be reduced. However, the position of married women did not improve until much later.

Abigail Adams never asked for the vote. Still the issue of voting by women came up from time to time. The New Jersey constitution of 1776 gave the vote to "all free inhabitants" who had a certain amount of property. That wording allowed both women and free blacks to vote. However, in 1807, New Jersey changed its constitution so women and blacks could no longer vote. Woman's suffrage, or the right of woman to vote, was still a long way off.

In the early years of the United States, there was great demand in Europe, especially in France, for information about the United States. Many French people visited the new Republic, and they often published books of their observations when they returned home. Some French writers even invented stunning accounts of the scenery and of Indian life in the United States without ever visiting North America.

The French reported with amazement that there were almost no poor people in the United States. Wages were high. One French traveler reported in surprise that he saw a man driving a cart while eating a turkey wing and a piece of white bread. In France, meat and white bread were luxuries for the very wealthy.

Most Americans could read and write, the travel writers reported, and all Americans were fascinated by politics. One writer was shocked to see a member of Congress riding in a coach seated next to a laborer. Most amazing of all, the laborer had voted for the member of the House, and the two men chatted about politics for the entire journey.

Still the Revolution brought some important changes for American women. Mothers won new respect because they raised the nation's children. To shape the future in that way, some women argued, was just as important as voting and holding public office. If mothers were to do a good job, they needed to be educated. Suddenly, special schools for girls started to appear. Many of the graduates of those schools later became champions of women's rights.

▶**2.** How did the position of American women change after the Revolution?

Reviewing Section II

Identify emancipation, Abigail Adams

Questions to Answer
1. What role did blacks play in abolishing slavery in the North?
2. What legal rights did married women have before 1800?

A Question to Think About How did slavery contradict the goals of the American patriots in the Revolution?

III. A Government for the Nation

The states needed to act together to support an army, win the war, and make treaties with other nations. They did those things at first through the Continental Congress. By 1776, it seemed important to establish the confederation in a more lasting way.

The Articles of Confederation

In June 1776, Congress set up a committee to draft a plan of union for the colonies. The **Articles of Confederation** were the result. The members of Congress made many

195

changes in the proposed Articles of Confederation before finally approving the document in November 1777.

Each of the states had to ratify, or approve, the Articles before it went into effect. Most of the states quickly gave their approval, but some of the smaller states were not satisfied with the document. Most of those states had no land claims west of the Appalachian Mountains. They feared that the states with such land claims might someday become very large and powerful. Seven states, including Virginia, New York, and Massachusetts, claimed vast amounts of land in the West. Those land claims were usually based on colonial charters.

Maryland refused to sign the Articles of Confederation until Virginia, which had the biggest land claims, **ceded** (sēd′əd), or granted, its western lands to Congress. Virginia gave Congress its land claims except for those to Kentucky, which it held until 1789. In return, Maryland ratified the Articles of Confederation. Government under the Articles began in 1781, the last year of the war.

Other states with land claims also gave them up. As a result, Congress took title to nearly 222 million acres between the Appalachians and the Mississippi River. Congress could sell that land to raise money.

▶**1.** Why did Maryland at first refuse to ratify the Articles of Confederation?

Government under the Articles

The Articles of Confederation created a "firm league of friendship" between the states, not a strong national government. In many ways, the powers of the national government under the Confederation were like those of the old Continental Congress.

Congress was still a one-house assembly. The states chose delegates to it each year.

Every state, big or small, had only one vote in Congress, as in the past.

Congress chose one of its members as a presiding officer, but no delegate could be president for more than one year in three. No person could be a delegate to Congress for more than three years in six. By limiting the number of years a person could hold office, the Articles limited the power of delegates.

The Articles also limited the powers of Congress. It could not tax the people. The states were fighting a war to keep Parliament from taxing them, and they were not ready to give that right to Congress. Nor would they let Congress regulate trade or raise an army. Congress could only ask the states for money and soldiers. If the states refused, there was nothing Congress could do.

▶**2.** What important powers did Congress lack under the Articles of Confederation?

A Step Forward

The Articles of Confederation were nonetheless an important step forward for the United States. Just to have the confederation defined in a written document was an improvement over the informal arrangements of the First and Second Continental Congresses.

The Articles also committed the states to a "Perpetual Union," one that would continue after the war was over. The Articles made Americans part of one large nation, not just thirteen smaller ones. The Articles said a citizen of one state had all the privileges of a citizen in any other state. As a result, people could travel freely and carry on business between the states.

Finally, the Articles separated the powers of the states from those of the nation. Congress had the "sole and exclusive right" to declare war and make peace, carry out foreign policy, regulate the value of money, fix weights and

Powers of the National Government under the Articles of Confederation

Power to	No Power to
• Pass laws with the consent of nine states	• Enforce its own laws
• Regulate the value of money	• Collect taxes or duties
• Establish weights and measures	• Regulate trade with foreign countries or between states
• Set up a postal system	• Raise an army
• Appoint military officers	• Set up national courts
• Declare war and make peace	
• Set up an army and a navy	
• Handle affairs with foreign countries	

Chart Study *List the powers of Congress under the Articles of Confederation.*

measures, and establish a post office. It had authority to decide disputes between states. The powers given to Congress were enough to make the United States one of the most powerful confederations in history.

▶**3.** What powers did the Articles of Confederation give Congress?

Accomplishments of the Confederation

Congress managed to accomplish a great deal under the Articles of Confederation. For one thing, it brought some order to the nation's financial affairs, which were in great confusion by the end of the war. Just to figure out who owed what to whom was a very difficult task.

Congress also created regular executive departments to help manage the country. In 1781, Congress set up the Departments of War, of Foreign Affairs, and of Finance.

▶**4.** What were some of the administrative achievements of the government under the Articles?

Land Ordinances Congress's most important achievement lay in the plans it made for the settlement of its western lands. It did that by laws, or **ordinances,** which Congress passed in 1785 and 1787.

The **Ordinance of 1785** set up a way of selling parts of the western territory to raise money. The territory would be surveyed and divided into townships 6 miles square. Each township was to be further divided into 36 lots, each 1 mile square. One lot in every township was reserved for public schools.

The **Northwest Ordinance of 1787** was even more important. It applied only to the area north of the Ohio River, east of the Mississippi, and south of the Great Lakes. That area was later called the Old Northwest.

The ordinance explained how that area would be governed. At first, the Northwest was divided into smaller territories, or districts. Each district was governed by a governor, a secretary, and three judges appointed by Congress. When a territory had a population of 5,000 free white males, it could send delegates to a local assembly. Once a territory had 60,000 free inhabitants, it could send regular delegates to Congress and set up a permanent constitution and a republican government. Then the territories could become states and members of the Union on equal terms with the original thirteen states. Eventually the states of Ohio, Indiana, Illinois,

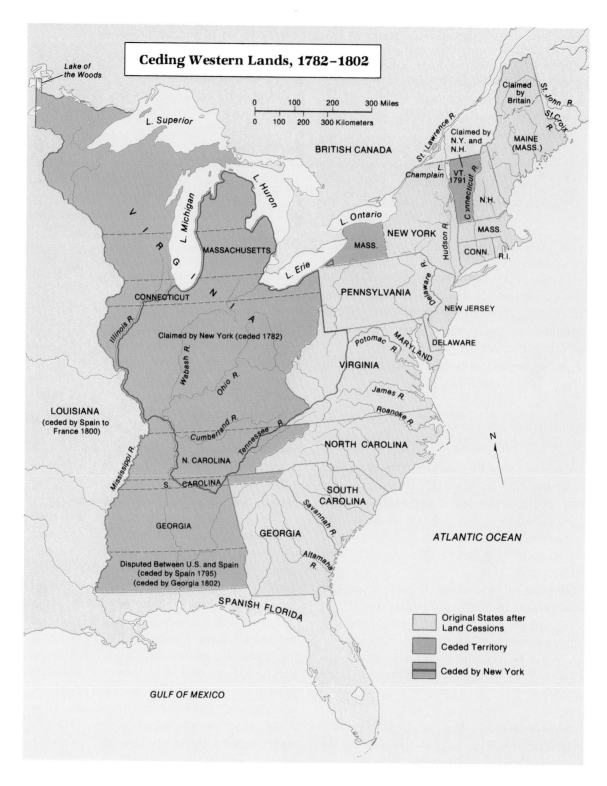

Ceding Western Lands, 1782–1802

Lake of the Woods

L. Superior

BRITISH CANADA

Claimed by Britain

St. John R.

St. Croix R.

St. Lawrence R.

L. Champlain

Claimed by N.Y. and N.H.

MAINE (MASS.)

Connecticut R.

VT. 1791

N.H.

L. Huron

L. Michigan

MASSACHUSETTS

L. Ontario

NEW YORK

MASS.

MASS.

CONN.

R.I.

L. Erie

Hudson R.

CONNECTICUT

V I R G I N I A

PENNSYLVANIA

NEW JERSEY

DELAWARE

Delaware R.

Illinois R.

Claimed by New York (ceded 1782)

Wabash R.

Ohio R.

Potomac R.

MARYLAND

VIRGINIA

James R.

LOUISIANA
(ceded by Spain to France 1800)

Cumberland R.

Tennessee R.

Roanoke R.

Mississippi R.

N. CAROLINA

NORTH CAROLINA

S. CAROLINA

SOUTH CAROLINA

GEORGIA

GEORGIA

Savannah R.

ATLANTIC OCEAN

N

Disputed Between U.S. and Spain
(ceded by Spain 1795)
(ceded by Georgia 1802)

Altamaha R.

SPANISH FLORIDA

GULF OF MEXICO

	Scale
0 100 200 300 Miles	
0 100 200 300 Kilometers	

Original States after Land Cessions

Ceded Territory

Ceded by New York

A member of General Anthony Wayne's staff made this painting of Wayne meeting with a group of Indians after the Battle of Fallen Timbers.

Michigan, and Wisconsin were formed from the Northwest Territory.

The ordinance also abolished slavery in the Old Northwest, guaranteed the settlers basic rights including trial by jury and religious freedom, and said "schools and the means of education" would be "encouraged."

The Northwest Ordinance of 1787 was a model for organizing other lands that the United States acquired later. Those lands would also be organized into states and made equal members of the nation rather than be held as colonies. For that reason, the Northwest Ordinance is one of the most important laws passed in American history.

▶5. What were the provisions of the land ordinances of 1785 and 1787?

The Indians of the Old Northwest The Ordinance of 1787 said "utmost good faith shall always be observed toward the Indians." It also stated that the Indians' lands and property would "never be taken from them without their consent."

From the start, the Indians were unwilling to give up their lands. Those who lived north of the Ohio River even formed a confederacy and refused to sell any land to people from the United States.

Most easterners, eager for land, poured across the Appalachians anyway. They soon clashed with the Indians. To protect the newcomers, General Joseph Harmar led an army in the 1790's against the Indian confederacy, which was led by Little Turtle, a

◀**Map Study** *Which state claimed the largest amount of western territory? How many states claimed land along the Mississippi River?*

199

IMPROVE YOUR SKILLS
Using Map Insets

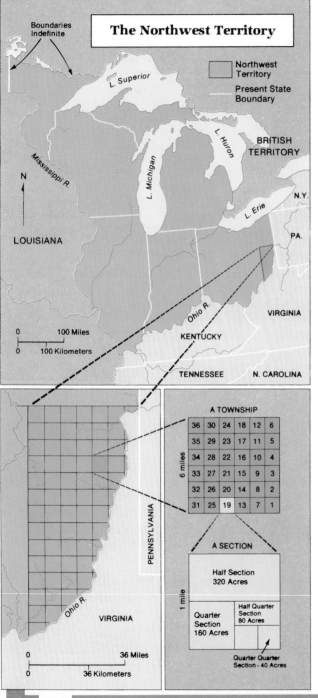

The Northwest Territory

Boundaries Indefinite

Northwest Territory

Present State Boundary

L. Superior

L. Michigan

L. Huron

BRITISH TERRITORY

N.Y.

L. Erie

PA.

Mississippi R.

N

LOUISIANA

VIRGINIA

Ohio R.

KENTUCKY

0   100 Miles

0   100 Kilometers

TENNESSEE   N. CAROLINA

PENNSYLVANIA

Ohio R.

VIRGINIA

0   36 Miles

0   36 Kilometers

A TOWNSHIP

36	30	24	18	12	6
35	29	23	17	11	5
34	28	22	16	10	4
33	27	21	15	9	3
32	26	20	14	8	2
31	25	19	13	7	1

6 miles

A SECTION

Half Section 320 Acres

1 mile

Quarter Section 160 Acres

Half Quarter Section 80 Acres

Quarter Quarter Section - 40 Acres

The Ordinance of 1785 set up the method used to sell land in the Northwest Territory. The map shows the Northwest Territory. It also shows a small area of land bordered by the Ohio River, Pennsylvania, and Virginia. That small area has been enlarged and reproduced near the larger map. It is an inset to, or a part of, the larger map. The inset map gives information about how townships were divided. Yet another inset shows the division of one section of land in a township. Use the large map and the insets to answer the following questions.

1. What area is shown on the large map?
2. How many sections of land are in a township?
3. A township is laid out in a square. How long is each of its sides? How many square miles make up a township?
4. How many acres are in one section of a township?
5. How many acres are in a half section of a township?

Miami Indian. Little Turtle defeated Harmar. Then Little Turtle defeated another, larger army led by Major General Arthur St. Clair.

In 1792, the United States sent yet another general to defeat the Indians. General Anthony Wayne finally broke the power of the Indian confederacy at the Battle of Fallen Timbers (near Toledo, Ohio) in August 1794. By the Treaty of Greenville, the Indians gave up their claims to all but a small corner of land in the Northwest Territory.

▶**6.** How did the Indians of the Old Northwest lose their lands?

Problems under the Confederation

Though Congress made good use of the powers it had, more and more problems arose because of the powers it lacked. Once the war ended, Americans were eager to buy British goods again. However, Britain was no longer willing to buy American products. Nor would it let the Americans sell to their old customers in the British West Indies. Without that trade, Americans could not export enough to pay for their imports. Congress was unable to help because it had no power over trade.

Partly as a result of Britain's trade rules, the United States went into a period of **depression** from 1784 to 1786. A depression is a time when businesses sell fewer products and have less money to start new projects. Many people lose their jobs.

▶**7.** How did Britain cause economic problems for the United States?

The Barbary Pirates American merchants needed to find new ports for trade. They began, for example, to trade with countries along the Mediterranean. Even there, however, the weakness of Congress was a problem.

The Mediterranean Sea swarmed with pirates from countries in northern Africa, called the **Barbary States.** They included Tripoli, Tunisia, Algeria, and Morocco. Many European nations paid the rulers of the Barbary States for protection against the pirates. The United States did not have the money to buy such protection. It did not have a navy to protect its merchant ships, either. So pirates captured American ships and sold their officers and sailors as slaves. Again, Congress could do nothing.

▶**8.** How did the Barbary States cause problems for the United States?

Trouble in the Northwest Congress faced problems of a different sort in the Old Northwest. In the Treaty of Paris, the peace treaty that ended the American Revolution, the British had promised to give up their posts along the Great Lakes and the St. Lawrence River. Later they refused to do so because they claimed the American states had violated the peace treaty.

The treaty said Congress would "earnestly recommend" that the states give Loyalists back their property, which Congress did. But many states refused to comply. Some states also passed laws interfering with the collection of debts owed to the British from before the Revolution.

The states were in the wrong. Their headstrong actions clearly interfered with Congress's "sole and exclusive power" to negotiate treaties and carry on foreign policy. However, Congress was helpless. It could not force the states to act more responsibly.

▶**9.** Why did Britain refuse to give back the posts it held in the Northwest?

Spain and the Old Southwest Meanwhile Spain stirred up trouble in the Old Southwest, the area south of the Ohio River between the Appalachian Mountains and the Mississippi River. After the war, many Americans moved to those lands. By 1790, there were over 100,000 new settlers in what became the states of Kentucky and Tennessee.

Most of the settlers were farmers. They grew corn, wheat, and tobacco and raised cattle and hogs. They did not want to haul those goods across the Appalachians to market. Instead, they wanted to ship their crops and cattle down the Mississippi River to the port of New Orleans.

After the French and Indian War, Spain took control of the west bank of the Mississippi and New Orleans. In 1784, Spain closed the Mississippi to all trade by Americans unless they were willing to become subjects of the Spanish king. Some Westerners were tempted. Congress could only watch and hope.
▶10. How did Spain cause problems in the Old Southwest?

The Power of the States The way the states were acting was also disturbing. Not only did they ignore the Treaty of Paris, but they also ignored Congress. They often refused to raise money for Congress or even to send delegates there. It looked for a time as though Congress might disappear.

By the late 1780's, many Americans thought something had to be done. They wanted to increase the strength of the national government so it could enforce its rights and powers. Then the national government could check the power of the states.
▶11. How did the conduct of the states raise support for a stronger national government?

Reviewing Section III

Identify Articles of Confederation, ceded, ordinances, Ordinance of 1785, Northwest Ordinance of 1787, Joseph Harmar, Little Turtle, Arthur St. Clair, Anthony Wayne, Battle of Fallen Timbers, Treaty of Greenville, depression, Barbary States

Questions to Answer
1. What were two of the accomplishments made by Congress under the Articles of Confederation?
2. What were two of the weaknesses of the national government under the Articles?

A Question to Think About What might have happened if the original states had tried to hold the western lands as colonies?

IV. From Confederation to Constitution

Virginia called for a meeting of the states at Annapolis, Maryland, to discuss ways to solve the nation's trade problems. Too few delegates attended the meeting in September 1786 for it to do much. However, before going home, the delegates called another, larger meeting to be held at Philadelphia in May 1787. The purpose of the meeting was to strengthen the national government. Congress joined in the call for a convention "for the sole and express purpose of revising the Articles of Confederation."

Shays's Rebellion
While plans for the new convention were being made, a crisis occurred in Massachusetts. That state had retired, or taken out of circulation, most of its wartime paper money. What gold and silver was available went to pay for British imports. Then, during the depression, bankers and other creditors demanded that debts be repaid. But debtors could not raise the necessary money. So the creditors went to court to seize their debtors' farms and other property.

This woodcut shows Daniel Shays, leader of the farmers' rebellion against taxation in western Massachusetts, with one of his officers, Job Shattuck.

Desperate farmers rose up in the fall of 1786 and forced the courts to close. They did not mean to overthrow the government. They only wanted to win time until a new legislature met. Then they expected to get relief through new laws.

In January 1787, a group of such farmers under Daniel Shays tried to seize ammunition from the federal armory at Springfield. They were driven off by Massachusetts troops. Shays fled to Vermont. What is known as **Shays's Rebellion** soon came to an end.

The disorder in Massachusetts made many people nervous about the future of the country. It seemed to them that the American Republic was beginning to fall apart just as earlier republics had. Leaders like George Washington thought that a more powerful national government could prevent disorders. Such men saw the Philadelphia convention as a last chance to save the Republic.

▶**1.** What was Shays's Rebellion?

The Constitutional Convention

All of the thirteen original states except Rhode Island sent delegates to the **Constitutional Convention** at Philadelphia. Although there were 74 elected delegates, only 55 men actually attended most sessions. They met for 16 long, hard, hot weeks at the Philadelphia State House. Those who remained for the whole time understood the historic importance of their work.

William Birch made this engraving of the Philadelphia State House three years after the Constitutional Convention was held there.

The 55 delegates were among the most distinguished citizens of the young nation. Over half of them had served in the Continental Congress. Seven had been state governors. Among the group, George Washington was the best known and the most respected. Benjamin Franklin at 82 was the oldest delegate. Most of the other delegates were relatively young. They had grown up during the Revolution. Those young men of the American Revolution thought clearly and in a fresh way about government.

▶**2.** What sort of people were the delegates to the Constitutional Convention?

Getting Started On May 25, the delegates met for the first time. They chose Washington to preside over the convention. They also decided to hold their sessions in secret so they could express their views as freely as possible. Dirt was spread on the cobblestones to muffle the noise of traffic outside.

Then, for five or six days a week, often for seven hours a day, the delegates argued and compromised their way toward a government different from—and better than—what anyone had expected. We know what took place only because some members kept private notes on the proceedings. James Madison of Virginia kept especially complete notes.

▶**3.** How do we know what went on at the Constitutional Convention?

The Task Defined Most of the delegates agreed that the national government needed more power. However, they disagreed about how to give it more power. Madison thought the convention should write an entirely new constitution. His views shaped the **Virginia Plan,** which was presented to the convention soon after it met. The Virginia Plan called for a bicameral legislature, an executive, and a national judiciary.

Other people thought that such a major change would never be accepted by the country. Their views shaped the **New Jersey Plan,** which was presented in mid-June. The New Jersey Plan looked more like a revision of the Articles of Confederation, but it would have created a much stronger national government. The New Jersey Plan gave the new government the power to raise taxes and regulate trade. Its laws would be "the supreme law" of the land.

The delegates decided to use the Virginia Plan as the basis for their work. That meant that Madison's views had won.

▶**4.** What plan did James Madison present to the convention?

The Great Compromise   Before the convention could proceed with its work, it had to decide how the states would be represented in the legislature of the new government. Delegates from certain small states thought that each state, large or small, should have the same number of representatives. Delegates from the larger states said that the number of representatives a state had should be based on its population.

For a long time, neither side was willing to give in. Then, on July 17, the convention agreed to the **Great Compromise.** Each state would have two votes in the upper house of the new legislature, the Senate. Representation in the House of Representatives, the lower house of the legislature, would be based on a state's population.

▶**5.** What was the Great Compromise?

Gouverneur Morris was responsible for writing most of the final draft of the Constitution.

The Three-Fifths Compromise   There was still another problem about representation to be solved. The southern states wanted to count slaves as part of their population in determining representation in the House of Representatives. That would give them more seats. The northern states did not want slaves to be counted. Again a compromise—the **Three-Fifths Compromise**—settled the issue. Three fifths of the slave population would be counted for purposes of representation and taxation. That agreement was tied to another clause allowing Congress to end the slave trade after 20 years.

▶**6.** What was the Three-Fifths Compromise?

Separation of Function   By adopting the Virginia Plan, the convention decided that the new government would be a balanced one. However, its power would no longer be divided as it was in Britain and in the Massachusetts constitution. Instead, power would

James Madison

Very often people who come best prepared to a meeting have the most power. At the Constitutional Convention of 1787, the delegate who came best prepared did indeed turn out to be a powerful leader. The delegate's name was James Madison.

At first glance, James Madison did not seem a powerful man. Frail and sickly, he stood barely five feet six inches tall and weighed only a hundred pounds. His bushy eyebrows and scraggly hair almost hid his bright blue eyes. Even in his speech, he was quiet and restrained. But underneath his quiet exterior, James Madison was a man of action and thought.

James Madison was born on March 6, 1751, in the Virginia Piedmont. He spent his childhood roaming the lush acres of the Madison plantation. His mother taught him to read and write. His father taught him the importance of serving his community.

By age 11, James had read all the books in his father's house. Then he studied with private tutors before going off to New Jersey's Princeton College in 1769. After graduating, he returned home and studied law for a time. But he never became a lawyer. Instead, Madison turned his energies to serving his country.

James Madison did indeed serve his country. In 1776, he helped get a clause in the Virginia Bill of Rights that said that men could no longer be denied the right to vote because of their religious beliefs. (At this time, women and blacks could not vote at all.) In 1787, he attended the Constitutional Convention in Philadelphia. Many of his opinions about government became part of the Virginia Plan, which the convention used in its new plan of government.

In the years after the convention, Madison continued to serve his country—first in Congress; then as secretary of state; and finally in 1809, as the nation's fourth President.

As President, Madison was, of course, new to the job. This was not the case for his wife Dolley, who had acted as White House hostess to widower Thomas Jefferson.

Madison had married Mrs. Dolley Todd, a widow, in 1794. As First Lady, Dolley Madison dazzled Washington with formal dinners, afternoon teas, and informal lawn parties. Her grace and confidence at social events helped her shy husband immensely.

Mrs. Madison's gaiety, however, could not dissolve the many concerns and issues that Madison faced as President. In 1812, he led the nation in its second war against Great Britain. The country's victory in 1815 earned Madison the title of the little President who had tolerated no nonsense from the world's strongest empire.

In 1817, at the end of his second term, the President and Mrs. Madison returned to their Virginia home. Dolley faithfully nursed her ailing husband until his death in 1836.

be divided among three parts of the government which were defined by their function. Those parts were the legislative, the executive, and the judiciary (jü dish′ ē er′ē).

No person could serve in more than one of those parts at one time. No part could be a government by itself. The legislature could pass laws but could not enforce them. The executive could enforce laws but could not enact them by itself. The judiciary could conduct trials but could not make laws or punish the guilty. Each part of the government needed the other parts. In that way, the powers of the government were limited.

▶7. How was power to be divided in the new Constitution?

The Parts of the Government The convention made many improvements in the Virginia Plan. The Constitution it wrote put the legislative power in Congress. Members of the House of Representatives would be elected for two-year terms by the people of their states. Senators would be elected for six-year terms by the state legislatures.

The executive power was entrusted to a powerful President. He or she was commander in chief of the army and navy. The President could negotiate treaties and appoint many officials with the consent of the Senate. He or she could even veto acts of Congress, though a two-thirds vote of Congress could put a law into effect despite the President's veto.

The convention did not want the President to be dependent on Congress for his or her job. It thought the people would not know the candidates well enough to choose the President. So it set up a system known as the **electoral college** to elect the President. However, the Constitution also said that the President could be removed from office for "treason, bribery, or other high crimes and misdemeanors."

The Constitution said little about judiciary power, which was placed in a Supreme Court and any other courts Congress chose to create. It did say that as long as judges remained on their "good behavior," they could not be thrown out of office. Nor could their salaries be reduced. In that way, the convention tried to make judges independent enough to do things that might displease the Congress and the President.

▶8. How were the judges made independent of Congress and the President?

The States and the Nation The new Constitution created a **federation.** That is, it divided power between a central, or federal, government and the states.

The powers of the federal government were clearly spelled out in the Constitution. Congress kept the powers it held under the Articles of Confederation. It could also collect taxes, raise an army, and regulate trade. Certain powers were denied to the states. They could not, for example, tax imports or make treaties with other countries. However, the states kept all powers not given to the nation or denied the states.

That division of power had to be respected because the Constitution was declared "the supreme law of the land." All federal and state officers had to swear to support the new Constitution.

▶9. How did the Constitution create a federation?

The Amending Process The delegates realized that changes might be necessary in the Constitution. So they wrote rules for changing, or **amending,** it. An amendment to the Constitution can be proposed by a two-thirds vote of Congress or by a specially called constitutional convention. A proposed amendment becomes part of the Constitution when it is ratified by three-fourths of the state legislatures or by the people in three-fourths of the states. The delegates purposely made the amending process difficult so that any changes to the Constitution would be carefully thought out.

▶**10.** How can the Constitution be changed?

Reviewing Section IV

Identify Shays's Rebellion, Constitutional Convention, James Madison, Virginia Plan, New Jersey Plan, Great Compromise, Three-Fifths Compromise, electoral college, federation, amending

Questions to Answer
1. What powers did the Constitution give the national government that it did have under the Articles of Confederation?
2. What powers did the Constitution give the states?

A Question to Think About How did the Constitution help to solve the problems of the government under the Articles of Confederation?

V. Ratifying the Constitution

The last part of the Constitution told how it could be ratified. It said that when conventions of the people in nine states approved the Constitution it would go into effect.

Federalists and Anti-Federalists

The supporters of the Constitution were called **Federalists.** They knew ratification would not be easy. The opponents of the Constitution were called **Anti-Federalists.** They thought the Constitution gave too much power to the central government. Probably a majority of the people agreed with them.

▶**1.** Who were the Anti-Federalists? Who were the Federalists?

The State Conventions

The Framers knew that the state legislatures were unlikely to approve the Constitution. That was one reason they had the Constitution sent to state conventions for approval. Ratification by popular conventions also meant that the Constitution would be the work of the people as well as the Framers.

Many of the Framers were Federalists. Therefore, they said the Constitution had to be approved by nine states because they thought nine states would ratify it quickly. Then it would be hard for Virginia and New York, where Anti-Federalists were strong, to turn it down. For states not to ratify the Constitution once it was going into effect would mean cutting themselves off from the United States.

The Federalists' plan worked. By the middle of June 1788, Delaware, Pennsylvania, New Jersey, Georgia, Connecticut, Massachusetts, Maryland, and South Carolina had approved the Constitution. New Hampshire, the ninth state, ratified on June 21, 1788. Then, after a long and emotional debate, Virginia added its approval on June 26.

Attention turned to New York. James Madison, John Jay, and Alexander Hamilton wrote 85 essays in defense of the Constitution for New York newspapers. Those essays, called *The Federalist Papers*, remain today one of the most thorough discussions of the Constitution ever written.

REDEUNT SATURNIA REGNA.

On the erection of the Eleventh PILLAR of the great National DOME, we beg leave most sincerely to felicitate " OUR DEAR COUNTRY."

The FEDERAL EDIFICE.

The Massachusetts Centinel *printed this cartoon in an effort to convince North Carolina and Rhode Island to ratify the Constitution.*

When the New York convention assembled, Federalists dragged out the debate, hoping for news of a favorable decision in Virginia. Finally, on July 2, a dispatch rider brought Hamilton a letter from Madison with a certificate that Virginia had ratified. It still took four weeks before New York decided to become part of the new United States.

In the end, all thirteen of the original thirteen colonies ratified the Constitution. However, North Carolina did not ratify it until November 1788. Rhode Island did not ratify until May 1790.

▶**2.** What was the Federalist plan for ratification of the Constitution?

Toward a Bill of Rights

The Anti-Federalists criticized the Constitution because it did not contain a bill of rights. Most state constitutions had such bills. They stated the rights of the people and safeguarded their liberties. The Anti-Federalists insisted that the Constitution have a bill of rights. The Federalists agreed. Therefore the

first Congress under the new Constitution prepared 12 amendments to the Constitution and sent them to the states for approval. Ten of the amendments were passed. They are known as the **Bill of Rights.**

The Constitution marked a great advance in American government. It set up a strong federal republic. Americans began life under their new national government determined to make their new Republic survive.

▶**3.** What is the Bill of Rights?

Reviewing Section V

Identify Federalists, Anti-Federalists, *The Federalist Papers,* Bill of Rights

Questions to Answer
1. Why did the Federalists hope to get nine states to ratify the Constitution before Virginia and New York voted on the issue?
2. Which were the last two states to ratify the Constitution?

A Question to Think About Did the Federalists take unfair advantage in writing the rules for ratifying the Constitution?

IMPROVE YOUR READING
Main Ideas/Details

The purpose of this exercise is to give you further practice in identifying main ideas and supporting details.

In items 1 to 5, the main ideas from subsections in the first three parts of Chapter 10 are given. Your task is to provide supporting details.

1. The main idea for "The Massachusetts Constitution" (page 193): The Massachusetts Constitution set up a balanced form of government.
2. The main idea for "Freeing the Slaves" (pp. 193–194): After the Revolution, some important steps were taken toward giving slaves their freedom.
3. The main idea for "Rights for Women" (pp. 194–195): Women did not have the same rights as men.
4. The main idea for "The Indians of the Old Northwest" (pp. 199–201): The Indians of the Old Northwest were unwilling to give up their lands.
5. The main idea for "Problems under the Confederation" (pp. 201–202): Congress, under Articles of Confederation, did not have the power to solve some of the nation's problems.

In items 6 to 10, supporting details of some main ideas found in sections III–V in Chapter 10 are provided. Your task is to identify the main idea they describe.

6. Details about "Spain and the Old Southwest" (pp. 201–202):
   a. Westerners wanted to ship their goods on the Mississippi.
   b. Spain closed the Mississippi to all trade by Americans.

7. Details about "Shays's Rebellion" (pp. 202–203):
   a. Shays and his followers tried to take ammunition from the Springfield armory.
   b. Shays fled to Vermont.

8. Details about "The Amending Process" (pp. 207–208):
   a. An amendment to the Constitution can be proposed by a two-thirds vote of Congress or a constitutional convention.
   b. An amendment becomes part of the Constitution when ratified by three-fourths of the state legislatures or by the people in three-fourths of the states.

9. Details about "The State Conventions" (pp. 208–209):
   a. Nine states were needed to ratify the Constitution.
   b. Some states opposed the Constitution.
   c. In the end, all thirteen states ratified the Constitution.

10. Details about "Toward a Bill of Rights" (page 209):
    a. Anti-Federalists insisted that the Constitution have a bill of rights.
    b. Most state constitutions contained a bill of rights.

CHAPTER 10 REVIEW

Vocabulary Check
Write a definition for each word.

1. Confederation
2. Constitution
3. Ratify
4. Emancipation
5. Amending

Fact Check
Match each term in column I with the phrase that best describes it in column II.

Column I
1. Executive
2. Legislative
3. Judicial
4. Constitutional Convention
5. Federalists
6. Three-Fifths Compromise
7. Virginia Plan
8. Anti-Federalists
9. Federation
10. Bill of Rights

Column II
a. Opponents of the Constitution
b. Part of government that enforces laws
c. A list of rights and liberties protected by the Constitution
d. Part of government that makes laws
e. Meeting of delegates called to change the Articles of Confederation
f. Plan that proposed a two-house national legislature
g. Supporters of the Constitution
h. Part of government that conducts trials
i. System by which powers are divided between national and state governments
j. Plan for counting slaves for a state's representation in Congress

Time Check
On a separate sheet of paper, put the following events in chronological order.

1. The Constitution becomes the law of the land.
2. The First Continental Congress passes an agreement to end the slave trade.
3. New York ratifies the Constitution.
4. Massachusetts has a new constitution.
5. Spain closes the Mississippi to trade by Americans.

Skills Check
Use the maps on page 200 to answer the following questions.

1. What lakes form the northern boundary of the Northwest Territory?
2. What three states border the Northwest Territory on the east?
3. How many acres are there in a quarter section of land?
4. What fraction of a section is 40 acres?
5. What river forms the western boundary of the Northwest Territory?

Think and Write
1. Why did most states give more power to the legislature than to the governor in their new constitutions?
2. What important changes took place for black Americans after the Revolution?
3. Why is the Northwest Ordinance one of the most important laws in the history of the country?
4. Explain the provisions of the Great Compromise.
5. Why did many Americans want a bill of rights added to the Constitution?

Chapter 11

How the Government Works

The Capitol has been changed and enlarged many times since President George Washington laid the cornerstone of the building on September 18, 1793.

The Constitution has been the supreme law of the United States for over 200 years. Today the United States is very different from what it was when the Constitution first went into effect. Despite rapid growth and many changes in the nation, the Constitution still serves it well.

The Constitution is not a long document. In fact, it contains only about 5,000 words. The Framers of the Constitution described the basic goals of the government in the introduction, called the Preamble. Then they set out a broad outline for how the government would work in Articles I to VII. They did not fill in many details. Over time, the Congress, the courts, and the people have added details and defined the exact meaning of some of the terms. The last part of the Constitution contains 26 amendments, or changes, that have been added to the document over the years. This chapter describes how the federal government set up under the Constitution operates today.

1600

Viriginia's House of Burgesses formed, 1619
Mayflower Compact, 1620

1650   Maryland's Act Concerning Religion, 1649

1700

1750

First Continental Congress ends slave trade, 1774

Declaration of Independence, 1776

Massachusetts Constitution, 1780

Articles of Confederation take effect, 1781

The Constitution takes effect, 1788

1800

I. Basic Principles

The Framers of the Constitution built their new form of government on several basic principles. In the United States, the people are sovereign. The sovereign people enacted the Constitution, which is why it begins, "We the people of the United States . . . do ordain and establish this Constitution . . ." In the government created by the Constitution, the people's will is expressed through elected representatives. The powers of government are limited. Power is also balanced among the three branches of government and between the nation and the states.

A Democracy and a Republic

The government of the United States is today often called a **democracy.** A democracy is a government in which the people rule. The Founding Fathers preferred to call the United States a **republic.** In a republic, the people rule not directly but through representatives. The United States can also be called a **representative democracy.** Leaders who are elected by the people to run the day-to-day business of the government represent the people. At each election, the people have the opportunity to select new representatives.

▶**1.** What is a representative democracy?

Limited Government

The Framers of the Constitution did not want an all-powerful national government. So they carefully limited its powers.

The powers of government have increased in many ways since 1789, but there are still things it cannot do. These are listed in Article 1, Section 9, and in the the first ten amendments to the Constitution, which are called the Bill of Rights. Government cannot, for example, suspend the right of *habeas corpus* (hā′bē əs kôr′pəs). That means the government cannot hold people in jail without having a legal reason for doing so. Congress cannot pass **bills of attainder.** Those are laws designed to convict or punish a specific person or group of people. Congress cannot pass *ex post facto* laws which would punish people for acts they had done before the laws took effect. It cannot interfere with freedom of speech or of the press.

▶**2.** What are some of the limitations the Constitution places on the government?

Chart Study *How has the Thirteenth Amendment added to the growth of freedom?*

The Growth of Freedom

1791	Bill of Rights
1865	**13th Amendment** abolishes slavery.
1868	**14th Amendment** makes blacks citizens and also guarantees equal protection of the law to all persons. The **14th Amendment** also forbids states to deny any person "life, liberty or property without due process of law."
1870	**15th Amendment** guarantees freed slaves the right to vote.
1913	**17th Amendment** provides for the direct election of senators.
1920	**19th Amendment** gives women the right to vote.
1961	**23rd Amendment** gives residents of Washington, D.C., the right to vote.
1971	**26th Amendment** gives 18 year olds the right to vote.

A Federalism: The Division of Powers

One of the main problems faced by the Framers was the need to balance the power between the national government and the states. The Framers did not want an all-powerful central government like that of Great Britain. Neither did they want all-powerful state governments. By dividing power between the states and the national government, the Constitution created a **federal system.** The division of power between two levels of government is also known as **federalism.**

In the American federal system, neither level of government gets its power from the other. Both levels exist solely to serve the people. Each level of government is equal in that the people give both an important but separate set of responsibilities to perform. The states take care of local matters. The national government takes care of matters that affect the whole nation.

▶**3.** What is the concept of a federal system?

Expressed and Implied Powers The first three articles of the Constitution describe what powers are **delegated,** or given, to each branch of the federal government. Article 1, Section 8, lists some of the powers of Congress. Article II sets down the functions of the President. Article III states the powers of the Supreme Court.

The powers that are expressed, or stated specifically, in the Constitution are called **expressed powers.** Powers that the government needs to carry out its duties but that are not written down are called **implied powers.** For example, Congress has the expressed power to raise an army. It is understood that Congress has the implied power to raise an air force as part of the nation's armed forces.

The Declaration of Independence and the Constitution are on display at the Exhibit Hall of the National Archives.

▶**4.** What are expressed powers of the government? Implied powers?

Powers of the States The Tenth Amendment to the Constitution protects the powers that have been reserved for the states. **Reserved powers** are powers that only the states have. Such powers include the right to set up a school system, pass marriage and divorce laws, and create local governments.

Powers that the states share with the national government are called **shared powers.** The states, like Congress, can levy taxes, define crimes, and punish criminals.

Like Congress, the states are denied certain powers. Article I, Section 10, says that the states cannot grant titles of nobility or pass bills of attainder and *ex post facto* laws. Nor can they do things that only the national government can do, such as make treaties.

▶5. What are some of the reserved powers of the states?

The Supremacy of the Constitution

The Constitution divides power between the national government and the states. But Article VI clearly states that the Constitution is the supreme law of the nation. Therefore, no state can pass any law that conflicts with the Constitution or with any treaty or law passed under the authority of the Constitution. All state officers must swear an oath to support the Constitution before they take office.

▶6. What is the supreme law of the United States?

Reviewing Section I

Identify democracy, republic, representative democracy, *habeas corpus*, bill of attainder, *ex post facto* laws, federal system, federalism, delegated, expressed powers, implied powers, reserved powers, shared powers

Questions to Answer
1. How does the government of the United States reflect the will of the people?
2. How are the powers of the national government limited?

A Question to Think About What are some federal laws that affect your life? What are some state laws that affect your life?

II. How the National Government Works

The Framers of the Constitution divided power between the states and the national government. They also divided power among the three branches of the national goverment: the legislative branch, the executive branch, and the judicial branch. The powers and duties of each branch are described in the Constitution.

Congress

Article 1, Section 1, of the Constitution states "All legislative powers . . . shall be vested in a Congress of the United States." That means the Congress has the duty to make laws for the nation.

Thousands of bills, or proposals for laws, come before Congress every year. Not all become laws. However, many do become laws and touch our lives in many ways. Congress can, for example, declare war, raise taxes, build dams, aid schools, create jobs, or set aside lands for public parks.

The Constitution sets up a two-house, or bicameral, legislature consisting of the Senate and the House of Representatives. The Senate is made up of two members from each state. Membership in the House is based on the number of people in each state according to the latest census. At first, the number of seats in the House grew with each census as the population of the country grew. However, in 1912 the number of seats was fixed at 435. The Senate has 100 members.

The Framers also wanted to make sure that Congress would consider each new law very carefully before passing it. So all bills must pass both the Senate and the House of Representatives before being presented to the President for consideration.

▶1. What kind of legislature did the Framers create?

Qualifications for Congress Almost any adult citizen can seek election to Congress. The Framers set only a few requirements. To run for the House, a person must be at least 25 years old, a citizen for 7 years, and a resident of the state in which he or she is running for office. To run for the Senate, a person needs to be 30 years old, a citizen for 9 years, and a resident of the state in which he or she is running for office. The term of office for House members is 2 years. Members of the Senate serve a 6-year term.

The House has always been regarded as the people's house. Because members of the House serve for only two years, the people have more control over House members than over senators. Members of the House of Representatives serve districts defined in part by population. A state may have many such districts.

For many years, senators were elected by the state legislatures. That was changed in 1913 by the Seventeenth Amendment, which called for direct election of senators. Although each state has two senators, each senator does not represent a different part of the state. Both senators represent the whole state.
▶**2.** What qualifications are required of a candidate for the House? For the Senate?

Powers of Congress Article 1, Section 8, lists the powers delegated to Congress. Each house of Congress also has its own special powers. Only the House of Representatives has the power to **impeach**, or accuse, the President and other national officials of not carrying out their duties. Once the House impeaches an official, it is the job of the Senate to act as a court. It decides whether the official is guilty or innocent.

President Ronald Reagan is shown here giving his State of the Union address to members of both houses of Congress.

All bills to raise revenue, or taxes, must start in the House. All other types of bills can start in either the House or the Senate. The Senate has the sole power of "advice and consent." That means the Senate must give its approval to all treaties and presidential appointments.

At times, Congress can even get involved in the election of the President and Vice President. If no candidates get a majority of the electoral vote in the November election, Congress chooses the President and the Vice President.

In addition to the powers spelled out in the Constitution, the Framers also gave Congress some unspecified powers. Article I, Section 8, states that Congress shall pass "all laws necessary and proper" to fulfill its responsibilities. That so-called **elastic clause** grants Congress a wide range of implied powers, which are not spelled out in so many words. Congress, for example, has the power to regulate commerce among the states. Congress uses that power to pass laws about wages and safety conditions in many industries because their products are sold across state lines. Congress has used its power over interstate commerce to build highways and establish a national speed limit of 55 miles per hour.

▶**3.** What powers does the elastic clause of the Constitution give Congress?

How a Bill Becomes a Law The main duty of Congress is to make laws for the nation. How does Congress make a law?

A bill, or proposal for a law, becomes a law when it gets a majority vote in both houses of Congress and is signed by the President. That sounds simple enough. However, things are rarely as simple as they first appear. This section describes the major steps in passing an ordinary bill.

A bill can be introduced in either the House or the Senate, except for money bills, which always begin in the House. Let us assume that a member of the House introduces a bill. The bill goes first to the appropriate House **committee** for review. A committee is a small group of House members who consider similar sorts of bills. There are also committees in the Senate. A committee can hold public

IMPROVE YOUR SKILLS
Using a Flow Chart

A flow chart is a diagram that shows the step-by-step process by which something happens. A flow chart often summarizes information that would otherwise take many words to explain.

The flow chart on page 219 shows part of the process of a bill becoming a law. Use it to answer the following questions.

1. Explain what each symbol in the flow chart stands for.

2. What happens if the Senate passes a bill in a form different from that of the House of Representatives?
3. What happens to a bill after a joint committee has reached a compromise?
4. What must happen to the joint committee's compromise bill before it can be sent to the President?
5. What must the President do to the bill to make it a law?

How a Bill Becomes a Law

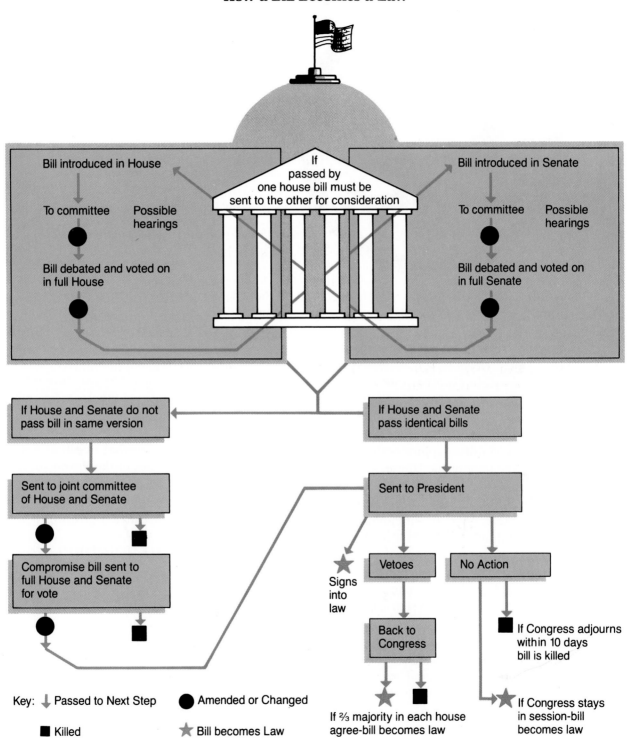

Bill introduced in House

To committee   Possible
                hearings

Bill debated and voted on
in full House

If passed by one house bill must be sent to the other for consideration

Bill introduced in Senate

To committee   Possible
                hearings

Bill debated and voted on
in full Senate

If House and Senate do not
pass bill in same version

If House and Senate
pass identical bills

Sent to joint committee
of House and Senate

Sent to President

Compromise bill sent to
full House and Senate
for vote

Signs
into
law

Vetoes

No Action

Back to
Congress

If Congress adjourns
within 10 days
bill is killed

Key: ↓ Passed to Next Step   ● Amended or Changed

■ Killed   ★ Bill becomes Law

If ⅔ majority in each house
agree-bill becomes law

If Congress stays
in session-bill
becomes law

219

The Great Seal has been the symbol of the United States for more than 200 years.

hearings so that interested persons can express their views for or against the bill. It can also call in expert witnesses to give information it needs. The committee may then amend, or change, the bill. The committee may table, or reject, the bill, or it may approve it. If the committee approves the bill, it then goes to the floor of the House. There the bill is debated, and a vote is taken.

If the bill is passed by the House, it is sent to the Senate. There the bill follows the same route it followed in the House. Any changes made in the Senate, however, mean that the bill is no longer the same bill that the House approved. For a bill to become a law, it must pass the Senate and the House in exactly the same form.

If the Senate passes a different version of the bill, a joint committee of House and Senate members will meet. Their job is to iron out differences between the House version and the Senate version. The new version is known as a compromise bill.

If a compromise bill is agreed upon, it is sent back to both the House and the Senate for approval. If the compromise bill clears both houses, it is then sent to the President to be signed. The President can sign the bill so that it becomes a law. However, the President may decide instead to **veto,** or reject, the bill, which usually kills it. The House and the Senate can override a President's veto by a two-thirds vote in each house. That does not often happen.

▶**4.** What are the major steps in creating a new law?

The President and the Executive Branch

Congress passes the laws. The President sees that the laws are executed, or put into effect. Article II, Section 1, of the Constitution states, "The executive power shall be vested in a President of the United States of America." The Framers of the Constitution did not define exactly what they meant by *executive power.* Over the years, however, that term has come to mean very broad powers.

How did the office of President gain such power? The answer to that question lies in part in the many roles of the President. Not all of those roles were as important in the 1790's as they are today. Indeed, much of this book will be about the growing power of the President.

▶**5.** What is the major duty of the President?

Chief Executive The President is in charge of all the executive departments and agencies in the national government. Since the time the Constitution was written, the size and scope of the executive branch has grown. Today more than 3 million people work in the executive branch.

As the nation's chief executive, the President can issue **executive orders.** Those are orders that have the effect of law. The President simply says, in effect, "I want this done." As long as the order is constitutional and not against any existing national law, it will be done. President Harry S Truman, for example, ended racial discrimination in the armed forces by signing an executive order. No act of Congress was needed.

The power to issue executive orders is not mentioned specifically in the Constitution. However, to fulfill the responsibilities of their office, Presidents have found it necessary to issue such orders.

▶**6.** What is an executive order?

Chief of State The President is the head of the United States. As chief of state, the President can, for example, represent the United States at international meetings, the crowning of a new king or queen, and the funeral of another head of state. When heads of other nations visit the United States, it is usually the President who plays host to them.

▶**7.** What is the President's role as chief of state?

Chief Diplomat As a diplomat, the President directs our foreign policy. The President can also make treaties for the United States with the consent of two thirds of the Senate. The President also has the power to nominate ambassadors. Here again the consent of the Senate is needed.

▶**8.** What is the President's role as chief diplomat?

Commander in Chief Somewhere on the wall of every American military base, you will find a portrait of the President. It is there to remind the military leaders who the boss is. Under the Constitution, the President is commander in chief of all branches of the United States armed forces.

The papers of most modern Presidents are stored in libraries such as the Kennedy Library.

Although only Congress can declare war, until 1973 the President had almost unlimited power to authorize military actions without declaring war. That year Congress passed the War Powers Act. It said the President could not send American troops to fight in a foreign country without informing Congress. Nor could the President keep them there for more than 60 days without Congress's approval. That law limited considerably the President's war-making power.

The President can use the armed forces to enforce a federal law anywhere in the country. The President can also call a state militia into national service.

▶**9.** What is the President's power as commander in chief?

Chief Legislator Although Congress has power to enact laws, the President may offer proposals and suggestions to Congress. The Constitution says that the President "shall from time to time give to the Congress information of the state of the Union . . ." By tradition, the President delivers a state-of-the-Union address to Congress once a year. In that speech, the President outlines a broad program of action for Congress to debate. The President also has the power to veto bills passed by Congress.

▶ **10.** How does the President function as chief legislator?

Head of a Political Party   Soon after it ratified the Constitution, the United States developed a system of political parties. Almost every President has been a member of a political party. Each party nominates a candidate for President, tries to get the candidate elected, and also supports the candidate's programs.

The President's role as head of a political party is closely related to his or her role as chief legislator. The President hopes members of his or her own political party in Congress will work to pass the legislation he or she suggests. In return, the President must work with party leaders and support their interests.

▶ **11.** How does the President aid a political party?

Qualifications and Term of Office   Who is eligible to fill all these roles and be President? The Framers said only that the President must be at least 35 years old, a resident of the United States for 14 years, and a native-born citizen. There is no mention of such things as sex, race, or level of education or of wealth.

The President is elected for a four-year term of office. Until 1951, there was no limit to the number of terms a President could serve, although no President except Franklin D. Roosevelt ever ran for more than two terms. He was elected four times. Then, in 1951, the Twenty-Second Amendment was passed. The amendment says that the President may serve only two terms.

It is possible that a President may serve for ten years. That could happen if a President dies or becomes disabled and the Vice President or next official in line takes over and fills out a term as President of less than two years. Then that same person may serve for two full terms as President in his or her own right.

▶ **12.** What is the usual limit on a President's years in office?

Electing the President   The Framers thought that the people would not know much about presidential candidates. Many of the Framers were afraid to let the people vote for the President directly. Instead, the people vote for **electors** who, in turn, elect the President. The Framers thought the electors would actually select the President. However, by 1800,

Thomas Nast created these as symbols of the Democratic and Republican parties.

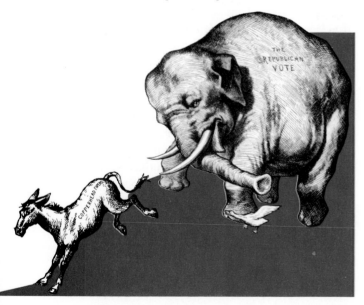

when strong political parties had appeared, the electors began to pledge to follow the choices of a political party.

Here is how the electoral system works today. Once the parties nominate their candidates, the race is on. The parties draw up a slate, or list, of electors. Those electors are pledged to their party's candidates for President and Vice President. The number of electors a state has is equal to the number of representatives and senators the state has in Congress.

On the first Tuesday after the first Monday in November, the people vote for their candidates. That is called the **popular vote.** The popular vote in each state decides which party's slate of electors will get to vote for the President and Vice President. If, for example, the Republican candidate wins in New York, then all of New York's 36 electoral college votes will go to the Republican slate of electors. We know after election day which candidates won the popular vote and usually also who will be the next President and Vice President. However, only in December when the electoral votes are cast and counted are the winners of the election officially declared to be President-elect and Vice President-elect.

If no candidates have a majority of electoral votes for President, the election goes to the House of Representatives, where, for this election, each state has one vote. The House chooses from among the top three candidates in electoral college votes. If no person receives a majority of electoral votes for Vice President, the Senate must decide who the next Vice President will be. Each senator has one vote, and a majority is required to win. The Senate selects from the two candidates who won the largest number of votes in the electoral college.

▶**13.** How does the electoral college function in presidential elections?

The Supreme Court

The third branch of the government is the judicial branch. Article III, Section 1, of the Constitution states, "The judicial power of the United States shall be vested in one Supreme Court, and in such inferior [lower] courts as the Congress may . . . establish."

Under the Articles of Confederation, there was no national court system. Each of the thirteen states could interpret the laws as each state saw fit. The result was chaos. The Framers wanted to avoid such confusion. Thus, they called for one Supreme Court which would be the final word on the law.

▶**14.** Why did the Framers set up a Supreme Court?

How the Court Works   The Supreme Court is today made up of one Chief Justice and eight associate justices. Decisions in the Supreme Court are made by majority vote. A Supreme Court with nine justices was not required by the Constitution. That number was set by Congress. The Constitution did say, however, that the justices would hold their office "during good behavior." That means the justices have their jobs for life unless they are impeached and found guilty of the charges. They can therefore make unpopular decisions without fear of being voted out of office.

Almost all the cases that the Supreme Court hears come to it on appeal from lower federal courts and the highest state courts. That means that the case was first tried in a lower court but the verdict of the lower court was appealed to the Supreme Court. The Supreme Court cannot hear all the cases that are sent to it. The justices usually select cases that involve some important question about the meaning of the Constitution.

▶**15.** What sorts of cases are heard in the Supreme Court?

President Reagan appointed Sandra Day O'Connor to the Supreme Court. She is shown here with the eight other members of the highest court in the land.

Other Courts The Supreme Court is the court of last resort. Once the Supreme Court hears a case, its decision is final. It can change or modify its position on what the Constitution means. But no other court can hear a case after the Supreme Court has given its judgment.

There are many other courts in the nation. The Judiciary Act of 1789 set up three circuit courts and a district court for each state. Since that time, Congress has added other courts as the needs of the nation have grown. There are also state courts. The system of national and state courts is another example of federalism.

▶**16.** What courts are there in the United States in addition to the Supreme Court?

Separation of Powers

The division of power among the executive, legislative, and judicial branches of government is called the **separation of powers.** No person can hold a position in more than one of those branches at one time. However, the actual functions of the three branches are not and cannot be completely separate. For example, the President acts as a legislator by proposing new laws or issuing executive orders. The Supreme Court sometimes acts as a legislative body too. Sometimes it issues instructions on what people must do that are legally binding, much like laws passed by Congress.

▶**17.** What is meant by separation of powers?

Checks and Balances

The Framers did not want any one of the three branches to acquire too much power. So, the Framers made sure that each branch would have a check on the other two branches. We call this system **checks and balances.** The power of each branch is balanced by the powers of the other branches.

▶**18.** What is meant by checks and balances?

Checks by the President The President checks Congress by vetoing bills that Congress has passed. The President checks the judicial branch by granting pardons and reprieves to persons convicted of crimes.

▶**19.** How does the President check Congress and the Supreme Court?

Checks by Congress Congress checks the executive branch by controlling the purse strings. Only Congress can appropriate and spend money. Congress can also override a President's veto. It can reject treaties and appointments made by the President. It has the power to impeach and try a President or other officials in the executive branch.

Congress can check the judicial branch by impeaching and trying judges. Congress also can propose amendments to the Constitution if it does not like rulings made by the Supreme Court. That happened when the Supreme Court ruled that an income tax was unconstitutional. Congress responded by proposing the Sixteenth Amendment. Approved in 1913, it made an income tax constitutional.

▶**20.** How does Congress check the President and the Supreme Court?

Chart Study *How does the executive branch check the Congress?*

Checks and Balances in the Federal Government

Executive Branch
President

May check the Judicial Branch by
Granting pardons to those who are convicted of federal crimes

May check Congress by
Vetoing bills passed by Congress
Sending messages to Congress
Appealing to the people

Legislative Branch
Congress

May check the President by
Impeaching the President
Overriding a veto
Refusing to approve presidential appointments
Approving or failing to approve treaties

May check the Judicial Branch by
Impeaching judges
Changing the number of justices on the Supreme Court
Proposing an amendment to the Constitution if the Supreme Court finds a law unconstitutional

The Judicial Branch
Supreme Court

May check the President by
Interpreting laws and treaties
Ruling that laws and executive acts are unconstitutional

May check Congress by
Interpreting laws and treaties
Declaring laws unconstitutional

Checks by the Supreme Court The Supreme Court can check the executive branch by declaring executive orders unconstitutional. The Supreme Court can check the legislative branch by declaring laws passed by Congress unconstitutional. This power is known as the power of **judicial review.** Judicial review was not spelled out in the Constitution, but it has become the one great check of the Supreme Court on Congress and the President.
▶**21.** How does the Supreme Court check Congress and the President?

Reviewing Section II——————

Identify impeach, elastic clause, committee, veto, executive orders, chief of state, commander in chief, electors, popular vote, separation of powers, checks and balances, judicial review

Questions to Answer
1. How does each of the three branches of government check the others?
2. How does a bill become a law?

A Question to Think About Is the electoral college working as the Framers intended?

III. Our Living Constitution

The Constitution has often been described as a living document. That means it can change with the times. Because it can change, the Constitution still serves Americans today despite the enormous changes the United States has undergone since 1787.

Formal Change

The Framers knew that they could not foresee all the problems that the government might face in the future. So they added Article V to the Constitution. That article outlines the ways the Constitution can be amended, or changed, when the need arises.

An amendment to the Constitution may be proposed in two ways. It can be proposed by a two-thirds vote in both houses of Congress. It can also be proposed by a national convention called by two thirds of the state legislatures. An amendment may be ratified by three fourths of the state legislatures or by special conventions in three fourths of the states. Two things are worthy of note about the amendment process. The first is the strong emphasis on federalism. That is, both Congress and the states participate. The second

is that there is no need for the President's signature anywhere in the process.

Since the Constitution was adopted, there have been thousands of proposals to amend it. Only 26, however, have been ratified.
▶**1.** In what two ways may amendments to the Constitution be proposed?

The Bill of Rights

The ability of the Constitution to respond to change was tested during the fight over ratification. Many states wanted the Constitution to contain a bill of rights—a list of freedoms guaranteed to American citizens. So, in 1791, the first ten amendments—the Bill of Rights—were added to the Constitution.

When people today think of the Constitution, they often think of the Bill of Rights. That is because the Bill of Rights protects individual rights.
▶**2.** What is the Bill of Rights?

Informal Change

The Constitution has been amended 16 times since the Bill of Rights. Informal changes

The Bill of Rights

1st Amendment ● Guarantees the freedom of religion, speech, and the press. Also guarantees the right of citizens to assemble peacefully in groups and to send petitions to the government.

2nd Amendment ● Allows each state to keep and arm a militia. The rights of individual citizens to keep weapons are regulated by federal and state laws.

3rd Amendment ● The government cannot house soldiers in a private home in peacetime without the owner's consent. During a war, special laws may allow the government to use private houses for soldiers.

4th Amendment ● Government officials can search Americans or their houses only with a warrant issued by a judge stating what it is that the officials are looking for.

5th Amendment ● No American can be held in a federal court without being charged by a grand jury. A grand jury is a group of 23 people who hear in secret the charges against the accused and then decide if the person should be tried in court. No person can be tried twice in federal courts for the same crime. People cannot be forced to give evidence against themselves that will help prove their guilt. Persons accused of a crime have the right to a fair trial by proper procedures. The government cannot take a person's property for public use without giving the owner a fair price.

6th Amendment ● A person accused of a crime has the right to be informed of the charges against him or her and the right to a speedy and public trial by jury. Witnesses for and against the accused can be ordered to appear in court to give evidence. The accused is entitled to confront the witnesses and to be represented by a lawyer.

7th Amendment ● If property worth more than $20 is disputed in federal court, the parties involved may choose to have a trial by jury.

8th Amendment ● Before a trial, a person accused of a crime may be released from jail after paying a sum of money, called bail, to the court. The bail is returned when the accused comes to trial. The amount of bail set may not be excessive. If the accused is found guilty, no excessive, cruel, or unusual punishments may be assigned.

9th Amendment ● Americans have other rights that are not listed in the Constitution, and the government may not deny them those rights.

10th Amendment ● Those powers not assigned to the federal government are assigned to the states or the people.

also alter the government. For example, the President's Cabinet is now a key feature of American government. The Cabinet is not mentioned specifically in the Constitution. But the Constitution in no way restricted such a development. As a result, when the need was felt for a presidential cabinet, it could develop freely. It is the flexibility of the Constitution that has enabled it to serve the nation so well for so long.

▶ **3.** How does the Constitution change informally?

Reviewing Section III

Identify   Article V, the Bill of Rights

Questions to Answer
1. Why did the Framers make rules about amending the Constitution?
2. What has allowed the Constitution to last so long?

A Question to Think About   Why have so few amendments been passed in over 200 years?

IMPROVE YOUR READING
Mapping

One way to help yourself remember information is to outline, or map, the ideas you are studying. When you map information, you make a diagram, or a design, of the major topic and the ideas related to it.

Here is how to map. First, when you read a section of a chapter, select the major topic of the section. Write it in the middle of a piece of paper and draw a circle around it. Then decide on the subtopics, or related ideas. Write these on lines connected to the major topic. Next, find the details. Write the details on lines connected

to ideas, or subtopics, they support. When you finish mapping, you have a convenient summary or diagram of what you have read.

Below is a partially completed map related to the section "The President and the Executive Branch." (pages 220–223) Copy the map on a piece of paper. Then complete the rest of the map. You will probably have to reread the section to do this task.

When you finish the map, read another section of this chapter or of another chapter and develop your own map.

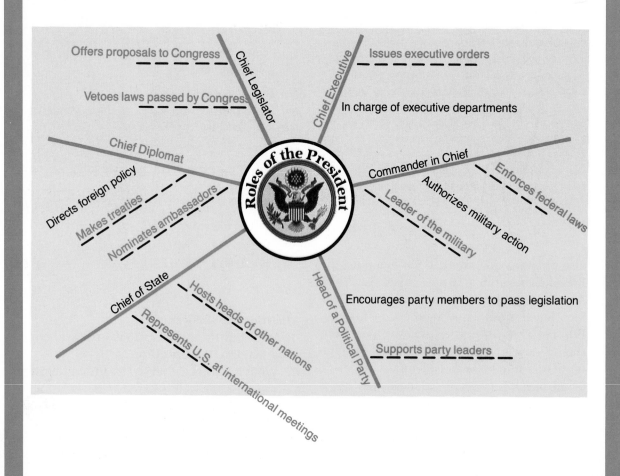

CHAPTER 11 REVIEW

Vocabulary Check
Write a short definition for the following words.
1. Democracy
2. Republic
3. Federal system
4. Impeach
5. Veto

Fact Check
On a separate sheet of paper, fill in the word or words that best complete each of the following sentences.

1. The supreme law of the United States is the _____.
2. Powers that are specifically stated in the Constitution are called _____.
3. Powers that the government needs to carry out its duties but are not written in the Constitution are called _____.
4. Laws that punish people for acts they have committed before the laws went into effect are called _____.
5. Powers that belong only to the states are called _____.
6. Powers that both the states and the national government have are called _____.
7. Presidential orders that have the effect of law are called _____.
8. The division of power among the executive, legislative, and judicial branches of government is called _____.
9. The system by which each branch has to share power with others and has a check on the other two branches is called _____.
10. The power of the Supreme Court to declare a law unconstitutional is called _____.

Who Has the Power?
The following is a list of powers that belong to the President, the House of Repesentatives, the Senate, or the Supreme Court. On a separate sheet of paper, tell which part or parts of the national government has the power described in each statement.

1. To declare war
2. To approve presidential appointments
3. To declare a law unconstitutional
4. To consider tax bills first for the national government
5. To grant pardons and reprieves

Skills Check
Use the flow chart on page 219 to answer the following questions.

1. In which house of Congress can bills be introduced?
2. Where does a bill go after it is introduced in the House?
3. How can a bill become a law if the President vetoes it?
4. What happens to a bill if the President does not act on it within the last ten days of a congressional session?
5. What happens to a bill if the President takes no action and Congress stays in session?

Think and Write
1. Describe the type of government the Framers set up under the Constitution.
2. What is meant by separation of powers?
3. Explain how a bill becomes a law.
4. Describe five important roles the President of the United States must fill.
5. Name one check each branch has on the other two branches of government.

Chapter 12

Establishing the Republic:
The 1790's

At the left of the painting, Martha Washington is shown standing on a platform during a reception given in her honor in New York City in 1789.

Soon after the Constitution was put into effect, Americans, including many of those who helped write the Constitution, began to divide into two political groups. Members of one group called themselves Republicans. Others called themselves Federalists. Those two groups were the first national political parties in the United States. However, they were very different from the political parties that were started in later times.

The Republican and Federalist parties were both working to save the American Republic from what they saw as its enemies. Those two parties did not last long. However, they gave shape and character to American politics in the 1790's.

1780

Washington becomes President, 1789
French Revolution begins, 1789

1790 — Hamilton's *Report on Public Credit*, 1790

Washington issues Proclamation of Neutrality, 1793

Jay's Treaty, 1795
Pinckney's Treaty, 1795

Adams elected President, 1796

Congress passes the Alien and Sedition Acts, 1798

1800

Jefferson elected President, 1801

12th Amendment added to the Constitution, 1804

1810

I. Starting the Government

General George Washington was the unanimous choice as the first President of the United States. He did not seek the office, but he did not refuse it. He was aware that he had no experience in running a government and would have preferred to stay home at Mount Vernon, his plantation in Virginia. However, he thought that if the people wanted him, he had to serve.

In 1789, at the age of 57, Washington became President. The job he took on was much harder than he had expected.

The First Inauguration

On April 30, 1789, Washington took the presidential oath of office from the second-story balcony at Federal Hall in New York City. Then he delivered the first inaugural address to both houses of Congress.

As President, Washington tried to act in a way that brought dignity and respect to his office. He often did that by imitating the head of state he knew best, the British king. Washington sometimes rode through New York on a white horse with a saddle of leopard skin trimmed with gold or in a splendid coach pulled by white horses. Outside his mansion stood uniformed guards with powdered wigs.

Congress, too, had to decide how to behave. Its members sometimes imitated British practices. John Adams even wanted members of Congress to call Washington "His Highness, the President of the United States and Protector of the Rights of the Same."

Some people worried that the federal government was turning into a monarchy with Washington as the new king. They opposed any imitation of Britain and wanted simplicity in government. Such people won the debate over how the president of a republic ought to be addressed. Washington was to be called Mr. President.

▶**1.** Why did some people worry that the federal government was turning into a monarchy?

The First Congress

The first Congress had a tremendous amount of work to do. One of the most pressing problems facing the young nation had to do with money.

The Constitution provided an outline for the government. The first Congress had to fill in the details. It also had to write a bill of rights.

▶**2.** What major problems awaited the first Congress?

Raising Money The Constitution gave Congress the right to raise money to support the United States government. So in July 1789, Congress imposed duties on certain imported goods and also on shipping. Those duties raised enough money to meet the needs of the new government very well.

▶**3.** How did Congress raise money to support the government?

Executive Departments The Constitution said the President could "require the opinion, in writing, of the principal officer in each of the executive departments, upon any subject relating to the duties of their respective offices." Congress decided to keep the Departments of War, Foreign Affairs, and Treasury that had been set up under the Articles of Confederation. However, Congress changed the name of the Department of Foreign Affairs to the Department of State. It also set up the office of Attorney General to advise the

The building on the right, known as Government House, was built in New York City as a presidential mansion before the government moved to Philadelphia.

President on matters of law and the office of Postmaster General to run the postal service.

In September 1789, Washington appointed Alexander Hamilton as secretary of the treasury. He persuaded Thomas Jefferson to become the first secretary of state. Washington's other executive appointments were less notable.

Washington worked with his heads of departments separately in the early years of his **administration,** or presidency, carefully keeping the decision-making power to himself. Only later did the heads of departments develop into a **cabinet,** or team of presidential advisors.

The Constitution also said the President could nominate all officers of the United States, though they required the Senate's approval before taking office. Did the President also need the Senate's approval before removing them from office? After hard debate, Congress agreed that the President could dismiss government officers on his own. Some people said that too much power was being given to the President. However, Congress decided that the departments of government should answer to the President.

▶**4.** What department heads did Congress set up under the new government?

Creating a Court System In September, Congress turned to the federal courts. The **Judiciary Act of 1789** set up a Supreme Court consisting of a chief justice and 5 associate

Highlighting People
Alexander Hamilton

He was a revolutionary in the true sense of the word. He was an independent thinker who was not afraid to differ when other people agreed. At the Constitutional Convention of 1787, his aristocratic ideals clashed greatly with the republican ideals of the other delegates. Yet he was willing to put aside his differences and support a plan for government that he did not totally agree with.

Alexander Hamilton was born in 1755 on the island of Nevis in the West Indies. Ten years after his birth his father moved the family to St. Croix, an island in what is now known as the Virgin Islands of the United States. Shortly afterward Mr. Hamilton abandoned his family. The 11-year-old youth had to go out to work.

Fortunately Alexander's employers recognized his talents. In 1772, they collected money from local people to send Alexander to the King's College (later Columbia) in New York City. Alexander vowed to pay them back by making something of his life. The American Revolution gave him his chance.

At King's College, Alexander wrote a stirring pamphlet on behalf of the American cause. He soon became a leader of the revolutionary movement. His career progressed even further when George Washington chose him as his secretary and aide in 1777. In time, Hamilton became like a son to the childless general.

While serving under Washington, Hamilton began to develop his ideas about government. He saw the confederation as hopelessly weak and feared it would not be strong enough to survive. He favored a strong national government, one in which the states had little power.

In many ways, Hamilton never understood his adopted country, where most people felt great devotion to their state. At the Constitutional Convention of 1787, he admitted to Madison, "No man's ideas are more remote [from the final draft of the Constitution] than my own." Even so, he worked closely with Madison and the others to get the Constitution ratified. Then he worked to strengthen the new nation as secretary of the treasury.

In 1795, Hamilton resigned as treasury secretary because of personal problems. However, he continued to take an active role in public life, making friends as well as enemies wherever he went. One of those enemies was an ambitious, arrogant man named Aaron Burr.

Aaron Burr was Vice President under Thomas Jefferson. Hamilton disliked the policies of both men, but he favored and voted for Jefferson over Burr as President. Burr never forgot the insult. On June 11, 1804, Aaron Burr challenged Alexander Hamilton to a duel. Hamilton accepted. The next day, June 12, Hamilton died from Burr's gunshot wound. The nation had lost one of its most dedicated leaders.

justices. The act also set up 13 district courts (courts where federal cases are first heard) and 3 circuit courts (courts to which federal judges travel to try cases). The act said that the Supreme Court could review the decisions of state courts. The Supreme Court could **nullify,** or cancel, any state law that violated the Constitution, other laws, or treaties of the United States.

▶**5.** What were the provisions of the Judiciary Act of 1789?

Hamilton's Financial Plans

Congress had worked quickly to solve some of the nation's immediate problems. It had raised money for expenses of the government. However, the country still faced great financial trouble. The job of straightening out the finances belonged to Secretary of the Treasury Alexander Hamilton. The House asked Hamilton to prepare plans for the nation's income and **credit,** that is, its good standing among those who could lend money. The disputes that arose over Hamilton's financial plans led to the first political parties in the nation.

▶**6.** Whose job was it to prepare plans for the nation's income and credit?

"The Report on Public Credit" Hamilton presented a daring "Report on Public Credit" to Congress in January 1790. The United States, Hamilton told Congress, owed over $65 million to people at home and in Europe. He proposed that the debt be paid in full. The United States had to uphold its credit by showing that it could and would pay the nation's debts.

Most members of Congress agreed that the foreign debt had to be paid. However, many disagreed over how to pay back the money owed to United States citizens. During the war, the government had sold bonds to people. Each bond was a promise that the government would return the purchase price of the bond with interest. Many bonds were given as pay to soldiers in the Continental Army.

During the hard days of the Revolution, most people who held bonds had been forced to sell them. **Speculators,** people who buy things at a low price in the hope of later selling them at a much higher price, bought the bonds at a mere fraction of their original cost. Some members of Congress did not think that speculators should be rewarded. Why should they be given full face value for bonds plus interest that they had bought for less than full value?

▶**7.** Why did some members of Congress not wish to pay in full that part of the federal debt owed to speculators?

Madison's Proposal Madison proposed that full value be paid only to those who had bought or received the bonds in the first place and still had them. Others would be paid back at about half the original cost of the bonds. The difference between the amount paid to them and the original cost would be given to citizens who had been forced by need to sell their bonds at a price that was lower than they had originally paid.

Madison's proposal failed because it was too complicated for the government to manage at that time. It also failed because there were a lot of speculators in Congress and they wanted to get full value for the bonds they held.

Hamilton believed that anyone who held a bond should be paid its full value. He understood that the government needed the support of people with money to spend and invest. At some time in the future, the United States would want to borrow from those people. That was what maintaining public credit was about. Hamilton also hoped such persons would use the money to help develop the nation's manufacturing strength.

▶**8.** Why did Hamilton want to pay full value to bond owners?

Assuming State Debts Another part of Hamilton's "Report on Public Credit" also caused great debate. He proposed not only that the nation should pay off, or fund, its own debt but also that it should **assume,** or take responsibility for, the remaining $25 million owed by the states. That would increase the importance of the nation for creditors everywhere.

Some states still had large debts to pay off. Those states thought Hamilton's assumption proposal was a wonderful idea. States that had already paid off all or most of their debts reacted differently. They had suffered to pay off their own debts, and they did not want to help pay off other states' debts.

About the time Congress was debating Hamilton's proposal, Congress was also deciding where to locate the nation's capital. Hamilton saw a chance to arrange a bargain. Four members of Congress whose districts were near the Potomac River agreed to support Hamilton's proposal for the assumption of state debts. In return, the decision was made to locate the national capital in Philadelphia for ten years, and then, from 1800, at a new site on the Potomac River between Maryland and Virginia. The proposal became law in August 1790.

▶**9.** Why did Hamilton want the nation to assume state debts?

A National Bank Four months later, Hamilton gave a second report to Congress that was even more hotly debated than his report on credit. This time he recommended the establishment of a national bank. In 1789, there were only three banks in the entire country. Hamilton thought there ought to be a central bank to take care of the government's money and to lend funds to the government when necessary. Notes issued by the bank would circulate as the nation's currency. Hamilton said that Congress should give the bank a **charter,** a legal document that would allow a bank to operate for 20 years and set rules for its operation. The federal government should supply one fifth of the $10 million that the bank would need to start operating. The federal government would also appoint one fifth of the bank's directors.

Hamilton's plan for a national bank had many advantages. It would help the government carry on its business, and by giving the country a reasonably sound currency, it would help private business too. However, many people questioned whether the Constitution allowed Congress to set up a bank.

Congress passed the bank bill. President Washington was not sure whether he should sign the bill or veto it. He asked the members of his Cabinet for their opinions.

Jefferson urged Washington to veto the bank bill. He said the bank bill was unconstitutional. The Constitution said Congress could do what was necessary and proper to exercise its legal powers. A bank might be useful, Jefferson said, but since it was not necessary, Congress could not set one up. Those who thought as Jefferson did were said to follow a **strict construction,** or narrow interpretation, of the Constitution.

Hamilton, on the other hand, replied that the bank would help the government collect taxes, regulate trade, and even provide for the common defense—powers the Constitution specifically gave to the federal government. Since the Constitution did not forbid Congress to create a bank and a bank would

This engraving of the First Bank of the United States was made in 1799. The bank was located on Third Street in Philadelphia.

help the government to do what the Constitution allowed, then Congress could set up the bank. People who favored Hamilton's position were said to have a **broad construction,** or loose interpretation, of the Constitution.

Washington was not sure which side was right. Because he thought he should support Hamilton as secretary of the treasury on financial issues, Washington signed the bank bill in February 1791.

▶ **10.** Why did Jefferson oppose the national bank?

The Report on Manufactures Hamilton submitted a third report to Congress, but it did not fare as well as his first two. He pro-

posed a plan for developing American manufacturing. He urged Congress to put a high tax on foreign goods imported into the country. Such a tariff, he believed, would encourage the growth of American manufacturing. Then Americans would not need to import so many goods from other countries.

Farmers opposed this idea. They feared they would have to pay more for the goods they bought. They also feared that other nations would respond to the new American duties by buying fewer American products such as tobacco, rice, and wheat. Besides, opponents of the bill argued, the United States was supported by duties on shipping. If imports were cut back, how would the government support

itself? The opposition was so strong that Hamilton's plan was defeated in Congress.
▶11. Why did farmers oppose Hamilton's plans to help manufacturing?

Reviewing Section I

Identify administration, cabinet, Judiciary Act of 1789, nullify, credit, speculators, assume, charter, strict construction, broad construction

Questions to Answer
1. What problems did Hamilton attempt to solve with his proposals to Congress?
2. What is the difference between broad construction and strict construction of the Constitution?

A Question to Think About Why did Washington and the members of Congress spend time on such minor issues as how to address the President?

II. Foreign and Domestic Policy

By 1791, many people were becoming worried over the plans of Hamilton and his supporters. Even people like James Madison who helped write the Constitution thought that Hamilton was putting too much power in the national government.

By 1792, Hamilton's opponents began to call themselves **Republicans.** They did so to indicate that they were working to save the Republic from people like Hamilton. The supporters of Hamilton called themselves **Federalists,** like the original supporters of the Constitution. They thought the conflict caused by the Republicans was itself a danger to republican government.

Foreign Policy Issues

The differences between the Republicans and the Federalists grew after 1790 over issues

The first political buttons worn in the United States showed support for George Washington during his first term as President.

Americans watched the French Revolution with interest. The moderate revolutionaries, who began the French uprising in 1789, repealed many of the special privileges of the nobles and issued a constitution for France. Still they kept King Louis XVI on the throne.

Other European kings, fearing the revolution would spread, went to war and tried to defeat the French. By 1792, France was at war with Austria, Prussia, Britain, and other countries.

Because the war went badly for France at first, a group of radicals, the Jacobins, were able to seize power. They deposed the king and set up a republic. Later they executed the king and thousands of other enemies of the state before the Reign of Terror ended.

From 1795 to 1799, a group called the Directory ruled France. It called on the hero of the hour, General Napoleon Bonaparte, for help in controlling the country. Napoleon overthrew the Directory and eventually crowned himself emperor of France.

The history of the First French Republic was like that of many other republics. Disorder and violence led to its eventual downfall. That made many Americans even more worried about the future of their own Republic. The Federalists, for example, called members of the Republican Party Jacobins. They also predicted that President Jefferson would become an American Napoleon. However, Jefferson proved that those critics were wrong in his two terms in office.

---

of **foreign policy,** that is, over how the United States should carry on its relations with the rest of the world.

▶**1.** What is foreign policy?

The Question of France In the 1790's, it seemed that Britain would soon declare war on France. That raised touchy problems, since the United States had had a treaty of alliance with France ever since 1778. France had helped the United States win its independence from Britain.

In July 1789, however, the French began a revolution of their own. They ended the rule by kings and nobles and set up a republic. Unlike the American Revolution, however, the French Revolution led to widespread violence. The king and many others were killed, and their property was seized. Control

of the nation slipped from one group to another.

Hamilton wanted the United States to cut itself off from France entirely. He said that the treaty with France was with the French king. Since there was no French king anymore, there was no alliance either.

Jefferson, Washington's secretary of state, saw the issue differently. He had been the American ambassador to France for five years and held deep affection for the French people. Not even the worst abuses of the French Revolution changed his mind. The treaty, he argued, was with the French nation, and so it remained in effect no matter who ruled the country.

Jefferson hoped to avoid offending the French, but he did not want the United States to go to war with Britain. Jefferson thought

IMPROVE YOUR SKILLS
Using Primary Sources

A primary source is a piece of evidence about the past that comes from that period of time. Diaries, letters, journals, and photographs are examples of primary sources. Primary sources are often the most reliable sources of information you can find about an event.

The following are excerpts, or parts of statements, made by Thomas Jefferson and Alexander Hamilton. Jefferson and Hamilton disagreed on many issues. One of those issues was the French Revolution. Read the excerpts and then answer the questions.

Hamilton

. . . There was a time when all men in this country entertained the same favorable view of the French Revolution. At the present time, they all still unite in the wish that the troubles of France may terminate [end] in the establishment of a free and good government; and dispassionate, well-informed men must equally unite in the doubt whether this be likely to take place under the auspices [guidance] of those who now govern . . . that country. But agreeing in these two points, there is great and serious diversity of opinion as to the real merits and probable issue [outcome] of the French Revolution.

Jefferson

In the struggle which was necessary, many guilty persons fell without the forms of trial, and with them some innocent. These I deplore as much as anybody, and shall deplore some of them to the day of my death. But I deplore them as I should have done had they fallen in battle . . . time and truth will rescue and embalm [preserve] their very liberty for which they would never have hesitated to offer up their lives. The liberty of the whole earth was depending on the issue of the contest, and was ever such a prize won with so little innocent blood?

1. What kind of government did Alexander Hamilton hope the French people would end up with?
2. What did Hamilton suggest about the people in power in France?
3. What did Thomas Jefferson say about the innocent people who were killed during the French Revolution?
4. Describe Hamilton's attitude toward the French Revolution.
5. Describe how Jefferson reacted to the killing of innocent people during the French Revolution.

that the United States should get something from Britain in exchange for its promise of **neutrality** (nü tral'ə tē), a promise not to take sides. Britain still held forts in the Northwest which it had promised to evacuate in 1783. Westerners complained that the British encouraged the Indians to fight American settlers. Jefferson hoped to use the neutrality issue to solve those problems.

▶2. What differing positions did Hamilton and Jefferson take over the alliance with France?

Washington Proclaims Neutrality

In April 1793, Washington issued a Proclamation of Neutrality. It said that the United States was at peace with both Great Britain and France. The proclamation ordered the citizens of the United States not to become involved in the war.

▶**3.** What was the Proclamation of Neutrality?

Citizen Genêt Washington's position may have been influenced by the minister France sent to the United States to win support for the French Republic. Citizen Edmond Charles Genêt (zhə nā') arrived in the United States on April 8, 1793. He was one of the most obnoxious and outrageous foreign visitors who ever came to the United States. As soon as he arrived, he began to hire Americans to serve as privateers for France. He also tried to organize armies to attack Spanish and British territories in North America.

In June, Jefferson notified Genêt that his actions were improper and that the privateers he had hired could not sail from the United States. Genêt promised to stop, and then he broke his word. Finally, the United States had to insist that France recall Genêt. France relieved Genêt of his post, but he requested permission to stay in the United States and, later, became a citizen.

Jefferson was embarrassed by the Genêt affair. He was also angered by Washington's neutrality proclamation and by his failure to bargain with Britain. It seemed clear to Jefferson that Hamilton was directing American foreign policy more than he was. So he resigned his position as secretary of state as of December 1793.

▶**4.** Who was Citizen Genêt?

Jay's Treaty Even before Jefferson left office, however, it seemed as though the United

John Jay was a strong supporter of the Constitution and pushed for its ratification.

States might go to war with Britain. In December 1793, the British started to seize American ships trading with the French West Indies. Many Americans also suspected that the British were responsible for Indian attacks on settlers in the Northwest Territory.

Many Americans clamored for war. In some cities, mobs attacked British sailors. Young men began to form volunteer militia companies. People across the country demanded that Britain somehow be punished for its acts. To avoid war, Washington sent a special mission to London under John Jay to bargain with the British.

Unfortunately, Jay had little to bargain with. Therefore, he did not win much for the United States. The British agreed to give up their posts in the Old Northwest as long they could continue to trade with the Indians there. The British also agreed to allow some American ships to trade in the West Indies. The United States had to promise not to compete with the British by selling basic products such as sugar, molasses, and cotton in other parts of the world.

Several other claims were referred to special **commissions,** groups of people appointed to do special tasks. One commission decided how much the British owed the Americans for ships seized in 1793. Another commission decided how much of the money Americans owed to Britons from before the Revolution should now be paid back.

On several other points, the British refused to give in at all. They would not promise to stop seizing American sailors and forcing them to serve in the British navy. The British refused to honor the rights of American neutral ships in time of war. They also refused to pay back southern planters for slaves taken during the Revolution.

Jay's Treaty, as this agreement of 1795 was called, was very unpopular in the United States. However, the Senate approved the treaty (except for the section on the West Indian trade) to avoid war with Britain. Washington signed it for the same reason. The public outcry did not, however, please the President.

▶**5.** What were the major provisions of Jay's Treaty?

Pinckney's Treaty Jay's Treaty had one good effect. It made Spain think the United States and Britain might be planning to work together in a way that threatened Spanish Louisiana. So Thomas Pinckney, the American minister to Spain, was able to negotiate a treaty with Spain that was very advantageous to the United States.

Pinckney's Treaty of 1795 won for Americans the right to ship goods freely on the Mississippi. It also won the **right of deposit** at the port of New Orleans. That meant Americans could unload and store their goods at New Orleans before loading them onto oceangoing ships. Spain also recognized the Mississippi and the 31st parallel as boundaries between its lands and those of the United States. Both countries agreed to keep the Indians within their territories from entering the other country's lands.

The parts of the treaty that dealt with the Mississippi were very important because they satisfied settlers in the West, and the West was growing. Kentucky had, in fact, become in 1792 the second new state to join the Union. (Vermont was the first; it became a state in 1791.) In 1796, Tennessee also became a state.

▶**6.** What were the major provisions of Pinckney's Treaty?

The Whisky Rebellion

During the war scare and the furor over Jay's Treaty, the division between Republicans and Federalists grew. Then events in western Pennsylvania also widened the gap between the two groups.

Back in 1791, Congress had passed a tax on whisky. News of the law set off protests in the backcountry where farmers found it much easier to haul their corn to market in the form of whisky than in the form of bulky grain. In the summer of 1794, "whisky boys" in the Monongahela (mə non′ gə hē′lə) Valley of Pennsylvania rose up to resist the law. They even tried to stop a federal marshal from arresting farmers accused of not paying the tax.

President Washington, on Hamilton's advice, decided such opposition to the law had

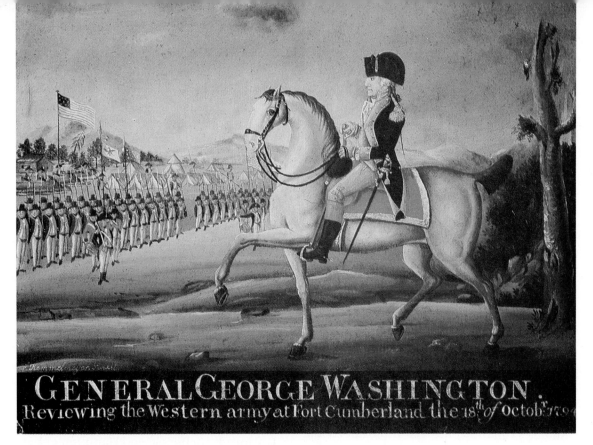

GENERAL GEORGE WASHINGTON.
Reviewing the Western army at Fort Cumberland the 18ᵗʰ of Octobᵣ 1794

The Whisky Rebellion came to an abrupt end when President Washington led federal soldiers against the rebels.

to be put down. He did not want another Shays's Rebellion. He summoned 15,000 militiamen from Pennsylvania and other states to stop the riots. For a while, Washington himself led those soldiers. However, by the time the soldiers arrived in western Pennsylvania, the trouble was mostly over. The ringleaders were arrested. But later, Washington pardoned them.

Washington thought his response to the rebellion made an important point. It showed that the United States would not allow organized resistance to the law. In a republic, citizens can work to change laws through their votes. Otherwise they must obey them. The Republicans saw the rebellion somewhat differently. They said that liberty was in

danger whenever a government called out the army against its own people.

▶ **7.** What caused the Whisky Rebellion?

The Election of 1796

Soon after the Whisky Rebellion, the Republicans and Federalists were in a battle over the election of 1796. Washington could have remained as President, but he decided to retire at the end of his second term. He announced his intention in his farewell address to the nation.

Washington used the address to give his country advice. He told Americans that the nation should always pay its debts and that it should avoid permanent political allia with European countries. Above all, he warned that the country should avoid the dangers of political parties. Their battles, he said, could cause the Republic to fail.

Obviously, Washington did not consider himself a member of a political party. He and other Federalists felt that they were only speaking for the national government.

▶**8.** What were the major points of Washington's farewell address?

The Candidates The presidential election of 1796 was the first in which there were party candidates. The candidates were chosen by the members of each party in Congress. The Republicans ran Thomas Jefferson for President and Aaron Burr of New York for Vice President. The Federalist candidate for President was John Adams.

Hamilton was not happy with the choice of Adams. However, Hamilton managed to get Thomas Pinckney of South Carolina as Adams's running mate. Hamilton hoped that Pinckney would become President. That was possible because of the way the electoral college voted. Each elector cast two votes, without saying which was for President and which for Vice President. Pinckney was a Southerner. Hamilton hoped that some southern Republican electors might vote for Pinckney rather than for Burr. In that way, Pinckney could

end up with more votes than Adams and become President.

▶**9.** Who were the candidates in the election of 1796?

The Outcome Adams's friends in New England also understood the electoral system. Several of them refused to vote for Pinckney so that Adams would be sure to have the most votes. In the end, Adams won 71 votes, Jefferson 68, Pinckney 59, and Burr 30. Federalist Adams became President and Republican Jefferson became his Vice President.

▶**10.** Why did Hamilton's plan to make Pinckney President fail?

Reviewing Section II——————

Identify Republicans, Federalists, foreign policy, neutrality, commissions, Jay's Treaty, Pinckney's Treaty, right of deposit, Whisky Rebellion

Questions to Answer

1. How did Jefferson and Hamilton disagree about relations with France?
2. How did Republican Jefferson become Vice President under Federalist President Adams?

A Question to Think About How did ratification of the Constitution affect Washington's response to the Whisky Rebellion?

III. The Administration of John Adams

No one ever expected candidates from two different parties to become President and Vice ~sident. In designing the election system, ~ers did not know the country would ~~ with tickets or lists of can- ~tely, Adams and Jefferson ~They were, however, very ~nother.

Adams and Jefferson

John Adams, the new President, was born in Braintree, Massachusetts, in 1735. Benjamin Franklin once described Adams as "always an honest man, often a wise one, but sometimes, and in some things, absolutely out of his senses." Others just said Adams was quick-tempered and insecure.

John Trumbull made this painting of John Adams (left), the second President of the United States. Charles Peale painted Thomas Jefferson, the third President.

Jefferson was born in Albemarle County, Virginia, in 1743. His father was a wealthy planter. Although shy, Jefferson was self-confident and likeable.

The two men did not look at all alike. The red-haired Jefferson was tall and angular, Adams short and chunky.

Their careers brought Adams and Jefferson together often. Both served in the Continental Congress where they favored independence. Then, in the 1780's, both served their country as diplomats in Europe.

Jefferson did not try very hard to win the election of 1796. In fact, if he and Adams had received the same number of votes in the electoral college, Jefferson wanted the Republicans to vote for Adams. "Adams has always been my senior," Jefferson said.

Adams and Jefferson set out in 1797 to overcome party divisions. Adams tried to please the Republicans in his inaugural address. However, he made one big mistake. He kept some members of Washington's Cabinet. Most of those men were not very good at their jobs. Worse yet, all of them took their orders from Alexander Hamilton, who had resigned from the Cabinet in 1795. So Hamilton had an important influence on Adams's administration.

As a result, Adams and Jefferson drifted farther apart. During the administration of John Adams, in fact, the Republicans and Federalists squared off against each other as they had never done before.

▶**1.** Why was it a mistake for Adams to keep Washington's Cabinet?

New Problems with France

The two parties fought again over the issue of France. The French were not pleased with Jay's Treaty. It seemed to them, quite correctly, that the United States was favoring Britain over France. So France started seizing American ships on their way to England and announced that it would no longer honor the neutrality of American ships. Then in 1797, the French seized about 300 American ships. The French refused to work with the American minister to France and even threatened to arrest him.

Adams dealt with the crisis by appointing a team of three diplomats to work things out. The three were Charles Cotesworth Pinckney of South Carolina (the brother of Thomas Pinckney), John Marshall, a Federalist from Virginia, and Elbridge Gerry, an old friend

This cartoon, printed in 1799, shows the French government as a five-headed monster trying to bribe the American diplomats.

of Adams from Massachusetts. Meanwhile, Adams prepared for a possible war. Jefferson and the Republicans feared that those preparations would anger the French and make peace even less likely.

▶**2.** Why did a war with France seem likely in 1797?

The XYZ Affair The three diplomats appointed by Adams tried to meet with Charles Maurice de Talleyrand, the French foreign minister. However, the American diplomats immediately ran into problems. Talleyrand kept the Americans waiting for several weeks. Then, in January 1798, he sent three men to tell the Americans that no talks could take place until the Americans paid him a $250,000 bribe and loaned several million dollars to France. "Not a sixpence," said Pinckney, and the negotiations fell through.

The Republicans in Congress did not believe the diplomats' story. Adams let them see the diplomatic reports, except for the names of the three French agents, whom he called X, Y, and Z. The whole country became outraged over what became known as the **XYZ Affair.** "Millions for defense, but not one cent for tribute" became a national slogan. It meant that the United States could not be forced to give money to any nation. In July 1798, Congress canceled the treaty of 1778 and so ended the alliance with France.

▶**3.** Why did the XYZ Affair enrage the Americans?

An Undeclared Naval War Some Federalists wanted to declare war on France immediately. They also wanted to build up the American army. Instead, Adams argued that the United States needed a strong navy to protect its merchant ships. In May 1798, he talked Congress into setting up a Department of the Navy. The decision came none too

This painting shows the armed American merchant ship Planter *fighting off an attack by a French privateer during the undeclared war with France.*

soon. From 1798 to 1800, the Americans and the French were involved in an undeclared war at sea.

▶**4.** When did the United States fight an undeclared naval war with France?

The Alien and Sedition Acts

The Federalists in Congress took advantage of the war scare to strengthen their political party. They managed to pass a series of measures known as the **Alien** (ā′lyən) **and Sedition** (si dish′ən) **Acts** that were designed to reduce support for the Republicans.

The Alien Acts, passed in July 1798, were aimed at immigrants. Federalists thought that immigrants were likely to join the Republican

Party as soon as they became citizens. So the Federalists made it harder for immigrants to become citizens. The new laws said immigrants had to live in the United States 14 years before becoming citizens. In the past, an immigrant could become a citizen in just 5 years. The new laws also gave the President the power to **deport,** or expel from the country, any immigrant he considered dangerous.

The Sedition Act was meant to put down all opposition to the Federalists. The act made any effort to oppose federal laws illegal. It also outlawed the writing, speaking, or publishing of false, scandalous, or malicious statements against the President, Congress, or the government. Basically, any criticism of the President or the government became illegal. Punishments included prison terms and heavy fines.

▶5. How did the Alien and Sedition Acts harm the Republicans?

The Virginia and Kentucky Resolutions

The Republicans were sure that the Sedition Act was unconstitutional. It violated the rights of free speech and assembly, which were protected by the Bill of Rights. However, the Republicans knew that they would get no help from the courts. Both Presidents Washington and Adams had appointed all the justices, and, naturally, they had appointed good Federalists.

In fact, Federalist judges enforced the Sedition Act. For example, Matthew Lyon, a Republican congressman from Vermont, publicly criticized the President while campaigning for reelection. A Federalist judge convicted Lyon of sedition, fined him $1,000, and sent him to prison for four months. (Lyon was reelected anyway.)

Since they could not turn to the courts, Madison and Jefferson decided to turn to the state legislatures. Jefferson wrote a set of resolutions that was passed by the Kentucky Legislature. Madison wrote a similar set that was accepted by the Virginia Assembly.

The **Kentucky Resolutions** of November 1798 said that each state could decide whether a new federal law violated the Constitution. Kentucky found the Sedition Act "altogether void and of no force" because it went against the Constitution.

The **Virginia Resolutions** said that a state had a duty to stop the federal government from taking on powers not given to it by the Constitution.

Virginia and Kentucky tried without success to get the backing of other states. The Alien and Sedition Acts were repealed or eventually expired. However, the important issue of whether states could stop acts of Congress from being enforced, or nullify them, was not settled. That issue would reappear at later times in the nation's history.

▶6. What issue did the Virginia and Kentucky resolutions raise?

Adams Takes Charge

John Adams finally acted forcefully and bravely to end the threat of war and the problems it caused. In January 1799, he received a letter from Talleyrand that said an American envoy to France would "be received with the respect due to the representative of a free, independent, and powerful nation." In February 1799—without asking his Cabinet's advice—Adams asked the Senate to confirm his nomination of William Vans Murray as a special diplomatic envoy to France.

That was a very courageous thing to do. By taking a step toward peace, Adams pulled the rug out from under those Federalists who were trying to use the war scare to crush the Republicans. The Murray mission was successful. It got the French to recognize the neutrality of American ships and ended French attacks on American commerce.

By 1799, Adams also understood that his Cabinet was loyal to Hamilton, his enemy. He asked the worst offenders to resign. Adams finally won control of his own administration. However, that had taken him too long.

▶7. How did Adams end the war scare?

The Election of 1800

Adams was proud of his first term as President and confident of winning the election of 1800. He, however, had lost the support of many

Federalists by appointing Murray and ending the war scare. The Republicans organized their supporters carefully to defeat Adams. The Republican candidates were Thomas Jefferson for President and Aaron Burr for Vice President.

Once again, the results of the election were unexpected. Adams and Charles Pinckney, the Federalist candidate for Vice President, lost. Adams won only 65 electoral votes and Pinckney 64. The Republican candidates, Jefferson and Burr, each had 73 votes. The electoral college's procedures still made it impossible for its members to vote separately for President and for Vice President.

Technically Jefferson and Burr were tied. Which of them would be President? Burr was ambitious. Rather than stepping aside for his party's presidential candidate, Burr thought that he could get enough Federalist support to become President. The decision was thrown into the House of Representatives, which voted 35 times before finally electing Jefferson in February 1801. Jefferson won in part because Hamilton told the Federalists that Jefferson was less dangerous than Burr.

In 1804, the Constitution was amended so such confusion would not happen again. The **Twelfth Amendment** required that the electoral college vote separately for President and Vice President.

Jefferson tried to heal the wounds between Federalists and Republicans in his inaugural address. "We are all Republicans," he said; "we are all Federalists." His words were a call for unity and a prayer for the end of party conflict.

John Adams was not there to hear Jefferson's speech. He was deeply hurt and humiliated by his defeat and so hurried home to Massachusetts before inauguration day. It would be ten years before he and Jefferson once again became friends. Then they began

John Vanderlyn painted this portrait of Aaron Burr, Vice President from 1801 to 1805.

to exchange letters, sharing memories and ideas in a spirit of mutual respect and admiration that lasted until their deaths. Strangely enough, both men died on the same day in the same year—July 4, 1826.

▶**8.** What was unusual about the presidential election of 1800?

Reviewing Section III

Identify XYZ Affair, Alien and Sedition Acts, deport, Kentucky Resolutions, Virginia Resolutions, Twelfth Amendment

Questions to Answer
1. What were the results of Adams's appointment of Murray as envoy to France?
2. What problem did the Twelfth Amendment solve?

A Question to Think About What problems might develop if the states could nullify federal laws?

249

IMPROVE YOUR READING
Context Clues

All readers come across new or unusual words. Sometimes when reading we also meet familiar words that have a meaning different from the one we know. For example, you know that a cabinet is a case or cupboard that usually has shelves and doors. However, in this chapter, *cabinet* has a different meaning. *Cabinet* refers to the group of people appointed by the President to give advice on important issues.

How can we figure out what unfamiliar words mean? One way, of course, is to consult the dictionary. Often we do not have to do this because writers give us context clues. That is, they help us figure out the meaning of a word by the way it is used. By noting that, we can find a meaning that makes sense.

Writers can also provide us with different types of context clues. In this chapter, the author often provides direct definitions of unfamiliar words. The definition is usually set off by commas. Here is an example from this chapter. "Speculators, people who buy things at a low price in the hope of later selling them at a much higher price, bought the bonds . . ." The word *speculator* means a person who is willing to take a business risk. The phrase *people who buy things at a low price in the hope of later selling them at a much higher price* was set off with commas. This context clue is a direct definition.

In this exercise, select the correct meaning for each of the italicized words. Look for the direct definition.

1. Washington worked with his heads of departments separately in the early years of his *administration,* or presidency, carefully keeping the decision-making power to himself.
   a. service in the army
   b. performance of presidential duties
   c. legal action

2. Only later did the heads of departments develop into a *cabinet,* or team of presidential advisors.
   a. stereo system
   b. chest of drawers
   c. heads of departments who serve as advisors to the President.

3. He proposed not only that the nation should pay off, or fund, its own debt, but also that it should *assume*, or take responsibility for, the $25 million owed by the states.
   a. judge
   b. take over
   c. give up

4. The new laws also gave the President the power to *deport*, or expel from the country, any immigrant he considered dangerous.
   a. bring in
   b. put in jail
   c. expel

5. Several other claims were referred to special *commissions*, groups of people appointed to do special tasks.
   a. people appointed for special tasks
   b. members of the armed forces
   c. workers in courts

CHAPTER 12 REVIEW

Vocabulary Check
On a separate sheet of paper, write the letter for the definition of each numbered item.

1. Cabinet
2. Credit
3. Speculators
4. Assume
5. Charter

a. Group of presidential advisors
b. People who buy things at a low price in the hope of later selling them at a much higher price
c. To take responsibility for something
d. Standing with those who lend money
e. A legal document that allows a business to operate and sets rules for it.

Fact Check
On a separate sheet of paper, complete each of the following sentences.

1. Hamilton's supporters called themselves _____ because they favored ratification of the Constitution.
2. Jefferson's and Madison's friends called themselves _____ because they defended the Republic against enemies.
3. Congress passed the _____, which set up a Supreme Court made up of a chief justice and five associate justices.
4. Hamilton's _____ proposed that the nation pay its debts in full.
5. Hamilton hoped that _____ would be elected President in 1796.
6. _____ resigned his Cabinet position because he disagreed with Washington's neutrality proclamation.
7. By the terms of _____, Americans got the right to ship goods on the Mississippi.
8. (a) The Republican candidate for President in 1796 was _____. (b) The Federalist candidate was _____.
9. The _____ made it difficult for immigrants to become United States citizens.
10. The _____ said that each state could decide if a new federal law violated the Constitution.

Time Check
On a separate sheet of paper, put the following events in chronological order.

1. George Washington becomes President.
2. Congress passes the first Judiciary Act.
3. The French Revolution begins.
4. Farmers in western Pennsylvania rebel.
5. Pinckney negotiates a treaty with Spain.

Skills Check
Use the information on page 240 to answer the following questions.

1. What is a primary source?
2. Give three examples of primary sources.
3. Why do historians use primary sources?
4. Compare Hamilton's and Jefferson's views on the violence of the French Revolution.
5. Why did Jefferson support the revolution?

Think and Write
1. Why did Hamilton favor taxes on imports?
2. What European nations caused problems during Washington's presidency?
3. Why were many Americans opposed to Jay's Treaty?
4. What did Washington accomplish by putting down the Whisky Rebellion?
5. Why was the Twelfth Amendment added to the Constitution?

Chapter 13

Establishing the Republic:
The Jeffersonians

In this William Birch watercolor, the north wing of the Capitol is shown as it looked in 1800.

In March 1801, Thomas Jefferson took the oath of office in the nation's new capital, Washington, D.C. Located on the Potomac River and in the District of Columbia (D.C.), it was named after the first President. The city was planned by Major Pierre-Charles L'Enfant, a French engineer who fought in the Revolutionary War.

In 1800, when the federal government first moved to Washington, the city still looked like a muddy frontier town. The President's house was unfinished. In fact, many of the city's buildings were only half built.

Washington was obviously no place for would-be kings or noblemen. It was just right, however, for the pared-down style Jefferson brought to the presidency. It was right, too, for the next two Presidents, Jefferson's fellow Virginians James Madison and James Monroe. Those three Presidents—the Jeffersonians—took the nation through some dark times that saw the destruction of Washington itself at the hands of a foreign enemy. By the time the Jeffersonians left office, however, Americans were more secure in their independence and confident—for the moment—that their Republic would endure.

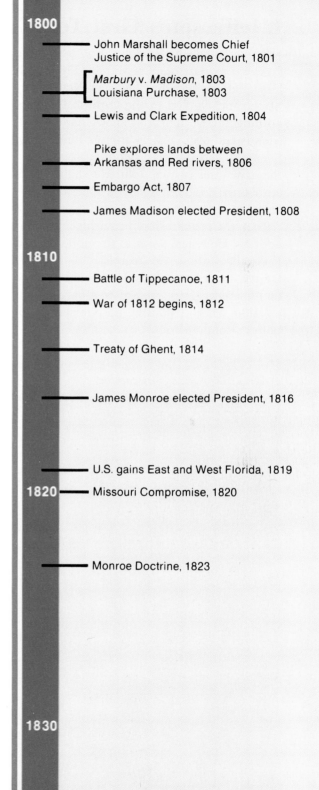

1800

John Marshall becomes Chief Justice of the Supreme Court, 1801

Marbury v. *Madison*, 1803
Louisiana Purchase, 1803

Lewis and Clark Expedition, 1804

Pike explores lands between Arkansas and Red rivers, 1806

Embargo Act, 1807

James Madison elected President, 1808

1810

Battle of Tippecanoe, 1811

War of 1812 begins, 1812

Treaty of Ghent, 1814

James Monroe elected President, 1816

U.S. gains East and West Florida, 1819

1820 Missouri Compromise, 1820

Monroe Doctrine, 1823

1830

I. Jefferson's First Term

Jefferson made his inauguration as simple an event as possible. On March 4, 1801, Jefferson left his boarding house on New Jersey Street and walked to the Capitol. He wore nothing fancy. Jefferson shook hands with friends and well-wishers after arriving at the Senate. There he was sworn into office by the new Chief Justice, John Marshall, a Federalist with whom Jefferson had some differences of opinion.

Then the new President gave his inaugural address. He reached out to Republicans and Federalists alike. He promised that in the United States one President could replace another peacefully even after a hard-fought election. There would be no punishment of political opponents.

Thomas Jefferson admired Natural Bridge in Virginia, shown at the right of this painting.

The New Administration

When Jefferson came into office, he intended to cut back the already modest national government of the Federalists. He wanted a "wise and frugal government" that would leave Americans free to manage their own affairs. On the other hand, he thought it best to avoid sudden changes. As a result, he kept many of Hamilton's economic programs. He did not interfere with the funding of the national and state debts. Nor did he try to end the First Bank of the United States.

▶**1.** What sort of government did Thomas Jefferson want for the United States?

Cutting the Debt Jefferson did not, however, share Hamilton's fondness for the national debt. Jefferson said the debt helped bankers and other rich people and hurt workers and farmers, whose taxes paid the interest on the debt. A really free country, Jefferson thought, would owe nothing to anyone. So he and his new secretary of the treasury, Albert Gallatin, decided to pay off the national debt.

To do that, the costs of government had to be trimmed. First, Jefferson and Gallatin cut the budget of the army. Jefferson did not believe in keeping armies in peacetime. He reduced the navy's budget even more, and he sent fewer diplomats to European nations.

▶**2.** Why did Jefferson try to trim the cost of government?

The Tripolitan War Jefferson's desire to save money drew the country into a small war. Over the previous 10 years, the United States had paid about $2 million so African pirates would leave American ships alone. Jefferson thought that money had better uses. He sent a naval squadron to the Mediterranean Sea to protect American merchant ships.

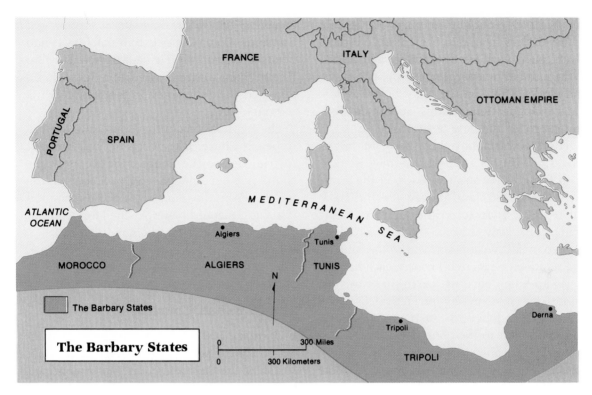

Map Study *Name the Barbary States. In which of the states was the port of Derna? Which European country is closest to the Barbary States?*

In 1803 and 1804, the navy blockaded the harbor of Tripoli, whose sultan, or leader, had demanded money from the United States. American marines also seized the port of Derna (der'nə), in Tripoli. Americans won that war in 1805, but the United States continued to make payments to countries along the Barbary Coast until 1816. The Tripolitan War showed, however, that a free country needed to be able to defend itself.

▶**3.** What was the Tripolitan War?

New Appointments Jefferson appointed Republicans to his Cabinet. Almost all the other jobs in the federal government were held by Federalists. They had been appointed by the two Federalist Presidents, Washington and Adams.

In his inaugural address, Jefferson had promised not to punish people for their politics. Still he felt that those who worked under his department heads had to respect Republican ideas. So Jefferson removed 105 Federalists from office and put Republicans in their places.

▶**4.** Why did Jefferson replace Federalist officeholders?

Jefferson and the Midnight Judges

Washington and Adams had appointed only Federalists to the courts. Those were the judges who had enforced the Alien and Sedition Acts against Republicans. On top of that, in the final days of his administration, Adams had signed a new law, the Judiciary

Act of 1801. It reduced the number of Supreme Court justices from 6 to 5, created 16 circuit courts each with its own judge, and added to the number of federal marshals, attorneys, and clerks. Then, on the night before Jefferson's inauguration, Adams appointed Federalists to all the new positions.

Jefferson was annoyed by those "midnight judges." With his support, the new Republican Congress promptly repealed the Judiciary Act of 1801 and passed the Judiciary Act of 1802. It restored the number of Supreme Court justices to six—so Jefferson could hope to make one appointment to the court—and set up only six circuit courts, each headed by a Supreme Court justice. In that way, the circuit courts created by the Federalists came to an end. The jobs of the justices that Adams had appointed to the courts ended as well.

Other Federalist judges had their jobs for life so long as they remained on their "good

John Marshall was one of the most respected Chief Justices to serve on the Supreme Court.

behavior." However, the Republicans thought Supreme Court Justice Samuel Chase had behaved improperly. He had convicted several Republicans under the Sedition Act and had attacked the Jefferson administration while in court.

The Republicans in the House managed to impeach Chase. But, when he was brought to trial before the Senate, the Republicans could not get enough votes to convict the justice. From that time on, it was understood that judges could be impeached for criminal conduct only, not for their politics.

▶**5.** Why were Republicans unhappy with the makeup of the courts in 1801?

The Marshall Court

In January 1801, John Adams appointed an extraordinary person, John Marshall, as Chief Justice of the Supreme Court. Marshall helped to strengthen the court. Jefferson disliked Marshall's Federalist politics, but it was impossible to find fault with the quality of his mind. He remained on the court until 1835, bringing it a prestige it had not had before.

Like Jefferson, Marshall was a Virginian and modest in his ways, a lover of simple pleasures. Marshall had a talent for writing crisp, clear court decisions. He used that talent to write some very important Supreme Court opinions.

▶**6.** Who was John Marshall?

The Marbury Decision In 1803, Marshall wrote the majority opinion in the case of *Marbury* v. *Madison*, the first case in which the Supreme Court declared an act of Congress to be unconstitutional. The case was brought to court by William Marbury, one of Adams's midnight appointments. Marbury had never received his commission—a written order appointing him to office. He wanted the court to force Jefferson's secretary of state, James Madison, to deliver it to him. The court agreed that Marbury had a right to the commission. However, the court said that it could not order Madison to deliver the commission. The Constitution did not give the court that right. That made a section of the Judiciary Act of 1789, which said the court could issue such orders, unconstitutional. Marbury had based his case upon that section of the law.

The decision was a clever one. Although Marshall was critical of Madison, he did not try to make Madison deliver Marbury's commission. Marshall feared that Madison would refuse to obey a court order to deliver the commission. That would have made the court seem weak. Instead Marshall strengthened the court by assuming the power of judicial review. He insisted on the right to review the constitutionality of all laws.

▶**7.** Why is the case of *Marbury* v. *Madison* important?

McCulloch v. Maryland Marshall's court supported the power of the nation whenever it could. In the case of *McCulloch* v. *Maryland* in 1819, the court struck down a Maryland law that tried to tax the Second Bank of the United States, which Congress had created in 1816. Laws passed by Congress under powers given it by the Constitution were the supreme law of the land, Marshall said. A state law could not interfere with a federal law. Moreover, Marshall said that Congress could do anything to carry out its duties that the Constitution did not specifically forbid it to do. That was exactly what Hamilton had said in defending the First Bank of the United States.

▶**8.** What did the decision in *McCulloch* v. *Maryland* say about the Constitution and state laws?

The Louisiana Purchase

A chain of unlikely events made Louisiana, an enormous stretch of land west of the Mississippi along with New Orleans, part of the United States. First, Spain secretly gave all of Louisiana to France in 1800. Meanwhile, in October 1802, Spanish officials at New Orleans said Americans could no longer deposit, or unload and store, their goods at New Orleans before shipping them out to other countries. Westerners were very upset. They needed use of the Mississippi and the port of New Orleans. Jefferson was just as worried. Whatever European country controlled New Orleans, he said, was a natural enemy of the United States.

Jefferson tried to solve the problem by having Robert R. Livingston, the American minister in Paris, buy New Orleans. If France had also gained title to West Florida, Jefferson told Livingston to try to buy that too. Jefferson sent James Monroe to help with the negotiations.

▶**9.** Why did Jefferson want to buy New Orleans?

The French Offer By the time Monroe arrived in Paris in April 1803, the French had already offered to sell not just New Orleans but all of Louisiana to the United States. They made that offer because the leader of France, Napoleon Bonaparte, needed money.

Napoleon had spent a great deal of money on another French possession in the Americas. In 1801, he had sent 20,000 soldiers to put down a rebellion in Santo Domingo, a small island in the Caribbean Sea. France owned part of the island. Spain controlled the rest. Slaves there under the black leader Toussaint L'Ouverture (tü san' lü ver tyr') had risen up and declared the independence of the island from France. The rebels and tropical diseases killed almost the entire French army.

This painting of New Orleans was made shortly after the Louisiana Purchase. By 1810, it had become one of the ten largest cities in the country.

Now Napoleon wanted to go to war with Britain again. Since the Louisiana Territory would be difficult and expensive to defend, Napoleon decided to sell it to the Americans. ▶10. Why did Napoleon want to sell the Louisiana Territory?

Authority for the Purchase Livingston and Monroe had no authority to buy Louisiana, but they could not pass up such an offer. They bargained a little, and the French accepted their bid of $15 million for all of Louisiana. That was not much more than they were authorized to pay for New Orleans alone.

The boundaries of the territory were not well defined. However, they went as far west as the Rocky Mountains. The **Louisiana Purchase** doubled the size of the nation.

The deal was not finalized in France, however. The Senate still had to approve the treaty, and the House had to approve the use of public funds for the purchase.

Jefferson worried because the Constitution did not give Congress the right to buy new territory. He wanted to propose an amendment to the Constitution giving it that power before asking Congress for its approval. However, Livingston and Monroe were afraid that Napoleon might change his mind if Congress did not act quickly. So Jefferson decided to go ahead. The Senate approved the treaty, the House of Representatives voted to pay for the purchase, and then Jefferson signed the treaty.
▶11. Why did Jefferson worry about buying Louisiana?

Lewis and Clark Explore the West

Even before the Louisiana Purchase, Jefferson had encouraged Congress to spend money for exploring the West. Jefferson thought that Americans should know more about the great continent of North America. In January 1803, Congress voted to fund an expedition to travel up the Misssouri River and then west to the Pacific Ocean.

The lands west of the Mississippi were then still ruled by Spain. Jefferson assured the Spanish minister that the expedition was a scientific one, meant only to advance the study of geography.

▶ **12.** Who funded exploration of the West?

Lewis and Clark Set Out Jefferson appointed as leaders of the expedition the 32-year-old Meriwether Lewis, who first learned wilderness skills in the Blue Ridge Mountains of Virginia, and a 28-year-old scout and soldier named William Clark. Clark's older brother, George Rogers Clark, was the hero who had captured Vincennes during the Revolution.

Congress instructed Lewis and Clark to make maps of the areas they visited. They were also to keep careful records of animal and vegetable life and of minerals and soils they saw on their journey. Congress also said the explorers should speak with Indian leaders they met about trade with the United States.

The Lewis and Clark expedition, consisting of 48 men, set out from St. Louis in the spring of 1804. Among the expedition's members was a black man named York, a slave owned by Clark. During the expedition's travels, York was of great interest to many Indians who had never seen a black person before.

By fall, the expedition had traveled up the Missouri River to present-day North Dakota. There the explorers built Fort Mandan, named after the nearby Mandan Indians, where they spent the winter. The next April, 16 members

Easterners were very interested in drawings of plants collected by the Lewis and Clark expedition.

of the group returned to St. Louis. They carried with them Clark's report on the expedition's findings up to that time and a fine collection of plants and animals.

▶ **13.** What route did the Lewis and Clark expedition follow to North Dakota?

To the Pacific The other members of the expedition turned west. They had added an important new member to the expedition, a woman named Sacajawea (sak′ə jə wē′ə). Lewis and Clark had actually hired her husband, a French fur trader. Sacajawea and her infant son went along. Sacajawea was a Shoshone (shō shō′nē) Indian who had been captured by a Dakota tribe. Now she promised to lead the explorers to her homeland in the northern Rockies. Her very presence with the expedition was helpful. Because the expedition traveled with a woman and an infant, Indian groups assumed they came in peace.

In June 1805, the explorers came to the Great Falls of the Missouri, where the river falls 80 feet. It took them a month to carry their goods around the falls. Then they continued to where three rivers—which they named the Madison, Jefferson, and Gallatin—joined to form the Missouri. They took the northernmost of those rivers to the land of the Shoshone Indians, whose chief, Sacajawea discovered, was her brother! The Shoshone gave Lewis and Clark horses and guides to help them cross the Rocky Mountains.

Finally, on November 15, 1805, they arrived on the banks of the Pacific Ocean, "the object of all our labours, the reward of all our anxieties." On the way back, they explored much of present-day Montana before turning down the Missouri toward St. Louis, where they arrived on September 23, 1806.

The Lewis and Clark expedition not only increased knowledge of the plants, animals, and peoples of North America but also let people know how far it was across the continent. The reports and maps of the expedition became more important when the land they visited became part of the United States.

▶**14.** What role did Sacajawea play in the Lewis and Clark expedition?

Zebulon Pike Before Lewis and Clark returned, Jefferson planned more expeditions. The most notable was Zebulon Pike's unsuccessful search for the source of the Mississippi from 1805 to 1806. In 1806 and 1807, Pike explored the western lands between the Arkansas and the Red rivers. He saw the mountain that is named for him, Pikes Peak.

▶**15.** Who was Zebulon Pike?

Reviewing Section I

Identify John Marshall, midnight judges, Samuel Chase, *Marbury* v. *Madison*, *McCulloch* v. *Maryland*, Toussaint L'Ouverture, Louisiana Purchase, Meriwether Lewis, William Clark, Sacajawea, Zebulon Pike

Questions to Answer

1. How did Justice John Marshall's decisions increase the power of the national government?
2. How did the Louisiana Purchase come about?

A Question to Think About How did the Judiciary Act of 1802 change the system of courts in the nation?

II. Jefferson's Second Term

The voters showed they approved of Jefferson's actions during his first term. In the election of 1804, he and his running mate, George Clinton of New York, received 162 out of 176 electoral votes.

It looked for the moment as though conflict between political parties was at an end. However, Jefferson's second term was full of trouble, and party conflict grew once more.

The Fate of Aaron Burr

Jefferson was pleased to have a Vice President he trusted after four years of Aaron Burr in

that office. After Burr tried to steal the presidency in 1800, Jefferson cut him off from all influence in the government.

By 1804, however, Burr was in the thick of a mysterious plot involving a group of New England Federalists. They wanted to split the northern states from the United States. Their exact plan remains unclear, but it seems Burr was to begin the movement by getting himself elected governor of New York in 1804. Alexander Hamilton worked hard to make sure Burr lost the election.

After his defeat, Burr challenged Hamilton to a duel. Duels, in which two people shoot

The map on this page shows the routes taken by the Lewis and Clark expedition and by Pike when they explored the Louisiana Purchase and the West. Follow the routes carefully to answer the questions.

1. What river did Zebulon Pike explore between 1805 and 1806?

2. In what direction did Louis and Clark travel to reach the source of the Missouri River?
3. (a) In what direction did Pike travel from St. Louis to Sante Fe? (b) What mountains did Pike explore along the way?
4. What river did Pike follow in 1806?
5. How far did Lewis and Clark travel from St. Louis to Fort Mandan?

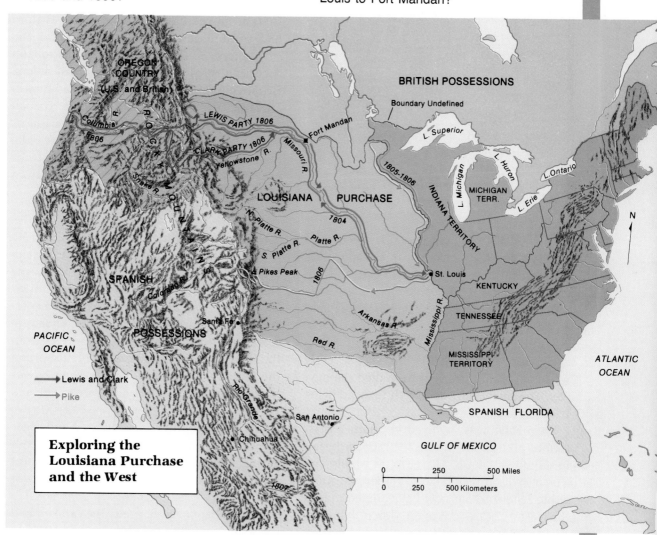

Exploring the Louisiana Purchase and the West

Americans protested impressment by making up songs such as "The American Sailor Boy."

for treason. Burr was saved, however, by John Marshall, who served as judge in Burr's trial. The Constitution said conviction for treason requires a confession or the testimony of two witnesses to an open act of treason. No such evidence was available, Marshall noted. So Burr went free.

▶**1.** How did Alexander Hamilton die?

Trouble with Britain

Meanwhile, the United States and Great Britain moved closer to war. Great Britain had trouble getting enough sailors for the royal navy. So the British continued to stop American ships and seize, or **impress,** sailors. Britain claimed that it only impressed British citizens. However, sometimes the British seized British-born United States citizens or native-born Americans. In any case, the practice was an insult to the nation.

▶**2.** Why did the British impress sailors from United States ships?

at each other following strict rules, were used to settle questions of honor in Europe. They were illegal in many American states. Hamilton did not believe in dueling. Yet he accepted Burr's challenge. The duel was held at Weehawken, New Jersey, on July 11, 1804. Hamilton fired his pistol into the air. However, Burr took careful aim and severely wounded Hamilton. Hamilton died the next day. The shady Burr fled south to avoid being tried for murder.

Soon Burr was involved in another mysterious plot. In the summer of 1806, he began to sail down the Ohio River to the Mississippi River with 60 men. One of the conspirators wrote Jefferson that now Burr wanted to lead the western states out of the Union. Jefferson decided Burr was guilty and had him tried

The Leopard *and the* Chesapeake   Congress protested British impressment of American seamen in 1806. Then, in June 1807, the *Leopard*, a British ship, stopped the United States ship *Chesapeake* inside American territorial waters. The *Leopard* demanded to search the American ship for deserters from the British navy. The *Chesapeake* refused, and the *Leopard* opened fire. The *Chesapeake* was badly damaged, 3 Americans were killed, and 18 wounded.

The entire country was outraged and eager for war. However, the United States was not strong enough to defend itself. Because of Jefferson's budget trimming, the navy was very weak.

▶**3.** What happened between the *Leopard* and the *Chesapeake*?

Exports to France and Britain, 1790-1815

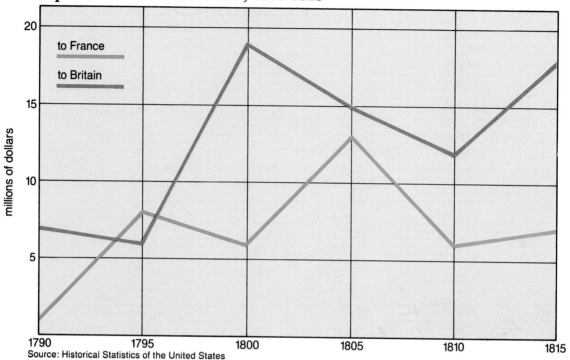

Graph Study In what year was the value of exports the highest? The lowest?

New Restrictions on American Trade

Britain soon began interfering more directly with American trade. First, a British court decided Britain could seize American ships bringing goods to Europe from the French West Indies. Then, in 1807, Britain blockaded France and imposed more restrictions on American ships. Napoleon replied that France would seize neutral ships that obeyed the British restrictions. In other words, American ships carrying goods to Europe were in danger from both France and Britain.

The threat to the American economy was serious. During the long wars in Europe, which had begun in 1793, American ships had taken over much of the shipping between European countries and their American colonies. That trade had brought growth and prosperity to many parts of the country.

▶4. How did Britain and France restrict American trade?

The Embargo In December 1807, Congress, at Jefferson's urging, passed the **Embargo Act.** It outlawed all exports of American goods. It also forbade American ships to trade with foreign nations. Jefferson hoped those measures would force France and Britain to respect American rights.

The Embargo Act did more harm to American trade than anything France or Britain had done. The embargo destroyed the booming businesses of merchants and shippers, who said the law was unconstitutional. A

263

brisk smuggling trade grew, especially by way of Canada. Many smugglers felt there was no harm in ignoring a law that was unconstitutional.

Jefferson and Congress responded with laws to stop the smuggling. Those laws violated many basic civil rights. Jefferson had become so caught up in enforcing the embargo that he brought more trouble to the country than even a war was likely to bring. By 1809, New Englanders were talking about leaving the Union. Opposition to the embargo was so strong that by March 1809, in the last days of his presidency, Jefferson was forced to sign a bill repealing that measure.

"Within a few days I retire to my family, my books and farms," he wrote a friend. "Never did a prisoner, released from his chains, feel such relief as I shall on shaking off the shackles of power."

▶**5.** Why did the Embargo Act cause more trouble for American shippers than Britain and France caused?

Reviewing Section II

Identify impress, *Leopard*, *Chesapeake*, Embargo Act

Questions to Answer
1. How did Britain interfere with the rights of United States citizens?
2. Why did the Embargo Act do so much damage?

A Question to Think About When citizens of the United States think a law is unconstitutional, what can they do legally to remedy the situation?

III. James Madison, President

Despite the unpopularity of Jefferson's embargo, another Republican from Virginia easily followed him into the White House. James Madison won the election of 1808 and became the nation's fourth President. Like Jefferson, Madison hoped to keep the United States out of war. In Madison's administration, the danger of war came not just from Europe but also from Indians in the West.

Tecumseh's Confederation

Many Indians who lived east of the Mississippi River were tired of being pushed off their lands. By 1808, Indians east of the Mississippi River had ceded more than 100 million acres of land to the government of the United States. Sometimes the Indians sold the land for a fair price. More often, the Indians did not understand the terms of the treaties they signed. Sometimes they were deliberately tricked. Now the Indians decided to band together to stop the loss of more land.

Two powerful Shawnee Indians, Tecumseh (tə kum′sə) and his brother Tenskwatawa (ten skwä′tä wä), who was known as The Prophet, led the fight. They tried to bring together in a confederation all the Indians south of the Great Lakes and east of the Mississippi. The confederation was strongest, however, in the Old Northwest.

Against Tecumseh, a brilliant leader, stood the governor of the Indiana Territory, William Henry Harrison. He had little respect for the Indians or their customs, although he recognized Tecumseh's strength as a leader. Harrison was willing to trick or cheat the Indians if he got their land as a result.

In the summer of 1811, Tecumseh went south to try to win the support of the Creek

Tecumseh, a tall, proud Shawnee leader, was born not far from present-day Columbus, Ohio, around the year 1765. As a young boy, he saw his father killed by American colonists. As a young man, he saw American settlers take over the hunting grounds of his ancestors in one treaty after another.

Of all the Indian chiefs, only Tecumseh objected to the treaties. He believed that like the air and the water, the land belonged to everyone. He argued that no single Indian leader had the right to sign peace treaties on behalf of all the Indians.

By 1808, Indians living east of the Mississippi River had given up more than a million acres of land to the United States government. Often the Indians did not understand the treaties they were signing. Often they were tricked or bribed into signing them.

Tecumseh believed that Indians could be strong if they followed the old ways of life and worked together. He believed that only by uniting could the Indians stop the taking of their lands.

Tecumseh wanted to form a confederation of all the Indians south of the Great Lakes and east of the Mississippi. To gain support, he and his brother traveled from their home in Ohio to almost every Indian group east of the Mississippi. Tecumseh used his skill as a speaker to try to convince the Indians to join together. Time and time again he recited from memory the terms of every treaty ever signed and when it had been broken.

William Henry Harrison, governor of the Northwest Territory and Tecumseh's hated enemy, described the great Indian leader this way:

> The obedience and respect that the followers of Tecumseh pay him is really astonishing . . . [He is] one of those uncommon geniuses

that spring up occasionally to produce revolutions and overturn the established order of things . . . If it were not for the vicinity of the United States, he would be the founder of an empire that would rival in glory Mexico or Peru.

In 1811, Tecumseh's cause suffered a bitter setback. In that year, William Henry Harrison marched against a large Indian settlement near Tippecanoe Creek in Indiana. Tecumseh was not there to see the bloody defeat.

A few months later the War of 1812 began. It was then that Tecumseh saw his chance for revenge. The Indian leader joined forces with the British against the Americans. With his help, the British captured Detroit in the first year of the war and stopped the American invasion of Canada.

Tecumseh's success was short-lived. He was killed in battle the next year. Dreams of an Indian confederation ended with his death. The cause of Indian unity had lost its most forceful leader.

Indians. Harrison saw his chance to attack the Indians in Indiana. He marched to a large Indian settlement on the Wabash River near Tippecanoe (tip'ə kə nü') Creek in Indiana. The Prophet led the beseiged Indians, but the Indians lost after a bitter fight on November 7, and Harrison's troops destroyed their town.

The Battle of Tippecanoe made Harrison a hero to many people, but it did not destroy the Indian confederation. In fact, it made relations between Tecumseh and the Americans even worse. If the United States went to war with Great Britain, Tecumseh would clearly take the British side.

▶**1.** What were the results of the Battle of Tippecanoe?

Steps to War

War between the United States and Britain seemed likely, but Madison and Congress still hoped to find a way to prevent it. After repealing the embargo, Congress passed a law in 1809 that allowed Americans to trade with all nations except Great Britain and France. The law, called the **Nonintercourse**, or no trade, **Act** promised to reopen trade with Britain and France as soon as they ended restrictions on American shipping.

▶**2.** What were the provisions of the Nonintercourse Act?

Macon's Bill Number Two In 1810, Congress tried still another variation on the same policy. Macon's Bill Number Two removed all restrictions on trade. However, if either France or Britain decided to honor American rights, the United States promised to impose restrictions on trade with the other country.

Napoleon saw his chance. He announced on November 1, 1810, that he would repeal French restrictions on American shipping. Actually France continued to seize American ships. However, Madison took Napoleon at his word and stopped American trade with Britain in February 1811.

Eventually—on June 23, 1812—Britain also decided to honor American shipping rights, but it was too late. Though the news had not reached Britain, on June 1, 1812, Madison had asked Congress to declare war. By imposing rules for American trade and by impressing United States citizens, Britain was treating the United States as if it were still a British colony. The ability of the Republic to protect its citizens was at issue. Indeed, independence itself seemed to be at stake.

▶**3.** How did Napoleon take advantage of Macon's Bill Number Two?

Congress Votes for War Congress had to vote on Madison's proposal for war. A group of young Republican congressmen including Henry Clay of Kentucky and John C. Calhoun of South Carolina were so eager for war that the Federalists called them **war hawks.** Most of the war hawks represented frontier areas of the nation.

Clay and Calhoun and the other war hawks belonged to a new generation of Americans born during the Revolution. They were outraged by Britain's unwillingness to respect the independence of the United States. They also suspected that the British were behind the nation's troubles with the Indians of the Old Northwest. War, they decided, was the only way to defend the rights and the honor of the United States. They also hoped to drive the British out of Canada and make it part of the United States.

The war hawks had their way, and Congress voted for war. The country was far from united in support of the war, however. All the votes for war were cast by Republicans. Many people, especially Federalists, thought war was unnecessary. New Englanders and people living in cities were concerned about the damage to trade and business that a war would cause. Some people opposed the war because they felt the United States was not strong enough to challenge Britain.

The President's enemies called the conflict Mr. Madison's war. However, they were not strong enough to defeat him in his bid for a second term as President in 1812.

▶4. Why did the war hawks favor war?

The War of 1812

Britain was much better prepared for war than the United States. Britain's army had about 300,000 men; that of the United States had about 11,000. The British navy had over 700 ships, including about 150 large "ships of the line" and the slightly smaller warships called frigates. The American navy had only about 16 or 20 ships and the largest of them were frigates. Considering how much weaker the United States was, it did not do badly.

▶5. How did the United States Army and Navy compare to the British army and navy?

The War at Sea The United States did not have many ships, but three of its frigates—the *Constitution*, the *United States*, and the *President*—were mighty vessels. Once a British shot bounced off the side of the *Constitution*. From then on, the ship was called *Old Ironsides*, though its sides were made of oak.

In ship-to-ship fights, those American frigates did well against the British. For example, the *Constitution* battled the British *Guerriere* (gər ē′ər) off the coast of Maine in August 1812. The cannon of the *Constitution* literally smashed the British ship to pieces.

Map Study *During the War of 1812, how many battles were fought in 1814? Where did they take place? Who won the Battle of Thames?* ▶

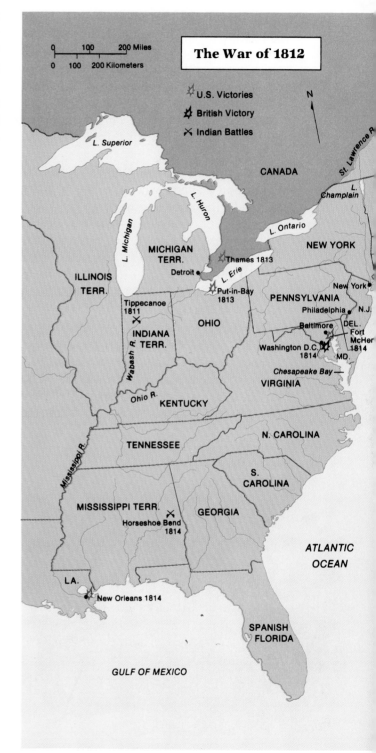

The War of 1812

☆ U.S. Victories
⚔ British Victory
✕ Indian Battles

The naval victories of 1812 did a lot for American pride. They did not, however, contribute much toward winning the war. The navy, in fact, did most for the American cause on the Great Lakes, where it worked closely with land forces.

▶6. What success did the United States frigates have against British ships?

The Campaign against Canada The Great Lakes and Canada were the logical places for the United States to wage war with Britain. In 1812, Americans invaded Canada. However, the invasion was a miserable failure. The British took the American fort at Detroit and several other forts. By the spring of 1813, the British held about half of the Northwest Territory.

The United States Navy, however, had some success on the Great Lakes. First, on September 10, 1813, Captain Oliver Hazard Perry destroyed the British squadron at Put-in-Bay on the northern shore of Lake Erie. Perry, only 28 years old at the time, had volunteered

This lithograph shows portraits of the naval heroes of the Battle of Put-in-Bay, 1813.

for service on the Great Lakes because he could not get a good position on an ocean-going vessel. His report on the battle at Put-in-Bay was simple. "We have met the enemy," he said, "and they are ours." Perry's victory gave the United States control of Lake Erie.

Next, General William Harrison and 3,500 American soldiers forced the British to abandon Fort Detroit and then defeated the British at the Battle of the Thames on the fifth of October. There the great Indian leader Tecumseh died while fighting for the British. Soon after, his Indian confederation fell apart. Having won back what they lost in 1812, the Americans gave up the effort to take Canada.

▶7. What was the outcome of the war in Canada?

The British Invasion In the next phase of the war, the British took the offensive. In the spring of 1814, they at last defeated Napoleon at the Battle of Waterloo. That meant the British could turn their full force against the United States.

The British blockaded most American ports early in the war. Then, in August 1814, they sailed into Chesapeake Bay and landed near Washington, D.C. On the night of August 24, they marched into Washington and burned several public buildings including the Capitol and the White House. President Madison was in Virginia. His wife, Dolley, escaped only minutes before the British arrived, taking a portrait of George Washington and important state papers with her.

The British did not try to hold Washington. Instead, they moved on to attack the city of Baltimore farther up Chesapeake Bay. On September 13, they began firing on Fort McHenry at the entrance to Baltimore's harbor. All that day and night the bombing continued. Luckily, the British ships were too far away to do much damage.

Hyacinthe Laclotte, a member of the Louisiana militia, was an eyewitness to the Battle of New Orleans. He later made this painting of the battle.

One of the witnesses to the bombing was Francis Scott Key, an American who had boarded a ship held by the British to ask for the release of a prisoner. Key was held by the British during the attack on Fort Mc-Henry. He watched the British bombs and rockets through the night. Then, in the morning, he saw the American flag still waving over the fort. Key was so proud that he wrote a poem called "The Star Spangled Banner." It later was set to music and became the national anthem of the United States.

The British were not able to take Fort McHenry. They pulled their ships out of the Chesapeake, and sailed to the West Indies.

▶8. What inspired Francis Scott Key to write "The Star Spangled Banner"?

The War in the Southwest   The last important campaign of the war was in the Old Southwest. There a Tennessee militia captain named Andrew Jackson won a string of memorable victories in 1814. First, he turned against the Creek Indians who were attacking American settlements. The Creek were influenced by Tecumseh and British agents who operated from Florida. Jackson and his militia defeated the Creek Indians in March 1814 at the Battle of Horseshoe Bend in Alabama. Then Jackson forced the Creek to give up about two thirds of their land and to retreat into the southern and western parts of Alabama. Next, Jackson captured the Spanish town at Pensacola, Florida. The British could not use it as a base any longer. Finally, he

269

marched overland to fight the British army at New Orleans.

There the British had brought a strong army from the Caribbean. On December 23, Jackson heard that the enemy was only seven miles away. Quickly he assembled an army of regular soldiers, militia, a unit of free blacks from New Orleans, civilians, and even some pirates. Jackson had his men build a defense line behind piles of dirt and bales of cotton.

The British commmander ordered an open attack on Jackson's troops. Jackson's men, safely under cover, mowed down the attackers. Over 2,000 British but only 8 Americans were killed in the Battle of New Orleans on January 8, 1815.

Finally the Americans had something to celebrate. Jackson became a national hero. His victory came, however, two weeks after the war officially ended, although no one in New Orleans knew it at the time.

During the war, a team of American diplomats had been negotiating with the British. The Americans had little success until the British became alarmed by the American victories on the Great Lakes. On December 24, 1814, they signed a peace treaty.

▶9. Who won the Battle of New Orleans?

The Hartford Convention

While Jackson was winning victories in the Old Southwest, Federalists in New England were trying to figure out other ways of stopping the war. New Englanders had opposed it from the beginning. The embargo and the war had ruined their businesses, they claimed.

In an effort to find a solution to their problems, delegates from several New England states met at a convention in Hartford, Connecticut, from December 15, 1814, to January 5, 1815. The **Hartford Convention,** in its final report, called for a set of constitutional amendments that would protect New England's interests.

When the report of the convention was released, however, the country was celebrating Jackson's victory at New Orleans. As a result, the convention seemed mean-spirited and small-minded. It became a great embarrassment to the Federalist party and to New England politicians for many years.

▶10. What was the Hartford Convention?

The Peace of Ghent

The peace agreements signed at Ghent (gent), in Belgium, on December 24, 1814, ended the War of 1812. The treaty settled none of the issues over which the war was fought. Still, most Americans felt that the United States had won the war. After all, it had lost no territory. Moreover, it had defeated Tecumseh and the western Indians. Above all, American independence had been defended.

Later agreements settled several old conflicts between Britain and the United States. The first, in 1815, removed many obstacles to trade between the two countries. Then, in 1817, the **Rush-Bagot Agreement** said that both Britain and the United States would cut back the number of ships they kept on the Great Lakes. As a result of those and later agreements, the boundary between the United States and Canada is today the longest unfortified boundary in the world.

Another agreement in 1818 set the northwestern boundary of the Louisiana Purchase and provided for joint British and American occupation of the Oregon Country over the next ten years. All those agreements were carried out in a friendly spirit. Bad feelings between Britain and the United States were, it seemed, over at last.

▶11. What agreements did the United States make with Britain in 1817 and 1818?

A New Economic Policy

The war showed how much the country needed a national bank. Without a national bank, the government had trouble financing the war. Also, since the First Bank of the United States closed down in 1811, a jumble of different currencies had circulated through the country. Only counterfeiters, people who print fake money, seemed to benefit from the confusion. So, in 1816, Madison asked Congress to create the Second Bank of the United States. The proposal had few opponents, and Congress passed the needed legislation.

Madison also encouraged Congress to pass a new protective tariff, one that would encourage the growth of manufacturing. He also asked Congress to support internal improvements like roads to tie the parts of the country more closely together. Once the Republic was no longer in danger, even the Republicans, it seemed, were ready to use the government to develop the nation's economy.

▶12. What three economic measures did Madison ask Congress to pass?

Reviewing Section III

Identify Tecumseh, Tenskwatawa, William Henry Harrison, Battle of Tippecanoe, Nonintercourse Act, Macon's Bill Number Two, war hawks, Oliver Hazard Perry, Francis Scott Key, Fort McHenry, Battle of Horseshoe Bend, Battle of New Orleans, Hartford Convention, Rush-Bagot Agreement

Questions to Answer
1. What caused the War of 1812?
2. What were the major battles in the war?

A Question to Think About What did the United States gain from the War of 1812?

IV. The Era of Good Feelings

In 1816, James Monroe easily won the presidential election. Monroe was the third Virginian Republican in a row to be elected President of the United States.

There was so little opposition to Monroe that one Boston newspaper said the country was living in an "Era of Good Feelings." That became the name of the nation's postwar period, which lasted through 1820.

Acquiring Florida

During his administration Monroe added East and West Florida to the United States. By the War of 1812, Spain, which regained title to Florida in 1783, was losing control of the region. As a result, Seminole Indians were able to raid southern Georgia and Alabama from bases in Florida. In 1818, General Andrew Jackson led an army of 3,000 American soldiers and 2,000 Indian allies into Florida to fight the Seminole. Although he found no Seminole to fight, he seized Pensacola and the town of St. Marks on the Gulf of Mexico, threw out the Spanish governor, and raised the American flag over the territory. He also tried and executed two British subjects whom he accused of turning Indians against the United States. Jackson, of course, had no right or authority to do any of those things.

Monroe's secretary of state, John Quincy Adams, managed to use Jackson's victories to advantage in his negotiations with the Spanish minister, Luis de Onis. In 1819, the **Adams-Onis Treaty** gave both East and West Florida to the United States.

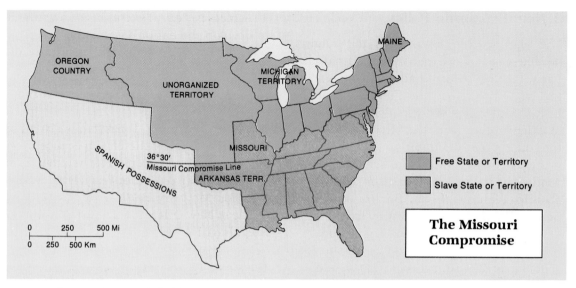

The Missouri Compromise

Free State or Territory

Slave State or Territory

Map Study *At what parallel of latitude was the Missouri Compromise line? Were most of the states above that line free states or slave states?*

The treaty also defined the western boundary of the Louisiana Purchase. It zigzagged from the mouth of the Sabine River on the Gulf of Mexico north along the Red and Arkansas rivers to the 42nd parallel. Then the boundary shifted west all the way to the Pacific. The Adams-Onis Treaty gave the United States a clear boundary that stretched all the way across the North American continent. It also strengthened the claim of the United States to the Oregon Country. Adams had done very well for his country.

▶**1.** What were the boundaries established by the Adams-Onis Treaty?

The Missouri Compromise

About the same time that the Adams-Onis Treaty was signed, a crisis arose over the admission of new states to the Union. Ohio (1803), Louisiana (1812), Indiana (1816), Mississippi (1817), Illinois (1818), and Ala-

bama (1819) had all entered the Union as states. By late 1819, there were 11 free and 11 slave states. Then Missouri asked to be admitted to the Union as a slave state. Northerners objected because it would give the slave states a majority in the Senate.

The issue was resolved by a law proposed by Senator Henry Clay that Congress passed in 1820. The law was known as the **Missouri Compromise.** Under its terms, Congress agreed to admit Missouri to the Union as a slave state and Maine as a free state. In that way, there would still be equal representation of slave and free states in the Senate. Moreover, the compromise defined a line through the Louisiana Territory at 36°30′ north latitude. With the exception of Missouri, all new states north of that line would be free states. New states south of that line could have slaves if their people so chose.

▶**2.** What were the provisions of the Missouri Compromise?

The independence movement in South America began in Venezuela. The people of South America revolted against Spanish rule. Simôn Bolívar, leader of the revolution, dreamed of setting up a republic like the United States that would include all of Spain's colonies in South America.

Between 1810 and 1821, Bolívar led an army in a series of wars against the Spanish. By 1821, his army had defeated the Spanish in Venezuela and the territory of Colombia.

While Bolívar was leading the revolutionary army in the northern part of South America, José de San Martín was leading the revolt in southern South America. San Martín planned to smash Spain's center of power in Peru. To reach Peru, San Martín's army crossed the Andes Mountains from Argentina into Chile and attacked Peru from there. San Martín took the Spanish by surprise and won a great battle. By 1818, San Martín's army had defeated the Spanish in Chile.

The Spanish were still not ready to give up. Bolívar offered to help San Martín. However, they disageed over the steps that should be taken to drive the Spanish from the rest of South America. Rather than divide the independence movement, San Martín resigned. By 1824, Bolívar's army had defeated the Spanish in all of South America.

One by one, the newly freed colonies set up their own governments. The new nations were grateful to the United States when they learned that President Monroe had issued the Monroe Doctrine, warning other nations to leave them in peace.

The Monroe Doctrine

The United States was proud and confident in the 1820's. It was ready to help some of its neighbors in the Western Hemisphere. In the early nineteenth century, revolutionaries rose up throughout Central and South America. They fought against Spanish rule and in time established their own republics. In 1823, the United States became the first country outside of Latin America to recognize officially those new nations.

Then the United States went further. Rumors circulated that various European countries were going to take back former colonies in South America. At the same time, Russia, which had claimed Alaska for some time, extended its claims to much of present-day British Columbia in Canada.

President Monroe believed that the United States should be a leader in world affairs. In his final message to Congress on December 2, 1823, President Monroe announced a new American policy that later became known as the **Monroe Doctrine.** He said that no new colonies could be created in the Americas. He also demanded that European countries stay out of the affairs of newly independent American nations. In return, he promised that the United States would not interfere with any established European colonies in the Western Hemisphere or in the internal affairs of European nations.

273

UNITED STATES

ATLANTIC OCEAN

EMPIRE OF MEXICO

REPUBLIC OF HAITI

CUBA

SANTO DOMINGO

BRITISH
HONDURAS

HONDURAS

JAMAICA

PUERTO
RICO

GUATEMALA

EL SALVADOR

NICARAGUA

COSTA RICA

BRITISH GUIANA

VENEZUELA

DUTCH GUIANA

FRENCH GUIANA

GREATER COLOMBIA

ECUADOR

Boundary Undefined

N

PERU

EMPIRE OF BRAZIL

UPPER PERU
(BOLIVIA,
Independent, 1825)

PACIFIC OCEAN

PARAGUAY

PROVINCES
OF RIO DE
LA PLATA

CHILE

URUGUAY
(Independent, 1828)

Colonies of European Nations

United Provinces of Central America

**New Nations in
Latin America, 1823**

◄ *Map Study*   *Name three European colonies along the northern coast of South America. When did Bolivia become independent?*

Monroe's announcement had little effect at the time. The United States was not yet in a position to defend its brave new policy. However, the Monroe Doctrine was a sign of the nation's self-confidence in the Era of Good Feelings.

►**3.** What were the major provisions of the Monroe Doctrine?

Reviewing Section IV

Identify   Era of Good Feelings, Adams-Onis Treaty, Missouri Compromise, Monroe Doctrine

Questions to Answer
1. What conflict did the Missouri Compromise solve?
2. Why did President Monroe issue the Monroe Doctrine?

A Question to Think About   Why did the Missouri Compromise seem logical at the time it was adopted?

IMPROVE YOUR READING
Cause-Effect and Paraphrasing

You have already learned about cause and effect relationships. A cause is the reason something happens. An effect is something that is produced by the cause.

You probably recognized several cause and effect relationships in this chapter. Parts of some of the cause and effect relationships from the chapter have been paraphrased below. To paraphrase is to say something in a different way.

Your task in this exercise is to complete the statements following. You will find that either the cause or the effect is missing from the statement. The page where the relationship is discussed is provided for you.

1. Since Jefferson did not want to make sudden changes when he became President, he _____ (p. 254)
2. Jefferson did not share Hamilton's desire for a national bank because _____ (p. 254)
3. Because Jefferson believed that a free country should owe nothing to anyone, he _____ (p. 254–255)
4. Republicans tried to impeach Supreme Court Justice Samuel Chase because _____ (p. 256)
5. Chief Justice Marshall said that Maryland could not tax the Second Bank of the United States because _____ (p. 257)
6. Because France needed money and the Louisiana Territory was difficult to defend, Napoleon _____ (p. 257)
7. Indian groups felt members of the Lewis and Clark expedition came in peace because _____ (p. 259)
8. The British impressed American soldiers in 1806 because _____ (p. 262)
9. The *Constitution* was given the nickname *Old Ironsides* because _____ (p. 267)
10. As a result of the Battle of New Orleans, _____ (p. 270)

CHAPTER 13 REVIEW

Vocabulary Check
Match each of the events in column I with the phrase that explains it in column II.

Column I
1. Embargo Act
2. Hartford Convention
3. Adams-Onis Treaty
4. Missouri Compromise
5. Monroe Doctrine

Column II
a. Agreement by which the United States gained both East and West Florida
b. Meeting of delegates from several New England states
c. Agreement by which the number of free and slaves states was kept equal
d. Law forbidding all exports of American goods
e. Statement warning European countries to stay out of the affairs of the newly independent American nations

Fact Check
On a separate sheet of paper, write the name of the person described in each phrase below.

1. President who appointed the midnight judges
2. Chief Justice of the Supreme Court who greatly strengthened the court
3. President who purchased the Louisiana Territory from France
4. Leaders of the expedition between the Missouri River and the Pacific Ocean
5. Explorer of the land between the Arkansas and the Red rivers
6. President who urged Congress to pass the Embargo Act
7. Indian leaders who brought many Indian groups in the Old Northwest into a confederation
8. Leaders of the war hawks
9. Author of "The Star Spangled Banner"
10. President who added East and West Florida to the United States

Time Check
On a separate sheet of paper, put the following events in chronological order.

1. Americans win the war against Tripoli.
2. The United States buys Louisiana.
3. Monroe issues the Monroe Doctrine.
4. President Madison asks Congress to declare war on Great Britain.
5. Congress passes the Embargo Act.

Skills Check
Use the map on page 261 to answer the following questions.

1. What rivers did Lewis and Clark travel on to reach the Pacific Ocean?
2. Who explored the Yellowstone River?
3. In which direction is Santa Fe from St. Louis?
4. (a) When did Lewis and Clark begin their expedition? (b) When did Clark return?
5. Name the four cities shown on Pike's route.

Think and Write
1. How did Jefferson's desire to save money help draw the United States into war?
2. What power did Chief Justice Marshall's decision in *Marbury* v. *Madison* establish?
3. Why did President Madison ask Congress to declare war on Great Britian?
4. Why did Tecumseh try to unite the Indians of the Old Northwest?
5. Why was the Monroe Doctrine issued?

REVIEWING UNIT 4

Reviewing the Facts I.

On a separate sheet of paper, write the name of the person described in each of the phrases below.

1. Second President of the United States
2. Indian leader who defeated General Joseph Harmar in the 1790's
3. Oldest delegate at the Constitutional Convention
4. President who did not consider himself a member of a political party
5. First secretary of the treasury
6. Secretary of state who supported the French Revolution
7. American minister to Spain who negotiated the treaty giving Americans use of the Mississippi River
8. President who asked Congress to declare war on Britain in 1812
9. John Adams's appointee as Chief Justice of the Supreme Court
10. President who warned European countries to stay out of the affairs of the newly independent American nations

Reviewing the Facts II.

On a separate sheet of paper, fill in the word or words that best complete each of the following sentences.

1. The three branches of government are the ____, ____, and ____ branches.
2. The ____ explained how the lands north of the Ohio River to the Mississippi would be governed.
3. People in a ____ participate in government by voting for representatives who run the government.
4. The ____ is the supreme law of the land.
5. The ____ clause of the Constitution allows Congress to do what is "necessary and proper" to carry out its other rights and duties.
6. Hamilton belonged to the ____ Party. Jefferson belonged to the ____ Party.
7. ____ was the first case in which the Supreme Court declared that a law was unconstitutional.
8. President Jefferson purchased ____ from France and gave Westerners use of the ____ River.
9. The British burned many buildings in Washington, D.C., during the ____.
10. By the ____ Treaty, the United States gained East and West Florida from Spain.

Reviewing Ideas

1. Describe some of the weaknesses of the Articles of Confederation.
2. Explain what is meant by the concept of balanced government.
3. What is meant by a federal system of government?
4. Explain what is meant by loose construction and strict construction of the Constitution.
5. Why did the United States and Great Britain go to war again in 1812?

UNIT FIVE

The New Nation Grows and Changes

The first half of the nineteenth century was a time of tremendous growth. From the original 13 states along the Atlantic coast, the nation had expanded to the Pacific Ocean. Inventions and new means of transportation, such as the Chesapeake and Ohio Canal shown here, brought great changes to the way Americans lived and worked.

Chapter 14

A Time of Growth

This lithograph of Lowell, Massachusetts, in 1834 shows the spread of mills along the Merrimack River, where 11 years before there had only been farms.

The United States was a much bigger country in 1826 than it had been 50 years earlier when it declared its independence. Eleven new states had been added to the original thirteen. The small nation of the Revolutionary Era, nestled between the Atlantic Ocean and the Mississippi River, now stretched all the way to the Rockies. The 2.5 million citizens of the United States in 1776 had grown to 11.5 million by 1826. There were also impressive changes in the American economy, that is, in the ways Americans supported themselves and in the amount of wealth they had.

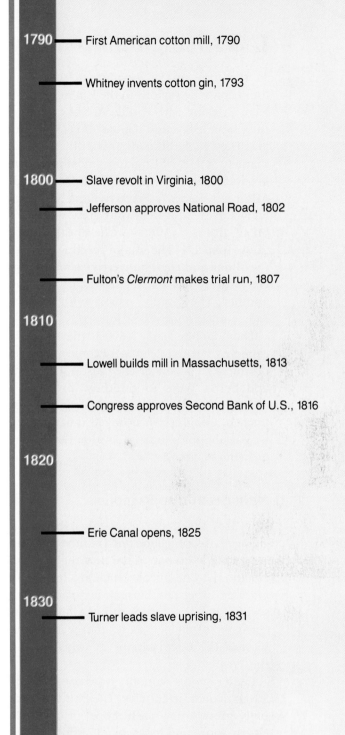

1790 — First American cotton mill, 1790

Whitney invents cotton gin, 1793

1800 — Slave revolt in Virginia, 1800

Jefferson approves National Road, 1802

Fulton's *Clermont* makes trial run, 1807

1810

Lowell builds mill in Massachusetts, 1813

Congress approves Second Bank of U.S., 1816

1820

Erie Canal opens, 1825

1830

Turner leads slave uprising, 1831

1840

I. A Changing Economy

At the time of the Revolution, there were four economic regions in the United States— New England, the Middle Atlantic colonies, the Chesapeake, and the Carolinas and Georgia. They each differed in what they grew or made to sell. New England's most important products were ships and fish. The Middle Atlantic colonies of Pennsylvania, New York, New Jersey, and Delaware grew wheat and other grains, while the Chesapeake region grew tobacco. The major products of the Carolinas and Georgia were rice and indigo. Only rarely did the regions trade with one another. They traded mostly with the West Indies and countries in Europe.

Then, in the early 1800's, the American economy began to change. People found new products to produce. They also found faster and better ways to get those products to market. New, larger economic regions were formed. Congress encouraged those changes by passing laws to help develop the nation's growing economy.

family-size farms where farmers grew a variety of agricultural products. These new economic regions, unlike the older ones, traded with one another.

Why did the economy of the United States change? The Revolution was partly responsible. The war took the United States out of the British economic system. That forced Americans to find other ways to get the products they needed. As new opportunities arose, Americans found many different ways to take advantage of them.

The economic changes of the 1800's added to Americans' wealth and changed their way of life. Those changes moved Americans toward a newer, richer world of store-bought food and factory-made clothes. Also, because the United States is a republic in which power rests with the people, the massive changes in American life had a powerful effect on American politics.

▶**1.** What new economic regions were formed in the early 1800's?

New Economic Regions

By 1826, the major economic regions had changed. New England and the other northern states made up one of the new regions—the North. The Chesapeake, the Carolinas, Georgia, and other southern states made up the second region—the South. A third region consisted of the new states that were formed west of the Appalachians. It was known as the West.

Each region's economy was based on a different economic activity. The South increasingly grew a new cash crop, cotton. In the North, more and more people were involved in manufacturing, especially of cloth made from southern cotton. The West had many

The American System

President James Madison was eager to encourage the growing and changing economy. Therefore, he adopted economic policies that were similiar to the earlier policies of Alexander Hamilton. By 1816, such policies no longer seemed so dangerous to him as they had in the 1790's.

Madison asked Congress to set up a new national bank. Congress approved a charter for the Second Bank of the United States in 1816. Madison also asked Congress to approve a **protective tariff,** a tax on goods coming into the country. It was to protect new industries in the United States from foreign competition. He hoped that measure would encourage the growth of manufacturing. Congress agreed. It passed a protective tariff in 1816.

Madison also asked Congress to pay for roads that would link together different parts of the country. In supporting such internal improvements, Madison followed an example set earlier by Thomas Jefferson. In 1802, Jefferson as President had signed a law for the building of a "National Road" from Cumberland, Maryland, across the Appalachians to Wheeling, Virginia.

Senator Henry Clay of Kentucky later called the government's program of a national bank, a protective tariff, and internal improvements the **American System.** Those measures, he thought, would strengthen the Union by tying the nation's sections more closely together.
▶**2.** What was the American System?

Reviewing Section I

Identify protective tariff, American System

Questions to Answer
1. Name the new economic regions and tell what each produced.

Residents of New York City could shop at Leonard Bond's Hat Store on Chatham Street.

2. How did the government encourage the growth of new industries?

A Question to Think About Why did Madison find Hamilton's economic policies less dangerous in 1816 than in the 1790's?

II. The South

The American Revolution forced the South to change. During the colonial period, the plantations in the Chesapeake, the Carolinas, and Georgia sold their products directly to Britain. But after independence, Britain was no longer so willing to buy American products. Nor were other European countries interested in increasing their purchases. Sales of tobacco, which made up one third of all American exports in the late colonial period, did not grow at all after the Revolution. Exports of rice, which had made many South Carolinians rich in the mid-eighteenth century, actually went down between 1770 and the early 1790's. Clearly, the southern economy was in trouble. Southerners needed a new product to sell.

The Lure of Cotton

There was, as Southerners knew, a growing demand for cotton. The demand came especially from Britain. There several new **technological developments,** improvements in the mechanical tools people use, had led to great growth in manufacturing. No industry was more affected than the **textile,** or cloth, industry. Some of the new inventions made it possible to make cloth entirely of cotton for the first time. Before the new machines, cotton yarn broke easily so it had to be combined with linen to make cloth.

The new machines caused great social changes. Before their invention, people spun and wove cloth in their homes. The machines, however, were big and heavy. Also, they were driven by water power. So mills began to appear in Britain, where people wove thousands of yards of cotton cloth using powerful looms and other recent inventions.

Eli Whitney received a patent for his cotton gin on March 14, 1794.

The demand for cotton skyrocketed. Yet British farmers could not grow the crop. Their country was too cold for cotton plants. As a result, British factory owners bought ever increasing amounts of cotton from other countries: 2.5 million pounds in 1760, 22 million pounds in 1787, and 366 million pounds 50 years later in 1837.

▶**1.** What caused cotton to become an important crop in the 1800's?

The Cotton Gin Much of the American South was warm enough to grow cotton. In fact, Americans grew some cotton for export on the Sea Islands off the coast of South Carolina and Georgia. There farmers could grow long-staple cotton, cotton whose fiber, or staple, was long and from which the seeds were relatively easy to remove. However, long-staple cotton did not grow well in other parts of the South. Farmers in those sections could grow only short-staple cotton, which had sticky seeds that were very difficult to remove. If only someone could figure out how to get the seeds out of short-staple cotton, the South would have a valuable new cash crop.

Eli Whitney, a Connecticut inventor, did just that. He learned about the problem on a visit to Georgia. By 1793, he had constructed a machine called a **cotton gin.** With it, one person could turn out 50 pounds of cleaned cotton a day from the short-staple plants.

▶**2.** How did Eli Whitney make the production of short-staple cotton profitable?

The Spread of Cotton The cotton gin transformed the southern economy. Throughout Georgia and large parts of South Carolina, Southerners began to grow cotton. Gradually, cotton plantations spread farther west to the rich lands in what became the new states of Alabama, Mississippi, Louisiana, and Arkansas and to parts of Florida. The population

During the last half of the eighteenth century, Great Britain's economy went through a period of rapid and dramatic change. The change affected not only the kinds of goods that were produced but also how and where they were produced. Those changes came about so quickly and so altered the lives and the work of the people that they created an Industrial Revolution.

The Industrial Revolution refers to the changes that took place in the way goods were produced. Before the revolution, most goods were produced by hand at home. After the revolution, most goods were produced in factories by power-driven machines.

The Industrial Revolution was made possible because of four great inventions. In 1765, James Hargreaves built a mechanical spinning wheel for making cotton thread, called the spinning jenny. In 1768, Richard Arkwright invented a spinning machine called the water frame. It made a much stronger thread. Then, between 1774 and 1779, Samuel Crompton invented the spinning mule. It combined features of both the spinning jenny and the water frame. Both Arkwright's and Crompton's machines required more power than horses or water wheels could produce. In 1785, James Watt invented a steam engine that was powerful enough to drive the new machines.

The new inventions and the growth of factories led to a new way of life for people in Great Britain. Before long, the Industrial Revolution spread to the United States and other countries around the world as well. As a result, great changes also took place in those countries.

of those new states grew dramatically. There were only 371,125 people in those five states in 1820. By 1850, there were over two million, and by 1860, over three million people lived there. By then, cotton planters were also pushing into Texas. Meanwhile, American production of cotton went from 3,000 bales in 1790 to 4,500,000 bales in 1860.

▶**3.** How did the cotton gin stimulate the growth of new southern states?

The Problems Cotton Brought

Cotton answered the South's need for a product it could sell. However, the massive spread of cotton plantations brought other problems to the South. For one thing, Southerners became dependent on one crop. In parts of the upper South, farmers still grew wheat and tobacco for export. Rice and sugar were still grown in certain areas along the coast of South Carolina, Georgia, and Louisiana. But everywhere else, cotton was "king." That is, it became by far the South's major product. As a result, the welfare of the South was tied, by and large, to cotton prices.

▶**4.** What problem was created by the growing importance of cotton in the South?

Supply and Demand The price of cotton went up and down. That was in part because every time prices went up Southerners pushed west, opening up new farming areas. It took a while for them to get set up, put in their crop, harvest it, and send their cotton to market. As more and more cotton reached the market, planters often found that they had produced more cotton than manufacturers were willing to buy. Whenever **supply** is greater than **demand**—that is, when there is more of some product offered for sale than buyers are ready to take—prices fall.

Cotton prices stayed low until textile manufacturing grew enough to handle all of the cotton that came from the areas under cultivation in the South. Then prices went up again. As they rose, more people decided to push to new lands where cotton could be grown, and the whole process started over again. The rise and fall of cotton prices caused Southerners much grief.

5. Explain how supply and demand for cotton affected cotton prices.

The Old South The expansion of cotton growing had sad effects on the older southern states, whose fields had often been growing crops for over 100 years. Planters often decided not to go to the expense of fertilizing their fields or shifting crops to keep the soil fertile. Many found it cheaper to move to the rich, unused soil in the West. As a result, the population of states in the Old South did not grow as rapidly as that of the rest of the country.

▶**6.** What effect did the expansion of cotton production have on the older southern states?

Cotton and Slavery

The expansion of cotton also tied the South ever more tightly to the institution of slavery. At the time of the Revolution, when the northern states began to end slavery, many Southerners assumed that, in time, slavery would die out in the South too. But cotton gave the South a new reason for keeping its slaves. Indeed, the demand for slaves increased as new lands were opened in the Old Southwest. Yet the supply was limited. In 1808, Congress ended the slave trade. No new slaves could be imported. As a result, the price of slaves tripled between 1820 and 1860. In short, too much money was involved for planters to give up their slaves easily. By 1850, there were 3 million black Americans in the country. Six out of seven of them were slaves.

▶**7.** Why did the price of slaves increase so rapidly between 1820 and 1860?

The Great Migration The expansion of cotton growing and of slavery into the new states of the Old Southwest caused a crisis of the first order for American slaves. Planters there had to buy slaves from older slaveholding states, since they could no longer import slaves from Africa or the West Indies. Between 1810 and 1860, well over two million blacks were forced to move from North Carolina and the Chesapeake, areas which were not well suited for growing cotton, to the newer slaveholding states along the Gulf of Mexico and the Mississippi River.

That great migration separated husbands from wives, children from parents. The slaves paid a terrible price in human pain for profits that went, in the end, to other Americans.

▶**8.** How did the expansion of cotton growing to the Old Southwest affect slaves?

The Lives of Slaves Whether slaves moved to the Old Southwest or stayed in the South, life was difficult for them. Their way of life differed somewhat depending on where they lived. Slaves living in the city had more freedom than those living in the country. Though most city slaves worked as household servants or as common laborers, slaves could also be found doing almost any kind of work, skilled or unskilled, that had to be done. Sometimes owners hired out their slaves to work for others. In fact, not all blacks in cities were slaves. New Orleans, for example, had a large community of free blacks.

The lives of slaves in the rural areas differed if they lived on small farms or on large plantations. Slaves on small farms often

This sculpture (left) was made by a slave in the 1800's. Because iron was so costly and the time needed to make the statue so great, it was probably made secretly. The sketch by Lewis Miller (top) shows slaves working in Virginia.

worked side by side with their owners. That was not true on large plantations, where slaves usually worked with other slaves. The owners of large plantations wanted to make their plantations as **self-sufficient** as possible. That is, they tried to produce what they needed on their own plantations. As a result, slaves not only grew cotton but also food for themselves and their owners. Some slaves learned to be blacksmiths or to do other skilled tasks.

Wherever they lived, slaves were restricted by laws that were much like those of the 1700's (see page 133). In fact, as time went on, slave laws became harsher in some ways. In the 1800's, for example, some states made it illegal to teach slaves to read.

▶**9.** How was the life of slaves living in cities different from the life of slaves in rural areas?

Owning Slaves In spite of the South's growing dependency on slave labor, two thirds of all white southern families had no slaves. Those that had slaves did not always have very many. Over half of the southern slave owners had fewer than five slaves. Only 1 in about 8 southern slave owners had 20 or more slaves. In short, big plantations were rare. But the owners of these plantations had the most power in the Old South.

▶**10.** What percentage of the people in the South owned slaves?

Slave Revolts All southern whites, whether or not they owned slaves, were afraid of slave uprisings. Several actual uprisings fed their fears. In August 1800, over 1,000 slaves met outside Richmond, Virginia and began to march on the city before being stopped. A

287

series of other plots followed in Virginia and the Carolinas.

In 1831, the most famous slave revolt occurred in Southampton County, Virginia. A black slave named Nat Turner and his followers killed 60 whites before the uprising was put down.

▶11. Why were most Southerners afraid of slave uprisings?

Other Effects of Slavery   The existence of a large slave labor force had other consequences. For one thing, the slave system discouraged **urbanization,** the development of towns and cities.

Towns and cities are usually centers for buying and selling. However, almost all of the South's slaves lived outside the **market economy.** That is, they were removed from the world of trade. What they grew belonged to other people, and they did not earn wages for their labor. Profits from the cotton trade went mostly to a few great planters who could send away for whatever goods they wanted.

Cities also develop as processing centers, where the raw materials grown or mined nearby are prepared for sale. However, since cotton could be ginned right on the plantations, the South did not need processing centers for cotton. Richmond, Virginia, did develop as a processing center for tobacco and for iron that was mined nearby.

Richmond, however, was very unusual. Most of the South's cities, such as New Orleans, Mobile, Savannah, Charleston, and Baltimore, were sea or river ports that served as shipping centers. Of those cities, only New Orleans grew rapidly in the early 1800's.

Slavery also helped keep the South from developing a school system. Rich planters did not see a need for local schools. They hired tutors for their own children or sent them away to private schools. Certainly they saw no reason to educate slaves. In fact, owners did not want their slaves to learn how to read. Reading could open a whole new world of ideas to slaves that would be dangerous to slave owners.

Poor white Southerners were especially hurt by the lack of schools. In 1840, the percentage of white people who could neither read nor write was over three times higher in the slave states than in the free states.

▶12. What negative effects did slavery have on the South?

Reviewing Section II

Identify   technological developments, textile, Eli Whitney, cotton gin, supply, demand, self-sufficient, Nat Turner, urbanization, market economy

Questions to Answer
1. What made cotton a profitable cash crop in the 1800's?
2. What problems did cotton cause for the South?

A Question to Think About   How might the economy of the South have been different if Whitney had not invented the cotton gin?

III. The North

The American Revolution also forced the North to change. Its markets were disrupted like those of the South. People in New England and the Middle Colonies had sold fish, grain, and other food to the British West Indies. Now that trade was entirely cut off. So in the 1780's, northern merchants began to develop new markets. Their greatest opportunity came, however, because of European wars from 1793 to 1814.

Thomas Hornor drew this busy scene of New York City in 1836. It shows the variety of shops that catered to the needs of the city's growing population.

The Carrying Trade

Countries at war could not easily send out ships to bring goods like sugar, coffee, cocoa, and spices to Europe from the Americas. However, the United States was neutral. So American ships took over that trade.

The profits of the carrying trade were so great that the cities of the North began to grow dramatically. Between 1790 and 1810, the population of Boston went from about 18,000 to 33,000. Philadelphia grew from about 42,500 to nearly 92,000, and New York almost tripled in size, increasing its population from about 33,000 to 96,000. The growth of American commerce also led to the growth of banks, insurance companies, and other businesses that served the shippers.

Then what looked like disaster struck the growing shipping industry. After Britain and France refused to allow American ships to sail freely, Jefferson issued an embargo that held American ships in port. The British blockade during the War of 1812 had the same effect. Traders with money in hand could not use that money to outfit their ships for new voyages.

Some such traders decided instead to make some of the goods that Americans could not get from Europe because of the embargo, or later, the blockade. For the moment, those American products had a **protected market.** That is, they did not have to compete with European manufacturers.

Americans made cloth because they could easily get cotton from the South and because cloth was something they could readily sell. The number of American cotton mills, most of which were in the North, grew rapidly after 1808. Some of the new mills went out of business once the War of 1812 ended. Others found they could hold out against the competition of European textiles. Congress helped them by passing protective tariffs. Because they added to the cost of imported goods, the tariffs made it easier for American manufacturers to compete with the foreign-made goods that came into the country.

▶**1.** How did the growth of the carrying trade in the North affect other businesses there?

Early Factories

Americans had long been interested in the wonderful devices the British had developed for spinning thread and weaving cloth. Moses Brown, a Rhode Island businessman, was the first American to build a factory like those in Britain. He put up a cotton mill in Pawtucket, Rhode Island, in 1790. It had a ma-

This nineteenth-century print shows workers making cotton cloth in a textile mill.

chine for spinning thread just like those in Britain. Samuel Slater, a British immigrant, had built the machine from memory.

Only thread was made in the Pawtucket factory. Brown then gave the thread to people who wove cloth from it in their homes. That was known as the **putting-out system.**

Later, mills combined the spinning of thread with the weaving of cloth. That was true at the new mill constructed in 1813 at Waltham, Massachusetts, by Francis Cabot Lowell and a group of people known as the Boston Associates. The Waltham mill used both modern spinning machines and power looms to produce cheap, rough cloth that had many uses. The mill was very successful. Sales rose from $3,000 to $300,000 a year between 1814 and 1823. The investors in the mill made a fine profit of 20 percent.

The number of mills increased, at first slowly and then more rapidly, in the 1820's and 1830's. Cotton mills and other factories were founded not just in New England but in New York and, to some extent, in Pennsylvania.

▶**2.** How did the cotton mill built by Francis Lowell differ from the one built by Moses Brown?

The Lowell Experiment Who worked in the mills? Brown and Slater used lots of children. Their first mill had a work force of seven boys and two girls, all between seven and twelve years old. Later, as more mills opened, owners sometimes put entire families to work, especially families with many children.

Francis Lowell had another idea. He decided to use young New England farm women in his mill. They could work for a few years and then leave to marry and raise families. In that way, Lowell hoped to avoid creating a class of poor people such as those who worked in the ugly mills of English cities.

By 1823, the Boston Associates had built a model factory town at Lowell, Massachusetts, 27 miles from Boston. By 1850, it had become the leading textile center in the United States.

To attract young women workers and to reassure their parents, the factory owners provided safe living quarters. At Lowell, the factory girls lived together in boarding houses under the watchful eyes of older women. The girls worked 12 hours a day, 6 days a week. Activities were provided for the rest of their waking hours. They had to attend religious services. Evening lectures and other cultural events were also available. The girls even had their own newspapers, of which the most famous was the *Lowell Offering*.

To be a mill girl was a fine thing—at the beginning of the factory system. The girls had a chance to make a little money on their own and to be independent for a few years. Women had long made cloth at home for their families, so mill work was not altogether different from their traditional tasks. Long as the factory hours were, some of the girls wrote that they had never known such ease.

Every effort was made to keep the town of Lowell healthy and handsome. Small gardens and potted plants brightened the factory complex and helped it blend in with the New England countryside. Visitors, often from abroad, traveled to Lowell regularly in the 1830's. Many could not get over how attractive it was compared to European industrial cities.
▶**3.** What was life like for the mill workers in Lowell?

Lowell Changes With time, however, conditions at Lowell changed. As competition became keener, owners and overseers made the women work harder and faster. When owners cut wages in 1834 and 1836, the women workers went on strike.

In the 1840's, the women workers organized and sent petitions to the state legislature. They wanted a law limiting the workday in Massachusetts factories. One of their popular songs went like this:

> But if I still must wend my way,
> Uncheered by hope's sweet song,
> God grant that, in the mills, the day
> May be but ten hours long.

The effort for a ten-hour day was not successful, but it was important anyway. When the Lowell women became involved in public affairs, they broke with traditional women's roles in a daring way.

Some mill owners grumbled about that break with tradition. They decided that New England women were a troublesome lot. Also, as the number of mills at Lowell grew, there were not enough New England-born women willing to go there and work. Gradually, the owners turned to poor Irish immigrants. They hired whole families. Those families lived in shacks, not boarding houses. Lowell was becoming like the factory towns of Britain.
▶**4.** How did conditions in Lowell change?

The Spread of Industry

The growth of the textile industry led to the development of other industries. A whole new machinery industry, for example, grew out of the textile industry. It supplied machines to mills and to other factories.

Other industries developed in similar ways. The clothing industry grew, especially after the mid-1840's when Elias Howe, Jr., who once worked in a Lowell machine factory, invented the sewing machine. Shoes, clocks, and guns were also increasingly produced in factories.

5. What new industries were started as a result of the textile industry?

Lucy Larcom

Lucy Larcom, mill worker and author, was born in Beverly, Massachusetts, on May 25, 1824. Her youth was spent in "a happy home, with stories of the ocean echoing around the fireside . . ."

In 1835, when Lucy was eleven, her merchant father died, leaving the family almost penniless. Shortly afterward Mrs. Larcom moved with some of her younger children to Lowell, Massachusetts. There she had been hired as a supervisor of a dormitory that housed mill girls.

It wasn't long before Lucy herself became a mill girl. In an article entitled "Among Lowell Mill Girls" that appeared in 1881 in *The Atlantic Monthly*, she wrote:

Work began at five o'clock on summer mornings, and at daylight in the winter. Breakfast was eaten by lamplight during the cold weather; in summer, an interval of half an hour was allowed for it, between seven and eight o'clock. The time given for the noon meal was from a half to three quarters of an hour. The only hours of leisure were from half past seven or eight to ten in the evening . . .

During those two evening hours, when it was too cold for the girls to sit in their rooms, the dining-room was used as a sitting-room, where they gathered around the tables, and sewed, and read, and wrote, and studied. It seems a wonder, to look back upon it, how they accomplished so much as they did in their limited allowance of time. They made and mended their own clothing . . . They . . . took books from the libraries, went to singing-schools, meetings, concerts, and lectures, watched at night by a sick girl's bedside, and did double work for her in the mill, if necessary. And on Sundays they were at church, not differing in appearance from other young women. Strangers who had been sitting beside them in a house of worship were often heard to ask, on coming out, "But where were the factory-girls?"

Lucy Larcom's writings reflect the pride she felt in being a mill girl. In her own words, the important thing was "to keep the surroundings of any community thus formed free from all that could be harmful to personal character, and leave it open in every direction to pure and healthful influences." It was Lucy's belief that the Lowell of the late 1830's and 1840's measured up to these standards.

In 1846, after working in the mills for ten years, Lucy Larcom left Lowell. The later years of her life were spent attending college, teaching, and writing. She died in 1893 at the age of 69.

Power Sources The early mills were powered by water. The first factories were always built by a swift-moving river. The rivers were used to turn the factory's water wheels, which in turn operated its machines. Later, Americans used steam power. Steam is produced by bringing water to the boiling point. The steam is then used to provide the power to run machines. Steam power allowed owners to build their factories anywhere.

▶**6.** What source of power was used to run the machines in the early mills?

Machines The use of power machines enabled Americans to lower the cost of producing goods. Workers in the United States had always earned more than workers in other countries. So the high cost of labor in the United States had always hampered American manufacturing. Now workers using machines could produce much more in less time than those who did their work by hand. Since workers were paid by the hour, labor costs went down. Also the cost of paying machine workers was spread over a much larger quantity of goods.

▶**7.** How did the use of machines help to lower of the cost of factory-made goods?

Interchangeable Parts The growth of new American industries also involved the development of a system of **interchangeable parts.** That is, some manufactured articles such as guns or clocks were made up of parts so alike in size and shape that they could be interchanged, or used in place of each other. With such a system, some workers could make one part, others another part. Then, in the end, all the different parts could easily and quickly be assembled, or put together.

The use of interchangeable parts had several results. It speeded up the manufacturing process. It also allowed manufacturers to hire unskilled workers to do limited, simple tasks. Factory owners benefited from this because they paid unskilled workers much lower wages than skilled laborers.

Legend has it that Eli Whitney invented the system of interchangeable parts when he made guns for the United States government in the 1790's. Evidence suggests, however, that the system may have begun earlier in Sweden and France.

The first Americans to use interchangeable parts were gun makers. The government armory at Harpers Ferry, Virginia, seems to have been making guns with interchangeable parts by about 1820. Whitney's plant at New Haven, Connecticut, used a lot of modern equipment but not a system of interchangeable parts. How can we be sure? Some people have tried taking apart the guns Whitney made. The parts of one gun cannot be easily used on another.

That the system of interchangeable parts began in Europe is not strange. Most of the machines Americans used had been invented in Europe. Then Americans changed them to suit their needs. Above all, they tried to find more ways to cut labor costs. They developed, for example, machines that would feed strands of fiber to spinning machinery automatically, without the help of people. Americans went so far in the use of power-driven machines and interchangeable parts to cut back labor costs that by the 1850's, those techniques were known to the world as the **American System of Manufacturing.**

▶**8.** Why were manufacturers so willing to use interchangeable parts?

A Growing Market

Large-scale manufacturing could grow in the United States because there were enough people to buy the goods factories turned out.

The country's population increased over eight times between 1790 and 1860, going from 3.9 million to 31.5 million. The size of American families began to decline in the 1800's. Still, families had enough children to keep the population growing. Immigrants also added to the population.

The Irish came in great numbers after their potato crops failed during the 1840's. They were joined by Germans who arrived in the 1830's and 1840's. The Germans came with more money and skills than the Irish. German immigrants tended to become farmers, artisans, or shopkeepers rather than factory workers. Because they had money, the Germans could go west. The Irish, on the other hand, stayed in the eastern cities where they first landed. Other immigrants came from Britain. They, too, were generally professional people or skilled workers. By 1860, over a quarter of all the free, white adult men in the United States were immigrants.

▶9. What caused the population of the United States to increase so rapidly in the 1830's and 1840's?

Ferdinand Reichardt made this painting of steamboats on the upper Mississippi River in 1857.

The Transportation Revolution

Factory owners faced one big problem in making the growing population consumers for American-made goods. Americans were spread over a large area. Already by 1840, over a third of the people in the United States lived beyond the Appalachians. How could goods be brought to them?

▶10. What problem did factory owners face as Americans continued to move west?

Roads Americans built roads through the mountains in the early 1800's. The most famous of those was the **National Road,** or Cumberland Road. The national government helped to build it. It began at Cumberland, Maryland, and went through the mountains of southern Pennsylvania and on to what is today Wheeling, West Virginia. Eventually, it went all the way to Vandalia, Illinois.

▶11. What important road did the government help build in the 1800's?

Steamboats Some goods could be shipped along the Atlantic coast, then up the Mississippi River to the West. It was, however, difficult to travel upstream until the development of the steamboat. James Watt, a Scot, built the first steam engine in the 1760's. It was more than 40 years later before someone found a way to use it to power a boat.

In 1807, Robert Fulton, an artist, designed the first practical steamboat, which he called the *Clermont*. Others called it Fulton's Folly. However, Fulton had the last laugh when his boat successfully sailed up the Hudson River from New York City to Albany.

Four years later, in 1811, Nicholas Roosevelt, who had worked with Fulton, built the *New Orleans* at Pittsburgh. The trip from there to New Orleans used to take four to six weeks. With the steamboat, it took only two weeks. Soon steamboats began sailing

Bar graphs are very similar to line graphs. To read a bar graph, first look at the title and key to see what the graph is about. Then look at the horizontal axis and the vertical axis to see what years the graph covers and what numbers each segment of the bar represents.

There are some things you should check when looking at a bar graph to be sure it is not distorted. The bars should be the same width so that one does not appear larger than another. The divisions on the horizontal and vertical axes should be consistent.

Study the graph and then answer the questions which follow.

1. What is the title of the graph?
2. What years are covered in the graph?
3. In what year shown was Irish immigration highest?
4. In what year shown was German immigration highest?
5. Is the average number of immigrants higher in the years shown for Irish or German immigrants?

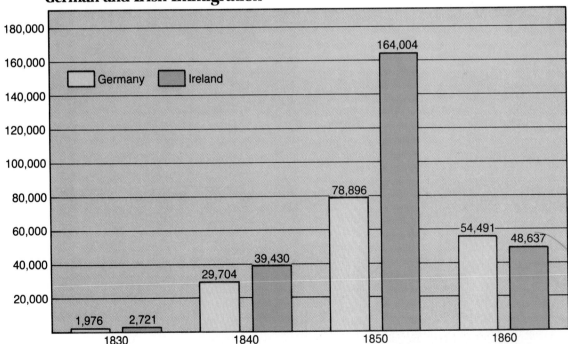

German and Irish Immigration

Source: Historical Statistics of the United States

up the Mississippi in record time. By the 1840's, there were over 500 steamboats working on that great river.

▶12. How did the steamboat improve travel by water?

Canals At first, most western goods went down the Mississippi River to New Orleans. Then they could be shipped out to ports along the Atlantic coast, which made for a very long trip. A whole new era began, however, in 1825 with the opening of the **Erie Canal.** It was a deep ditch 363 miles long, filled with water that connected the Hudson and Mohawk rivers in New York to Lake Erie.

The Erie Canal was the wonder of its time. Soon other canals were built, thousands of miles of them by the 1840's. Many of them connected the rivers of the Ohio Valley with the Great Lakes, creating an uninterrupted water route between western farms and New York City.

With the building of canals, the costs of transportation fell. In 1817, before the canals were built, it cost over 19 cents per mile to ship a ton of goods between Buffalo and New York City. By the late 1850's, it cost less than a penny. So traffic on the canals grew rapidly.

▶13. Why was the Erie Canal especially important to the western farmers?

Map Study *Name the canal that connected the cities of Evansville, Indiana, and Toledo, Ohio. In which cities did the Erie Canal start and end?*

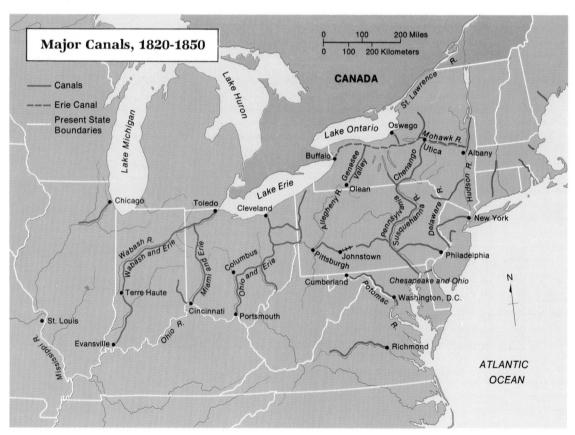

The Lemon House on the Allegheny Portage Railroad Line in Pennsylvania was an inn and station house. Passengers waited there for trains.

Railroads   Then another great marvel began to replace canals—railroads. The first American railroad, the Baltimore and Ohio, was started in 1828. It soon became clear that the great trains with their sputtering, steam-powered engines had advantages over the canals. They were cheaper and faster than boats, could go almost anywhere, and did not have to stop when water froze over in the winter. As a result, Americans quickly laid down tracks. By the late 1850's, the railroads were carrying even more freight than was being shipped through the canals.

These new systems of internal improvements amounted to a transportation revolution. The roads, steamboats, canals, and railroads tied the nation together into one economic community. The building of new transportation systems also encouraged the growth of manufacturing. The creation of railroads, for example, spurred the development of the American iron industry by creating a great demand for iron.

▶**14.** What made railroads a better form of transportation than boats?

Reviewing Section III

Identify   protected market, Moses Brown, Samuel Slater, putting-out system, Francis Cabot Lowell, Boston Associates, the *Lowell Offering*, Elias Howe, Jr., interchangeable parts, American System of Manufacturing, National Road, James Watt, Robert Fulton, *Clermont, New Orleans,* Erie Canal

Questions to Answer
1. What are some of the inventions and manufacturing techniques that stimulated the growth of northern industries?
2. How was the economy of the North different from that of the South?

A Question to Think About   Would the rapid growth of industry in the North have been possible if there had not been a revolution in transportation? Give reasons for your answer.

297

IV. The West

The West of the early nineteenth century was an enormous place stretching through all the lands west of the Appalachians from the Great Lakes in the north to the Gulf of Mexico in the south. The first large group of western settlers had pushed through the Cumberland Gap into Tennessee and Kentucky in the late 1700's. Southerners settled those states and others farther south where cotton could be grown. They also took up land in the southernmost parts of the Ohio Valley. There they grew corn and wheat. Settlers from New England and the Middle Atlantic states moved west a little later, settling the Old Northwest and nearby areas. They helped bring many new free states into the Union—Ohio (1803), Indiana (1816), Illinois (1818), Michigan (1837), Iowa (1846), Wisconsin (1848), and Minnesota (1858).

The Westerners and What They Wanted

What were the Westerners like? Some, no doubt, were loners who went west to get away from other people. Such people did not have the West to themselves for long. By far the more typical Westerners, it seems, were young married couples. They went west to claim good farmlands and grow foodstuffs to sell. As a result, they tried to settle in places where they could get their crops to market and buy the things they needed.

First, the settlers took up lands along the rivers such as the Ohio that fed into the Mississippi. Those rivers formed a great natural transportation system, a vast waterway that served as the West's first great link with the outside world. Later, settlers took up lands near canals and then along railroad lines. Rich farmlands farther inland, far from transportation routes, did not attract the settlers. Those lands remained empty.

▶**1.** Where did people moving west settle?

The Growth of Cities in the Northwest

Outside of the cotton growing Southwest, most Westerners were involved in a market economy. From the beginning, Northwesterners intended to grow wheat and corn for sale and to buy other things that they needed. The income they earned was spread through the population fairly evenly. As a result, towns with stores grew up through the grainbelt, that is, those parts of the West where wheat and corn were grown.

The agricultural products of the Northwest had to be **processed,** or changed from their original form into another form, before they were sold. That was not easily done on individual farms. Therefore, grain mills were established at central places. There wheat was made into flour. Before long, some of those commercial and processing centers grew into important cities—Cincinnati, Cleveland, Detroit, St. Louis, and later, Chicago, Indianapolis, Milwaukee, Minneapolis, and St. Paul.

▶**2.** What stimulated the growth of cities in the Northwest?

A Diversified Economy

The development of cities distinguished the agricultural Northwest from the agricultural Southwest. So too did the differences in their economic development. Indeed the economy of the cotton growing Southwest was so similar to that of the Old South that people began to refer to both areas as simply the *South.*

Increasingly too, the word *West* referred to the Northwest alone. The West developed a far more **diversified economy** than the South did. A diversified economy is one in which money is made by producing a variety of different products. Wheat and corn remained the West's main products, along with flour, whiskey, and meat products (bacon, ham, salt pork) from animals fed on corn. The section also shipped lead from Missouri, copper from Michigan, and iron from western Pennsylvania and, later, from northern Minnesota.

A whole series of businesses sprang up to serve farmers in the West—stores, machine and tool shops, newspapers, and so on. Farmers there also proved to be far more open to the new farming devices than were Southerners. Westerners quickly adopted iron and then steel plows and mechanical reapers. Factories were established in cities such as Chicago and Dayton to produce the new farm machinery.

▶**3.** How did the people in the West earn their living?

The West in National Politics

The development of the West was important for American politics. In the early nineteenth century, most of the new states west of the Appalachians were settled by Southerners. Then the North complained that it was becoming a minority in national politics. In those days, threats of **secession**—that is, of withdrawing from the United States—came from the New England states and New York. Later, as more and more people moved to the West and it grew in strength, the South began to feel left out. Always the West was the issue. Which of the older parts of the country would it support—the South or the North?

S. Holmes Andrews's painting of St. Paul, Minnesota, shows the city in 1855.

While the West sent its goods down the Mississippi, it had important economic ties to the South. The South, however, was never an important market for western foodstuffs, since, by and large, it could feed itself. A far more promising market for western products lay in the North. There it became necessary to import more and more food as people left their farms to work in cities or factory towns. With the development of direct east-west trade routes by canals and railroads, the economic ties between the North and the West became even stronger.

In time, the South felt endangered by the close ties that were developing between the North and the growing West. It felt increasingly cut off from the rest of the nation.

Obviously, the creation of economic links between the sections did not always make the nation more unified. In some ways, it tended to pull it apart. As a result, holding the Union together continued to challenge politicians in a time when, at last, a Westerner had become President: Andrew Jackson.

▶**4.** Why was the South concerned about the growing ties between the North and the West?

299

Identify processed, diversified economy, secession, Andrew Jackson

Questions to Answer

1. How did the economy of the Old Southwest differ from that of the Old Northwest?

2. What caused the South to feel threatened by the North and the West?

A Question to Think About What effect did the development of the new economic regions—the North, South, and West—have on the country?

IMPROVE YOUR READING
Fact and Opinion

When you read about people or events that have shaped history, it is important to evaluate what you read. One way to do that is to consider whether a statement is a *fact* or an *opinion*.

A *fact* is a statement that we can accept with reasonable certainty as being true. We can prove that a statement is a *fact* by finding evidence to show that the information is true. For example, the following statement is a *fact:* "The United States won 83 gold medals in the 1984 summer Olympics." We can check that statement in newspapers or magazines or by consulting the members of the United States Olympic Committee.

An *opinion* is a statement of what a person thinks about something. Evidence cannot be found to prove that what a person thinks about something is the truth and therefore a fact. When a person makes a judgment about something, that person is stating an *opinion*. For example, the following statement is an *opinion:* "The 1984 Olympic events were the most exciting events in Olympic history." Because it is impossible to find evidence that supports the truth of that statement, you can be sure that it is someone's *opinion*, not a *fact*.

The statements below are about events discussed in the chapter. Read each statement carefully and decide whether each is *fact* or *opinion*. Number the paper 1 to 10 and write either fact or opinion next to each number.

1. At Madison's request, Congress set up the Second Bank of the United States.
2. James Madison was the best President the nation had ever had.
3. Americans were more skilled at growing cotton than the British.
4. Eli Whitney invented the cotton gin.
5. Between 1820 and 1860, the price of slaves tripled.
6. Families enjoyed working together at the Lowell Mill.
7. Women workers at the Lowell Mill went on strike when their wages were cut.
8. The majority of people in the South did not own slaves.
9. Elias Howe, Jr., invented the sewing machine in the mid-1840's.
10. Many slaves were pleased to move into the new states that were formed out of the Old Southwest.

CHAPTER 14 REVIEW

Vocabulary Check

Write a short definition for each of the following words.

1. Protective tariff
2. Technological developments
3. Market economy
4. Urbanization
5. Interchangeable parts

Fact Check

Match each name in column I with the event, place, or object that is associated with it from column II.

Column I

1. Robert Fulton
2. Nat Turner
3. Elias Howe, Jr.
4. Francis Cabot Lowell
5. Eli Whitney

Column II

a. Cotton gin
b. Sewing machine
c. Slave revolt in Virginia
d. *Clermont*
e. Mill town in Massachusetts
f. Pawtucket, Rhode Island
g. Steam engine
h. Spinning mule

Time Check

On a separate piece of paper, put the following events in chronological order.

1. Minnesota becomes a state.
2. The slave trade becomes illegal.
3. The first railroad in the United States is started.
4. Fulton designs the *Clermont*.
5. The Erie Canal opens.

Skill Check

Use the map on page 296 to answer the following questions.

1. What was the shortest water route between Evansville, Indiana, and New York City in the 1840's?
2. What canal linked Cumberland, Maryland, to Washington, D.C.?
3. What river did that canal follow?
4. What did Buffalo, New York; Evansville, Indiana; and Portsmouth, Ohio; have in common?
5. In which cities did the Wabash and Erie Canal start and end?

Think and Write

1. Describe the three economic regions of the United States in 1826.
2. Why did Senator Clay favor the government measures he called the American System of Manufacturing?
3. How did the invention of the cotton gin affect the population of the Old South?
4. Explain how supply and demand affected the price and production of cotton.
5. What role did the growth of population and new methods of transportation play in the development of manufacturing?

Chapter 15

A New Era in Politics

During the presidency of Andrew Jackson, Americans became greatly interested in politics. This painting shows the interest and enthusiasm for the inauguration of President William Henry Harrison in 1841.

The Era of Good Feelings that followed the War of 1812 did not last long. It gave way to another era, one that took its name from Andrew Jackson of Tennessee. Politics became a great national game in the Age of Jackson. The existence of opposing parties became acceptable as it had not been in the days of Washington and Jefferson. The Age of Jackson was a time, too, when the office of the President took on a power and importance it did not have in earlier years.

Jackson did not cause all the changes in American politics that were part of the Age of Jackson. He benefited from changes that had been going on ever since the Revolution. His own achievement lay in understanding those changes and in using them to support his power as President.

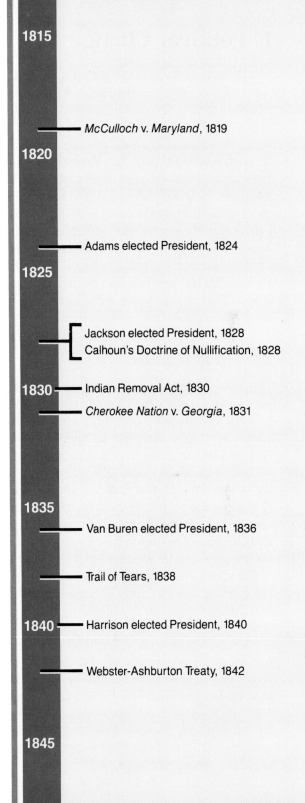

1815

McCulloch v. *Maryland*, 1819

1820

Adams elected President, 1824

1825

Jackson elected President, 1828
Calhoun's Doctrine of Nullification, 1828

1830 — Indian Removal Act, 1830
Cherokee Nation v. *Georgia*, 1831

1835

Van Buren elected President, 1836

Trail of Tears, 1838

1840 — Harrison elected President, 1840

Webster-Ashburton Treaty, 1842

1845

I. Political Change

The American Revolution set up a republic, not a democracy. For people such as James Madison, the difference between a republic and a democracy was very important. In a republic, Madison said, the people rule through representatives. In a democracy, they rule directly. Only very small places like towns in New England could be called democracies in Madison's sense of the word.

In time, however, the influence of the American people on the federal government increased. In that sense, the Republic of the United States became increasingly democratic. That change made a big difference in American politics and government.

Toward Democracy

The most important step in making American government and politics more democratic was a result of changes in requirements for the **franchise**, that is, the right to vote. The Constitution let the states decide who could vote for members of the House of Representatives, the only part of the federal government elected by the people directly. (Senators were chosen by the state legislatures, which also had the power to decide how to appoint the state's presidential electors.)

The states did not allow all people to vote. Blacks, whether slave or free, could not vote. Nor could women. Not even all white men could vote in the late eighteenth century, since most states said voters had to own a certain amount of property. The amount of property—usually land—that a man had to hold varied from place to place. Some states even allowed artisans and others without landed property to vote. Still, the state requirements limited the **electorate,** the body of people who could vote.

▶**1.** What were the qualifications for voting in the late eighteenth century?

Suffrage Reform Pennsylvania began to extend the franchise in 1776 by allowing all male taxpayers to vote. Other states followed Pennsylvania's example. However, a taxpaying qualification for the vote raised all kinds of practical problems. New York, for example, allowed all male taxpayers to vote in 1821. Then it discovered that by lowering or ending state taxes it would also **disenfranchise** large numbers of men (that is, take away their right to vote). Therefore, in 1826, New York changed its requirements again. All male citizens of adult age who lived in the state could vote, and that became known as **universal manhood suffrage.** However, despite the word *universal*, black males still could not vote.

By the late 1820's, adult white men in most states could vote. By the 1850's, all of the states had adopted universal (white) manhood suffrage.

▶**2.** Explain why universal manhood suffrage was not really universal in the 1850's.

Interest in Politics To qualify for the vote was one thing; to use it was another. Even in the colonial period, many men who could vote did not bother to do so. How could their interest be sparked? By the growing number of newpapers, for one thing. But nothing made people more interested in voting than political controversies. And nothing spurred political controversies better than political parties.

▶**3.** What helped to get people more interested in voting?

A New Party System A new kind of political party began to develop in the 1820's. Its members won local elections by carefully organizing supporters. Loyalty to party became a first principle of politics to such men who fought hard to win votes and to win office. If their candidates lost, they just worked harder to win the next time. They could be friendly with their opponents—as, for example, baseball players might be friendly with the members of another team.

These new party members were thus very different from the old Federalists and Republicans, who felt that members of the opposing party were a threat to the survival of the nation. The new-style politicians were also more comfortable with political parties. They accepted parties as a regular, continuing part of American politics.

The new parties sought above all to win votes. In recruiting voters, they roused interest in politics and increased the number of people who voted. The development of political parties and the widening of the franchise went hand in hand.

▶**4.** How were members of the new political parties different from the old Federalists and Republicans?

Direct Election Meanwhile, more and more officials were elected directly by the people. For example, many states changed their rules so that governors were elected by the people rather than by state legislatures.

By 1828, the people, rather than the state legislatures, were also electing members of the electoral college in all states but South Carolina. What difference did the change make? It allowed the President to claim a special place in national government because he alone represented all the people of the United States. Moreover, the people decided who would be President. In the late 1820's, the people finally determined that their hero—not the hero of the politicians in Washington—

Ralph Earl, constant companion of Jackson, made this portrait of the new President in 1833.

would be President. Their hero was Andrew Jackson.

▶**5.** What changes took place in the way governors and members of the electoral college were chosen in the 1800's?

Andrew Jackson

Jackson had a reputation as the champion of the common man, the man without great wealth or social standing. After all, Jackson came from humble beginnings. He was born in 1767 to a family of poor Scotch-Irish immigrants living in the back country of North Carolina. As a teenager, he fought in the Revolutionary War. By the time the war ended, all other members of his family had died. So he had to make his own way in life. Jackson taught school for a time, though he was poorly educated. His spelling was always very bad. Then he became a lawyer, and moved west to what soon became the new state of Tennessee.

There Jackson defended **creditors,** or money lenders, against **debtors,** those who borrowed money. That was strange for a champion of the common man, who was more often a debtor than a creditor. Jackson also became a **land speculator.** That is, he bought cheap land in the West hoping to sell it at a higher price when settlers finally moved in. Those

Andrew Jackson (center) is shown at a ball given in his honor by John Quincy Adams.

settlers naturally hated land speculators. Soon Jackson had enough money to build a plantation, the Hermitage, and to buy a large number of slaves.

Clearly, Andrew Jackson was no common man except in his humble origins. He was, however, an example of what an able man without privileges might become in the United States. Jackson was repeatedly elected to public office. Voters chose him to represent them at the Tennessee constitutional convention in 1796. Then he became the first representative from Tennessee to serve in the House of Representatives (1796–1797). He became a senator in 1797. The following year he gave up his Senate seat to become a judge in the Tennessee Supreme Court. He held that position until 1804.

Jackson also became a military hero. He won the admiration of Westerners for his victory over the Creek during the War of 1812. The whole nation celebrated his triumph at New Orleans in 1814. His wild invasion of Florida four years later added to his popularity. When Jackson toured the United States in 1819, Americans turned out in hordes. They wanted to see the man they named Old Hickory. He was called that because he seemed as tough as the hardest of American hardwood trees.

▶**6.** What offices and honors did Andrew Jackson win?

The Election of 1824

In 1824, the Tennessee legislature proposed Jackson for President. His candidacy caught on in a way no one had expected. A ground swell of support from the people gave him more votes than any other candidate received. That had never happened before. It was a sign of the times, a sign that a new era had arrived in American politics.

Jackson did not win the election of 1824 despite the fact that he received the most votes. John Quincy Adams, the son of John Adams and secretary of state to President Monroe, became President. The way Jackson lost the election added to his popularity, undermined Adams's presidency, and ensured Jackson's victory four years later.

President James Monroe did not nominate his successor, as both Jefferson and Madison had done. As a result, the fight for the presidency was wide open in 1824. John Quincy Adams had the support of New England. Kentucky's Henry Clay, the speaker of the House of Representatives, hoped for the Westerners' votes. John C. Calhoun of South Carolina, Monroe's secretary of war, appealed to the South. Jackson was the only candidate with a nationwide following.

The Republicans in Congress ignored all four men. They met and nominated Monroe's secretary of the treasury, William H. Crawford. The supporters of the other candidates refused to support Crawford and attacked the **caucus,** the group of party members who met to select a candidate, as undemocratic. Indeed, 1824 was the last year in which a congressional caucus nominated a presidential candidate.

From there on, the election became a horse race. Calhoun dropped out of the race early. Crawford and Clay lagged far behind the top two candidates. When the votes were counted, Jackson came in first with 43 percent of the popular vote. Adams was second, and Crawford third. However, none of the candidates won a majority of the electoral votes. As a result, the election had to be decided in the House of Representatives, where each state would have one vote.

Clay was out of the race but still a powerful man in the House. He favored Adams over Jackson and for an honorable reason. Adams, like Clay, believed in a federal government that actively promoted the nation's growth. Jackson was of a different mind. Like Jefferson, he thought the national government should interfere very little in the nation's affairs. Indeed, Adams and Clay were men who were gradually coming together in the new National Republican or Whig Party. Jackson and men who shared his views were part of the Democratic-Republican or, as it was soon called, the Democratic Party.

Clay convinced his supporters to back Adams, and Adams won the election. The new President appointed Clay as his secretary of state in 1825. The supporters of Jackson were outraged. Adams had defeated Jackson, they said, because of a corrupt bargain between Adams and Clay, by which Clay provided votes for Adams in return for a cabinet office. The election of 1824 was hardly over before that of 1828 had begun.

▶7. Why did Jackson lose the election of 1824?

President Adams

Unfortunately, John Quincy Adams, who was an experienced diplomat and a brilliant secretary of state, was not a very good President. He had lots of ideas about how the federal government could promote "the common good." He thought the federal government should support internal improvements such as roads and canals. He also wanted to establish a national university and an astronomical observatory in Washington.

Adams's ideas were perhaps ahead of their time. In any case, he had no idea whatsoever how to get his program through Congress. He was hesitant to make deals and to organize his supporters. The Jacksonians, who had no such hesitation, outmaneuvered him.

▶8. Why was Adams unsuccessful at getting his program through Congress?

John Quincy Adams was the first son of a former President to also become President.

The New Politics

Meanwhile, the Jacksonians prepared for the election of 1828, building support for Jackson among the planters of the South and the workers and small farmers of the North. Jackson himself organized a central party committee to oversee his campaign. At the same time, his supporters founded newspapers to bring their case to the people. Local Hickory Clubs passed out leaflets and organized parades, rallies, and barbecues. Such a program cost money—perhaps a million dollars, a great amount in 1828. The new politics were obviously not for poor people.

The new politics were also rough and not always honest. In the campaign of 1828, there was a good bit of mudslinging, that is, of crude and often untrue accusations hurled at the candidates. Jackson's opponents made much of the fact that he had unknowingly married his wife Rachel before she was legally divorced from her first husband.

▶**9.** How did Jackson's supporters prepare for the election of 1828?

The Results of the Election

When the election results were in, Jackson had won 647,000 popular votes to Adams's 508,000, and 178 electoral votes to Adams's 83. The new democratic politics had, moreover, brought out the voters. Over 56 percent of the adult white males cast ballots in the election of 1828. That was over twice as many as in 1824.

▶**10.** What were the results of the 1828 election?

Reviewing Section I

Identify franchise, electorate, disenfranchise, universal manhood suffrage, creditors, debtors, land speculator, John Quincy Adams, John C. Calhoun, William H. Crawford, caucus

Questions to Answer

1. How did government become more democratic during the early 1800's?
2. How did the new political parties of the 1820's try to win the elections?

A Question to Think About What did Jackson's election as President demonstrate about who could become President of the United States?

II. The Presidency of Andrew Jackson

On March 4, 1829, the day of Jackson's inauguration, Washington was a different city than it had been when Thomas Jefferson was inaugurated 28 years earlier. The buildings that were then unfinished had been built, destroyed by the British, and built again, better than before. The city, its people bragged, had 91,665 feet of brick pavement. Still mud seemed to be everywhere on that late winter day in 1829, as crowds pushed into the city to see their man made President.

The Inauguration

The people thronged outside the Capitol where Jackson, dressed in a plain black suit, took the oath of office and made his inaugural speech. Then they followed him to the White House, pushed their way into the reception rooms, helped themselves to food, and tramped, as tradition has it, with their muddy boots on the fine carpets and even climbed on silk-covered chairs to get a better look at the new President.

Some said the scene at the inauguration announced the beginning of mob rule. In fact, the inauguration party was not much different than receptions given by earlier Presidents. Nor was Jackson, the man of the West, very different in outward style from the Presidents before him. The man had a dignity that was fully in keeping with the office he held.

▶**1.** How did Americans celebrate the inauguration of their new President?

Robert Cruikshank's painting shows the hundreds of Jackson supporters who supposedly invited themselves to Jackson's inaugural reception.

Jackson's Appointments

What was new in 1829 was the new President's right to speak as the special representative of the American people. Jackson understood that fact and made the most of it. He appointed men to his Cabinet from those parts of the country that had supported him. Jackson appointed Martin Van Buren of New York as secretary of state. His other appointees were not exceptional men. Unlike Presidents before him, however, Jackson felt free to replace Cabinet members with men of his own choosing.

Jackson, however, did not depend on his Cabinet for advice. He depended instead on what his opponents called a **kitchen cabinet,** an informal group of his friends.

▶**2.** Who were Jackson's real advisors during his presidency?

Jacksonian Democracy

What did the Jacksonian Democrats stand for? Large numbers of them favored slavery, although slavery was not an issue discussed openly in politics. Jackson owned slaves, and so other slave owners though he was "safe." Generally Jacksonian Democrats preferred a small federal government, while their opponents generally favored a larger, more active government. However, the parties of Jackson's time did not have firm stands on the issues. Members of the same party often disagreed on questions of policy. They agreed mainly in wanting to get members of their party into office.

Because parties had no open and consistent stand on the issues, it was not entirely clear what they would do with the office once they won it. Nor was it clear what the people expected from their candidates. Jackson, for example, increased his popularity in office even while doing things that his opponents thought would destroy him. It was not what Jackson did, it seems, but why he did what he did that increased his strength. Very often he explained his policies as ways to give the common man a fairer chance in life. That aim and the arguments Jackson used were important parts of Jacksonian democracy.

▶**3.** What policies did the Jacksonian Democrats stand for?

Government Offices Jackson recognized that not all people were equal. Some were more talented than others, for example. Such differences were natural. Jackson insisted, however, that the United States government must not give to any person or group artificial advantages that it did not give to other people or groups.

Jackson saw that one way the federal government might give some people such advantages was through appointments to public office. In Jackson's first message to Congress, he said that public office was supposed to be a way of serving the people, not of helping individuals advance their careers or wealth.

Jackson said, too, that no man should be allowed to hold a government office for a long time. Jackson did not think that government service required any experience or special training. He said that federal offices required only men of intelligence to fill them. Such people could be found among the poor as well as the rich and well educated.

▶**4.** What were Jackson's views on who was qualified for public office?

The Spoils System In a practical sense, Jackson's policy justified turning out government workers who had held office under Adams and appointing good Democrats to their places. That practice of rewarding supporters with political offices was known as the **spoils system.** Certainly Jackson saw nothing wrong

Through the first half of the nineteenth century, serious American artists tried to find a way to express the American identity in their paintings. However, American artists were dependent on Europe for training and ideas. Most trained American artists were known for their portraits. Few Americans were interested in painting landscapes.

The Hudson River School was the name given to the first group of American artists who developed a uniquely American style of landscape painting in the late 1820's and 1830's. Unlike European landscape artists, who painted peaceful countrysides, the artists of the Hudson River School showed the wild, untamed beauty and grandeur of canyons, rivers, and other natural landscape features. Their works reflected the intense patriotism of Americans of their time.

At first, the artists painted scenes of the Hudson River Valley in New York. Later, like many other Americans, artists became interested in the West. They traveled far beyond New York to other parts of North America.

Among the most famous of the Hudson River School artists are Thomas Cole, Thomas Doughty, Asher B. Durand, and later, Albert Bierstadt and Frederick E. Church. Those artists created some of the finest landscape paintings ever done by Americans. See page 446 for an example of Albert Bierstadt's work.

---

in using his powers to increase the strength of his party.

In fact, however, Jackson replaced only about 20 percent of federal officeholders in 8 years as President. What he did was, in short, less important than what he said.

▶**5.** What was the spoils system?

The Maysville Veto

Jackson used a similar argument to explain his 1830 veto of the Maysville Road Bill. That bill said that the federal government would help pay for a 60-mile road in Kentucky from the town of Maysville to Lexington.

Like Presidents Madison and Monroe, Jackson thought the federal government had no business supporting internal improvement projects that were local, not national, in character. The Maysville Road, Jackson noted, was exclusively within the limits of one state.

Even among Kentuckians, he said, the road would give advantages to some men but not all, which was just what he opposed in his spoils system statement.

▶**6.** Why did Jackson oppose the Maysville Road Bill?

The Bank War

The greatest example of Jackson's opposition to the government's granting artificial distinctions to certain men, and the one that had the most far-reaching effects, was his personal war against the Second Bank of the United States.

The charter of the Second Bank of the United States, which Congress approved in 1816, was good for 20 years. As a result, it did not have to be renewed until 1836. In general, the bank fulfilled the purposes for which it had been created. It provided a safe

George Tattersall's nineteenth-century watercolor clearly shows the poor condition of the nation's roads.

place for the government to keep its money. It sold bonds for the government. It loaned money to business people and so helped them finance the country's economic development. It also gave the country a sound national currency. The bank even helped keep state banks operating in a responsible way.

There was no doubt, however, that the bank had tremendous economic power. It controlled a good part of the country's credit (its borrowing power) and its **specie**, or gold and silver.

All that power was, moreover, held by people who were under very little government control. The bank was quite simply a private business. Opponents of the bank said that since the bank loaned money or paid fees to many important politicians, it was corrupt.

▶**7.** What services did the Second Bank of the United States provide to the country?

Jackson's Doubts Jackson had his own doubts about the bank. He questioned both the constitutionality and the usefulness of the bank. In 1819, the Supreme Court had said the bank was constitutional by its decision in the *McCulloch* v. *Maryland* case. However, Jackson was not a man to let the Court do his thinking for him. "I have read the opinion of John Marshall," he said, "and could not agree with him."

Jackson, in fact, had little love for any bank. Nor did he like paper money, which the bank printed. He preferred gold and silver because he thought hard money did not change in value. Still, Jackson was unwilling to push the issue before the bank's charter came up for renewal. He thought that would probably happen only after the election of 1832.

▶**8.** What were Jackson's views on the national bank?

Nicholas Biddle   At the time, Nicholas Biddle was president of the Second Bank of the United States. He no doubt understood the country's money and banking needs better than Jackson. However, Biddle was not a good politician. He was also the kind of man Jackson most disliked and mistrusted. Born into a wealthy Philadelphia family, Biddle was well educated and moved easily among the wealthiest and most privileged people of eastern society.

On the advice of Clay and Webster, Biddle took the President on. He applied for a new charter four years before the bank's old charter ran out. The renewal bill easily passed in Congress and even won the support of many Democrats. Jackson just dug in. The bank is "trying to kill me," he told Van Buren, "but I will kill it." He vetoed the bill to recharter the bank on July 10, 1832.

▶**9.** What happened to the renewal bill for the Second Bank of the United States?

Jackson's Veto Message   In his veto message, Jackson questioned the bank's constitutionality. He also questioned the wisdom of putting so much power "in the hands of a few men irresponsible to the people." Above all, Jackson attacked the notion that the federal government should give such special privileges to a handful of people. Over a quarter of the bank's stockholders, he noted, were foreigners. The rest were "a few hundred of our own citizens, chiefly of the richest class." That was unfair. The laws of the nation should not add artificial distinctions to the natural distinctions that separate person from person.

▶**10.** Why did Jackson veto the renewal bill for the Second Bank of the United States?

The Election of 1832   The bank's supporters thought Jackson had done himself in by vetoing the charter renewal. They made the

Nicholas Biddle went down to defeat in his "Bank War" against President Jackson.

bank a big issue in the campaign of 1832, in which Henry Clay was the National Republican candidate. Clay's supporters even handed out thousands of copies of Jackson's veto message. Their efforts only increased the President's popularity. Equal opportunity for rich and poor was a powerful principle at that time. So the people in 1832 reelected Jackson with a majority of the popular votes and 219 electoral votes to Clay's 49.

▶**11.** What effect did Jackson's veto of the bank renewal bill have on the results of the election of 1832?

The Bank's Last Stand   Once reelected, Jackson moved in against the bank. He decided to take the government's funds out of the bank. He had to get rid of two secretaries of the treasury before he found one—Roger Taney—who was ready to do that for him. Taney paid the government's expenses out of funds already in the bank. He made all deposits into dozens of state banks or "pet banks" as Jackson's enemies called them. Unfortunately, the state banks were not as safe and reliable as the Second Bank of the United States had been.

Then the bank's supporters struck back. In 1834, they managed to get a resolution through the Senate that criticized the President for removing government deposits from the bank and exercising powers not given to him by the Constitution. It took three years before the Jacksonians could get that resolution removed from the Senate's records. The National Republicans also started calling Jackson "King Andrew I." They began calling themselves members of the Whig Party, after the party formed by Englishmen who wanted to limit the power of the king in the 1600's.

Biddle also carried on the fight against Jackson, but in an irresponsible way. He called in loans issued by the bank and cut back on new loans. He had to do so because he did not have government funds anymore. But he went further than he had to in hope that the complaints of businessmen would force Jackson to back down. Instead, Biddle lost many supporters. In 1836, the bank received a charter from Pennsylvania and remained in business until 1841. Then it was forced to close.

▶**12.** How did Roger Taney help Jackson in his war against the bank?

The Specie Circular The state banks issued so much paper currency that it declined in value. Some of that paper money was being used to buy government lands. As a result, in July 1836, Jackson issued his Specie Circular, a decree that said that in the future government lands would have to be paid for with gold or silver. Clearly, the President and his anti-bank and hard money policies—right or wrong—had won the day.

▶**13.** Why did Jackson issue his Specie Circular?

The Nullification Crisis

Jackson was a strong nationalist, deeply devoted to the United States as a nation. Nothing made that clearer than his actions during the Nullification Crisis, which occurred at the same time as the Bank War.

The crisis began in South Carolina. The state's economy was in trouble in the 1820's. Its land produced less cotton than in the past. What cotton it did grow earned less as the price of cotton fell from 31 cents a pound in 1818 to 8 cents in 1831. The reasons were clear. South Carolina's soil was worn out after years of use, and the growing supply of cotton from the new states of the Old Southwest was driving down cotton prices.

Carolinians, however, had another explanation: the federal tariff. The duties imposed by the tariff on imported goods had been increasing. In 1816, the tariff averaged 25 percent of the value of imported goods. By 1824, the average had risen to 33.33 percent. Then, in 1828, came what the Carolinians called the Tariff of Abominations. The average duty rose to 50 percent of the value of imports.

The American manufacturers who were helped by the tariff were mainly in the North. All the tariff did for Southerners, the Carolinians said, was to raise the price of goods they had to buy. The tariff also cut the amount of goods foreign countries could sell in the United States. That meant it also cut the amount of cotton those foreign countries could buy from southern planters. In both ways,

Political cartoons are one kind of primary source. Political cartoons are not necessarily meant to be funny. They are usually drawn to express a point of view about a person or event.

To understand a political cartoon, try to identify all the characters. Read the caption and the writing in the cartoon. Then ask "What is the cartoonist trying to say?"

Look carefully at the cartoon and answer the following questions.

1. Who is the character in this cartoon?
2. How is he dressed?
3. What does he hold in his hands?
4. What items are on the floor?
5. What is the cartoonist trying to say?

BORN TO COMMAND.

OF VETO MEMORY.

HAD I BEEN CONSULTED.

KING ANDREW THE FIRST.

the South was hurt while the North benefited. That was not fair. The Carolinians even said the protective tariff was unconstitutional.

The argument had a Jacksonian flavor. After all, Jackson thought the government should avoid helping some people at the cost of others. In fact, Jackson had mixed feelings about the tariff. However, once the Carolinians argued that a state could nullify, or refuse to obey, an act of Congress, they lost Jackson's sympathy.

▶14. Why did Carolinians oppose protective tariffs?

Nullification In 1828, John C. Calhoun, Jackson's Vice President, secretly developed the doctrine of nullification in an essay entitled "The South Carolina Exposition and

Protest." That essay was adopted by the South Carolina legislature and published without revealing the name of its author.

The states, Calhoun argued in his essay, had come together to create the federal government. (By "the states" he did not mean the state governments. He meant the people who lived within the boundaries of the various states.) So states had a right to decide whether the federal government was acting properly. If that government took on powers not granted by the Constitution, the people of a state could "interpose" by calling a new convention. There the state's people could declare the unconstitutional act null and void within the borders of their state. If the other states disagreed, they could amend the Constitution to make it clear that the federal government had the power under dispute.

▶**15.** What were Calhoun's arguments in support of nullification?

Calhoun's Reasons Calhoun did not want to destroy the Union with his doctrine of nullification. In fact, he hoped one day to become President. Calhoun proposed nullification because some people in South Carolina were already proposing to secede, or leave the Union. If the right of the states to nullify federal laws was established, Calhoun thought, it would seldom have to be used. The very threat of nullification would make Congress more careful and respectful of the rights of states. That would help end the threat of secession.

▶**16.** What were Calhoun's reasons for proposing nullification?

Reactions to Nullification The doctrine of nullification found few supporters outside South Carolina in the late 1820's and early 1830's. The Senate considered the doctrine fully in 1830, when South Carolina's Senator Robert Y. Hayne defended nullification in a debate with Senator Daniel Webster of Massachusetts, a great orator. Webster questioned whether the Union could survive if the states were permitted to decide if and when they would obey federal laws. He ended with an eloquent statement of his belief in the Union's lasting character: "Liberty and Union, now and forever, one and inseparable!"

Calhoun, as Vice President, was presiding over the Senate during the debate. He was silent except for one interruption of Webster. By then, it was no longer a secret that he was the man who was behind South Carolina's arguments.

▶**17.** What were Daniel Webster's views on the states' right to nullify federal laws?

Jackson and Calhoun Jackson already had trouble with Calhoun. One disagreement was over a social matter. John Eaton, who became Jackson's secretary of war, married Peggy O'Neil Timberlake, the beautiful daughter of an Irish tavernkeeper. The wedding took place only four months after the death of her first husband. Floride Calhoun, the Vice President's wife, refused to associate with Peggy Eaton. The other cabinet wives followed suit.

Jackson sympathized with the Eatons and resented Floride Calhoun's snobbery. Jackson's wife Rachel had experienced attacks like those on Peggy Eaton. The December before Jackson's first inauguration, Rachel had died—from the pain suffered in the campaign of 1828, some said. Jackson also learned that Calhoun, as secretary of war under James Monroe, had condemned Jackson's 1818 invasion of Florida.

The two men squared off against each other over nullification more than any other issue. Jackson first announced his position against nullification—and Calhoun—at the Democratic Party's Jefferson Day dinner in April

1830. Called upon to offer a toast, the President stood up, looked at Calhoun, and said "Our Union—it must be preserved." All eyes turned toward Calhoun, whose hands shook so much that the wine in his glass splashed over the sides. Then he rose, pale-faced, and offered his answer, "The Union. Next to our liberties, most dear."

▶ **18.** What issues did Jackson and Calhoun disagree over?

The Crisis The real nullification crisis came in 1832, after Jackson signed a new tariff bill that kept some duties high. Then South Carolina called a convention that declared the tariffs of 1828 and 1832 "null, void, and no law." Within weeks, Jackson issued a proclamation that rejected the arguments for nullification.

Henry Clay added to his reputation as the Great Compromiser by designing a compromise tariff bill that would gradually reduce duties. In March 1833, Congress passed both the compromise tariff and a force bill which gave the President power to use the army and navy to enforce federal laws if that became necessary.

South Carolina gave in. It accepted the compromise tariff and withdrew its nullification ordinance. To save face, however, it nullified the Force Bill. Jackson had the good sense to overlook that bit of spite. He could be generous. He had won again.

▶ **19.** How did Henry Clay help to bring the nullification crisis to an end?

Indian Removal

Jackson faced less opposition in his efforts to send those Indians who remained east of the Mississippi farther west. At that time, most people in the United States thought that replacing Indians with white settlers

This Mathew Brady photograph of Peggy Eaton was taken long after the controversy she caused.

served the interests of progress and civilization. The best thing that could be done for the Indians, Jackson thought, would be to save them "from their wandering habits," to make them, in effect, settled farmers like Americans of European descent. Even if the Indians changed their ways, Jackson thought it was for their own good that they be moved away from white settlements. Few people publicly questioned his views except for the Indians themselves.

After the death of Tecumseh (tə kum′sə) in 1813, the ability of the Indians to protect their lands declined considerably. By the 1820's, only a handful of groups held out. Jackson set out to break their resistance.

▶ **20.** Why did Jackson favor Indian removal?

Robert Lindneaux's famous painting shows the Cherokee on the "Trail of Tears" during their forced march west from Georgia to Oklahoma.

The Cherokee Among the hardest to defeat were the Cherokee, many of whom lived in northwest Georgia. They had become much like their white neighbors. They were settled farmers who lived in European-styled houses. They published newspapers in their own language. They even had a written constitution for their Cherokee Nation.

When the state of Georgia tried to seize their lands, the Cherokee took their case to the Supreme Court. The Court supported them. In *Cherokee Nation* v. *Georgia* (1831), John Marshall said that the Indians could lose title to their land only if they gave it up voluntarily. In a second case, *Worcester* v. *Georgia* (1832), Marshall said that Georgians could not even enter Cherokee lands without the Indians' permission.

Jackson, however, refused to help the Cherokee, even though it is the President's duty to enforce the law. "John Marshall has made his decision," he supposedly said. "Now let him enforce it."

▶ **21.** How did the Cherokee Nation fight to keep their land?

Trails of Tears In 1830, Congress passed an Indian Removal Act, which gave the President power to move the Indians west of the Mississippi. Federal agents met with the Choctaw (chok'tô) Indians of Mississippi and Alabama. They offered the Indians free land in the West, help in moving there and in settling their new homeland, and yearly payments afterward. The Choctaw agreed. Between 1831 and 1833, about 15,000 headed west. The trip was badly managed, in part because the government tried to cut its costs. Many Choctaw died along the way.

Those Indians that did not agree to leave were forced to go. The Creek of Alabama were pushed west by the United States Army

John Ross, Cherokee leader, was born in 1790 near Lookout Mountain, Tennessee. Both of his parents were Scotch, but his mother was also one-fourth Cherokee. Although Ross was only part Cherokee, he always put his Cherokee identity first. The Cherokee name he used was *Cooweecoowee*, meaning "white bird."

As a child, John was taught at home by a private tutor. Later he attended the private Kingston Academy in Tennessee. In 1809, a United States Indian agent gave Ross his first assignment working with the Cherokee. Ross's calm, confident manner quickly won him their respect and support. In 1817, when he was 27, he won a place on the National Council, a major governing body of the eastern Cherokee. By the age of 38, he had become their chosen leader.

Ross became leader of the Cherokee nation in 1828—the year Andrew Jackson became President. Unlike earlier Presidents, Jackson saw the Cherokee as a threat to white settlers. He resented their prosperous farms and businesses, and he disliked their independence.

Jackson set out to remove the Cherokee from their ancient lands. For ten years, Ross led the Cherokee in their fight to stay in their homeland. His efforts, however, met with failure. In 1838, federal troops rounded up the Cherokee and forced them to begin their long march west.

The journey from Tennessee and Georgia to Oklahoma was a thousand miles long. Over 4,000 Cherokee, including Ross's wife, died of exhaustion and disease. Still the Cherokee people did not give up. As soon as they arrived in Oklahoma, they once again chose Ross as their leader. They looked to him for comfort and hope.

Ross immediately organized a great meeting for all the Indians who had been moved far from their homes. More than 17 different groups

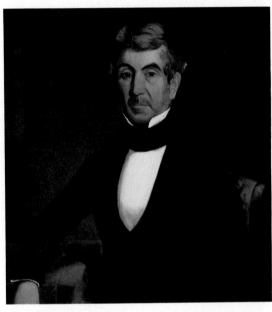

attended. Many groups had fought one another in the past. Ross asked them to put aside their differences. He then said:

> Brothers: When we see that our people have been compelled to remove to a new and distant country, we cannot help but feel sorry; but we should not despair of once more enjoying the blessings of peace in our new homes.
>
> Brothers: By this removal, tribes that were once separated by distance have become neighbors . . . Let us then act that peace and friendship may be forever preserved and that we may always live as brothers of the same family.

Ross's dreams of unity for his people did not come true. Still he continued to work for the Cherokee. He died at the age of 76 during a trip to Washington. He had gone there to work out the terms of a new treaty for the Cherokee after the Civil War.

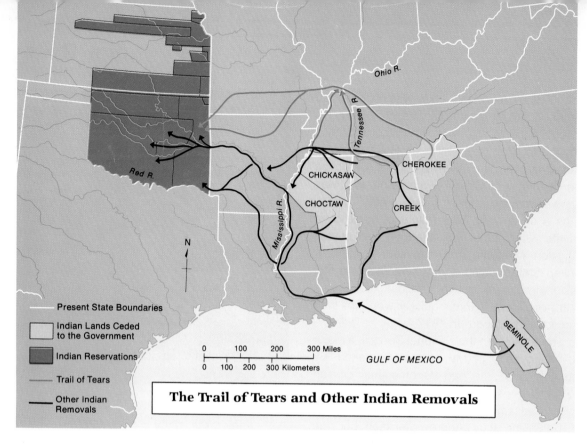

The Trail of Tears and Other Indian Removals

Legend:
- Present State Boundaries
- Indian Lands Ceded to the Government
- Indian Reservations
- Trail of Tears
- Other Indian Removals

Map Study *Name the Indian groups whose removal routes are shown on the map. Which of those groups traveled the farthest north?*

in 1836. The following year the Chickasaw were also forced out.

And the Cherokee? Some were willing to go and signed a treaty with the United States in 1835. But when the time came to leave, most Indians wanted to stay. Finally, in 1838, the army made them march to Oklahoma along the so-called Trail of Tears. Many families had to leave all their possessions behind. About 4,000 of the 15,000 Cherokee died on the westward journey.

▶22. Why was "Trail of Tears" a good name for the westward journey of the Indians?

The Indian Wars Only one small group of Seminole Indians in Florida under Chief Osceola (os′ē ō′lä) held out successfully. They

fought so well that the United States lost 1,500 soldiers and $20 million before it finally gave up on the so-called Second Seminole War (1835–1842).

The Sac and Fox, led by Chief Black Hawk, were not as successful as the Seminole. They tried to return to their homes in Illinois. The United States Army, helped by local militia, drove them back across the Mississippi in the Black Hawk War of 1832.

By the time Jackson left office, most of the eastern Indians had been moved west of the Mississippi or were about to be moved there. Jackson was proud of that fact.

▶23. How successful were the Seminole, Sac, and Fox Indians in their efforts to resist moving west?

320

Jackson's Achievements

Few Americans today are proud of their country's treatment of the Indians. For that reason, it is sometimes hard to understand why Jackson is often named among the country's greatest Presidents. After all, except for removing the Indians, what did he do? Mostly he kept the government from doing one thing or another—from helping build the Maysville Road, for example, or rechartering the Second Bank of the United States.

Jackson's achievement lay above all in his use of presidential power. He took charge as no President had before him. He had no hesitation about firing Cabinet members when they did not do what he wanted.

Moreover, Jackson used the veto power more than all the previous Presidents combined. He did not use the veto only when he thought a measure was unconstitutional as George Washington advocated. He also vetoed measures for political reasons or just because he did not like them. Congress could, of course, override a presidential veto if two thirds of its members voted to do that. But no presidential veto was overridden by Congress until 1866.

Finally, Jackson showed his strength in the way he stood up to South Carolina during the nullification crisis.

Jackson was the country's first strong President, one who showed those who came later what could be made of the office of the President. Jackson was so strong a President because he was a strong person. He was not called Old Hickory for nothing. Jackson was also a skilled politician. Above all, however, he was a strong President because he could claim special power as the spokesman for all the people of the United States. That was something no President before him could do.

▶**24.** How did Jackson strengthen the office of the President?

Reviewing Section II

Identify Martin Van Buren, kitchen cabinet, Jacksonian Democrats, spoils system, Maysville Road Bill, specie, Nicholas Biddle, Roger Taney, Specie Circular, Robert Y. Hayne, Daniel Webster, John Eaton, *Cherokee Nation* v. *Georgia*, *Worcester* v. *Georgia*, Indian Removal Act, Trail of Tears, Chief Osceola, Chief Black Hawk

Questions to Answer
1. How did Jackson fight against rechartering the Second Bank of the United States?
2. What was the Nullification Crisis?

A Question to Think About Is the term *Jacksonian democracy* an appropriate one to describe Jackson's actions during his two terms as President? Give reasons for your answer.

III. Democrats and Whigs

Jackson finished his second term in 1837. The new kind of politics that started with his campaigns did not end, however. The Democratic and Whig (formally the National Republican) parties survived and continued to battle, seeking always new ways to win votes and get into office.

The Rise of Party Conventions
Starting in 1831 and 1832, American political parties began selecting presidential candidates in a new way. **Party conventions** made up of representatives from local party organizations met to nominate candidates for President and Vice President. The new system

was not necessarily more democratic than the old congressional caucuses. A handful of professional politicians could still have considerable power over conventions. At least, though, the conventions were more open and involved a wider range of people.

▶1. How were candidates for President and Vice President selected after 1832?

Martin Van Buren

In 1836, the Democratic convention nominated Martin Van Buren for the presidency. The Whigs did not hold a convention. Instead, they ran three men for the presidency, hoping to throw the election into the House of Representatives. The strategy failed. Van Buren won 170 electoral votes to 124 for his various opponents.

Van Buren came from a modest family in New York State. Like Jackson, he had made his fortune as a lawyer. His claim to fame came from his role as a founder of the modern American party system.

Like few other men of his day, Van Buren understood the usefulness of parties. He said they were a necessary part of free government. Parties helped keep the people interested in government. The existence of an organized opposition also helped to keep persons in power from doing dangerous things. Finally, parties helped hold the country together. For example, Democrats in the South and in the North worked together for the good of their party, which was national, not for their sections alone.

▶2. Why did Van Buren believe that political parties were good for the nation?

Hard Times

Van Buren's presidency, however, was nothing to brag about. The good times that graced the last years of Jackson's administration did not carry over into Van Buren's.

After 1831, prices had begun to rise—including those of cotton, which may have helped to quiet down the Carolinians. It was a prosperous period, and states, privately owned businesses, and land speculators all took out loans to finance various activities. Many of the loans came from the growing number of state banks.

Then suddenly, two months after Van Buren took office, prices fell. Banks called in their loans. That is, the banks asked for immediate repayment. The great boom ended with the Panic of 1837. The panic settled into a deep depression in which businesses closed down and many people lost their jobs. The depression lasted through Van Buren's presidency and into the mid-1840's.

Van Buren probably made things worse. In 1840, he convinced Congress to pass the **Independent Treasury Act.** Under its terms, the government put its money into government run "subtreasuries" located in cities across the nation. By so doing, Van Buren hoped to keep the government's money safe and to prevent private banks from misusing that money. However, because the state banks no longer received government funds, they could make fewer loans to business people. Loans might have helped businesses get going again and put people back to work.

▶3. How did Van Buren's Independent Treasury Act worsen the depression?

The Log Cabin Campaign

The Democrats ran Van Buren for the presidency again in 1840; but because of the depression, the Whigs smelled victory. They nominated for President the closest thing they had to a military hero, William Henry Harrison of Ohio. He had attacked Tecumseh's people and won the Battle of Tippecanoe. A Southerner, John Tyler, was their candidate for Vice President.

Harrison came from a fairly wealthy Virginia family and lived in a great mansion in Ohio. The Whigs, however, made him sound like a poor frontier farmer. When someone sneered that Harrison would be contented in a log cabin with a barrel of hard cider, the Whigs turned the criticism into a compliment. Log cabins and cider barrels became symbols for their candidate. In fact, during the campaign it became a disgrace to have anything but humble origins.

In other ways, too, the Whigs tried to outdo the Democrats. They attacked Van Buren as a man of high tastes who wasted the public's money. They held parades, barbecues, and mass meetings, and above all they shouted their slogans: "Van, Van is a used-up man," and "Tippecanoe and Tyler, too!" These worked. Harrison won 234 electoral votes. Van Buren won only 60 electoral votes.
▶**4.** What kind of campaign did the Whigs run against the Democrats in 1840?

President Tyler

The Whigs got Harrison into office, but their victory was short-lived. Harrison, 68 years old when elected, caught pneumonia and died in 1841 a month after taking office. Tyler became President. He proved to be a strange Whig. He vetoed one proposal after another that Whigs supported, including internal improvements and a new national bank. In fact, Tyler lost almost all the support of his party. Only his secretary of state, Daniel Webster, stuck with him, at least for a while.

Webster was deep at work on the **Webster-Ashburton Treaty** of 1842, which settled the northern border between the United States and British territory (except for Oregon). Once

The Whig Party used this flag during their campaign for the presidency in 1840.

the treaty was settled, Webster resigned from the Cabinet too.

In 1844, with the Whig Party still badly split, the Democrats were once again able to capture the presidency for their candidate, James K. Polk.

Still, the Log Cabin campaign of 1840 was of lasting importance. In that campaign, both major parties carried on a lively battle in every part of the country. The two-party system was definitely at work in the United States. The parties pulled out the voters—80 percent of the electorate cast ballots in 1840. (A 50 percent turn-out is considered pretty good today.) Nothing showed better the triumph of democracy in the Age of Jackson.
▶**5.** Why was Tyler not considered a faithful party member?

Identify Party conventions, Panic of 1837, Independent Treasury Act, John Tyler, Webster-Ashburton Treaty, James K. Polk

Questions to Answer
1. What strategy did the Whigs use in an effort to win the presidency in 1836?

2. Why was the Whig Party's victory in the election of 1840 considered to be a short-lived victory?

A Question to Think About Why is the Log Cabin election of 1840 important in the history of American politics?

IMPROVE YOUR READING
Outlining

A good way to organize and remember information is to make an outline of the main ideas and supporting details. The basic form of an outline appears on this page.

I. Major Topic
   A. Subtopic
   B. Subtopic
      1. Related Detail
      2. Related Detail
         a. Detail
         b. Detail
II. Major Topic

This is a partially completed outline of section I. (pages 304–308). On a separate sheet of paper, complete the outline and fill in the missing main ideas and details from the chapter.

I. Political Change
   A. Toward Democracy
      1. The most important step in making American government more democratic was a result of changes in the right to vote.

2. Most states gave the vote only to white men who owned a certain amount of property.

   a. Suffrage Reform
      1. Pennsylvania led the way in 1776 by giving all male taxpayers the right to vote.
      2. _____
   b. Interest in Politics
      1. Newspapers sparked an interest in voting.
      2. _____
   c. A New Party System
      1. _____
      2. _____
   d. Direct Election
      1. _____
      2. _____

B. Andrew Jackson
   1. _____
   2. _____
   3. _____

CHAPTER 15 REVIEW

Vocabulary Check
Write a short definition for each of the following words.

1. Specie
2. Kitchen cabinet
3. Franchise
4. Electorate
5. Caucus

Fact Check
On a separate piece of paper, write the word or words that best complete each of the following sentences.

1. The _____ was the route followed by the Cherokee when they were forced to leave their homeland.
2. President Jackson defended the _____, a way of thanking supporters by giving them jobs in government.
3. In 1776, Pennsylvania reformed the franchise by allowing _____.
4. People who bought land cheaply hoping to sell it later at a much higher price were called _____.
5. Andrew Jackson's nickname was _____.

Time Check
On a separate piece of paper, write the letter of the event that occurred first in each of the following pairs of events.

1. a. New York passes a law allowing universal manhood suffrage.
   b. Pennsylvania allows all male taxpayers to vote.
2. a. Tecumseh dies.
   b. William Henry Harrison becomes President

3. a. Clay becomes secretary of state under John Quincy Adams.
   b. Van Buren runs for President.
4. a. Jackson vetoes the bill to recharter the Second Bank of the United States.
   b. The Supreme Court decision in *McCulloch* v. *Maryland* finds the Bank of the United States constitutional
5. a. The Supreme Court hears the case *Cherokee Nation* v. *Georgia*.
   b. The Cherokee are forced to move to Oklahoma.

Skill Check
Use the map on page 320 to answer the following questions.

1. What is the map about?
2. Approximately how many miles did the Cherokee travel on the Trail of Tears?
3. In what direction did they travel?
4. Which two Indian groups had to cross parts of the Gulf of Mexico?
5. Approximately how many miles did the Seminole travel?

Think and Write
1. How did political parties change elections in the early 1800's?
2. Why was Andrew Jackson a popular President?
3. Assess Jackson's response to the the Supreme Court decision *Cherokee Nation* v. *Georgia* in terms of checks and balances.
4. Were Jackson's critics justified in calling him "King Andrew"? Why or why not?
5. Why was nullification a threat to the future of the United States?

Chapter 16

An Age of Reform

During the Second Great Awakening, large numbers of American Protestants attended revival meetings like the one shown in this 1838 lithograph.

In the early nineteenth century, the American economy was developing rapidly, and the nation's politics were changing in important ways. Why should change stop there? Some Americans, known as reformers, wanted to go further. By conscious effort, reformers believed, people could build a better world. Some reformers started model communities to show how to build such a world. Others worked to help unfortunate people of one sort or another. They founded schools, hospitals, and prisons. During this age, or time of reform, people also began to work for more rights for women. Above all, however, reformers worked to free the slaves.

Each of the reform causes was different from the others. But the same people often worked for several different causes. Many reformers also shared certain basic beliefs that help explain why they were reformers.

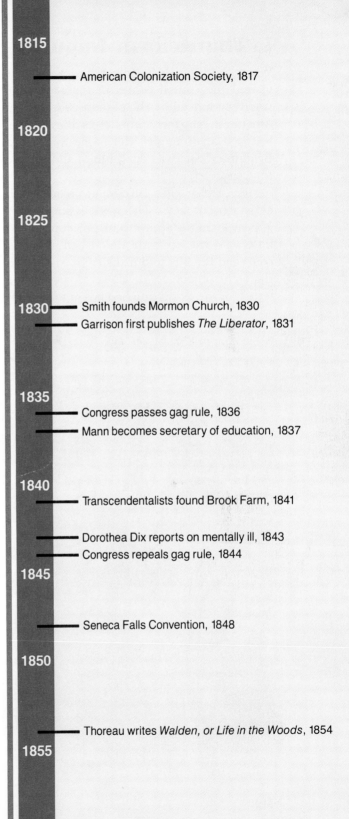

1815

American Colonization Society, 1817

1820

1825

1830 — Smith founds Mormon Church, 1830
— Garrison first publishes *The Liberator*, 1831

1835

Congress passes gag rule, 1836
Mann becomes secretary of education, 1837

1840

Transcendentalists found Brook Farm, 1841

Dorothea Dix reports on mentally ill, 1843
Congress repeals gag rule, 1844

1845

Seneca Falls Convention, 1848

1850

Thoreau writes *Walden, or Life in the Woods*, 1854

1855

I. The Reform Impulse

When the English novelist Charles Dickens visited the United States in the 1840's, he was very moved by the patient efforts of an American reformer, Samuel Gridley Howe, to teach a young girl. Her name was Laura Bridgman. She was deaf, blind, and unable to speak.

First, Howe gave Bridgman objects such as spoons or keys. The word *spoon* or *key* appeared on the appropriate object in raised letters. Howe took the labels off and encouraged the girl to put the right word with the right object. Next, Howe separated the letters of the words and had her put the right

Some reformers had great success teaching blind and deaf children.

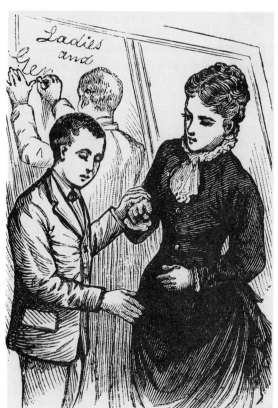

letters together to make the proper labels. The process was very mechanical.

Then suddenly, Howe said, "the truth began to flash upon her. She understood that here was a way by which she could herself make up a sign of anything that was in her mind, and show it to another mind." Her face lighted up "with a human expression." From that moment, Howe said, he saw that "the great obstacle was overcome." He would be able to help the girl.

Howe was the founder of a famous school for the blind, the Perkins Institute in Boston. He was also involved in other reform causes. His work with Laura Bridgman showed clearly what lay behind the cause of reform at that time.

Howe spent hundreds of hours teaching the girl. What could she ever do with her life that would be worth the time Howe devoted to her? That did not matter to him or to other reformers like Howe. Laura Bridgman's human spirit was valuable beyond measure.

That belief in the value of all human beings was the basis of Howe's idealism. In one way or another, it affected all the major reforms of Howe's day.

Religion and Reform

The reformers' belief in the power and importance of human beings came out of American Protestantism. It arose during a period of **revival,** or intense religious feeling.

The **Second Great Awakening,** as this period of revival is called, started in Kentucky and Tennessee soon after 1800 and then spread to other places. It was very different from the First Great Awakening, which swept through the colonies in the 1730's and 1740's.

In the earlier revival, preachers like the Reverend Jonathan Edwards of Connecticut stressed human weakness in the face of God's overpowering strength. Instead, preachers in the Second Awakening taught that human efforts were important. By trying hard, people could earn a place in heaven. If individuals could win a place in heaven, surely they could also transform the world.

Not all people swept up by the Second Awakening became reformers, and not all reformers came out of the Second Awakening. But many did. Schools founded by revivalists such as Lane Seminary and Oberlin College in Ohio became centers of reform. Their graduates went out to try to win salvation both in heaven and on earth.

▶1. How was the Second Awakening different from the Great Awakening of the 1700's?

Transcendentalists

The ideas that inspired reformers could also be seen among a group of writers and thinkers known as **transcendentalists.** Many transcendentalists lived in Concord, Massachusetts. Among them was Henry David Thoreau (thə rō'). In 1845, Thoreau went to live by himself at nearby Walden Pond, which he wrote about in his book *Walden, or Life in the Woods* (1854).

The essayist Ralph Waldo Emerson was another well-known transcendentalist thinker. Emerson believed that God was in every human being. Also, each person was unique, created by God for a purpose that could not be fulfilled by anyone else. A belief in the value of all people, in fact, was widely shared by Americans of that time and helps explain why they thought every person, however disabled or degraded, was worth saving. Such a belief was obviously at work in Howe's efforts to teach Laura Bridgman.

▶2. What beliefs did Thoreau and Emerson share with Howe and other reformers?

Reviewing Section I

Identify Samuel Gridley Howe, Laura Bridgman, revival, Second Great Awakening, transcendentalists, Henry David Thoreau, *Walden, or Life in the Woods*, Ralph Waldo Emerson

Questions to Answer
1. Why did Howe devote so much time to Laura Bridgman?
2. What message did the preachers of the Second Great Awakening spread?

A Question to Think About How did ideas about human life inspire reformers?

II. The Road to Change

Reformers of the early 1800's tried to save individuals in a variety of ways. Many thought the best way of doing so was to found communities that would serve as models for change. Other reformers started institutions like prisons, hospitals, or schools to help people. Still others worked to fight evils such as drunkenness.

Communal Experiments

Reformers who started model communities tried new ways of organizing work and family life or new forms of property holding. In that way, reformers hoped to give individuals more freedom to develop their best qualities.

▶1. Why did some reformers build model communities?

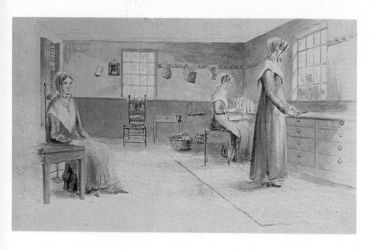

Members of a Shaker community are shown packing and labeling medicines they made for market.

The Shakers Actually, there were some model communities in North America even before the Revolution. For example, the Shakers, a religious group, began founding such communities after their leader, Mother Ann Lee, arrived from England in 1774.

The Shakers did not marry and have children. As a result, their communities could grow only by attracting new members. The group reached its height between 1820 and 1860. At that time, there were 20 Shaker settlements in 8 states that included altogether about 6,000 people.

Shakers lived a simple life of hard work broken by the ritual-like dances that became part of their tradition. The communities supported themselves by farming, and selling craft products, seeds, and medicines.

▶**2.** How did the Shakers support themselves?

Brook Farm Several new kinds of model communities were started in the early 1800's. One of the best known was Brook Farm, founded at West Roxbury, Massachusetts, in 1841 by a group of transcendentalists. The group of 20 at Brook Farm included the family of Louisa May Alcott, who wrote *Little Women* and *Little Men*. Nathaniel Hawthorne, a great American novelist, also lived for a time at Brook Farm. The experiment was discontinued because few of the group knew anything about farming and the community could not support itself.

▶**3.** Why was the Brook Farm community a failure?

The Mormons One of the most successful communities was founded by the Church of the Latter Day Saints, also known as the **Mormon Church.** Joseph Smith founded the church in 1830 in upstate New York. Smith said an angel revealed to him the location of golden tablets. On those tablets were words that he translated and published as the *Book of Mormon.*

Smith's followers first settled in Ohio and then moved to Missouri. In 1839, they began a cooperative society at Nauvoo, Illinois. There they did very well. By the mid-1840's, the town had 15,000 people.

Their neighbors were not, however, happy to have the Mormons nearby. Their hostility deepened when Smith announced that the Mormons were to practice polygamy. That is, each man was to take several wives. Smith was arrested and thrown in jail. A mob murdered him there on June 27, 1844, and then attacked Nauvoo itself.

The group's brilliant new leader, Brigham Young, decided to lead the Mormons to another new home in the valley of the Great Salt Lake in Utah, which was in Mexican territory. There he hoped his people would be free to live as they chose. That was not to be. The Mormons, however, prospered. Their close-knit, hard working communities proved especially suited to life in the West. Mormons, who no longer practice polygamy, remain a powerful force in Utah today.

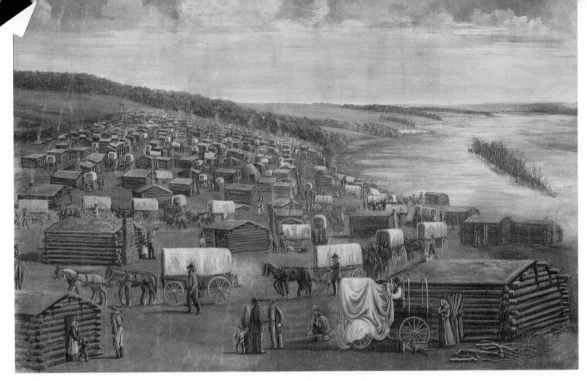

A group of Mormons, on their way to Utah during the winter of 1846–47, set up a temporary city along the bank of the Missouri River.

▶**4.** Why did Brigham Young lead the Mormons into Mexican territory?

Reforming Prisons and Asylums

Some reformers founded prisons, reformatories, insane asylums, poor houses, orphanages, and other such institutions. They set out to help the least fortunate members of society. To save such people would surely show that God lives in every human being. Among such reformers was Dorothea Dix.

▶**5.** Why did some reformers found reformatories, orphanages, and other such institutions?

Helping the Mentally Ill Dorothea Dix fought to create special hospitals for the mentally ill. Her crusade began when she was asked to teach Sunday School to some prisoners in Cambridge, Massachusetts. She

Dorothea Dix's work on behalf of the mentally ill led to reform in many states.

found to her surprise that people who were mentally ill were locked in unheated, unclean jail rooms with criminals. Dix decided to find out how the mentally ill were treated in other parts of Massachusetts.

After two years of study, Dix reported to the Massachusetts legislature. She found the mentally ill, she declared in 1843, "in cages, closets, cellars, stalls, pens! Chained, naked, beaten with rods, and lashed into obedience!"

Dix and other reformers had great success in setting up special hospitals for the mentally ill. By the 1850's, there were such hospitals in 28 states. There, the reformers believed, the insane could be cured. First, however, they had to be separated from the rest of the world and made to live a very ordered life. The new hospitals or asylums were much like another institution reformers founded—prisons.

▶ **6.** How did Dorothea Dix help people with mental disorders?

Prisons In the eighteenth century, convicted criminals were most often fined or sentenced to some physical punishment. They might be whipped in public, for example. After the Revolution, laws changed so that criminals were often punished by having to serve time in jail. It was not until the 1820's, however, that big prisons were built. They reflected perfectly the ideas of their founders.

Prison reformers thought that prisoners had to be separated from all evil influences in order to be turned into good citizens. Prisoners also needed to discover the good within themselves. As a result, reformers suggested that prisons be built in the countryside away from the distractions of the city. In the new prisons, prisoners were kept by themselves in individual cells or small rooms.

At one of the first of the new prisons, Auburn State Prison in New York, the inmates had to follow very rigid rules. They had to march to work in step with their heads turned to the side so they could not even look at each other. The cells at Auburn were only seven feet high, seven feet wide, and three feet long. Prisoners were allowed to work with others only during the day. They stayed alone in their cells at night.

At Eastern State Penitentiary near Philadelphia, another model prison, the cells were larger. However, the convicts never left them for the entire length of their sentences. While in prison, they could talk with nobody from the outside world except prison officials and chaplains.

The reformers believed that not just criminals but all Americans needed to learn habits of order and discipline. But they failed to create prisons that would reform criminals and hospitals that would cure the mentally ill. The criminals sent to the new prisons tended to be the most hardened wrongdoers. The mentally ill sent to the new hospitals were the ones most in need of care. They also included a growing number of immigrants, especially the Irish, for whom the reformers did not have much concern.

Before long those institutions became simply **custodial.** That is, they became places where criminals and others could be locked up and kept off the streets. They also became crowded and dirty. Nowhere did the reformers fail so badly.

▶ **7.** Why did the new prisons fail to turn criminals into good citizens?

Public Schools

In 1800, there were no public school systems in the United States except in New England. Even in New England, children attended school for only a few years. All that started to change after Massachusetts established a

Certificates of merit, such as the one shown here, were awarded for outstanding work. This one was for faithfulness and good behavior.

state board of education in 1837 and made the reformer Horace Mann its secretary.

▶**8.** What part of the country had a public school system in 1800?

Horace Mann Mann believed strongly in public education. Unless the country prepared its children to be good citizens, he argued, "then our Republic must go down to destruction." Like the men who founded Lowell, Mann was especially afraid that a permanent class of poor people might form in the United States. Education, he thought, would help avoid that. It was therefore necessary to educate all the country's children.

Mann's arguments were helped by the spread of suffrage to all adult white males. Many believed that all white males, at least, needed an education so that they could vote intelligently. Changes in the northern economy also increased the need for people who

could read and write and whose minds were open to new ideas.

▶**9.** Why did Horace Mann believe so strongly in public education?

Mann's Reforms Mann did more than talk about reforming education. He lengthened the school year in Massachusetts to six months, started a state-supported training school for teachers, and increased teachers' pay. He also added to the number of high schools in the state and changed the subjects those schools taught. Before, high schools had taught subjects like Latin and Greek. Mann instead emphasized arithmetic, science, geography, and American history. Many other states followed the example of Massachusetts, especially those in the North and the Old Northwest.

Mann did not accomplish as much as he had hoped. Many poor families had to put their children to work at an early age so that they could help buy food and pay the rent. Such families did not send their children to school. Catholic immigrants also feared that the public schools would make their children into Protestants. As a result, they began to start their own schools.

By 1860, there were still only about 300 public high schools in the nation, and one third of those were in Massachusetts. The students who attended high school were generally well-off. Girls may have benefited the most from the new high schools. If they chose, they could go on to become school teachers, the one profession that was actually opening up to women in those years. In Massachusetts, 39 percent of the teachers were female in 1840—and 86 percent 25 years later. In other states, teaching school was also becoming a woman's profession.

▶10. What changes did Mann make in public education in Massachusetts?

Women and Reform

Most Americans of the nineteenth century thought that women were more moral than men. In fact, women were considered the guardians of the nation's morals. Because morality and religion are so closely related, it seemed proper for women to become more active in church affairs after the Great Awakening. From there, many went on to work in various reform movements.

▶11. Why were women considered to be the guardians of the nation's morals?

From Home to Church   In the 1800's, middle-class white women had more time to devote to the church. American families were smaller than they had been in the past, and children stayed at school for more hours each week. Women no longer had to spin and weave like their grandmothers, either. They could buy ready-made clothes and other store-bought goods. The flood of Irish immigrants meant that many middle-class households could hire low-paid Irish servants. Many of the women joined prayer groups, missionary societies, or charitable groups.

▶12. Why could middle-class white women devote more time to church activities in the 1800's?

From Church to Reform   By the mid-1830's, many middle-class Protestant women began moving from church activities into various reform groups. Dorothea Dix, for example, first became interested in the mentally ill while teaching a Sunday school class at a jail. In general, women lent their help to reform movements that had some importance for them and for the home.

▶13. How did women decide what kind of reform movements to support?

Temperance   Many women joined in the **temperance** movement. The movement was started to convince Americans to drink less alcohol or to drink none at all. Temperance had a special meaning for women. Many wives and children were harmed by husbands and fathers who drank too much. Of course, drunkenness obscured the good qualities of human beings.

The temperance movement was popular, too, because it served the needs of an industrializing society. In earlier times, workers were sometimes paid part of their wages in rum or beer. But a factory worker who had been drinking alcohol could ruin a machine or cause a serious accident. That would make that worker less able to support a family.

The temperance reformers were very successful. They made a major change in American life. In 1830, Americans drank five gallons of alcohol **per capita** (for each man, woman, and child.) By the mid-1840's, that figure had dropped to two gallons.

▶**14.** What was the temperance movement?

Reviewing Section II

Identify Shakers, ~~Mother Ann Lee~~, Brook Farm, Louisa May Alcott, Nathaniel Hawthorne, Mormon Church, Joseph Smith, Brigham Young, Dorothea Dix, custodial, Horace Mann, temperance, per capita

Questions to Answer
1. What were some of the problems of the new model communities started in the 1800's?
2. What kinds of reform movements were started in the 1800's?

A Question to Think About Why do you think women became so interested in reform movements?

III. The Crusade against Slavery

Women also worked hard at the one reform that perhaps more than any other changed American society, a reform that in time drew in many people who once worked in other causes. That reform was abolition, the effort to end slavery.

The American Colonization Society

When Andrew Jackson first became President, the American antislavery movement was in trouble. Whites centered their efforts to end slavery around the **American Colonization Society,** founded in 1817. The society tried to convince slaveholders to free their slaves. Then the society proposed to ship freed blacks out of the country. In 1822, for example, a colony of free American blacks was "planted" in Liberia on the west coast of Africa. Those efforts at colonization suggested that blacks could not become part of American society. Black Americans, both slave and free, male and female, disagreed.

Colonization was a losing battle for other reasons too. The slave population of the

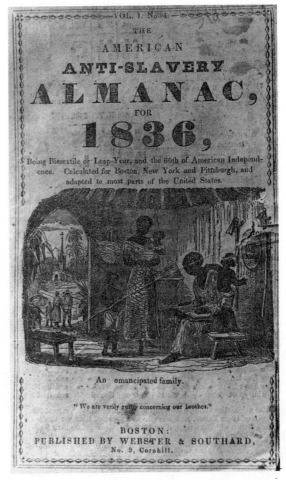

The American Anti-Slavery Almanac *pointed out the benefits of emancipation.* ▶

335

United States was growing rapidly. The 694,000 slaves in the United States in 1790 had grown to about two million by the 1820's. Meanwhile, the amount of slave territory had almost tripled.

▶**1.** What plan did the American Colonization Society propose for free blacks?

Abolition

There were also about 50 local black antislavery societies in the United States by 1830. The free blacks who belonged to those groups helped fugitive slaves—those who ran away from their owners. The black antislavery societies argued that the slaves should be freed, or emancipated, immediately. Such blacks helped found the **abolitionist movement,** which was led by William Lloyd Garrison, a white reformer.

▶**2.** Why did black antislavery societies support the abolitionist movement?

William Lloyd Garrison Garrison was born in Newburyport, Massachusetts, in December 1805. When he grew up, Garrison became a

Harriet Tubman (left) is shown here with some of the slaves she led to freedom.

journalist and worked on a temperance newspaper.

In 1827, Garrison met Benjamin Lundy, a New Jersey Quaker who favored colonization. In the fall of 1829, Garrison went to Baltimore to help Lundy edit his newspaper, the *Genius of Universal Emancipation.* Garrison's attacks on slaveholders were so severe that he was thrown in jail for one of his editorials. Then he moved to Boston and, on January 1, 1831, began to publish his own newspaper, *The Liberator.*

Garrison demanded that slavery should be abolished, or ended, at once. *The Liberator* spoke for those antislavery people known as **abolitionists.**

▶**3.** Who was William Lloyd Garrison?

Garrison's Stand Garrison sounded more than a little like a revivalist preacher. Indeed, Garrison and the abolitionists attacked slavery not just because it contradicted American principles but because it was a sin. Like the revivalists, they called on both Northerners and Southerners to repent and to free the land of the sin called slavery.

Garrison minced no words. "I will be as harsh as truth, and as uncompromising as justice," he said in the first issue of *The Liberator.* On the subject of emancipation, he said, "I do not wish to think, or speak, or write with moderation . . . I am in earnest— I will not equivocate—I will not excuse—I will not retreat a single inch—AND I WILL BE HEARD."

Garrison argued that free blacks should have rights like those of white Americans. The New England Anti-Slavery Society, which Garrison organized in 1832, and the American Anti-Slavery Society of 1833 accepted both women and blacks as members. Three members of the American Anti-Slavery Society's executive committee were black.

At this antislavery meeting in the 1840's, men and women show their support for views expressed by the speakers.

▶**4.** What were Garrison's views on slavery?

Black Abolitionists One of the best known black abolitionists was Harriet Tubman, a Maryland slave who escaped to freedom in the North. She risked her freedom 19 times by returning to the South to help hundreds of other slaves escape.

Frederick Douglass was another well-known black abolitionist. He told the story of his life as a slave in his autobiography, which was first published as an abolitionist pamphlet. That so brilliant a man could be held in bondage made the wrongfulness of slavery clear. A powerful writer and speaker, Douglass became the most important black leader of his day.

▶**5.** In what ways did Harriet Tubman and Frederick Douglass fight against slavery?

Opposition to Abolition The abolitionists had many opponents, even in the North. In 1835, Garrison was dragged through the streets and almost killed by a mob in Boston. On the same day another mob in Utica, New York, broke up a meeting of the New York State Anti-Slavery Society. In 1837, Elijah Lovejoy, who published an antislavery newspaper, was murdered while trying to save his press from a mob in Alton, Illinois.

As mobs in the North tried to silence the abolitionists, others in the South burned abolitionist writings brought there through the mails. Even President Jackson favored a law

Highlighting People
Sojourner Truth

Sojourner Truth had a mission. She believed that God had chosen her to travel from place to place and speak out against the evils of slavery. No one knew those evils better than she did. Sojourner Truth had been born a slave.

Sojourner Truth was born in the late 1790's in Ulster County, New York. She was named Isabella at birth. During her first thirty years, she had several owners and at least five children. When two of her daughters were sold, Isabella fled from her owner. One year later, in 1828, the state of New York banned slavery. Isabella was free.

In 1829, Isabella and two of her children went to New York City to find work. She stayed there for 14 years. During this time, she lived in several religious communities and claimed to have had many mystical experiences. The most powerful one took the form of voices that told her to take the name of Sojourner Truth and travel east to preach.

In 1843, Sojourner set out. She spoke wherever people would listen—at church meetings, in parks, on the streets. Her message was simple. She urged people to show their love for God by being kind to one another. As she traveled, she supported herself by working as a housemaid or caring for the sick.

In time, her reputation as a powerful speaker spread. In Northampton, Massachusetts, she met abolitionists William Lloyd Garrison and Frederick Douglass. They asked Sojourner to join them. From then on, she spoke at anti-slavery meetings throughout the Northeast and Midwest, describing her life as a slave.

In 1851, a friend invited her to speak at a women's rights convention in Akron, Ohio. At the convention, Sojourner listened as a clergyman spoke out against the right of women to vote. He claimed that women should be denied that right because they were weak and helpless. Sojourner's response shamed him into silence.

> That man over there says women need to be helped into carriages and lifted over ditches, and to have the best place everywhere. Nobody ever helps me into carriages or over puddles, or gives me the best place. And ain't I a woman?
>
> Look at my arm. I have ploughed and planted and gathered into barns ... And ain't I a woman? I could work as much and eat as much as a man—when I could get it—and bear the lash as well. And ain't I a woman?

In 1864, at the age of 67, Sojourner Truth visited Abraham Lincoln in the White House. After the war, she stayed in Washington for several years, finding jobs and housing for former slaves. In her eighties, she began to travel again, trying to persuade people that Congress should set aside government land for freed slaves. Sojourner Truth was nearly a century old when she died in Battle Creek, Michigan. Her funeral was the largest ever held in the town.

that would make it illegal to send abolitionist materials through the mails.

In 1836, Congress adopted a **gag rule** by which all the petitions against slavery were automatically set aside without debate. What, then, of the right of free speech and the right of petition? Former President John Quincy Adams, now a member of the House of Representatives, led the fight against the gag rule and managed to get it repealed in 1844.

Gradually, the abolitionists seemed to be standing for the basic civil rights of all Americans. That attracted still more people to the movement. By 1840, there were over 2,000 local abolitionist societies in the United States. They had over 200,000 members.

▶**6.** How did their opponents try to stop the abolitionists?

The Movement Divides

Soon, however, differences of opinion among abolitionists caused the movement to divide. Many people opposed to slavery objected to Garrison's radical demands. Some were outraged by his willingness to let women play an important public role in the abolitionist movement. Others were horrified by his bitter verbal attacks on churches that failed to oppose slavery.

A more moderate group of abolitionists in New York broke with Garrison in 1840. They founded what they called the American and Foreign Anti-Slavery Society. Some of those who disagreed with Garrison decided to work against slavery through politics. They founded the Liberty Party, which ran an abolitionist, James G. Birney, for President in 1840.

After the split, Garrison became even more extreme in his arguments. He decided that slavery continued only because the Constitution supported it. If there was a major slave uprising in the South, he noted, northern troops would help put it down. As a result, he condemned the Constitution as "a covenant with death and an agreement with hell," and urged the free states to secede from the Union. In 1843, the Massachusetts Anti-Slavery Society voted 59 to 21 in favor of disunion! Thereafter "No Union with Slaveholders" became a slogan among the Garrisonian abolitionists.

▶**7.** Why did some abolitionists leave the movement headed by Garrison?

Douglass's Stand

Frederick Douglass disagreed. If the North left the Union, he asked, how could it help free the slaves? At first, the Garrisonians had set out to free the slaves, but their new policy, Douglass said, would leave the slaves to free themselves.

Douglass's unhappiness with the abolitionists had been building for several years. Garrison's followers were more ready to treat blacks as equals than most Americans, but even they had a long way to go. They were uncomfortable, for example, with Douglass's polished manner of speaking. "People won't believe you ever were a slave, Frederick, if you keep on this way," one white abolitionist told him. "It is not best that you seem too learned."

Why should Douglass have to take directions from such people? To him and to other blacks, life among the abolitionists seemed at times too much like the old days on the plantation, with white antislavery leaders taking the place of overseers.

Blacks were also interested in practical problems like getting jobs. They got little help from the abolitionists with that problem. More and more, it seemed, blacks had to speak for themselves. They had their own newspaper, *The Colored American*, published

Abolitionist reformer Frederick Douglass also fought for women's suffrage.

in New York. Then Douglass began another journal, *Frederick Douglass's Paper*, in Rochester, New York.

Garrison argued strongly against black separatism. But for Douglass and others like him who fought both southern slavery and northern prejudice, that change was necessary. Blacks had to declare their independence of white leaders before they could realize their own strength as people.

▶ **8.** Why did Douglass feel he had to break away from the Garrisonian abolitionists?

From Abolitionism to Feminism

Some white women also became increasingly discontented among the abolitionists. In 1837, two sisters from South Carolina, Angelina and Sarah Grimké, gave a series of antislavery lectures in New England. That caused an uproar since the audiences included men. Women, their critics said, should not speak

★★ The United States and the World ★★★★★★★★★★★★★★★
The Start of the Women's Rights Movement

In 1840, British abolitionists called for a World Anti-Slavery Convention to be held in London. They invited abolitionists from other countries to attend. Among the members of the American contingent were Lucretia Mott and her husband James, Wendell Phillips and his wife Ann, and Henry Stanton and his bride Elizabeth Cady Stanton.

Although the women were eager to attend the convention, they were uncertain how they would be received in London. Still, they looked forward to the opportunity to represent their country in the fight against slavery. The British, however, were shocked at the idea of women taking part in the convention.

Wendell Phillips decided to lead the fight to admit women delegates to the convention. As he prepared his arguments, Ann Green Phillips told her husband, "No shilly-shallying Wendell! Be brave as a lion!" The issue was hotly debated for hours. When the vote was finally taken, the male delegates had overwhelmingly voted to exclude the women.

Lucretia Mott and Elizabeth Cady Stanton discussed the situation. They were so angered by the convention's action that they pledged to work for women's rights for the rest of their lives. Eight years later, they organized the first women's rights convention in the United States. It was held on July 19–20, in Seneca Falls, New York.

in public and certainly not before men. Garrison defended the Grimkés. He was very advanced on the "woman question." But many abolitionists seemed to be on the other side.

The Grimkés, who had devoted themselves to the cause of the slaves, suddenly understood that they, too, were the victims of injustice. They became **feminists,** defenders of the rights of women. Men and women had the same rights and the same duties, feminists insisted. They attacked the whole idea that women should be subordinate to men. Others soon joined them in their cause.

In 1848, Elizabeth Cady Stanton and Lucretia Mott, both of whom had worked against slavery, organized the first convention in support of women's rights. It was known as the Seneca Falls Convention because it met in Seneca Falls, New York. The convention issued a "Declaration of Sentiments and Resolutions" modeled after the Declaration of Independence.

The declaration said, "The history of mankind is a history of repeated injuries and usurpations on the part of man toward woman, having in direct object the establishment of an absolute tyranny over her." It complained that men had denied women the vote, made women submit to laws to which the women had not consented, made married women "in the eyes of the law civilly dead", taken away women's rights to property, and denied women the chance for a "thorough education." It demanded that women immediately be given "all the rights . . . which belong to them as citizens of the United States."

Women did not get all of those rights. In the years before 1860, married women won some control over their property, but not much else. They would not get the vote until "ladies" like those at Seneca Falls could get together with working women, like the mill

Elizabeth Cady Stanton (left) and Susan B. Anthony led the early women's rights movement.

girls at Lowell. But of the feminists, only Susan B. Anthony, another former abolitionist, was much interested in working women.

▶**9.** What rights did women demand in the "Declaration of Sentiments and Resolutions"?

Reviewing Section III

Identify American Colonization Society, abolitionist movement, William Lloyd Garrison, Benjamin Lundy, *Genius of Universal Emancipation, The Liberator,* abolitionists, Harriet Tubman, Frederick Douglass, gag rule, Angelina and Sarah Grimké, feminists, Elizabeth Cady Stanton, Lucretia Mott, Seneca Falls Convention, Susan B. Anthony

Questions to Answer
1. What was the abolitionists' viewpoint on the issue of slavery?
2. Why did the abolition movement split apart?

A Question to Think About How did the role women played in the abolitionist movement encourage the rise of feminism?

341

Reading a Primary Source

Following is a selection from the *Seneca Falls Declaration of Rights and Sentiments*. Read the selection and answer the questions which follow.

When, in the course of human events, it becomes necessary for one portion of the family of man to assume among the people of the earth a position different from that which they have hitherto occupied, but one to which the laws of nature and of nature's God entitle them, a decent respect to the opinion of mankind requires that they should declare the causes that impel them to such a course.

We hold these truths to be self-evident: that all men and women are created equal . . .

The history of mankind is a history of repeated injuries and usurpations on the part of man toward woman . . . To prove this, let facts be submitted to a candid world.

He has never permitted her to exercise her inalienable right to the elective franchise.

He has compelled her to submit to laws in the formation of which she has no voice . . .

He has taken from her all right in property, even to the wages she earns . . .

(From *History of Woman Suffrage,* Elizabeth C. Stanton, et al., eds., Vol. I, New York, 1881, pp. 70–73.)

1. Why do you think the authors of the Seneca Falls Declaration modeled their document on the Declaration of Independence?
2. Review the Declaration of Independence. Who is the "He" cited for wrongs against the colonists?
3. Who is the "He" cited for wrongs in the Seneca Falls Declaration?
4. What are the wrongs "He" has committed against women in the selection quoted?
5. The following is a quotation from historian Thomas Bailey. "The Seneca Falls meeting, which launched the modern women's rights movement, not surprisingly became the object of scorn and denunciation from press and pulpit." Is it a primary source?

IV. Reform and Politics

Many reformers tried at first to win change through the power of persuasion. But after a while, the reformers turned to the government for help. Temperance advocates, for example, first tried to persuade people to give up drink. Then they fought for laws that would limit or end the sale of liquor. Similarly, those who opposed slavery first tried to persuade slave owners to give up their slaves. Then some fought for legal change.

Because the reformers supported an active government, one that intervened to bring about change, they tended to support the Whig Party. Those who opposed reform often became Democrats. Among the strongest opponents of reform were immigrants, especially the Irish.

Nativism

The Irish had good reason for thinking the reformers were not their friends. Many reformers were attracted to **nativism,** an anti-immigrant movement that began to grow in strength in the 1830's. What upset the nativists was, above all, the fact that so many newcomers were Catholics. The nativists published the most scandalous and false stories to discredit the Catholic Church. Catholics, especially Irish Catholics, were justly outraged.

▶**1.** What was the nativist movement?

The Irish and Politics

Logically, the Irish supported the Jacksonian Democrats. They brought that party a lot of strength. That was in part because some states allowed immigrants to vote even before they were citizens. The Irish tended to stick together and vote together. Large groups of Irish lived in states with large numbers of electoral votes such as Massachusetts and New York. The Irish early discovered those advantages and learned to use them. The increasing importance of Irish Catholics in politics was therefore a sign of their Americanization.

What did the Irish do with their power? In time, they would use it for many causes. For the moment, however, they used it to vote against their enemies. They also tried to get government jobs for relatives and friends. The nativists thought such practices were corrupt and un-American. However, the Irish were right in line with the policies of Andrew Jackson, the creator and defender of the spoils system.

▶**2.** How did the Irish use their political power?

Slavery and Politics

That the Democrats were "soft" on slavery did not bother the Irish at all. If the slaves were freed, after all, they would be fighting for the very jobs that kept some food on Irish tables. In any case, it was comforting for the Irish to know that some people were even worse off than they were.

The Democrats did not, of course, advocate any national programs to strengthen southern slavery. They just wanted to keep the issue out of national politics. The growing strength of the abolitionists made that increasingly hard to do. But what finally undermined the Democratic effort was something else, a series of events in the Far West that once again brought a great new block of territory under the government of the United States.

▶**3.** Why did many of the Irish support the Democratic Party?

Reviewing Section IV

Identify nativism

Questions to Answer
1. Why did most reformers support the Whig Party?
2. Why were Democrats pleased to have the support of Irish voters?

A Question to Think About Why did the Irish dislike and distrust most reformers?

IMPROVE YOUR READING
Categorizing

The reform movement grew out of people's desire to find solutions to some of the problems Americans faced in the early 1800's. A good way to understand and remember those reforms is to categorize them according what the problem was, who was involved, why they took place, and the solutions offered by the reformers.

The chart below will help you categorize the information discussed in the chapter. Some of the problems discussed in the chapter have been listed for you. On a separate sheet of paper, copy the chart and fill in the missing information. You may need to refer back to the chapter to complete the chart.

Problem	Leader or Leaders	Why Reformers Called for Change	Solution Offered by Reformers
Lack of Education for the Handicapped			
Poor Treatment of the Mentally Ill			
Illiteracy			
Drunkenness			
Slavery			
Women Denied Full Rights			

CHAPTER 16 REVIEW

Vocabulary Check
Match each term in column I with the phrase that describes it in column II.

Column I

1. Transcendentalists
2. Feminists
3. Abolitionists
4. Temperance
5. Nativism

Column II

a. People who worked for an immediate end to slavery
b. An anti-immigrant movement
c. A group of writers and thinkers including Thoreau and Emerson
d. Defenders of the the rights of women
e. Movement started to convince Americans to drink less alcohol

Fact Check
On a separate piece of paper, write the name of the person or persons described in each of the sentences below.

1. He wrote about living alone at Walden Pond in Concord, Massachusetts.
2. He founded the Perkins Institute, a school for the blind.
3. She was a former slave who guided other slaves to freedom.
4. She wrote *Little Women* and *Little Men* and lived briefly at Brook Farm.
5. A former slave, he became the most important black leader of his day.
6. This radical abolitionist published *The Liberator*.
7. She worked to improve the care of the mentally ill.
8. These two women organized the convention in Seneca Falls in 1848.
9. This educator wanted public education for all students.
10. He led the Mormons to Utah.

Time Check
On a separate piece of paper, put the following events in chronological order.

1. Joseph Smith founds the Mormon Church.
2. The Seneca Falls Convention meets.
3. Brook Farm begins.
4. Horace Mann becomes secretary of the Massachusetts State Board of Education.
5. The American Anti-Slavery Society begins.

Skills Check
On a separate piece of paper, decide which of the following items is a primary source. Give reasons for your choices.

1. An issue of *The Liberator*
2. A biography of Henry David Thoreau illustrated with pictures of Walden Pond
3. Frederick Douglass's autobiography
4. A film about the Mormons' journey to Utah
5. A letter from Lucretia Mott

Think and Write
1. What effects did the Second Great Awakening have on American life?
2. Show how a belief in the value of human life affected reformers in many fields.
3. Why did women become involved in the reform movements of the 1800's?
4. Why did black abolitionists feel that they had to speak and act for themselves?
5. Why did most Irish immigrants distrust the reform movements?

Chapter 17
Claiming the West

In the 1830's and 1840's, wagon trains were a common sight on the Oregon Trail. This painting shows a wagon train crossing a river.

West of the Mississippi lay a land unfamiliar to people who knew only Europe or the eastern United States. First came the Great Plains, an enormous grassland three to four hundred miles wide that stretched from Canada south to Texas. Farther west lay the Rocky Mountains. The Rockies were the very backbone of the continent, beginning in

Alaska and stretching all the way south to Mexico. Just getting through them to the lands beyond was a problem.

The best way through the Rockies was discovered by an explorer and fur trapper named Jedediah Smith. In 1824, he used an almost level passageway between the northern and southern Rockies in western Wyoming. He and other fur trappers called it South Pass.

Soon families of pioneers followed the paths the trappers had blazed, starting farms and building homes in the Far West. The settlers moved to lands that were not clearly owned by the United States. Many of them hoped that the flag would soon follow them and that their efforts would help the country grow. Before much time had passed, those dreams came true.

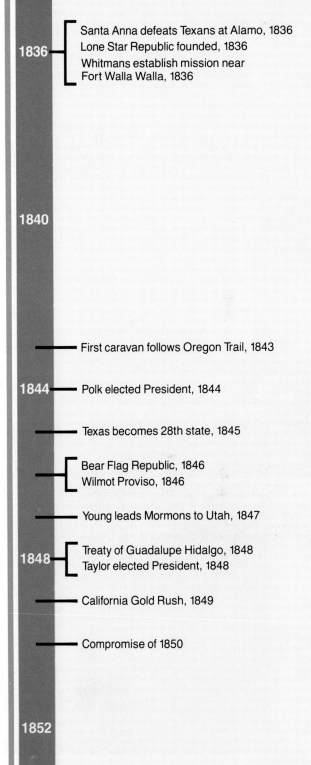

I. The Westward Movement
    Texas
    The Texas Revolution
    Oregon
    New Mexico and California
    Utah

II. Manifest Destiny and the Mexican War
    Manifest Destiny
    The Election of 1844
    Taking Texas and Oregon
    The Mexican War

III. Slavery Enters Politics
    The New Southern Argument
    The North Defends Free Labor
    The Election of 1848
    Crisis in the West
    Toward Compromise

Timeline:

1836
- Santa Anna defeats Texans at Alamo, 1836
- Lone Star Republic founded, 1836
- Whitmans establish mission near Fort Walla Walla, 1836

1840

- First caravan follows Oregon Trail, 1843

1844
- Polk elected President, 1844

- Texas becomes 28th state, 1845

- Bear Flag Republic, 1846
- Wilmot Proviso, 1846

- Young leads Mormons to Utah, 1847

1848
- Treaty of Guadalupe Hidalgo, 1848
- Taylor elected President, 1848

- California Gold Rush, 1849

- Compromise of 1850

1852

I. The Westward Movement

In the 1820's and 1830's, there was still plenty of good farming land to be taken up in places such as Iowa, Wisconsin, and Minnesota. Those lands, however, were too far north for growing cotton. Cotton planters spread into Arkansas and Florida. Then they began looking for other lands where cotton would grow. They found such lands in Texas.

Texas

Texas belonged first to Spain and then, after 1821, to Mexico. The United States offered to buy Texas, but Mexico was unwilling to sell. So it remained part of Mexico.

Although Mexico would not sell Texas, it did open the territory to immigrants from the United States. It hoped that this would enrich Mexico and protect its people from the Indians to their north. The Mexican government made agreements with men known as **empresarios** (em prä sä′ryoz) who promised to bring at least 200 families into Texas within a stated amount of time. Empresarios were granted large tracts of land—66,774 acres for every 200 families brought in.

It was not hard to attract people to Texas. An empresario could sell a rancher over 4,000 acres very cheaply. Farmers could buy 177 acres of good farmland cheaper than they could in the United States. However, most families decided to raise cattle rather than farm crops. Immigrants were freed from taxes for six years. Mexico insisted, however, that the immigrants be or soon become Roman Catholics. They also had to become citizens

F. J. Rothhaas made this watercolor of a house he designed for George Allen. Allen and his five brothers founded the city of Houston, Texas.

of Mexico within three years from the time they bought land.

▶**1.** Under what conditions did immigrants move to Texas?

Stephen Austin Some of the people who flocked to Texas accepted those terms in good faith. For example, Stephen F. Austin, who was one of the first empresarios, fully intended to keep his part of the agreement. He wrote a friend that he was "determined to fulfill rigidly all the duties and obligations of a Mexican citizen."

As an empresario, Austin was enormously successful. He brought about 750 families to Texas. Their successes encouraged others to come. By 1830, there were between 25,000 and 30,000 people in Texas, of whom only 4,000 were native Mexicans. Most of the rest came from the United States. Few of them were willing to learn Spanish or to become Mexican citizens. They were also unhappy when Mexico adopted laws that said they could not bring slaves into Mexican territory. The new laws also said that many slaves already in Texas would be freed when their owners died. There were about 1,000 slaves in Texas in 1830.

▶**2.** What made Stephen Austin a successful empresario?

Mexico's Reaction The Mexican government soon discovered that the Americans were ignoring the new laws on slavery. Furthermore, almost none of them—not even Stephen Austin—had become Catholic. Therefore the government changed its policy. In 1830, it announced that people from the United States could no longer settle in Texas. It also decided that slaves could no longer be brought to any part of Mexico. At the same time, the Mexican government put heavy duties on goods from the United States. It also did all it could to get native Mexicans, even criminals, to move to Texas, and stationed Mexican soldiers near the American settlements.

▶**3.** Why did the Mexican government change its policy in Texas?

The Texas Revolution

Unrest throughout Mexico, including Texas, led to a change in government. In 1834, General Antonio López de Santa Anna took charge of the country. At first, many Texans thought he would end the restrictions placed on them by the old government. The Texans prepared petitions for Santa Anna. However, when Stephen Austin took them to Mexico City in 1834, he was arrested and held in Mexico for eighteen months.

By the time Austin returned to Texas in 1835, the people of Texas had already adopted a temporary constitution and were governing themselves.

▶**4.** How did the Americans in Texas respond to the new Mexican policies?

The Alamo Santa Anna decided to put down the Texas rebels, as Mexico's rulers called them. In February 1836, he led 4,000 Mexicans against the Alamo mission in San Antonio. There 187 Texans held out for two weeks before they were killed on March 6.

In spite of their losses at the Alamo, Texans did not give up. Indeed, the fight had only begun. Four days before the Alamo fell, Texas had declared its independence, established the **Lone Star Republic,** and made Samuel Houston, a former governor of Tennessee, commander of its regular army.

▶**5.** What happened at the Alamo in 1836?

Independence for Texas The Texans' big victory came on April 21, 1836, at the Battle of San Jacinto (san' jə sin'tō) on the western

The heroic stand of the Texans at the Alamo inspired other Texans to "Remember the Alamo." They went on to defeat the Mexicans and to win independence.

bank of the San Jacinto River near Galveston. Shouting "Remember the Alamo!" Houston and his men destroyed the Mexican army in 15 minutes, killing or capturing about 1,100 Mexican soldiers. Among them was Santa Anna. The Texans forced him to sign a treaty giving Texas its independence. Mexico refused to honor that treaty, but it made no further attempt to conquer Texas.

With their war for independence ended, the Texans confirmed their new constitution in September 1836. Then they rewarded Sam Houston for his service by making him the first president of the new Texas Republic. The voters also told their new president to seek **annexation** to the United States. That is, they wanted Texas to become part of the United States.

▶ **6.** How did Texas win its independence?

The Annexation Issue Not everyone in the United States wanted Texas to be annexed. The Texas constitution allowed slavery. Many Northerners were against admitting another slave state to the Union. Northerners also feared that Texans in Congress would vote against tariffs and other measures designed to help the North. Others thought that by annexing Texas, the United States might provoke a war with Mexico.

Jackson was still President in 1836, and he wanted Texas to join the Union. But Jackson was also a good politician. He understood how explosive the slavery issue was. There was no way Texas could be annexed without a big debate over slavery. Moreover, 1836 was an election year. A battle over Texas might hurt the Democrats' chances of winning. So Jackson did not urge Congress to

Houston, Texas—one of the state's largest and most prosperous cities—bears the name of one of the state's most famous people. Yet this famous Texan was not from Texas at all. He was born hundreds of miles away in Virginia.

Sam Houston was born near Lexington, Virginia, in 1793. When he was 14, his father died, and his mother moved her nine children to a farm in Tennessee. Two years later, Sam went to work as a clerk in the village store. But he hated the dull work of the business world. The world of the Cherokee Indians who lived across the river appealed to him much more.

During his time with the Cherokee, Sam developed a great love and respect for their way of life. He stayed with them three years before leaving to serve under Andrew Jackson during the War of 1812. After the war, his friendship with Jackson led to his appointment as a Cherokee agent.

In 1818, Houston resigned from the army to study law. As a lawyer, Sam's energy and genius for drama quickly attracted attention. Within a year, he was elected district attorney. Within three years, he was elected to Congress. Finally, in 1827, he became governor of Tennessee.

In 1829, Houston's wife of three months left him. Shocked by her sudden departure, he resigned his post as governor and moved west to become an Indian trader.

By 1833, Houston was living in Texas, working as an agent for the Cherokee. As each day passed, it became more certain that war between Mexico and the Texans would break out. To many Texans, Sam Houston, with his enthusiasm and confidence, seemed a natural leader. In 1836, they made him commander in chief of their army.

On April 20, 1836, Houston led a force of 783 against an equal force of Mexicans led by Antonio de Santa Anna at San Jacinto. After a minor

skirmish, the two small armies retreated to watch and wait. The second day, over 500 Mexicans arrived. Sam struck that same afternoon. In a battle lasting only 15 minutes, Sam Houston's forces wiped out the Mexican army.

Houston's victory forced Santa Anna to recognize the independence of Texas. In October of the same year, Houston became president of the Republic of Texas. Nine years later, in 1845, Texas became the twenty-eighth state to join the Union.

In the years that followed, Houston served Texas first as a United States senator and then as governor in 1859. Two years later, at the start of the Civil War, Texas voted to leave the Union. Houston disagreed. His enemies branded him a coward and forced him to leave office.

The 68-year-old Houston retired to his farm in Huntsville, Texas. There he died two years later, hated by many of the Texans he had served so well.

annex Texas. He did not even recognize its independence or send a representative there until the very end of his term in office. Jackson's successor in the White House, Martin Van Buren, also refused to recommend annexation. For the time, then, Texas was left to make its separate way.

▶**7.** Why did Jackson and Van Buren refuse to recommend the annexation of Texas?

Oregon

At about the same time the annexation of Texas became an issue, some Americans became interested in annexing the Oregon Country. Oregon stretched from the Rocky Mountains in the east to the Pacific Ocean in the west and from 42° north latitude to 54° 40′ north latitude. North of that line was Alaska, which was claimed by the Russians, whose fur traders had set up an outpost there in 1784.

▶**8.** Where was the Oregon Country?

American and British Claims
Before the 1830's, Russia, Spain, Great Britain, and the United States all claimed the Oregon country. By the 1830's, however, only Great Britain and the United States still contended for the area. The claims of both nations rested on the right of discovery.

The American claim was based in part on the voyage of a New England sea captain, Robert Gray. His trading ship *Columbia* sailed up the mouth of the Columbia River in 1792. Gray named the river after his ship. Before long, other New England merchants seeking furs for the China trade were visiting the Oregon coast regularly. After Lewis and Clark explored the area from 1804 to 1805, even more traders came. Many worked for John Jacob Astor. He built a trading post named Astoria in Oregon between 1811 and 1813.

Great Britain's claim was at least as strong as that of the United States. Sir Francis Drake visited Oregon in 1579. Captain James Cook explored the area in the 1770's. Alexander Mackenzie, a British fur trader, traveled overland to Oregon in 1793.

Since both countries had strong claims, it seemed sensible to divide Oregon between them. But along what line? The two countries tried unsuccessfully to decide that issue in 1818. Then they agreed to let citizens of both countries occupy the land together for ten years. Nine years later they decided to let that arrangement go on indefinitely. Either country, however, could end the agreement on one year's notice.

▶**9.** How did Britain and the United States each support its claim to the Oregon Country?

Traders and Missionaries
In the early 1800's, most of Oregon was left to Britain's Hudson Bay Company, which had a trading post called Fort Vancouver where the Columbia joins the Willamette River. There the company bought furs from the Indians.

Some Americans tried a new way of getting furs in the 1820's. The Rocky Mountain Fur Company, based in St. Louis, sent out its own trappers. They collected furs throughout the winter and then came together in the summer to be paid for their work. Soon American mountain men like Jedediah Smith were tramping through Oregon and other parts of the Far West.

Then, in 1833, a report spread through the East that the Indians of the Pacific Northwest wanted to be instructed in the Christian religion. The report was wrong, but it led several religious groups to send missionaries there. Perhaps the most famous missionary was Marcus Whitman, a trained doctor, who, along with his wife Narcissa established a mission near Fort Walla Walla in 1836.

Whalers were among the first Americans to reach the Pacific coast. Their visits strengthened the United States claim to the Oregon Country.

Whaling was very dangerous, but it was also highly profitable. People used whalebone to make corsets, fishing rods, umbrellas, and many other items. Whale oil was used in lamps and to make candles.

Whaling became an important industry once sailors discovered that they could find large numbers of whales if they traveled far enough out into the ocean. At first, crews hunted whales just off the Atlantic coast. Then, in 1712, a sudden storm swept a whaling ship far out to sea. There the crew came upon a school of whales. They killed one and brought it back.

Other whalers then ventured farther out in the ocean in search of the valuable creatures. Hardy whaling crews set out from Nantucket, New Bedford, New London, and other New England ports. Year after year they went farther and farther south until they finally rounded Cape Horn at the southern tip of South America and sailed into the Pacific Ocean.

As the whalers moved farther from their home ports, they sailed into areas never or seldom before seen by Europeans or Americans. They came to the Sandwich Islands—later called the Hawaiian Islands—in the South Pacific. Some even sailed to the Cape Verde Islands, off the west coast of Africa. Those islands were owned by Portugal.

The Whitmans and other Protestant missionaries did not make many converts among the Indians. They did, however, send back east news of the rich farming lands in the Northwest.

▶10. Why did Marcus and Narcissa Whitman go to Oregon in the 1830's?

On the Oregon Trail By the 1840's, "Oregon Fever" was spreading through the East. Large numbers of settlers made the long westward trip. They did not travel alone but moved in long caravans, or groups of covered wagons pulled by horses or oxen. At night, the wagons were pulled into a closed circle with the animals inside. That way the pioneers could defend themselves against attacks by Indians who did not want outsiders on their lands.

The first great caravan set out in 1843 under the leadership of Peter H. Burnett. It included 1,000 men, women, and children from western Missouri, Ohio, Illinois, Kentucky, and Tennessee. They brought 5,000 cattle and oxen with them. The caravan traveled west in 2 columns of 60 wagons each. In one column were people without many animals. The other column—the cow column—was for those who had to move more slowly because they brought herds of cattle.

The caravan followed the **Oregon Trail.** The Whitmans opened part of that route on their way to Oregon in 1836. In fact, Marcus Whitman served as a guide for the first caravan. He was on his way back to Oregon after a meeting with church leaders in the East. Whitman led the caravan along the Missouri River northwest to the Platte River, and then along the Platte, North Platte, and Sweetwater rivers to South Pass. Once the wagon train went through the Rocky Mountains, it could follow the Snake and Columbia rivers all the way to the Pacific coast.

A wagon train slowly makes its way west on the Oregon Trail.

The Oregon Trail was a far easier route than the one Lewis and Clark had taken along the Missouri River. Food and water were available all along the way, and the Oregon Trail could be traveled easily by wagon until the train reached Fort Hall on the Snake River. From there on, the land was rugged. As the going got hard, travelers often threw away furniture and other goods to lighten their loads.

The train was 2,000 miles long, and the journey took many months. The group Whitman guided in 1843 left Independence, Missouri, in May. It arrived in the Willamette Valley late in the fall. Still the pioneers of 1843 showed that large groups of people traveling together could reach Oregon.

▶ **11.** What made the Oregon Trail a good route west?

The Oregon Territory By 1846, there were about 6,000 Americans in Oregon, mostly in the Willamette Valley. Although they had received considerable help from the Hudson Bay Company, they wanted to be governed by the United States. As early as 1843, the settlers adopted a form of government for the Oregon Territory that was to remain in effect, they said, "until such time as the United States of America extend their jurisdiction over us."

Those settlers outlawed slavery in Oregon. As a result, many Southerners did not want the Oregon Territory to join the Union. More important, before the United States could annex Oregon, it had to settle its northwest border dispute with Great Britain.

▶ **12.** Why did Southerners oppose having Oregon in the Union?

New Mexico and California

Texas and Oregon were not the only parts of the Far West that attracted Americans. Many were also interested in New Mexico and California. However, both territories belonged to Mexico.

▶ **13.** To what nation did New Mexico and California belong?

New Mexico In the 1820's, as settlers started pouring into Texas, American traders were opening a profitable trade with the Mexican settlement at Santa Fe. It and other New Mexican towns were hundreds of miles from Mexico City, the center of trade for Mexico. So when the Americans arrived in Sante Fe, they found people eager to buy manufactured goods. The Mexicans were also eager to sell gold, silver, and hides. Soon a profitable trade sprang up.

Each spring, American traders, traveling in small groups, left Independence, Missouri. They traveled along the Oregon Trail for about 40 miles. Then the **Santa Fe Trail** cut southward to the Arkansas River and west to Santa Fe. Some traders took a shortcut to the Cimarron River and then on to New Mexico.

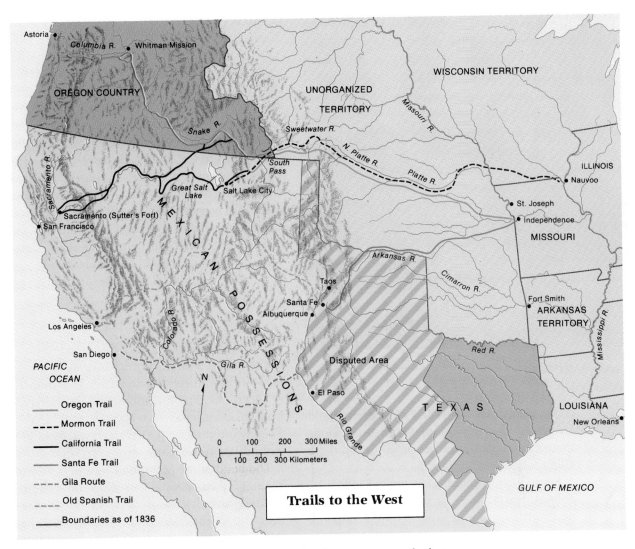

Astoria • • Whitman Mission
Columbia R.

OREGON COUNTRY

Snake R.

WISCONSIN TERRITORY

UNORGANIZED
TERRITORY

Missouri R.

Sweetwater R.

N. Platte R.

Platte R.

Sacramento R.

South
Pass

Great Salt
Lake

Salt Lake City

Sacramento (Sutter's Fort)
San Francisco

MEXICAN POSSESSIONS

ILLINOIS
• Nauvoo

• St. Joseph
• Independence

MISSOURI

Arkansas R.

Taos •

Santa Fe •
Albuquerque •

Cimarron R.

Los Angeles •

Colorado R.

San Diego •

PACIFIC
OCEAN

Gila R.

N

• El Paso

Fort Smith
ARKANSAS
TERRITORY

Mississippi R.

Red R.

Disputed Area

T E X A S

LOUISIANA

New Orleans •

Rio Grande

0   100   200   300 Miles
0 100 200 300 Kilometers

——— Oregon Trail
- - - - Mormon Trail
——— California Trail
——— Santa Fe Trail
- - - Gila Route
- - - Old Spanish Trail
~~~ Boundaries as of 1836

Trails to the West

GULF OF MEXICO

Map Study   *Where does the Mormon Trail begin and end? Name two trails that begin at the same city. Near what trail was the Whitman Mission?*

The traders made Americans more aware of New Mexico. Some Americans even thought that it ought to become a part of the United States.

▶ **14.** Describe the route of the Santa Fe Trail.

California Many more Americans were eager to annex California. They spoke glowingly of the splendid harbors at San Diego and San Francisco. Some dreamed of building cattle ranches along the coast similar to those the Mexicans had started. Others were more interested in starting farms in the fertile river valleys tucked between California's rugged mountain chains.

The first Americans to visit California came by ship. American whalers in the Pacific Ocean used to stop in California for food and

355

Mexicans in California had created a distinctive culture by 1846.

Trail. It was the same as the Oregon Trail through South Pass. Then California migrants cut southwest across the Nevada desert and over the Sierra Nevadas toward the Pacific coast at San Francisco. Most of them never got that far. Instead, they started farms in the Sacramento Valley.

By 1846, there were between 500 and 800 Americans in California. However, they were outnumbered ten to one by native Californians. But Mexican rule over the area was weak and was regularly upset by local revolts. Some Americans saw that weakness as an opportunity. It could help them make California a part of the United States.

▶**15.** What made California attractive to Americans?

Utah

Some of the westward migrants were members of the Church of the Latter Day Saints, or Mormons. The Mormons had been driven from their settlements in Missouri and Illinois. They wanted to keep as far away as possible from other Americans.

The head of the Mormon Church, Brigham Young, led his people to a place no one else wanted, the dry lands west of South Pass near the Great Salt Lake. A less promising area was hard to imagine. One early arrival described it as "a broad and barren plain . . . the paradise of the lizard, the cricket and the rattlesnake." To the east, however, lay the Wasatch Mountains, which branched out from the main body of the Rockies. Young saw the possibility of catching the streams that tumbled down from the mountains and carrying their water to the fields below.

Young led the first group of Mormons to their new home in 1847. Before long, they had built great irrigation channels to carry water to their fields and literally made the

fresh water. By the 1820's, New England trading ships were also making regular stops there. Occasionally traders or sailors on those ships settled in California.

Some Europeans also settled in California. John A. Sutter, a Swiss immigrant, received an enormous grant of land in the Sacramento Valley from the Mexican government between 1839 and 1841. He hoped other Swiss immigrants would settle on his estate, which he called New Helvetia. When the Swiss failed to come, Sutter tried to persuade Americans headed for Oregon to change their course and make their homes in California. Sutter became one of many California boosters who advertised, and sometimes exaggerated, its glories to attract settlers.

In the 1840's, Americans began arriving in California not by sea, as was true earlier, but overland. They followed the **California** desert bloom. They managed not just to survive but to do well because the Mormons worked together in a cooperative way under the direction of their church's leaders. They also benefited from the growing stream of migrants to California, who often stopped at Salt Lake City to buy food and supplies.

▶ **16.** Why did the Mormons settle in Utah?

Reviewing Section I

Identify empresarios, Stephen F. Austin, Santa Anna, the Alamo, San Antonio, Lone Star Republic, Samuel Houston, San Jacinto, annexation, John Jacob Astor, Marcus and Narcissa Whitman, Oregon Trail, Santa Fe Trail, John Sutter, California Trail, Brigham Young

Questions to Answer
1. What prompted the Texas Revolution?
2. What attracted Americans to Oregon, New Mexico, California, and Utah?

A Question to Think About How were the causes of the Texas Revolution similar to the causes of the American Revolution?

II. Manifest Destiny and the Mexican War

As late as the 1820's, many Americans thought the boundaries of the United States could go no farther west than the Rocky Mountains. By the 1840's, however, a new idea began to spread. It was, some Americans now argued, the **Manifest Destiny** of the United States—that is, its clear, God-given fate—to expand even further.

Manifest Destiny

The term *Manifest Destiny* was first used in the summer of 1845 by John L. O'Sullivan, an editor of a literary journal called the *Democratic Review*. He believed it was the nation's destiny to expand. Members of the Whig Party were almost entirely opposed to expansion. The Democrats, however, became caught up in expansionism.

The nation's growth, O'Sullivan thought, would happen peacefully. People who lived beyond the borders of the United States would revolt from the governments that ruled them. Then, like the Texans, they would ask to be annexed to the United States.

How far should the country expand? Some said to the Pacific. Others said the nation would someday cover all of North America, including Canada, Mexico, and Central America. All the supporters of Manifest Destiny agreed, however, that the growth of the United States meant a growth of freedom for the people under its rule.

During the 1840's, the territory governed by the United States grew enormously. It did so, however, in a different way from the way the early supporters of Manifest Destiny expected.

▶ **1.** What is the meaning of *Manifest Destiny*?

The Election of 1844

Martin Van Buren, the Democrat who lost the presidency to the Whigs in 1840, fully expected to be his party's candidate again in 1844. But Van Buren—like the Whig candidate, Henry Clay—refused to support the annexation of Texas. As a result, the Democrats nominated James K. Polk of Tennessee, who favored expansion and annexation.

Then the Democrats adopted a **platform,** a statement of policies for which a party stands. The Democrats' platform demanded the annexation of Texas and said that the United States had a "clear and unquestionable" right to *all* of Oregon. The Democrats campaigned with the slogan "Fifty-four forty or fight!" They meant that the United States should fight Britain if necessary to get all of Oregon up to its northernmost boundary.

Polk was the first "dark horse" candidate. In other words, he was the first presidential nominee who was not considered a serious candidate before his party's convention. Polk was born in North Carolina and then moved to Tennessee where he became—like Andrew Jackson before him—a successful lawyer and planter. He served in the Tennessee legislature and as governor of that state.

In 1844, Polk faced two other candidates—the Whig candidate, Henry Clay, and James G. Birney of the new, antislavery Liberty Party. Polk won more popular votes than Clay or Birney and easily won the election.

President Polk was a good Jacksonian. He vetoed several bills for internal improvements and opposed protective tariffs. His administration was responsible for getting through Congress a tariff bill that lowered duties. But Polk was a more ardent expansionist than Jackson. His support of expansion caused important changes even before he took office.
▶**2.** In what ways was Polk a Jacksonian President?

Taking Texas and Oregon

In the spring of 1844, President Tyler tried without success to get the Senate to approve the annexation of Texas. After the November election, he tried again, arguing that by electing Polk, the voters had decided in favor of expansion. This time Congress agreed. It approved a resolution admitting Texas to the Union. Tyler signed the resolution in March 1845, just before leaving office. In December 1845, Texas became the nation's twenty-eighth state.

Getting Oregon was more complicated because Great Britain also claimed the territory. The Democrats wanted all of Oregon. Polk proposed a compromise—divide the territory at 49° north latitude. When the British refused, Polk persuaded Congress to end the joint occupation agreement. War seemed a real possibility. Then the British gave in. The land between the Columbia River and the 49th parallel did not seem worth fighting for. The British insisted, however, on keeping all of Vancouver Island. They also won the right to use the Columbia River.

Polk sent the proposed treaty to the Senate, which approved it in June 1846. If the Senate had not done so, the United States might have found itself at war with two countries. A war with Mexico had already begun.
▶**3.** How did Britain and the United States compromise over Oregon?

The Mexican War

Mexico was not happy about the United States' decision to annex Texas. Differences between the two countries might have been resolved, however, if the United States had been content to keep the boundaries of Texas as they had been under Spanish rule. In those days, its western boundary extended only to the Nueces (nü ā′səs) River. The Americans, however, insisted that Texas went farther west—all the way to the Rio Grande.

In addition to the Rio Grande border of Texas, Polk also wanted New Mexico and California. He sent a diplomat, John Slidell of Louisiana, to Mexico City to negotiate the Texas boundary and to offer to buy New

When those Americans who wanted to annex all of the Oregon Country shouted the slogan "Fifty-four forty or fight!" they were referring to a parallel of latitude. Parallels of latitude are imaginary lines that circle Earth. Their purpose is to help us precisely locate places on Earth.

The starting point for measuring parallels of latitude is the equator. It is the imaginary line which is exactly halfway between the North Pole and the South Pole. The equator is labeled 0° latitude. All places north of the equator are north latitude. The places farthest away from the equator are the poles. The North Pole is 90° north latitude. The South Pole is 90° south latitude.

The areas between the equator and the poles are divided by parallels of latitude. They are called parallels because they are always the same distance apart. There are 90 lines of north latitude between the equator and the North Pole. There are also 90 lines of south latitude between the equator and the South Pole.

For even greater precision in locating places, the area between lines of latitude is subdivided into 60 more lines called minutes ('). Degrees and minutes of latitude are often written like this: 54°40' N.

Use the map and the information above to answer the following questions.

1. About how many minutes of latitude separate 54°40'N from 55°N?
2. About how many degrees of latitude separate 49°N from the equator?
3. At about what latitude was the southern boundary of the Oregon Country?
4. At about what latitude was the Boundary Line of 1846?
5. At about what latitude is Spokane?

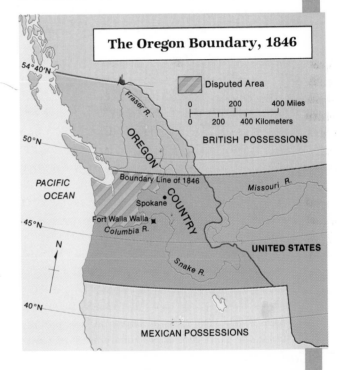

The Oregon Boundary, 1846

Mexico and California. By the time Slidell arrived at the Mexican capital in December 1845, the Mexicans knew about his mission. They were outraged. No government official would talk with him.

▶ 4. What was Slidell's mission in Mexico?

Taylor in Mexico When Polk heard about Slidell's failure, he sent American troops led by General Zachary Taylor to the disputed area between the Nueces River and the Rio Grande. Later that spring, a group of Mexican soldiers crossed the Rio Grande and met the

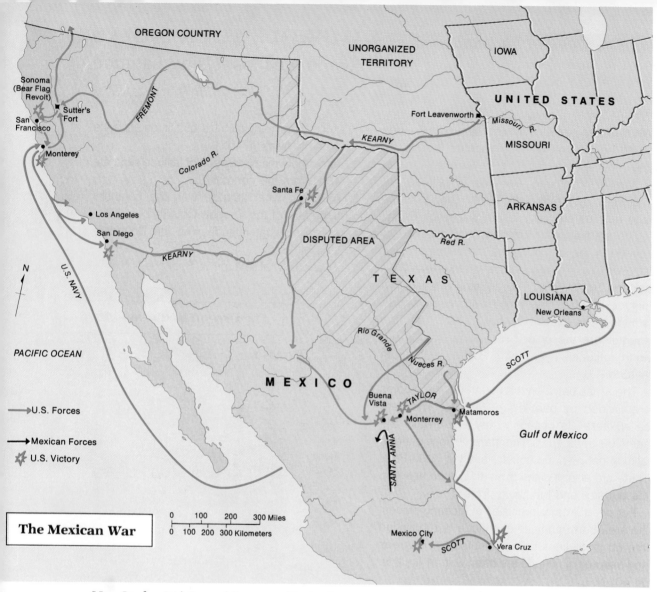

OREGON COUNTRY

UNORGANIZED TERRITORY

IOWA

UNITED STATES

Fort Leavenworth

MISSOURI

Missouri R.

Sonoma (Bear Flag Revolt)

Sutter's Fort

San Francisco

Monterey

KEARNY

ARKANSAS

Santa Fe

Colorado R.

DISPUTED AREA

TEXAS

Los Angeles

San Diego

KEARNY

Red R.

LOUISIANA

New Orleans

N

U.S. NAVY

PACIFIC OCEAN

Rio Grande

Nueces R.

M E X I C O

SCOTT

Buena Vista

TAYLOR

Matamoros

Monterrey

Gulf of Mexico

→U.S. Forces

→Mexican Forces

✺U.S. Victory

SANTA ANNA

The Mexican War

0 100 200 300 Miles
0 100 200 300 Kilometers

Mexico City

SCOTT

Vera Cruz

Map Study *Did General Scott travel by land or water to Matamoros? What city lies along Colonel Kearny's route from Fort Leavenworth to San Diego?*

American soldiers. In the fight that followed, 16 Americans were killed or wounded.

"American blood," Polk told Congress on May 11, had been shed on "American soil." He claimed that Mexico had begun a war. Of course the Mexicans did not see it that way. They thought that the Americans were wrongfully on Mexican soil. Two days later Congress approved a declaration of war.

The United States won the Mexican war in three campaigns. First, General Taylor led his army across the Rio Grande and took the city of Matamoros (mat ə mōr′əs). Then he went on to defeat the Mexican garrison at Monterrey (mon tə rā′) to the west of Matamoros. Taylor became a hero to the American people, who called him Old Rough and Ready. After he defeated Santa Anna at the

Battle of Buena Vista (bwā′nə vis′tə) (February 1847), the war in northern Mexico was over.

▶**5.** How did Taylor conduct the war in northern Mexico?

Kearny in New Mexico In the next campaign, the Americans captured New Mexico and California. Colonel Stephen W. Kearny started west from Fort Leavenworth, Kansas, in the summer of 1846 with 1,700 American soldiers. By August, they had taken Santa Fe. Then Kearny declared that all of New Mexico belonged to the United States. Leaving a part of his army in New Mexico, he headed for California. There he found that most of his work had been done for him. John C. Frémont was partly responsible for that.

▶**6.** What part did Stephen Kearny play in the Mexican War?

The Bear Flag Republic Frémont, a captain in the American Army, had led an exploring party of 65 men into California in 1845. Known as the Pathfinder, Frémont was a popular writer who had published many reports of his travels.

Mexican authorities were nervous about having an American army officer in their territory. In 1846, they told Frémont to leave. He started to go. Then he and his men defied the Mexicans and took over some land not far from John Sutter's estate in the Sacramento Valley.

Nearby American settlers thought Frémont's action meant that the United States government was ready to support them if they revolted. They rose up in June 1846—even before they heard about the war with Mexico. They threw off Mexican authority and proclaimed the **Bear Flag Republic.** They also seized the town of Sonoma north of San Francisco Bay. Meanwhile, the American

The Bear Flag of California was raised in 1846. The Republic lasted only one month.

Navy landed at Monterey, south of San Francisco, and raised the American flag. By the time Kearny arrived much of California was already controlled by Americans. Now he had only to put down some opposition in the south.

▶**7.** Why did Americans in California proclaim the Bear Flag Republic?

Scott Ends the War Mexico agreed to the loss of California and New Mexico only after a third American military campaign. In March 1847, General Winfield Scott landed near the city of Vera Cruz (ver′ə krüz′) on the Gulf of Mexico. He took the city and slowly made his way to the capital of Mexico. The American Army entered Mexico City on September 14, 1847. After a fierce battle, Mexico surrendered.

▶**8.** What was Winfield Scott's role in the Mexican War?

The Treaty of Guadalupe Hidalgo The war officially ended with a treaty signed at Guadalupe Hidalgo (gwa′dl üp′ hi dal′gō), Mexico, on February 2, 1848. Under its terms, the United States agreed to pay all the claims American citizens had against the Mexican government and to give Mexico $15 million.

On September 14, 1847, General Scott and his army rode in triumph into the great public square in Mexico City.

In return, Mexico gave up New Mexico and California and accepted the Rio Grande as the Texas border. In short, the treaty gave the United States one third of the land that had been Mexico's before the war.

When Polk was elected, the United States covered about 1,788,000 square miles. When he left office in 1849, it included another 1,204,000 square miles. A nation that was once nestled along the Atlantic suddenly stretched "from sea to shining sea."

▶**9.** What were the terms of the Treaty of Guadalupe Hidalgo?

Reaction to the War The Mexican War was very unpopular in certain parts of the country, especially the Northeast. Even some believers in Manifest Destiny opposed the war. John L. O'Sullivan, for example, wanted the United States to expand by peaceful means, not by force. But the Mexican War was so successful in bringing new land under the Stars and Stripes that many opponents found it hard to remain critical.

Still, some groups of people were unhappy with the Treaty of Guadalupe Hidalgo. The Mormons—who went west to get away from other Americans—suddenly found themselves in the United States again. So did many Indians. Those Mexicans who made their homes in California or New Mexico were also uneasy. The treaty protected their right to keep their language and customs, but many were suspicious of the Americans. They feared those parts of the treaty would not be enforced.

There was also an important group of people in the older states of the nation who were suspicious of the treaty. Their reason was different. They thought it might give American slavery a new lease on life.

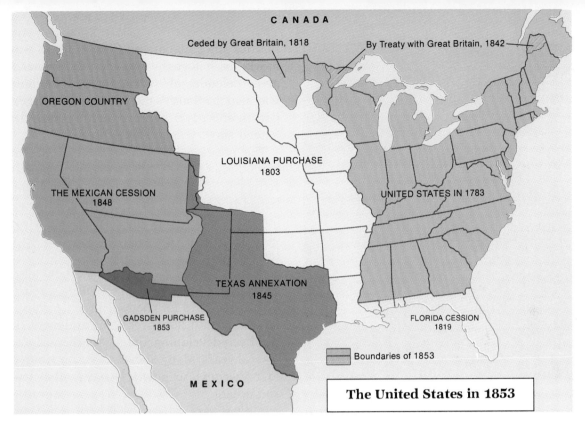

CANADA

Ceded by Great Britain, 1818

By Treaty with Great Britain, 1842

OREGON COUNTRY

LOUISIANA PURCHASE
1803

THE MEXICAN CESSION
1848

UNITED STATES IN 1783

TEXAS ANNEXATION
1845

GADSDEN PURCHASE
1853

FLORIDA CESSION
1819

Boundaries of 1853

MEXICO

The United States in 1853

Map Study *In what year did Texas become part of the United States? What name was given to the land the United States won from Mexico?*

▶**10.** What groups of people were not pleased with the results of the Mexican War?

Reviewing Section II————————

Identify Manifest Destiny, James K. Polk, platform, Zachary Taylor, Battle of Buena Vista, Stephen W. Kearny, John C. Frémont, Bear Flag Republic, Winfield Scott, Treaty of Guadalupe Hidalgo

Questions to Answer
1. Describe the three major campaigns of the Mexican War.
2. What were the results of the Mexican War?

A Question to Think About How might the war with Mexico have been different if the conflict with Britain over Oregon had not already been settled?

III. Slavery Enters Politics

In the years between the Missouri Compromise of 1820 and the 1840's, most Americans thought slavery should be kept out of politics. Andrew Jackson and his followers tried especially hard to prevent the issue from coming up. Even in the North, many wise and respectable people considered slavery a dangerous subject. They thought Northerners should avoid offending the slave states. Northerners should not set one section of the

Senator John C. Calhoun was one of the South's leading defenders of slavery.

country against another or interfere with the profitable trade between the North and South. As a result, there was a great silence on slavery.

The abolitionists were the first to break that silence. Then came the great expansion of the 1840's. The country had to decide whether the lands it won in the Mexican War would be slave or free. As the debate raged in the Senate, the line between the North and the South became sharper.

The New Southern Argument

In the 1830's, some Southerners developed a new argument in support of slavery. John C. Calhoun stated the South's position in 1837. Slavery, he said, was "good—a positive good." Calhoun, a South Carolinian born in 1782, had played an important role in American politics since he entered Congress as a war hawk just before the War of 1812. He was a great defender of the nation. But Calhoun was also the South's most prominent spokesperson and never more so than when he defended slavery as a positive good.

The position he took was very different from that of earlier Southerners like Thomas Jefferson. They had regretted slavery and hoped it would one day disappear. Calhoun, however, said it was a fine thing. As a class of laborers, he argued, southern slaves were much better off than northern factory workers. Their owners took care of sick and aged slaves, but heartless factory owners left such workers to care for themselves.

Calhoun did not invent this argument. It had been developing among Southerners for several years. Many Southerners contributed to it—writers, scientists, lawyers, ministers, and others.

▶**1.** What was the new southern argument in favor of slavery?

The North Defends Free Labor

Northerners were quick to defend themselves against southern criticism. Any traveler could see that the South was poor, with many people wearing rags and living in shacks, while the North showed signs of prosperity everywhere. Why were Northerners so much better off? Because, or so the northern argument went, its labor was free. Factory workers could work hard, save money, and one day start their own businesses or buy their own farms.

The defenders of free labor were, of course, critics of the South. Slave labor was anything but free, and the slave system, they argued, was why so many Southerners were poor. People worked hard only when they saw a chance to better their lives. What chance did slaves have to improve their lives?

Poor southern whites also suffered from the effects of slavery, the Northerners said. They were taught that work was the lot of slaves. As a result they, too, were unwilling to work hard.

▶ **2.** What was the free labor argument against slavery?

The Wilmot Proviso The northern arguments for free labor assumed that land was available in the West where workers could buy farms. That land, or soil, had to be free of slavery, the argument went, because free laborers would never go where labor was degraded by slavery.

For that reason, David Wilmot, a Democratic congressman from Pennsylvania, proposed his famous **Wilmot Proviso** in August 1846. Under the terms of the proviso, slavery would be forbidden in any lands won from Mexico. The proviso passed the House of Representatives twice but was defeated in the Senate, where the South remained strong. Though it never went into effect, the Wilmot Proviso was important. It provoked heated debates and made clear that the issue of slavery was back in American politics.

▶ **3.** What did the Wilmot Proviso say?

The Free Soilers The **Free Soilers,** unlike the abolitionists, did not hesitate to become involved in politics. In fact, their arguments were designed to appeal to as many voters as possible. Unlike the abolitionists, they did not condemn slavery as a sin. They talked about its economic effects and said very little about helping slaves. Instead, they defended the rights of free white workers. In that way, they could appeal to the many Northerners who tried to avoid contact with blacks. The new states of the Old Northwest Territory, for example, refused to allow free blacks to settle there. Where there were communities of free blacks, as in Boston, black children were forced to go to separate schools so they did not mix with white children.

▶ **4.** How did the Free Soilers attract voters?

The Election of 1848

The nation's major political parties were divided in 1848. Many northern Democrats supported the Wilmot Proviso. Meanwhile, Calhoun and many southern Democrats insisted that Congress had no right to keep American citizens from going west and bringing their slaves with them.

When President Polk announced that he would not run for a second term, the Democrats tried to overcome divisions at their convention by nominating Lewis Cass of Michigan. He was a Northerner who opposed the Wilmot Proviso. They also adopted a platform that said nothing about slavery. The strategy did not work. The Free Soil Democrats were so angry that they left the convention.

The Whigs chose Zachary Taylor, the hero of the Mexican War, as their candidate. Taylor lived in Louisiana, and he owned slaves. The Whigs tried to avoid taking a stand on slavery by writing no platform at all. Again, the strategy did not work. Many Whigs who opposed slavery—Conscience Whigs—decided they could not support Taylor.

The Free Soil Democrats and the Conscience Whigs organized a new **Free Soil Party** in Buffalo, New York, in August 1848. They nominated Martin Van Buren for President and Charles Francis Adams, the son of John Quincy Adams, for Vice President.

The Free Soil Party's platform demanded that slavery be kept from the territories. It also proposed federal support for internal improvements and called for a homestead law that would give settlers free farms from federal lands in the West. The new party claimed it stood for "Free Soil, Free Speech, Free Labor, and Free Men."

Taylor won the election with about 1.3 million votes to Cass's 1.2 million. The Free Soil Party candidates received only 291,000 votes. Still, it won over four times as many votes as the Liberty Party received four years earlier. The Free Soil Party also elected 12 congressmen. That was a very good beginning for a party less than three months old.

▶**5.** What were the parties and issues in the election of 1848?

Crisis in the West

While eastern politicians argued, the new lands in the West remained unorganized. Congress delayed in creating the Oregon

Miners had a hard job separating gold from ore, rocks containing valuable metal.

Territory for two years because the proposed constitution banned slavery there.

Then, in 1847, the Whitmans and 12 other settlers were murdered by a group of Cayuse Indians. As the news spread through the East, public sympathy rose for the Oregonians. Surely they deserved better support from the United States. Finally, in August 1848, Congress approved plans to organize the Oregon Territory.

▶**6.** What prompted Congress to set up the Oregon Territory?

Gold in California Before long, California also needed a territorial government. The crisis there started in January 1848, with the discovery of gold about 40 miles from John Sutter's fort. Right away miners started rushing in from the Pacific coast. By 1849, thousands of **forty-niners** moved to California in the hope of becoming rich. They came from eastern sections of the United States, from Europe, Asia, and even Australia.

Some of the forty-niners traveled overland, while others sailed around the tip of South America then north along the Pacific coast. A few even trudged across the thick rain forests of Panama to get to California faster. Some forty-niners did strike it rich. But many lost all of their profits through drinking or gambling.

▶**7.** Why did the forty-niners move to California?

A Constitution for California By late 1849, California's population had grown to 100,000 people. They badly needed a regular government. Theft and murder were widespread, and the American Army could not handle the situation. Something had to be done.

If Congress could not act, President Taylor decided he would. He told the people living in California and New Mexico to meet, adopt constitutions, and then ask Congress to admit them into the Union. They did not have to wait for Congress's permission, Taylor said. Californians drafted and approved a constitution by October 1849. The constitution forbade slavery. That, Taylor thought, solved the crisis. All Congress had to do was accept California into the Union.

▶ **8.** What did President Taylor tell the people of California and New Mexico?

Toward Compromise

Taylor was wrong. The question of admitting California and New Mexico to the Union set off one of the most bitter Congressional fights in American history. It seemed as if the Union might splinter.

The debates involved three great senators, each at the end of his career—Clay, Calhoun, and Webster. Henry Clay, the Great Compromiser was 73 years old in 1850. He had run for President three times (1824, 1832, and 1844) but never won. Clay had had a long career in Congress. He had helped frame the Missouri Compromise of 1820 and the Compromise Tariff of 1833, which helped end the nullification crisis.

Now Clay tried again to save the Union through compromise. He proposed, in January 1850, that California be admitted to the Union as a free state and that the rest of the land won from Mexico be organized into territories without any restriction on slavery.

Clay appealed to antislavery forces by proposing that slaves would no longer be bought and sold in the District of Columbia. He appealed to those in favor of slavery by proposing a stronger **Fugitive Slave Law,** by which federal authorities would help slaveholders capture runaway slaves. He also proposed that Congress declare that it had no power to interfere with the interstate slave

Henry Clay tries to win support from his fellow senators for the Compromise of 1850.

trade. Clay warned that unless the nation worked out these differences, the South would leave the Union and there would be a "furious, bloody" civil war.

The debates over Clay's proposals were long and emotional. On March 4, the dying Senator Calhoun of South Carolina sat while a friend read his speech for him. The North caused the crisis, he said, by warring against southern rights. Southern rights must be respected or the South would resist.

Three days later the great New England orator Daniel Webster took the floor of the Senate. "I speak," he said, "not as a Massachusetts man, nor as a northern man, but as an American." He asked all sides, but especially the North, to give in so that the Union might be saved.

▶ **9.** What were Clay's compromise proposals?

Douglas Wins the Compromise Despite Webster's plea, Congress would not approve the package. Finally Stephen Douglas, a young senator from Illinois, took Clay's place as leader of the compromisers. By appealing to small groups and juggling votes, Douglas managed to get Clay's proposals through the Senate not as a group, but one by one. Moderates and Southerners, for example, voted

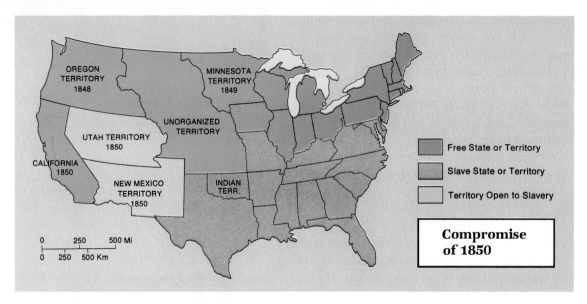

OREGON
TERRITORY
1848

MINNESOTA
TERRITORY
1849

UTAH TERRITORY
1850

UNORGANIZED
TERRITORY

CALIFORNIA
1850

NEW MEXICO
TERRITORY
1850

INDIAN
TERR.

☐ Free State or Territory

☐ Slave State or Territory

☐ Territory Open to Slavery

**Compromise
of 1850**

0   250   500 Mi

0   250   500 Km

Map Study *How many free states were in the Union in 1850? How many slave
states? Was California a free state or a slave state?*

for the Fugitive Slave Law, while moderates
and northern antislavery senators voted to
get California accepted as a free state.

In July, President Taylor, who opposed the
compromise, died in office. His successor,
Vice President Millard Fillmore of New York
supported it. He signed each of the various
bills of the Compromise of 1850 once they
had gone through Congress.

▶10. How did Douglas get the Compromise
of 1850 through Congress?

Effects of the Compromise Many people
hoped that the compromise would heal the
divisions in the nation caused by the issue
of slavery. Two years later, voters rejected
the Whig candidate, General Winfield Scott,
who refused to endorse the compromise, and
elected instead the Democratic candidate,
Franklin Pierce of New Hampshire. Pierce
ran on a platform that not only supported
the compromise but promised to resist all
future agitation over slavery. Moreover, the

Free Soil Party won only half as many votes
in 1852 as it had won in 1848. It seemed
possible that the crisis over slavery was over,
and the Union had been saved.

▶11. Why did General Winfield Scott lose
the election of 1852?

Reviewing Section III

Identify John C. Calhoun, David Wilmot,
Wilmot Proviso, Free Soilers, Louis Cass, Free
Soil Party, Martin Van Buren, Charles Francis
Adams, forty-niners, Fugitive Slave Law,
Millard Fillmore, Franklin Pierce

Questions to Answer
1. Why did the acquisition of new territories
   cause problems for the nation?
2. How did Northerners defend themselves
   against southern charges that slaves were
   better off than northern factory workers?

A Question to Think About What problems
were likely under the Compromise of 1850?

368

In previous Improve Your Reading exercises, you learned about reading for main ideas and details. You found out that a general statement about a topic is the main idea. You also learned that the specific facts and examples related to the main idea are called details.

Your task in this exercise is first to choose the statement that is the main idea. Then, select the accurate supporting detail. Next, select the inaccurate supporting detail. Finally, change the inaccurate detail to an accurate detail.

The first item has been done for you.

1. Refer back to the topic "Stephen Austin" on page 349.
   a. Stephen Austin did not intend to fulfill his obligations as a Mexican citizen.
   b. About 750 families came to Texas with Austin.
   c. Stephen Austin was a successful empresario.

The main idea is "c." The accurate detail is "b." The inaccurate detail is "a." It should read: Stephen Austin fully intended to fulfill his obligations as a Mexican citizen."

2. Refer back to the topic "The Alamo," on page 349.
   a. About 500 Texans fought at the Alamo.
   b. Texans were defeated at the Alamo.
   c. After the Alamo battle, Texans continued to seek independence.

3. Refer back to the topic "The Annexation Issue" on pages 350 and 352.
   a. Because of disagreements regarding the annexation of Texas, the Lone Star Republic was left on its own.
   b. Jackson wanted Texas to be annexed.
   c. Van Buren did not urge Congress to annex Texas.

4. Refer back to the topic "Taylor in Mexico" on pages 359–361.
   a. Taylor defeated Santa Anna in 1867.
   b. Taylor led the United States to victory in the Mexican War.
   c. Taylor's role in the war earned him the title Old Rough and Ready.

5. Refer back to the topic "The Treaty of Guadalupe Hidalgo" on pages 361–362.
   a. The Mexican War officially ended with the signing of the Treaty of Guadalupe Hidalgo.
   b. The Treaty of Guadalupe Hidalgo was signed on February 2, 1848.
   c. One of the terms of the Treaty of Guadalupe Hidalgo was for the United States to give Mexico $5 million.

6. Refer back to the topic "Gold in California" on page 366.
   a. Thousands of forty-niners rushed to find gold in California.
   b. Forty-niners came from the United States, Europe, Asia, and Australia.
   c. Few forty-niners lost all of their profits through drinking or gambling.

CHAPTER 17 REVIEW

Vocabulary Check
Write a short definition for each of the following words.

1. Empresarios
2. Annexation
3. Manifest Destiny
4. Platform
5. Forty-niners

Fact Check
On a separate piece of paper, complete each of the following sentences.

1. One of the fur trappers and explorers who discovered the South Pass through the Rockies was _____.
2. After holding out for two weeks against Santa Anna, 187 Texans were killed at the _____.
3. Texans declared their independence from Mexico and set up the _____ Republic.
4. The _____ set up a mission near Fort Walla Walla in 1836.
5. Americans started a profitable trade center at the New Mexican town of _____.
6. The Democratic presidential candidate who supported the annexation of Texas and claimed all of Oregon for the United States was _____.
7. Old Rough and Ready, _____, was an American hero in the Mexican War and later became President.
8. Americans in California proclaimed the _____ Republic in 1846.
9. John C. Calhoun argued that the institution of slavery was a _____.
10. The series of laws which ended the debate over the status of slavery in California and New Mexico are called the _____.

Time Check
On a separate sheet of paper, put the following events in the order in which they occurred.

1. Texans are defeated at the Alamo.
2. Californians proclaimed the Bear Flag Republic.
3. Gold is discovered in California.
4. Congressman David Wilmot proposes the Wilmot Proviso.
5. Texas is admitted to the Union.

Skills Check
Use the map on page 355 to answer the following questions.

1. Which trails shown on the map followed the Platte and North Platte rivers for part of their route?
2. Which trail ended at Los Angeles?
3. Which trail followed the Arkansas River for part of its length?
4. Where does the California Trail split from the Mormon Trail?
5. About how many miles was the journey from Salt Lake City to Sacramento?

Think and Write
1. Why did the idea of Manifest Destiny appeal to many Americans?
2. What were the claims to the Oregon Country of Great Britain and the United States?
3. Describe the three campaigns of the Mexican War.
4. Why were the Mormons unhappy with the results of the Mexican War?
5. What were the key elements in the Compromise of 1850?

REVIEWING UNIT 5

Reviewing the Facts I.

On a separate piece of paper, write the name of the person or persons described by each of the sentences below.

1. He invented the cotton gin.
2. Called "Old Hickory," he was a war hero and a popular President.
3. Vice President who argued for the doctrine of nullification.
4. He founded the Mormon Church.
5. These two women organized the Seneca Falls Convention.
6. A leading black abolitionist who broke from Garrison's leadership.
7. He was the first president of the Republic of Texas.
8. These missionaries helped publicize the rich farmland of Oregon.
9. The Mexican War began during this President's administration.
10. He was called the Great Compromiser.

Reviewing the Facts II.

On a separate piece of paper, fill in the word or words that best complete each of the following sentences.

1. The nation was divided into three economic regions around 1830: the _____, the _____, and the _____.
2. The economic rule of _____ and _____ caused the price of cotton to rise and fall.
3. The Lowell experiment involved the use of _____ as factory workers.
4. American government became more _____ as more people were allowed to vote.
5. President Jackson vetoed the charter of the _____.
6. The Cherokee traveled on the _____ from their homeland to Indian territory west of the Mississippi.
7. The _____ was organized to stop Americans from drinking alcohol.
8. People who sought an immediate end to slavery were called _____.
9. By the 1840's, many Americans believed that it was the _____ of the United States to expand.
10. Under the _____, California was admitted to the Union as a free state, and Congress passed the Fugitive Slave Law.

Reviewing Ideas

1. Explain why protective tariffs both hurt and helped American businesses.
2. Describe how slavery affected the development of the South throughout the 1840's.
3. What is meant by the term Jacksonian Democracy?
4. How had the lives of middle-class American women changed by the 1830's?
5. Why did Americans differ on the issue of the Mexican War?

UNIT SIX

Division and Reunion

During the 1850's, Northerners and Southerners could not find a way to re-solve their differences over slavery. Those differences brought on a civil war. Union General George McClellan is shown here looking over his camp at Cumberland Landing, Virginia. When the war ended, the nation faced the difficult task of reconstruction.

Chapter 18

The Nation Divides:
The 1850's

By the 1850's, the plantation system had become an important part of the Southern way of life. By 1860, most Southerners were ready to fight to defend it.

Franklin Pierce gave his first message to Congress in December 1853. He said the Compromise of 1850 had given new life to our institutions and restored peace and security to the public mind. Like many other Americans, he believed that the issue of slavery had been settled for good. He was wrong. Before long, divisions over slavery returned to the center of national politics.

This time it proved impossible to resolve the differences between North and South through political compromise. As politics failed, violence arose. Increasingly, the North and the South pulled away from each other.

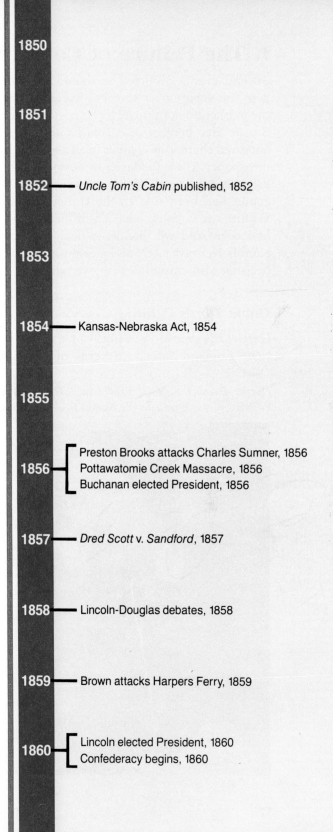

1850

1851

1852 — *Uncle Tom's Cabin* published, 1852

1853

1854 — Kansas-Nebraska Act, 1854

1855

1856 — Preston Brooks attacks Charles Sumner, 1856
Pottawatomie Creek Massacre, 1856
Buchanan elected President, 1856

1857 — *Dred Scott* v. *Sandford*, 1857

1858 — Lincoln-Douglas debates, 1858

1859 — Brown attacks Harpers Ferry, 1859

1860 — Lincoln elected President, 1860
Confederacy begins, 1860

I. The Failure of Compromise

Several events occurred in the 1850's that kept the debate over slavery alive. One was the publication of a novel by Harriet Beecher Stowe. Her book, *Uncle Tom's Cabin*, first appeared chapter by chapter in an abolitionist newspaper. Then, in March 1852, it was published in book form. Within one year, 305,000 copies had been sold in the United States. Within a few years, over 2.5 million copies had been sold worldwide. A new law, the Kansas-Nebraska Act, and a Supreme Court decision also caused debate over slavery.

Uncle Tom's Cabin

Harriet Beecher Stowe came from a religious New England family. Several of her 13 brothers and sisters became famous as writers, ministers, or leaders of the antislavery movement. However, none of the Beecher children had a greater impact on their time than Harriet. Her book showed how slavery hurt the family, an institution she and other Americans of her time considered sacred. *Uncle Tom's Cabin* helped its readers understand how truly horrible the slave system was by making them feel the fears and pains of slaves.

Uncle Tom's Cabin was also an attack on the Fugitive Slave Law, an important part of the Compromise of 1850. This law required the federal government to help slaveholders catch runaway slaves. Stowe knew about fleeing slaves firsthand. Stowe was born in

Harriet Beecher Stowe's novel Uncle Tom's Cabin *won many converts to the antislavery movement in the North. It also aroused resentment in the South.*

135,000 SETS, 270,000 VOLUMES SOLD.

UNCLE TOM'S CABIN

FOR SALE HERE.

AN EDITION FOR THE MILLION, COMPLETE IN 1 Vol., PRICE 37 1-2 CENTS.
" " IN GERMAN, IN 1 Vol., PRICE 50 CENTS.
" " IN 2 Vols., CLOTH, 6 PLATES, PRICE $1.50.
SUPERB ILLUSTRATED EDITION, IN 1 Vol., WITH 153 ENGRAVINGS,
PRICES FROM $2.50 TO $5.00.

The Greatest Book of the Age.

Connecticut but lived her adult life in Ohio. That state was the "land of the free" for many blacks who tried to escape across the Ohio River from the South. She and her husband, Calvin Stowe, once hired a black girl who claimed to be free. Then a slaveholder appeared who said the girl was his. Calvin Stowe and Harriet's brother, Henry Ward Beecher, helped the girl escape.

▶ **1.** Why was *Uncle Tom's Cabin* important?

IMPROVE YOUR SKILLS
Understanding a Primary Source

Below are two selections from *Uncle Tom's Cabin.* Although it is a work of fiction, *Uncle Tom's Cabin* had such a strong effect on its readers that historians study it as a document of its time, or a primary source. Read each selection and answer the questions. In the first selection, Eliza, a beautiful young slave woman, has just learned that her small son, Harry, has been sold to a slave dealer. She has decided to run for freedom. Stowe asks her readers:

> If it were *your* Harry, or *your* Willie, that were going to be torn from you by a brutal trader, tomorrow morning . . . and you had only from twelve o'clock until morning to make good your escape,—how fast could *you* walk? How many miles could you make within those few brief hours with the darling . . . the sleepy head on your shoulder,—the small, soft arms trustingly holding on to your neck?

In this scene, one of the most important characters in the novel, Eliza, reaches the shore of the Ohio River. She is waiting for a boat to take her across the icy river when the slave trader spots her.

> A thousand lives seemed to be concentrated in that one moment to Eliza. Her room opened by a side door to the river. She caught her child, and sprang down the steps towards it. The trader caught a full glimpse of her . . .

and . . . he was after her like a hound after a deer. In that dizzy moment her feet to her scarce seemed to touch the ground, and a moment brought her to the water's edge. Right on behind they came; and . . . with one wild cry and flying leap, she vaulted sheer over the turbid current by the shore to the raft of ice beyond . . .

The huge green fragment of ice on which she alighted pitched and creaked . . . With wild cries and desperate energy she leaped to another and still another . . . stumbling,—leaping,—slipping . . . Her shoes are gone,—her stocking cut from her feet,—while blood marked every step; but she saw nothing, felt nothing, till dimly . . . she saw the Ohio side, and a man helping her up the bank.

1. What makes these selections different from a newspaper account of a slave's escape across the Ohio River?
2. Would illustrations drawn in 1980 for a new edition of *Uncle Tom's Cabin* be primary sources?
3. How does Stowe make the reader care what happens to Eliza?
4. To what group of people in particular does Stowe appeal in the first selection?
5. What attitude toward slave traders does this passage suggest?

The Fugitive Slave Law

Many Northerners, like Harriet Beecher Stowe, thought that the Fugitive Slave Law of 1850 was unfair. Under the terms of the law, blacks who were accused of being runaway slaves had to appear before federal commissioners. The accused slaves did not have the benefit of jury trials, nor could they testify in their own behalf. Moreover, if the commissioners decided that an accused black was a slave, they received a fee of $10. If the commissioners decided a person was free, they received only $5. So the law encouraged the commissioners to decide that the accused blacks were slaves.

What could Northerners do about the law? Vermont passed a set of **personal liberty laws** in 1850. Those laws helped accused slaves obtain a lawyer and made it illegal to use state or local jails to hold them. In that way, the laws made it harder for slaveholders to get back runaway slaves.

Soon other free states followed Vermont's example. In some cases, Northerners went even further. They charged with kidnapping or false arrest any Southern slaveholders who entered free territory in search of slaves. Sometimes Northern crowds rescued accused slaves from the authorities.

If Northerners refused to honor the laws of Congress, it made no sense for Southerners to try to defend their interests through Congress. What use was compromise if the results of such compromise were ignored?

▶**2.** How did some Northerners work against the Fugitive Slave Law?

The Kansas-Nebraska Act

From the start, people knew the Fugitive Slave Law would be unpopular in the North. No one, however, expected there to be more trouble over slavery in the West.

The Missouri Compromise of 1820 seemed to settle that issue for lands acquired by the Louisiana Purchase. It said that, except for the state of Missouri, slavery could not be established in lands north of an imaginary line at 36° 30′ north latitude. South of that line, slavery would be legal.

Then the Compromise of 1850 seemed to settle the issue for lands won in the Mexican War. Under its terms, California entered the Union as a free state. The rest of the land from Mexico was organized into the territories of New Mexico and Utah. In time, each of them would enter the Union "with or without slavery, as their constitution may prescribe."

In short, unless the United States got still more land, the issue seemed to be closed. That was a great relief to most people.

▶**3.** Which compromises seemed to settle the issue of slavery in the territories?

Senator Douglas's Bill In January 1854, Stephen Douglas reopened the issue of slavery in the territories. He introduced a bill called the **Kansas-Nebraska Act** to organize two new territories, Kansas and Nebraska. Both territories were part of the Louisiana Purchase and lay north of the 36° 30′ line. Under the terms of the Missouri Compromise, slavery would be outlawed there.

Douglas's bill proposed that the people of Kansas and Nebraska, like those of New Mexico and Utah, be allowed to decide for themselves whether their states would be free or slave. Letting the people of the territories decide for themselves about slavery was known as **popular sovereignty.**

▶**4.** What were the provisions of the Kansas-Nebraska Act?

Douglas's Reasons Douglas thought he had good reasons for reopening the slavery issue. He wanted Kansas and Nebraska settled.

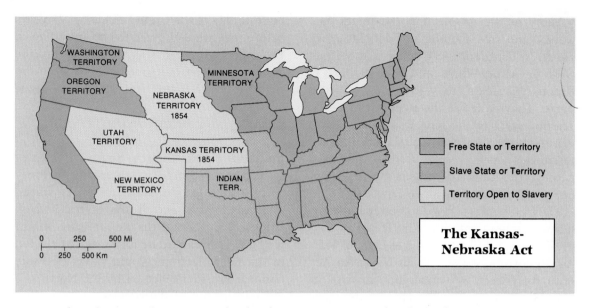

Map Study *When were the Kansas and Nebraska territories organized? Which of the two territories was closer to the slave states?*

Douglas thought it would be good for the country if there were "a continuous line of settlements" from east to west.

Douglas had another reason for his action. If Kansas and Nebraska were settled, there was a good chance that a proposed transcontinental railroad, one that ran from the Atlantic to the Pacific coast, would be built along a northern route. The eastern end of the railroad would be at Chicago. That would be very good for Douglas's home state of Illinois. Douglas thought his proposal was so good that it would even help his chance of becoming President in 1856.

Douglas realized that the Kansas-Nebraska Act had no chance of being passed by Congress without the support of some Southerners. He also knew that Southerners would not vote for the organization of territories where slaves could go. Douglas hoped popular sovereignty would satisfy members of Congress from the South. When it did not, Douglas was even willing to repeal the Missouri

Compromise. From his point of view, the line drawn by the Missouri Compromise made little practical difference, anyway. Cotton could not be grown in states that lay so far to the north, so he thought slaveholders would not go there. Douglas also hoped to get the slavery issue out of Congress once and for all by moving that decision into the territories and states.

Seldom has anyone been so wrong. Douglas brought slavery right back into national politics. With it came all the anger and division that had supposedly been resolved in 1850.
▶**5.** Why did Stephen Douglas reopen the issue of slavery?

The Election of 1856

It did not take long to see how mistaken Douglas was. The Kansas-Nebraska Act had barely been signed into law by President Pierce when demonstrations against it and its author began in the North.

Many of the people opposed to the law were Democrats, members of Douglas's own party. In February 1854, some of them met with one-time Whigs and Free Soilers in Ripon, Wisconsin, to start a new political party. They called it the **Republican Party.** The founders of the new Republican Party were against the spread of slavery into the territories. As a result, Republicans condemned the Kansas-Nebraska Act. They also opposed the Fugitive Slave Law.

The Democrats refused to nominate Douglas or to renominate Franklin Pierce as their presidential candidate in the election of 1856. As supporters of the Kansas-Nebraska Act, both men were too unpopular to win the election. It took 17 ballots before the Democratic Convention found its candidate— James Buchanan of Pennsylvania. The Democratic platform, nonetheless, stood behind the Kansas-Nebraska Act as "the only sound and safe solution of the slavery question."

▶ **6.** What was the platform of the new Republican Party?

The Results By 1856, the Republican Party had become the second most powerful political party in the United States. The Democrat's candidate, Buchanan, defeated the Republican candidate, John C. Frémont. Still, Frémont won over 1.3 million votes. He also won 114 electoral votes to Buchanan's 174. That was a remarkable achievement for the candidate of a new political party.

The third most popular political party in 1856 was the American or "Know-Nothing" Party. The party got its name because its members were very secretive. When asked about the party, a member's usual reply was "I know nothing." The Know-Nothing Party opposed Catholics and immigrants. It asked that all Catholics and foreigners be barred from public office. It wanted immigrants to be residents of the United States for 21 years before they were allowed to become citizens. The party's power was, however, on the downturn. Many of its members would eventually join the Republican Party, making it even stronger.

▶ **7.** Who won the election of 1856?

Southern Fears From a Southern point of view, the strength of the Republican Party was a bad sign. Frémont carried 11 states, all in the North, and all free states. In fact, it looked as though the Republicans might well get their candidate for President elected in the next election. Would slavery be safe under a President elected by the North?

The question of the presidency was especially important, since the South had already lost control of the Senate. With the admission of California to statehood, there were 16 free states and 15 slave states in the Union. Each state, of course, had two senators. When Minnesota and Oregon became states in 1858 and 1859, respectively, the free state majority in the Senate increased.

▶ **8.** Why were Southerners alarmed by the election of 1856?

The Dred Scott Decision

Even if Congress and the presidency were controlled by opponents of slavery, the South could turn to the Supreme Court for protection of what it saw as its constitutional rights. In 1857, a case came before the Supreme Court that some, including President Buchanan, hoped would settle the issues that divided North and South. Unfortunately, the case—*Dred Scott* v. *Sandford*—was very complicated, and the Supreme Court's decision divided Americans even more.

Dred Scott was a slave who had been bought in Missouri, which was a slave state,

Pictures of Dred Scott, his wife, Harriet, and his daughters, Eliza and Lizzie, appeared in Frank Leslie's Illustrated Newspaper *in 1857.*

by an army doctor, John Emerson. Later, Emerson took Scott to Illinois, a free state, and then to Wisconsin territory, which was also free under the terms of the Missouri Compromise. Eventually, Emerson and Scott returned to Missouri. After Emerson died, Scott claimed to be a free man because he had once lived in a free state and in a free territory.

Scott won his first court case but lost when the decision was appealed to the Missouri State Supreme Court. In the meantime, title to Scott passed to Emerson's brother-in-law, John F. A. Sanford (whose name was misspelled in the official court records). Because Sanford lived in New York and Scott in Missouri, Scott's lawyers decided to bring the case before federal courts. Eventually, the Supreme Court agreed to hear the case.

▶**9.** Why did Scott claim to be free?

The Issues The Court had three major issues to settle: (1) Did Scott have a right to bring his case into federal courts? Scott had that right only if he were a citizen of the United

States. So the Court had to decide whether or not blacks were citizens of the United States. (2) Had Scott become a free man by living for a time in a free state and in a free territory? Scott's claim was based in part on the time he spent in Wisconsin. Wisconsin was free territory only if Congress had the right to exclude slavery from the territories. Congress had acted as if it had that right in 1820 when it passed the Missouri Compromise. But (3) was the Missouri Compromise constitutional?

▶**10.** What issues did the Supreme Court face in the Dred Scott case?

The Decision Each of the nine Supreme Court justices wrote a separate opinion on the case. That is highly unusual and made it difficult to understand just what the court decided on some of the issues.

The opinion written by the Chief Justice of the United States, Roger Taney, is generally taken to speak for the majority of the justices. Taney said that (1) blacks were not citizens of the United States. Several of the other justices, however, avoided that issue, making it unclear whether Taney's statement represented a majority opinion.

The Supreme Court was clearer in deciding that (2) Scott had not become free by living in a free state. Six justices agreed on that point, though for different reasons. The Court also decided that (3) the Missouri Compromise was unconstitutional. To prohibit slavery in territories under Congress's jurisdiction was, Taney said, to deprive persons of property without the due process of law. The Fifth Amendment to the Constitution did not allow Congress to do that.

▶ **11.** What did the Supreme Court decide on the three major issues that were part of the Dred Scott case?

The Freeport Doctrine

The Dred Scott decision set off a storm of controversy. The decision became a major issue in the election of members to the Illinois legislature in 1858.

At that time, members of the state legislatures still elected United States senators. So voters were choosing state legislators who, in turn, would elect a senator. In this particular election, it was clear that Democratic legislators would vote for Senator Stephen A. Douglas, who was running for reelection. Republican legislators would vote for a Republican lawyer named Abraham Lincoln. The two candidates held a series of public debates throughout the state. They are known as the **Lincoln-Douglas Debates.**

During one of the debates, at Freeport, Illinois, Lincoln asked Douglas an important question on the issue of slavery: Was there any way the people of a territory could keep slavery from their land before they were organized into a state?

Yes, said Douglas. All they had to do was refuse to pass a **slave code.** A slave code was a set of laws that defined a slave's status and the rights of a slave owner and provided for the enforcement of the owner's rights. No slaveholder would bring slaves into a territory without such laws. Douglas's answer became known as the **Freeport Doctrine.**

Douglas won the election and returned to the Senate. The Freeport Doctrine, however, lost him many friends in the South. What he said was true, and Southerners knew it. But if the people of a territory could so easily keep out slavery, what good was the Dred Scott decision? The South wanted recognition of the right of slaveholders to bring their property with them into any part of the nation. The Dred Scott decision seemed to give them that recognition. Then the Freeport Doctrine took it away.

▶ **12.** What was the Freeport Doctrine?

Reviewing Section I

Identify Uncle Tom's Cabin, Harriet Beecher Stowe, personal liberty laws, Kansas-Nebraska Act, popular sovereignty, Republican Party, James Buchanan, Know-Nothing Party, *Dred Scott* v. *Sandford*, Roger Taney, Lincoln-Douglas Debates, slave code, Freeport Doctrine

Questions to Answer

1. Why did Southerners fear the strength of the Republican Party?
2. How was the election of 1856 a victory for the new Republican Party?

A Question to Think About Why did Stephen Douglas's plan to get the issue of slavery out of national politics backfire?

The startling difference in their appearance is clear in these photographs of Stephen Douglas and Abraham Lincoln. Douglas stood just over five feet tall. Lincoln was almost six feet four inches tall.

II. A Rising Tide of Violence

Government and politics are peaceful ways of resolving differences. Many Southerners, however, decided that Congress could not protect their rights. The President and the Supreme Court also seemed unreliable.

At the same time, many Northerners were becoming unhappy with the government. The Kansas-Nebraska Act and the Dred Scott decision seemed gravely wrong. Some Northerners worried that the country was being taken over by a slave conspiracy.

The frustration on both sides led to violence over the slavery issue in the 1850's. From the Kansas frontier to the floor of the United States Congress and in the foothills of Virginia, opponents and supporters of slavery tried to resolve their differences by force. The violence of the 1850's settled nothing. It only made matters worse.

The Fight over Kansas

The war over slavery first broke out in Kansas. To the east of Kansas is Missouri, a slave state. Hundreds of people raced from Missouri to Kansas in the hope of making it a slave state. Others rushed to Kansas in the hope of keeping it free of slavery. Nebraska, which lay farther north and had no slave state nearby, saw no such trouble.

Proslavery voters in Kansas managed to elect the territory's delegate to Congress in the fall of 1854. The next spring, they elected most members of the territory's new legislature. There was, however, a great deal of cheating in those elections. Many well-armed Missourians crossed the border, voted illegally, and then went home again.

The proslavery legislature passed a number of harsh laws in support of slavery. A person could be given a two-year prison term just for questioning the slave system. Anyone convicted of encouraging slaves to run away or rebel could be put to death.

▶**1.** Which side seemed to have the majority in Kansas?

The Topeka Constitution   Antislavery voters in Kansas were so outraged by the actions of the legislature that they organized their own government in the fall of 1855. They drew up a document known as the **Topeka Constitution.** It outlawed slavery in Kansas after 1857. The group also elected its own legislature and a delegate to Congress.

Kansas then had two governments, one supporting slavery and one against it. The first was organized under the laws of the United States but was based upon elections that did not honestly represent the people of Kansas. The other was illegal under United States law but represented the wishes of most of the settlers.

▶**2.** What was the Topeka Constitution?

Bleeding Kansas   Before long, violence broke out. Small groups of armed men from Missouri wandered through Kansas threatening the settlers from the North. The antislavery people organized to defend themselves.

A Kansas man named John Brown decided it was time for antislavery people to seek revenge for the raids. In May 1856, he led seven men (including four of his sons and a son-in-law) to a proslavery settlement at Pottawatomie (pät ə wat'ə mē) Creek. They took five men from their cabins and murdered them, leaving their bodies as a warning to others who supported slavery.

In revenge, some Missourians attacked, among other places, Brown's settlement at Osawatomie (ōs ə wat'ə mē). Many free state

On September 13, 1856, proslavery and antislavery forces clashed in the Kansas Territory. S. J. Readers, an eyewitness, made this sketch of the battle.

supporters condemned the **Pottawatomie Creek Massacre**. They could not, however, stop the spilling of blood.

▶**3.** What happened at the Pottawatomie Creek Massacre?

The Lecompton Constitution Congress could not settle the Kansas disputes. The House of Representatives voted to accept the Topeka Constitution and so make Kansas a free state. However, the Senate would not agree.

In 1857, elections were held in Kansas to choose delegates to a new constitutional convention. Because the antislavery settlers did not like the way the election was set up, they refused to vote. As a result, most of the delegates at the convention, which met at Lecompton, Kansas, were supporters of slavery. They wrote the **Lecompton Constitution**, which allowed slavery in Kansas. The constitution was ratified by the people of the territory, but, again, the opponents of slavery refused to vote. Most settlers in Kansas were still against slavery.

Nonetheless, in 1858, President James Buchanan asked Congress to admit Kansas to the Union as a slave state under the Lecompton Constitution. The Senate agreed, but Republicans in the House of Representatives voted the proposal down.

▶**4.** What was the Lecompton Constitution?

The Attack on Charles Sumner

The debate over Kansas was impassioned in both houses of Congress. In the Senate, the fight became so heated that one senator was nearly killed.

In May 1856, Senator Charles Sumner of Massachusetts made a speech called "The Crime Against Kansas." The speech was so long that it took two days to read. In the course of his speech, Sumner made some nasty remarks about Senator Andrew Butler of South Carolina, who was a supporter of the slave system.

That was too much for Congressman Preston Brooks, who was Butler's cousin. So, on

American artist Winslow Homer made this lithograph showing Preston Brooks attacking Charles Sumner in the Senate chamber.

May 22, Brooks went to the Senate chamber, walked up to Sumner's desk, and began beating Sumner with a heavy cane. Before the beating was over, Sumner was unconscious. His injuries were so severe that he could not return to the Senate for three and a half years. Sumner's empty seat became a shrine to those opposed to slavery. Meanwhile, Brooks became a hero to Southerners who were tired of being insulted by Northerners.

That such an ugly incident took place in the Senate chamber was bad in itself. That otherwise decent people cheered after it happened was worse. Those developments showed again that reasoned talk was giving way to angry violence.

▶**5.** How did Southerners respond to the attack on Senator Sumner?

Harpers Ferry

In 1859, the violence moved to the South. This time, some Northerners cheered the man responsible for the violence, John Brown.

After the Pottawatomie Creek Massacre, Brown continued to lead the free state settlers of Kansas in battles with their opponents. He traveled to places such as Boston and New York to raise money for the free state forces in Kansas. Meanwhile, he did what he could to help runaway slaves.

Brown decided to carry his war against slavery into the oldest slave states. He established his base at a farm in Maryland about four miles from the town of Harpers Ferry, Virginia. On the night of October 16, 1859, he led a party of 18 men, including 5 blacks, across the Potomac River into Virginia. They seized the federal arsenal at Harpers Ferry, where ammunition and guns were stored. Brown had expected the slaves of the area to join him and his followers. None did.

Two days later, the United States Marines under Colonel Robert E. Lee arrived and recaptured the arsenal. One marine was killed along with four local people (including the mayor of Harpers Ferry and a free black). Ten of Brown's followers also died in the fighting. Brown was captured and tried for treason against the state of Virginia and for inciting a slave uprising. After being convicted of both crimes, he was hanged at Charlestown, Virginia, on December 2, 1859.

What had Brown intended to do? He claimed that he was only trying to help slaves escape to Canada. The evidence suggests,

The 1850's were part of a period called the Victorian Age. It was named after an extraordinary ruler of Great Britain, Queen Victoria. She was crowned in 1837 when she was an 18-year-old girl. She reigned for 63 years. During Victoria's time as queen, Great Britain expanded abroad.

In the United States, the middle class created its own "Victorian Age" in architecture, household furnishings, clothing, and manners. People in the North and the South followed those styles.

American Victorians liked to be surrounded by plenty. Their houses were decorated with useless towers and arches, many windows, big porches, and ornate trim called gingerbread.

Inside their houses, Victorians stuffed rooms with furniture, pictures, scarves, plants, lamps, and statues. The goal in furnishing a Victorian room was to leave only enough room for a person to turn around.

The Victorians liked plenty to eat too. A formal dinner contained twelve separate courses. Fortunately, the Victorians did not admire thin figures in men or women.

Victorians wanted to be proper in all things. Although Queen Victoria was considered the ultimate authority on correct behavior, etiquette books were often consulted.

The forms of proper behavior were, of course, sometimes different in Great Britain from those in the American Republic. But the shared tastes and styles during the Victorian Age suggested that the United States and Great Britain still had some close ties with one another. ·

---

however, that he wanted to start a revolution that would destroy slavery in the South. He and his followers had collected about 400 guns and 950 pikes (pointed iron sticks) at their Maryland farm. They even had a plan for governing the South after they conquered it. The plan would have put power in the hands of a commander in chief named John Brown.

▶**6.** What happened during Brown's raid on Harpers Ferry?

Northern Reactions Brown and his raid on Harpers Ferry impressed a number of important people in the North. They were struck by his moral firmness and his willingness to sacrifice himself for others. Abolitionists such as Wendell Phillips cheered Brown's attempt.

That Brown broke the laws of the United States and of Virginia made no difference to them. Brown, they said, was following God's law. That Brown's understanding of God's law was unlike that of most Americans made no difference. Brown's supporters called him a martyr, saying he gave up his life for a holy cause.

However, most people disagreed. Among them were leading Northern politicians of both major political parties. Both Abraham Lincoln and Stephen Douglas condemned Brown's actions. Slavery was wrong, Lincoln said, but that did not justify "violence, bloodshed, and treason." Most Northerners condemned the attack on Harpers Ferry.

▶**7.** What were the reactions of people in the North to Brown's raid?

During the course of his life, John Brown was many things to many people. To some, he was a hero who led slaves to freedom. To others, he was a violent madman whose actions contributed to the start of the Civil War.

John Brown was born in Torrington, Connecticut, in 1800. He came from an old New England family whose ancestors may well have arrived on the *Mayflower*. When he was very young, he moved with his family to Hudson, Ohio. It was there that John spent his childhood.

John disliked spending time in school. Instead, he preferred the freedom of being outdoors. During the War of 1812, he loved the long hours he spent on the trail, driving beef cattle for the army. Later he worked for his father as a tanner.

In 1820, Brown married Dianthe Lusk. She had seven children before she died in 1831. Within a year, Brown married his second wife, May Anne Day, a girl of 16. Brown had 13 children with this wife.

Like his father, John was a drifter, moving from one town to another. In the late 1830's,

he borrowed heavily to invest in land and then lost what he had borrowed after the Panic of 1837. He tried to get himself out of debt by organizing new businesses, but they too failed. As a result, Brown and his family lived in poverty.

Brown was in his fifties when the idea of using force to free slaves came to him. He had always supported the antislavery movement. Now the desire to help slaves became an obsession. His sons were also committed to the antislavery movement. When five of his sons moved to Kansas in 1855 to help keep the territory from becoming a slave state, Brown followed them.

Brown and his sons soon attracted a large following. Armed with knives and rifles, the group terrorized the countryside. In the spring of 1856, the terror turned to murder when Brown and his followers killed five Southerners at Pottawatomie Creek.

Many people believed that Brown was mad. There was, in fact, some insanity in Brown's family. But Brown insisted that he knew what he was doing. "Slavery," he said, "is a great wrong against God and humanity. As a result, it is right to fight it."

In 1857, Brown began to collect arms and men for an invasion of the South. For almost two years, he thought of nothing else. His efforts ended with an attack on the federal arsenal at Harpers Ferry, Virginia. In the end, 10 of Brown's small force of 18 lay dead or dying. Among those men were two of Brown's sons.

On December 2, 1859, John Brown was hung. A Kansas farmer commented, "He (Brown) will trouble them more when his coffin's nailed down." The Kansas farmer was right. In the North, John Brown became a hero and an inspiration to the antislavery forces. In the South, his memory was a constant reminder of what the slave states could expect if they remained in the Union.

Southern Reactions The South heard only those Northerners who sang John Brown's praises. What Brown had done terrified the Southerners. Among the documents captured from Brown were maps of the South with strange marks here and there. Did those marks perhaps indicate places where Brown's followers planned to start slave uprisings?

A wave of terror swept through the South. Suddenly, any Northerner who happened to be in the South was suspected of being a follower of Brown. Mobs attacked sailors, peddlers, even teachers who had lived in the South for years. Those mobs were taking the law into their own hands much as Brown had done. As a result, violence continued to spread and the rule of law was weakened.

On the day he was hanged, John Brown made a brief statement. "I . . . am now quite certain," he said, "that the crimes of this guilty land will never be purged away but with Blood." He had done much to make that prediction come true.

▶8. How did Southerners react to Brown's raid on Harpers Ferry?

Reviewing Section II

Identify Topeka Constitution, John Brown, Pottawatomie Creek Massacre, Lecompton Constitution, Charles Sumner, Preston Brooks, Harpers Ferry

Questions to Answer
1. Why did a war over slavery break out in Kansas in 1856?
2. What were the major results of John Brown's raid?

A Question to Think About Why did popular sovereignty fail to resolve the issue of slavery in Kansas?

III. The Secession Crisis

The nation was already divided by the time of John Brown's raid on Harpers Ferry. After that event, division spread even further. First the Democratic Party, the one remaining national party, divided into Northern and Southern wings. Before long, the Union itself was in peril.

The Election of 1860

The Democratic Party met in Charleston, South Carolina, in April 1860. The Southern delegates were ready to test their power. A delegate from Alabama declared that the party must take the position that "slavery was right." It must call for a national slave code, to be passed by Congress, that would protect slavery in the territories.

The Northern Democrats would not do that. As a result, delegates from eight Southern states left the convention. Those Democrats met alone and named their own candidate, John C. Breckinridge from Kentucky. The Northern Democrats eventually supported Stephen Douglas.

The Republicans met in Chicago in May. Their platform firmly stated that slavery should not be brought into the territories. In states where the slave system was established, however, it should be left alone. The Republicans condemned the "Missouri ruffians" who had caused so much trouble in Kansas, and the raid on Harpers Ferry. They supported a federal homestead act that would give free land to settlers. They also favored the building of a transcontinental railroad and higher tariffs to protect American industry. Finally, after three ballots, they chose as their presidential candidate Abraham Lincoln, the man who had lost to Douglas in the Illinois senatorial election of 1858.

Lincoln faced three other candidates—Douglas, the Northern Democrat; Breckinridge, the Southern Democrat; and John Bell of Tennessee. Bell was nominated by a new party, the Constitutional Union Party, which

This engraving shows Lincoln, his wife Mary, son Robert, and younger son Tad. The portrait is of Lincoln's son Willie, who died at the age of 12.

stood for "the Constitution of the country, the Union of the States, and the enforcement of the laws."

Lincoln easily won the election of 1860. He had 180 electoral votes, more than all the other candidates together. He also had more popular votes than any one of the other candidates. There was only one problem. Almost all of Lincoln's supporters were in the North. ▶**1.** Who were the candidates for President in 1860?

The President-Elect

The man who won the election of 1860 was an enemy of slavery, but not of the South. In fact, Abraham Lincoln was born in a slave state and lived much of his life in the company of Southerners.

Abraham Lincoln's family had its roots in New England, like those of Harriet Beecher Stowe and John Brown. His ancestors had moved to Pennsylvania, then to Virginia, where Lincoln's parents were born, and then to Kentucky. There Abraham was born on February 12, 1809. His father soon moved to another part of Kentucky, then went to Indiana, and later to Illinois.

The family was never well off. Abraham was ambitious and bright, but spent little time in school as a boy. In Illinois, he did odd jobs, like splitting rails, and studied law. In time, he became a good lawyer, the husband of Mary Todd Lincoln, and the proud father of three sons.

The voters of Illinois elected him to the state legislature many times and finally sent him to the United States House of Representatives for a term from 1847 to 1849. In those years, Lincoln was a Whig and an admirer of Henry Clay. While in Congress, Lincoln opposed the Mexican War even though most people in Illinois favored the war. That stand made him so unpopular that he did not run for reelection.

▶**2.** What political offices did Abraham Lincoln hold before 1860?

Lincoln Returns to Politics Lincoln returned to politics as an opponent of the Kansas-Nebraska Act. He ran for the Senate as a Republican in 1858. Though he lost the election to Douglas, the campaign made him nationally well-known.

Lincoln was a politician who wanted to win elections. Illinois was a free state, but its southern counties were settled by people from the South. Therefore, to win elections a politician in Illinois had to appeal to both sides on the slavery issue. Lincoln's experience in Illinois prepared him well for national politics. By 1860, he had taken a stand that would, he hoped, satisfy the North without losing the South.

Lincoln believed in the Declaration of Independence, the Constitution, and the Republic. Preserving the nation was to him a sacred trust. He also believed in democracy and the rule of law. For those reasons, he condemned the raid on Harpers Ferry and said that Americans should obey the Fugitive Slave Law.

▶**3.** Why did Lincoln believe Americans should obey the Fugitive Slave Law?

Lincoln's Views on Slavery Slavery, Lincoln said, was wrong, even a "monstrous injustice." But he understood how hard it would be to end slavery in a satisfactory way. White Americans, he thought, were unwilling to accept free blacks as equals. If the slaves were freed and kept as underlings, would they be much better off? For Lincoln, as for many Americans in both the North and South, the real problem was what would happen to blacks if slavery were ended.

The slave system had to be respected, Lincoln said, in states where it was already established. He insisted, though, that slavery not be allowed to spread farther. Like other Americans of his time, Lincoln thought that if slavery did not spread it would eventually die out. He made that point in a famous speech in 1858. "I believe the government cannot endure permanently half slave and half free," he said. "It will become all one thing, or all the other."

Clearly, Lincoln would do all he could under the Constitution to keep the nation from becoming all slave. That stand was not enough to make Lincoln an abolitionist. It was, nonetheless, too antislavery for Southerners to accept. By 1860, unless people were ready to say slavery was good, they were considered enemies of the South.

▶**4.** How did Lincoln think slavery would end in the United States?

Secession

South Carolinians had talked about leaving the Union since at least the 1820's. As soon as they heard about Lincoln's election, they called a state convention. It met in Charleston on December 20, 1860, and declared "the Union . . . between South Carolina and other states under the name of 'The United States of America' . . . hereby dissolved."

▶**5.** What was the first state to secede from the Union?

The Confederacy Begins By the beginning of February 1861, six other states—Georgia, Alabama, Florida, Mississippi, Louisiana, and Texas—had followed South Carolina's lead. The seceded states sent delegates to Montgomery, Alabama. There the **Confederate States of America,** or **Confederacy,** was formed. The delegates adopted a constitution

On February 18, 1861, Jefferson Davis was inaugurated president of the Confederacy.

and elected Jefferson Davis of Mississippi as president and Alexander Stephens of Georgia as vice president.

Not everyone in the South supported secession. Even the new president of the Confederacy, Jefferson Davis, was hesitant about leaving the Union. Yet when Mississippi voted to secede, Davis supported its decision.

▶6. Who was president of the Confederacy?

Why the Confederate States Seceded The Confederate states seceded from the Union to protect slavery. The seven so-called cotton states that seceded first were those that had the highest percentage of blacks in their populations. When convention delegates in those states explained why they were leaving the Union, they spoke almost entirely of threats to slavery.

The Mississippi convention argued that the people of the North urged slaves to run away and interfered with their recapture under the Fugitive Slave Law. Northerners had even encouraged the raid on Harpers Ferry. South Carolina added that Northerners had condemned slavery as sinful, allowed the founding of abolition societies, and elected to the presidency a man "whose opinions and purposes are hostile to slavery."

The complaints of Southern states went back several years. Their current actions, however, reflected a mood of great fear that set in after the raid on Harpers Ferry. Those fears worsened after Lincoln's election. He was, they said, a "black Republican," an enemy of the South and its slave system.

▶7. Why did the Confederate states secede?

Lincoln Takes Charge

Lincoln did not take office until March 4, 1861. In the time between the election and his inauguration, the country remained in the hands of President James Buchanan and Congress.

When the Confederacy began taking over federal forts and arsenals in the South, Buchanan did nothing until it was too late to make a difference. As a result, many Southerners thought they would be allowed to leave the Union peacefully.

Spring approached and attention turned toward the new President. What would he do? Lincoln stayed in Illinois, watching events but saying little. When he did speak, he came out against compromise. "Stand firm," he advised, "especially on keeping slavery from the territories."

Finally, it was Inauguration Day, March 4, 1861. Lincoln gave his well-prepared inaugural address at the Capitol. He once again assured the Confederacy that he would not interfere with slavery in the states where it already existed. "I believe I have no lawful right to do so," Lincoln said, "and I have no

Five days after Jefferson Davis's inauguration, Abraham Lincoln took the oath of office as the sixteenth President of the United States.

inclination to do so." He denied that states had any lawful right to leave the Union and promised to enforce federal authority "in all the States." Lincoln also said that he would use his power "to hold, occupy, and possess the property, and places belonging to the government . . ." He was referring to federal forts and arsenals in the South. Lincoln would not, however, invade the South, nor would he use more force than necessary.

The issue of civil war therefore lay, he said, with the people of the South. "The Government will not assail *you*. You can have no conflict, without being yourselves the aggressors." Lincoln's address ended with an appeal to the country's shared history, to "the mystic chords of memory" that would one day again "swell the chorus of the Union."

To the seceded states, Lincoln's decision to hold and occupy federal property within the Confederacy meant war. The question was no longer if it would occur, but when and where the fighting would begin.

▶ **8.** What points did Lincoln make in his first inaugural address?

Reviewing Section III

Identify John C. Breckinridge, John Bell, Constitutional Union Party, Confederate States of America, Jefferson Davis

Questions to Answer
1. What was the Republican Party's platform in 1860?
2. What was Lincoln's position on slavery before the election of 1860?

A Question to Think About What might have happened if Buchanan had tried to stop the Confederates from taking federal forts and arsenals?

IMPROVE YOUR READING
Drawing Conclusions

We can learn a great deal about people by their actions and words. When we observe the way people act and listen to what they say, we can draw conclusions about them.

If a person does not smile very often and complains about almost everything, we might conclude that he or she is basically unhappy. If a person complains or shouts frequently, we might conclude that he or she has a bad temper.

We can also draw conclusions about the opinions of other people from their actions and words. After reading about Congressman Preston Brooks in this chapter, we can probably conclude that he strongly disagreed with what Senator Charles Sumner had to say in his "Crime against Kansas" speech. That is true; Sumner's speech included unpleasant remarks about Brooks's cousin, Senator Andrew Butler. It also attacked the slave system that Brooks supported.

In this exercise, you are to draw conclusions about the opinions held by various people described in this chapter. Each statement is paired with the name of a historical figure. Consider what you learned about the people in this chapter. What were their beliefs? How did they act? Decide whether you think the individual would have agreed or disagreed with the statement that appears below his or her name. Number your paper from 1 to 10. Write either "agree" or "disagree" next to each number. Be prepared to give reasons for your answers.

1. Harriet Beecher Stowe
   "Human beings are all the same. It does not matter what the color of their skin is."
2. Stephen Douglas
   "Each state should decide for itself whether or not to permit slavery."
3. Dred Scott
   "Freedom is worth a struggle."
4. Justice Taney
   "Slaves who enter free states should consider themselves free citizens."
5. John Brown
   "Those who support slavery should fear for their lives."
6. Abraham Lincoln
   "People who live in states where slavery is legal should not be forced to give up their slaves."
7. Jefferson Davis
   "Secession is wrong. We should support President Lincoln."
8. John C. Frémont
   "Slavery should not spread into new territories."
9. John C. Breckinridge
   "The nation needs a slave code."
10. John Bell
   "Enforcing the laws of our country is necessary at all costs."

CHAPTER 18 REVIEW

Vocabulary Check
Match each term in column I with the phrase that best explains it in column II.

Column I

1. Republican Party
2. Know-Nothing Party
3. Slave code
4. Popular sovereignty
5. Constitutional Union Party

Column II

a. New party in the election of 1860
b. Laws defining the status of slaves and the rights of slave owners
c. Party that was opposed to Catholics and immigrants
d. Letting the people of an area decide for themselves whether or not to allow slavery
e. Party founded to oppose the spread of slavery into the territories

Fact Check
On a separate sheet of paper, write the name of the person described in each of the sentences below.

1. She wrote *Uncle Tom's Cabin*.
2. He won the presidency in 1860.
3. He introduced the Kansas-Nebraska bill in Congress.
4. A slave who sued for his freedom because he had lived in a free state.
5. He led the raid on Harpers Ferry.

Time Check
On a separate piece of paper, put the following events in the proper chronological order.

1. Missouri Compromise
2. Fugitive Slave Law
3. Topeka Constitution
4. *Dred Scott* v. *Sandford*
5. Harpers Ferry

Skills Check
Use the map on page 379 and the map of the United States in the atlas to answer the following questions.

1. Which territories were opened to slavery by the Kansas-Nebraska Act?
2. What free territories are shown on the map?
3. What present-day states (or parts of states) were carved from the Nebraska Territory?
4. What states (or parts of states) were carved from the New Mexico Territory?
5. What states (or parts of states) were carved from the Utah Territory?

Think and Write
1. How did Senator Douglas create controversy over slavery?
2. What stand did the Republican Party take on the issue of slavery in 1860?
3. Why did slaveholders think that the federal government would no longer protect their rights in the 1850's?
4. Why did Lincoln insist that the Fugitive Slave Law be obeyed?
5. What serious problem did Lincoln think would arise if slavery was ended?

Chapter 19

The Civil War

The sky is ablaze with exploding mortar shells as Confederate soldiers in Charleston, South Carolina, fire the first shots of the Civil War.

In the spring of 1861, attention in both the North and the South turned to Fort Sumter in Charleston Harbor. It and Fort Pickens in Florida were the only forts within the seceded states that remained in federal hands. However, it looked as though Fort Sumter would soon fall to the Confederacy. Its commander, Major Robert Anderson, needed supplies.

By March, when Lincoln took office, Anderson was becoming desperate. Unless supplies came soon, he would have to surrender.

President Lincoln discussed the situation with his advisers. After delaying for a month, he made his decision. On April 6, Lincoln told the governor of South Carolina that he intended to supply the federal garrison at Fort Sumter with food. He did not intend to send ammunition or additional soldiers there. Five days later, before the supply ships arrived, South Carolina demanded that Major Anderson surrender immediately. Anderson asked that he be allowed, for honor's sake, to surrender only when his supplies ran out. His request was turned down.

At 4:30 A.M. on April 12, Confederate guns opened fire on Fort Sumter. The shelling continued for 34 hours before Anderson surrendered. The Civil War had begun.

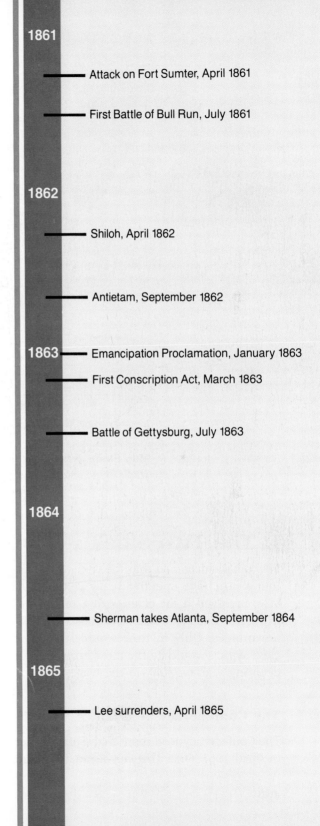

1861
Attack on Fort Sumter, April 1861
First Battle of Bull Run, July 1861
1862
Shiloh, April 1862
Antietam, September 1862
1863 Emancipation Proclamation, January 1863
First Conscription Act, March 1863
Battle of Gettysburg, July 1863
1864
Sherman takes Atlanta, September 1864
1865
Lee surrenders, April 1865

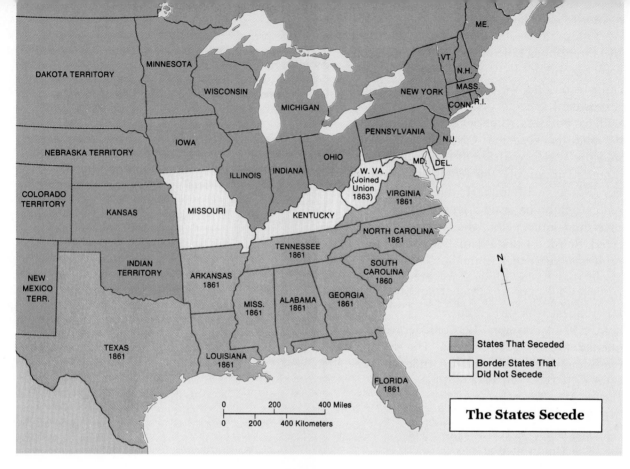

Map Study *Which was the first state to secede? Which state joined the Union in 1863? Which states seceded in 1861?*

I. The Two Sides

Few people dreamed that the war would last four years. The opening years of the Civil War involved a lot of adjusting to the unexpected. Each side had advantages and disadvantages. Only in time would it become clear which would be the most important in deciding who would win the war.

The Confederacy at War

The Confederacy won more than Fort Sumter in April 1861. Once the war began, it gained several new states. Within a matter of days, Virginia seceded. Soon Arkansas, Tennessee, and North Carolina followed. They brought with them into the Confederacy some of the best officers in the United States Army, including Robert E. Lee, whom Lincoln had asked to command the Union army, and Joseph E. Johnston.

The new Confederate states were all **border states.** That is, they were all near the border that separated free and slave states. The border states had fewer slaves than the states that seceded earlier and were more divided over the question of secession.

Once the war began, people in the border states had to decide whether they would fight with or against the Confederacy. For many it was a very hard decision. Robert E. Lee, for example, had attended the United States Military Academy at West Point and had strong ties to the Union. After his home state of Virginia seceded, however, he supported the Confederacy. "I could not," he explained, "raise my hand against my birthplace, my home, my children."

Many people in the border states decided differently and fought with the Union, and not all the border states seceded. There were Northerners in the Confederate army as well.

▶1. What border states seceded after the attack on Fort Sumter?

Confederate Weaknesses Lee's decision and that of the four border states that joined the Confederacy brought considerable strength to the Confederate states. The Confederacy had, however, a number of weaknesses. One lay in its government. Confederates were determined to protect **states' rights.** That is, they were dedicated to preserving the powers of the states from interference by their new national government. But carrying on a war effectively demands a strong central government. The determination of the states to control their own affairs made it harder for the Confederacy to raise the money and troops it needed to fight the war.

Another weakness came from the fact that only a minority of white Confederates owned slaves. The Confederacy was fighting to protect its slave system, but the cost of the war fell largely on people who owned no slaves—or so it seemed to them.

In 1862, the Confederate Congress passed a law that required all white men between the ages of 18 and 35 to serve in the army for 3 years. A rich man, however, could pay someone else to serve in his place. Also, one white man on each plantation with 20 or more slaves did not have to fight. The Confederate Congress hoped in that way to avoid slave uprisings. The task of fighting the war fell on white men who were too poor to own more than a few slaves and who could not pay someone else to fight for them. Those men often resented having to serve in "a rich man's war and a poor man's fight." Such discontent greatly weakened the Confederate commitment to the war.

▶2. Why did people living in the Confederate states who had little money resent having to fight in the war?

Jefferson Davis At first, Jefferson Davis seemed to be a more impressive president than Abraham Lincoln. He was better educated and had more experience in both government and war. Like Lincoln, Davis was born in Kentucky. He later graduated from Transylvania University in Lexington, Kentucky. He then went on to the United States Military Academy at West Point. He fought in the Mexican War and was secretary of war under President Franklin Pierce. Davis also served in the United States House of Representatives and in the Senate.

As president of the Confederacy, Jefferson Davis's flaws soon became obvious. They were especially important because the president of the Confederacy had a six-year term of office.

One of Davis's weaknesses was that he was not a very good politician. He lacked Lincoln's ability to get along with people. Davis quarreled often with the members of his Cabinet and he also had a great deal of trouble getting the support he needed from the Confederate Congress.

Jefferson Davis was a former member of the U.S. Congress and secretary of war.

Davis was also a rather poor military leader. He had trouble making the Confederacy's military officers work together. He also decided that the Confederacy should merely defend itself against invaders and not attack the enemy in the North. A defensive strategy would mean Confederate soldiers had to travel less far, which would save money. It also meant they would be fighting for their homes in familiar places, which would give them strength. In time, Davis thought, the Union would give up.

A defensive strategy works well where the defenders have time on their side. As it turned out, however, the Confederacy did not have time. A long war increased the discontent of the nonslaveholders who were doing so much of the fighting. The Union, moreover, had the men, equipment, and economic strength to carry on a long war.

To win, the Confederacy had to bring the war to the North. By doing so, it hoped to break the Union's will to fight and convince foreign countries to support the Confederacy. Almost a year and a half had passed before Davis learned that his defensive strategy was not enough for victory.

▶**3.** What were Jefferson Davis's weaknesses as a leader?

The Union at War

The Union shared many of the problems faced by the Confederacy. Like the Confederacy, the Union faced internal discontent as the war dragged on. The Union, however, had many strengths the Confederacy did not have. The Union had a much larger population. It also had over 80 percent of the nation's manufacturing capacity and a far more extensive railroad network than the Confederacy. Just how much difference those advantages would make was not clear in 1861. By 1865, their importance was obvious. They let the Union raise and equip more men and move them from place to place more rapidly than the Confederacy could ever do.

Above all else, though, the Union had the advantage of being led by Abraham Lincoln. His strengths as a President in wartime turned out to be far greater than anyone could have predicted. When Lincoln saw what had to be done, he did it. He was also able to get the support he needed.

▶**4.** What were some of the Union's advantages at the beginning of the war?

Lincoln and the Border States The war's outcome, Lincoln quickly understood, would turn on what happened with the border states. He suspected that the outbreak of fighting would drive some of them to the Confederacy. That explains his caution over supplying Fort

Graphing Comparative Resources

The bar graph below compares the resources of the Union and Confederate states in 1860. One part of the bar shows the Union's resources. The other part of the bar shows the Confederacy's resources.

The graph below shows the resources of the two sides as ratios. A ratio shows the relationship of one number to another. For example, the Union's factory production was in the ratio of 10 to 1 to that of the Confederacy. That means for every 10 items produced in Union factories, Confederate factories produced 1 item. The graph does not show exactly how many items each side had of each category. Rather, it shows how many more or less each side had.

Study the graph and answer the questions that follow.

1. (a) What color represents the Union? (b) The Confederacy?
2. How many miles of railroad track did the Union have for every one mile of track in the Confederacy?
3. Of the items illustrated on the chart, for which was Confederate production higher than Union production?
4. Draw a bar to illustrate the following ratio: naval ship tonnage, Union:25; Confederate:1.
5. Draw a bar to illustrate the following ratio: textile goods production, Union:14; Confederate:1.

A Comparison of the Union and Confederacy, 1861

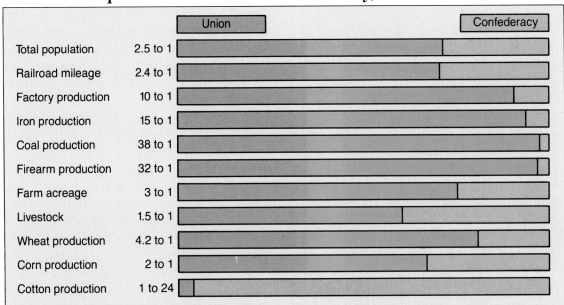

	Union	Confederacy
Total population	2.5 to 1	
Railroad mileage	2.4 to 1	
Factory production	10 to 1	
Iron production	15 to 1	
Coal production	38 to 1	
Firearm production	32 to 1	
Farm acreage	3 to 1	
Livestock	1.5 to 1	
Wheat production	4.2 to 1	
Corn production	2 to 1	
Cotton production	1 to 24	

Source: The Times Atlas of World History, New Jersey, 1978

Sumter. In part, because of Lincoln's skill and decisiveness, only four of the eight border states actually joined the Confederacy.

Delaware had never seriously considered secession. Less than 2 percent of its people were slaves, far fewer than in any other slave state. Maryland was more of a problem. If it sided with the Confederacy, the District of Columbia would be surrounded by enemy territory. So Lincoln gave no ground to Confederate sympathizers in Maryland.

When a mob in Baltimore attacked Massachusetts troops on the way to Washington, D.C., on April 19, Lincoln put the state under military law and suspended the right of habeas corpus. (That right protects people from being arrested when there is no solid evidence against them.) Lincoln then had public supporters of the Confederacy put in jail. As a result, when a proposal that the state secede was brought before the Maryland legislature, it was voted down.

In Missouri and Kentucky, Lincoln worked closely with local Union supporters. Without his care and understanding, both states would almost certainly have seceded. Union Loyalists in Kentucky knew they could never get their state to fight the Confederacy, so they asked only that it remain neutral. That was all right with Lincoln. He kept Union recruiting officers out of the state and even let Kentucky trade with the Confederacy. Lincoln was also careful not to threaten slavery in the border states for fear of driving them into the Confederacy. He understood that the West would be important to a Union victory and that Kentucky in particular would be critical in winning the West.

▶5. How did Lincoln keep Maryland, Missouri, and Kentucky from seceding?

Building a Navy   In other areas, too, Lincoln acted forcefully after the surrender of Fort Sumter. On April 19, he ordered the United States Navy to blockade the Southern coast. That was meant to cut off the Confederacy's trade with other countries. The navy was, however, too weak to police the 3,550 miles of Confederate coastline. Therefore, even before Congress met, Lincoln and his secretary of the navy, Gideon Welles, began a major program to build up and modernize the navy.

The program started by Lincoln and Welles was very successful. Yet the navy was never able to stop the Confederate trade entirely. Throughout the war, small Confederate ships known as blockade runners darted out to sea to buy goods in the Bahamas, Bermuda, or Cuba and then slipped home again.

▶6. Why did Lincoln strengthen the navy?

Building Up the Army   After the attack on Fort Sumter, Lincoln issued a call for 75,000 soldiers to serve for three months. Throughout the North, volunteers rushed to join the army while the excitement was still high. Lincoln soon sensed, however, that the war would be longer than most people expected. So he called for 42,000 more volunteers to serve for three years in the regular standing United States Army. At the time, he did not have a legal right to do that. But when Congress met the following July, it readily approved Lincoln's action.

▶7. Why did Lincoln call for over 40,000 volunteers to serve three years in the regular United States Army?

Lincoln as Head of State   Lincoln had enough faith in his own powers of leadership to appoint some powerful men to his Cabinet. He made William Seward secretary of state. Seward had been his main opponent for the Republican presidential nomination in 1860. Salmon P. Chase, who also hoped one day to be President, became secretary of the treasury. After Lincoln's first secretary of war proved unable to handle the job, the President appointed Edwin M. Stanton to the position. Stanton proved to be very capable. In general, Lincoln's Cabinet was much stronger than the cabinet put together by Jefferson Davis.

The Union lacked, however, the strong military officers that guided the Confederacy in the opening years of the war. So responsibility for the conduct of the war fell back on Lincoln himself as commander in chief. Lincoln had little experience in that area.
▶**8.** What did Lincoln's choices for his Cabinet show about him?

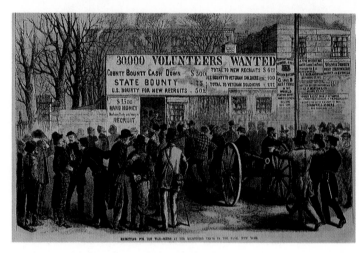

At the beginning of the war, Northern volunteers rushed to sign up to defend the Union.

Reviewing Section I

Identify border states, Robert E. Lee, states' rights, Gideon Welles, William Seward, Salmon P. Chase, Edwin M. Stanton

Questions to Answer
1. What were some of the weaknesses of the Confederacy?

2. How did Lincoln handle the border states that stayed in the Union?

A Question to Think About Which of Lincoln's strengths was the most important for a leader of a country at war?

★★★★★★★★★★★★★★★★★ The United States and the World ★★
A Letter from Siam

It is often difficult for people living in one country to imagine life in a very different sort of place. During the Civil War, the king of Siam (now known as Thailand) learned a little about Abraham Lincoln. The king also learned that elephants were popular in the United States, and that some camels had been sent to the United States from Arabia. That gave him an idea.

The king sent Lincoln a letter with a very generous offer. The king offered to send several pairs of young elephants to the United States from his country. Then he gave detailed instructions regarding the care of the elephants. He stated, "When they arrive in America do not let

them be taken to a cold climate . . . but let them with all haste be turned out to run wild in some jungle suitable for them, not confining them any length of time." He explained that after a while the elephants will become large herds that can be caught, tamed, used to carry heavy loads, and travel through uncleared woods and matted jungles.

Although President Lincoln was very busy during the Civil War, he still found time to write a polite response to the king of Siam. Lincoln declined the offer of elephants because he knew that the climate of the United States was not suited for such animals.

II. The First Two Years of War

In the nineteenth century, war was like football, though, of course, more deadly. The two armies lined up against each other on a field. There was an exchange of fire. Then one or both sides moved forward. When the two lines met, the soldiers attacked their enemies with the bayonets attached to their guns. The idea was to force the other side's soldiers to break their line and run away or, if possible, to destroy the enemy's army.

The two sides spent a lot of effort fighting in northern Virginia in 1861 and 1862. The most important actions of those years were, however, fought in the West, especially in Kentucky and Tennessee.

The Anaconda Plan

When the war began, General Winfield Scott was commander of the United States Army. "Old Fuss and Feathers," as he was called, was 75 years old in 1861 and in no shape to lead an army in the field. But he knew exactly how the Union could defeat the Confederate States.

First, Scott said, the Union should set up a blockade, cutting the Confederacy off from the outside world. Then the Union should win control of the Mississippi River, which would separate Texas, Arkansas, and Louisiana from the rest of the Confederacy. Once that was done, the Union should attack the remainder of the Confederacy from several sides, taking territory and moving inland, gradually tightening the Union's hold. His scheme was named the **anaconda plan** after the large snake that coils around its victim, slowly squeezing it to death. Union victory, Scott predicted, would require at least two or three years and an army of several hundred thousand men.

In 1861, however, most Union supporters, including many members of Lincoln's Cabinet, expected a quick victory. Scott, they said, was out of touch with reality. Just send an army into northern Virginia to defeat Lee and take the new Confederate capital at Richmond, they said, and the war would be over.

Lincoln established a blockade but rejected the rest of Scott's advice. He listened instead to those who thought a quick victory was possible and ordered a Union army into northern Virginia. In the end, however, the war proved that Scott was far wiser than his critics believed he was.

▶**1.** What was the anaconda plan?

The War in the East, July 1861–September 1862

Hundreds of people came down from Washington, D.C., to see the first and, they thought, the last major battle of the war on July 21, 1861. They even brought lunches so they could picnic on the gently sloping fields east of Bull Run, a slow stream in Virginia about 30 miles south of Washington. But the battle, the first Battle of Bull Run, did not turn out as the Union expected.

The Union army under General Irwin McDowell did well at first. It looked, for a time, as though it would break the Confederate line. But the Confederates, inspired by Virginia troops under Brigadier General Thomas J. Jackson, held firm. ("There is Jackson standing like a stone wall," the cry went out. Ever after that he was known as "Stonewall" Jackson.) When more Southern troops arrived, McDowell's soldiers broke rank and ran toward Washington over a road clogged with civilians who understood the picnic was over. Fortunately for the Union, the Confederate army did not give chase. However, the number of deaths on both sides shocked the country.

After the Battle of Bull Run, the Union troops dug in for a long, hard fight. Lincoln appointed George C. McClellan as the new commander of the Union's Army of the Potomac. At the time, McClellan seemed a wise choice. He had already driven Confederate troops out of western Virginia, where most people opposed secession. (In 1863, West Virginia entered the Union as a separate state.) McClellan's men trusted him, and he, in turn, did all he could to protect them. Unfortunately, that kept him from going into battle until everything seemed perfect.

▶**2.** Why was the outcome of the first Battle of Bull Run a surprise for the Union?

The Peninsular Campaign McClellan spent the winter of 1861–1862 training his 150,000 soldiers. In the spring, he took most of his men down the Potomac to the Chesapeake Bay. They landed on the peninsula between the James and York rivers in Virginia and turned to the northwest, toward Richmond. McClellan thought the Confederates were much stronger than they were. As a result, he moved very slowly and cautiously, insisting that he needed more troops.

By June, McClellan still had not reached Richmond. That month, General Robert E. Lee became commander of the Confederate Army of Northern Virginia. Determined to save Richmond, Lee, with Stonewall Jackson's help, moved against McClellan in a series of battles known together as the Seven Days' Battles (June 26–July 2).

Although the Confederates had fewer men than McClellan, they managed to drive the Union forces back to Harrison's Landing on the James River. There, with the help of Union gunboats, McClellan held out until Lee finally

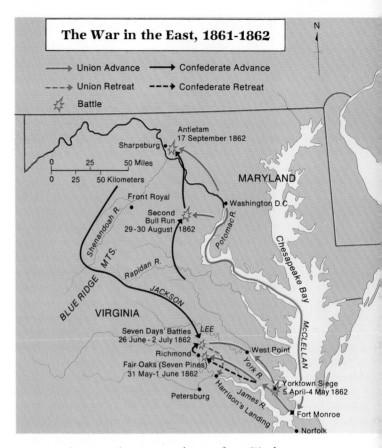

Map Study *Was the Union advance from Washington, D.C., to Fort Monroe by land or by water? Which battle was fought after the Yorktown siege?*

withdrew. In the fighting, the Union had lost 15,000 men, the Confederacy 20,000. But clearly the Confederates had gained the upper hand.

▶**3.** Who won the Seven Days' Battles?

The Second Battle of Bull Run Though the Peninsular Campaign was over, Lincoln still hoped the Union could take Richmond. He called in troops from the West and ordered McClellan to join General John Pope in a new attack on the Confederate capital.

Lee had plans of his own. He decided to destroy Pope's army before McClellan could

Robert E. Lee, the Confederacy's most talented general, was admired by soldiers on both sides.

get there. The armies of Pope and Lee met on the old battlefield of Bull Run on August 29 and 30. Lee had his way. The Confederates drove Pope back toward Washington and saved Richmond a second time.

▶ **4.** Who won the second Battle of Bull Run?

Antietam Lee was not content with saving Virginia. He and Jefferson Davis decided it was time to carry the war into the North. So Lee and his army crossed the Potomac River into Maryland and pushed north toward Pennsylvania. Meanwhile, his right-hand man, Stonewall Jackson, captured the federal arsenal at Harpers Ferry, Virginia, early in September. Jackson's victory brought the Confederacy a considerable amount of much-needed equipment.

Then, on September 13, something extraordinary happened. One of McClellan's men found a few cigars in an abandoned Confederate camp. They were wrapped in a dispatch from Lee. It revealed that Lee and Jackson were separated for the moment. For once, McClellan acted quickly, hoping to defeat Lee before Jackson rejoined him. He attacked Lee again and again on September 17 at Antietam Creek near the town of Sharpsburg, Maryland. Help, however, arrived in time to save Lee's army. Even so, McClellan might have won with just one more attack. But he did not make that attack or even pursue the retreating Confederate army.

That day at Antietam was the bloodiest single day of the war. The Union lost 13,000 men and the Confederacy almost 11,000. Blackened, swollen bodies lay scattered over what was, and would again be, peaceful farmland. The battle, however, ended Lee's remarkable advance of 1862.

▶ **5.** What was McClellan's mistake at the Battle of Antietam?

The War in the West, September 1861–December 1862

The war went much better for the Union in the West during 1861 and 1862. Success there was due largely to an unlikely Union officer by the name of Ulysses Simpson Grant. By the fall of 1861, Grant was in command of a large Union army in Cairo (kā′ rō), Illinois, where the Mississippi and Ohio rivers meet.

Grant crossed the Ohio in the fall of 1861 to secure Kentucky for the Union. Then he joined forces with Commodore A. H. Foote of the navy who had a set of gunboats under his control. They took Fort Henry on the Tennessee River on February 6, 1862. Ten days later, after a fierce battle, Grant took Fort Donelson on the Cumberland River. Control of the Tennessee and Cumberland rivers was important to the Union because those rivers looped down through the heartland of the Confederacy. Soon Nashville fell, and the Confederate army under General Albert S. Johnston retreated into northern Mississippi.

▶**6.** Where were Forts Henry and Donelson?

Shiloh Grant followed Johnston. He made camp at a place called Pittsburg Landing near the Mississippi-Tennessee line. There, on April 6, near the Shiloh meetinghouse, Johnston attacked. The fighting was confused on the first day of battle. Johnston was killed, but the Union forces were very nearly defeated anyway. Soon more troops arrived to help Grant. By the night of April 7, the Union forces were in control, and the Confederate army pulled back.

The loss of life at Shiloh was enormous. Of the 63,000 Union soldiers who fought at Shiloh, 13,000 died. The Confederacy lost 11,000 of its 40,000 soldiers. Grant was blamed for the Union's death toll. Some Union supporters insisted that he be replaced. Lincoln, who was having trouble getting McClellan to act, refused. "I can't spare this man," the President said. "He fights."

▶**7.** Why did Lincoln refuse to remove Grant from command after the Battle of Shiloh?

Taking the Mississippi River The Union won other great victories in the West in the spring of 1862. The navy's David Farragut crashed his fleet through the Confederate defenses and took the city of New Orleans on April 25. Then he captured Baton Rouge. Meanwhile, Union gunboats came down the river and took Memphis, Tennessee.

Before long, the Union controlled all of the Mississippi River except for a stretch of about 250 miles from Vicksburg, Mississippi, south to Port Hudson. Vicksburg was the critical Confederate stronghold. It lay on high lands near a hairpin turn in the river. Grant tried

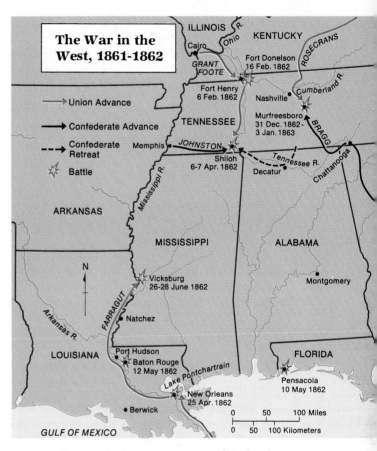

Map Study *In which state were most of the battles in the West fought? Who led the Union advance in Louisiana?*

to capture the city several times in late 1862. He failed, so Vicksburg remained in Confederate hands.

Meanwhile, Confederate General Braxton Bragg almost succeeded in capturing Kentucky and Tennessee. Then, on December 31, he met the Union army near Murfreesboro in Tennessee. After a desperate battle, Bragg retreated. The battle accomplished little for either side. Bragg had lost at least 10,000 men, the Union 13,000. The war in the West, like that in the East, was at a standstill.

▶**8.** How much of the Mississippi River did the Union control by the spring of 1862?

Identify Winfield Scott, anaconda plan, Bull Run, "Stonewall" Jackson, George McClellan, Seven Days' Battles, Antietam, Ulysses Simpson Grant, ~~Fort Henry, Fort Donelson~~, Shiloh, ~~David Farragut~~, Vicksburg, ~~Murfreesboro~~

Questions to Answer
1. Describe the war in the East through the fall of 1862.
2. Describe the war in the West through 1862.

A Question to Think About What parts, if any, of the anaconda plan had the Union put into effect by the end of 1862?

III. Toward Union Victory

By 1863, Lincoln had decided to take a step that would increase people's commitment to the war effort. He made the war something more than a fight to save the Union. He made it a crusade to free the slaves.

The Arguments for Emancipation

From the time the war began, many people had urged Lincoln to free the slaves. They argued that it was not worth so much suffering just to bring the Confederacy back into the Union. After all, it might just secede again at some later time to defend its slave system. The Union would never be safe until slavery was ended. Also, if Lincoln freed the slaves, they could be used to fight for the Union.

Lincoln had been very careful about the slavery issue for fear of losing the support of the border states. His caution, however, upset many people. Frederick Douglass, for example, said the border states were holding the Union back from doing what it should.

Lincoln was also afraid that the British might help the Confederacy become a separate nation. Because Britain bought much of the South's cotton, it had strong economic ties with the Confederacy. Lincoln could, however, undermine British sympathy for the Confederacy by freeing the slaves. Antislavery feeling was too strong in Britain for that country to support a fight for slavery.

▶1. After the war began, what arguments were offered in favor of freeing the slaves?

The Question of Legality Did Lincoln have power to free the slaves in the Confederacy? On the day he took office, he said he did not. That, however, was before the war began. Lincoln thought a President had much greater powers during wartime than in peacetime. He was not afraid to use those powers. If it were necessary to free the slaves to win the war, he could do it, he decided. However, it was not wise to announce such a step when the Union armies seemed to be losing, as was the case through the late summer of 1862.

▶2. Why did Lincoln think he had the power to free the slaves?

The Emancipation Proclamation On September 22, 1862, five days after the Union victory at Antietam, Lincoln announced that all persons held as slaves in those states still in rebellion on January 1, 1863, would be freed. He kept his promise. On New Years Day, Lincoln issued the **Emancipation Proclamation**. It said that all slaves in the rebellious states were "then, thenceforward, and forever free." Slaves in the border states that sided with the Union were not affected. Nor were slaves in parts of the Confederacy that had already been conquered and were being governed by the Union army. In fact, the Emancipation Proclamation freed no slaves. It only promised freedom to those in states still under the Confederacy when federal authority was reestablished there.

Lincoln's step was nonetheless extremely important. The Union war effort became a fight to free the slaves. That brought new strength to the Union even as it increased the Confederacy's will to resist. The Emancipation Proclamation kept Britain from supporting the Confederacy. It also opened the way for the use of black soldiers in the Union army.

Northern free blacks had volunteered for service early in the war but were turned down. Blacks had fought bravely in both the Revolutionary War and the War of 1812. Now they would be allowed to serve in the Civil War. By the end of that war, some 180,000 blacks had fought in the Union army. Their courage at battles such as Port Hudson on the Mississippi earned them the respect and gratitude of the Union.

▶3. What did the Emancipation Proclamation promise?

Conscription and the Draft Riots The availability of blacks for military service was important because by 1863, the Union was hard pressed for soldiers. In fact, it was so hard pressed that on March 3, 1863, Congress passed the first **Conscription Act.** It allowed the President to conscript, or draft, men between the ages of 20 and 45 into military service. Exemptions were allowed only for those who could pay $300 or hire someone to enlist for three years in their place.

Resentment against the draft was great, especially among immigrants and ordinary

Sergeant J. L. Balldwin of Company G, 56th U.S. Colored Infantry, was one of the 180,000 black soldiers who fought to defend the Union.

workers who had no great desire to sacrifice themselves on the slaves' behalf. Many such people took part in the terrible New York City Draft Riots. The violence there began on July 13, 1863, when the first people drafted under the new system were supposed to be chosen. For days mobs went through the streets attacking shops, houses, and people. Altogether 128 people were killed, most of them black. Part of the Union army had to be taken from the battlefield to restore peace in the city.

▶4. What was the Conscription Act?

Women and the War

As the war called up more and more men in both the Union and Confederacy, women found themselves facing new responsibilities.

In the South, planters' wives and daughters learned how to manage their plantations. Women on smaller farms plowed the ground and grew their food. In the North, farmers' wives sometimes had new farm machinery that allowed them to do as much work as many men using hand tools.

In both the Union and Confederacy, women also took paying jobs as government workers or in industry. On both sides, a few women served as spies. Many more were nurses. At first, however, women were not welcome in military hospitals. Clara Barton, who later founded the American Red Cross, and Dorothea Dix worked to change that situation. The large numbers of wounded soldiers also made women's help necessary. The North set up a training program for nurses under Dr. Elizabeth Blackwell, the first American woman to graduate from medical school. The Confederacy officially accepted women as nurses in September 1862.

▶ **5.** What new roles did women take on during the Civil War?

The War in the East, December 1862–July 1863

In November 1862, Lincoln named Ambrose Burnside to replace McClellan. By mid-December, Burnside had attacked the Confederate army at Fredericksburg, Virginia. The Union lost 12,000 soldiers, twice as many as were lost by the Confederates. That was not a promising beginning.

As a result, Lincoln appointed still another commander in the East, "Fighting" Joseph Hooker. Hooker, however, only narrowly avoided losing his entire army of 130,000

◀ *Clara Barton (top) organized a training program for nurses to help wounded Union soldiers. Pauline Cushman served as a spy for the Union.*

This painting shows Union soldiers attacking Confederate troops at Seminary Ridge in Gettysburg, Pennsylvania. The battle was a Union victory.

men to Robert E. Lee and Stonewall Jackson at the Battle of Chancellorsville in Virginia on May 3. Lee and Jackson had only half as many troops as Hooker. After the battle, Jackson was accidently shot by one of his own soldiers. His death was a terrible loss to the Confederacy.

In June 1863, Lee decided once again to bring the war into the North. He headed again toward Pennsylvania. As Hooker chased after Lee, he complained about one thing or another and finally resigned his command on June 28. Lincoln then appointed General George Gordon Meade as head of the Army of the Potomac. Meade continued the chase after Lee.

Almost by accident, the armies met near Gettysburg, Pennsylvania, on July 1, 1863.

Map Study *Approximately how many miles is it from Frederick to Gettysburg? In what direction did the Confederate and Union armies advance?* ▶

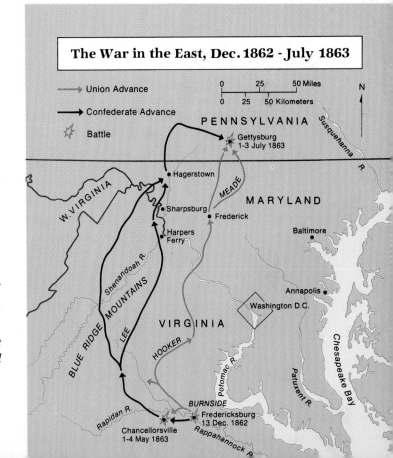

The War in the East, Dec. 1862 - July 1863

→ Union Advance
→ Confederate Advance
☆ Battle

0   25   50 Miles
0   25   50 Kilometers

N

PENNSYLVANIA

Gettysburg
1-3 July 1863

Susquehanna R.

W. VIRGINIA

Hagerstown

MEADE

MARYLAND

Sharpsburg

Frederick

Baltimore

Harpers
Ferry

Shenandoah R.

BLUE RIDGE MOUNTAINS

LEE

HOOKER

VIRGINIA

Annapolis

Washington D.C.

Chesapeake Bay

Potomac R.

Patuxent R.

Rapidan R.

BURNSIDE

Fredericksburg
13 Dec. 1862

Chancellorsville
1-4 May 1863

Rappahannock R.

Meade put his men in a very strong line along what was known as Cemetery Ridge. The Confederates faced them from Seminary Ridge, almost a mile away.

On July 3, the Confederate **artillery**—the big guns that could be shot at the enemy from a distance—hit the Union line. Then Lee sent 15,000 men under General George Pickett charging toward the center of the Union line. Pickett's men made it to the Union line—but then their attack failed because the Union guns mowed them down. Finally, on July 4, Lee sadly moved back toward home. He had lost about 25,000 men. The Union had lost almost as many men, but it had won a great battle.

▶ **6.** How successful was the Union army in the East from December 1862 to May 1863?

The War in the West, July 1863–March 1864

On the day before Lee left Pennsylvania, the Union won an even greater victory in the West. On July 4, Grant finally took Vicksburg. Together Gettysburg and Vicksburg marked a turning point in the war. From then on, the Union kept winning.

Next the Union took Port Hudson to the south of Vicksburg. The Union then held the entire Mississippi River. That meant the Confederate states farther west could be kept from sending men and supplies to support the Confederate states east of the Mississippi.

Grant's star was rising. Lincoln made him commander of all the Union armies west of the Appalachians. That meant he had to take charge of the situation in Tennessee. There, in late September, the Confederate army under General Bragg had almost defeated the Union forces in the Battle of Chickamunga. Grant now headed for Chattanooga where other Union armies joined him.

The Battle of Chattanooga on November 24 and 25 was a great victory for the Union. It was brilliantly planned and executed by Grant. He drove the Confederates into Georgia and showed Lincoln that the Union had, at last, the general he had been seeking. In March 1864, the President made Grant commander of all Union forces, and so Grant remained for the rest of the war.

▶ **7.** What was the turning point of the war?

Grant's Plan

Now Grant moved to the East. He left his old Western command in the able hands of General William Tecumseh Sherman. On both fronts, Grant decided, the Union could win by wearing down the Confederacy.

Grant showed what he meant in a series of terrible battles fought during May and early June on the blood-soaked fields of northern Virginia. Grant pounded Lee in the battles of the Wilderness, Spotsylvania Court House, and Cold Harbor. The costs were appalling, but still Grant kept coming back. "I propose to fight it out along this line," he told Lincoln, "if it takes all summer."

Finally Grant turned toward Petersburg, a railroad center 20 miles south of Richmond. There he began what became a nine-month-long siege of the town. If he took Petersburg, Grant could cut the Confederate capital off from the rest of the South. By the time he settled in near Petersburg, however, Grant had lost 60,000 men in only a month or so of fighting. Those men could be replaced. Lee had lost half as many, but his men proved impossible to replace.

Meanwhile Sherman fought as doggedly in the West as Grant fought in the East. As Sherman moved south from Chattanooga toward Georgia, he fought several battles with the Confederates. The Confederacy was on

Like Abraham Lincoln, Ulysses Simpson Grant came from humble origins. He was born on April 27, 1822, in a two-room cabin in Point Pleasant, Ohio. His mother was a hardworking woman of few words. Grant resembled her more than he did his father, who was a self-taught man with a great deal of ambition.

Ulysses's father saw to it that his son attended school from the time he was 6 years old. When Ulysses was 17, his father got him an appointment to the United States Military Academy. Reluctantly, Ulysses agreed to go.

Ulysses won few honors at West Point. Although he disliked the military, he stayed in the army after he graduated in 1843. Two years later, in 1845, he was sent off to the Mexican War. It was a war he strongly disapproved of.

Despite such feelings, Grant gained valuable experience as an officer and a fighter during the war. As soon as the war ended, he went to St. Louis, Missouri, where he married his sweetheart, Julia Dent.

Ulysses stayed in the army for six years following his marriage. During part of that time, he was stationed away from his family in a lonely outpost in Oregon Territory. There were rumors that Grant drank heavily. He received a warning from his commanding officer and resigned shortly afterward.

In 1854, after 11 years in the army, Grant returned to his family. The next years of his life were difficult. He failed at almost everything he tried. People would cross the street to avoid talking to him for fear he would ask for money.

The firing on Fort Sumter in 1861 changed his life—for the better. He quickly enlisted in the army. The Union badly needed West Point graduates with military experience. By the war's end, Grant had become the greatest general in the Union army.

What made Grant great? To begin with, he was brave. In times of danger, he had an almost inhuman calmness. He was also willing to take chances. At West Point, students learned that armies were expensive and hard to replace. Therefore a good officer did not take chances.

Grant did not agree. He knew that the Union had more men than the Confederacy. He knew too that the Union could equip its armies. For these reasons, Grant felt that it was all right to take risks. "Find out where your enemy is," he said. "Get at him as soon as you can. Strike at him as hard as you can and keep moving."

Grant was rewarded for his military success. He became secretary of war in 1867 and President of the United States two years later.

Although Grant's two terms were marred by scandal, he fascinated people. They eagerly bought Grant's *Personal Memoirs*, which he finished writing a week before his death on July 23, 1885. Those two volumes had an honored place in thousands of Union homes.

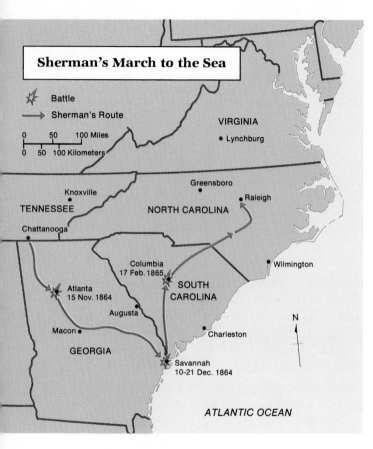

Sherman's March to the Sea

Battle

Sherman's Route

0   50   100 Miles

0   50   100 Kilometers

VIRGINIA
• Lynchburg

Greensboro •

• Raleigh

Knoxville

TENNESSEE   NORTH CAROLINA

Chattanooga

Columbia
17 Feb. 1865

Wilmington •

Atlanta   SOUTH
15 Nov. 1864   CAROLINA

Augusta

Macon •   • Charleston   N

GEORGIA

Savannah
10-21 Dec. 1864

ATLANTIC OCEAN

Map Study *Which three Southern cities shown on the map are located along the Atlantic coast? About how many miles was Sherman's march?*

the defensive, and Sherman gained ground slowly. The fighting in northern Georgia was especially hard. But finally, on September 1, 1864, the city of Atlanta fell to Sherman.

▶ **8.** How did Grant believe the Union could defeat the Confederacy?

The Election of 1864

Not everyone was as willing as Grant to pay the deadly price of a Union victory. Criticism of President Lincoln and the war reached new heights as the death tolls continued to mount in mid-1864.

Most critics of Lincoln were Democrats who had long been sympathetic to the Confederacy. As Northerners became ever more tired of the war, the Democrats' hopes for victory in the election of 1864 increased. They nominated for President George C. McClellan, the one-time commander of the Union Army of the Potomac. The Democratic platform said the war was a "failure" and called for an immediate end to the fighting.

Even some Republicans criticized Lincoln. They thought he had assumed too many powers that should have been left to Congress. They also said he was too hesitant in supporting the rights of free blacks and too kindly toward the Confederacy in general. Those **Radical Republicans** supported John C. Frémont for the presidency.

Lincoln ran in 1864 as the candidate of the so-called National Union Party. It hoped to win some pro-Confederate votes by nominating Andrew C. Johnson of Tennessee for Vice President. When Tennessee had joined the Confederacy, Johnson had remained loyal to the Union.

By August, Lincoln's opposition was so strong that he expected to lose the election. However, Sherman's victory in Atlanta helped boost Lincoln's popularity. In the end, he was elected to a second term with a large majority in the electoral college (212 to 21). He had, however, won only a small majority of the popular vote.

▶ **9.** Why did the Democrats think they might defeat Lincoln in 1864?

Sherman's March to the Sea

Soon after the election, Sherman marched out of Atlanta, leaving the city in flames. On he moved toward the Atlantic, burning houses and private property over an area 60 miles wide. He wanted to break the spirit of the

Confederate people, and so make it impossible for the Confederacy to carry on the war. He was fighting a new kind of war in which armies turned against civilians as well as enemy soldiers—total war, it has been called. Sherman was not disturbed by the suffering he caused. "War is cruel," he said.

In December he captured Savannah, which he also burned. Then Sherman turned north and marched through the Carolinas.

By this time, the Confederate cause was hopeless. On April 2, Lee abandoned Petersburg and the Confederate government left Richmond, which had finally fallen into Union hands. The next day, flames swept through Richmond, leaving ruins where a proud city once stood.

▶10. Why did Sherman burn houses and destroy private property during his long march to the sea?

Lee Surrenders

Finally, on April 8, Lee decided to surrender. The next day, he met Grant at a private home in the little village of Appomattox Court House. Lee wore a new dress uniform and a jewel-studded sword. Grant had no sword and wore an unbuttoned private's shirt and a dirty officer's coat.

The two generals chatted a little about old times. Then Grant wrote out the terms of surrender. They were generous. He asked Lee to have his men lay down their arms and go home. Those who did so, Grant promised, would not be bothered further by the federal government. Neither Confederate officers nor enlisted men would be hanged for treason. Grant was willing for soldiers to die to end the war. When the war was done, however, he wanted no more killings. It was then time to heal. He even let the Confederate soldiers take their horses or mules home with them.

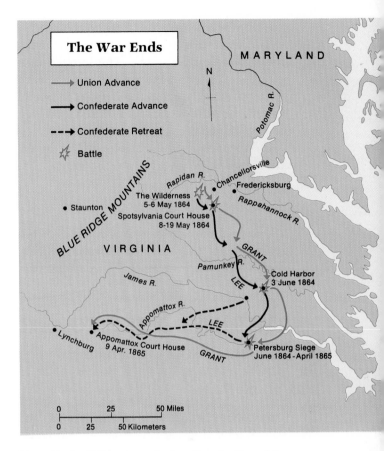

Map Study *What were the last four battles of the Civil War? Who led the Union advance to Appomattox? Who led the Confederate advance?*

▶11. What were the terms of surrender that Grant gave to Lee?

The Results of the War

The most important effects of the war were the most obvious ones. First and foremost, it saved the Union. Even the Confederacy was willing to admit that secession was no longer a possibility. Americans could stop worrying, as they had since the days of the Revolution, that their Republic would split into pieces and disappear. Second, the war freed millions of slaves in those parts of the nation where slavery had been most securely established. Slavery could not last much longer in the other parts. The freeing of so many slaves was an enormous step forward for American freedom. Just what it would mean for black Americans remained, however, to be decided.

▶12. What were the obvious effects of the Civil War?

Reviewing Section III

Identify Emancipation Proclamation, Conscription Act, Clara Barton, Elizabeth Blackwell, ~~Ambrose Burnside~~, Fredericksburg, Joseph ~~Hooker~~, Chancellorsville, ~~George Meade~~, Gettysburg, artillery, Vicksburg, ~~Port Hudson~~, Chickamunga, Chattanooga, William Tecumseh Sherman, Radical Republicans, Appomattox Court House

Questions to Answer
1. Why did Lincoln issue the Emancipation Proclamation?
2. How did Grant and Sherman believe the war had to be fought?

A Question to Think About Why was the Civil War more horrible than wars the nation had fought previously?

IMPROVE YOUR READING
Comparison/Contrast

This chapter focuses on people, places, and events related to the Civil War. As you know, the war involved the Confederacy and the Union. In previous chapters you have done exercises that involved comparing (noting similarities) and contrasting (noting differences). The exercise below is designed to give you more practice by comparing and contrasting various aspects of the Civil War.

The following statements are based on information contained in Section I of the chapter (pages 398 to 403). For each statement, choose the word or words that will make the statement accurate. The first statement has been done for you. Write your answers on a separate sheet of paper.

The Confederacy had a *(a) strong (b) weak* president, while the Union had a *(c) strong (d) weak* one.
Answers: (b) weak (c) strong

1. A long war favored the *(a) Confederacy (b) Union* because it had greater economic strength and more men to fight.
2. Both the Confederacy and the Union faced *(a) external (b) internal* discontent.
3. At the beginning of the Civil War, the Confederacy had *(a) strong (b) weak* military leadership, while the Union had *(c) strong (d) weak* military leadership.

The statement below is based on information contained in Section II (pages 404 to 408).

4. From 1861 to 1862, the *(a) Confederacy (b) Union* had an edge in the war in the West, while the *(c) Confederacy (d) Union* had an edge in the war in the East.

The statement below is based on information contained in Section III (pages 408 to 416).

5. Grant lost *(a) more (b) fewer* men than Lee in the battles of May and June 1864.

CHAPTER 19 REVIEW

Vocabulary Check

On a separate sheet of paper, write a short explanation of each of the following terms.

1. Border states
2. States' rights
3. Anaconda plan
4. Emancipation Proclamation
5. Artillery

Fact Check

On a separate sheet of paper, write the name of the person, battle, or town described in each of the sentences below.

1. He was the president of the Confederate States of America.
2. He led the Union's Army of the Potomac during the Peninsular Campaign.
3. He was Commander of the Confederate Army of Northern Virginia.
4. She worked as a nurse during the Civil War and later founded the American Red Cross.
5. He became head of all the Union forces after the Battle of Chattanooga.
6. He marched to the sea from Atlanta, burning houses and private property.
7. The Union was surprised when it did not win this first battle of the war.
8. About 60,000 Union soldiers died in this nine-month-long battle.
9. Stonewall Jackson was killed after this battle in Virginia.
10. These two battles marked a turning point in the war.

Time Check

On a separate sheet of paper, put the following events in chronological order.

1. President Lincoln issues the Emancipation Proclamation.
2. Grant takes Petersburg.
3. Confederates fire on Fort Sumter.
4. Congress passes the Conscription Act.
5. Lincoln is elected for a second term.

Skills Check

Use the maps in this chapter to answer the following questions.

1. Approximately how many miles did the Union forces travel from Washington, D.C., to Fair Oaks? (See map, page 405)
2. (a) In what direction did Lee travel from Chancellorsville to Gettysburg? (b) Name three cities he passed on his route to Gettysburg. (See map, page 411)
3. (a) In what direction did Sherman travel to reach Savannah? (b) In what direction did he move from Savannah to Raleigh? (See map, page 414)
4. For approximately how many miles did Grant follow Lee from the Wilderness to Appomatox? (See map, page 415)
5. In what state did the Civil War end? (See map, page 415)

Think and Write

1. Contrast the resources and leadership of the Union and Confederacy at the beginning of the war.
2. How did Lincoln use his powers as chief executive in the border states?
3. Why did Lincoln issue the Emancipation Proclamation?
4. What was new about the way Grant and Sherman viewed war?
5. How did the war change women's roles?

Chapter 20

Reconstruction and the New South

This painting of New Orleans in 1883 shows that cotton was still the South's most important crop for many years after the Civil War.

The growing number of dead soldiers was a cause of great pain to President Lincoln. In a speech at Gettysburg, Pennsylvania, on November 19, 1863, he said the Union soldiers died to show that a nation "conceived in Liberty, and dedicated to the proposition that all men are created equal" could endure. Then, as the war dragged on, he began to think that it happened because God willed it. In his second inaugural address, Lincoln suggested that God sent "this terrible War" to punish both sides for the "offense" of slavery.

Lincoln promised to end the war "with malice toward none, with charity for all." But Lincoln did not live to finish that work. He was shot on April 14, 1865, at Ford's Theater in Washington, D.C., by an actor and Confederate sympathizer named John Wilkes Booth. Lincoln died the next morning. Responsibility for rebuilding the nation—for its **reconstruction**—fell to others.

I. Presidential Reconstruction
Lincoln and the Confederates
Andrew Johnson's Reconstruction

II. Congress Takes Over
Radical and Moderate Republicans
Congress and the President

III. Reconstruction in the South
What the Republicans Did
White Southerners' Complaints
The Ku Klux Klan
The Election of 1872
The End of Reconstruction

IV. From Slavery to Sharecropping
The Revival of Plantations
Sharecropping
The Reign of King Cotton

V. From Slavery to Segregation
A Loss of Rights
Booker T. Washington's View
The Views of W.E.B. Du Bois

VI. The New South
Encouraging Industry
The Limits of Development
The Boll Weevil Causes Change

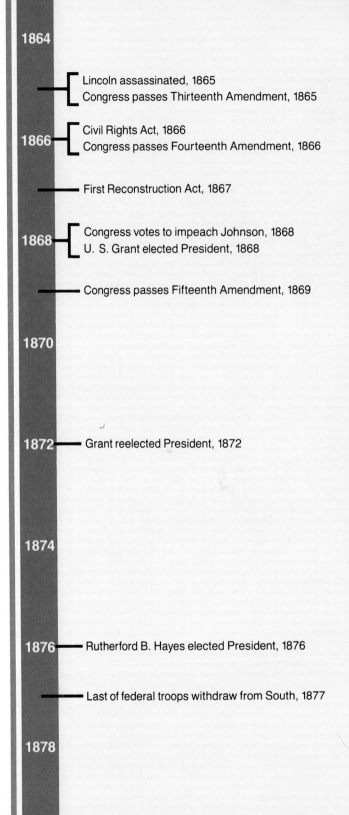

1864

Lincoln assassinated, 1865
Congress passes Thirteenth Amendment, 1865

1866
Civil Rights Act, 1866
Congress passes Fourteenth Amendment, 1866

First Reconstruction Act, 1867

1868
Congress votes to impeach Johnson, 1868
U. S. Grant elected President, 1868

Congress passes Fifteenth Amendment, 1869

1870

1872 — Grant reelected President, 1872

1874

1876 — Rutherford B. Hayes elected President, 1876

Last of federal troops withdraw from South, 1877

1878

Richmond, Virginia, the first capital of the Confederacy during the Civil War, was in ruins when the war ended.

I. Presidential Reconstruction

Some of the important issues of reconstruction, or rebuilding, had to be decided in Washington, D.C. How would the defeated Confederate states be brought back into national politics? What demands would the victorious Union make? Even before his death, Lincoln began to deal with those issues. After Lincoln's assassination, the Vice President, Andrew Johnson, took over. Within a few years, however, Congress was defining the rules by which the former Confederate states would become functioning parts of the nation.

Lincoln and the Confederates

Long before the war ended, Union armies advanced into parts of the Confederacy. The areas they took came once again under federal jurisdiction. In early 1862, Lincoln set up military governments in Louisiana, Arkansas, and Tennessee. He also began planning ways to set up regular governments there that were loyal to the Union. Lincoln wanted to "bind up the nation's wounds," not to make them worse. He also wanted to achieve a "just and lasting peace."

▶**1.** Where did President Lincoln set up the first military governments for states that had been part of the Confederacy?

Lincoln's Plan Lincoln announced his plan for handling the defeated states in a proclamation issued on December 8, 1863. He offered a full pardon to all but a very few people involved in the rebellion. To be pardoned, citizens of the former Confederate states would have to take an oath of loyalty to the Constitution. They would also have to swear to support the Emancipation Proclamation and all other acts of Congress concerning ex-slaves. Moreover, a state of the Confederacy could take its place in the Union and in Congress when the number of citizens equal to 10 percent of the voters in 1860 had taken the oath and organized a government. Louisiana and Arkansas quickly set up governments under Lincoln's plan.

▶**2.** What did Lincoln demand before a Confederate state could take its place in the Union?

The Thirteenth Amendment   The **Thirteenth Amendment** was passed by Congress in January 1865. It outlawed slavery everywhere in the United States. Lincoln thought that blacks should also be given full rights as citizens. By "assisting to save the life of the Republic" on the battlefield, Lincoln said in 1864, blacks had "demonstrated in blood their right to the ballot." Lincoln believed, however, that the nation's duty to blacks would be fulfilled by the states.

▶**3.** What did the Thirteenth Amendment outlaw?

Congress Disagrees   Congress thought Lincoln was too easy on the South. It said no state should be allowed to set up a new government until people equal to a majority of its voters in 1860—not just 10 percent—had taken oaths of loyalty. Congress also wanted all those who had held office under the Confederacy to be kept from voting or holding office under the postwar governments.

Those provisions were part of the **Wade-Davis Bill,** which Congress passed in July 1864. Lincoln vetoed it, and Congress could not get the necessary two-thirds vote to put the bill into effect despite his veto. It could, however, get enough votes to pass the **Wade-Davis Manifesto** which said that Congress, not the President, should set the rules for reconstruction. Congress also refused to accept representatives from the governments set up in Louisiana and Arkansas.

▶**4.** In what ways did Congress's Wade-Davis Bill differ from President Lincoln's plan for reconstruction?

Andrew Johnson's Reconstruction

With Lincoln's death, power passed to his Vice President, Andrew Johnson. Johnson was the only senator from the Confederate states who took the Union side in the Civil War. That recommended him strongly to Lincoln, who made Johnson the military governor of Tennessee in 1862 and then his running mate two years later. Lincoln hoped that Johnson, a lifelong Democrat, would attract the votes of some pro-war Democrats in the election of 1864. A man like Johnson was, however, likely to have even more trouble than Lincoln working with the Republicans in Congress.

▶**5.** Why did Lincoln select Johnson as his running mate?

Johnson's Plan   Johnson outlined his reconstruction program in proclamations issued in the months after he took office. He asked that Confederates take oaths of loyalty to the Union. Then any property seized from them during the war (except, of course, for slaves) would be returned. Some Confederates, including those who owned more than $20,000 worth of property and those who held high office in the Confederacy, had to receive a special pardon from the President. Johnson also demanded that the new state governments refuse to pay Confederate war debts, repeal all secession laws, and ratify the Thirteenth Amendment.

In some ways, Johnson's reconstruction plan was stricter than Lincoln's. Johnson, however, did not enforce it strictly. He pardoned many high Confederate officials. He also failed to look closely at the records of the new governments "reconstructed" under

This cartoon shows President Johnson mending Uncle Sam's coat, which was torn by the Civil War.

his presidency. For example, Mississippi did not ratify the Thirteenth Amendment. South Carolina "repealed" secession without suggesting in any way that it had been wrong from the first. None of that bothered Johnson, who wanted the Union back together as soon as possible. He did not even mind when Georgia elected the old Confederate Vice President, Alexander H. Stephens, to the Senate.

▶6. What was President Johnson's plan for reconstruction?

Black Codes Congress reacted differently to the new state governments. Many members were not pleased with Johnson's handling of reconstruction. The final blow came when the Southern states passed **black codes**—laws to regulate the ex-slaves that seemed very much like the old Southern slave codes. Those laws said blacks could not own guns or meet together after sunset. They could be put in prison if they had no jobs. At least one state, South Carolina, said blacks could practice no trade except that of a farmer or a servant. If such laws were allowed to stand, it seemed as if the Civil War had accomplished nothing, and the Union dead had died in vain.

▶7. What were black codes?

Reviewing Section I

Identify reconstruction, Thirteenth Amendment, Wade-Davis Bill, Wade-Davis Manifesto, black codes

Questions to Answer
1. What did Congress think of Lincoln's reconstruction program?
2. How did Johnson's reconstruction program differ from Lincoln's?

A Question to Think About Why did members of Congress want to control the reconstruction process?

II. Congress Takes Over

By the time Congress met in December 1865, every Confederate state except Texas had set up new governments under Lincoln's or Johnson's reconstruction program. Congress refused to admit the senators and representatives sent to Washington by those states.

Radical and Moderate Republicans

Most of Johnson's opponents in Congress were Republicans, but some were more radical than others. The Radical Republicans wanted to protect the rights of the former slaves and to punish the Confederacy for its crimes. The

Radicals thought that former slaves should get the vote because that was right, and because they would vote for Republican candidates. Some thought Congress should seize the land of the Confederate planters and give it to their slaves.

Among the best known Radical Republicans were Representative Thaddeus Stevens of Pennsylvania and Senator Charles Sumner of Massachusetts. Sumner said the old Confederate states had given up all their rights under the Constitution when they left the Union. As a result, Congress could treat those states as it chose.

The Radicals did not, however, control Congress. They had to work with the **Moderate Republicans.** The Moderates agreed with the Radicals on the need to protect the rights of freed slaves and to protect the interests of their party in the South. They were less anxious, though, to punish the South and thought Congress had less power than Sumner claimed. They were also less rigid in their views and more willing to compromise. Lincoln had been a Moderate Republican. Another of them, Senator William Pitt Fessenden of Maine, was made chairman of the Congress's Joint Committee on Reconstruction.

▶**1.** What were the differences between Radical and Moderate Republicans?

The Freedmen's Bureau The first measure recommended by the Joint Committee on Reconstruction was the New Freedmen's Bureau Bill, which Congress passed in February 1866. The **Freedmen's Bureau** was first set up by Congress in March 1865 to care for ex-slaves who were wandering through the South. The Bureau helped feed and clothe the freed men and women and helped them find work. It also set up schools, often run by Northern women, to teach the crowds of black adults and children who so desperately wanted to learn to read. The New Freedmen's Bureau Bill tried to give that agency the power to bring cases in military courts against anyone who interfered with the ex-slaves civil rights.

▶**2.** What was the Freedmen's Bureau?

The Civil Rights Act The Committee recommended a **Civil Rights Act** to make clear what civil rights the freed slaves had. It was passed by Congress in April 1866. Blacks, it said, were citizens of the United States and had the same civil rights as all other citizens. (Congress had to make that clear in law because of the Dred Scott decision.)

The Republicans did not consider either the New Freedmen's Bureau Bill or the Civil Rights Act extreme. Still, President Johnson

This 1866 engraving shows a schoolroom in a Freedmen's Bureau School in Virginia.

vetoed them both. Congress managed to get the necessary two-thirds vote to pass them over Johnson's veto.

▶**3.** What was the purpose of the Civil Rights Act?

The Fourteenth Amendment Even members of Congress were not sure that the Civil Rights Act was constitutional. As a result, Congress voted to pass the **Fourteenth Amendment** to the Constitution in June 1866. That amendment defined United States citizenship in a way that included blacks. It said the states could not limit the "privileges and immunities" of United States citizens, deny anyone "life, liberty, or property, without due process of law," or deny anyone "the equal protection of the laws."

The amendment also said that certain ex-Confederates could never again hold state or federal office unless they were pardoned by Congress. It said the debts made by the Confederate states during the Civil War were no longer valid. It said that the whole black population of a state would be used to figure its representation in Congress, rather than the three-fifths of the slave population previously used. If, however, the states did not allow blacks to vote, their representation would be reduced accordingly. In other words, the power of the ex-Confederate states would not be allowed to increase unless they let blacks vote.

Since the amendment had to be ratified by three-quarters of the states to become law, some Southern legislatures would have to ratify it. Only Tennessee did so, however. Congress promptly allowed Tennessee's senators and representatives to take their seats.

▶**4.** What were the provisions of the Fourteenth Amendment?

The Republican Majority President Johnson encouraged the Southern states to oppose the Fourteenth Amendment. Then he declared open war against the Republicans in Congress.

★★ The United States and the World ★★★★★★★★★★★★★★★★
The Statue of Liberty

One of the symbols of the United States is the Statue of Liberty in New York Harbor. This great copper statue was a gift to the people of the United States from the people of France. It was a gesture of friendship to celebrate the hundredth anniversary of the Declaration of Independence in 1876. The French people donated about $250,000 for the statue, which was presented to the Minister of the United States in Paris on July 4, 1884. President Grover Cleveland dedicated the monument on October 4, 1886. It was unveiled before representatives of both countries.

The French sculptor Frederic Auguste Bartholdi designed the statue, which was called *Liberty Enlightening the World*. Alexander Gustave Eiffel, who built the Eiffel Tower in Paris, built the supporting framework.

In 1903, a poem written by Emma Lazarus was inscribed on the pedestal of the statue. The poem contains the famous lines, "Give me your tired, your poor, your huddled masses yearning to breathe free." Lazarus was an American poet who spent much of her time organizing relief programs for the thousands of Jews emigrating from Russia.

He actively campaigned against them in the congressional elections of 1866.

The voters, however, did not agree. In the election of 1866, the voters sent so many more Republicans to Congress that the Republicans held two-thirds of the seats in both the House and Senate.

▶ **5.** What were the results of Johnson's campaign against the Republicans?

The First Reconstruction Act (1867) With such an outpouring of support, the Republicans took control of reconstruction. On March 2, 1867, they passed a **Reconstruction Act** that returned the former Confederate states to military rule. It divided the ten "unreconstructed" states into five military districts. The army once again took charge.

To restore civilian rule, the people of the ex-Confederate states had to elect delegates to conventions. All adult males were to be allowed to vote for the delegates. No one could participate in the conventions who could not hold office under the Fourteenth Amendment. The constitutions set up by the conventions had to guarantee the vote to blacks and ratify the Fourteenth Amendment. Congress would then review each state's case and decide whether to end military rule and allow the representatives of the "reconstructed" states to take their seats in Congress. Johnson vetoed the Reconstruction Act, but Congress passed it over his veto.

▶ **6.** What were the provisions of the Reconstruction Act of 1867?

Congress and the President

Members of Congress grew more suspicious of Johnson in 1867. They feared that he might undercut Congress and maybe even overthrow the government. So Congress passed a law that made the President and secretary of state

President Johnson receives a summons of impeachment from the sergeant-at-arms of the Senate.

issue military orders only through the general of the Army, U.S. Grant. Congress also tried to protect its friends in government by forbidding the President to dismiss from office anyone who had been appointed with the Senate's approval unless the Senate also approved the dismissal. Johnson did not think that law, the **Tenure of Office Act,** was constitutional. He fired Secretary of War Edwin Stanton without the Senate's consent.

At that point, the Republicans in Congress had had enough. In February 1868, they voted to impeach Johnson. Under the Constitution, a majority of the members of the House of Representatives can decide to bring charges against the President. Then the Senate meets to consider those charges. Two-thirds of the

425

senators must agree to find a President guilty before he can be removed from office.

The House impeached Johnson for several "high crimes and misdemeanors in office," especially for violating the Tenure of Office Act. The Senate, however, failed by one vote to convict the President. The House's charges simply did not hold water. It turned out, for example, that the Tenure of Office Act did not affect Stanton since he had been appointed by Lincoln, not Johnson.

▶7. On what grounds did the House impeach Johnson?

The Election of 1868 In 1868, the Republicans in Congress helped to elect a President with whom they could work. The Republican candidate, Ulysses S. Grant, won the election. The votes of Southern blacks played an important part in the Republican victory. That encouraged Republicans to go further in securing black suffrage.

▶8. Why were the Republicans willing to work harder for black suffrage after 1868?

The Fifteenth Amendment In February 1869, the Republican-dominated Congress passed the **Fifteenth Amendment** to the Constitution, which said states could not deny anyone the vote "on account of race, color, or previous condition of servitude." States that still had not complied with Congress's reconstruction requirements had to ratify the Fifteenth as well as the Fourteenth Amendment. However, the Fifteenth Amendment had its greatest effect on the North, where most states still denied the vote to blacks. The Republicans thought it was right that those blacks, too, should vote—especially since their votes were likely to help the Republicans in future elections.

▶9. Why did the Fifteenth Amendment have its greatest effect in the North?

Reviewing Section II

Identify Thaddeus Stevens, Charles Sumner, Moderate Republicans, Freedmen's Bureau, Civil Rights Act, Fourteenth Amendment, Reconstruction Act, Tenure of Office Act, Fifteenth Amendment

Questions to Answer

1. What rights did blacks gain from the Civil Rights Act and the Fourteenth and Fifteenth Amendments?
2. What did Republicans do after they took control of reconstruction?

A Question to Think About Why did the Framers of the Constitution make it difficult to remove public officials from office?

III. Reconstruction in the South

By 1870, all the old states of the Confederacy had adopted constitutions acceptable to Congress. That might have been the end of reconstruction. However, a large number of white Southerners did not see it that way. For them, the first elected governments of those "reconstructed" states were almost as unacceptable as the military governments they replaced. Those first governments were controlled by Republicans. Not until the Democrats took office again in the Southern states did the South consider itself saved from the evils of reconstruction.

What the Republicans Did

The time when Republicans ruled the South is sometimes called **Radical reconstruction**.

The word "radical" suggests basic change of an extreme sort. To give blacks a share of power was certainly a basic change in the way the South was ruled. The Republicans also brought a number of other changes to the South, reforms of a sort that were made in the North much earlier. For one thing, they started the first public school systems in the South. They also built new hospitals and orphanages and began to reform the criminal justice system.

Meanwhile, the new state governments rebuilt those vast parts of the South that were destroyed in the war. They also tried to lay the basis for further economic growth. The Republican governments, for example, used large amounts of tax money to help railroad companies lay tracks throughout the South.

No government could do so much without spending a lot of money. The costs of government in the "reconstructed" states grew by leaps and bounds under the Republicans.

As a result, the tax burden throughout the South was about four times as great in 1870 as it had been in 1860. Taxes, moreover, rested on people who owned property—members especially of the old planter class.

▶1. Why did taxes greatly increase during reconstruction?

White Southerners' Complaints

The critics of Republican reconstruction claimed that their taxes were high mainly because the new state governments were run badly and, even more, because tax money was being stolen. There was some basis for that complaint. **Corruption,** the misuse of public money by officials especially for their own benefit, did exist under the Republican governments of the South. It also existed, however, under the governments that came before them and under the Democratic governments that followed. In fact, corruption

Among the first black members of Congress were (left to right) Senator Hiram Revels of Mississippi, Congressmen Benjamin Turner of Alabama, Robert De Large of South Carolina, Josiah Walls of Florida, Jefferson Long of Georgia, Joseph Rainey and R. Brown Elliot from South Carolina.

was a national problem during reconstruction. President Grant's administration was troubled by several cases of corruption.

Southern critics also said their state governments were too often run by people born in the North. Those Northerners were called **carpetbaggers** because they supposedly carried cheap suitcases covered with carpet material. After they stuffed those bags with whatever they could steal, Southerners said, the carpetbaggers would return to the North. Republicans born in the South were called **scalawags** by their enemies. The name suggested that they were good-for-nothings. Generally, they were people who had opposed secession. That was their greatest "crime."

Many white Southerners opposed the new governments because under them blacks voted and held office. As a result those Southerners (and some Northerners) referred to the period of Republican rule as "black reconstruction." Blacks did not, however, control the Republican governments. They made up a majority of the state legislature only for a few years in one state, South Carolina. There were no black governors anywhere in the South, and only three black lieutenant governors. Some blacks elected to office were poorly prepared for their duties. But a remarkable number had managed to receive a good education in Canada and the North and were very able officials.

▶**2.** What were some of the complaints about reconstruction governments?

The Ku Klux Klan

Those former Confederates who hated Republican reconstruction had many ways of opposing it, even when they could not vote. They sometimes refused to have anything to do with local white Republicans. With blacks, pressure took more violent forms. Whites sometimes burned down the schools for blacks founded by the Freedmen's Bureau and attacked the teachers and students.

One group dedicated to controlling blacks through violence and threats of violence was the **Ku Klux Klan**. It was founded in Pulaski, Tennessee, in 1866 by a group of young people. Within a few years, the Klan grew into an organization with branches in several Southern states. Klan members often covered their faces and wore long robes and pointed hats on their "night visits" to blacks. In 1870 and 1871 Congress passed laws against the Klan. Officially, the Klan then disbanded. In fact, however, it merely operated more secretly or broke up into groups with different names. All those groups had the same purpose: to re-establish white rule in the South. They whipped people and were willing even to kill. Many black officials lost their lives to the "night riders." Whites who helped blacks were also in danger from the Klan.

▶**3.** What was the Ku Klux Klan?

The Election of 1872

By 1872, even some Republicans were criticizing the Grant administration's continued interference in the South. Grant was re-elected President anyway. The Democrats, however, won a majority in the House of Representatives and took control of 23 states. The voters seemed to be tiring of the Republicans and their insistence on supporting black rights in the South.

▶**4.** What did the election of 1872 suggest about voters' attitudes?

The End of Reconstruction

Reconstruction finally ended as a result of the presidential election of 1876. The Republican candidate that year was Rutherford

B. Hayes of Ohio. The Democrats ran Samuel J. Tilden, the governor of New York. Tilden won the popular vote, but the electoral result was unclear. Returns were under question in four states—Florida, Louisiana, Oregon, and South Carolina. Without the vote of those states, Tilden would be one vote short of victory.

To resolve the problem, Congress set up an electoral commission. It decided to award the election to Hayes. Democrats went along with that decision in return for certain favors. The Republicans had to promise: (1) to remove all federal soldiers from the South; (2) to appoint at least one Southerner to Hayes's Cabinet; and (3) to grant federal money for internal improvements in the South.

So it was that in 1877 the last federal troops were finally withdrawn from the South. Already Democrats had taken over the governments of several ex-Confederate states. Then in 1877, Democrats took over the last Southern states where Republicans still held power—Florida, Louisiana, and South Carolina. The South, including its millions of newly-freed blacks, was once again under the control of those Southern whites who had ruled it before, in the days when slavery was legal.

▶5. What events brought about the end of reconstruction?

President Grant and his wife Julia (right) entertain friends at their summer cottage.

Reviewing Section III

Identify Radical reconstruction, corruption, carpetbaggers, scalawags, Ku Klux Klan, Rutherford B. Hayes, Samuel Tilden

Questions to Answer
1. What were the major objections to Radical Reconstruction?
2. What promises did Republicans make in return for Hayes's election to the presidency in 1876?

A Question to Think About What motivated Republican reconstruction policies?

IV. From Slavery to Sharecropping

Southern blacks wanted to be free. They also wanted to own the land they farmed. However, at the war's end, the lands of the Confederacy were returned to their white owners. The freed men and women had to house themselves, raise their children, and provide for the old. How, above all, would they support themselves?

The Revival of Plantations
Many slaves left the plantations for good, especially if their former owners had been cruel. Often, however, the slaves ended up right back on plantation land, working for their former owner or for another planter.

For a year or two after the war, planters tried to hire black farm workers for a set

Many Southern blacks became sharecroppers when the Civil War ended. Share-cropping allowed the former slaves to live together with their families.

wage plus housing and food. Those workers were forced to sign contracts that kept them from leaving the plantation. The freed men and women did not like the system at all. It was too much like slavery.

The planters did not like it, either. They had to pay the same wages to their workers in good years and in bad. The bad years came first. Cotton prices were low in 1866–1867, and many crops failed the next year for lack of rain. Planters feared they would be ruined if they had to keep paying workers while their own incomes remained so low.
▶1. Why were planters reluctant to hire black workers for a set wage?

Sharecropping

By the late 1860's, the South had found another way to use its lands, a way that answered the needs of both ex-slaves and planters—in the short run. It was called sharecropping. Under that system, black and sometimes white families farmed small parts of the old plantations. In return, these families, or sharecroppers, agreed to give their landlord, the one-time planter, a share of their crop.

The landlord had the right to watch over the way sharecroppers ran their farms and to say just which crops they should plant. Landlords generally said the land had to be used for growing cotton. The sharecropping system gave ex-slaves a chance to live with their families on rented plots of land, rather than in slave quarters.
▶2. What was the advantage of the sharecropping system to the ex-slaves?

The Crop Lien System Although sharecropping gave many freed slaves a chance to live with their families, sharecropping had some serious disadvantages. For one thing, sharecroppers were never out of debt. They started out owing half their crops to their landlords. Before their crop came in, their families had to be fed and clothed. So sharecroppers borrowed from local storekeepers, buying their supplies on credit. The storekeepers were often the landlords or relatives of the landlords. And they, too, insisted that their debtors grow cotton.

When buyers finally paid their bills, they paid not just the price of the goods but also additional money, or **interest,** as the cost of the loan. The interest often amounted to 60 percent of the amount of goods bought on credit. Sometimes the rate of interest was even higher.

Storekeepers asked the sharecroppers to put up a share of their crop as security on the loan. They received a claim, or lien, on the borrowers' future crops. When farmers sold their crops, they had to pay the storekeepers right away. That system of credit was known as the **crop lien system**.

▶**3.** What was the crop lien system?

The Cycle of Debt Sharecroppers got only about half the return on their crops, and the crop lien system meant a good part of that went to pay their loans at the store. In years when the crop was poor, a family's share of the crop might not even be enough to pay off its debts. Then the debts would be carried over into the next year—when more interest would be added to the bill. Soon it became almost impossible for poor farmers to make any profit at all.

The sharecroppers were, of course, legally free. Some, indeed, were whites who had never been slaves. But white or black, they became caught in a debt system that gave them little freedom of choice and little hope for the future.

▶**4.** How did sharecroppers become trapped in debt?

The Reign of King Cotton

What was bad for the sharecropper was also bad for the South as a whole. Its economy became dependent on one crop, cotton. In 1859, the South grew 5.4 million bales of cotton. By 1900, it was growing 10 million bales per year.

As the amount of cotton grown went up, however, the prices went down. The prosperity of the entire South fell with cotton prices, because it grew so little else.

The South did not even grow enough food for its people. It had to buy more and more food from other parts of the country. Growing so much cotton was also hard on the land. Like the tobacco plant, cotton tended to use up the soil's fertility, that is, its ability to grow things well.

The poor farmers of the South kept farming in old ways, with hoes and mules. At most, they bought fertilizer because it increased their harvest. But Southern farmers did not buy machines like farmers in the North. Poor Southern farmers had no money to invest in such things. Their plots were too small to make good use of machines, anyway.

▶**5.** What bad effects did dependence on cotton have on the South?

Reviewing Section IV

Identify sharecropping, interest, crop lien system

Questions to Answer
1. How did the sharecropping system change the economy of the South?
2. Why did the sharecropping and crop lien system entrap poor families?

A Question to Think About Families that did the best in the South after the Civil War were both planters and store owners. Why?

Making Generalizations from Statistics

Historians are often less interested in a specific piece of data, like the price of a pound of cotton in a given year, than in the picture of trends given by many pieces of data looked at together. The changes in the price of a pound of cotton over 10 years may show a significant trend. The price of a pound of cotton when compared with the total amount of the harvest may be even more significant. A *generalization* is a broad statement based on facts or data.

The chart shows the acreage, production, and price for cotton annually from 1880 to 1890. Study the figures carefully. Think about what you have read in this chapter about agriculture in the South after the Civil War. Then answer the questions that follow.

Date	Acreage Harvested	Pounds of Cotton	Price per Pound
		(in thousands)	
1880	15,921	6,606	$ 9.83
1881	16,483	5,456	$10.66
1882	15,638	6,949	$ 9.12
1883	16,295	5,713	$ 9.13
1884	16,849	5,682	$ 9.19
1885	17,922	6,576	$ 8.39
1886	18,370	6,505	$ 8.06
1887	18,739	7,047	$ 8.55
1888	19,520	6,938	$ 8.50
1889	20,191	7,473	$ 8.55
1890	20,937	8,653	$ 8.59

Source: Historical Statistics of the United States

1. In what year did the price of a pound of cotton exceed $10?
2. Was the production for that year greater or less than the production for the previous year?
3. From 1880 to 1890 did the number of acres harvested generally increase or decrease?
4. From 1880 to 1890 did the price of cotton generally increase or generally decrease?
5. From the information on the chart, write a generalization about the relationship between the price of cotton and the number of acres harvested.

V. From Slavery to Segregation

The economy of the South was not the only thing to change there after the war. Its social system changed too. Before the war, slaves lived in close contact with their owners' families. But after emancipation, the South gradually adopted a system of **segregation,** by which blacks and whites were separated from each other. A society is segregated when, for example, blacks and whites live in different neighborhoods, attend different schools, and travel in different railroad cars or in different parts of the same railroad car.

Before the Civil War, segregation was well established in the North. Eventually the South developed a system of segregation far more extreme than anything the North had known.

Segregation did not, however, happen right away. It was a system that developed slowly over a long period of time. Segregation in the South began, at first, through choices made by both blacks and whites. Blacks no longer wanted to live under the watchful eyes of whites. They therefore pulled away—living with family members on their own small farms or in black settlements. To be able to do such things was, for blacks, an exercise of their freedom. However, blacks felt that separation had to be by choice. So blacks opposed efforts to make them ride in separate railroad cars.

A Loss of Rights

After reconstruction ended, usually upper-class, native, white Southerners took charge of state and local governments. Those people were members of the Democratic Party, and were called **Redeemers** because they redeemed the South from Republican rule.

As long as Southerners like themselves controlled their states, the Redeemers saw no reason to take away the privileges blacks had won since the Civil War. The Redeemers even tried to win the support of black voters—with some success. As a result, blacks continued to vote in the South long after the last Northern soldiers went home. Blacks also held some seats in state legislatures as late as the 1890's and were even appointed to minor government posts by Redeemer governors, such as Wade Hampton of South Carolina.

▶**1.** How did Redeemers deal with blacks?

Disenfranchisement Then suddenly, blacks lost the vote in one Southern state after another. Their **disenfranchisement**, or loss of the vote, happened in several ways. Some states established a **literacy test** for the vote.

Voters had to read and explain the Constitution in a way that satisfied the voting registration officials. Those officials were white and were generally unwilling to say that any black, even college graduates, had passed the test.

Other states used **grandfather clauses**. Louisiana began the practice in 1898 when it said people could vote without taking a literacy test if their father or grandfather had voted in state elections before 1867. Of course, no blacks could vote before 1867 in Louisiana—or in any other state that adopted such a grandfather clause.

Some states relied on **poll taxes** to weed out black voters. As early as 1877 Georgia made each voter pay a tax of $1 or $2. Other states followed Georgia's example. The poll taxes were not high, but few blacks were able to pay them.

None of these measures explicitly denied people the vote "on account of race, color, or previous condition of servitude," which was forbidden by the Fifteenth Amendment.

Some blacks became well-to-do after the Civil War. This family gathers in the parlor.

Still, they hit blacks the hardest. In the 1890's, before those disenfranchisement measures were widely adopted, some 73 percent of all adult men voted in the South. Ten years later, after the disenfranchisement measures went into effect, only 30 percent voted. In short, Southern democracy came into very bad times after 1890.

▶ **2.** In what ways did Southern states stop blacks from voting?

The Spread of Segregation At about the same time blacks were losing the vote, segregation spread more widely in the South. That system, moreover, no longer depended on individual choices. It was imposed by law.

Laws requiring segregation on railroads were first passed by the Southern states west of the Appalachians. Then they were adopted in the Old South. Soon separate waiting rooms were required for blacks and whites. Other laws forced blacks to sit in the back of streetcars.

Blacks and whites could not work in the same room or use the same entrances, doors, stairs, or washrooms. Not only were schools segregated, but blacks and whites could not even use the same textbooks.

That extreme form of segregation set in after 1900, about 25 years after the end of reconstruction. Violence against blacks also increased at that time. **Lynching,** the practice of executing a person without a legal trial, reached a new height. Lynchings were much more common in the South than the North. Most of the victims of Southern lynch mobs were black.

▶ **3.** In what ways did segregation spread in the South?

The Reasons for Change Why suddenly after about 1890 did white Southerners take away the blacks' vote, begin an extreme form of segregation, and attack blacks with more illegal violence? There is no easy answer to that question. It is, however, clear that some whites in the South would have done almost anything to keep blacks down. Those whites were held in check by several forces. However, by the 1890's, each of those forces had lost its effectiveness.

The Redeemers, for one thing, had helped to hold white racism in check. But several scandals in Redeemer governments cost them votes. Then, in the 1890's, their black supporters seemed to be abandoning them and joining an alliance with poor whites. So the Redeemers stopped defending blacks. In fact, they adopted racist arguments in an effort to win white votes. Redeemers also helped disenfranchise blacks. That, they thought, was better than having blacks vote for their opponents.

Several federal laws had also once checked white racism. They were passed during reconstruction. But by the 1890's, the Supreme Court robbed one law after another of its force. In 1876, the Supreme Court said that the Fourteenth Amendment protected black rights against the states but not against individuals. If, then, some private person interfered with the constitutional rights of blacks, there was—or so it seemed—nothing the United States could do.

In the 1890's, the Supreme Court went further. It approved the new discriminatory measures being adopted in the South. Its most important decision was in the case *Plessy* v. *Ferguson* of 1896. There the Court said it was all right if a state required segregated railroad facilities as long as facilities were equal for blacks and whites. The doctrine of "separate but equal" remained in force until the 1950's. The courts let white Southerners set up separate facilities but did little to make sure the facilities for blacks were equal to

Booker T. Washington started Tuskegee Institute in Alabama as a trade school. Students learned skills such as carpentry (right). However, some also studied academic subjects, like the students in this algebra class (left).

those for whites. And in 1898, the Court approved a Mississippi plan for disenfranchising blacks.

Obviously the Supreme Court was not working to limit racism. Instead, it seemed to encourage it. The Supreme Court acted as it did, moreover, with the support of Northern opinion. Most Northerners had become tired of intervening in the South on behalf of blacks. Blacks held boycotts and protests against segregation laws in several Southern cities. For the most part, however, their protests were not successful.

▶ **4.** What actions of the Supreme Court hurt blacks?

Booker T. Washington's View

A black leader named Booker T. Washington achieved fame by proposing a way of dealing with segregation. Booker T. Washington was a former slave who had worked his way through Hampton Institute, a school for blacks in Hampton, Virginia. Hampton Institute stressed trades and skills. Eventually, Washington became a teacher there. Before long, he was asked to start a similar school, Tuskegee Institute, in Alabama. Washington thought that his life had changed rapidly for the better. With hard work and determination, he believed that other blacks could do the same thing.

Washington became a leading speaker for his people and was known and respected throughout the United States. He believed that if blacks were to succeed in the South, they had to win the support of Southern whites. To win and hold that support, he publicly backed the values and attitudes of whites whenever he could. He was even willing to suggest that blacks were not ready to vote or hold office. "It is at the bottom of life we must begin," he said about his fellow blacks, "not at the top."

Therefore, Washington recommended that blacks not study law, politics, languages, or

Highlighting People
Booker T. Washington

In 1881, Booker T. Washington founded and became principal of one of the most famous industrial schools of all times—Tuskegee Institute. During his lifetime, he also advised two Presidents on racial problems and helped get several blacks appointed to office in the early 1900's. Yet this famous black educator did not begin his life among educated people. Rather, he was born a slave in a one-room cabin on a Virginia plantation.

Booker T. Washington was born in 1856, five years before the start of the Civil War. As a young boy, he had a strong desire to learn, but it was against the law for anyone to teach a slave to read or write. His mother shared Booker's ambitions for him, and she spent many hours praying that she and her children might be free.

In 1863, her prayers came true when President Lincoln issued the Emancipation Proclamation. Shortly afterward, she moved her children to a small town near Charleston, West Virginia. For the first time in his life, Booker slept in a bed.

Freedom changed his life in other ways as well. It was no longer against the law for him to learn to read or write. His mother got him a copy of *Webster's Blue-back Spelling Book,* and he became the only black person for miles around who could read. He then spent every spare moment studying.

During these early years, he overheard a conversation about a school for blacks called Hampton Institute. In 1872, at the age of 17, he set out alone on the long 500-mile journey to Hampton.

Booker stayed at Hampton Institute for three years before graduating in 1875. For the next several years, he worked at a variety of jobs, including waiter, teacher, and mason.

In 1881, Washington at the urging of several interested people started Tuskegee Institute in Alabama. He believed that blacks could benefit most from learning a specific trade, such as carpentry or farming. The institute was founded with this in mind.

On the first day of school, 40 students attended. Most of them were so poor that they had barely enough food to eat. Classes were held in a run-down building near a church that was used as a kind of gathering place.

Washington devoted his life to the institute. He traveled throughout the country, raising funds for the school and speaking to groups about education and race relations. Often he ate and slept in the homes of the people he was trying to help. In 1901, he recorded his life's work in an autobiography. He called it *Up from Slavery.*

Booker T. Washington died in 1915. By the time of his death, Tuskegee Institute had more than a hundred buildings, owned 2,000 acres of land, taught 38 trades, and employed almost 200 teachers. Today a bronze statue on the Tuskegee campus stands as a tribute to its founder.

literature. Instead, they should learn to work well with their hands, he said. At Tuskegee, for example, blacks learned to make good bricks. If a man made the best bricks in his area, Washington thought, his skill would be respected despite his race.

In 1895, Washington was invited to speak at the opening of an international exhibition in Atlanta, Georgia. He was the only black speaker. The audience was mostly white. He used the occasion to urge Southern whites to hire native blacks as workers. In return, Washington seemed to promise that blacks would cause no strikes. He even seemed to accept segregation. "In all things that are purely social," he said, "we can be as separate as the fingers, yet one as the hand in all things essential to mutual progress." Washington's promise that blacks would accept separate but equal treatment in exchange for jobs and education became known as the **Atlanta Compromise**.

▶**5.** What was the Atlanta Compromise?

The Views of W.E.B. Du Bois

Not all blacks agreed with Washington. One of Washington's most eloquent critics was a black man named W.E.B. (William Edward Burghardt) Du Bois. Born in Massachusetts in 1872, Du Bois studied at Fisk University and at Harvard.

Du Bois did not insist, as did Washington, that things were getting better for blacks all the time. In his book, *The Souls of Black Folk*, published in 1903, Du Bois attacked Washington's views and made a striking prediction. "The problem of the twentieth century," he said, "is the problem of the color-line."

Du Bois thought blacks should get as much education as they could. He also said blacks should keep politically active and fight for their civil rights. In 1905, Du Bois helped

W. E. B. Du Bois believed that college-educated blacks should lead the fight against segregation.

to launch the **Niagara Movement**, a group that worked to end both discrimination and segregation.

▶**6.** What was the Niagara Movement?

Reviewing Section V————————

Identify segregation, Redeemers, disenfranchisement, literacy test, grandfather clauses, poll taxes, lynching, *Plessy* v. *Ferguson*, Booker T. Washington, Atlanta Compromise, W.E.B. Du Bois, Niagara Movement

Questions to Answer
1. What methods were used to disenfranchise blacks in Southern states?
2. What forces led to segregation and violence against blacks?

A Question to Think About Why was the doctrine of "separate but equal" unlikely to insure equal treatment?

437

The South had begun to industrialize after the Civil War. Atlanta, Georgia, shown here in the 1880's, had become a center of manufacturing and trade.

VI. The New South

Many Southern whites were as hopeful of the future as blacks when the Civil War ended. They, too, looked forward to a time of great opportunity. They saw no reason why the South could not develop a growing, thriving economy, like that of the North. It was time, they said, to start building a New South. However, for a number of reasons, the South did not industrialize. By 1900, dreams of a New South had failed.

Encouraging Industry

Henry W. Grady, the editor of the *Atlanta Constitution*, was one of the greatest boosters of the New South. He called for a South that would no longer be simply agricultural. Instead, it would be a place of cities and factories and business opportunities.

Many were eager to take advantage of some of the changes the Civil War had forced on the South. During the war, for example, cities had begun to grow. Richmond's population increased two and a half times during the war years. Other cities like Mobile, Atlanta, and Selma also grew dramatically. Meanwhile, the South began to manufacture things that it had once purchased from Northern states. Of course, the South did not become an industrial power overnight. It had, however, made a beginning. Why not build on that beginning once the war was over?

State governments were more than willing to cooperate. They did all they could to attract Northern investors and to encourage the economic development of the South. With their encouragement railroads grew even faster in the South than in the North during the 1880's.

Railroads gave the iron mines in Tennessee, Virginia, and Alabama a way to get their ore to market, so the mines also increased production at a great rate. By 1898, Birmingham, Alabama, was the third greatest shipping point for pig iron in the world and the greatest in the United States. The number of cotton mills grew in the Carolinas, Georgia, and Alabama.

▶1. How did state governments encourage industry in the South by the 1890's?

The Limits of Development

Nonetheless, the South remained very different from the North in 1900. Far more of its people were still involved in farming; far fewer of them lived in cities. Above all, the South was poor. Its people earned only about half of what the average American earned.

Railroad rates set in the North were partly to blame for discouraging the growth of Southern industries. It was very expensive to ship manufactured goods out of the South. Better rates were offered on raw materials that would be processed in the Northeast. Therefore, Southerners had a much greater incentive to produce raw materials.

The South also had trouble raising the money necessary to develop new industries. Credit was hard to come by except through retail merchants; and the rates of interest in the South were discouragingly high. Many of the profits from Southern industries—even from the textile mills—made their way into the pockets of Northern investors. Few Southerners benefited.

What the South did gain from the new industries was jobs; but most jobs were very poorly paid. Workers in the textile mills earned about fifty cents per day—half what workers earned in the North. Women, who made up 40 percent of the labor force in the mills, earned less, and children, 25 percent of the work force, earned as little as ten or twelve cents a day. Most factory jobs were not open to blacks.

The factories did allow at least some white families to leave their farms. But they soon found that factory work was not much better than sharecropping. Mill owners or managers took the place of landlords. The company store took the place of the rural stores with their high-priced credit. Workers found themselves unable to get out of debt. To make ends meet, whole families had to march off to the mill in the early morning. Children could not attend school. For people such as they, the "opportunities" of Southern industry were not very promising at all.

▶2. In what ways were factory jobs like sharecropping?

The Boll Weevil Causes Change

Before the South could even begin to catch up with the rest of the country, however, more people had to stop farming. Then they would have to find better ways of making a living either in the South or elsewhere.

Change came at first in the shape of a quarter-inch long bug, the boll weevil. The female weevil lays its eggs in cotton plants during the spring. After they hatch, the grubs eat the developing cotton and destroy much of the crop. Boll weevils lived in Mexico for years. The weevil first attacked Texas cotton about 1892. Then the weevil moved north and east throughout the cotton growing areas of the South.

All along the path of the weevil poor farmers were forced off the land. Thousands of them migrated north. There they could at least hope to find some other form of unskilled work. Farmers who stayed in the South planted new crops like peanuts or soybeans.

The tyranny of King Cotton was over, but not the stubborn poverty of the post-Civil War cotton kingdom. As late as the 1930's the South remained, according to the President of the United States, the nation's "number one economic problem." Only after the Second World War, in fact, did anything like Henry Grady's New South emerge in the rich lands of the old Confederacy.

▶**3.** What effects did the boll weevil have on the South?

Reviewing Section VI

Identify ~~Henry W. Grady~~, boll weevil

Questions to Answer

1. What was the dream of the New South?
2. What stopped the South from becoming an industrial region?

A Question to Think About ~~In what way did the boll weevil help~~ the South?

In Their Own Words

The Gettysburg Address, November 19, 1863

Fourscore and seven years ago our Fathers brought forth, on this continent, a new nation, conceived in Liberty, and dedicated to the proposition that all men are created equal.

Now we are engaged in a great civil war, testing whether that nation, or any nation so conceived and so dedicated, can long endure. We are met on a great battlefield of that war. We have come to dedicate a portion of that field, as a final resting place for those who here gave their lives that that nation might live. It is altogether fitting and proper that we should do this.

But, in a larger sense, we can not dedicate—we can not consecrate—we can not hallow—this ground. The brave men, living and dead, who struggled here, have consecrated it, far above our poor power to add or detract. The world will little note, nor long remember what we say here, but it can never forget what they did here. It is for us the living, rather, to be dedicated here to the unfinished work which they who fought here have thus far so nobly advanced. It is rather for us to be here dedicated to the great task remaining before us—that from these honored dead we take increased devotion to that cause for which they gave the last full measure of devotion—that we here highly resolve that these dead shall not have died in vain—that this nation, under God, shall have a new birth of freedom—and that government of the people, by the people, for the people, shall not perish from the earth.

Abraham Lincoln

If somebody says something to you that is unclear, you would probably ask, "What do you mean?" The person would then *paraphrase*, or restate, what he or she has just said. If the person carefully paraphrases the statement, it will be easier for you to understand.

Here is an example. "If we do not capitulate on this issue we are unlikely to resolve the argument." Do you understand the statement? If the statement is restated in this way it will probably be clearer: "Let's give in so we can reach an agreement."

When you read complex sentences and paragraphs, you can make the meaning clearer by paraphrasing. Ask yourself, "What, in simple English, was the writer saying?" When you paraphrase you may have to look in the dictionary for the meanings of words that are difficult to understand. This is especially true when there are no context clues to help you with the meaning.

Column A contains statements from The Gettysburg Address. Column B contains a paraphrase of each statement. Your task is to decide if the original statement from Column A means the same as the paraphrased statement in Column B. Be sure to give reasons for your decisions. If necessary use a dictionary to help make the decisions. Write your answers on a separate piece of paper.

Column A

1. Fourscore and seven years ago our Fathers brought forth on this continent, a new nation, conceived in Liberty, and dedicated to proposition that all men are created equal.

2. Now we are engaged in a great civil war, testing whether that nation, or any nation so conceived and so dedicated, can long endure.

3. We are met on a great battlefield of that war. We have come to dedicate a portion of that field, as a final resting place for those who here gave their lives that that nation might live. It is altogether fitting and proper that we should do this.

4. But, in a larger sense, we can not dedicate—we can not consecrate—we can not hallow—this ground. The brave men, living and dead, who struggled here, have consecrated it, far above our poor power to add or detract.

5. The world will little note, nor long remember what we say here, but it can never forget what they did here.

Column B

1. Eighty-seven years ago the United States was established as a free country where all its people had equal rights.

2. The purpose of this civil war is to see who is stronger, the North or the South.

3. It is appropriate for us to bury on this battlefield those who fought for our country's freedom.

4. We cannot honor this ground. Those who have fought here already have honored it more than we can.

5. The world will always remember what we said here and what the soldiers did here.

CHAPTER 20 REVIEW

Vocabulary Check
Write a short definition for each of the following terms.

1. Corruption
2. Carpetbaggers
3. Sharecropping
4. Segregation
5. Interest

Fact Check
On a separate piece of paper, fill in the word or words that best complete each of the following sentences.

1. The process of rebuilding the Union after the Civil War was called _____.
2. Congress set up the _____ to take care of former slaves.
3. Andrew Johnson was _____ by the House of Representatives in 1864.
4. The _____ was a secret organization that tried to control blacks by violence and threats.
5. The _____ Amendment defined citizenship in a way that included blacks.
6. _____ led the Niagara Movement.
7. The _____, upper–class, native, white Democrats, at first tried to win the support of black voters but later adopted racist arguments.
8. In the 1896 case of _____, the Supreme Court established the doctrine of "separate but equal" facilities for whites and blacks.
9. Henry Grady called for a _____ with industry, larger cities, and many jobs.
10. The _____ finally ended the reign of King Cotton in the 1890's.

Time Check
On a separate piece of paper, put the following events in chronological order.

1. Lincoln is shot.
2. The Thirteenth Amendment is passed by Congress.
3. Congress passes a Civil Rights Act.
4. The Freedmen's Bureau is set up.
5. Congress passes the Fifteenth Amendment.

Skills Check
Use the illustrations in this chapter to answer the following questions.

1. (a) Who is the central figure in the cartoon on page 422? (b) What is he shown doing?
2. Look at the illustration on page 423. Do you think the artist approved or disapproved of the Freedmen's Bureau? Why or why not?
3. Look at the illustration on page 425. To what situation does it refer?
4. Why is the illustration on page 430 considered to be a primary source?
5. Look at the photographs on page 435. (a) What do you think the photographer thought of the people portrayed? (b) What tells you the photographer's feelings?

Think and Write
1. How did Lincoln's view of the seceded states differ from the Radical Republicans' view?
2. Which bills passed by Congress during reconstruction helped blacks?
3. How did reconstruction end?
4. What state laws and Supreme Court decisions allowed the system of segregation to become established in the South?
5. Why did the South remain primarily agricultural after the Civil War?

REVIEWING UNIT 6

Reviewing the Facts I.

On a separate piece of paper, write the name of the person described in each of the sentences below.

1. Her abolitionist novel was popular in the United States and other countries as well.
2. The Supreme Court ruled that this slave was not a citizen of the United States.
3. He led attacks on Pottawatomie Creek and Harpers Ferry.
4. He was defeated by Senator Douglas in 1858 but became President in 1860.
5. She founded the American Red Cross.
6. He led the Confederate army through most of the Civil War.
7. This President was impeached.
8. A former general, he became President in 1868.
9. This leader said blacks should seek education, work in politics, and work for civil rights.
10. He became President on the condition that federal troops leave the South.

Reviewing the Facts II.

On a separate piece of paper, fill in the word or words that best complete each of the following sentences.

1. Some Northerners helped runaway slaves escape, violating the _____.
2. Allowing the citizens of territories to decide for themselves whether or not to allow slavery was called _____.
3. For a period of time, the _____ Territory had two governments, one proslavery, the other antislavery.
4. Lincoln made sure that the _____ did not secede in part by not threatening slavery there.
5. _____ was the critical Confederate stronghold on the Mississippi River.
6. Lee's thrust into Pennsylvania was stopped by the Battle of _____ in July 1863.
7. Sherman believed in _____, war in which armies turn against civilians as well as enemy soldiers.
8. The rebuilding of the nation after the Civil War is called _____.
9. The members of Congress who wanted to punish the former Confederate states and who thought that Congress could pass any laws it wished for those states were called _____.
10. The _____ forced Southern farmers to replace cotton with other crops.

Reviewing Ideas

1. What major events led to the outbreak of the Civil War?
2. Why did Southerners think in 1860 that the federal government would not protect their interests?
3. What good things did reconstruction accomplish on a national and state level?
4. How were blacks disenfranchised in the South after reconstruction?
5. How did the sharecropping system work?

UNIT SEVEN

Change and Expansion

In the years prior to the Civil War, the United States was a nation of farmers. After the war, inventions and new ways of producing goods brought great changes. By 1900, more and more Americans and millions of newly arrived immigrants began to settle in cities. This painting of New York City in 1895 shows some of the inventions that were changing ways of life in the nation.

Chapter 21

The New West

Miners, cowboys, and farmers brought great changes to the West. Albert Bierstadt tried to evoke the grandeur and vastness of the West.

In the late 1870's, about 20,000 southern blacks left the South to take up new lands and a new life in Kansas. They were known as Exodusters, a name created from the word *exodus*, which means a mass departure. Later many more blacks would leave the South, but the Exodusters had a special role to play. Along with thousands of other Americans from both North and South, they helped settle the last great section of the West.

The story of the West in the late nineteenth century, like that of the South, is one of great change. Lands once passed over by settlers were claimed first by miners and ranchers, then by farmers. The newcomers caused great changes in the lives of those proud Indians who had long lived on the Plains and in the mountains of the American West.

I.   Claiming the Drylands
The Miners' Frontier
The Cowboys' Frontier

II.   The Farmers' Frontier
The Transcontinental Railroad
Life on the Great Plains

III.   The Indians' Last Stand
The Plains Indians
New Weapons
Indian Policy and Indian Wars

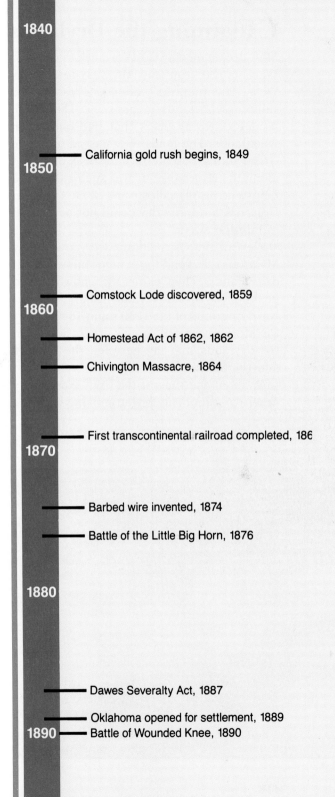

1840

1850 — California gold rush begins, 1849

1860 — Comstock Lode discovered, 1859

— Homestead Act of 1862, 1862

— Chivington Massacre, 1864

— First transcontinental railroad completed, 186

1870

— Barbed wire invented, 1874

— Battle of the Little Big Horn, 1876

1880

— Dawes Severalty Act, 1887

— Oklahoma opened for settlement, 1889

1890 — Battle of Wounded Knee, 1890

I. Claiming the Drylands

Most people moving westward before the Civil War hopped from the Midwest to the Far West. The pioneers had good reasons for skipping the lands in between. They were used to farming fields that had once been woodlands. The lands they passed over, the Great Plains, had no trees to speak of except along the riverbanks. It was such a dry land that some people called it the Great American Desert. A land that dry could not be farmed in familiar ways.

West of the Great Plains were the Rocky Mountains. Beyond those mountains lay still drier lands. Then came the snow-covered peaks of the Sierra Nevadas. Of all the westward migrants of the 1830's and 1840's, only the Mormons dared to make their homes on the drylands that lay between the Rockies and the Sierras.

At about the time of the Civil War, many Americans suddenly began moving onto the

This photograph, taken in 1852, shows prospectors mining gold in Auburn, California.

drylands. They came from three directions. Some came from the West Coast in search of gold and other valuable minerals. Others moved northward from Texas in search of grazing lands for cattle. Before long, still other pioneers began moving westward into Kansas, Nebraska, and other parts of the Great Plains to farm. With the claiming of the Plains, the westward movement, which was so important a part of the American past, came to an end.

The Miners' Frontier

The California gold rush of 1849 drew thousands of people from all over the world to the Far West. Then a series of other discoveries sent miners hurrying eastward.

In 1858, gold was discovered in the Pikes Peak country of Colorado. The next year, more "finds" were made in Boulder and Denver. In 1859, the fabulous **Comstock Lode,** one of the richest deposits of gold and silver of all time, was discovered at Virginia City, Nevada. Then one find followed another in western Nevada. Thousands of miners hurried there hoping to strike it rich.

Once people bothered to look, they found gold in Arizona at Tucson and Prescott (1860 and 1862) and in Idaho (1860). The "rushes" spread to Montana in 1862. Some of the richest mines lay near Butte. They held not only gold but also silver, copper, and zinc in immense amounts. More gold turned up near South Pass in Wyoming in 1864, and before long the population of Wyoming began to grow. There were enough people living in the Far West for Congress to organize the new territories of Nevada and Colorado in 1861, Arizona and Idaho in 1863, Montana in 1864, and Wyoming in 1868. Nevada became a state in 1864.

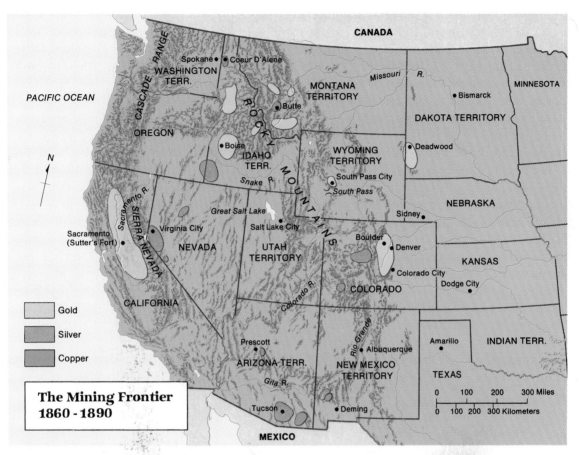

CANADA

PACIFIC OCEAN

CASCADE RANGE

Spokane • Coeur D'Alene

WASHINGTON TERR.

ROCKY MOUNTAINS

MONTANA TERRITORY

Missouri R.

MINNESOTA

• Butte

• Bismarck

OREGON

• Boise

IDAHO TERR.

Snake R.

DAKOTA TERRITORY

• Deadwood

WYOMING TERRITORY

• South Pass City
South Pass

NEBRASKA

Sacramento R.

SIERRA NEVADA

Great Salt Lake

Salt Lake City

Sidney •

• Virginia City

Sacramento (Sutter's Fort) •

NEVADA

UTAH TERRITORY

Boulder

• Denver

KANSAS

CALIFORNIA

• Colorado City

Dodge City •

Colorado R.

COLORADO

Gold

Silver

Copper

Prescott •

ARIZONA TERR.

Rio Grande

• Albuquerque

Amarillo •

INDIAN TERR.

NEW MEXICO TERRITORY

TEXAS

Gila R.

Tucson •

• Deming

0   100   200   300 Miles

0   100 200 300 Kilometers

The Mining Frontier 1860-1890

MEXICO

Map Study *Which of the states or territories shown on the map had the largest gold mining area?*

▶ **1.** Where did miners find gold and silver after the California gold rush?

The Miners' Code The miners came from many different countries. Among them were people from China, Mexico, and almost every European country, as well as Indians and American-born whites and blacks.

Most of the miners were men. In 1880, there were three men to every adult woman in Colorado, Nevada, and Arizona. The women were important. They made family life possible, and in general, had a settling effect on the communities where they lived.

Most prospectors worked lands that belonged to the United States. Their claims to the land and its gold depended on unofficial codes or rules that the miners agreed to among themselves. Those rules said, for example, that a miner could claim only one piece of mining land at a time. If that land was not worked for a week, someone else could take it over.

The camps where miners lived often had other rules. The miners chose officials, including a sheriff. Sometimes they set up courts to try people accused of crimes. The courts' punishments were often fairly mild.

A person convicted of a minor crime might, for example, be whipped or forced to leave the camp. Worse offenders, such as murderers or horse thieves, might be hung.

Despite the miners' homespun law, mining camps were rough places. Most people there were looking for quick riches. Some lost their money as fast as they made it by gambling or drinking in saloons.

The camps were also short-lived. One day they were bustling little towns. The next day the gold was gone and all the miners raced off to stake new claims at a fresh site. Left behind were the famous ghost towns with their empty, dust-blown buildings. Such ghost towns were scattered throughout the mining country. Some camps, however, became proper cities. Last Chance Gulch in Montana, for example, eventually grew into the city of Helena.

The miners' frontier reached the Black Hills of South Dakota in the 1870's. There, in the areas so dry and rocky that they are called "badlands," the mining frontier—complete with robbers, saloons, and gamblers—flourished briefly. Then suddenly, the day of the individual miner passed, and mining became a regular business.

▶**2.** What was life like in the mining camps?

Mining Lodes The lone miners who first worked the new mines gathered the gold that was loose or near the earth's surface. They did not have the machines or help to reach the gold that lay buried in **lodes,** that is, in veins of rock made up of gold and another mineral, quartz. So, when the surface gold was gone, large companies with money to buy equipment and hire workers took over. The owners were investors in the East who hoped to make their fortune without ever leaving home.

A company wanted to have legal title to the land it mined. So in 1866, Congress passed

A lonely cowboy on the Matador Range in Texas watches over a herd of cattle that he is bringing to rail lines in Lubbock, Texas.

the Mineral Land Act that set rules for claiming land for mining.

▶**3.** When did large companies begin mining?

The Cowboys' Frontier

To the pioneers, the Great Plains were a poor place to farm. However, their vast stretches of grassland had long provided food for herds of buffalo and wild horses. In fact, in the southwestern part of Texas, cattle that descended from animals brought by the Spanish multiplied until they became something of a nuisance. By 1860, there were about five million head of longhorn cattle in Texas.

By the mid-1860's, those cattle gave ambitious Texans a chance to make their fortune. The demand for meat was rising in the growing cities of the East. The problem was getting Texas cattle to those markets. The solution to that problem was the **long drive** from Texas to the Midwest.

For the long drive, huge herds of 2,000 to 2,500 steers were collected in Texas. Then they were driven northward under the care of a dozen or so cowboys along cattle trails several hundred miles long. The trails stretched to "cow towns" such as Wichita, Dodge City, and the greatest of them all, Abilene. From such towns, the cattle were shipped to the East by railroad.

Some years after the Civil War, ranchers discovered that longhorn cattle could live much farther north on the Plains. So ranchers spread into Colorado, Wyoming, Montana, and Idaho. Cattle from the northern Plains also had to be driven to railroad lines.

▶**4.** What was the long drive?

Home on the Range Cowboys herded cattle on long drives from the 1860's through the 1880's. The first American cowboys were Southerners in Texas. Mexicans, who had

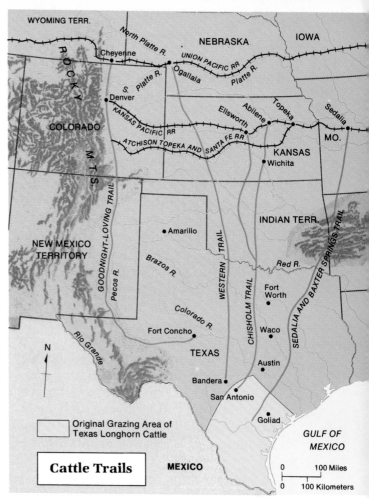

Map Study *Name the trail that connected Bandera, Texas, to Ogallala, Nebraska. What cities were connected by the Goodnight-Loving Trail?*

been in the cattle business for centuries, taught the newcomers how to herd cattle from a horse's back. The American cowboys also imitated the gear and clothing of the Mexican cowhands, called *vaqueros* (vä ker'ōz). The cowboys' hat, high-heeled boots, rope, and saddle were all Mexican in origin. Many cowboys were Mexican Americans, and as many as a quarter of all cowboys were black.

It took skill to herd cattle. Cowboys had to drive the cattle slowly or the animals lost too much weight. At night, the cowboys had to keep the herd together. The cowboys also had to guard against stampedes and rustlers.

▶**5.** Where did American cowboys learn to herd cattle?

The Roundup Cowboys had plenty of work to do when they were not driving cattle. Ranchers on the Great Plains let their herds graze on the open ranges or grasslands. There were no fences. Cowboys "rode the line" between one range and another to try to keep the herds separate. However, some animals always got mixed up in the wrong herd.

For that reason, the famous **roundup** came to be. Once each year, usually in the spring, all the ranchers in an area got together and sorted out their animals. All the new calves were branded, or marked with a hot iron, to show to which herd they belonged. Another roundup was held each fall to figure out which steers were fat enough to be sold.

The roundups were organized by local ranchers' associations, which provided a kind of voluntary government much like that in the mining camps. The associations could not, however, stop violence from breaking out between ranchers and Mexican American sheepherders who drove their herds north from the Southwest. Ranchers claimed that sheep ruined the grass by grazing too close to the ground and that cattle would not graze on land where sheep had passed.

▶**6.** What was the roundup?

The End of the Trail In the mid-1880's—twenty years or so after it all began—the era of the long drive and the roundup suddenly ended. Cattle ranching became less profitable. Beef prices dropped in 1885 from around $30 to $35 to about $8 to $10 per head. Then many ranchers lost half or more of their herds in the bitterly cold winters of 1885–1886 and 1886–1887.

Other more basic changes also brought about the end of the open range. The animals best able to survive on the grasslands of the Great Plains were the Texas longhorn cattle. However, eastern customers found that the meat from those cattle was too tough. To produce more tender meat, ranchers had to pay attention to breeding, which meant they could no longer let their cattle mingle with the cattle of other ranchers. They bought new stock and watched over it carefully on privately owned, fenced-in ranches. Ranchers made good use of an important new invention of 1874—barbed-wire fence. Farmers moving onto the Great Plains also fenced their lands with the same thorny wire. Once fences went up, the long drives of the 1860's and 1870's were no longer possible.

By the late 1880's then, cattle ranching, like mining, was becoming a regular business. Cattle were bred and raised on enormous ranches, sometimes stretching over thousands of acres. One of the greatest of them, the King Ranch in southwestern Texas, covered more than a million acres and held over 100,000 head of cattle.

Meanwhile, railroads pushed into the ranch lands. The long drive was no longer necessary.

▶**7.** Why did ranchers begin buying land and fencing in their stock?

Reviewing Section I

Identify Comstock Lode, Butte, Helena, lodes, longhorn cattle, long drive, roundup

Questions to Answer
1. What was the miners' code?
2. How did ranching become a regular business?

A Question to Think About Why did mining companies insist on having a legal title to the lands they mined?

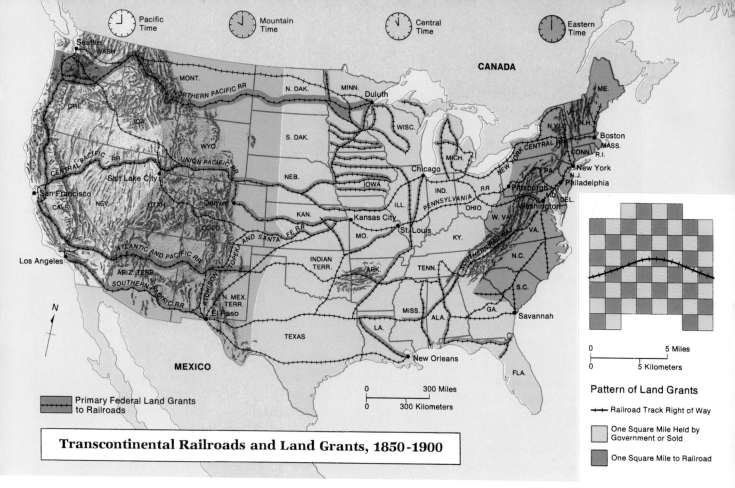

Time Zones (labels on map)

Pacific Time — Mountain Time — Central Time — Eastern Time

CANADA

MEXICO

Primary Federal Land Grants to Railroads

0 — 300 Miles
0 — 300 Kilometers

0 — 5 Miles
0 — 5 Kilometers

Pattern of Land Grants

+—+ Railroad Track Right of Way

One Square Mile Held by Government or Sold

One Square Mile to Railroad

Transcontinental Railroads and Land Grants, 1850-1900

Map Study *Name the four time zones that are shown on the map. Which territory does the Atchison, Topeka, and Sante Fe Railroad cross?*

II. The Farmers' Frontier

The growth of farming in the United States after the Civil War was astounding. In the 30 years between 1870 and 1900, more land was made into farms than in all the previous 250 years. That happened because railroads were available to move people west and ship farm products east.

The Transcontinental Railroad

For many years, Americans had dreamed of a **transcontinental** railroad, one that went all the way from the Atlantic to the Pacific. It was finally built after the Civil War.

Two railroad companies built the transcontinental railroad. The Central Pacific Railroad laid tracks stretching eastward from California. It used many Chinese immigrants on its crews. The Union Pacific Railroad laid track stretching westward from Omaha, Nebraska. Many Irish immigrants worked for the Union Pacific. Americans of all races and nationalities, including Mexican Americans and blacks, also worked on the project. The

453

Railroad workers and officials gathered on May 10, 1869, at Promontory Point, Utah, to celebrate the completion of the first transcontinental railroad.

two sets of tracks met at Promontory Point in Utah. There on May 10, 1869, officials hammered in a last, golden spike with a silver hammer.

Before long, other railroads crisscrossed the country. Among them were the Great Northern; the Denver and Rio Grande; the Atchison, Topeka, and Santa Fe; and the Southern Pacific. Americans could then travel from coast to coast in about a week. The same trip had taken the pioneers who settled California and Oregon several months.

▶ **1.** When was the first transcontinental railroad completed?

Land Grants The federal government gave the new railroads considerable help. That help came in the form of cheap loans and, more important, land grants.

The government gave railroads land on both sides of the tracks—some 20 to 40 square miles of land for each mile of track laid. The railroad lands came in square plots. Next to them lay plots held by the government. A map of the railroad plots and the government plots looked like a checkerboard. Some states also granted lands to the railroads to encourage their development.

▶ **2.** How did the national and state governments encourage the railroads?

Selling the West Those enormous tracts of land were not much good to the railroads unless they were sold. By selling their land, the railroad companies, in fact, made money in two ways. They made money from both the sale itself and from the business new settlers gave the railroads. As a result, the railroads worked hard to attract settlers.

The railroad companies set up land offices in the East where they offered land in the West at good prices. That was just the beginning. They were willing to sell on credit and to loan settlers money for food and supplies. Some railroads promised to carry whole families and goods to their new homes in the West absolutely free. The Burlington Railroad even offered to let people buy round trip

Chinese Workers Seek the Golden Mountain

Between 1850 and 1882, almost 200,000 men from China left their families and sailed for *Gum Shan*, or the Golden Mountain. That was the name the Chinese gave to California after the discovery of gold there in the 1840's.

Political turmoil in China, higher taxes, a severe drought, and crop failure led daring Chinese to make the four to six week ocean crossing. The men who made the trip did not intend to stay in the United States. They thought that in a few years they could make enough money on the Golden Mountain to return to China and live in ease for the rest of their lives. Very few women made the trip because respectable Chinese women did not leave their houses.

In the 1850's, some of the first Chinese to reach the United States did return to China with great fortunes. That encouraged more men to try their luck in the United States. Most of them did not make fortunes. However, they lived frugally in order to send as much money as possible to their families in China.

The Chinese had great respect for the family. One reason the Chinese did not intend to stay in the United States was that they could not leave the graves of their ancestors untended.

Thousands of Chinese were recruited to work on the Central Pacific Railroad. They carved out much of the railbed through the Sierra Nevadas.

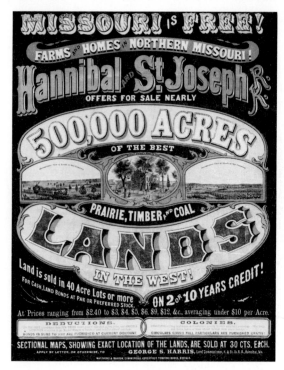

Railroad posters such as the one shown here encouraged people to buy land in the West.

tickets at a reduced price if they wanted to go out and have a look at land that they were thinking of buying.

Nor did the railroads limit their appeals to Americans. Railroad companies also set up offices in Europe to encourage people there to immigrate and settle in the West. In that way, the railroads helped bring large numbers of Swedes, Norwegians, Danes, and Germans to the United States.

The railroads' descriptions of the West made it sound like heaven. Farming the Great Plains, they claimed, was easier than farming lands that first had to be cleared of trees. Farmers on the Great Plains seemed almost certain to make money. As a result, people were willing to borrow money to go there. Banks and lending institutions multiplied in the West.

Since they wanted people to settle in the West, the railroads explained how people could get land from the government. The federal **Homestead Act of 1862** allowed heads of families to have 160 acres of public land almost free if they lived on it for five years. Another federal law, the Timber Culture Act of 1873, granted 160 acres to farmers who promised to grow trees on a quarter of it.

Unfortunately, most of the public land available was 20 miles or more from the railroad tracks. Settlers wanted to be nearer the tracks so they could more easily send their crops to market. So they were more attracted to the railroad lands they had to buy than to those they could get almost free from the government.

The railroads were very successful in attracting settlers. The population of Kansas shot up from 365,000 to 996,000 in the 1870's. Nebraska's population grew from 123,000 to 452,000—an increase of more than 250 percent. Meanwhile, people began settling in the Dakotas. The population of the Great Plains states kept growing in the 1880's.
▶3. How did the railroads try to attract settlers to the West?

Life on the Great Plains

The new settlers found that life on the Great Plains was not as easy as the railroads had promised. Before the Civil War, pioneers in Kansas and Nebraska had claimed the lands along streams where trees grew and water was available. The new settlers were moving into an area where the annual rainfall was normally less than the minimum necessary to farm by ordinary methods (about 20 inches). The eastern edge of that area ran from the Dakotas south through Nebraska, Kansas, Oklahoma, and into Texas. It also stretched westward to the Rockies.

456

Homesteader Moses Speese and his family pose in front of their sod house. It was located near the town of Westerville, Nebraska.

Life on the dry Plains was very hard. Powerful winds blew across the treeless lands. In the winter, those winds carried bitter cold air south from the Arctic. In the summer, they swept hot, dry air northward from Mexico. Rivers that flooded from rain and melting snow in the spring could disappear altogether in the summer. Then terrible fires might sweep across the dried-out grass, destroying everything in their path. Huge clouds of grasshoppers could darken the sun on a bright August day, then settle down to eat everything in sight, from the crops in farmers' fields to the laundry on their clotheslines.

Finding and saving water was a constant problem on the Great Plains. Settlers hoarded rainwater or carted barrels of water home from faraway streams. Such water, however, often carried "prairie fever," or typhoid. It was better to dig a well, although that was sometimes an almost impossible task. Farmers considered themselves lucky if they had to dig down only 40 or 50 feet before finding water. More often, the water was 200 or 300 feet under the ground.

Shelter was another problem. There was not enough wood or stone for a house, so farmers dug holes into the sides of hills and made their houses there. Other farmers built houses of **sod,** chunks of prairie grass and its roots. Fuel was also scarce for the settlers. While the buffalo lasted, people burned dried buffalo manure or "chips." In the days of open-range cattle grazing, farm families used the dried manure of nearby herds. Sometimes they burned sunflower stalks, or rolled-up hunks of hay, or corncobs. None of those were entirely satisfactory.

In time, farmers found ways to live on the Great Plains. They used barbed wire to fence

457

Highlighting People
Willa Cather

To many people, life on the Nebraska prairie brings to mind the name of author Willa Cather. Willa Cather came to Nebraska as a pioneer. She was born in Rock Creek County, Virginia.

Willa Cather was born in 1873, the first of seven children. When she was nine, Willa's parents decided to leave Virginia and join her grandparents on their ranch in Nebraska. Willa and her family lived on the ranch for two years. During much of this time, her mother was too ill to watch over the children closely. To their delight, the older children had the run of the countryside.

Willa delighted in the wild Nebraska countryside and its people. Her neighbors came from Sweden, Bohemia, Germany, and Russia. The young girl visited their sod homes (see above) and listened eagerly to their tales of tragedy and triumph. Visions of blizzards, hunger, and prairie fires filled her head.

When Willa was 11, her father gave up ranching and moved his family to the small town of Red Cloud. To many people, Red Cloud would have seemed a dull, lifeless place in which to live. But to Willa, it was a constant source of amazement. Tucked away in her cozy attic room, she spent long hours dreaming and thinking. Perhaps much of what she wrote later on in life was first conceived in that room.

Willa did not spend all of her life in Nebraska. When she was 22, she moved away from home to take a job writing play reviews in Pittsburgh, Pennsylvania. Although she visited Nebraska time and time again, she never again lived there. Instead, memories furnished her with the material that she later included in her novels and stories about prairie life. In her books *My Antonia* and *O Pioneers* we hear once again the voices of the brave men and women who settled the West.

Willa Cather died in New York City in 1947. She was 74 years old.

Sometimes historians turn to fiction, or stories about imaginary people and events, for help in understanding a time period or an event. Although a writer of fiction uses his or her imagination to create events and characters, sometimes a piece of fiction is based on fact. Fiction is important to the historian, however, not for its factual content but for the way a skillful writer can capture people's feelings or provide a new way of viewing an event.

O.E. Rölvaag based his novel, *Giants in the Earth*, on his experiences as a Norwegian immigrant in South Dakota. His novel has been acclaimed for its interpretation of life on the Great Plains.

In the selection that follows, Beret, the mother of a Norwegian family traveling across the Plains to reach its homestead in the 1870's, thinks about the land. Read the selection and answer the questions following it.

In a certain sense, she had to admit to herself, it was lovely up here. The broad expanse stretching away endlessly in every direction, seemed almost like the ocean . . . It reminded her strongly of the sea, and yet it was very different . . . This formless prairie had no heart that beat, no waves that sang . . .

The infinitude surrounding her on every hand might not have been so oppressive, might even have brought her a measure of peace, if it had not been for the deep silence, which lay heavier here than in a church. Indeed, what was there to break it? Here no warbling sound of birds rose on the air, no buzzing of insects sounded; . . . the waving blades of grass that trembled to the faintest breath now stood erect and quiet, as if listening, in the great hush of the evening . . . it must have been over two weeks now since she had heard a bird sing! Had they traveled into some nameless, abandoned region? Could no living thing exist out here, in the empty, desolate, endless wastes of green and blue? How *could* existence go on, she thought, desperately? If life is to thrive and endure, it must at least have something to hide behind! . . .

From O.E. Rölvaag, *Giants in the Earth*, translated by O.E. Rölvaag and Lincoln Colcord (New York: Harper and Brothers, 1927, 1929), pp. 37–38.

1. What are some of the words Beret uses in her thoughts to describe the Plains?
2. What about the Great Plains does she find the most disturbing?
3. Why do you think Beret says that living things need something to hide behind?
4. Do you think Beret will be a successful pioneer? Why or why not?
5. Rölvaag went to South Dakota in 1899 where he attended school. He lived much of his life in Minnesota. Do you think his description of South Dakota in the 1870's is accurate? Why or why not?

their land. They brought in machines to drill wells, and used windmills to lift water up from deep under the ground. Meanwhile, farmers learned to grow lines of trees as windbreaks and found ways to stop prairie fires.

▶4. How did the farmers on the dry Plains find water, shelter, and fuel?

A New Way of Farming Building a house of sod was easier than growing crops on the

Farmers in Colorado are shown using a steam tractor and belt-driven thrashing machine to harvest wheat in the late 1800's.

dry Plains. In the 1870's and early 1880's, more rain than usual fell. Then in 1886, the rains stopped. In only two of the next ten years was there enough rain for farmers to grow crops. In five of those years, the crops failed almost entirely.

Gradually, Americans developed the techniques of **dry farming,** a way of growing crops in areas of low rainfall without irrigation. Dry farming demands special ways of plowing fields to keep moisture in the soil. It also involves growing types of plants that can thrive despite infrequent rainfall. In the southern Plains, for example, farmers learned to grow special strains of wheat, such as the Turkey Red variety brought to Kansas in the 1870's by immigrants from the dry lands of southern Russia. Turkey Red is a "winter wheat." That is, it is planted in the fall after the September rains. It grows through the winter even under light snow, then it shoots up in the spring when there is plenty of moisture from rain and melted snow. Winter wheat

can be harvested before the dry part of the summer.

Meanwhile, it became clear that farming on the Great Plains had to be done on a large scale. The plowing required by dry farming is best done by machines. Also, the enormous flat fields of the Great Plains were perfectly suited for farming by machine.

During the Civil War, people began to use new farm machines such as the McCormick reaper. After the war, other machines were invented to improve farming. With the use of such machinery, a wheat farmer could do in 3 hours what used to take 61 hours to do when only hand tools were available. Machinery, though, made sense only when it could be used on hundreds of acres.

▶**5.** What are some techniques that made it possible to farm on the Great Plains?

"In Kansas We Busted" Farmers who worked large tracts of land were successful on the Great Plains. What, then, happened

to the small-scale farmers? They had borrowed heavily in the 1870's and 1880's to buy land and supplies. Because many could not make the payments on their loans when their crops failed, their creditors took over the farms. Many settlers returned to the East, often on prairie wagons with signs that said such things as "In God we trusted, in Kansas we busted." Some failed farmers stayed on the Great Plains, becoming hired hands or, very often, **tenant farmers.** Tenant farmers rent land.

Tenant farming never became as widespread on the Great Plains as sharecropping did in the South. Still, by 1890, almost 37 percent of all farmers in Nebraska and over 35 percent in Kansas were tenants. By the late nineteenth century, the small-scale, independent farmer was going the way of the lone prospector and the open-range cowboy. Farming, like mining and cattle ranching, was becoming a big business.

▶**6.** How widespread was tenant farming on the Great Plains in the 1890's?

Reviewing Section II

Identify transcontinental, Homestead Act of 1862, sod, dry farming, tenant farmers

Questions to Answer
1. What role did the railroads play in settling the Great Plains?
2. Why did farming on the Great Plains become big business?

A Question to Think About Why did the federal government assist the railroads with land grants?

III. The Indians' Last Stand

The "New West" was not empty when the miners, the cowboys, and the farmers began to move there. The drylands of the West were home to about 223,000 of the 300,000 Indians who remained in the United States. In the northern parts of the Great Plains lived about 30 groups of Indians such as the Sioux (sü), Mandan, Gros Ventre (grō von′trə), Blackfoot, Crow, Cheyenne, Arapaho (a rap′ ə hō′), and Nez Perce (nez′ pers′). Farther south lived the Comanche, Apache, Ute (yüt), and Kiowa (kī′ō wə). Many of those Indians were skilled fighters, determined to keep outsiders from crossing their lands.

After the Civil War, citizens of the United States proposed not just to cross Indian lands but to take them over. That involved several major changes in the Indian policy of the United States government. It also provoked several decades of Indian wars.

The Plains Indians

Early Plains Indians gathered seeds and hunted animals on foot. Some groups grew food along the riverbeds that crossed the Great Plains. Then the Spaniards brought horses to the Americas. The horses thrived on the western grasslands. In time, they spread throughout the Great Plains, bringing great changes in the Indians' lives.

There were about 12 million buffalo on the Great Plains by the mid-nineteenth century. The Indians found it far easier to hunt those huge, clumsy animals on horseback than on foot. The Indians learned that the buffalo could provide almost everything they needed. They ate buffalo meat and used the animals' hides for clothing and to cover their tepees, or tents. They used buffalo manure for fuel. They even made the bones of the animals into tools. So the Indians gave up attempts

Artist George Catlin captured the way of life of the Plains Indians when buffalo still roamed freely.

to farm. They became **nomads,** people who move from place to place. The Indians followed the buffalo, always on horseback.

All the Indians on the Great Plains became superb riders. The Comanche were perhaps the best of all. Their wild horses were small and powerful. Comanche fighters could drop to the side so their horses shielded them from enemy fire, and then suddenly pull themselves up and drop to the other side. They could also fire a bow and arrow or throw a lance sitting straight up—or from under their horses' necks! Many Indians carried shields of buffalo skin strong enough to stop most bullets. They could shoot off 20 arrows with deadly force in the time it took to load a clumsy muzzle-loading rifle.

▶**1.** How did the horse change the Plains Indians' way of life?

New Weapons

If settlers were to defeat Indian warriors, they needed a small weapon that could be fired quickly from horseback. That need was filled by the revolver or "six-shooter." It was a pistol (a handgun) that could shoot six bullets before it needed to be reloaded. The revolver was invented by Samuel Colt in the 1830's and was later improved greatly.

The revolver alone did not ensure the defeat of the Indians. Hunters from the United States also weakened the Indians by destroying the buffaloes that supported their way of life.

The slaughter of the buffalo began in the late 1860's with the building of the transcontinental railroads. First the railroads hired a few sharpshooters such as "Buffalo Bill" Cody to kill buffalo so they would not block the tracks. Before long, passengers and railroad crews were shooting the animals for the fun of it. Then, in 1871, a tannery in Pennsylvania began offering up to $3 for a single buffalo hide. Suddenly, teams of hunters swarmed over the Great Plains. With amazing speed they killed millions of animals. By the mid-1880's, the great herds were gone.

Without the buffalo, the Indians survived only because of handouts from the government of the United States. In return, however, the United States gained the power to decide where and how the Indians would live.

▶**2.** How did hunters destroy the Indians' way of life?

Indian Policy and Indian Wars

Once the United States decided to open Kansas and Nebraska to settlement, it was no longer willing to let the Indians have free run of the Great Plains. So in 1851, it adopted a new policy. It decided to divide up the Great Plains, giving the various Indian groups certain defined pieces of territory. That was called the **concentration policy.** The Sioux Indians, for example, were concentrated, or grouped together, in the Dakota country north of the Platte River. In return for agreeing to live on the lands given them, the Indians received money and other gifts.

▶**3.** What was the concentration policy?

War in Colorado The Indians were promised that their new lands would be theirs forever. But "forever" did not last very long. In the late 1850's, thousands of miners moved onto lands of the Arapaho and Cheyenne. Federal agents tried to convince the leaders of those Indian groups to give up their claims and move to a small reservation in eastern Colorado. The Indian leaders agreed, but their followers did not. They waged a bitter war against miners, travelers, and other people intruding on their lands.

By the fall of 1864, however, the Cheyenne Indians, led by Black Kettle, were ready to make peace. Then, on November 28, a company of the Colorado militia under Colonel John M. Chivington surrounded a camp at Sand Creek where Black Kettle and 500 Cheyenne slept. At the break of dawn, the militia attacked, killing 450 men, women, and children.

The **Chivington Massacre** encouraged other Indians to continue their war for survival. It took another full year of war before the Cheyenne and Arapaho finally surrendered. At about the same time, the Kiowa and Comanche also gave up the lands that had been promised to them forever in 1851 and moved into a small area in northern Texas.

▶**4.** What happened at the Chivington Massacre?

The Sioux Wars Before long, war also broke out in the northern Plains. The Sioux of Minnesota had been placed on lands without access to good hunting grounds. As a result, they were starving. In the summer of 1862, they struck with deadly force against settlers in southern and western Minnesota. Some of the greatest bloodshed occurred at the little town of New Ulm, where German immigrants had settled. By December, the United States Army finally brought peace to the area.

A few years later, the Sioux farther west began to wage war because the United States planned to build a road through the lands given the Sioux in 1851. Worse still, the chosen route threatened to destroy the Indians' favorite hunting grounds in the foothills of the Big Horn Mountains. When the protests of Sioux leader Red Cloud were ignored, he and his warriors went to war in 1865 and again in 1866. Those conflicts ended only when the United States gave up its road plans. The Sioux then agreed to live on a reservation in the Dakota Territory. For the time, at least, they could still use their favorite hunting grounds.

▶**5.** What prompted the Sioux wars in Minnesota and the Dakotas?

The Small Reservation Policy Obviously the United States was no longer honoring its policy of 1851. It was no longer trying to concentrate the Indians on large blocks of land. Instead, in 1867, the United States officially adopted a new policy, known as the **small reservation policy.** Under that policy, the government set out to move the Indians onto small reservations in out-of-the-way areas that other settlers did not want.

The government also decided to move most of the Indians of the southern Plains onto reservations in the western part of the present-day state of Oklahoma. That entire area was then known as **Indian Territory.** It belonged to the Cherokee, Creek, Choctaw, Chickasaw, and Seminole tribes. The government had moved those groups to Indian Territory from the Southeast when Andrew Jackson was President. Now those groups lost part of their land once again.

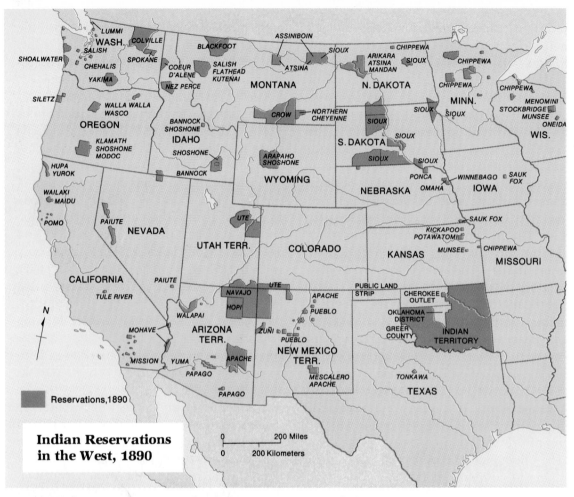

Indian Reservations in the West, 1890

Reservations, 1890

0   200 Miles
0   200 Kilometers

Map Study *Name three states that had reservations set aside for the Shoshone. In which territory did the Navajo settle?*

In 1871, the United States changed its policies one more time. It decided that it would no longer treat the various Indian groups as separate nations able to make treaties like the other nations of the world.

▶ **6.** What was the new government Indian policy of 1867?

Indian Resistance Few Plains Indians moved to new reservations peacefully. When the Indians refused to give up their old homes, the United States turned its army, under the old Civil War general, William Tecumseh Sherman, against them.

By 1874, Sherman won a kind of peace in the West. Then, in 1875, thousands of gold prospectors rushed onto Sioux lands in the Black Hills of Dakota. War began again. On June 25, 1876, warriors led by Sitting Bull killed all 265 men under General George A. Custer in the **Battle of the Little Big Horn,** also known as Custer's Last Stand.

Although the Indians won that famous battle, they lost the war. Within months, the

Sioux were forced to surrender. Then they sadly made their way back to their Dakota reservation.

▶ **7.** What happened at the Battle of the Little Big Horn?

The Nez Perce Even Indians who had been friends of the United States suffered. The Nez Perce Indians who lived in western Idaho were a peaceful people. When Lewis and Clark passed through their lands, they helped the explorers. Never, the Indians claimed, had any of the Nez Perce killed a white person. Why, then, did the United States want to remove them from the lands where their ancestors were buried? They refused to move onto a reservation until finally, in 1877, their leader, a man called Chief Joseph by whites, was forced to give in to the government's demands.

A group of Sioux pose in front of a building on the Pine Ridge Reservation in South Dakota.

Sitting Bull (left) defeated George Custer at the Battle of the Little Big Horn on June 25, 1876. Custer and all of the 265 men with him were killed.

465

While Chief Joseph led his people to the lands given them in Oregon, a few of his angry followers killed some white settlers. Chief Joseph decided that to avoid a war, he would take his people to Canada. They eluded the United States Army for 1,500 miles. When they were almost to the border, they stopped to rest. Then, in September 1877, the army appeared and a battle began. The Indians held out for four days before Chief Joseph surrendered. Chief Joseph was sent to a reservation in the Washington Territory. His people were sent to some of the poorest land in the southern part of Indian Territory.

▶ 8. Who was the leader of the Nez Perce?

Wounded Knee Many Indians longed for the world as it had been before they lost their lands and before the buffalo disappeared.

Their grief finally took religious form. The Dakota Sioux became caught up in the teachings of a religious leader named Wovoka (wo vo′kəh). If the Indians performed certain "ghost dances," he said, the white settlers and soldiers would disappear and the Indians would get their lands back. Those dances frightened settlers in nearby towns. The army was called in to end the dances. Finally, in the horrible Battle of Wounded Knee in 1890, American troops turned their guns on the Indians at the Black Hills reservation. They killed 200 men, women, and children.

▶ 9. Why was the army at Wounded Knee?

The "Reform" of Indian Policy Not all Americans approved of their country's Indian policy. One of the most critical was a woman named Helen Hunt Jackson. In 1881, she

In Their Own Words

Chief Joseph spoke on behalf of Indians.

. . . I have heard talk and talk but nothing is done. Good words do not last long unless they amount to something. Words do not pay for my dead people. They do not pay for my country, now overrun by white men. They do not protect my father's grave. They do not pay for my horses and cattle.

Good words do not give me back my children . . . . Good words will not give my people good health and stop them from dying. Good words will not get my people a home where they can live in peace and take care of themselves . . . . I only ask of the government to be treated as all other men are treated. If I cannot go to my own home, let me have a home in a country where my people will not die so fast. I would like to go to Bitter Root Valley (western Montana). There my people would be healthy; where they are now, they are dying. Three have died since I left my camp to come to Washington . . . .

We only ask an even chance to live as other men live. We ask to be recognized as men. We ask that the same law shall work alike on all men. If an Indian breaks the law, punish him by the law. If a white man breaks the law, punish him also.

Let me be a free man—free to travel, free to stop, free to work, free to trade where I choose, free to choose my own teachers, free to follow the religion of my fathers, free to think and talk and act for myself—and I will obey every law or submit to the penalty . . . .

North American Review, 128, April 1879

published an important book about Indian policy called *A Century of Dishonor.*

Reformers like Jackson did not think the Indians should be left to live in their own way. They wanted the Indians to live like other Americans. To do that, the Indians would have to give up their old loyalties to their nations and their leaders. They would have to stop being Indians.

The reformers wanted reservation lands, which were held by the Indians as a group, divided up into family plots. Then the Indians could become small-scale farmers.

With the encouragement of those who considered themselves friends to the Indians, Congress, in 1887, passed the **Dawes Severalty Act.** It ordered that each Indian group's lands be divided up among its members. The United States kept some control over the land for 25 years, however. Those who finally received a plot of land became citizens of the United States. The lands left over after small farms were given out were to be sold. The money was to be used to educate Indian children.

The law did not work out as the reformers had intended. Indians who had lived as hunters were unwilling to become farmers. They were generally cheated out of their lands in one way or another. Indians lost their group identity and communal way of life. Meanwhile, large tracts of lands once owned by Indians were opened to settlers. Even some 2 million acres in the southern Indian Territory were thrown open to land-hungry farmers. A signal was given on April 22, 1889, and the land rush began. Homesteaders called "boomers" and "sooners" ran in to claim their land. By 1890, Indian Territory was ready to become Oklahoma Territory.

The Dawes Act, in short, brought an end to most of the reservations. It left the Indians a poor, often landless people, living on food

On September 16, 1893, more than 50,000 "boomers" rushed to claim land in north-central Oklahoma after the government opened the territory for settlement.

and clothing handed out by the government of the United States. The Indians of the Great Plains could regard the "New West" only with sadness and anger. It was built at their expense.

▶10. Why did the Dawes Act have terrible effects on the Indians?

Reviewing Section III———————

Identify nomads, Samuel Colt, "Buffalo Bill" Cody, concentration policy, Black Kettle, Chivington Massacre, small reservation pol-icy, Indian Territory, Battle of the Little Big Horn, Chief Joseph, Battle of Wounded Knee, Helen Hunt Jackson, Dawes Severalty Act

Questions to Answer
1. How did government Indian policy change from 1851 to 1887?
2. Why was the Dawes Act unsuccessful?

A Question to Think About How would the United States be different today if the government had not changed its Indian policy in 1851?

IMPROVE YOUR READING
Context Clues/Variant Meanings

Sometimes in your reading you encounter words that have several different, or variant, meanings. When this happens, you must decide on the correct meaning. Often the words are common, so authors do not give direct definitions for them.

To decide on the proper meaning of words with variant meanings, you must look at the context, the sentence in which the word appears, to make a reasonable guess at the word's meaning. Of course, if you cannot guess the meaning of the word, you should look it up in a dictionary.

The word *plots* has several meanings. Some of its meanings are "points located on a map," "secret plans," and "measured pieces of land." See if you can use the context to decide on the correct meaning of *plots* in this sentence. "The railroad lands came in square plots." By noticing the reference in the sentence to *land*, you can conclude that the correct meaning of *plots* is "measured pieces of land."

Your task is to use context clues to decide on the correct meaning of each italicized word in the sentences below. Write your answer on a separate sheet of paper.

1. As miners looked for gold and silver, one *strike* followed another in western Nevada. *Strike* means (a) hit (b) work stoppage (c) discovery.
2. A company wanted to have legal *title* to the land it mined. *Title* means (a) right to possession (b) championship (c) name of a book.
3. Farmers learned to grow special *strains* of wheat, such as Turkey Red. *Strains* means (a) traces (b) stretches (c) kinds.
4. Federal agents tried to convince Indian leaders to give up their *claims* and move to a small reservation. *Claims* means (a) insurance payments (b) a right to something (c) state something as a fact.
5. Women made family life possible and in general had a *settling* effect on mining towns. *Settling* means (a) making quiet and orderly (b) sinking to the bottom (c) packing down.

CHAPTER 21 REVIEW

Vocabulary Check
Write a short definition for each of the following terms.

1. Lodes
2. Roundup
3. Sod
4. Dry farming
5. Nomads

Fact Check
Match each term or name in column I with the phrase that describes it in column II.

Column I

1. Exodusters
2. Helen Hunt Jackson
3. Comstock Lode
4. Long drive
5. Chief Joseph
6. Chivington Massacre
7. Tenant farmers
8. Homestead Act of 1862
9. Custer's Last Stand
10. Dawes Severalty Act

Column II

a. Law that divided Indian land into farms
b. Rich deposit of gold and silver in Nevada
c. Southern blacks who moved to Kansas in the 1870's
d. Incident in 1864 when 450 Cheyenne were killed at Sand Creek, Colorado
e. Method of bringing cattle from Texas to the Midwest
f. Law that offered heads of families 160 acres of almost free land
g. Battle of the Little Big Horn in 1876
h. People who work on land they rent from someone else
i. Writer who worked for Indian reform
j. Leader of the Nez Perce who tried to lead his people to Canada in the 1870's

Skills Check
Use the map on page 453 to answer the following questions.

1. What does this map show?
2. What does the checkerboard represent?
3. What do the four clocks represent?
4. Which railroad could be used to travel from Minnesota to Washington State?
5. Which railroad would a passenger have used to travel from Washington State to California?

Time Check
On a separate piece of paper, put the following events in chronological order.

1. The Central Pacific and Union Pacific railroads meet in Utah.
2. Oklahoma is opened up to homesteaders.
3. The United States adopts the small reservation policy.
4. The Battle of Wounded Knee takes place.
5. The Dawes Severalty Act is passed.

Think and Write
1. How had life on the Great Plains changed from about 1865 to about 1900 for miners, ranchers, farmers, and Indians?
2. What role did the railroads play in the settlement of the Great Plains?
3. What was life like for people in early mining towns and along the long drive?
4. How did the slaughter of buffalo change the way of life of the Plains Indians?
5. Why was the Dawes Act a failure?

Chapter 22

The Nation Industrializes

After the Civil War, industry began to expand. By the late 1800's, steelmaking had become a major industry.

Mining, ranching, and farming became big businesses in the West after the Civil War. In the late nineteenth century, large companies also began to take over manufacturing. As the nation's industries grew, work changed. In fact, industrialization, the growth of industry, touched the lives of all Americans. It affected the places where they lived, the clothes they wore, and even the food they ate.

I. **The Growth of Industry**
The Railroads
Carnegie Steel
Inventions Help Business
Businesses Compete
Government Regulates Business

II. **The World of Work**
The Early Unions
The American Federation of Labor
Strikes and Strikebreakers

III. **City Life**
Transportation and Industrial Centers
The Lure of the City
The New Immigrants
Women's Changing Role
Education

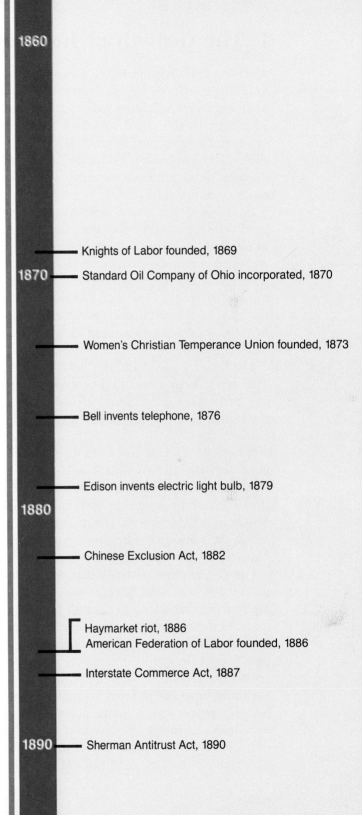

1860

Knights of Labor founded, 1869

1870 Standard Oil Company of Ohio incorporated, 1870

Women's Christian Temperance Union founded, 1873

Bell invents telephone, 1876

Edison invents electric light bulb, 1879

1880

Chinese Exclusion Act, 1882

Haymarket riot, 1886
American Federation of Labor founded, 1886

Interstate Commerce Act, 1887

1890 Sherman Antitrust Act, 1890

I. The Growth of Industry

After the Civil War, industry grew at an astounding rate in the United States. The value of American manufactures rose from less than $2 billion in 1860 to almost $5.5 billion in 1880, and it continued to grow. By 1890, for the first time in history, the value of American manufactured products exceeded the value of its farm products.

How could American industry grow so rapidly? One reason was that the United States had the natural resources—coal, iron, and other minerals—to support that growth. Americans had discovered some of those resources before the Civil War. Others, such as the iron ore of great Mesabi (mə sä′ bē) Range in Minnesota, were discovered soon after the war ended.

The country also had a large labor force. That labor force grew in the late nineteenth and early twentieth century as hundreds of thousands of immigrants entered the United States.

Industry benefited, too, from the talents of people in the United States who invented better ways to do things. It was also important that men and women in both the United States and Europe were ready and able to invest their money to help develop American industry.

The government of the United States did what it could to help. For example, it passed high tariffs that added to the cost of foreign manufactured goods in the United States. Such tariffs on foreign merchandise made it easier for American companies to sell their products at home.

Finally, American industry was able to grow because there was a large population of Americans willing to buy its products. The population of the United States grew from 31.5 million in 1860 to 63 million by 1890.

By 1900, the population was 76 million. Those American customers were, however, spread over an enormous land. Before they could buy the products of big, national companies, it was necessary to find a way to get goods to them easily and cheaply. That was accomplished above all by the railroads.

The Railroads

Railroads grew rapidly after the Civil War. There were only 31,000 miles of railroad track in the United States in 1850. Most of the country's railroad lines were very short. By 1900, the United States had 200,000 miles of railroad tracks—more than in all of Europe. The tracks tied together the major cities and sections of the nation.

As the railroads made it possible to get across the country faster, shipping costs also dropped. In 1865, it cost $3.45 to ship a barrel of flour to the east coast from a point 1,000 miles away. Twenty years later, it cost only 68 cents.

▶**1.** How did railroad growth affect travel time and shipping costs?

Standard Gauge and Time The railroads were the first big business in the United States. They were managed by company officers who worked from a central office but kept in touch with events all over the country. To serve their needs, the railroads had to **standardize** many practices throughout the country, that is, to make them alike.

For example, before the Civil War, the gauge, or distance between the rails, often was different for different railroad lines. That meant that trains built for the tracks of one railroad company could not run on the tracks of another line. The problem was solved by standardizing the gauges. In 1886, workers in the South moved one rail three inches nearer the other so their gauge would be the same as that in the North.

Time posed another problem for the railroads. There were so many different local time zones in the country that it was almost impossible to set time schedules that made sense everywhere. As a result, on November 18, 1883, the American Railway Association adopted four standard time zones, each with standard time one hour different from its neighbors.

▶**2.** How did the railroads standardize their gauges and time zones?

Money to Build the Railroads Building the railroads cost more money than anything Americans had done before. All the canals built between 1815 and 1860 cost $188 million. By 1859, the railroads had already cost over $1,100 million, and their greatest growth was yet to come. Canals were built mostly with money from state and local governments. Local, state, and national governments also helped build the railroads, but private citizens financed most of their growth.

The railroads were not owned by one person or even a small group of people. Few individuals or even groups had the millions of dollars needed to build a railroad. Those who did were unwilling to risk their fortunes on a venture that might fail. Instead, they formed **corporations,** companies that sold stock to the public. Each railroad was therefore owned by thousands of stockholders who each owned at least one share, or title to part of the company. The company's profits were divided so that each share of stock earned the same amount of money.

Stockholders hoped the company's profits would be high. They also hoped that the stock itself would rise in value so that they could

OUR STANDARD (GAUGE) ADOPTED ALL OVER THE UNION.

By converting to a standard track gauge, the major railroads of the nation were united.

sell their shares for more than they paid for them. The New York Stock Exchange grew in size and importance during the 1840's and 1850's mainly because it handled the millions of shares that railroad stockholders bought and sold.

▶**3.** Why did railroads become corporations?

Carnegie Steel

The railroads and other growing industries needed iron and steel. Andrew Carnegie was among those who decided to meet that need.

Carnegie was born in Scotland. He came to the United States with his parents in 1848,

Andrew Carnegie's steel mills helped the United States become a leading industrial nation.

when he was just 13 years old. Because his family was poor, Carnegie promptly went to work. First, he was a bobbin boy at a textile mill in Pennsylvania, and then a messenger at a Pittsburgh telegraph office. At the age of 17, he took a job with the Pennsylvania Railroad. He was bright and able, a good speaker and writer, and learned a great deal during his years with the railroad. He used that knowledge when he went into business for himself, producing iron and then steel.

Steel is much stronger than iron. It lasts 20 times as long. Steel had been very expensive before 1857 when an Englishman, Henry Bessemer, discovered a cheap way to make it. The **Bessemer process** involved shooting a blast of cold air through hot, melted iron. This process made the impurities

that weakened the iron burn away, and the iron became steel.

In 1872, Carnegie began building a huge steel plant near Pittsburgh. By cutting costs, he was able to lower the price of his steel. As a result, sales rose and profits grew. "Watch the costs," he always said, "and the profits will take care of themselves."

Carnegie plowed profits back into the company. He bought the mines that produced iron ore and the ships and railroad lines that carried the ore to his furnaces. He also built new plants and bought up those of his rivals.

Carnegie refused to sell stock to the public. Carnegie Steel remained a privately owned company. As a result, all the profits went to a handful of people, especially to Carnegie himself. In 1900, his profits amounted to nearly $25 million! In 1901, Carnegie sold his steel company, and it became part of the United States Steel Corporation. United States Steel was the nation's first billion-dollar corporation.

▶**4.** What were some of Carnegie's business methods?

Inventions Help Business

Growing businesses such as the railroads and Carnegie Steel needed information from far-away places as quickly as possible. They had to know where supplies for their industry were available and at what price. They had to know where their products were wanted and where too many of them were already on hand. Several inventions made that sort of quick communication possible.

Samuel F. B. Morse invented the telegraph in the 1830's. It sent messages through electric wires over great distances. The messages were in the form of signals that were changed into ordinary language according to a system known as Morse code. By 1861, telegraph lines were stretched all across the United States connecting the West with the East.

Cyrus W. Field wanted to go even one step further — to connect the United States to countries in Europe by telegraph. He succeeded in 1866. Later, he also laid cables to Asia and Australia so that telegraph messages could be sent to distant parts of the world.

▶5. How did Samuel Morse and Cyrus Field improve communication?

The Telephone   The next major advance in communication was Alexander Graham Bell's telephone. As a teacher of deaf people, Bell became interested in acoustics, the science of sound. On March 10, 1876, his experiments paid off. On that day, Bell sent an understandable message over telephone wires. In time, he improved the telephone and then offered to sell it to the Western Union Telegraph Company for $100,000. Western Union was not interested in Bell's "electrical toy," so Bell formed his own company. Then in 1885, its directors reorganized that company into the American Telephone and Telegraph Company.

▶6. Who invented the telephone?

Edison and the Business of Inventions   Like American Telephone and Telegraph, many companies were formed because of an invention. One man, however, made inventing a business in itself. Thomas Alva Edison started out as a telegraph operator. Soon he was finding ways to improve the telegraph, for which he was well rewarded by the telegraph company.

Then, in 1876, Edison opened an "invention factory" at Menlo Park, New Jersey. Inventions, Edison said, happened because people were trying to figure out how to do something. The inventions he was after were those that had business possibilities. Edison's inventions

In 1892, Bell made the first long-distance telephone call between New York and Chicago.

Because of his many inventions, Thomas Alva Edison was called the Wizard of Menlo Park.

475

include the phonograph, the electric storage battery, an electric locomotive, and a motion-picture projector. His most important invention, though, was the electric light bulb.

Electric arc lights were already used to light streets in Paris when Edison began his work. Unfortunately, the arc lights could not be dimmed and were not safe for use indoors. Factories and homes were still lit by kerosene or gas lamps. They were dangerous, and they smelled bad.

Edison decided to make light by passing electricity through a wire inside an airless glass container. The wire would glow but not burn because fire needs air. He worked at his project for two years, trying one kind of wire after another. Finally, in 1879, he got a bulb to burn for 40 hours. Then he worked on other parts of an electric lighting system. On New Year's Eve, 1879, Edison amazed visitors to Menlo Park by lighting it with 40 "incandescent bulbs," as he called them, all of which could be turned off and on at the flick of a switch.

▶**7.** What were some of Edison's inventions?

Businesses Compete

In one industry after another, companies used new methods to produce more products at a lower cost. Unfortunately, many of those companies were soon producing more of almost every product than Americans could buy. Even the railroads were overbuilt. As many as 10 different railroad lines ran between some cities. There just was not enough business for them all.

Some companies began to compete fiercely for customers. In doing so, each company hoped to force its rivals out of business. Companies might, for example, sell their goods or services for even less than it cost to produce them. In that way, companies

hoped to take away their rivals' customers, even at the risk of going bankrupt.

Some companies made special deals with the railroads that gave them advantages over rivals. The railroad companies often offered special rates to companies that shipped large amounts of goods with them. They also gave **rebates** to favored customers; that is, they refunded part of the shipping costs.

As prices dropped steadily between the 1870's and late 1890's, it was hard for all but the strongest companies to make ends meet. In fact, for every man like Carnegie who became a millionaire, hundreds of others went bankrupt.

▶**8.** Why did businesses compete so fiercely?

Pools People caught in fierce competition tried as hard as they could to end destructive practices and waste. For example, the railroad companies, the first to face cutthroat competition, began to make agreements with one another over the rates they would charge. Soon some railroad companies joined together in more formal groups known as **pools.** The companies in a pool divided business among themselves rather than fighting for customers. Members of the pool decided which railroad would serve which customers and how much pool members would charge.

Pools, however, only worked in good times. When business was bad, railroad companies ended up cutting rates to steal customers from one another.

▶**9.** How did business pools operate?

Rockefeller and the Holding Company John D. Rockefeller and the Standard Oil Company came up with a new way to reduce competition. Rockefeller was a successful dealer in grains and meat in Cleveland, Ohio. When oil was discovered in western Pennsylvania, only about 100 miles away, he went into the oil business. By 1863, Rockefeller owned a refinery which removed the impurities from crude oil so it could be burned as kerosene in lamps.

In 1870, Rockefeller's company was incorporated, or became a corporation. It was known as the Standard Oil Company of Ohio. Like Carnegie, Rockefeller watched his costs very carefully. He also found uses for the by-products of the refining process, which reduced waste and made money.

Rockefeller was a ruthless competitor. He did everything he could to gain an advantage over other refiners. He convinced the railroads to give rebates to his company. He made barrels to carry his oil and bought forests to make sure he had enough wood. He made the chemicals used in refining oil. He bought ships and railroads to carry it. Then Standard Oil began building a pipeline to carry oil to its customers.

Rockefeller hated such cutthroat competition. He wanted to bring companies together in a way that could avoid the costs and strain of competition. In 1882, a lawyer for Standard Oil found a way to do that. He reorganized that company as a **trust.** To form the trust, the shareholders of 40 different oil companies turned in their stock and received in return shares in the new Standard Oil Trust. All the companies, therefore, came under the control of a single board of trustees.

Ten years later, the Standard Oil Company gave up the trust agreement and became a **holding company** under the laws of New Jersey. The new company, Standard Oil of New Jersey, could hold stock in other companies even if they were not in New Jersey. The difference between a trust and a holding company was not great. Both brought different companies together in legal arrangements. Both ended competition between member companies.

John D. Rockefeller, Jr., snips off competing rosebuds to perfect his company's flower.

After the early 1880's, people generally used the term trust very loosely. Often they called all big businesses trusts. The word *trust* came to mean the same thing as **monopoly.** A monopoly is a company so big that it controls an entire industry. Those who do business with a monopoly have to do it on the monopoly's terms, whether they like it or not.
▶**10.** In what ways is a holding company similar to a trust?

Government Regulates Business

While business leaders were happy to see less competition, their customers were not as pleased. Many Americans felt that big business was abusing its power. They called for government regulation of business. Railroads were their first target.

Reformers said that railroad companies should not help big business at the expense of small business by offering special rates and privileges. They also protested the fact that rates were lower for goods shipped from a large city than for those shipped from a small town where there was less railroad competition. Farmers especially complained about such uneven rates.

▶11. What abuses by railroads did some people wish to change?

The Interstate Commerce Act Several states in the West passed laws that regulated the way railroad companies set rates. Then, in 1886, the Supreme Court ruled that only Congress could regulate **interstate commerce,** or the flow of goods between the states.

In 1887, Congress passed the **Interstate Commerce Act.** It said that railroad companies had to publish their rates. It also said that railroad companies could not give one shipper advantages denied to another and, in general, had to set "reasonable and just" rates. The act also outlawed pools designed to keep rates high. The law was to be enforced by an **Interstate Commerce Commission.** Unfortunately, this commission had to sue in the courts to get its decisions enforced. The courts almost always decided in favor of the railroad companies.

▶12. What was the Interstate Commerce Act?

The Sherman Antitrust Act As public resentment of monopolies increased, Congress passed the **Sherman Antitrust Act** in 1890. It made illegal any sort of combination of businesses that resulted in the "restraint of trade or commerce among the several States, or with foreign nations." It also outlawed efforts to monopolize trade. Similar laws were passed by the states. That explains why Standard Oil changed from a trust to a holding company. The company's lawyers hoped to get around the new laws.

Soon, however, a decision of the Supreme Court robbed the Sherman Antitrust Act of

its power to hurt big businesses. In the case of *United States* v. *E.C. Knight* (1895), the Court said that manufacturing was different from trade. As a result, one of the biggest manufacturing monopolies in the country, the American Sugar Refining Company, was not affected by the Sherman Antitrust Act.

After the Knight decision, smaller corporations merged at a rapid rate. They formed large trusts modeled after Standard Oil. The mergers continued right on into the early 1900's. They were often arranged by investment bankers, people who were experts on organizing companies and raising money from investors.

The greatest of the investment bankers was J. Pierpont Morgan, who wanted desperately to end the "waste" of competition. Morgan was one of the most powerful people in the United States from the 1880's until his death in 1913.

▶13. What made the Sherman Antitrust Act ineffective against big business?

Reviewing Section I

Identify standardize, corporations, Bessemer process, Cyrus Field, rebates, pools, John D. Rockefeller, trust, holding company, monopoly, interstate commerce, Interstate Commerce Act, Interstate Commerce Commission, Sherman Antitrust Act, J. Pierpont Morgan

Questions to Answer
1. What allowed the United States to become a great industrial nation?
2. In what ways did large companies try to avoid fierce competition?

A Question to Think About Why was the development of the railroads essential to the growth of industry in the United States?

II. The World of Work

Before the Civil War, the goal of most American workers was to own a farm or business of their own. Industrialization and the growth of big business made that goal more difficult to attain.

The growth of industry and big business changed the kind of work people did and the way workers lived. Those changes affected **white collar workers,** people who worked in offices or as sales persons. In the past such people often worked in close contact with a business owner. Now they more often worked within a **bureaucracy,** the complex network of people necessary to run a large corporation. The head of such a business could not know all the employees on a personal basis.

The growth of industry also caused great changes in the lives of **blue collar workers.** Those were people who worked with their hands, often in factories.

The Early Unions

The jobs of most factory workers required little skill. They worked at machines doing one small task over and over each day. There was not much satisfaction in such work.

The workday was long. In 1890, the average worker in a manufacturing plant worked ten hours per day, six days per week. In some industries, the hours were even longer. People in steel mills and breweries generally worked 12 hours per day, 7 days per week.

Wages, at least, were rising. The average worker in manufacturing earned $300 yearly in 1860 and $425 in 1890. Prices fell during those years, so **real wages**—the amount of goods and services people could buy with their income—went up even more.

However, few workers enjoyed any job security. They could easily be replaced. There were more people eager to work than there were jobs. Also, the increased use of machinery made the work itself more dangerous. The number of on-job accidents increased sharply. Many workers were killed. Others lost arms or legs. Businesses were not required to follow any safety rules. Disabled workers lost their jobs. Companies were not required to help them support themselves and their families.

▶**1.** What made life difficult for factory workers in the 1890's?

Unionization To company officials, employees were part of the cost of doing business. If the company wanted to hold out against its competitors it had to keep expenses down.

The new factory machines were often very dangerous to work with. Accidents were common.

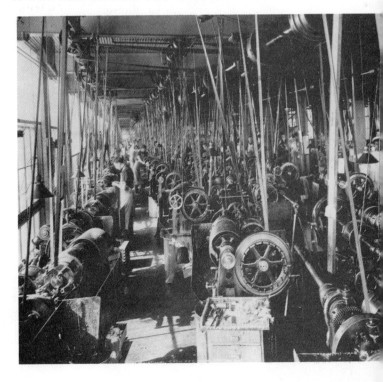

So companies tried to get employees to work very quickly for low wages.

Workers realized that they could hold out against demands to work long hours in unsafe conditions only if they all spoke with one voice. So some employees began to form **unions.** A union is an organization of workers who bargain with employers as a group.

Unions did not make a great deal of progress in the late nineteenth century for a number of reasons. Workers were divided among themselves by race and national origin. Workers born in the United States did not, for example, trust or understand workers from Poland or Russia. Another reason for the slow growth of unions was that the companies were extremely powerful and did all they could to crush the emerging unions.

▶**2.** What is a union?

Frank Farrell (standing left) introduces Terence Powderly at a union meeting in 1886.

The Knights of Labor One of the first large unions was the **Knights of Labor,** founded in 1869. It was made up of many smaller unions. The Knights tried to bring together all workers or "producers," including blacks, immigrants, and women into one major union. The Knights understood that the workers had to be organized to defend themselves against big businesses. Under the elegant Terence Powderly, who became Grand Master of the Knights in 1879, the union grew until it had more than 700,000 members in early 1886.

The Knights supported cooperation between employers and workers. They were against **strikes.** During a strike, workers refuse to work in an effort to force employers to give in to their employees' demands. Most leaders of the Knights dreamed of a day when employees would own the mines and factories where they worked. Those leaders were not very interested in helping workers fight for better hours and wages.

Local groups of the Knights did call some strikes and win some victories over the railroad companies. However, when some other union strikes failed, Powderly once again condemned strikes and labor violence. Some local unions then left the Knights, and its membership began to decrease.

▶**3.** What was the Knights of Labor?

The Haymarket Riot The **Haymarket riot** in Chicago also contributed to the Knights' decline. It occurred on May 4, 1886, when a great rally of working people met at Haymarket Square near downtown Chicago. The meeting was held to protest police actions during a strike at the McCormick reaper factory. As a line of police moved toward the Haymarket meeting, a bomb went off. It killed 7 police officers and wounded 67 others. Many union members were arrested. Eight were convicted of murder, though there was little evidence against them.

Several strikes occurred in other parts of the country at nearly the same time as the riot. Along with the Haymarket riot, such strikes turned many Americans against the unions. It seemed to such people that labor was causing terrible violence and disorder. Many manufacturers started associations to help each other fight off the demands of their workers. In many cities, strong militia companies were formed to keep the peace. Huge fortlike armories were built to store guns and give the militias places to drill.

▶**4.** Why did many Americans turn against unions?

The American Federation of Labor

As the Knights of Labor declined, another union managed to survive and grow. The **American Federation of Labor** (AFL) was founded in 1886. It was a loose alliance of national **craft unions,** unions that were open only to skilled workers such as machinists or plumbers. Most immigrants were not skilled workers, so AFL members were mostly native-born white American men. The AFL did not welcome female members. Unlike the Knights of Labor, the AFL worked for concrete gains such as shorter hours and higher pay.

The AFL's powerful leader, Samuel Gompers of the Cigar Makers' International Union, defended the workers' right to strike. In no other way, he said, could workers force employers to decrease hours and raise wages. Only when the unions became as strong as large businesses could the differences between the two be settled by reason rather than by force. Until then, strikes were necessary.

▶**5.** What were three differences between the AFL and the Knights of Labor?

Samuel Gompers was one of the organizers of the American Federation of Labor.

Strikes and Strikebreakers

In 1892, the AFL became involved in one of the nation's most famous strikes. An AFL union, the Amalgamated Association of Iron and Steelworkers, struck the Carnegie Steel Company's plant in Homestead, Pennsylvania, because the company lowered wages.

The head of the plant, Henry C. Frick, hired 300 private detectives from the Pinkerton detective agency to help him break the strike and the union. When the armed detectives arrived, angry workers attacked them. Sixteen detectives and workers died before the Pinkertons gave up. The strike, however, continued for another five months. Then the governor of Pennsylvania sent in the National Guard. The soldiers helped Frick bring in **strikebreakers,** people who would take the strikers'

The 15th U.S. Infantry was called in to protect Pullman trains from the striking workers.

jobs. The strike failed, and union membership dropped.

Federal troops were used again to end the famous **Pullman strike** two years later. The Pullman Company built sleeping cars for railroads. The strike occurred in the factory town that George Pullman built south of Chicago. Pullman's workers rented houses from the company and bought their food at company stores. When Pullman cut wages without cutting rents, his employees were unable to make ends meet. As a result, the desperate members of the American Railway Union decided to go on strike. That union was led by Eugene V. Debs, who was trying to organize workers throughout the railroad industry.

The strike won the support of union members throughout the nation. They showed their support by refusing to work on trains carrying Pullman cars. When the railroads tried to fire those workers, the strike spread. Soon

almost every railroad worker west of Chicago was on strike.

Then railroad executives got a court order against the strikers for "obstructing the railways and holding up the mails." (The mail traveled by train.) Soon the United States Army arrived to protect the mails. With the army's help, the owners soon broke the strike. Debs was thrown in jail for defying the court order.

As long as the government was so strongly on the employers' side, there was not much hope for the unions. That may be why only about 1 million out of 27.6 million American workers were union members in 1900. Employers found it all too easy to replace striking workers with hungry immigrants. That, of course, caused resentment, which divided the workers all the more. While workers remained divided, they remained weak. In fact, they were far weaker than they had been in the old days, when workers were skilled artisans and businesses were small.

▶**6.** How did the Homestead and Pullman strikes end?

Reviewing Section II

Identify white collar workers, bureaucracy, blue collar workers, real wages, unions, Knights of Labor, strikes, Haymarket riot, American Federation of Labor, craft unions, Samuel Gompers, strikebreakers, Pullman strike

Questions to Answer
1. What were some of the obstacles to the growth of unions?
2. How was the AFL different from the Knights of Labor?

A Question to Think About How effective were the unions formed between 1869 and 1886?

III. City Life

The growth of industry in the late 1800's went hand in hand with the growth of cities. Before the Civil War, factories were generally built in towns near swift rivers or waterfalls which were used to provide power to run the factories' machines. But in the late nineteenth century, factories used steam power. That meant factories could be built almost anywhere. Most were built near the growing centers of transportation.

By 1909, Chicago had become a center of trade and transportation. The city's streets were often crowded with street cars, trucks, and people.

Transportation and Industrial Centers

In the late 1800's, the older cities of the East with good water transportation and railroad lines surged in population. In 1890, over 1.5 million people lived in New York City.

In the West, newer cities sprouted up where water and rail routes met. Chicago, for example, was located on the southern shore of Lake Michigan, which was part of that great inland water system, the Great Lakes. Railroad lines from the East also connected with those from the West in Chicago. The city was almost entirely destroyed by fire in 1871, but it had about 500,000 people by 1880. Ten years later, its population had doubled, and it was the second-largest city in the United States. During the same 10 years, the twin cities of Minneapolis and St. Paul tripled in size. They were on the Mississippi River and also served as a center for the railroads that went to the Northwest.

Such cities grew rapidly because transportation centers were becoming industrial centers. Chicago became a meat-packing center. Minneapolis had flour mills. Milwaukee held many breweries, and Cleveland had oil refineries.

As cities grew, the United States became an urban nation. The one in six Americans who lived in a city after the Civil War had become one in three by 1900. A majority of all Americans made their homes in cities just 20 years later.

Most of the country's new city people were born on farms. Large parts of the rural countryside, especially in New York State and New England, declined in population as the cities grew. Most immigrants also were new to city life. They, too, had been farmers in their native lands. For such people, life in the city was very different from anything they knew. Even those born in the city often found urban life new and bewildering because the cities themselves were changing rapidly in the late nineteenth century.

▶**1.** Where did cities grow in the West?

The Lure of the City

As thousands of people rushed to the cities looking for work, new housing as well as new factories and offices had to be built. Land increased in value. Builders put up apartment buildings and other multifamily dwellings so that more people could live on a piece of land. Also, skyscrapers, buildings that could be built very high because they had skeletons of steel, began to appear.

Rapid growth brought many problems. Among those problems was sewage. At first, sewers ran through the streets in open gutters that endangered the public health. So new sewage systems were built.

The cities' dirt streets became deeply rutted from carriage wheels, which threw up dust or mud depending on the weather. So the roads were paved. At first, that was done with wood blocks or bricks or cobblestones. Then roads were covered with macadam, a surface of crushed stone, and later, with a new, cheaper material called asphalt. In 1887, Richmond, Virginia, became the nation's first city to use electric streetcars. Soon Boston began building the country's first subway system. New transportation systems allowed middle-class and wealthy people to work in the city but live in the suburbs where they could have houses with lawns. Meanwhile, gas and electric lights brightened city nights.

▶**2.** How did the cities solve the problem of sewage and poor roads?

City Attractions Skyscrapers, paved streets, electric lights, streetcars, and subways did more than create jobs. They made the cities exciting places to be. Shops selling foods from many countries — foods far more varied than those available on American farms — added to the appeal. The cities also had theaters, orchestras, and museums.

Then there were the great new downtown **department stores**. In those stores, customers found under one roof goods that could previously be found only in many separate shops. The department store seemed to be a wonderland where the ready-made products of American industry were laid out in ways that captured the buyer's eyes.

Newspapers thrived in the bustling cities. For only a penny, readers could buy one of the **yellow press** papers, named for the color of the cheap paper they used. Yellow press newspapers, such as the *New York World* or the *New York Journal*, featured sensational stories to catch readers' attention.

▶**3.** What were some city attractions?

The Neighborhoods Cities, like department stores, were made up of many separate parts, or neighborhoods. In the late nineteenth century, urban neighborhoods were very different from one another. Some neighborhoods were for the rich—Nob Hill in San Francisco, for example, or Chicago's Gold Coast along Lake Shore Drive. There, millionaires built expensive palaces with towers, libraries, and even art galleries. Other neighborhoods, sometimes only a few blocks away, were for the poor. There, several families lived in airless, dirty tenement houses. In such neighborhoods, crime and sickness flourished.

▶**4.** How did city neighborhoods differ?

The New Immigrants

Many immigrants clustered together in city neighborhoods. Such people were often unable to speak English and lacked the skills

City dwellers flocked to department stores where they could find a wide variety of goods.

This group of women waits for a bank to open in one of Chicago's Greek neighborhoods.

that could get them good jobs. As a result, they went to work in the nation's factories. They lived together where they could speak the languages they knew, buy familiar foods, and keep up the religious and social customs of their homelands. The cities offered immigrants the comfort of stores and churches where their own language was spoken.

▶**5.** Why did many immigrants stay in the cities?

New Nativism Some Americans were unhappy about the newcomers. They complained that the immigrants of the 1890's were different from those of earlier times. The majority of those earlier immigrants had come from Northern and Western Europe. Many of them had been educated and had money. Others were skilled in a trade. Except for the Irish, most were Protestant. Many earlier immigrants also spoke English.

After 1890, a large percent of the new immigrants were people from Southern or Eastern Europe. In the 1890's, Italians, Russians, Poles, and Turks flocked to the United States. Many of them had darker skin and hair than did the earlier immigrants. They were also different in language and customs from the peoples of Northern and Western Europe. Often the new immigrants were Catholics or Jews.

Some native-born Americans feared that the new immigrants would not **assimilate,** or become like Americans of earlier times. But as the children of immigrant families went to school, learned English, and picked up new customs, many of them became much like Americans whose families had been in the country for generations. Assimilation sometimes caused great pain as immigrant parents saw their children growing apart from them and their ways.

★★ The United States and the World ★★★★★★★★★★★★★★★★
The New Arrivals

During the late 1880's, thousands of people from Southern and Eastern Europe came to the United States. Most left their homelands because they could not earn a living and thought they could find greater opportunities in the United States. Some left to avoid Europe's constant wars. Others, such as Jews from Russia, left because of religious persecution.

Under Czar, or Emperor, Alexander II there was no tolerance for minority groups in Russia. The government wanted all peoples to speak Russian, worship in the Russian Orthodox Church, and give up their own customs in an attempt to become more Russian.

Since Jews would not give up their religion, the Russian government sometimes encouraged citizens to attack Jewish settlements. Mobs rode on horses through the villages killing families and burning homes and synagogues. Sometimes whole villages were destroyed during the raids. Ashes were all that were left behind of what were once close-knit communities. Many times the attacks occurred on holidays or during a joyous occasion such as a wedding.

Jews were not allowed to take part in the cultural life of Russia. They were not allowed to attend colleges or universities. Often jobs were not open to them. Many Jews, therefore, were eager to leave their homes to seek a new life and a better future in the United States. For those reasons, many Russian Jews were among the new arrivals.

The circle graph, like the line graph and the bar graph, is a way of illustrating statistical information. Circle graphs are especially useful when you want to compare percentages. The entire circle represents 100 percent, and smaller percentages are shown as portions of the circle graph.

Study the circle graphs below and answer the questions that follow.

1. (a) What information do the graphs show?
   (b) What years are covered by the graphs?
   (c) Where did you look to find the answers?
2. (a) Approximately what percent of foreign-born residents of the United States came from Eastern and Southern Europe in 1890?
   (b) Approximately what percent came to the United States in 1910?

3. The percentage of foreign-born residents of the United States from what area stayed about the same in 1890 and 1910?
4. Draw a circle graph showing the following information: in 1920, about 39 percent of foreign-born residents in the United States came from Northern Europe; 46 percent came from Eastern and Southern Europe; 13 percent came from other parts of the Americas; and 2 percent came from other parts of the world.
5. (a) You cannot make a generalization from the two graphs on this page and the graph you have drawn about changes in the number of immigrants coming to the United States from Eastern and Southern Europe between 1910 and 1920. Why not? (b) What generalization can you make from the information you have been given?

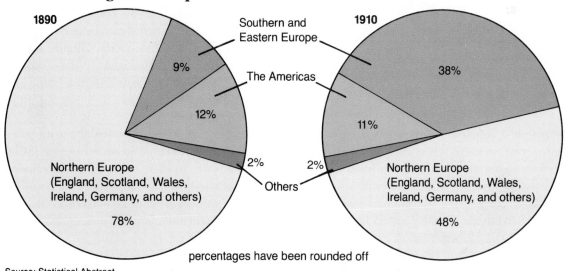

Foreign-Born Population of the U.S. in 1890 and 1910

percentages have been rounded off

Source: Statistical Abstract

Chinese immigrants owned many businesses in New York City's Chinatown.

Some native-born Americans wanted to reduce the number of new immigrants entering the United States. They formed nativist associations such as the Immigration Restriction League to pressure Congress to adopt laws limiting immigration.

▶**6.** Why were some Americans unhappy about the new immigrants?

Chinese Exclusion Americans opposed to immigration were not successful in their attempts to restrict immigration from Europe. They did, however, succeed in the case of the Chinese.

In 1880, there were about 75,000 Chinese workers in California. Most lived near one another in sections of cities called "Chinatowns." There they felt free to speak their own language and to carry on their traditions. However, the language and customs of the Chinese frightened some Americans. Other nativist Americans resented the Chinese because they worked for very low wages.

At the urging of the nativists, Congress passed the **Chinese Exclusion Act** in 1882. This act prohibited Chinese workers from entering the country.

▶**7.** What was the Chinese Exclusion Act?

Women's Changing Role

The growth of cities and industry changed the lives of women, especially those of white middle-class women. They had fewer children and, as a result of modern conveniences, had to do less housework than other women. For example, even medium-priced housing in cities had hot and cold running water. That in itself cut down the time necessary to do a family's laundry. Doing the family wash used to take a third of a woman's work time. By the 1890's, it could be done in a day.

At the time of the Civil War, most families ate home-baked bread. By 1890, nine out of ten city families ate store-bought bread. That meant a woman had to spend less time in the kitchen. Other time-saving conveniences were on their way. Electricity, Thomas Edison predicted, would "revolutionize the woman's world." It would free her from the home and let her devote her energies to "broader, more constructive fields."

What did women do with the time they saved from household labor? For one thing, they shopped. In their new role as **consumers,** as those who bought things for their families, women gained a new importance. Advertisements were increasingly designed to appeal to them.

▶**8.** Why did middle-class women have more leisure time in the 1890's?

During the late 1880's, many colleges for women were started. This photograph shows a chemistry class at Smith College in Massachusetts in 1880.

Club Women and Suffragists Many married middle-class women also joined clubs devoted to making the world a better place. The Woman's Christian Temperance Union (WCTU), which fought against drinking and other social problems, was founded in 1873. By 1890, it had about 160,000 members. Women also supported many social and charitable programs, such as the Young Women's Christian Association (YWCA), founded at Boston in 1866.

Soon women again demanded the vote. The National American Woman Suffrage Association worked hard to win for women the right to vote. Female workers for suffrage were called **suffragists.** Their first victory came in 1890 when women were given full voting rights in Wyoming. A handful of other western states followed Wyoming's lead, including Colorado (1893), Utah (1896), and Idaho (1896).

▶**9.** Why was the National American Woman Suffrage Association formed?

Working Women Although white, middle-class, married women were active in many social groups, they did not work for wages. That was not considered respectable. It was, however, considered fine for unmarried women to work and the jobs open to single women increased in the late nineteenth century. Poorer women worked in factories or as servants. Middle-class white women refused to do such work. They did, however, take jobs in department stores. They also became school teachers. Some learned to operate the typewriter, invented by Christopher L. Sholes in 1867. Women became telephone operators too.

Most of the jobs women got, however, offered little room for advancement. Teachers were women, but principals were men. Although women worked as department store clerks, cashiers, typists, and telephone operators, their bosses usually were men. Still, many women thought that a dead-end job was better than no job at all. And women

Jane Addams, social reformer and peace worker, was born in 1860 in a small town in north central Illinois. She adored her father, John Addams— a successful miller, banker, and community leader. She barely knew her mother, Sarah Addams, who died when Jane was two.

At 17, Jane left home for Rockford Seminary in Rockford, Illinois. She had hoped to attend Smith College in Massachusetts, but her father preferred a school closer to home. Jane admired Rockford's high standards and simple way of life. In a short time, students and teachers alike grew to admire Jane's spirit and intelligence.

In 1882, Jane received her degree from Rockford. She then enrolled in the Woman's Medical College of Pennsylvania. Six months later she became ill from a problem related to a curvature of the spine. She was forced to leave school and have an operation.

The next year was a difficult one for Jane. Her illness and the recent death of her father depressed her greatly. Her family encouraged her to lift her spirits by traveling. Following their advice, Jane left for Europe in 1883.

Jane's first trip to Europe lasted two years. While there, she visited the poor section of London's East End. The visit impressed upon her the need to help the poor.

Jane returned to Europe in 1887. Once again she spent time with the poor. This time she and a close friend — Ellen Starr—visited London's Toynbee Hall, a neighborhood center, or settlement house, where college students worked with the needy. The notion of helping the poor in this way appealed to the two young women. They decided to return to the United States and start a settlement house of their own.

By September 1889, Addams and Starr had found and rented Hull House, an old mansion in one of Chicago's poorest sections. Hull House quickly became a gathering place for neighborhood people. It offered classes, housed social clubs, and provided child care. Children who had previously roamed the streets or stayed locked inside while their parents worked now had a safe place to go.

In the beginning, Jane Addams paid for Hull House out of her own pocket. Later, she was forced to turn to the public for support. By the late 1920's, contributions to Hull House amounted to over $100,000 per year. Much of this money came from wealthy Chicago women.

Jane's success did not stop with Hull House. Rather, she went on to take an active role in public affairs. Her efforts resulted in the first eight-hour law for working women, the first state child-labor law, and the first juvenile court.

Four years before her death at the age of 75, Jane Addams shared a Nobel Peace Prize. It was one of the many honors given this woman who had helped so many people.

working as typists or experienced salespeople earned wages that compared well with those of many men. In a nation that often measured people by how much they earned, women began to count.

New educational opportunities also opened for young middle-class women. Oberlin College in Ohio and other colleges in the West were already admitting female students at the time of the Civil War. Then several colleges just for women were begun, including Vassar (1865), Smith (1871), Radcliffe (1879), and Bryn Mawr (1885).

Many female college graduates went on to work in the new **settlement houses,** such as Hull House in Chicago or Henry Street Settlement in New York. Settlement houses were centers for immigrants. There, the women helped set up libraries and nurseries, or they taught classes to immigrants (especially women). Work in the settlement houses concerned children and families and so did not seem to depart much from the traditional "women's sphere" in the home.

▶**10.** What jobs were opened to middle-class single women in the 1890's?

Education

Many children, especially the children of immigrants and poor people, held full-time jobs in the 1890's and early 1900's. Their chances of rising in life were limited. Real opportunity was saved for those who went to school.

In the late nineteenth century, the public school system grew. More and more states required that all children attend school for longer periods of time. More students attended high school than ever before. Classes were also begun for kindergarteners and for adults.

Higher education also changed. Before the Civil War, colleges taught the liberal arts, such as the classics and literature. Suddenly, new institutions of higher learning sprang up to teach subjects like business, science, and engineering.

The Morrill Act of 1862 gave states land to help them set up agricultural and mechanical schools. Many other new schools were built with contributions from business leaders. Leland Stanford, one of the builders of the Central Pacific Railroad, helped build Stanford University in California. Stanford University was long known as a school for mining engineers. Similarly, George Eastman, inventor of the Kodak camera and founder of the Eastman Kodak Company, donated millions to help build the Massachusetts Institute of Technology. The founding of such schools also changed American life. There were fewer opportunities for untrained amateurs. Professional training was required for many positions. Education was becoming the American way to a better future.

▶**11.** How did education change in the late 1890's and early 1900's?

Reviewing Section III

Identify department stores, yellow press, assimilate, Chinese Exclusion Act, consumers, suffragists, settlement houses, Morrill Act of 1862

Questions to Answer

1. Why did some Americans form the Immigration Restriction League?

2. How did life change for the American middle-class during the 1890's and early 1900's?

A Question to Think About Why did some Americans feel threatened by immigrants in the 1890's and early 1900's?

IMPROVE YOUR READING
Mapping Ideas

In Chapter 11 you learned how to map ideas as a study aid. Here is a review of the steps in mapping ideas:

1. Identify the major topic you wish to map.
2. Write it in a circle in the middle of a sheet of paper.
3. Identify the sub-topics to be mapped.
4. Write the sub-topics on lines connected to the circle.
5. Identify the details related to the sub-topics.
6. Write the sub-topics on lines connected to the details.

Below is a partially completed map related to the section "City Life" on pages 483–491 from Chapter 22. Copy the map on a sheet of paper. Then write in the correct sub-topics and details to complete the map.

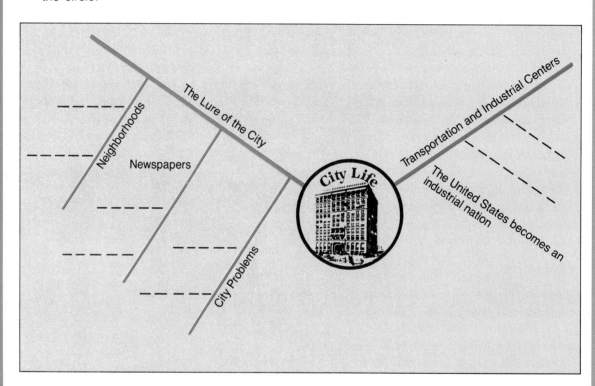

CHAPTER 22 REVIEW

Vocabulary Check
Write a short definition for each of the following words.

1. Corporations
2. Standardize
3. Rebates
4. White collar workers
5. Suffragists

Fact Check
On a separate sheet of paper, write the name or term that best completes each of the following sentences.

1. A corporation sells ____ of stock.
2. ____ became part of the United States Steel Corporation.
3. ____ made a profession of inventing.
4. ____ started Standard Oil Company.
5. Both trusts and ____ brought different companies together to end competition.
6. A ____ is a company so big that it controls an entire industry.
7. ____ is the flow of goods between states.
8. The amount of goods and services workers can buy with their wages are their ____.
9. Many of the new immigrants who arrived after 1890 came from the ____ and ____ parts of Europe.
10. Some female college graduates worked in ____, centers for immigrants.

Time Check
On a separate sheet of paper, put each of the following events in chronological order.

1. Congress passes the Sherman Antitrust Act.
2. Congress passes the Chinese Exclusion Act.
3. Police officers are killed and wounded at the Haymarket riot.
4. Steel workers go on strike at Homestead, Pennsylvania.
5. Congress passes the Interstate Commerce Act.

Skills Check
Look at the cartoon on page 477 and answer the following questions.

1. Who is the central figure in the cartoon?
2. What does the cartoonist think about that person?
3. How does the cartoonist think big business affects competition?
4. How does the cartoonist want people to respond to the drawing?
5. Write one sentence that states the message of the cartoon.

Think and Write
1. (a) What was needed for the United States to become an industrial nation? (b) How were those needs met?
2. How did work life change as a result of the growth of large corporations?
3. How did cities change after the Civil War?
4. (a) Who were the new immigrants of the 1890's? (b) Why did some Americans want to restrict their numbers?
5. How did industrialization lead to changes in womens' roles?

Chapter 23

Politics, Populists, and Imperialists: The 1890's

Fred Pansing's painting shows cruisers and battleships returning to New York City after their victory in the Spanish-American War.

The great changes that occurred in the American economy after the Civil War had important effects on American politics and government. For a time, the struggle between political parties seemed less interesting than the struggles between big corporations and their powerful leaders. But the issues people argued about—the tariff, for example, or American currency—were important. Generally those issues were decided in favor of wealthy business interests. Then, in the 1890's, people called Populists tried to make government act in ways that would give ordinary workers and farmers a greater share of the nation's wealth.

The growing economic power of the United States also changed its relations with the rest of the world. Trade and naval power became more important. Before the 1800's were over, the country had acquired territory in other parts of the world and sent its soldiers to fight wars far from the Americas. Suddenly, foreign affairs became an important part of American government.

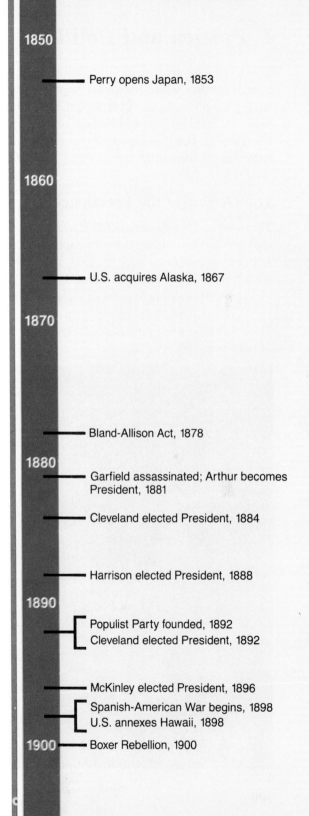

1850

Perry opens Japan, 1853

1860

U.S. acquires Alaska, 1867

1870

Bland-Allison Act, 1878

1880

Garfield assassinated; Arthur becomes President, 1881

Cleveland elected President, 1884

Harrison elected President, 1888

1890

Populist Party founded, 1892
Cleveland elected President, 1892

McKinley elected President, 1896

Spanish-American War begins, 1898
U.S. annexes Hawaii, 1898

1900 — Boxer Rebellion, 1900

I. Parties and Politics

The most powerful people of the late nineteenth century were outside the world of politics—people such as Andrew Carnegie and John D. Rockefeller. Compared to rich industrialists, the Presidents of the period did little worth remembering.

The Decline of the Presidency

There were many reasons for the decline of the presidency. After the impeachment of Andrew Johnson, power passed from the White House to Congress. From the 1870's to the 1890's were years of **laissez-faire**

These items are from the Cleveland-Harrison presidential campaign of 1888.

(les'ā fer'). *Laissez-faire* is a French phrase meaning "let people do as they wish." Americans who supported a *laissez-faire* approach thought government should interfere as little as possible in the nation's affairs. In fact, the national government did relatively little to affect the course of events in those years. When it did act, it supported those business interests that already had great power.

▶**1.** What does *laissez-faire* mean?

Presidential Elections

The two major political parties were evenly matched in the late 1800's. Election results were very close. The election of 1876 was, of course, so close that it had to be decided by the House of Representatives. Four years later, a Republican congressman from Ohio, James A. Garfield, defeated the Democratic candidate, General Winfield Scott Hancock, by only 7,018 popular votes.

The election of 1884 also was close. In that contest, the Democratic governor of New York, Grover Cleveland, defeated the Republican James G. Blaine of Maine by 62,683 votes. Cleveland carried the critical state of New York by a mere 1,149 votes.

In 1888, the wind shifted in the other direction, and Cleveland lost to the Republican, Benjamin Harrison of Indiana. Harrison's victory was short-lived. In 1892, Cleveland edged him out.

With elections so close, the presidency could pass back and forth between the Republicans and Democrats. Both parties were afraid to lose votes by taking strong stands on issues. As a result, it seemed to make little difference which party's candidate won the election.

That is not to say that there were no important issues in the late 1880's. There were some, and occasionally, members of the Republican and Democratic parties did take different stands on them.

▶ **2.** Why did the two major political parties seem so much alike in the late 1800's?

The Tariff The tariff was an important issue in late nineteenth-century politics. The United States first put a protective tariff on some foreign goods after the War of 1812. The tariff made those imported goods more expensive for American buyers and therefore helped the nation's growing industries. By the late nineteenth century, however, many American industries could hold their own against foreign competition. Still they were not ready to give up protective tariffs because tariffs allowed American makers to charge more for their products.

The tariff, however, made some people angry. Farmers had to pay higher prices for machinery and other manufactured goods. Yet, they had to sell their cotton, wheat, and corn in a world market that offered little or no tariff protection. Farmers wanted tariffs on manufactured goods to be lowered or ended altogether.

The tariff was an issue on which the major parties disagreed somewhat. Most Republicans supported high tariffs, while many Democrats wanted lower tariffs. In 1887, the Democratic President Cleveland made a strong plea for tariff reform. However, he could not get the Republican Senate to pass a tariff reform bill.

From 1889 to 1891, the Republicans controlled both houses of Congress, and Republican Harrison was in the White House. The Republicans used their power to pass the McKinley Tariff of 1890, named after Representative William McKinley of Ohio. The new law raised the average duty on imported goods to almost 50 percent of their value.

In the election of 1892, the Democrats promised to lower the tariff, and they did try. However, by the time their reform tariff was passed by Congress, the **protectionists** who favored high tariffs had tacked on some 600 amendments. In the end, the Wilson-Gorman Tariff of 1894 actually raised many tariffs, though it lowered the average rate.

Three years later, Congress passed the Dingley Tariff of 1897, which raised tariffs to a new high. So protectionism, that let business keep its tariffs and the profits they brought, won out. Even the Democrats had fought the tariff only half-heartedly.

▶ **3.** What groups favored a high protective tariff on manufactured goods? A low tariff?

Currency Another issue that aroused much debate concerned money. During the Civil War, the United States had issued almost $500 million in paper money. Those bills were printed in green ink, so they were called **greenbacks.** Greenbacks could not be exchanged for silver or gold money. They were worth less than **hard money** of the same face value, that included both coins and paper money printed in yellow ink that could be exchanged for gold. After the war, the government began to take the greenbacks out of circulation.

Retiring the greenbacks caused some discontent. It increased the value of the money that stayed in circulation. Since money was worth more, prices dropped. As a result, debtors had to pay back loans with money worth more than the money they had borrowed. Farmers were especially hard hit. Many were in debt because they had borrowed money to buy farm machinery.

A new political party, the National Greenback Party, adopted the cause of debtors and tried to keep greenbacks in circulation. The government, however, continued to retire the

Populists believed that prosperity would come with the free coinage of silver.

greenbacks until, by 1879, the remaining greenbacks were worth just as much as gold dollars. Then the greenback issue was dead. ▶**4.** Why did some people oppose the retiring of greenbacks?

Silver and the Gold Standard Debtors still wanted more money in circulation in the late 1870's. With the discovery of new mines in the West, more and more silver was available for minting into dollars and other coins. In 1873, however, Congress had voted to stop coining silver dollars. Within a few years, **inflationists,** those who wanted the value of money to drop so prices would rise, called for the "free and unlimited" coinage of silver.

The value of silver, they said, should be set at a ratio of 16:1. In other words, 16 ounces of silver should be worth as much as 1 ounce of gold.

The "free silver" people were so strong that Congress had to do something to please them. In 1878, it passed the **Bland-Allison Act,** which required the United States Treasury to buy between $2 and $4 million of silver each month and make it into coins. Meanwhile, because silver miners were having trouble selling the metal, the price of silver dropped. Therefore, miners too demanded the free coinage of silver. The political power of the free silver advocates increased when six new mining states joined the Union and sent representatives to Congress. Montana, Washington, and the two Dakotas entered the Union in 1889. Idaho and Wyoming became states in 1890.

In 1890, there were enough free silver advocates for Congress to pass the **Sherman Silver Purchase Act.** It forced the Treasury to buy 4.5 million ounces of silver each month—which was all the mines were producing—at the market price. Since silver was so plentiful, silver dollars were worth only 49 cents. So people exchanged their silver money for gold. Soon the treasury's supply of gold was running very low.

The new law frightened those people who wanted sound money. Among them was President Cleveland. He wanted the nation to stay on the **gold standard.** That meant he wanted gold to be the only metal used in deciding the value of American currency. In 1893, he persuaded Congress to repeal the Sherman Silver Purchase Act. His victory was expensive. It split the Democratic Party into "gold bugs" and "free silver" people, which hurt it in the election of 1896. The Republicans, on the other hand, generally supported the gold standard.

Debates over money were very emotional in the late nineteenth century. Both sides seemed to think that settling the money issue could solve all kinds of economic problems, which was not true. Probably, however, the inflationists were right in arguing that the United States needed a larger supply of money as its economy grew. They received that increased amount of money after 1898, when new supplies of gold became available. That permitted the minting of more gold—not silver. Only then did prices begin to rise.

▶**5.** Why did Cleveland oppose free silver?

Corruption Another issue that caused much talk was **corruption,** the use of government offices or government funds in ways that enriched individuals at the public's cost. There was a great deal of corruption in government and business in the late nineteenth century.

As cities grew, for example, city officials had to decide which company would run its streetcar lines or sell its people gas and electricity. Companies often bribed officials in exchange for such contracts. Another way companies rewarded corrupt officials was with "kickbacks," payments taken out of the huge profits companies received for their services.

New York City fell under the control of a group of corrupt politicians known as the **Tweed Ring,** after their leader "Boss" William Marcy Tweed. The Tweed Ring did all sorts of dishonest things. For instance, the taxpayers of New York City paid $11 million to build a courthouse that actually cost $3 million. The extra $8 million went into the pockets of Tweed and his followers. Before it was exposed in 1871, the Tweed Ring had stolen as much as $200 million from the public treasury.

Corruption occurred in cities partly because their governments were controlled by tight groups of politicians called **machines.** Power

Thomas Nast's cartoon "Who Stole the People's Money" appeared in Harpers Weekly *in 1871. It shows Boss Tweed (left) and members of the Tweed Ring.*

in a machine went from a boss such as Tweed at the top down through several levels of command, ending in the various wards, or neighborhoods.

The ward politicians worked hard at getting votes. They made sure they knew the people in their ward. The politicians helped immigrants settle into the city. Sometimes politicians gave baskets of food to needy families, or paid for funerals. Above all, the political machines were oiled by jobs. Without jobs to reward faithful supporters, the whole system would fail.

Of course, the machine was rewarded by votes. With the support of the cities' voters, machine politicians took control of urban government and sent people on to state and national offices too.

▶ **6.** How did political machines operate?

The Civil Service System   Corruption awoke the zeal of reformers. Such people were especially upset by the system of **patronage** that had become so well established in American politics. Patronage, the spoils system of Andrew Jackson's day, is the practice of giving out government jobs in return for political support.

The handing out of jobs to political supporters was well established long before the Civil War. On the national level, though, the patronage system caused new problems when the federal government began to grow. In 1830, there were 24,000 federal employees. By 1891, there were 166,000.

Whenever a new President came into office, much time was wasted deciding which government employees would be fired and who would take their places. Therefore, practical considerations supported the cause of reform.

A tragedy also supported reform. On July 2, 1881, President Garfield was shot by a disappointed office-seeker. Garfield died on September 19. Vice President Chester Arthur then became President. Arthur, who had been a machine politician himself, now joined those working for reform.

Arthur and the other reformers wanted a civil service system. That meant certain government jobs would be given only to people who did well on a written examination. Those qualified people would then keep their jobs even when a different political party gained control of the government.

In 1883, Congress passed the **Pendleton Act.** It set up a **Civil Service Commission** made up of three people, selected from both political parties. The commission was to conduct examinations to test people's knowledge and assign government jobs to those who did best on the tests. At first, only about 10 percent of all government jobs were civil service jobs. However, by 1900, the total had jumped to 40 percent.

▶ **7.** What were the major provisions of the Pendleton Act?

Reviewing Section I

Identify laissez-faire, James A. Garfield, Grover Cleveland, Benjamin Harrison, protectionists, greenbacks, hard money, inflationists, Bland-Allison Act, Sherman Silver Purchase Act, gold standard, corruption, Tweed Ring, William Marcy Tweed, machines, patronage, Chester Arthur, Pendleton Act, Civil Service Commission

Questions to Answer

1. What was the conflict over the tariff?
2. What was the conflict over currency?

A Question to Think About   How likely were people to support both tariff reform and the free coinage of silver?

II. The Populist Revolt

Although there was little difference in the 1880's between the Democrats and Republicans, there was one political party that took a distinctive stand on the issues. That party grew out of the farmers' discontent.

Farmers had much to complain about. The price of the crops they grew dropped steadily in the last decades of the nineteenth century. By 1889, corn was selling for so little that Kansas farmers were burning it for fuel. Southern farmers were actually selling cotton for less than it cost to grow it in the 1890's.

Crop prices fell in part because farmers were growing so much more than in earlier years. Government money policies also helped make the price of farm products fall. Meanwhile, farmers had to pay high prices for manufactured goods because of the tariff. The railroads added to the farmers' distress by charging what the farmers called unfair rates. Many farmers understood that there was only one way to fight these and other problems. They would have to organize.

The Grange and the Farmers' Alliance

Many farmers joined the Patrons of Husbandry, better known as the **Grange.** It was founded in 1867 by Oliver Hudson Kelley, a Minnesota farmer. At first, the local Grange was largely a social club for farm families.

Soon the Grange became more than a way to end the loneliness of farm life; it began to fight the railroads. The first state laws regulating railroad rates are called **Granger Laws,** though in fact many small business people also helped to get them passed. The Grangers also founded **cooperatives** through which they sold their crops and bought supplies as a group. The Grange had about 1.5 million members in 1874. Within a few years, however, its membership began to decline.

Meanwhile, another farmers' group began to grow. The **National Farmers' Alliance and Industrial Union** was founded in Texas during the mid-1870's. It spread through the South and many Plains' states including Kansas, the Dakotas, and Nebraska. In 1886, Dr. C. W. Macune became its leader.

Macune proposed a **subtreasury plan.** He wanted the government to store farmers' crops for them and to give the farmers loans for up to 80 percent of the value of the stored crops. Then farmers could wait until prices were right before they sold their harvest.

A critic of the Populists portrayed the Populist Party as a patchwork made by dreamers.

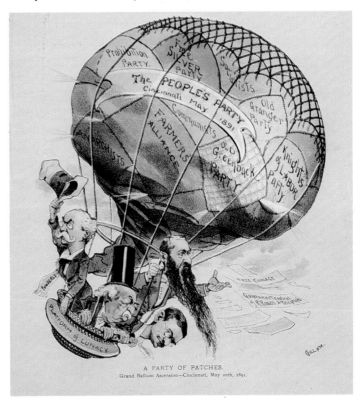

A PARTY OF PATCHES.
Grand Balloon Ascension—Cincinnati, May 20th, 1891.

In the meantime, they would have cash on which to live.

The Farmers' Alliance supported Macune's subtreasury plan. It also adopted a list of other demands in a meeting at Ocala, Florida, in December 1890.

The **Ocala** (ō kəl'ə) **Demands** called for the establishment of government subtreasuries and for the free coinage of silver along with other measures that would increase the amount of money in circulation. The Alliance members wanted tariffs removed from all "necessities of life." They asked, too, that land be taken from aliens, railroads, and anyone who was not actually living on it. They called for a graduated income tax, one that would increase with the size of a person's income. Their demands also included a call for "rigid, honest, and just" government control of transportation and communication networks. If that did not end abuses, the Alliance said, the government should take over the ownership of railroads and telegraph and telephone companies.

By 1891, the National Farmers' Alliance had about 2 million members. A separate Alliance for blacks had another quarter-million members. In 1890, the group managed to elect many governors, senators, representatives, and members of state legislatures. All promised to support the Alliance's program. As a result of the Alliance's success, members urged other groups to join them and form a new political party—the People's Party, also called the **Populist Party.**

▶**1.** What were some of the Ocala Demands?

The Populist Party

The new Populist Party was launched at a convention at St. Louis in February 1892. The National Farmers' Alliance was the most powerful group at the meeting. Other delegates came from the Knights of Labor and several reform groups, including the Greenbackers.

On July 4, 1892, the Populists chose General James B. Weaver, an old Greenbacker and officer in the Union army, as their candidate for President. Much of the party's platform repeated the Ocala Demands of 1890. The party platform made clear, however, that Populism was a movement of working people. It tried to unite factory workers and farmers, Northerners and Southerners, whites and blacks. It was a party of reform, not revolution, and it proposed to win its way through the ballot box.

Weaver received a million votes in the election of 1892. The Populists also elected 10 representatives, 5 senators, 3 governors, and about 1500 members of state legislatures.

▶**2.** What was the platform of the Populist Party in 1892?

Mary Elizabeth Lease of Kansas was one of the leaders of the Populist Party.

The Depression and Coxey's Army

In 1893, only a year after the national election, a depression began that was worse than any other the nation had known. By 1894, some 3 million people—about 1 out of 5 American workers—had lost their jobs. Homeless people took to the roads or slept on city streets. President Cleveland's only attempt to end the depression was to encourage Congress to repeal the Sherman Silver Purchase Act. That did not help the situation much.

A Populist named James S. Coxey of Massillon, Ohio, said the government should start a job program. He believed it should issue $500 million in legal paper dollars to pay people for working on the public roads. By that means, the jobless would get jobs, the public would get better roads, and the circulation of more dollars would help get other businesses going again.

Coxey collected an army of hundreds of people who marched from Ohio to Washington, D.C., in 1894 to petition for his program. The march was peaceful. But when its members met near the Capitol, armed police broke up the group. Coxey was thrown in jail for walking on the Capitol's lawn.

Coxey's army and some 1,400 strikes in 1894 convinced President Cleveland and many other people that the nation was falling apart. The Populists only added to their fears.

▶**3.** What was Coxey's army?

The Election of 1896

By 1896, President Cleveland was very unpopular even in his own party. Democrats from the silver-mining states of the West disliked his support for the gold standard. Other Democrats opposed his use of federal troops to end the Pullman strike. At the Democratic National Convention in Chicago during July

William Jennings Bryan failed in two attempts to win the presidency.

1896, Democrats dissatisfied with Cleveland found a powerful spokesman in a 36-year-old former member of Congress from Nebraska, William Jennings Bryan. There were no microphones then. However, Bryan's strong voice commanded silence, attention, and then cheers. His speech to the convention ended with a stunning cry against the gold standard: "You shall not press down upon the brow of labor this crown of thorns. You shall not crucify mankind upon a cross of gold."

The convention delegates followed Bryan's advice. They adopted a platform calling for the free coinage of silver. The Democrats also called for an income tax and attacked the tariff, the trusts, and even the Supreme Court. Then, on the fifth ballot, the delegates chose Bryan as its presidential candidate.

Finally the voters would have a choice between two major political parties that took

Newly elected President William McKinley is shown at his home in Canton, Ohio, after his successful "front porch campaign" in 1896.

different stands on the issues. In June, the Republican National Convention had come out in favor of the gold standard. William McKinley was the Republican presidential nominee. Many "gold Democrats" crossed party lines to support him.

The Republicans had no trouble getting contributions from bankers and other wealthy people. McKinley's campaign was organized by his faithful friend, Marcus Alonzo Hanna. He was the Republican boss of Cleveland, Ohio and a very wealthy man. With a fund of $3.5 million, Hanna printed tons of pro-McKinley posters and pamphlets and sent out hundreds of speakers to campaign for the Republican candidate.

Hanna also paid the travel expenses of some 750,000 people from different interest groups to McKinley's home in Canton, Ohio. There, the handsome McKinley and his wife, Ida, met visitors on the front porch of their modest house. In that way, McKinley, who was not a good orator, could avoid making speeches

to big crowds. McKinley's "front porch campaign" was obviously no cheap effort.

The situation put the Populists in a difficult spot. Populists from the West wanted to support Bryan. Southern Populists, however, did not want their party to merge with that of the Democrats. Eventually, the Southerners gave in, and the Populists supported Bryan.

Bryan also won the support of many other reformers. He had only $300,000 or so to spend on his campaign, but he traveled thousands of miles on trains, giving hundreds of speeches along the way. Bryan won almost a million more votes than those that put Cleveland in the White House four years earlier. That was not enough. McKinley won 600,000 more popular votes than Bryan and 271 electoral votes to Bryan's 176.

The results were important. Bryan did not carry a single industrialized state, and he did poorly in the cities. Clearly, he did not appeal to industrial workers as much as to farmers. There were some good reasons for that. To factory workers, the high tariffs that protected American industries also protected their jobs. Also, industrial workers were not in favor of free silver and other measures that would raise prices on agricultural goods. Such measures would increase the cost of the food they bought.

On issues such as the tariff and currency, then, the interests of farmers and workers often went in different directions. That hurt Bryan, the Democrat. It also meant that the Populist dream of pulling together the common people of the United States was likely to remain just that—a dream.

▶ 4. Who were the candidates in the presidential election of 1896? Who won?

Reviewing Section II

Identify Grange, Granger Laws, cooperatives, National Farmers' Alliance and Industrial Union, C. W. Macune, subtreasury plan, Ocala Demands, Populist Party, James B. Weaver, James Coxey, William Jennings Bryan, William McKinley, Marcus Alonzo Hanna

Questions to Answer
1. What was the platform of the Populist Party in 1892?
2. Why did factory workers vote Republican in 1896?

A Question to Think About What Populist demands are now law?

In Their Own Words
Bryan's Cross of Gold Speech, 1896

. . . The hardy pioneers who have braved all the dangers of the wilderness, who have made the desert to bloom as the rose . . . who rear their children near to Nature's heart . . . out there where they have erected schoolhouses for the education of their young, churches where they praise their Creator, and cemeteries where rest the ashes of their dead—these people, we say, are as deserving of the consideration of our party as any people in this country. It is for these that we speak . . . . We have petitioned, and our petitions have been scorned . . . we have begged, and they have mocked when our calamity came. We beg no longer; we entreat no more; we petition no more. We defy them . . . .

You come to us and tell us that the great cities are in favor of the gold standard; we reply that the great cities rest upon our broad and fertile prairies. Burn down your cities and leave our farms, and your cities will spring up again as if by magic; but destroy our farms and the grass will grow in the streets of every city in the country . . . .

. . . Having behind us the producing masses of this nation and the world, supported by the commercial interests, the laboring interests, and the toilers everywhere, we will answer our opponents' demand for a gold standard by saying to them: You shall not press down upon the brow of labor this crown of thorns, you shall not crucify mankind upon a cross of gold.

William Jennings Bryan

III. Expansion Overseas

After McKinley was elected President, the nation began to debate new issues—issues that concerned foreign policy. Throughout much of the 1800's, the United States had tried to avoid becoming involved in the affairs of other countries, especially those in Europe. That was not hard to do at a time when it took months to cross the Atlantic Ocean. But by the 1890's, steamships and telegraph cables were making contact between nations faster and easier.

Meanwhile, the United States was becoming one of the most powerful nations in the world. By 1880, it had more people than any industrial country except Russia. The United States also grew more wheat than any other nation. Ten years later, it led or nearly led the world in the production of coal, iron, and steel. It had become one of the world's richest nations. How exactly would the United States use its power? How would its growth as an industrial nation affect its relationship with other countries?

Opening Japan

Americans had been trading for many years with people in other parts of the world. As the United States became more industrial, that trade became even more important. It increasingly affected the nation's foreign policy. For example, the United States tried hard to open trade with Japan.

For over 200 years, Japan had closed its ports to ships from other nations. In the 1600's, European missionaries and traders were regularly visiting Japan. Their influence frightened the nation's leaders. They feared that Europeans would interfere with Japan's government. Therefore, in 1639, they strictly limited contact with the outside world. Their plan worked so well that most Westerners simply forgot about Japan.

In the 1800's, however, American interest in Japan grew. When shipwrecked sailors from American whaling vessels reached Japan, they were treated as criminals. Many Americans were outraged. They wanted the United States to protect those sailors. Other Americans wanted to trade with the Japanese.

In 1853, the United States government sent Commodore Matthew Perry to Japan to secure a trade treaty. To the surprise of many people, he was successful, partly because of his show of naval power. The fleet that Perry brought to Japan included four battleships. Eager to avoid war, Japan's leaders were more than willing to reconsider their policy.

Japanese artist Gessan Ogata made this painting of Commodore Perry arriving in Japan.

Japan was only the beginning. As the foreign trade of the United States grew, so did demands for a strong navy to protect that trade. In 1883, Congress ordered the building of several cruisers and five battleships. By 1900, the United States was the third strongest naval power in the world. As its ships sailed the oceans, they needed fueling stations far from home. That, too, increased American interest in the outside world.

▶**1.** How did the United States open Japan?

Acquiring Alaska

The United States quietly added a huge territory to its possessions when it acquired Alaska in 1867. Although there was little enthusiasm for the purchase, Secretary of State William H. Seward bought Alaska from Russia for $7.2 million. For about two cents an acre, the United States acquired a land rich in wood, minerals, and, as it turned out, oil. Seward had some trouble persuading the House of Representatives to approve the treaty. Some people thought it was silly to buy what they called "Seward's ice box" or "Seward's folly." Time showed how wrong they were. In 1959, Alaska became a state.

▶**2.** How did the United States acquire Alaska?

Positions on Imperialism

Because Alaska was in North America, it was not considered a colony. The question of whether or not the United States should acquire colonies in other parts of the world did, however, arise after the Civil War. Some Americans, known as **imperialists,** wanted the country to acquire colonies and, in general, to exert a greater influence on the world. They also thought the United States should get title to lands that could serve as bases

for the navy. Imperialists were often members of the Republican Party.

Other Americans disapproved of imperialism. They thought the United States should acquire no land outside the North American continent. They also thought it was against American traditions to take over another country by force and to rule its people without their consent. President Cleveland and many Democrats held that position.

▶**3.** What did imperialists believe about the acquisition of colonies?

Hawaii

In 1867, the same year in which Alaska was purchased, the United States took over the Midway Islands, which lie about 1,000 miles north of Hawaii. No one lived on the islands, so the event did not cause much notice.

Hawaii itself was another question. American ships had visited the Hawaiian Islands as early as the eighteenth century. Then missionaries moved there. Their children and grandchildren became sugar planters who sold most of their crop to the United States.

In 1875, the United States agreed to import Hawaiian sugar duty-free. Over the next 15 years, Hawaiian sugar production increased 9 times. Then the McKinley Tariff eliminated duties on sugar from other countries while giving special supports for American sugar producers. That caused an economic crisis in Hawaii. Obviously, Hawaiian sugar planters would be in a much stronger position if Hawaii were part of the United States.

Queen Liliuokalani (lē lē' ü ō kä lä' ē) became Hawaii's ruler in 1891. She refused to share power with American planters as earlier rulers had done. So the planters organized a revolution. With the help of 150 American marines, they forced "Queen Lil" to surrender—"to the superior force of the United

Queen Liliuokalani tried to limit the influence of foreigners in Hawaii.

States of America,'' as she said. Then the revolutionaries asked that Hawaii be annexed.

President Harrison was willing to oblige. In February 1893, he sent the Senate a treaty providing for Hawaii's annexation. In March, Cleveland became President for the second time. He asked the Senate to wait until he could get a report from an official he had sent to Hawaii. When the official reported that most Hawaiians were against annexation, Cleveland turned against it too.

The President asked the head of the revolutionaries, Sanford B. Dole, to return power to Queen Lil. But Dole—who later made a fortune in Hawaiian pineapples—refused. Instead, on July 4, 1894, the revolutionaries proclaimed Hawaii a republic. Like the Texans of an earlier day, they then sat back and waited. In time, they thought, the United States would welcome them. It did, but Hawaii did not become a state until 1959.

▶ **4.** How did Hawaii become a republic?

War with Spain

Those opposed to imperialism believed that they had won a victory in the case of Hawaii. The United States should not meddle in other countries' affairs, they said. Within a few years, however, the United States went to war to help Cuba win its independence from Spain. That war was a major victory for the imperialists.

Cuba was one of the last Spanish colonies in the Americas. The Cubans rose up against Spain in 1868, but their revolt failed. In 1895, they tried again to win their independence.

Most Americans hoped the Cubans would be successful. They followed the activities of the revolution in the yellow press. Those newspapers made the Spanish sound even more brutal than they were.

In January 1898, President McKinley sent the battleship *Maine* to Havana, Cuba, to protect American citizens. But on February 15, while still anchored in the harbor, the

The World *inflamed Americans with stories about the bombing of the* Maine.

Maine was ripped apart by a great explosion that killed 260 Americans. To this day, no one knows for sure what caused the blast. The press, however, blamed Spain. The cry "Remember the *Maine!*" went up, calling Americans to war.

On April 11, the President told Congress he had done all he could to end the terrible situation in Cuba. He asked permission to use force to bring peace to the island. Eight days later, Congress recognized Cuba's independence. On April 24, Spain declared war against the United States. Congress declared war on Spain the next day.

▶**5.** How did the bombing of the *Maine* lead to war?

The Reasons for War Congress made its intentions in Cuba clear by passing an amendment to its resolution declaring that Cuba was independent. The **Teller Amendment** said

the United States had no intention of taking over any part of Cuba. Yet imperialists saw the war as a chance for the United States to expand its power and to acquire naval bases.

Business people did not at first favor the war. In 1898, the United States had begun to pull out of the depression that began five years earlier. They feared the war would hurt the economic recovery.

However, American business leaders soon changed their minds about the war because they learned more about trade opportunities in China. In 1898, Germany, Russia, Britain, and France were busy dividing China into "spheres of influence" where their traders would have special rights. American sales in China were small but growing. Business writers noted that China, with its 400 million people, could easily buy up the surplus products of American manufacturers. To trade with Asia, American steamships would have

Map Study *What body of water is north and east of Cuba? Name two bodies of water that surround the Philippine Islands.*

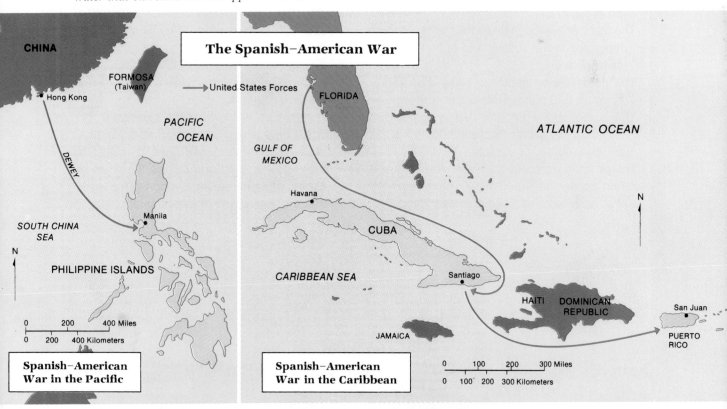

The Spanish–American War

Spanish–American War in the Pacific

Spanish–American War in the Caribbean

Propaganda consists of statements, drawings, even music designed to make people think in a certain way about a person or issue. Sometimes, but not always, propaganda uses lies and partial truths to shape people's opinions. Sometimes statements of propaganda are perfectly true and in support of worthwhile causes. Propaganda is not necessarily a bad thing—but it is important to be able to recognize it in all cases. Only then can a reader or listener make an objective judgment about the issue or person being discussed.

There are several types of propaganda. Among the most common are the following:

The *bandwagon* approach says "Everyone believes this and you should too."

The *card-stacking* approach presents only the facts and evidence that support one side of an argument.

The *transfer* approach takes the feelings people have about one subject and applies them to another subject.

The *name-calling* approach gives a person or object a bad name without giving evidence.

The *testimonial* approach has a well-known person make a statement either for or against an idea, object, or person.

The *glittering-generality* approach uses language that appeals to the emotions without backing it up with facts and can also exaggerate.

In the late 1890's, the yellow press printed sensational stories about conditions in Cuba and, in general, urged the country to go to war with Spain. The publishers and reporters often used propaganda to persuade their readers that war with Spain was necessary.

Read the following quotations and, on a separate sheet of paper, identify the kind of propaganda used in each.

1. When Spain sent General Weyler to Cuba in 1896 to put down the Cuban rebellion, the yellow press gave him the name "Butcher."
2. When the State Department received a letter from the Spanish Minister to the United States which criticized McKinley, the *New York Journal* published it under the headline "Worst insult to the United States in Its History."
3. After the sinking of the *Maine*, the *New York Journal* headline read, "The whole country thrills with war fever."
4. Another headline said, "The warship *Maine* was split in two by an enemy's secret infernal machines."
5. A *New York World* headline said that a "Dr. E. C. Pendleton, just arrived from Havana, says he overheard talk there of a plot to blow up the ship—Capt. Zalinski, the dynamite expert, and other experts report to the world that the wreck was not accidental . . . "

Teddy Roosevelt and his Rough Riders (left) as well as black cavalrymen helped capture Cuba in the Spanish-American War.

to have fueling stations along the way. Suddenly, business people began to understand what the imperialists were saying. The United States should acquire bases in Asia, and war with Spain, which owned the Philippine Islands, was one way to do that.

▶**6.** Why did events in China result in support for war with Spain?

The Philippines The first major battle of the **Spanish-American War,** the name given to the war with Spain, was fought in the Philippine Islands in the Pacific Ocean. The United States naval squadron in the Pacific was commanded by Commodore George Dewey. On receiving news of war, Dewey steamed out of Hong Kong for Manila Bay in the Philippines. There, on May 1, 1898, he won a victory that made him a great hero. Dewey's forces sank all ten ships of the Spanish fleet without losing any American lives.

That victory ended Spanish power in the Pacific. American and Filipino troops, led by General Emilio Aguinaldo (ä′gē näl′ dō), later took the city of Manila.

▶**7.** Who defeated the Spanish in the Philippines?

The War in Cuba Thousands of American men volunteered to fight in Cuba. Assistant Secretary of the Navy Theodore Roosevelt was an eager supporter of the war. He left his job in the Navy Department to become a lieutenant colonel in the army. Roosevelt organized the most famous regiment in the war, the **Rough Riders.** It included cowboys, Indians, police officers, and athletes—a strange assortment of people that Roosevelt drew together.

The United States was poorly prepared for the war. Soldiers were sent woolen uniforms to wear in the summer. Their food was often bad, and disease tore through the army camps. Volunteers were sent into combat with little or no training. Fortunately, the army had only a weak enemy to fight.

The war in Cuba did not last long. The Rough Riders and black and white soldiers led by General William Shafter helped to take San Juan Hill on July 1. Then the Americans held the highlands near the port of Santiago and could fire on the Spanish fleet below.

The Spanish commander decided to put out to sea. American battleships were waiting. After a four-hour battle on July 3, the Spanish fleet was destroyed. From that point, the war was really over. Two weeks later, the Spanish garrison at Santiago surrendered.

▶8. How did the Americans defeat the Spanish in Cuba?

"A Splendid Little War"   Meanwhile, on May 25, American ships on the way to the Philippines took over the Pacific island of Guam. Spanish officials there did not know a war was being fought. They thought the American shots were a salute, and they apologized because they had no ammunition to answer it.

On July 4, an American expedition also took over Wake Island, 2,300 miles west of Honolulu. By that time, the importance of Hawaii to the United States fleet in the Pacific had become clear. Congress voted to annex Hawaii on July 7. On July 25, the United States took over the Spanish island of Puerto Rico, which lay to the southeast of Cuba.

Secretary of State John Hay called it all "a splendid little war." It certainly was short, and the Americans won. But in a few months' time, 5,400 Americans had died. Only 379 had lost their lives in battle. The rest were killed by disease, such as malaria and yellow fever.

▶9. What territory did the United States take over during the war with Spain?

The Peace of Paris   What would the United States do with the lands it had won? Congress had promised not to take over Cuba. But what about the Philippine Islands? President McKinley struggled with the problem. Finally, as he later told a group of Methodist ministers, he decided that the United States could not give them back to Spain. That would be "cowardly and dishonorable." It could not give them to "commercial rivals" in Europe such as France or Germany. That would be bad business. The United States also could not leave the Filipinos to themselves because they were "unfit for self-government." So the United States would have to keep the islands. It would work to educate the Filipinos and to "Christianize" them. The President seemed to overlook the fact that many Filipinos were already Catholics.

The peace terms were decided in Paris in December 1898. In the Treaty of Paris, Spain agreed to give the Philippine Islands to the United States for $20 million. Spain also ceded Puerto Rico and Guam to the United States and gave up its title to Cuba.

The United States was not eager to release its hold on the Philippines. That became very clear in February 1899, when the Filipinos began an armed revolt against American rule. Led by Aguinaldo, the Filipinos fought bitterly until 1902. Then Aguinaldo was captured and imprisoned. The United States kept control of the Philippines until 1946.

The United States was also slow to give up its hold on Cuba. The American army remained in control there until 1902. It refused to leave the island until the Cubans agreed to a set of demands known as the **Platt Amendment.** Later those demands were included in the Cuban constitution and in a treaty with the United States.

The Platt Amendment said that Cuba could not enter into any foreign treaty that would

On July 1, 1898, Colonel Theodore Roosevelt led a group of American fighters up one of the hills that surrounded Santiago, Cuba. They had come to help Cubans revolt against their Spanish rulers. Only three years later, in 1901, the young colonel became the twenty-sixth President of the United States. At 42, he was the youngest man ever to serve as President.

Theodore Roosevelt was born in New York City in 1858. As a young child, he suffered terribly from asthma. His earliest memories were of sitting up in bed, gasping, while his father and mother tried to help him breathe.

At the age of nine, Teddie's father sent him to Maine to recover from a bad attack of asthma. During the trip, some boys teased him mercilessly because of his weak condition. Teddie vowed that never again would anyone be able to tease him because of his illness. He spent the remainder of his childhood building up his weak body in a gymnasium.

At 17, Teddie entered Harvard University. During his senior year, he met and married Alice Hathaway Lee. When he graduated, he still had not decided on a career. He tried law for a time before finding his true calling—politics.

In 1881, at the age of 23, Roosevelt was elected to the New York State Assembly. During his three terms in office, his intelligence and energy attracted the attention of many people. Soon he had a statewide reputation.

In 1884, Teddie's young wife and mother died only six hours apart. He spent the next two years working on a ranch he owned in North Dakota's badlands. There Teddie hunted buffalo and spent long hours tending cattle. The experience helped him recover from his tragedies.

Roosevelt returned to New York in 1886. That same year he married a childhood friend, Edith Kermit Carow. Two years later President Harrison

appointed him to the Civil Service Commission. From there, Roosevelt went on to serve as police commissioner of New York City and assistant secretary of the navy.

In 1898, America's war with Spain made Roosevelt a national hero. That same year he ran for and won the office of governor of New York. As governor, he successfully pushed for a wide variety of reforms. His biggest victory forced big business to pay higher taxes.

In 1900, Roosevelt ran for Vice President with McKinley. When McKinley won, Roosevelt took office, thinking he would live in the President's shadow. He was wrong. Only six months after the election, McKinley was assassinated.

When Roosevelt heard the news, he hurried back from a vacation. Six weeks later he became President. For the frail boy who had worked so hard to become strong, the greatest challenge of his life was about to begin.

Puerto Rico, Island Commonwealth

In just a short period of time, Puerto Rico went through several changes in government in the late 1800's. Having been a colony of Spain for hundreds of years, Puerto Ricans won a charter from Spain granting them some powers of self-government in 1897. Then the United States acquired Puerto Rico in 1898 at the end of the Spanish-American War.

Self-government was ended. Two years later, Congress passed the Foraker Act which set up a new government for the island. Key officials, such as the governor, were to be appointed by the President of the United States.

In 1917, Congress made Puerto Ricans citizens and set up an elective government there.

However, the island's status did not please all the people there. Some Puerto Ricans worked for statehood, while others worked for independence.

In 1950, Congress called for a constitution to be drafted and approved by the people of Puerto Rico. In 1952, Puerto Rico became a commonwealth. That means it is self-governing and associated with the United States by its own desire and consent. Puerto Rico is represented in the United States Congress by a resident commissioner. He is elected to a four-year term but has no vote. Debate about the future status of the island is still going on. Many Puerto Ricans hope the Commonwealth of Puerto Rico will one day become the fifty-first state.

threaten its independence. Cuba also had to agree to contract no debts it could not repay. Cuba agreed that the United States could intervene in Cuban affairs to preserve Cuban independence and maintain law and order. Cuba also promised to sell or lease to the United States lands for a naval or fueling station.

▶**10.** Why did the United States keep the Philippines?

The Anti-imperialists

The Treaty of Paris awoke widespread opposition. Its critics, the anti-imperialists, included former President Cleveland and other Democrats, labor leaders such as Samuel Gompers, industrial leaders such as Andrew Carnegie, the presidents of Harvard and Stanford, the social worker Jane Addams, and many leading writers. They had different and sometimes conflicting reasons for their opposition. All agreed, however, that it was wrong for the United States government to rule other people without those people's consent. Many doubted the Filipinos' ability to govern themselves. That made it hard for them to say the Philippines should just be made independent.

Opposition to the treaty was so strong that it passed the Senate with only one vote to spare. William Jennings Bryan helped get it through by persuading Democrats to vote for it. He was against taking over the Philippines but wanted peace. He thought the future of the islands could be decided in the election of 1900.

▶**11.** Who were some of the anti-imperialists?

China and the Open Door

During the Spanish-American War, Secretary of State Hay also kept an eye on China. Hay wanted to be sure that the European nations carving out spheres of influence there would allow the Americans their proper share of trade. So in September 1899, Hay wrote to the European countries that had footholds in China. In that **open door note,** he urged them to allow other nations equal access to trade in the areas they controlled. That is, tariffs, harbor duties, railroad charges, and the like should be the same for everyone. Recipients of Hay's letter said that if each other nation involved in China agreed to respect the open door policy, then their nation would too. Russia refused to consent, and Britain agreed only with conditions. Still Hay boldly announced that all powers had agreed, and their consent to the open door policy was "final and definitive"! Not many people were fooled.

Soon some young Chinese decided they had enough of Europeans in their land. They belonged to a group known as the Righteous,

Harmonious Fists, or the **Boxers.** They rose up in May 1900, attacking missionaries, business people, and Chinese Christians and destroying foreign-owned property. The foreigners rushed to their embassies in Beijing (bā′jing′). An army from several countries, including 2,000 Americans, went to help them and to put down the Boxer Rebellion.

Secretary Hay was worried that European countries would use their troops to increase their power over China. As a result, on July 3, 1900, Hay sent a second note to the European powers in China. It said the United States intended to protect all the trading rights mentioned in his first note, and also intended to prevent the dividing of China's land and government. This time all the other countries agreed.

Hay was also worried that the European countries would weaken China by forcing it to pay huge sums for European losses during

Map Study *When did the United States gain each of the following: Alaska, the Philippine Islands, the Hawaiian Islands, the Virgin Islands?*

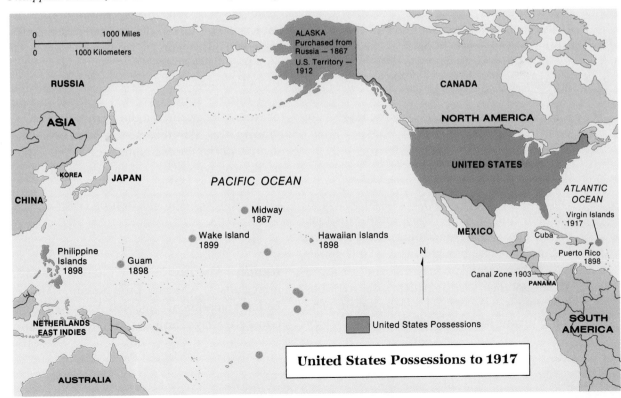

United States Possessions to 1917

A Japanese artist painted this picture of United States troops marching through Peking after the Boxer Rebellion.

the Boxer Rebellion. Hay was right. The sums paid by the Chinese were much larger than Hay thought proper. The United States eventually returned to China $18 million of the $25.5 million granted it for its losses. China was grateful. It used the money to educate Chinese young people at home and in the United States.

Events in China made clear that the United States had interests in parts of the world far from the Americas. And it was willing to use its army and its navy to protect those scattered interests.

▶**12.** What was Secretary of State Hay's concern in China?

The Election of 1900

Good times returned to the United States by election time in 1900. The Republicans took advantage of that, reminding voters that the Republicans had brought them a "full dinner pail." Their candidate for President was again McKinley. For Vice President, the Republicans nominated Theodore Roosevelt. The Republicans also bragged about the victory over Spain and the Republicans' efforts to get "new markets" for American goods through the policy of the open door.

The Democrats took a strong stand against imperialism and America's entry into world politics. They also endorsed free silver. Their candidate, Bryan, did even worse than in 1896. He received only 6.3 million votes to McKinley's 7.2 million. In the electoral college, McKinley won 292 votes to Bryan's 153. The Republicans also won strong majorities in both houses of Congress. Even farming and mining states, like Bryan's home state of Nebraska, went for the Republicans. Obviously, the "Populist Revolt" was over. The decline of the Populists meant that the cause of reform passed to other people in other places.

▶**13.** Who won the election of 1900?

Reviewing Section III

Identify Matthew Perry, William H. Seward, imperialists, Queen Liliuokalani, *Maine*, Teller Amendment, Spanish-American War, George Dewey, Emilio Aguinaldo, Theodore

Roosevelt, Rough Riders, John Hay, Platt Amendment, open door note, Boxers

Questions to Answer

1. Why did the United States become involved in the Spanish-American War?

2. What territory did the United States acquire between 1867 and 1898?

A Question to Think About Why did the purchase of Alaska seem different to most Americans than the purchase of the Philippine Islands?

IMPROVE YOUR READING
Prepositions and Conjunctions

Are little words easy to understand? Some are, especially when they represent something concrete. *Shoe* is an easy word because it is the written symbol for "covering for feet."

Other little words such as prepositions and conjunctions, however, do not stand for something concrete. Their function usually is to connect two ideas. If we fail to pay attention to these "connector" words, we may not understand the author's meaning.

Here is a list of "connector" words.

although	however	yet
but	rather than	though
while	even though	instead of

The purpose of the exercise that follows is to make you more aware of "connector" words. Your task is to replace the underlined connector word in each sentence with another connector word. You are not to change the meaning of the original sentence. You may, however, change the order of words in the sentence. You may also have to combine two sentences into one.

Here is a sample sentence. "*Even though* the Wilson-Gorman tariff raised many tariffs, it lowered the average rate." Notice that if a new "connector" word is used, the order of words in the sentence is often changed. "The Wilson-Gorman tariff raised many tariffs, *yet* it lowered the average rate."

1. *Although* there was little difference in the 1880's between the Democrats and Republicans, there was a political party that took a different stand on the issues.
2. Most Republicans were for high tariffs, *while* many Democrats wanted lower tariffs.
3. The Grange had about 1.5 million members in 1874. Within a few years, *however*, its membership began to decline.
4. *Although* there was little enthusiasm for the purchase, Secretary of State William H. Seward bought Alaska from Russia for $7.2 million.
5. The Cubans rose up against Spain in 1868, *but* their revolt failed.

CHAPTER 23 REVIEW

Vocabulary Check

On a separate sheet of paper, write a short definition for each of the following words.

1. *Laissez-faire*
2. Inflationists
3. Corruption
4. Patronage
5. Imperialists

Fact Check

On a separate sheet of paper, write the name of the person described in each of the phrases below.

1. Leader of a corrupt political ring in New York City in the 1860's
2. President who worked to set up a civil service system
3. Democratic candidate for President in 1896 known for his position against the gold standard.
4. He opened Japan to trade
5. Secretary of state who purchased Alaska
6. She surrendered Hawaii
7. President during the Spanish-American War
8. Filipino who opposed American control of the Philippines
9. Leader of the Rough Riders
10. Writer of the Open Door Note

Skills Check

Read each of the following statements. On a separate sheet of paper, identify the type of propaganda each statement uses, or write "no" if no propaganda is used.

1. "My campaign platform rests on American values, the American way of life, and fair play for all people."

2. "In my last term as your representative, I was present at 51 percent of all roll call votes. I visited in my district on each major holiday, and I made six important trips to investigate how successful resorts operate."
3. "My opponent missed 51 percent of the roll call votes during the last congressional session. My opponent was in the district to listen to the voters only 10 days last session. I visited voters on 35 days. My opponent took six week-long trips to Bermuda, the Bahamas, and other Caribbean islands. The only trip I took was to a hydro-electric project in the next state."
4. "A vote for me is a vote for justice."
5. "My opponent is corrupt."

Time Check

On a separate sheet of paper, write one important event that happened during each of the years listed below.

1. 1867
2. 1881
3. 1883
4. 1892
5. 1898

Think and Write

1. Why did free silver supporters want to have more money in circulation?
2. What reforms did the Populists support?
3. In what ways had the United States become a world power by 1900?
4. For what reasons did some people oppose expansion of the nation abroad?
5. Why did McKinley say that the United States had to maintain control of the Philippine Islands?

REVIEWING UNIT 7

Reviewing the Facts I.
Write the name of the person described in each of the sentences below.

1. He defeated Custer at the Battle of the Little Big Horn.
2. This leader of the Nez Perce tried to take his people to Canada in 1877.
3. She wrote *A Century of Dishonor* about the government's Indian policy.
4. He invented the telephone.
5. He invented the electric light.
6. He started Standard Oil Company.
7. He started the AFL.
8. Although the Populists also supported this Democratic presidential contender, he lost the election of 1896 to McKinley.
9. He was President during the Spanish-American War.
10. This naval hero sank the Spanish fleet in Manila Bay during the Spanish-American War.

Reviewing the Facts II.
On a separate sheet of paper, fill in the word or words that best completes each of the following sentences.

1. The Great American Desert is better known as the ____.
2. The long drive first went from ____ to "cow towns" such as ____.
3. Cowboys first learned how to tend cattle from ____.
4. The method of growing crops without irrigation in dry areas is called ____.
5. The ____ broke up the lands of Indian groups into small farms.
6. Companies in the same industry could form pools, ____, and ____ in order to avoid competition.
7. A ____ is an organization of workers formed to bargain with employers.
8. The ____ of the 1890's came from Southern and Eastern Europe.
9. ____ make imported goods more expensive and allow American manufacturers to sell products more cheaply in the United States.
10. ____ wanted the United States to acquire new territory and to take an active role in world affairs.

Reviewing Ideas

1. Nevada was organized as a territory in 1861 and had enough people to become a state in 1864. Why did its population grow so quickly?
2. How did mining, ranching, and farming become regular businesses in the West?
3. The United States had the necessary ingredients for becoming a great industrial nation. What were those ingredients?
4. (a) Secretary of State John Hay called the Spanish-American War a "splendid little war." Why? (b) In what ways was the war a terrible event?
5. Why did the Philippine Islands present a problem to President McKinley after the Spanish-American War?

UNIT EIGHT

Into the Twentieth Century

The twentieth century was a time of tremendous growth for the nation. The economic growth of the nation inspired this landscape by Charles Sheeler. The coming of the twentieth century also brought a growth in population and in cities and the extension of democracy. However, it also brought the United States for the first time into a war in Europe.

Chapter 24

Progressive Reform, 1900–1916

With the growth of cities, improved methods of transportation were needed. "The Green Car" by William Glackens shows a trolley car in New York City in 1910.

In the nineteenth century, almost all Americans believed in progress. It seemed to them that the nation was improving in many ways. It was gaining territory. Its population was increasing. The nation was also growing in wealth. Some Americans thought things would continue to improve if government maintained a *laissez-faire* approach and did not interfere in the affairs of its people. Others, however, said that the government should take an active part in shaping the nation's progress. Many people with that point of view became progressive reformers.

I. The Progressive Movement
The Reformers
The Muckrakers
La Follette and the Wisconsin Idea
Social Reform
Women's Suffrage
Limits to Progressive Democracy

II. Reform in the Cities
The Beginnings of Urban Reform
New Forms of City Government
Serving the Cities' People

III. Reforming the Nation
"TR"
Roosevelt and Big Business
Roosevelt and Labor
The Square Deal
Conservation
Taft as President
The Election of 1912
Woodrow Wilson, Progressive Democrat
The End of an Era

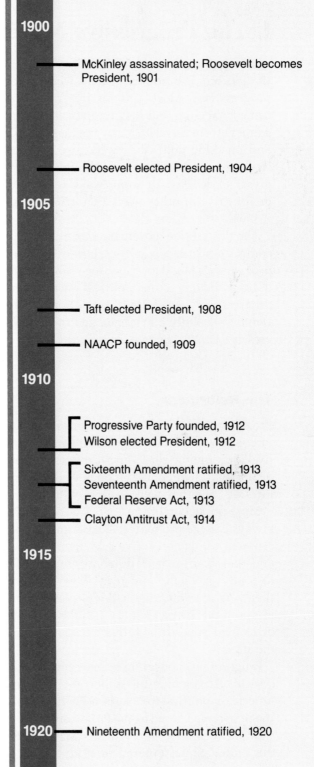

1900

McKinley assassinated; Roosevelt becomes President, 1901

Roosevelt elected President, 1904

1905

Taft elected President, 1908

NAACP founded, 1909

1910

Progressive Party founded, 1912
Wilson elected President, 1912

Sixteenth Amendment ratified, 1913
Seventeenth Amendment ratified, 1913
Federal Reserve Act, 1913
Clayton Antitrust Act, 1914

1915

1920 — Nineteenth Amendment ratified, 1920

I. The Progressive Movement

About 1900, a new wave of reform began in the nation. The new reformers were called **progressives.** Most progressive reformers came from cities, but they received important support from farmers. Many business people and machine politicians were also progressives of one sort or another. Though the progressives worked in some ways to expand democracy, in other ways they tried to cut it back.

The progressive movement was much more complicated than populism because not all progressives stood for the same reforms. Nor did they belong to one political party. Some progressives were Republicans. Some were Democrats. Only a few belonged to the Progressive Party that took part in the election of 1912.

The Reformers

Progressives did tend to have certain things in common. They were generally white, native-born, middle-class Americans. They were people who had enough money to live comfortably, but they were seldom wealthy.

More important, progressives were almost always college graduates. They wanted government to play an active role in public life, and they had great faith in people's ability to study problems and learn how to solve them. As a result, they created many commissions of experts to study public problems or to help govern the cities, the states, and the nation.

Progressivism began in the late nineteenth century. It remains an important force in American politics today. But its heyday—the time remembered as the Progressive Era—was between 1900 and World War I, which the United States entered in 1917.

▶**1.** What did progressive reformers have in common?

The Muckrakers

The **muckrakers** were people with the progressive spirit. They were reporters who wrote stories on public problems for popular magazines. Theodore Roosevelt, who did not like them, gave them their name. He meant to suggest that they were people who spent time digging in dirt when they could have been doing more glorious things. That was not really fair. Muckrakers generally did very careful research before writing their articles. They were, in fact, the nation's first investigative reporters.

McClure's was a magazine that printed many important muckraking articles. It sold for only ten cents per copy and was read by hundreds of thousands of people across the country.

One of *McClure's* best-known writers was Ida Tarbell. Her mother was a great supporter of women's rights. Under her influence, Tarbell decided to take advantage of the new opportunities opening to women in the late nineteenth century. She chose to have a career as a writer. Tarbell had already written several popular articles when *McClure's* asked her to study the oil industry.

Tarbell knew something about that subject, because she was born and raised in the oil-drilling country of western Pennsylvania. She spent a year learning more about the subject. Then *McClure's* published her "History of Standard Oil" in eighteen installments between November 1902 and the spring of 1904. During that time, the magazine's readership doubled. In her articles, Tarbell traced the beginnings of the oil industry and its takeover by John D. Rockefeller. Her accounts were based on a careful study of court records, government reports, interviews, and even company records.

Tarbell found much to admire in Standard Oil. But she sympathized with the owners of small companies taken over or destroyed by Rockefeller. She found many of his methods unacceptable. She said that when people acquire as much power as Rockefeller had, they use that power "to oppress and defraud the public."

Other muckrakers wrote on different topics. Lincoln Steffans studied the nation's cities and found that many of their governments were corrupt. His articles were published together as *The Shame of the Cities*. Later, he wrote about corruption in state governments.

▶ **2.** Who were the muckrakers?

La Follette and the Wisconsin Idea

The muckrakers presented the public with problems in need of solutions. But how could the people solve those problems? As Steffans had discovered, local and state governments were often controlled by political bosses or by corrupt interests. As long as that remained true, the people had little influence on public policy. So progressive reformers looked for ways to increase the power of the people.

▶ **3.** Why did progressive reformers wish to increase the power of the people?

Robert La Follette One of the most important progressive reformers was a politician from Wisconsin named Robert La Follette. He became governor of that state in 1900 and began a series of reforms that spread to many other parts of the nation.

La Follette's parents were pioneers who began life in Kentucky. There his grandfather had a farm right next to the farm of Thomas

Ida Tarbell was one of the reformers Theodore Roosevelt referred to as muckrakers.

Lincoln, Abraham's father. Like the Lincolns, the La Follettes moved to Indiana. Then they went on to the new state of Wisconsin, where their son, Robert, was born in 1855. As a boy, young La Follette worked on the family farm. Later, he put himself through the University of Wisconsin and became a lawyer in Madison, the state capital.

La Follette had a way of attracting attention. He was a short man with thick hair and a powerful, dramatic speaking style. He had the help, too, of his wife, Belle Case La Follette. She was also a lawyer and worked closely with her husband in both law and politics.

Although La Follette was a Republican, he acted as an independent. For example, he found that the state's government and its political parties were controlled in large part by the railroads and banks. So "Battling Bob,"

Robert and Belle La Follette (second and third from the right) are shown on a campaign train in 1900.

as he was called, campaigned for governor in 1900 on the promise of a new kind of government—one that would be honest, efficient, and devoted to the good of the public. He was elected in part because he had the support of farmers in areas of the state where the Grange and populists had been popular.

▶**4.** Why did La Follette think Wisconsin needed a new kind of state government?

The Wisconsin Reforms   As governor, La Follette supported measures that increased the power of the people. He fought for the **initiative,** by which voters themselves could propose new laws and force their state legislature to vote on them. La Follette also fought for the **referendum.** By that reform, laws could be placed on the ballot so the people could vote on them directly instead of letting the legislature make the decisions.

La Follette supported the **direct primary,** a special election in which voters who claim membership in one of the political parties choose their parties' candidates for office. Otherwise, politicians selected the candidates.

La Follette set up special state commissions to regulate railroad rates and banks. He made corporations pay a fairer share of state taxes. Wisconsin adopted a graduated income tax, so that the rich paid more than the poor. It passed laws to regulate working conditions and to make employers responsible for injuries that happened to workers on the job. La Follette and other Wisconsin progressives developed such laws with the help of experts from the University of Wisconsin. La Follette, in short, made his state "the laboratory of democracy." That is, it became a place where new ideas in government by and for the people were developed and tested.

▶**5.** How did the initiative and referendum give the people of Wisconsin a bigger voice in state government?

Progressive Reform Spreads   Before long, the "Wisconsin idea" of progressive government spread to other states. Iowa, Minnesota, the Dakotas, and many other states all had progressive governments.

The reforms adopted in those states varied. In general, however, progressives carried democratic reforms such as the direct primary, the initiative, and the referendum into many parts of the nation.

Progressives were also responsible for the **Seventeenth Amendment** to the Constitution of the United States. That amendment, ratified in May, 1913, said that United States senators would be elected directly by the people. In the past, state legislatures had selected the state's senators.

▶**6.** What change was made by the Seventeenth Amendment?

Robert La Follette and Belle Case La Follette

On December 31, 1881, a young woman named Belle Case and a young man named Robert La Follette were married. Well matched in background, interests, and values, each also had a great deal of respect for the other. Their marriage marked the start of a loving partnership.

Like her husband, Belle Case La Follette was born in a Wisconsin log cabin. The land she was born on had been cleared by her parents—Anton and Mary Case. From her parents, Belle inherited a great respect for hard work and a strong sense of self-reliance.

At the age of 16, Belle entered the University of Wisconsin. There she won many honors. She also met Robert La Follette, a young law student. Two years later the couple was married.

During the first year of married life, Belle La Follette developed an interest in law. Two years later, in 1883, she entered the University of Wisconsin Law School. The young mother became the first woman to get a law degree from that university. Although Belle never practiced law, she did help her husband's practice. She was his "wisest and best counselor."

In 1885, Robert La Follette became a United States congressman. Five years later he ran again but was defeated. For the next nine years, the La Follettes lived outside politics. During this time, Belle La Follette was able to devote herself to her own interests.

One issue Belle felt strongly about was that a woman, no matter what her station or stage in life, should take an active role in public affairs. Belle used her skill as a public speaker to lecture on this and related topics. Wherever she went, audiences admired her honesty and intelligence.

The La Follettes' private life ended in 1890 when Robert La Follette became governor of Wisconsin and began the series of reforms for which he became famous. Six years later, in 1906, he went to Washington as a senator.

In Washington, Belle and her husband created *La Follette's Weekly Magazine.* Its purpose was to provide a place for political debate. Belle La Follette edited a section of the magazine that focused on women and education. Over the next 20 years, her articles reflected the increasing role of women in influencing social reform.

The magazine was only one of Belle La Follette's many interests. She also supported women's suffrage, the improvement of race relations, and the cause of world peace. During World War I, she helped found the Women's International League for Peace and Freedom. When her husband died in 1925, many people urged her to complete his term in the Senate. Instead, Robert La Follette, Jr., filled his father's seat.

Belle La Follette lived for six years after her husband's death. When she died, the *New York Times* called her "the most influential of all American women who have had to do with public affairs in this country."

Social Reform

Progressives across the nation also followed Wisconsin's lead in passing laws designed to help workers and their families. By 1915, 25 states had laws making employers liable for on-the-job accidents. The progressives were also concerned about the more than three million American children—often younger than ten years—who held full-time or nearly full-time jobs in 1900. By 1916, the reformers had convinced several states to adopt laws forbidding child labor.

A number of states also passed laws to regulate working conditions. A few gave financial help to mothers raising children without the help of fathers. That program, **Aid to Families with Dependent Children** (AFDC), is still a part of the **welfare** program in many states. Welfare refers to government laws or programs designed to provide for the health and well-being of its citizens, especially those who are poor.

▶**7.** What kinds of social reforms did progressives make?

Women's Suffrage

Many progressives worked to give women the right to vote. The cause of women's suffrage gained ground steadily after 1900. The National American Woman Suffrage Association had about 13,000 members in 1893. By 1917, it had more than two million members, thanks in part to the work of its leaders, Anna Howard Shaw and Carrie Chapman Catt. Another such organization was Alice Paul's Congressional Union. That group also fought for women's suffrage.

As government became more interested in social issues such as the welfare of children and families, some people felt more strongly than ever that women should have the vote. The growing number of female workers also seemed to need the kind of legal protection that female voters would support.

By 1919, women had full voting rights in 15 of the 48 states. In 39 other states, women could vote in some elections. Finally in August 1920, the suffragists won ratification of the **Nineteenth Amendment** to the Constitution. The amendment said that "the right of citizens of the United States to vote" could not be limited or denied by state or federal governments "on account of sex."

▶**8.** What amendment gave women the right to vote?

Limits to Progressive Democracy

The progressives' belief in democracy was limited. Though they often fought for democratic reforms to take power from corrupt state legislatures, they did not entirely trust

These young boys worked long hours sorting coal in one of Pennsylvania's coal mines.

the people. They believed instead in government by trained professionals, such as those who served on government commissions. Such professionals, they thought, would defend the public's interests. That was not always true. In any case, government by experts is not government by the people.

▶**9.** Why was the progressive's reliance on experts in government not democratic?

The Cause of Blacks Progressive democracy was limited in other ways too. Most progressives were not interested in protecting the rights of black Americans. During the Progressive Era, blacks lost the right to vote in many parts of the South. Few people in the North objected. Southern states were among the first to adopt the direct primary, but they limited the right to vote in the primaries to white voters.

Segregation also spread in both the North and the South during the Progressive Era. That system of separating members of different races was applied to federal employees under the administration of a progressive President, Woodrow Wilson. "I have never seen the colored people so discouraged and so bitter as they are at the present time," Booker T. Washington said in 1913.

By then, many blacks had rejected Washington's leadership. Some of them fought for black rights through the Niagara Movement. In 1909, W.E.B. Du Bois and other blacks had also helped form the **National Association for the Advancement of Colored People** (NAACP). They were joined by a few white progressives, including Jane Addams, who were willing to fight actively against segregation and racism. The NAACP built up national, state, and local branches. It fought for black rights above all through the courts.

Du Bois was the leading spirit behind the NAACP. He was like white progressives in

Women in Ohio worked to win support for the Twenty-Third Amendment to their state constitution. It would give them the right to vote.

some ways. He depended on research and facts to support his cause. And he did not pin his hopes on ordinary black people. A "talented tenth" of American blacks, he thought, would lead the rest.

▶**10.** What was the NAACP?

Immigrants Some progressives blamed corruption in the cities on the immigrants who lived there. Those progressives tried to get laws passed to restrict immigration. They even got "expert" testimony to support their cause. Such laws, however, were not passed until the 1920's.

▶**11.** Why did some progressives wish to restrict immigration?

Reviewing Section I

Identify progressives, muckrakers, Ida Tarbell, ~~Lincoln Steffans~~, Robert La Follette, initiative, referendum, direct primary, Seventeenth Amendment, ~~Aid to Families with Dependent Children,~~ welfare, Nineteenth Amendment, ~~National Association for the Advancement of Colored People~~

do it
NAACP

Questions to Answer

1. What did most of the progressives have in common?
2. What reforms did La Follette support in Wisconsin?

A Question to Think About   Why were blacks and immigrants often excluded from progressive attempts to widen democracy?

II. Reform in the Cities

The progressives had great success in reforming state governments. They were also successful in reforming the nation's cities. There, long before they influenced the national government, progressive reformers enacted a rich variety of new programs.

The Beginnings of Urban Reform

In many cities during the 1890's and early 1900's, voters threw off corrupt politicians and elected candidates who promised to create honest governments. Hazen S. Pingree was, for example, a "reform" mayor in Detroit. Samuel "Golden Rule" Jones in Toledo, Ohio, Thomas L. Johnson in Cleveland, Ohio, and Seth Low in New York City also promised to stop corrupt practices.

However, reform governments did not last very long. They had trouble getting and holding the support of business people. Also the reformers were not generally as skilled in the art of politics as the "machine" politicians who were part of organizations that kept a strong hold on voters' loyalties. As a result, the bosses of political machines were soon back in power. It took a whole new way of looking at city government to root out or weaken the political machines.

▶1. Why did reform governments have trouble staying in power?

New Forms of City Government

Before 1900, the government of Galveston, Texas, was like that of many other cities. It had a mayor, a city council, and a board of aldermen. Then, in September 1900, a terrible tidal wave hit the city. Thousands of homes and businesses were destroyed. The old city government was clearly unable to cope with the disaster. Its power was just too divided for quick, effective action.

To deal with the emergency, the city adopted a new form of government. It set up a **city commission** of five people who each ran one of the city's major departments, such as the water department. The new government proved able to provide more services at a lower price than the old one had done. So the city commission form of government spread to other cities in Texas and then, in 1907, to Des Moines, Iowa. By 1913, more than 300 American cities had adopted the Des Moines plan.

Lockport, New York, chose a slightly different form of government in 1910. It also had an elected city commission to legislate for the city. But the executive power was given to an appointed city manager and a set of appointed department heads who served under the manager. Again, the **city manager** form of government spread, especially after Dayton, Ohio, adopted it in 1913. Six years later, 130 cities had governments modeled on the Dayton plan.

Business people were the most powerful supporters of these changes. Although at one time many business executives had worked with political machines, now they became reformers so that their cities could provide more services. Business people wanted paved streets, better water and sewage systems, electric lighting, and reliable fire and police departments. Cities could do such things cheaply and efficiently, the business people thought, if the cities were organized more like corporations.

The new forms of city government did not please everyone, however. The political machines did not like the new city governments because they cut the amount of patronage available to politicians. Other groups complained because they had no power in the new governments. Commissioners were usually elected at large, or by all the voters of a city, not just by those of a small neighborhood, or ward. As a result, many minority groups, who could win a majority of votes in a neighborhood or ward, but not in a citywide election, lost power.

The city commission and city manager plans never spread to the nation's biggest cities. There another new agency appeared— the **municipal research bureau,** which collected information on the city and its people. The bureau was meant to help the city government work in a more informed and businesslike way.

▶**2.** What were two new forms of city government?

Cities celebrated their growth with world's fairs. The 1904 World's Fair was held in St. Louis.

Serving the Cities' People

The new city governments found they could serve the needs not only of businesses but also those of the public. Many reformed city governments built playgrounds and parks. Some started other programs such as public milk inspection and health examinations for schoolchildren. They also passed several laws to regulate housing conditions.

Pressure for such reforms often came from settlement house workers or, as they came to be called, social workers. Like other progressives, social workers studied the cities and their people. They became experts on housing, drug addiction, diseases, and other

Social workers in many states helped to start nurseries, such as this one in New York for the children of working mothers.

served as head of the federal Children's Bureau.

Eventually, machine politicians realized that they had to support reform or they would lose votes. As the machines changed, they backed new kinds of candidates for office. In the old days, the machines were suspicious of college-educated people. But soon after 1900, New York's Democratic Party machine, called **Tammany Hall** after its meeting place, gave its full support to the young Robert Wagner. The son of poor German immigrants, Wagner had graduated from City College and become a lawyer. Tammany helped him win a seat in the state legislature. There Wagner helped pass some of the nation's first laws regulating factory conditions. Later Wagner served the people of New York in the United States Senate.

Tammany Hall also supported Al Smith, who helped Wagner fight for laws that would help poor working people in the cities. Smith later became the Democratic Party's presidential candidate in the 1928 election.

▶**3.** What caused machine politicians to realize they had to support reform?

city problems. Then they urged city governments to help solve those problems. Jane Addams, for example, pushed so hard for more frequent garbage collections in Chicago that she was made garbage inspector for a period of time.

Social workers often helped put into effect the measures they supported. For example, Florence Kelley, who worked with Addams at Hull House, helped write the first law regulating factories in Illinois. When the law was passed, the governor appointed Kelley factory inspector. Another Hull House worker, Julia Lathrop, became a member of the Illinois State Board of Charities. Later, she

Reviewing Section II

Identify city commission, city manager, municipal research bureau, Florence Kelley, Julia Lathrop, Tammany Hall, Robert Wagner

Questions to Answer
1. How were city governments organized under the city commission and city manager systems?
2. What was the role of social workers in urban reform?

A Question to Think About Why did machine politics change after 1900?

III. Reforming the Nation

Progressive reformers accused elected legislatures of corruption. The reformers also distrusted the courts because judges often struck down or weakened laws designed to regulate business and industry. As a result, progressive reformers worked mainly with the executive branch of state and local governments—with governors, mayors, or city managers. Once the reform cause touched the national government, it made the presidency more important than it had been since the days of Abraham Lincoln.

The United States got its first progressive President as a result of a tragedy. On September 14, 1901, President William McKinley died of gunshot wounds inflicted by an assassin. That same day, the Vice President, Theodore Roosevelt, took office as President. The presidency would never be the same again.

"TR"

"Teddy," or "TR," as the new President preferred to be called, was well-known. In 1898, the same year he led the Rough Riders in the Spanish-American War, Roosevelt was elected governor of New York.

Roosevelt was such a reformer that he scared the Republican Party bosses. They thought they had gotten him out of the way by making him McKinley's Vice President. Then TR became President.

Roosevelt was only 42 years old when he took the oath of office, which made him the youngest President in United States history to date. He was intelligent, educated, and had great confidence in himself and lots of energy. This man was not going to sit still for the next three or four years. He intended to use the power of the presidency.

▶1. Why were many Republicans unhappy to see Roosevelt become President?

Roosevelt and Big Business

The new President thought that large business corporations were necessary in the modern world. He therefore disapproved of reformers who attacked monopolies. Roosevelt also had no love for the muckrakers. On the other hand, he recognized that big businesses could do bad things. TR thought the government should decide what was right and wrong in

This portrait of President Theodore Roosevelt was painted in 1903.

business and should force companies to act in ways that served the public's interest.

▶**2.** What did Roosevelt think government's role should be with regard to business?

The Northern Securities Company The Supreme Court had ruled that the federal government had no power to regulate large manufacturing companies. TR wanted to challenge that ruling because he thought the federal government should be able to make some rules for business. In 1902, he had his attorney general bring a suit under the Sherman Antitrust Act against the Northern Securities Company. The Northern Securities Company was a $400 million holding company for several railroads in the Northwest. In 1904, the Supreme Court said that the company had to be broken up.

After that victory, Roosevelt was sometimes called a "trust-buster." His administration

Lion-tamer Roosevelt is shown trying to control some of the nation's trusts.

did bring cases against 43 big corporations. Roosevelt said, however, "We do not wish to destroy corporations," but to make them serve "the public good." He told business leaders that the government did not intend to attack all monopolies. It would bring suits against monopolies only if "they have done something we regard as wrong."

▶**3.** What did Roosevelt's suit against the Northern Securities Company accomplish?

Regulating Business Roosevelt wanted the government to regulate business in a way that made antitrust suits unnecessary. As a result, in 1903 he urged Congress to create a new department of the government, the **Department of Commerce and Labor.** It included a Bureau of Corporations that had power to study industries and report to the President on their activities. The President could release that information to the public. The pressure of public opinion, Roosevelt thought, would end a lot of wrongdoing.

Roosevelt also wanted the Interstate Commerce Commission to become more effective in regulating railroad companies. He supported the Elkins Act of 1903, a law that made rebates illegal. The Elkins Act also said railroad companies could not charge rates different from those on their published lists.

Three years later, Congress passed a stronger measure, the **Hepburn Act.** It increased the size of the Interstate Commerce Commission to five members and gave it more power. The Commission could actually set railroad rates. It could also make all railroad companies keep their accounts in the same way so they would be easier to watch over. In addition, the Commission was given power over sleeping car companies, oil pipelines, bridges, and ferries.

▶**4.** What new ways of regulating business did Roosevelt support?

Roosevelt and Labor

Roosevelt's attitudes toward labor were different than those of earlier Presidents. That became clear during a coal strike that began in May 1902. When the strike lasted into the fall, Roosevelt began to worry that there would not be enough coal for the nation that winter. So he called representatives of the labor union and the mine owners to the White House. He asked that both sides let their dispute be settled by **arbitration.** Then trained, objective people would listen to both sides and decide what to do to resolve the dispute.

The miners agreed to arbitration, but the owners refused. In fact, the owners wanted the government to order the miners back to work and, if necessary, send in the army to end the strike, as it had in the 1890's. Roosevelt was so angry at the owners' unwillingness to compromise that he threatened to take over their mines. Only then did the owners agree to let arbiters decide what should be done. The arbiters gave the workers a 10 percent wage increase and reduced their workday to 9 hours.

Never before had a President acted so positively toward labor. Roosevelt said he wanted to give the workers a **Square Deal**, a term he later applied to his programs in general. He meant that his programs would give all Americans, rich and poor, factory owners and workers, fair and equal treatment.

▶**5.** How did Roosevelt deal with the coal miners' strike of 1902?

The Square Deal

Roosevelt easily won the presidential election of 1904. He had almost a quarter million more popular votes than the Democratic candidate, Alton B. Parker of New York, and more than twice as many electoral votes.

In 1906, Roosevelt supported passage of two new laws, the **Pure Food and Drug Act** and a federal **Meat Inspection Act.** Under those laws, the federal government set standards for food and drugs that traveled across state lines before being sold.

The cry for such new laws was raised in part by writer Upton Sinclair. His novel, *The Jungle*, told of disgusting conditions in the meat-packing industry. Sinclair wrote his book to help the workers. Instead his book led to federal food inspection. "I aimed at the public's heart," Sinclair said, "and by accident I hit it in the stomach."

Many large meat-packing companies supported the new law. They willingly accepted federal inspection because they did business in more than one state. Before the new law was passed, they often had to deal with conflicting state laws. Federal meat inspection also helped the big packers sell more meat in foreign countries.

Roosevelt had less success with other Square Deal measures. He sent to Congress bills that he thought would help workers, but he could not get them passed. On one issue, however, Roosevelt battled for reform and won. That issue was **conservation,** the protection or preservation of the nation's natural resources.

▶**6.** What created a cry for reform of the food and drug industries?

Conservation

Roosevelt loved the outdoors. He worried about the future of the American wilderness. Early in his presidency, he began adding millions of acres to the national forests and parks. He also fought ranchers and lumber companies who were using the public lands for their own profit. His actions were not always popular.

Thomas Moran's painting "The Grand Canyon on the Yellowstone" helped to convince members of Congress to establish the Yellowstone National Park in 1872. Roosevelt added millions of acres to the nation's national parks.

In 1907, Congress passed a law preventing the President from adding to the public land in the West without the consent of Congress. Before that law went into effect, however, Roosevelt added 17 million more acres to the public reserves. By the time he left office, Roosevelt had added about 125 million acres to the national forests, and he had also claimed for the public many mineral beds and waterpower sites.

Roosevelt was willing to let the public lands be used and developed, but he insisted that they be used intelligently. As a result, he wanted experts to watch so that private developers did not waste natural resources. On that point he agreed with his chief advisor on conservation, Gifford Pinchot. Pinchot was the country's first professional forester.

The Roosevelt administration was even willing to use federal funds to help develop the West. It supported the **Newlands Act** of 1902, which said that money from the sale of public lands in the West and the Southwest would be used to build dams, reservoirs, and irrigation canals there. By 1915, $80 million had been spent on such projects. One of those projects, the dam on the Salt River in Arizona, was named for Roosevelt.

▶7. How did the Newlands Act reflect Roosevelt's beliefs about the use of public land?

Taft as President

In 1908, Roosevelt said he would not run again for President. He supported the Republican candidate, William Howard Taft of Ohio. A friend of Roosevelt, Taft easily beat the Democratic candidate, William Jennings Bryan. In 1909, TR went off to Africa to hunt big game.

Taft had been a judge, governor of the Philippines, and secretary of war under Roosevelt. Like the Presidents who served between Lincoln and Roosevelt, Taft was not interested in using presidential power to fight for reforms. Instead, Taft was inclined to let Congress and big business do whatever they wanted. That made him unpopular with Republican progressives. It got him into trouble with Roosevelt too.

Roosevelt was also outraged by a battle between Taft's secretary of the interior, Richard A. Ballinger, and Gifford Pinchot, who remained head of the Forest Service. Ballinger opened nearly one million acres of public land for sale. Roosevelt had seized those lands illegally, Ballinger said. Pinchot publicly criticized Ballinger's action. Then Pinchot accused Ballinger of profiting from a sale of public coal lands in Alaska. The controversy ended, in a way, when Taft fired Pinchot and a congressional committee found Ballinger innocent of any wrongdoing. But Pinchot appealed to Roosevelt, who returned to the United States in 1910. Before long, TR was complaining that Taft had "completely twisted around the policies I advocated and acted upon."

▶8. Why did the Ballinger-Pinchot controversy turn Roosevelt against Taft?

The Election of 1912

Roosevelt became so angry with Taft that he decided to run for President again in 1912. That year, he won all the Republican primary elections, but the Republican voters did not control their party. That control was in the hands of a group of leaders known as the "Old Guard." They saw to it that the Republican convention nominated Taft.

Claiming that the Republicans had sacrificed the people to the "interests," Roosevelt

William Howard Taft easily beat William Jennings Bryan in the election of 1908.

pulled his supporters together and formed a new party, the **Progressive Party.** It was also called the Bull Moose Party after Roosevelt told reporters that he felt "fit as a bull moose." The new party, of course, nominated TR for President in 1912.

Roosevelt ran on a program he called the New Nationalism. Government, he said, should regulate private property so that it is used in ways that serve the public interest. The platform he wrote for the Progressive Party in 1912 called for many reforms, including a graduated tax on incomes and on inheritances, payments to workers hurt in industrial accidents, an end to child labor, and the setting of minimum wages for women.

By splitting the Republican Party, however, Roosevelt practically gave the election to the

Colonial Africa

In 1909, after Taft's inauguration, Theodore Roosevelt went on safari to Africa. By 1900, almost all of Africa had been carved into colonies by European powers. The only two independent nations in Africa at that time were Ethiopia and Liberia. TR spent most of his time in Africa in a British colony called British East Africa. Today it is the country of Kenya.

Britain also controlled Egypt and the area that is Sudan today. It also had colonies in today's Uganda, South Africa, Botswana, Zambia, Zimbabwe, Malawi, Swaziland, and Lesotho. On the west coast of Africa, Britain controlled Nigeria and the countries now called Ghana, Sierra Leone, and Gambia.

France held a huge area of northwest Africa, including most of the Sahara. The king of Belgium personally owned a huge area called the Congo Free State. In 1908, he was forced to make that land a colony of Belgium. Today the Belgian Congo is the nation of Zaire.

Germany began its colonizing later than other nations. It took four widely separated areas: Togoland (Togo), Cameroon, German East Africa (Tanzania), and German Southwest Africa (Namibia). Spain, Italy, and Portugal also had African colonies.

After 1946, Africans began to demand their independence. Today no European nation has an African colony.

Democratic candidate, Woodrow Wilson, a progressive governor of New Jersey. In November, Wilson won a plurality of the popular votes, that is, more votes than any other candidate, but not a majority. In the electoral college, however, Wilson won the greatest majority in American history to that time—435 votes to Roosevelt's 88 and Taft's 8.

The election was a clear victory for progressivism. Both Wilson and Roosevelt ran as progressives, and together they had many more votes than Taft. After the election of 1912, the Democrats took control of both the House of Representatives and the Senate. They knew that if they did not move in a progressive direction, they could not hold the voters' support.

▶9. Why was the election of 1912 a clear victory for progressivism?

Woodrow Wilson, Progressive Democrat

The tall, scholarly man who took office on March 4, 1913, was as ready to use presidential power as Roosevelt had been. As a former professor of political science, he knew that the United States needed strong presidential leadership in the modern world. But what would he do with his power? Wilson's program was called the **New Freedom.** Once in the White House, Wilson fought for reform in three areas: the tariff, banking, and control of the trusts.

▶10. What was Wilson's program called?

The Tariff Wilson called a special session of Congress to reform the tariff. He even appeared before the Congress to make his case. He was the first President since John Adams

When historians consult primary and secondary sources, they often encounter different *points of view* on the same subject. Not everyone looks at an event in the same way.

When comparing two pieces of writing with different points of view, it is often useful to see where the two writers agree. It is also useful to see whether the writers are basing their discussions on facts or using the techniques of propaganda.

Read the following quotations in which Woodrow Wilson and William Howard Taft express different points of view about the initiative and referendum. Then answer the questions that follow.

Wilson

I believe that we are on the eve of recovering some of the most important [rights] of a free people, and that the initiative and referendum are playing a great part in that recovery . . . We have felt that in too many instances our government did not represent us . . . The initiative is a means of seeing to it that measures which the people want shall be passed—when legislatures defy or ignore public opinion. The referendum is a means of seeing to it that the representative measures that [people] do not want shall not be placed upon the statute book.

Woodrow Wilson, *The New Freedom* (1913), pp. 235–37.

Taft

Suppose [a measure placed on the ballot by the initiative] is voted in? It never has had the test of discussion and amendment that every law ought to have. I am not complaining of the movement that brings about this initiative and referendum for that is prompted by a desire to clinch the movement against corruption, on the theory that you cannot corrupt the whole people and that the initiative and referendum mean detailed and direct government by the whole people. But . . . the whole people will not vote at an election, much less at a primary.

W.H. Taft, *Ethics in Service* (1915), pp. 78–82.

1. How does Wilson define initiative and referendum?
2. Why does Wilson say those reforms are needed?
3. Taft offers two arguments against the initiative. What are they?
4. Which writer seems to have more faith in the people?
5. Based on the extracts you have read, does the following sentence reflect the point of view of Wilson or Taft: ". . . What is the initiative? In practice, it means that if 5 percent of the electorate can get together and agree on a measure, they shall compel all the rest of the electorate to vote as to whether it shall become law or not. There is no opportunity for amendment, for discussion."

This portrait of Woodrow Wilson was painted in 1921.

It could do so because, in February, 1913, the country had ratified the **Sixteenth Amendment,** which gave Congress the power "to lay and collect taxes on incomes."

▶**11.** What was the Sixteenth Amendment?

Banking Next, Wilson turned to reform of the banking system. Control of the nation's money had fallen into the hands of a small group of financiers on the East Coast. Progressives wanted the government to have more power over the "money trust."

The result was the **Federal Reserve Act** of 1913. That law set up a national banking system controlled by both private bankers and people appointed by the federal government. At the top of the system was a Federal Reserve Board that sat in Washington. Its members were appointed by the President. Under it were twelve local federal reserve banks controlled by those banks that belonged to the system. All national banks had to join, and state banks could join if they wanted to. Member banks had to put part of their assets, the wealth they held, into the federal reserve bank. The federal reserve banks could use those reserves to make loans to member banks. The interest rate on such loans—known as the **rediscount rate**—was set by the Federal Reserve Board. The loans were made in federal reserve notes, which became part of the national currency.

The Federal Reserve Act is one of the most important laws in American history. It finally gave the country a workable banking system that served public as well as private interests.

The Federal Reserve Board's right to set the rediscount rate on loans to banks gave it considerable power over the national economy. If it raised the rate, member banks had to raise the rate of interest they charged to their customers. Then fewer people would take out loans, which would "slow down"

to do so. As a result of Wilson's efforts, Congress passed the **Underwood Tariff** of 1913. It lowered tariff rates by about 8 percent and allowed many foreign goods, including iron and steel, to be imported duty free. Most of those goods, however, could already be produced more cheaply in the United States than they could be made abroad.

The lower tariff would reduce government's income. To make up for that loss, Congress approved a new, graduated tax on incomes.

the economy. If the Federal Reserve Board lowered the discount rate, it stimulated, or boosted, the economy by making it easier for businesses and individuals to borrow money to build new factories or homes or whatever. Decisions of the Federal Reserve Board also controlled the number of federal reserve notes in circulation. As a result, the country finally got a more flexible money system, which reformers had been demanding for years.

▶ **12.** What were the provisions of the Federal Reserve Act?

The Trusts Finally, Wilson turned to the problem of the trusts. He called for a new antitrust law. The **Clayton Antitrust Act** of 1914 outlawed many business practices that the old Sherman Antitrust Act did not mention. But when the Senate passed amendments that weakened the act, Wilson did nothing.

Instead, President Wilson pinned his hopes for business reform on the new **Federal Trade Commission** that Congress approved in September 1914. It took the place of Roosevelt's old Bureau of Corporations and had much greater power to regulate business and prevent unfair trade practices. The Federal Trade Commission could, for example, demand reports from corporations on their activities. It could even order companies to stop certain practices that the Commission considered unfair.

▶ **13.** How did Wilson deal with the problem of trusts?

The End of an Era

By the fall of 1914, Congress had passed new laws on the tariff, banks, and the trusts. Wilson thought his reform program was complete. However, he later pushed Congress to pass more reform measures as a campaign tactic for the election of 1916.

Under Wilson's leadership, Congress passed laws making it easier for farmers to get loans, setting an eight-hour workday for railroad workers, and outlawing child labor. However, the Supreme Court declared the child labor law unconstitutional. It had struck down many other progressive acts for the same reason.

Wilson then added a progressive voice to the Supreme Court in 1916 when he appointed an outspoken progressive named Louis Brandeis to the Court. Brandeis was the first Jew to serve on the Supreme Court.

Soon troubles in Europe attracted more attention than problems at home. As a result,

Louis Brandeis was one of the most distinguished justices to serve on the Supreme Court.

the Progressive Era came to an end in 1916, although its influence on American government continued. Government had taken on more power over the direction and quality of American life than ever before.

▶**14.** Who was Louis Brandeis?

Reviewing Section III

Identify Department of Commerce and Labor, Hepburn Act, arbitration, Square Deal, Pure Food and Drug Act, Meat Inspection Act, Upton Sinclair, conservation, Gifford Pinchot, Newlands Act, William Howard Taft, Richard A. Ballinger, Progressive Party, Woodrow Wilson, New Freedom, Underwood Tariff, Sixteenth Amendment, Federal Reserve Act, rediscount rate, Clayton Antitrust Act, Federal Trade Commission, Louis Brandeis

Questions to Answer
1. What major reform laws were passed while Theodore Roosevelt was President?
2. How did Wilson deal with reform of the tariff, banking, and trusts?

A Question to Think About In what way did Roosevelt and Wilson view their role as President differently from Taft?

IMPROVE YOUR READING
Fact and Opinion

You have learned that when you read history it is often necessary to determine when a statement is a fact and when a statement is an opinion.

A statement that can be verified, or checked for accuracy, is a fact. Factual statements are usually specific. A statement that cannot be verified is usually classified as an opinion. Often opinions express feelings.

The following statements are about events discussed in Chapter 24. Decide whether each statement is a fact or an opinion. Write your answers on a separate piece of paper.

1. The muckrakers wanted to cause trouble for business.
2. Ida Tarbell wrote for *McClure's* magazine.
3. Cities work most efficiently when they are organized like businesses.
4. Theodore Roosevelt added about 125 million acres to the national forests.
5. Roosevelt's claim to greatness as President rests on his actions for conservation.
6. La Follette was elected governor because he had the votes of farmers.
7. Female workers strongly supported the passage of the Nineteenth Amendment.
8. Du Bois was the leading spirit behind the NAACP.
9. Social workers often helped put into effect the measures they supported.
10. The conditions in the meat-packing companies were disgusting.

CHAPTER 24 REVIEW

Vocabulary Check
Write a short definition for each of the following words.

1. Initiative
2. Rediscount rate
3. Conservation
4. Welfare
5. Arbitration

Fact Check
On a separate sheet of paper, fill in the word or words that best complete each of the following sentences.

1. _____ reformers were almost always college graduates and had great faith in experts.
2. Theodore Roosevelt gave the _____, reporters who wrote stories for popular magazines on public problems, their name.
3. By the _____, laws can be placed on the ballot so voters could vote on them directly instead of letting the state legislature decide.
4. In the _____ form of city government, an appointed manager and department heads run the executive branch.
5. Theodore Roosevelt called the programs he worked for as President the _____.

Skills Check
1. Draw a circle graph to illustrate the electoral vote in the election of 1904: Roosevelt, 336; Parker, 140.
2. Draw a circle graph to illustrate the electoral votes in the election of 1908: Taft, 32l; Bryan, 162.
3. Draw a circle graph to illustrate the electoral votes in the election of 1912: Wilson, 435; Roosevelt, 88; Taft, 8.
4. Draw a bar graph to illustrate the popular votes in the election of 1912: Wilson, 6,293,454; Roosevelt, 4,119,538; Taft, 3,484,980.
5. Draw a line graph to illustrate the number of electoral votes received by William Jennings Bryan in three presidential elections: 1908, 162; 1900, 155; 1896, 176.

Time Check
On a separate sheet of paper, put the following events in the order in which they occurred.

1. Sixteenth Amendment is ratified.
2. Elkins Act is passed.
3. Seventeenth Amendment is ratified.
4. Nineteenth Amendment is ratified.
5. Pure Food and Drug Act becomes law.

Think and Write
1. What reforms did the progressive movement help bring about?
2. Describe three ways in which progressives expanded democracy.
3. Describe the city commission and city manager form of government.
4. How accurate is Theodore Roosevelt's nickname "trust-buster"?
5. How did the Federal Reserve Act provide for the regulation of banking?

Chapter 25

The United States and the World, 1900–1919

Artist J. F. Bouchor, an eyewitness to the event, made this painting of American troops arriving in Paris, France, in 1918.

During the Progressive Era, Theodore Roosevelt and Woodrow Wilson made the office of President more important by promoting reforms at home. Both Presidents also took an active role in foreign affairs. By so doing, they not only increased the power of the nation but also that of their office.

When Roosevelt used his power as President to bring about reforms at home, he had to fight many opponents. But in foreign affairs, he had a freer hand. Everyone agreed that it was the President's job to deal with other nations.

Woodrow Wilson acted in ways that were very much like those of Roosevelt. During his administration, the United States Army for the first time took part in a war in Europe, the war remembered as World War I.

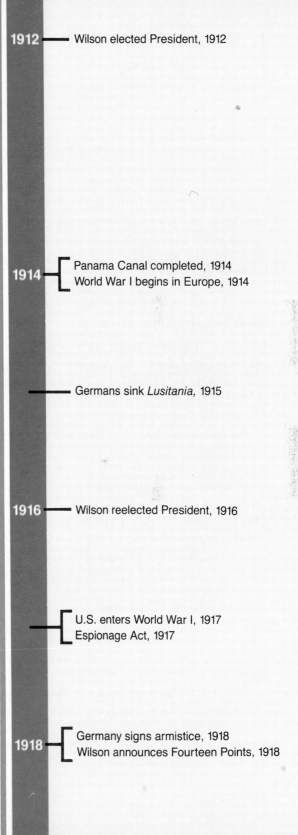

1912 — Wilson elected President, 1912

1914 — Panama Canal completed, 1914
World War I begins in Europe, 1914

Germans sink *Lusitania*, 1915

1916 — Wilson reelected President, 1916

U.S. enters World War I, 1917
Espionage Act, 1917

1918 — Germany signs armistice, 1918
Wilson announces Fourteen Points, 1918

I. Roosevelt and the World

When Vice President Roosevelt became President in 1901, he already had some strong ideas about his country's place in foreign affairs. Roosevelt wanted the United States to play an active role in the world. He thought that "civilized and orderly" nations such as the United States, Great Britain, and Japan had a duty to police the world and maintain order. To do that, he said, the United States should, in the words of an African proverb, "speak softly but carry a big stick." No nation could live in peace, he said, unless it was ready to fight.

Building the "Big Stick"

Roosevelt started to build his "big stick" by reforming the army. The Spanish-American War had shown that the army was outdated. So McKinley ordered his secretary of war, Elihu Root, to reorganize it. After McKinley's death, Roosevelt gave strong support to Root.

Root began his reform program by enlarging the army. He then set up officer-training schools and set strict standards for promoting officers from one rank to another. Root put American soldiers under professional officers, trained military experts who made their living as army officers. Finally, he put the entire army under a general staff, a group of top officers, and a chief of staff. In that way, he set up centralized control of the military.

Roosevelt had served as assistant secretary of the Navy, and the navy was dear to his heart. He continued the work of building a modern navy that had begun in the 1880's. The American fleet doubled in size during his presidency. By 1909, the United States Navy was the second strongest in the world, outdone only by Great Britain's.

To make sure the rest of the world knew about the naval strength of the United States, Roosevelt sent a fleet of ships around the world. It was known as the **Great White Fleet** because the ships were painted white.

Roosevelt used the nation's new military strength, especially that of the navy, to influence affairs throughout the world. That is why his way of dealing with world affairs is sometimes called **gunboat diplomacy.**

▶**1.** How did TR change the armed forces?

This flag commemorates the Great White Fleet's voyage around the world, 1907–1908.

The Panama Canal

One example of gunboat diplomacy was the way Roosevelt got land for the Panama Canal. By the time Roosevelt became President, many Americans, including Roosevelt, believed that the United States needed a canal somewhere in Central America to shorten the voyage between the Atlantic and Pacific coasts. Without a canal, ships making that trip had to sail all the way around South America.

The United States was not the only country eager for such a canal. As early as 1850, the United States and Britain had agreed that any canal in Central America would be a joint venture. But in 1901 the British said the United States could build and control a canal by itself. The ships of all nations would, however, have to be able to use the canal on equal terms.

Where would the canal be built? Some people argued for a route through Nicaragua (nik ə rä′gwə). Others preferred one through Panama. In the late 1800's, a French company had tried to build a canal in Panama. After ten years, the company gave up. It sent an agent, Philippe Bunau-Varilla (bü′nō vä′rē ya′), to Washington to convince the United States government to buy its claim. Then, in 1903, the President and Congress decided to use the Panama route and agreed to buy the French company's rights for $40 million.

The route through Panama was shorter than the one across Nicaragua. However, the land in Panama was more mountainous. It was also covered by thick rain forests.

▶2. Why did the United States want a canal in Central America?

Revolt in Colombia Before beginning work on the canal, the United States had to get permission from Colombia, which then ruled Panama. The United States offered to lease an area of land across Panama, which was called the **Canal Zone,** for 99 years. It would pay Colombia $10 million plus an annual rent of $250,000. Colombia refused the offer. Its government wanted more money.

Roosevelt was furious. So when a group of Panamanians and some people tied to the old French company—which would not be paid if the United States did not build its canal in Panama—plotted against Colombia, Roosevelt supported them. On November 2, 1903, he sent American warships to Panama. The revolt began the next day. Colombian troops sent to restore order in Panama could not land because of the American ships. Three days after the revolt began, the United States recognized a new nation, the Republic of Panama.

Soon Panama's minister to the United States—none other than Philippe Bunau-Varilla—arrived in Washington, D.C. It did not take long for him and Secretary of State John Hay to finish work on the **Hay-Bunau-Varilla Treaty.** By that agreement, Panama gave the United States perpetual use and control of a ten-mile-wide Canal Zone at about the same price Colombia had refused. The Senate approved the treaty in February 1904.

▶3. How did Roosevelt secure the Canal Zone for the United States?

Digging the Big Ditch Before work could begin on the Big Ditch, as the canal was called, the United States had to solve a problem that had defeated the French, that of disease. Malaria and yellow fever, the same diseases that had killed many Americans in Cuba during the Spanish-American War, had also killed tens of thousands of French canal workers.

By 1903, several doctors, including the American Walter Reed, had discovered that

This painting shows workers busily carving out one of the deep cuts along the route of the Panama Canal.

mosquitoes carried the germs that caused malaria and yellow fever. Those diseases could be prevented by draining pools of standing water where the insects bred.

After the Spanish-American War, Colonel William Gorgas had eliminated the mosquito in Cuba. Now the army sent him to Panama. Gorgas was tireless. He drained as much standing water as he could. The water he could not drain he covered with oil to seal the mosquitos' breeding places. He also cut grass, burned rubbish, paved streets, and covered the windows of houses with fine screens.

Then American builders arrived with great machines unlike anything the French had had to work with. Huge derricks, cranes, and steam drills spread over the site as work began on May 4, 1904.

The Panama Canal was a great triumph for American engineers. The work also required the labor of thousands of other people.

About 80 percent of the workers were West Indians. Many of the other workers were Italians and Spaniards.

The fifty-mile canal, which cost $375 million to build, was finally opened on August 15, 1914. No one was prouder of the Panama Canal than Teddy Roosevelt. "I took the Canal Zone and let Congress debate," he bragged.

▶4. What problem had to be solved before work could begin on the Canal?

The Roosevelt Corollary

The building of the Panama Canal made the safety and security of the Caribbean very important to the United States. Roosevelt was determined to maintain order and keep other nations out of that area. To do that, the President announced, in December 1904, a policy known as the **Roosevelt Corollary** to the Monroe Doctrine. (See pages 273 and 275.) A corollary is an addition that follows logically from another statement or doctrine. The Roosevelt Corollary said that the United States might have to use its power to stop wrongdoing by nations in the Western Hemisphere since the Monroe Doctrine kept other "civilized" nations from doing that job.

The President first applied his corollary in a crisis in the Dominican Republic, which shares the Caribbean island of Hispaniola with Haiti. The Dominican Republic had borrowed more money from Europeans than it could pay back. When it looked as though its European creditors were going to step in, the nation turned to the United States for help. The United States took over the Dominican Republic's customs houses for two years. In that time, it gave 55 percent of the customs duties it collected to the Dominican Republic's creditors. The Dominican Republic was allowed to keep the rest. In that way, Roosevelt satisfied both sides without risking war.

In 1906, however, Roosevelt used force to end a revolt in Cuba. In fact, American troops remained there until 1909.

▶ **5.** What did the Roosevelt Corollary say about the role of the United States in the Western Hemisphere?

Roosevelt as Diplomat

Although Roosevelt believed in carrying a "big stick" when dealing with other nations, he was also very good at "speaking softly." He showed his skills well on two very important occasions.

The first came in 1905 when Roosevelt was asked to help settle a dispute between France and Germany over their rights in Morocco, a country in North Africa. It looked for a time as if the Moroccan crisis might lead to a general European war. However, Roosevelt managed to get delegates from the Euro-

President Roosevelt meets with Russian and Japanese delegates at Portsmouth, New Hampshire.

pean countries to a meeting at Algeciras (al jə sir′əs), Spain. There the dispute was settled peacefully. The crisis itself is of less importance than the President's role. Never before had the chief executive of the United States been so involved in the political affairs of Europe.

Roosevelt was also concerned about maintaining peace in Asia. When war broke out between Japan and Russia in 1904, he tried very hard to arrange a peace that would not upset the balance of power in Asia. In the summer of 1905, he brought the two countries to a peace conference in Portsmouth, New Hampshire. In 1910, he received the Nobel Peace Prize for his work in ending the Russo-Japanese War.

▶ **6.** What disputes in Europe and Asia did TR help settle?

Dollar Diplomacy

Roosevelt thought President Taft would carry on his foreign policies. TR was disappointed. Instead of Roosevelt's gunboat diplomacy, Taft and his secretary of state, Philander C. Knox, used what some people called **dollar diplomacy.** That is, they tried to use American money to influence the foreign policies of other countries.

For example, Knox encouraged South American countries to borrow from the United States rather than from countries in Europe. That would, of course, lessen the chance of Europeans intervening in Latin American affairs. Sometimes Taft did use force to protect American investments. He sent United States soldiers into Nicaragua after a revolution broke out there in 1911. They stayed ten years. At the same time, United States bankers took charge of Nicaragua's finances. Such interventions, by arms or financial control, provoked great hostility against the United States throughout South America.

▶**7.** What was dollar diplomacy?

Reviewing Section I

Identify Elihu Root, Great White Fleet, gunboat diplomacy, Canal Zone, Hay-Bunau-Varilla Treaty, William Gorgas, Roosevelt Corollary, dollar diplomacy

Questions to Answer
1. How did the United States come to build the Panama Canal?
2. How did Roosevelt's foreign policy increase the role of the United States in the world?

A Question to Think About How did Roosevelt's foreign policy reflect his progressive beliefs?

II. Wilson and the World

When Woodrow Wilson became President in 1913, he had little experience and not much interest in foreign affairs. He was far more concerned about reforms at home. He did believe that moral principles, rather than power and wealth, should decide what should be done in the world. So he rejected both gunboat diplomacy and dollar diplomacy.

Moral Diplomacy

Wilson believed that the United States had a special role to play in God's plans for the world. He thought that God wanted the world to become a peaceful place where human rights were respected. That could only happen if people ruled themselves. Wilson thought that the United States, the most democratic nation in the world, had a duty to teach other nations how to govern themselves. It was not arms or wealth that made the United States strong, Wilson said. "The force of America," he insisted "is the force of moral principle." So the United States should practice **moral diplomacy** by working for the good of all the world, not just for its own selfish interests.

Wilson's belief in moral diplomacy inspired a lot of people. However, his confidence that he knew what was right for the United States and for other countries caused problems. Above all, he found it hard to make compromises. Politics, the art of getting things done in a democratic system, requires give and take. A President who cannot engage in politics risks not getting what he or she wants done.

▶**1.** How did Wilson think the United States could practice moral diplomacy?

The Mexican Revolution

Wilson's moral diplomacy first ran into serious trouble in Mexico. That country had long been ruled by a dictator, Porfirio Diaz (dē′as). In 1911, Diaz was overthrown by Francisco Madero (mä ₮Hā′rō) who promised democratic reforms. Early in 1913, however, a general named Victoriano Huerta (wer′tä) took over the Mexican government and then murdered Madero.

Wilson refused to recognize the government Huerta formed. He called it a "government of butchers." He hoped that Huerta's opponents, led by Venustiano Carranza (kar rän′sä), would come to power. Wilson even offered to send American troops to help Carranza overthrow the new government. Carranza turned down the offer. He wanted Mexicans to settle their own affairs.

▶**2.** Why did Wilson refuse to support Huerta as leader of Mexico?

Veracruz In April 1914, one of Huerta's officers arrested a few American sailors who went ashore at Tampico (tam pē′kō), Mexico. President Wilson responded by seizing Veracruz, an important Mexican port. A total of 19 Americans and 126 Mexicans died in the fight. Carranza said the United States government had no business taking Mexican territory. By late summer, Carranza was able to take control of the country. Only then did the United States pull its forces from Veracruz.

▶**3.** Why did the United States send troops to Veracruz, Mexico?

Pancho Villa's raid on American citizens caused President Wilson to send soldiers after Villa.

Chasing Pancho Villa The crisis in Mexico was not over. Since Carranza was unwilling to accept the leadership of the United States, Wilson for a time supported Francisco "Pancho" Villa (vē′yä), one of Carranza's opponents. Then in October 1915, Wilson changed his mind and recognized the Carranza government. Villa felt betrayed. In January 1916, he and his men stopped a train in northern Mexico and killed 17 United States citizens. Two months later, Villa and his men crossed the border and set fire to the town of Columbus, New Mexico.

Wilson sent a military force led by General John J. Pershing into Mexico after Villa. That was a clear violation of Mexico's rights. Pershing never caught Villa. The invasion succeeded only in further alienating Carranza. Eventually, in February 1917, Wilson ordered Pershing to return home.

▶ **4.** Why did Pershing lead United States troops into Mexico?

The Caribbean

Despite his emphasis on moral principle, Wilson often used arms to support American interests in the Caribbean. He sent marines into Haiti in 1916 to end a revolution there and protect American investments. The marines stayed until 1934. Wilson also used armed force to bring order to the Dominican Republic in 1916. That country was governed by the United States Navy until 1924. Finally,

Wilson forced Nicaragua to promise that it would allow no other country to build a canal through its land.

▶ **5.** In what countries did Wilson use arms to support American interests?

The United States and Europe

From 1914 on, Wilson and most other Americans focused their attention on events in Europe. A new crisis began on June 28, 1914, when an assassin killed Archduke Francis Ferdinand, the heir to the Austro-Hungarian throne, and his wife in the city of Sarajevo (sä'ə yā'vō). Sarajevo is today a city in Yugoslavia. The assassin had been encouraged by politicians in the nearby country of Serbia.

The assassination of Archduke Ferdinand and his wife (seated in the back of the car) was the spark that set off World War I.

In August, the Austrians invaded Serbia. Before long, all of Europe was involved in a war that came to be known as **World War I.** One nation after another was drawn into the fighting because it was tied to Austria or Serbia by an alliance, or treaty. Austria was part of an alliance that included Germany and, later, Bulgaria and Turkey. Those countries were known as the **Central Powers.** Serbia was part of an alliance that included the countries of Great Britain, France, and Russia. Its members were known as the **Allies.**

▶ **6.** What event led to the outbreak of World War I?

Germany's submarine warfare eventually brought the United States into World War I.

Links to the Allies Wilson quickly announced that the United States would remain neutral, favoring neither side. Americans, he said, should be "impartial in thought as well as deed." Not many Americans were. Americans of German descent favored the Central Powers. So did many Irish Americans. Ireland at that time was struggling for its independence from Great Britain, so many Irish in the United States did not want to help the British. On the other hand, Americans of British and French descent favored the Allies, as did most other Americans. To them, Britain and France seemed more like the United States in political traditions and principles. The Germans, on the other hand, seemed to stand for military rule. Democratic principle, in other words, seemed to favor the Allies.

Despite the policy of neutrality, the United States became more tied to the Allies. In 1916, the United States sold $275 million worth of goods to Britain and France, and only $29 million worth of goods to Germany.

▶ **7.** Why did most Americans favor the Allies?

Freedom of the Seas Wilson set out to defend American rights on the seas. That was not

an easy task. Britain wanted to stop Germany's trade with other nations. So the British blockaded northern European ports to keep supplies from reaching Germany. The British also seized the cargoes of neutral ships bound for Germany, and they mined the North Sea to destroy ships there.

The Germans fought back against the blockade. They used submarines, which they called "undersea boats," or **U-boats.** International law said an attacker had to warn passengers on a neutral ship before firing. The Germans did not do that. In fact, the rule made no sense in submarine warfare, which was based on surprise attack. If a submarine rose to the surface to warn a ship, then the ship could easily sink the sub. Wilson, however, insisted that the Germans strictly honor the traditional rules of the sea.

▶ **8.** In what ways did Britain and Germany infringe other countries' right to free use of the seas?

War Deferred The U-boat problem became a crisis on May 7, 1915. On that day, a German

The Rise of Germany

Before the nineteenth century, the German nation did not exist. A powerful Austria along with hundreds of smaller states led by princes and nobles made up the so-called Holy Roman Empire. By the end of the eighteenth century, however, one of those states, Prussia, whose capital was Berlin, used its powerful army to take over more land. Soon it began to rival Austria.

In 1814 and 1815, Europe's leaders assembled at the Congress of Vienna to work out a peace settlement at the end of a long series of wars caused by Napoleon. The Congress set up the German Confederation, a union of 39 German-speaking states in which Austria and Prussia remained rivals.

In 1862, Otto von Bismarck became prime minister of Prussia. He led Prussia into wars that further increased Prussia's territory and power. After defeating Austria and then France, Bismarck convinced the southern German states to join a united German empire under Prussian leadership. On January 18, 1871, Wilhelm I of Prussia was declared kaiser, or emperor, of Germany.

Bismarck was the first chancellor, or head of government. He served until he was dismissed by the new kaiser, Wilhelm II, in 1890. The new kaiser was jealous of Bismarck's power. By then, Germany was already becoming a powerful industrial nation. Kaiser Wilhelm's plans to increase the influence of Germany were a major cause of World War I, which broke out in 1914. The United States entered that war three years later in April 1917.

---

submarine sank the *Lusitania*, a British passenger liner. Almost 1,200 people died, including 128 Americans.

The Germans believed that the attack was justified. The ship carried ammunition for the Allies, which it was not supposed to do. Also, the Germans had published warnings to passengers in New York City newspapers before the liner sailed.

Wilson, however, protested strongly against the assault on a passenger ship. He said the "sacred . . . rights of humanity" were involved. The Germans agreed to pay for the American losses and promised to attack no more ocean liners without warning.

In March 1916, the Germans broke that promise. They sank a French steamer, the *Sussex*, which was carrying its passengers, including some Americans, across the English Channel. Again Wilson protested. Again the Germans gave in. They signed the **Sussex Pledge,** promising to sink no more merchant ships without warning. But they also insisted that the United States make Great Britain observe the rules of international law. Most Americans were relieved. They did not want to go to war.

▶**9.** What actions of the Germans almost caused the United States to declare war in 1915 and 1916?

The Election of 1916

"He kept us out of war" was an important slogan in Wilson's campaign for reelection in 1916. He needed all the help he could get.

The Republican candidate for President, Charles Evans Hughes, had many supporters. Hughes had been a reform governor of New York and also a Supreme Court Justice. Even Theodore Roosevelt, whom the Progressive Party tried to nominate again for the presidency, gave his support to Hughes.

Wilson managed to carry the election, though it was very close. He won 9.1 million popular votes to Hughes's 8.5 million, and took 277 electoral votes to Hughes's 254. The election hinged on the results in California, where Wilson won by only 3,773 votes.

▶10. How did Wilson use his foreign policy in the campaign of 1916?

Into the War

After the 1916 election, Wilson made new efforts to end the war. In January 1917, he called for a "peace without victory." A peace without winners and losers would prevent anger and resentment on the losing side. Wilson also said that for the peace to last, countries had to be ruled by governments their own people had chosen. The peace would also have to be guarded by a new organization of nations.

Wilson assumed that the United States would help negotiate the peace treaty. The Germans, however, said that they wanted no neutral parties at the peace table. Then, on January 31, 1917, they announced that Germany would resume unrestricted submarine warfare. That is, despite their earlier promises, they were going to attack all ships on the high seas, whether the ships belonged to neutral nations or to those countries actually at war. During the next two months, one ship after another fell victim to the German U-boats.

The Germans knew that their actions would bring the United States into the war. But

This Wilson campaign truck shows many of the Democratic slogans of 1916.

they thought they could win the war before the United States sent in troops. Since 1914, the Germans had been fighting on two fronts, or two places of conflict. On the **Eastern Front,** the Germans were fighting the Russians. The Russians were, however, beginning to give in by 1917. As a result, the Germans thought they could turn their full force toward the **Western Front,** where they were fighting the French and the British, and win a quick victory.

▶11. Why did the Germans think they could defeat the French and British before the United States entered the war?

The Zimmermann Note Great Britain was eager to have the United States join the Allies. So the British were pleased when, in February 1917, they intercepted a telegram from the German Foreign Secretary Arthur Zimmermann addressed to the German minister in Mexico. If the United States and Germany

555

went to war, Zimmermann said, the minister should try to make an alliance with Mexico. Then Germany would help Mexico get back its "lost territory in New Mexico, Texas, and Arizona." The British quickly decoded the telegram and gave it to the United States government. On March 1, 1917, Wilson released the **Zimmermann note** to the public. It led to a great wave of anti-German feeling in the United States.

▶**12.** What was the Zimmermann note?

Making the World Safe On April 2, 1917, Wilson asked Congress to declare war. The United States had no quarrel with the German people, he said. It was opposed only to their government, which had "thrown aside all considerations of humanity and of right." Wilson stressed that the United States "had no selfish ends to serve" by entering the war. "The world," Wilson said, "must be made safe for democracy." In short, the United States would enter the "Great War" in Europe not for power or for wealth but to uphold a moral principle. Within days, huge majorities in both houses of Congress approved the war resolution.

▶**13.** Why did Wilson say the United States should enter the war?

Reviewing Section II

Identify moral diplomacy, Porfirio Diaz, Francisco Madero, Victoriano Huerta, Venustiano Carranza, Pancho Villa, John Pershing, Archduke Francis Ferdinand, World War I, Central Powers, Allies, U-boats, *Lusitania*, Sussex Pledge, Charles Evans Hughes, Eastern Front, Western Front, Zimmermann note

Questions to Answer
1. How did President Wilson try to end the war after the 1916 election?
2. What led the United States to declare war on Germany?

A Question to Think About In what ways was the sinking of the *Lusitania* like the sinking of the *Maine*?

III. The War and the Peace

As early as 1916, Congress had passed bills proposed by President Wilson to build up the military. Still, the nation was not ready when war came. To get the nation's fighting forces, economy, and its people organized for war drew on all the managerial skills Americans had developed over the past few decades.

Building the Military

Wilson insisted that conscription, or the draft, be used to raise soldiers for the United States Army. Only in that way would the nation have enough troops. The rich had to serve as well as the poor. Before the war was over, almost three million men were drafted. Another two million served voluntarily.

General Pershing became head of the **American Expeditionary Force** (AEF), the troops that the United States sent to Europe. Pershing was a professional soldier. As such, he insisted that no troops be sent into battle until they were thoroughly trained.

Because of Pershing and the professionalization of the army during the Progressive Era, the American performance in World War I was very different from what it had been in the Spanish-American War. When Teddy Roosevelt tried to organize a volunteer regiment like his old Rough Riders, the army refused to accept his unit. There was no place for amateurs in the AEF.

The United States Navy also played an important part in the war. American ships laid mines to destroy German U-boats and in other ways fought off the submarine threat. United States ships also traveled across the sea in **convoys,** or groups of ships, to protect merchant vessels. The convoy system reduced losses dramatically.

▶**1.** Why did Wilson insist that men be drafted into the army?

The War at Home

The war affected every part of life in the United States. The government geared up the economy to produce more and more goods for the war effort. It also tried to influence public opinion to favor its policies. To do those things, the federal government took on more power than ever before.

▶**2.** Why did the power of the federal government grow during World War I?

The War Boards To organize the nation's economy in support of the war required central direction. So President Wilson set up several **war boards** to organize the production and distribution of crucial goods that were needed for the war.

In March 1918, Bernard M. Baruch, a wealthy financier, became head of the War Industries Board. It was set up to oversee American manufacturing. Baruch got some of the nation's best business leaders to help him. They served the war effort, but they served the interest of business too. Corporate profits went up by leaps and bounds during the war.

Meanwhile, the War Labor Board tried to prevent strikes and other disputes that might tie up wartime production. The Labor Board also fought for an eight-hour workday and equal pay for women who did the same work as men. Female workers were very important to the war effort. About 40,000 women took over the jobs of men who had been drafted.

In addition, the War Labor Board supported the right of workers to organize, or join unions. Membership in the American Federation of Labor (AFL) doubled during the war years. Wages also rose, but not by nearly as much as corporate profits.

The most famous of the war boards was the Food Administration. Its head was a mining engineer and businessman named Herbert Hoover. His job was, first of all, to

Hoover's campaign to get Americans to produce more and eat less was a great success.

Eat less and let us be thankful that we have enough to share with those who fight for freedom

UNITED STATES FOOD ADMINISTRATION

557

Highlighting People
John J. Pershing

On April 2, 1917, President Woodrow Wilson declared war on Germany. One month later Secretary of War Newton Baker gave General John Pershing complete control of American forces in Europe. The secretary gave the general two orders: "one to go and one to return." Pershing did both.

John Pershing, known to his family and friends as Jack, was born the first of six children in 1860 in Laclede, Missouri. When he was 17, money problems in his family forced Jack to take a job teaching in a local school. Jack liked teaching and decided to make it his career.

Through careful budgeting, Jack was able to save enough money to enroll in a nearby teacher's training college. While there, he happened to come across a newspaper ad announcing admission tests to the United States Military Academy, known as West Point. He took the tests, hoping to receive a free education.

To his surprise, Jack passed the tests and entered the academy. In a short time, he knew that he had found his true calling. He remained loyal to the army all his life.

Pershing graduated from West Point in 1886. Following graduation, he fought in the Indian Wars in the Southwest, taught military techniques at the University of Nebraska, and served in Cuba during the Spanish-American War. Later he went to the Philippines, where he helped put down a local revolt.

Pershing's skill in the Philippines attracted the attention of President Theodore Roosevelt. In 1906, the President rewarded the 46-year-old captain by making him brigadier general.

After his promotion, Pershing served for a time in the Philippines before returning to the United States. There, in 1915, tragedy struck. A fire killed his wife and three daughters.

Shortly following this tragedy, Pershing was given the assignment of tracking down the Mexican rebel Pancho Villa. Although Pershing never caught the rebel, his efforts impressed yet another President—President Wilson.

In 1917, Wilson made Pershing head of the American Expeditionary Force in Europe. It was as leader of this force that Pershing gained his greatest fame.

From the beginning, Pershing had very strong ideas about the role of American forces in Europe. British and French commanders wanted to use American troops to replace the dead and wounded in their own forces. Pershing refused to do that. He thought that a fresh, unified American army would keep American morale high and hurt German morale. He was right on both accounts.

In 1918, Pershing came home as the most honored soldier in American history. He received the title General of the Armies, a title previously held only by George Washington. General Pershing died in 1948.

increase the amount of food the nation produced. He accomplished that goal without much trouble, since farmers were well-paid for increasing their crops.

Hoover also wanted Americans to change their eating habits so that more food could be sent to Europe. To do that, he brought his campaign right into American homes. He organized voluntary "meatless Tuesdays" and "wheatless Wednesdays." Hoover used catchy slogans like "Food will win the war." Americans responded with great enthusiasm to Hoover's campaign.

▶**3.** What was the work of the war boards?

Propaganda The government also sponsored a great campaign to increase support for the war through **propaganda,** measures designed to shape people's opinions. (See page 510 for more information on propaganda.) A Committee on Public Information under George Creel printed tons of pro-war materials. It also placed advertisements in magazines, put up posters, sent out speakers, and even made films to drum up support for the war.

Unfortunately, the committee campaigned not just for the war, but against Americans who had doubts about the war. Such Americans included many reformers who thought the United States should improve life at home before it began reforming the world. Some Americans of German and Irish descent opposed their country's role in the war. Such people had a right to their opinions so long as they did nothing to undermine the war effort, but propaganda made them appear to be un-American.

Soon war propaganda made the Germans into "Huns," evil enemies of all that was good and right. Anything connected with Germany became suspect, including the German language and even music written by German composers.

War posters, such as the one shown here, helped to win support for the war.

▶**4.** What did the Committee on Public Information do?

Regulating Loyalty Amid growing suspicion and distrust of those who opposed the war, President Wilson tried to protect the nation from spies and traitors. Some of his measures deprived citizens of their civil liberties.

On Wilson's request, Congress passed an Espionage Act in 1917. It set fines and prison terms not just for spies but for anyone who interfered with the war effort. In 1918, Congress passed a Sabotage Act and a Sedition Act. The two laws allowed the government to punish people merely for saying anything "disloyal . . . or abusive" about the United States government or the flag. In many cases, the definition of *disloyal* was very loose. Citizens were arrested for passing out antiwar petitions, for example.

The government also tried to stamp out a radical union, the **International Workers of the World** (IWW) or "Wobblies." The army was used to put down IWW strikes in copper mines and lumber camps. The Wobblies acted illegally, so some government officials thought, in slowing down the war effort. However, the government used questionable evidence to deport or jail union members.

Where the goverment was slow to act, individuals or groups took it upon themselves to find and punish people they suspected of favoring Germany in the war. Among those were people who had criticized the war boards or the Red Cross. German Americans were fired from their jobs and even attacked by mobs. In short, civil liberties were all but forgotten.

▶ **5.** In what ways did the government attempt to protect the nation from spies and traitors?

Millions of soldiers lost their lives fighting in the trenches spread across Europe.

The War in Europe

By May 1918, the United States had 500,000 soldiers in France. Those soldiers and the Americans who followed helped to end a war that was particularly horrible. In all, about 1,390,000 American soldiers fought in active combat. A total of 2,084,000 American soldiers were sent to France.

In 1914, the German army had swung west through Belgium and almost made it to Paris. Then the Allies stopped them. For years, the war was in a stalemate—neither side could move.

All along the Western Front the Germans and the Allies fought each other from long **trenches,** or ditches dug into the ground to protect the soldiers from enemy fire. There the soldiers lived, night and day. The trenches were damp and dirty and often filled with rats. Attempts to break through the trenches caused terrible losses. Soldiers from one side would go "over the top" and rush toward the enemy's trenches often to be killed by machine-gun fire. Thousands might be killed in a day. Artillery shells buried many soldiers in the trenches. Poison gas left others dead or burning with pain. Still neither side could break through the other's line. The land between the trenches became a scarred desert, burned to the ground by exchanges of fire. The lines stretched all the way from the North Sea southward through France to Switzerland.

As the war went on, it spread into the sky, where airplanes were used in combat for the first time. Some "ace" pilots such as Eddie Rickenbacker, who shot down 26 German planes, became great heroes.

▶ **6.** How did soldiers fight from the trenches?

The Fighting The United States could not get many troops to Europe before 1918, and

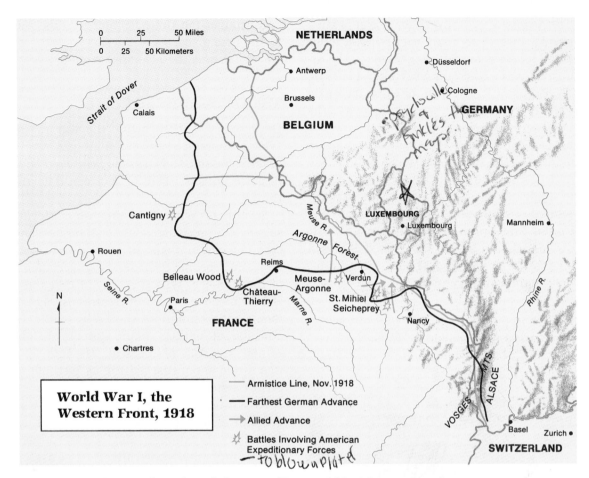

Map Study *What river flows through the cities of Rouen and Paris? Approximately how far is Château-Thierry from Paris?*

when they finally arrived, the Allies were in desperate need of their help. In March 1918, the Russians, as a result of a revolution in November 1917, made peace with the Germans. Because the Russians were no longer a threat, the Germans could turn their full force toward the Western Front.

General Pershing insisted that the American forces fight separately, not as part of the British or French armies. That upset the Allies. Still, American troops helped hold back a German attack at Château-Thierry (shä tō′ ty rē′) near Paris in May 1918. Then they helped fight off the Germans at Reims (rēmz). Before long, the Allies were able to mount their own attack. The American First Army under General Pershing took a position in the south of France near the town of St. Mihiel (san mē yel′). Then, from mid-September, it pushed back the German troops. The worst of the fighting took place in the Argonne (är′gon) Forest to the northwest of St. Mihiel. Slowly, the Allies pushed the Germans eastward.

▶**7.** What were some of the major areas where American troops fought in World War I?

The Armistice   Finally, as the line of fighting moved toward Germany itself, the Germans asked for an **armistice,** or cease-fire. The armistice was signed on November 11, 1918. The Germans, in effect, admitted to the world that their cause had become hopeless. The war was finally over.

American troops had fought only about six months of the war's four years. Only 48,909 Americans were killed in battle, compared to 4,000,000 British, French, and Russian soldiers. Nonetheless, the part played by the United States was critical to the Allies. It was enough to assure the United States a place at the peace table. That was important. It was one of the reasons President Wilson

These black soldiers are awarded the Distinguished Service Cross for bravery in World War I.

had brought the United States into the war in the first place.

▶**8.** When was the armistice signed?

The Fourteen Points

On January 8, 1918, while the war raged, Wilson announced his complete peace program. It became known as the **Fourteen Points** because Wilson asked for fourteen different things.

Several of Wilson's points were specific suggestions on changing national borders and creating new nations. In general, however, he wanted people to be led by governments of their choice. Wilson also said that there should be no more secret treaties. All agreements between nations should be public. In addition, all nations should support an "absolute" freedom of the seas. He said, too, that trade should be as free as possible of tariff barriers.

To Wilson, the most important point was the fourteenth. It called for a "general association of nations" that would protect "great and small states alike." That association, or **League of Nations,** as it was called, would keep the peace by encouraging its members to solve problems by negotiating.

The peace settlement Wilson suggested was generous to the losers. Wilson did not want to punish the German people or their allies. He offered Germany an equal place among nations in the postwar world. The generosity of Wilson's program was, in fact, one of the reasons the Germans were so ready to sign an armistice in November 1918. The promise of a world where justice reigned and the misery of war would be no more was as welcome to the battle-weary Germans as it was to other Europeans.

▶**9.** What were the major provisions of Wilson's Fourteen Points?

The Versailles Conference

The peace conference began in January 1919 at the splendid Palace of Versailles (ver sī′) near Paris. It was such an important meeting that President Wilson decided to attend himself. When he arrived at Paris, he was welcomed by the most enormous crowd of cheering people ever assembled in France.

All the countries who met at Versailles were Allies. Germany was not represented. Neither was Russia, which had made its peace with Germany. David Lloyd George, the British prime minister, was there, along with Georges Clemenceau (klem′ən sō′), the president of France, and Vittorio Orlando (or lan′dō), the Italian prime minister. (Italy had joined the Allies after the war began.) With Wilson, these three men made up the **Big Four.**

Unlike Wilson, the other members of the Big Four were determined to make Germany pay for the war. They were not committed to Wilson's Fourteen Points. They had won the war and now wanted some reward for their victory.

The treaty written at Versailles blamed Germany for the war and said the Germans would have to pay **reparations.** That is, they would have to repay the Allies for their losses. Just how much Germany would have to repay was decided by a special commission. It set the sum at $33 billion, far more than Germans believed they could afford. That measure caused just the resentments Wilson had hoped to avoid.

Some of Wilson's other hopes for the peace treaty were also lost. The British would not even discuss freedom of the seas. Free trade was another lost cause. Wilson wanted to end secret treaties and diplomacy, but most of the Versailles talks were secret. Furthermore, many of the Allies had already made secret agreements to divide up Germany's colonies.

This painting shows the signing of the Treaty of Versailles in the beautiful Hall of Mirrors.

Wilson was somewhat more successful in creating independent nations in Eastern Europe. Yet even there, problems remained. The new boundary lines did not always exactly reflect the people's choices, but they were probably better than the old boundaries.

Most important, though, the conference agreed to a League of Nations. Five large nations—the United States, Britain, France, Italy, and Japan—would be the permanent members of its Executive Council. The League would also have a General Assembly at which representatives of 42 allied and neutral nations would meet. Germany was obviously going to be left out. Still, Wilson put his hopes in the League of Nations. What problems there were in the Treaty of Versailles, he thought, could be fixed up by the League.
▶**10.** What were the major points of the Treaty of Versailles?

IMPROVE YOUR SKILLS
Comparing Cartoons

Cartoonists, like writers, express their points of view about issues. As writers frequently have conflicting points of view, so also do cartoonists. Look at the cartoons on this page and answer the questions that follow.

1. What is the topic of these cartoons?
2. Why does the creator of the cartoon on the bottom left think the United States made a mistake in not joining the League of Nations?
3. (a) Who are the figures in the cartoon on the bottom right? (b) Why does the creator of that cartoon think the United States should not join the League?
4. The cartoon on the top right appeared in a British magazine, while the other cartoons appeared in United States newspapers. What point of view is expressed by the cartoon on the top right?

5. (a) How do you think Americans reacted to the cartoon on the top right? (b) Why do you think they reacted that way?

The Fight for the Treaty

Wilson quickly learned that his troubles were not over when he left Europe. He still had to get the treaty ratified by the United States Senate. That was not going to be easy. In the congressional elections of 1918, Wilson had asked the voters to support Democrats. Instead, Republicans won a majority in both houses of Congress.

The election results meant that Wilson would have to get the treaty through a Republican Senate. By asking voters to support only Democrats, he had driven away Republicans who had supported the war and his peace program. Wilson cut himself off from such Republicans even more by inviting none of them to the conference in Versailles. Those were very serious political mistakes, and they cost Wilson dearly.

The Senate might have approved the treaty anyway. Of the 96 senators, 49 were Republicans. But only 14 of them would not support the treaty in any case. Those senators simply did not want the United States to become so involved with Europe. Among them were several old progressives, such as Hiram Johnson and Robert La Follette.

Most Republicans, however, were willing to vote for the treaty with changes, called reservations, that would clarify or limit the obligations of the United States. They were led by Henry Cabot Lodge, chairman of the Senate Foreign Relations Committee.

Lodge thought the United States should take an active part in the world. However, he wanted to be sure that in joining the League of Nations, the United States would not undermine the powers of Congress in foreign affairs. He wanted to assure, for example, that no American soldier could be ordered to fight without Congress's consent. Most of the Allies were, it seems, willing to accept the "Lodge reservations."

President Wilson, however, would not give an inch. He believed that the reservations expressed by Senator Lodge would so weaken the league that it would become powerless. The Senate, Wilson said, had to accept the whole treaty as it was agreed on at Versailles or none of it. Moral principle and the people of the world were on his side, Wilson thought, so the Senate would have to give in. Wilson even went on a speaking tour across the United States to increase popular support for the League. He attracted large, cheering crowds. But it was still the Senate, not the people, that had to approve the treaty.

Then, after a speech at Pueblo, Colorado, on September 25, 1919, tragedy struck. A blood vessel broke in Wilson's brain. He was rushed back to Washington near death. For months, he was so ill that only his doctors, his wife, and his closest advisers were allowed to see him. They kept all bad news from reaching him. During his illness, Wilson became even more rigid, and ever more self-righteous than before.

The treaty came up for approval in the Senate on November 19, 1919. Wilson ordered the Democratic senators to vote against the treaty if it was tied to any reservations. They did as he said. As a result, a proposal to pass the treaty with reservations failed. Next the Senate voted on the treaty without reservations. Again, it failed to pass.

The United States never approved the Treaty of Versailles, and it never joined the League of Nations. In October 1920, the Senate ratified separate treaties with Germany, Austria, and Hungary. That brought an end to Wilson's great dream. His failure was the greater because the hopes he raised had been so grand.

▶11. What mistakes did Wilson make in his attempt to have the Treaty of Versailles ratified?

Identify American Expeditionary Force, convoys, war boards, ~~Bernard Baruch~~, Herbert Hoover, propaganda, ~~Committee on Public Information~~, Espionage Act, Sabotage Act and Sedition Act, ~~International Workers of the World~~, trenches, ~~Chateau-Thierry~~, ~~Reims~~, ~~St. Mihiel~~, ~~Argonne Forest~~, armistice, Fourteen Points, League of Nations, Big Four, reparations, ~~Henry Cabot Lodge~~

Questions to Answer

1. How did government grow during World War I?
2. What parts of the Treaty of Versailles met Wilson's expectations? What parts disappointed him?

A Question to Think About Why is it more difficult to defend personal liberty in wartime than in peacetime?

IMPROVE YOUR READING
Using Sequence

A previous reading skills exercise (page 185), discussed the signal words that writers use to help their readers understand the order in which events happened. Signal words, such as "before" and "after," are especially helpful when a sentence mentions events out of chronological order. Here is an example of that sort of sentence: "Before building the Panama Canal, the United States gained control of the Canal Zone." The building of the Panama Canal happened after the United States gained control of the Canal Zone.

Following are two paragraphs from this chapter and a list of events described in them. Read the paragraphs. Then, on a separate sheet of paper, write the events in the order in which they occurred.

Before beginning work on the canal, the United States had to get permission from Colombia, which then ruled Panama. The United States offered to lease an area of land across Panama, which was called the **Canal Zone,** for 99 years. It would pay Colombia $10 million plus an annual rent of $250,000. Colombia refused the offer. Its government wanted more money.

Roosevelt was furious. So when a group of Panamanians and some people tied to the old French company—which would not be paid if the United States did not build its canal in Panama—plotted against Colombia, Roosevelt supported them. On November 2, 1903, he sent American warships to Panama. The revolt began the next day. Colombian troops sent to restore order in Panama could not land because of the American ships. Three days after the revolt began, the United States recognized a new nation, the Republic of Panama.

1. The United States recognizes the Republic of Panama.
2. President Roosevelt sends American warships to Panama.
3. The United States offers to lease the Canal Zone from Colombia.
4. A group of people plotted against Colombia.
5. A revolt against Colombia began in Panama.

CHAPTER 25 REVIEW

Vocabulary Check
On a separate sheet of paper, fill in the word or words that best completes each of the following sentences.

1. During much of World War I, soldiers fought from damp and dirty _____.
2. Germany used _____ to fight back against the British blockade.
3. American ships traveled in groups, which were called _____, during the war.
4. The cease-fire, or _____, ending World War I was signed on November 11, 1918.
5. The Treaty of Versailles forced the Germans to pay _____ to repay losses by the Allies.

Fact Check
On a separate sheet of paper, write the name of the person associated with each of the following terms or phrases. A person may be associated with more than one term.

1. "Speak softly but carry a big stick."
2. Gunboat diplomacy
3. Dollar diplomacy
4. Moral diplomacy
5. The Big Ditch
6. Pursuit of Pancho Villa
7. American Expeditionary Force
8. Food Administration
9. Committee on Public Information
10. Fourteen Points

Skills Check
Use the map on page 561 to answer the following questions.

1. What is the subject of this map?
2. Approximately how close had the Germans come to Paris?

3. Château-Thierry is located on what river?
4. In what direction is Cantigny from Seicheprey?
5. How many miles is Reims from Verdun?

Time Check
On a separate sheet of paper, put the following events in the order in which they occurred.

1. The Senate approves the Hay-Bunau-Varrilla Treaty giving the United States use and control of the Canal Zone.
2. TR issues the Roosevelt Corollary.
3. An assassin kills Archduke Francis Ferdinand and his wife in Sarajevo.
4. German torpedos sink the *Lusitania*.
5. The armistice ending World War I is signed.

Think and Write
1. Compare the ways Presidents Roosevelt and Wilson thought the United States should deal with other nations.
2. What actions of Presidents Roosevelt, Taft, and Wilson caused hostility in Central and South America?
3. How did the war boards organize the home front for the war effort?
4. Why did Wilson hope for a peace without victory to end World War I?
5. Why did many Americans oppose joining the League of Nations?

Chapter 26

The 1920's

Carnivals, such as the one shown here by artist John Sloan, were extremely popular in the 1920's.

The 1920's were years of many different moods. Once World War I ended, the United States suffered terrible waves of fear. Those fears were inspired in part by events abroad, especially in Russia. For a time, the nation seemed to be at war with itself as Americans turned against other Americans.

Then the hard times that came with the war's end gave way to a new prosperity. With that change arrived a kind of happiness as Americans enjoyed the many new products that became available for their convenience and amusement.

The idealism of the pre-war and early war years seemed to disappear from public life in the 1920's. World War I had not, after all, made the world safe for democracy in Europe or at home. Tired of great campaigns to improve the world, many Americans lost interest in politics. That mood also passed with the election of 1928.

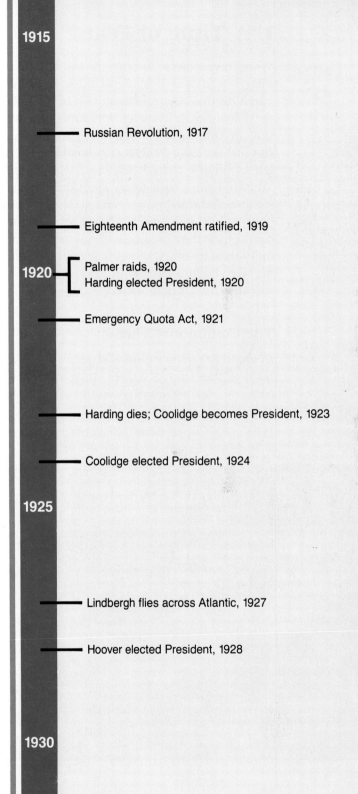

1915

Russian Revolution, 1917

Eighteenth Amendment ratified, 1919

1920
Palmer raids, 1920
Harding elected President, 1920

Emergency Quota Act, 1921

Harding dies; Coolidge becomes President, 1923

Coolidge elected President, 1924

1925

Lindbergh flies across Atlantic, 1927

Hoover elected President, 1928

1930

I. A Time of Fear

Waves of fear swept through the United States after World War I. Many of those fears began with the Russian Revolution of 1917. At first, the revolutionaries replaced Russia's czar, or king, with a democratic government. But in November 1917, the Communist Party, led by Vladimir Ilich Ulyanov, who called himself Lenin, took over. The Communists set up a **dictatorship,** a government in which one person or a group of people rule the country as they choose without regard for individual liberties. In many ways, the Communist dictatorship in Russia seemed to threaten the United States.

The Communist Threat

Communists oppose **capitalist** economies like that of the United States. In a capitalist economy, farms, stores, factories, and other businesses are owned by private citizens who try to earn profits. The Communists say that capitalists, the people who own the businesses, make their profits at the expense of their workers.

In 1848, Karl Marx, a German writer and historian, outlined Communist beliefs in a book called the *Communist Manifesto*. Marx called on the workers of the world to rise up and throw off their capitalist rulers. Then they could begin a Communist economic system in which the people together owned all the "means of production" and operated them for their own good. Lenin and other Communist leaders said that they followed the teachings of Karl Marx, although in fact, they added a further belief to Marx's ideas. Only a small, disciplined party could carry out the necessary revolution, they said, and to do that might require imposing a dictatorship.

President Wilson thought from the start that the Communist government in Russia was a challenge to the United States. Americans believe in private property and in a free enterprise system, which allows individuals to make their own economic decisions. Americans also place a high value on democratic procedures and on a government that protects their civil liberties.

In part because he opposed the new Communist government, Wilson was willing to send 15,000 American troops to Russia in 1918. Some European governments also sent troops. Wilson said the troops were there to protect Allied supplies and Russian railroads from the Germans. The American soldiers stayed until 1920. They did not accomplish much except to anger the Communist government.

▶ **1.** How does the capitalist economic system differ from the system outlined by Marx?

Many people suspected of being Communist supporters were deported during the Red Scare.

The Russian Revolution of 1917 created a new, powerful Communist nation. The results of that revolution have been felt throughout the world.

The revolutionary movement in Russia began in the early 1800's. By 1894, when Nicholas II became czar, the idea of revolution had won the support of the educated middle class, the workers, and the peasants.

Several revolutionary parties competed for followers. One of those parties, the Social Democrats, accepted the ideas of Karl Marx, who believed that city workers, not peasants, would create the revolution. In 1903, the Social Democrats split. Lenin became the leader of the Bolshevik, or majority wing, which was the more radical group. It insisted that only dedicated revolutionaries could join the party.

In 1905, Russia fought and lost a war with Japan, which hurt Russia's already troubled economy. Then in 1914, Russia entered World War I. The war exhausted Russia. By 1917, the Russian armies had mutinied and Nicholas II was overthrown. Then a struggle for power began between the moderate revolutionaries and the Bolsheviks. The Bolsheviks seized power in November 1917 and began to organize a Communist state.

In 1918, anti-Communist Russians, called Whites, tried to overthrow the new government. Despite aid from other countries, including the United States, the Whites failed. The Communists were in control and tightened their dictatorship. They set up a new government. In 1922, Russia became the Union of Soviet Socialist Republics (USSR), or the Soviet Union. The cost of the new government was enormous. Millions of Russians had died and the economy was in ruins.

Problems for the newly formed nation continued. In 1924, Lenin died. By 1929, Josef Djugashvili, who called himself Stalin, defeated Lev Bronstein, who called himself Trotsky, in a bitter struggle for control of the country.

Stalin became the "iron man" of the Soviet Union. He took even more dictatorial power than Lenin had held. Stalin ordered the killing of thousands of people in purges in the 1930's. He led the Soviet Union through World War II, and died in 1953.

The Red Scare

In 1919, the Russian Communists set up the Communist International, or Comintern. The declared purpose of this international organization was to encourage revolution throughout the world. In 1922, the Communists organized the territory of the Russian Empire into the Union of Soviet Socialist Republics, often called the Soviet Union.

Developments in the Soviet Union, along with some events within the United States, frightened many Americans. It seemed to those Americans that their country was full of **subversives**—people who were secretly trying to undermine the government of the United States.

During early postwar years, many states passed sedition laws that made it a serious offense to work for revolution. Then they threw people accused of subversion in jail. Sometimes mobs took the law into their own hands, beating up and even lynching people whom they thought were Reds, as Communists were called. That episode in United States history is called the **Red Scare.**

▶**2.** What was the Red Scare?

Bombs Americans' fears of subversives were strengthened by a rash of bombs that were sent or planted in the United States in 1919 and 1920. In late April 1919, a total of 38 packages containing bombs were mailed to prominent people such as J.P. Morgan, John D. Rockefeller, and the Attorney General of the United States A. Mitchell Palmer. Only one person, the servant of a senator from Georgia, was hurt by the bombs. Although no one knew who sent the bombs, suspicion fell on Communist subversives.

There were other bombs too. One blew up on the night of June 2, 1919, in front of Palmer's house in Washington. The worst explosion occurred at lunchtime on September 16, 1920, on Wall Street in New York, the very center of American capitalism. Hundreds of people were hurt, and 33 died. Again, no one ever found out for sure who was responsible.

▶**3.** What bombing incidents made people fear subversives?

Strikes After the war, the nation was troubled by serious labor disputes. Many Americans thought the strikes were the work of Communists, since Communist doctrine called for workers to revolt. In fact, only a few union members, such as members of the IWW, wanted to change the American system. Most workers were interested only in "bread and butter" issues like hours and wages.

During the war, many workers had joined unions and won some increase in wages. Then, when the war ended, prices went up. By 1919, the country was in a period of **inflation.** Inflation is a time when prices rise because money and credit become available but there are fewer goods to purchase. The inflation of 1919 and 1920 made it harder for workers to make ends meet. When employers refused to raise wages and even tried to take away benefits won by workers during the war, the unions called strikes.

In February 1919, a famous strike began in Seattle, Washington. It started among shipyard workers, but spread until almost all work in the city came to a halt. The city was paralyzed. The mayor of Seattle, Ole Hanson, got the United States marines to keep the city going. Then the strike failed.

In September 1919, the police in Boston, Massachusetts, went on strike. Volunteers tried to keep order. They failed. Thieves and looters ran loose through the streets. But again, both city and state officials stood firm. "There is no right to strike against the public safety by anybody, anywhere, any time," said Massachusetts Governor Calvin Coolidge. The strike in Boston, like the one in Seattle, failed. The city hired new police officers to replace the strikers.

No workers in the United States had better reason to strike than the steelworkers. In 1919, many of them still worked 12 hours a day, 7 days per week. Sometimes steelworkers put in 96 hours a week while most Americans put in 48 hours. As a result, the steelworkers organized and asked for shorter hours and higher wages. When owners refused their demands, steelworkers called a massive strike. It failed, as did most later strikes of the period.

There were about 3,600 strikes involving more than four million workers in 1919. Employers had little trouble associating the strikers with Communists and getting the government to help fight them. As a result, the strikes of 1919 and 1920 failed so badly that it took the labor movement more than ten years to recover.

▶**4.** Why did the strikes of 1919 and 1920 frighten many Americans?

The Palmer Raids Attorney General Palmer feared and hated Communists. In early January 1920, he ordered a series of raids, called the **Palmer raids,** on suspected subversives. More than 6,000 people were arrested and thrown in jail. There they remained for weeks, but no charges were brought against them. The government's failure to file formal charges violated their constitutional rights. Later, most of those arrested were released. But 500 suspects who were not United States citizens were deported—that is, shipped out of the country.

▶**5.** What were the Palmer raids?

Sacco and Vanzetti The Red Scare reached new heights with the arrest and execution of Nicola Sacco (sak ō′) and Bartolomeo Vanzetti (van zet′ē). In May 1920, they were accused of robbing and killing a paymaster in South Braintree, Massachusetts. Both men were Italian immigrants. Both were also **anarchists.** Anarchists believe the world would be a better place with no government at all.

The evidence against Sacco and Vanzetti was not strong, and they defended themselves eloquently. Although they won the support of many Americans, they were convicted. On August 23, 1927, they died in the electric chair. Many thoughtful people were convinced that they were innocent and died because of prejudice against immigrants and anarchists.

▶**6.** What did some people believe was the reason for executing Sacco and Vanzetti?

Immigration Restriction There had been attempts since the 1890's to limit immigration from Southern and Eastern Europe. After World War I, support for such immigration

The Museum of Modern Art

Artist Ben Shahn painted Sacco and Vanzetti as they waited to hear the jury's decision.

restriction grew rapidly. The development was fueled by the idea that immigrants were often subversives. In 1914, the peak year of immigration to the United States, 1,218,480 immigrants had entered the country. Between 1905 and 1914, the one million mark had been crossed six times.

Then in 1921, Congress approved passage of the **Emergency Quota Act.** It said only 357,000 immigrants could come to the United States each year. The law also said the number of immigrants from any country could be no more than 3 percent of the number of people from that country already in the United States in 1910.

Three years later, Congress passed yet another law, the **National Origins Act.** It cut the number of yearly immigrants to 164,000 per year. It said *no one* could come to the United States from countries in Asia such as China and Japan. The number of immigrants from countries in Europe could be no more than 2 percent of those already in the United States in 1890.

The law greatly limited the number of immigrants from Southern and Eastern Europe. Before 1890, most immigrants had come from the British Isles and Germany. By basing new immigration on the population in 1890 instead of 1910, the law made it harder for people from Eastern and Southern Europe to enter the United States. It was much easier to immigrate from countries such as Britain or Germany. In fact, the quota for many Northern European countries—the number of immigrants allowed from those countries—was often higher than the number of people who wanted to come.

The laws of 1921 and 1924 ended the massive flow of immigrants to the United States. In the future, Congress cut the number who could come even further. The United States

Members of the KKK gather in Washington, D.C., in 1925 to win support for their cause.

remained a land of opportunity, but fewer foreigners could take advantage of those opportunities. Often those who wanted to come most to the United States found it the hardest to do.

▶**7.** How did Congress limit the number and nationalities of immigrants who could enter the country in the 1920's?

The Ku Klux Klan Even after the worst of the Red Scare had passed, many Americans remained distrustful of anyone different from themselves. That distrust led to the revival of the Ku Klux Klan (KKK). The original KKK terrified newly freed blacks in the post-Civil War South. It had died out in the 1870's. Then, in 1915, the organization was revived. It had members throughout the United States and was very strong in Indiana and other parts of the Middle West.

Like the old Klan, the new KKK used terror to control blacks. The new Klan, however, was also directed against immigrants, Catholics, and Jews. Sometimes the KKK threatened people or boycotted their businesses. Sometimes it used violence, punishing its victims with whippings, arson, and even lynchings. By 1924, the KKK had four million members. Then its leaders began quarreling with one another and membership declined.

▶**8.** What was the difference between the old Klan and the new?

Racial Conflict

The KKK tried, with some success, to make use of racial conflict brewing in the North. Southern blacks began to move north in the 1880's as the boll weevil spread through the South, ruining the cotton crop. Then, after 1910, the wave of **migration,** or movement from one place to another, grew dramatically.

Black artist Jacob Lawrence made a series of paintings showing black migration. This one is entitled "The Migrants Arrive in Great Numbers."

About 40,000 blacks left the South between 1900 and 1910, but 227,000 left between 1910 and 1920. In the 1920's, the movement grew even more—about 445,000 blacks migrated. Most of the newcomers sought jobs in northern cities.

Many of the newcomers were willing to work for lower wages than white workers. In fact, some blacks were brought to the North as strikebreakers. As a result, few were welcomed by Northerners.

In 1917, white mobs in several cities attacked blacks. The violence became worse in 1919. That year, there was a full week of rioting in Chicago. When peace was finally restored, 38 people were dead and a large part of the city was in ashes. Racial violence also exploded in other cities. In the end, the fighting left about 120 Americans dead and many more homeless.

The riots were a sad welcome home for the 400,000 blacks who had served in the United States Army during World War I. Many of those soldiers supported organizations that were fighting for black rights, such as the NAACP.

Some blacks gave up hope of finding a better future in the United States. A half million of them joined the Universal Negro Improvement Association. Its leader was Marcus Garvey, a black from Jamaica. Garvey wanted American blacks to found a new nation in Africa where he would be their ruler. Although Garvey's descriptions of the great African civilizations of the past increased the pride of black people, few blacks made the move to Africa. They had long since become Americans.

▶9. Why did many blacks move to the North between 1880 and the 1920's?

IMPROVE YOUR SKILLS
Using Tables

In the early 1900's, thousands of black Americans left the South looking for a better life in other parts of the country. Their migration caused a decrease in population in some states, and an increase in others. Tables are a good way to show shifts in population.

The table below shows changes in the black population of various states between 1910 and 1920. The figures with a minus sign (−) show a loss of population. Look at the footnote at the bottom of the table. It explains the number that appears next to New Hampshire and South Dakota.

On a separate sheet of paper, answer the following questions.

1. Which state had the largest decrease in population?
2. Which state had the largest increase in population?
3. What change in the black population took place in Vermont?
4. About how many more people emigrated to Michigan than to Indiana?
5. What kind of graph (circle, bar, or line) would best illustrate the data from the chart?

Changes in Black Population, 1910 to 1920
(In Thousands)

State	Pop.	State	Pop.	State	Pop.
The North		**The South**		**The West**	
Maine	0.1	Delaware	-0.6	Montana	-0.1
New Hampshire	(^{1})	Maryland	7.0	Idaho	0.3
Vermont	-0.9	Virginia	-27.2	Wyoming	-0.6
Massachusetts	6.9	West Virginia	15.5	Colorado	0.7
Rhode Island	0.6	North Carolina	-28.9	New Mexico	4.1
Connecticut	5.3	South Carolina	-74.5	Arizona	5.8
New York	63.1	Georgia	-74.7	Utah	0.4
New Jersey	24.5	Florida	3.2	Nevada	-0.1
Pennsylvania	82.5	Kentucky	-16.6	Washington	1.1
Ohio	69.4	Tennessee	-29.3	Oregon	0.7
Indiana	20.3	Alabama	-70.8	California	16.1
Illinois	69.8	Mississippi	-129.6		
Michigan	38.7	Arkansas	-1.0		
Wisconsin	2.2	Louisiana	-51.2		
Minnesota	2.1	Oklahoma	0.8		
Iowa	3.9	Texas	5.2		
Missouri	27.2				
North Dakota	-0.1				
South Dakota	(^{1})				
Nebraska	5.2				
Kansas	5.4				

(^{1}) less than 50

Source: Historical Statistics of the United States

Reviewing Section I

Identify dictatorship, Communists, capitalist, Karl Marx, Communist International, subversives, Red Scare, inflation, Calvin Coolidge, Palmer raids, Nicola Sacco, Bartolomeo Vanzetti, anarchists, Emergency Quota Act, National Origins Act, migration, Marcus Garvey

Questions to Answer
1. Why did communism and Communists seem to pose a threat to the United States in the 1920's?
2. Why did the labor movement lose ground in the early 1920's?

A Question to Think About What contributed to racial tension after World War I?

II. The Roaring Twenties

By 1921, the worst of the Red Scare and the racial violence was over. In that year, too, the economy of the United States began a period of impressive growth. In the course of the 1920's, the **gross national product,** the total amount of goods and services produced in the United States, went up by 40 percent.

As the nation became more prosperous, many Americans found that they had to spend less time at work. Industrial workers often had to work only five and a half days a week by the late 1920's. Many white collar workers even received paid vacations each year. Wages also rose. After they paid for food and shelter, many Americans had money left over. They found new ways to use their extra time and money.

New Products for Consumers

Americans went on a spending spree in the 1920's. There were many new products they could buy. As a result, the 1920's became a great age of consumerism, a time when people were preoccupied with buying things. American life was changed in many ways during the great buying spree of the 1920's.
▶**1.** What is an age of consumerism?

The Automobile The new consumer product that had the greatest impact on American life was, perhaps, the automobile. It was invented long before the 1920's. In fact, 2.5 million automobiles were already on American roads in 1915. In the 1920's, however, automobiles came within the reach of ordinary people. That change came about because of the work of Henry Ford.

Ford grew up on a farm in Michigan but hated farm work. In 1887, he moved to Detroit

Workers at a Ford plant are shown putting cars together on an assembly line.

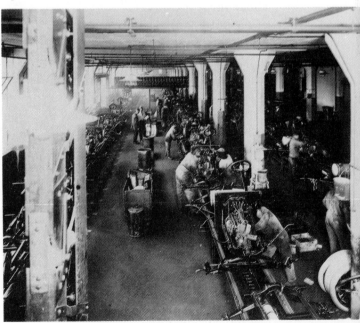

and took a job in a machine shop. At the same time, he worked to fulfill a dream. He wanted to build a car that most Americans could afford.

Five years after he founded the Ford Motor Company in 1903, Ford brought out the first Model T car. It sold for $850. Then, in 1913, Ford established the first moving **assembly line.** Before that, a car remained in one place while it was being built. Many different workers went there to work on it. With an assembly line, the car was moved from one worker to another. Each worker performed one operation on many cars from the same place. The assembly line allowed Ford to cut the time it took to build a car. Before the assembly line, it took 12.5 hours of work to put a car together. Afterwards, it took only 1.5 hours.

Saving time was saving money. By 1925, the Ford Motor Company was producing a new car every ten seconds. That year the price tag for a Model T had fallen to $290. Even a factory worker earned that much in about three months.

▶**2.** What is an assembly line?

A Nation on Wheels The boom in automobile-making meant that more steel, rubber, and glass had to be produced. Better roads were built, and restaurants sprang up along those roads. So did motels, places where both people and their cars could spend the night. Of course, the petroleum business also grew, since without gasoline the new car-owners could go nowhere.

Where did people want to go? They wanted to go to and from work, for one thing. With the automobile, people no longer had to work within walking distance of their jobs or even along the cities' streetcar lines. More and more Americans moved to sprawling suburbs just outside the city.

▶**3.** What changes did the automobile bring to the United States?

Radio and Movies In the 1920's, entertainment became an industry. The first radio station in the United States to broadcast presidential election results was KDKA in Pittsburgh. The first of those broadcasts was in 1920. At that time, almost no one owned a radio. But by 1929, 12 million families had radio sets. Local stations and two national stations, the National Broadcasting Company (NBC) and the Columbia Broadcasting Company (CBS) competed for listeners. Often millions of people listened to the same broadcast. As a result, the radio helped tie Americans together.

The movies also helped link Americans because people living in different sections of the country saw the same films. The movies

Charlie Chaplin was one of the nation's best-known actors in the 1920's.

were not as new as radio. Silent films had been around since the early 1900's. Never before, however, were film stars as adored as they were in the 1920's. Americans rushed to see movies featuring their favorite actors and actresses. Stars such as Mary Pickford, Greta Garbo, Rudolph Valentino, and Charlie Chaplin were known to almost everyone. Then, with *The Jazz Singer*, a movie of 1927, the "talkies" were born. By the 1930's, millions of Americans were going to the movies every week.

▶**4.** How did radio and movies tie the country together?

Fads and Sports

The Twenties was a time of many fads. New games and heroes appeared with a rush of publicity and then faded from view. Americans played board games such as mah-jongg or worked crossword puzzles. They tried out new dances or learned to play new games such as miniature golf. Some even tried to sit on flagpoles longer than anyone else.

▶**5.** What were two of the fads popular in the Twenties?

Sports The most excitement, however, was reserved for sports. The 1920's was the "Golden Age of Sports." Professional baseball became the national game. People across the country cheered when Babe Ruth came to bat. At first a pitcher for the Boston Red Sox, Ruth became an outfielder after joining the New York Yankees. He hit 60 home runs in 1927 and 714 in all before he retired.

There were heroes in other sports as well. Boxer Jack Dempsey, tennis player William Tilden, and golfer Bobby Jones were just a few of those new heroes. There were female sports stars, too. Gertrude Ederle became the first woman to swim the English Channel.

The Golden Age of Sports created celebrities like tennis star Helen Wills.

Helen Wills won more major tennis championships than any other woman in the world. She won her first United States women's tournament in 1923.

▶**6.** Who were some of the sports stars of the 1920's?

Aviation The most enthusiastic response to any hero of the 1920's went to Charles Lindbergh, the first person to fly alone, nonstop across the Atlantic Ocean. In December 1903, two brothers, Wilbur and Orville Wright, managed to keep a plane airborn for almost a minute. They made their famous flight on the beach at Kitty Hawk, North Carolina. At the time Charles Lindbergh of Minnesota was just 2 years old. Only 24 years later, he made his famous flight.

Lindbergh's plane, *The Spirit of St. Louis*, took off in the rain from a muddy field near New York City on May 20, 1927. He brought

the plane down at the Le Bourget airport near Paris 33 hours later. Immediately he became the idol of millions. The President sent a cruiser to bring him home. Crowds turned out to cheer him wherever he went.
▶**7.** Who was Charles Lindbergh?

Opportunities for Women

Although married women still seldom worked outside their homes in the 1920's, more and more single women had jobs. By 1930, close to 11 million women held paying jobs. Most women continued to be employed in offices as typists and clerks. About 2 million women worked in factories, although many factory jobs were closed to women. More than a million women worked in professions such as nursing and teaching. Some became college professors, musicians, authors, editors, reporters, and artists.

The lives of married women who did not hold jobs outside their homes also changed. Women bought more washing machines, vacuum cleaners, and other appliances that made doing housework faster and easier. The use of such labor-saving machines could spread because by 1928 two-thirds of all American families had a source of energy, electricity, in their homes. Those families were, however, more likely to live in cities than on farms. The release of rural women from the worst drudgery of housework was yet to come.

In the 1920's, some young women, especially college students and young working women, found a new way to assert their freedom from "old-fashioned" restrictions. They became **flappers.** They cut their hair, raised their skirts, rolled their stockings, started wearing makeup, and learned to do the latest dances that were sweeping the nation.
▶**8.** Who were the flappers?

The new styles worn by these flappers were very popular during the 1920's.

The Arts in the 1920's

Many writers found a great deal to criticize in Americans' new ways of life. They opposed the bigotry and racism of the 1920's. They said the United States had become too materialistic, that is, it valued things more than ideals. In his novel *Main Street*, published in 1920, Sinclair Lewis tried to show how much was lost as Americans gave in to consumerism. And in *The Great Gatsby*, published in 1925, F. Scott Fitzgerald wrote about the emptiness of material success.

Some writers left the United States. The poet T.S. Eliot, for example, lived most his adult life in England. Other writers went to Paris. Many moved to New York City's Greenwich Village, a part of Manhattan, where their simple way of life showed their contempt for American materialism.

On the other end of Manhattan, in Harlem, lived another group of writers and artists with a different message. Black writers of the **Harlem Renaissance** such as Langston Hughes, Countee Cullen, and Claude McKay wrote with pride of their race and their African heritage.

Black musicians had, perhaps, an even greater influence on their time. They created **jazz,** a form of music so popular that the 1920's were sometimes called the Jazz Age.

Jazz was invented by black musicians in New Orleans in the 1800's. Its roots lay in the days of slavery. By the 1920's, jazz was popular with blacks and whites alike. Jazz musicians such as Louis Armstrong and King Oliver improvised, or made up their melodies as they went along. Jazz remains one of the most important contributions Americans have made to the world of music.

▶**9.** How did blacks contribute to the arts in the 1920's?

Prohibition

Life in the 1920's was shaped in part by the **Eighteenth Amendment** to the Constitution, which Congress had approved during World War I. It is called the Prohibition Amendment because it outlawed, or prohibited, the "manufacture, sale, or transportation of intoxicating liquors." The amendment was the greatest triumph of the temperance movement which began before the Civil War.

The amendment was ratified in January 1919. The same year, Congress passed the Volstead Act. That law set down rules for enforcing Prohibition beginning in 1920 and defined "intoxicating liquors" in a way that included beer as well as stronger drinks like whiskey.

Many Americans refused to obey the law. Manufacturing and selling alcohol became a

The poetry of Langston Hughes is admired by Americans of all racial backgrounds.

huge illegal business. Americans paid as much as $2 billion a year to bootleggers who made whisky illegally or smuggled it across the border from Canada.

▶**10.** What was Prohibition? When did it begin?

Reviewing Section II

Identify gross national product, Henry Ford, assembly line, Charles Lindbergh, flappers, Harlem Renaissance, jazz, Eighteenth Amendment, Prohibition

Questions to Answer
1. Name three ways the automobile changed the way Americans lived.
2. What were some of the ways Americans spent their increased leisure time in the Twenties?

A Question to Think About Why was the Eighteenth Amendment unsuccessful?

III. Politics: From Harding to Hoover

Americans of the 1920's, the writer F. Scott Fitzgerald once said, had "no interest in politics at all." The Presidents of the time did not increase interest in public affairs. Leaders who believed government could help make a better world seemed to fade from public life. Those who led the nation believed more often, like Thomas Jefferson, that government was best when it did the least.

The Election of 1920

In 1920, Democrats nominated for President the governor of Ohio, James M. Cox. His running mate was Franklin D. Roosevelt, a cousin of Theodore Roosevelt and Wilson's assistant secretary of the navy.

The Republican candidate was chosen by the party's bosses. They wanted someone they could control, and they settled on a good-natured senator from Ohio, Warren Gamaliel Harding. The editor of a paper in Marion, Ohio, Harding had served in both the Ohio state legislature and the United States Senate without doing anything worth remembering. For Vice President, the Republicans chose Calvin Coolidge, the Massachusetts governor who had refused to give in to striking Boston police officers.

Harding did not promise much in his campaign. The voters, it seemed, did not want much. They elected him President with 60 percent of the popular vote.

▶1. Who won the election of 1920?

President Harding's Cabinet

Warren Harding had the good sense to know he was not qualified to be President. He was handsome and easygoing, and he was happy enough to do whatever other Republicans wanted him to do. He could not manage the government of the United States. Instead he delegated responsibility to others.

Harding appointed some talented people. His secretary of commerce, Herbert C. Hoover, and secretary of state, Charles Evans Hughes, were both able, successful Cabinet members.

The most powerful member of Harding's Cabinet was the secretary of the treasury, Andrew Mellon, a millionaire from Pittsburgh. Mellon said, "Government is just a business." By that he meant it should trim its costs as much as possible. Mellon thought that government should encourage business and wealthy people to spend. As a result, he worked to lower the taxes for corporations and rich people. Mellon also hoped to help business by the Ford-McCumber Tariff of 1922. It raised tariffs to a new high level.

Unlike Hoover, Hughes, and Mellon, many of Harding's appointees were old political friends. They used their offices mainly to enrich themselves.

It took a few years before the scandals of Harding's administration became known. Harding's secretaries of the interior and of the navy had leased the rich oil lands held by the government at Teapot Dome, Wyoming, and Elk Hills, California, to private interests. In return, they received hundreds of thousands of dollars in bribes. Eventually, one member after another of Harding's administration was exposed for having misused his office in that way. Several went to jail.

When the extent of corruption was first revealed in the summer of 1923, a tired and worried Harding took a trip to Alaska and the West. He died of a heart attack on August 2 in San Francisco.

▶2. Why were many of Harding's appointments unfortunate?

President Coolidge

Vice President Calvin Coolidge was in Vermont when he received the news of Harding's death. There, in the family kitchen, by the light of a kerosene lamp, his father, who was a justice of the peace, administered the oath of the office of President to Coolidge.

A small town boy from New England, Coolidge had worked his way through college. He became a lawyer and moved to Massachusetts. There he entered state politics and eventually became governor. He did little in office to distinguish himself except during the Boston police strike. Coolidge brought no great strength of mind to the White House. He was honest, though, and his morals were above question.

The voters loved him. In the election of 1924, they gave Coolidge 15.7 million votes— 54 percent of the total—compared to 8.3 million for his Democratic opponent, John W. Davis, a Wall Street lawyer.

There was also an old-style reform candidate in the 1924 presidential race. A newly formed Progressive Party ran Robert La Follette, now nearly 70 years old but as much a fighter for his causes as ever. He was against child labor. He favored conservation, greater taxes for the rich, and the rights of labor. He won 4.8 million votes but carried only his home state of Wisconsin. The Progressive Party disappeared after La Follette died the next year.

Coolidge was called "Silent Cal" because he said very little in public. Once a woman told him she had bet a friend she could get him to say more than three words to her. "You lose," he answered. He also did very little during his presidency. His daily naps became something of a joke.

Coolidge supported fully the world of business that was bringing so many riches to the American consumers. "The business of

Harding used campaign posters that showed him to be a loyal American in the election of 1920.

America is business," he once said. In other words, the government should help business so business could give jobs and pay to workers. His thoughts fit those of Andrew Mellon, who remained head of the Treasury Department. With Coolidge's blessing and the help of Congress, Mellon continued to cut the taxes for the rich and reduce the activities of the federal government.

▶**3.** What did Coolidge mean when he said, "The business of America is business?"

The Election of 1928

Many expected Coolidge to win a second term easily. However, as the 1928 election approached, Coolidge made a brief, surprise announcement. "I do not choose to run," he said. Suddenly, the silence ended. The election

President Coolidge (left) and Herbert Hoover are shown relaxing in California.

of 1928 was more noisy and exciting than any since William Jennings Bryan and William McKinley fought it out in the 1896 presidential election.

The election of 1928 pitted two competent, energetic candidates against each other. The differences between the two candidates were sharply drawn. On one side was a Republican who believed that government could best serve the nation's interest by working closely with business. On the other side was a Democrat who had fought for laws to protect workers and the poor.

▶4. Why was the election of 1928 exciting?

Herbert Hoover The Republicans chose as their candidate in 1928 a talented man of action, Herbert Hoover. Hoover served as secretary of commerce under both Harding and Coolidge. He made the Department of

Commerce a center of activity in those otherwise do-little administrations.

The future progress and the prosperity of the country, Hoover believed, would come through cooperation between industries. As a result, he encouraged businesses to join trade associations and to draw up industrial codes that would help them avoid "wasteful" competition with one another. He worked, too, for cooperation between business and labor and even got the steel industry to adopt the eight-hour workday, something that the strikes of 1919 failed to do. He became interested in measures businesses might adopt that would help keep the economy on a steady course, avoiding the panics and depressions of earlier days. Obviously, his faith lay with private business, but he was more willing than most Republicans to see the government play a much more active role in helping business build a better world. Hoover was, in fact, something of a progressive reformer, 1920's style.

▶5. What sorts of reforms did Hoover work for during his presidency?

Al Smith The Democratic candidate was a progressive of an older sort. Alfred E. Smith was born to Irish Catholic parents in a tenement house on New York's East Side in 1873. He was smart and he had charm and a sense of humor. He made his career as a politician supported by Tammany Hall, the Democratic machine in New York City. Smith became a Democratic leader of the state assembly at Albany. He served with Robert Wagner on the state's factory investigating commission. Together they helped get a series of new factory and labor laws through the legislature. Clearly, Smith's brand of progressivism did not rest on faith in big business. Smith wanted governments to work more actively to protect the workers and the

IMPROVE YOUR READING
Using Categories

You have read about many important people in this chapter, people who made contributions in different fields such as politics, music, sports, and entertainment. One way to help yourself remember so many names is to make a chart. On a separate sheet of paper, make a chart with the following headings: **Politics, Arts and Entertainment, Sports,** and **Other,** like the one shown below. Then write each of the following names under the correct category. Use your completed chart to help you review the chapter.

Henry Ford
A. Mitchell Palmer
Gertrude Ederle
Greta Garbo
Babe Ruth
Sacco and Vanzetti
Helen Wills
King Oliver
Andrew Mellon
Marcus Garvey
Langston Hughes
Herbert Hoover
Warren Harding
Al Smith
Calvin Coolidge
Charles Lindbergh
Jack Dempsey
Louis Armstrong

Politics	*Arts and Entertainment*	*Sports*	*Other*

CHAPTER 26 REVIEW

Vocabulary Check
Write a short definition for each of the following words.

1. Dictatorship
2. Capitalist
3. Subversives
4. Inflation
5. Anarchists
6. Migration
7. Gross national product
8. Assembly line
9. Flappers
10. Jazz

Fact Check
On a separate sheet of paper, fill in the word or words that best complete each of the following sentences.

1. According to _____ teachings, a nation's workers should together own its farms, stores, and factories.
2. During the _____, many Americans feared that Communist subversives were causing bombings and strikes.
3. During the _____, more than 6,000 suspected subversives were arrested.
4. _____ and _____ were immigrant anarchists who were executed for murder on what some people felt was insufficient evidence.
5. The Emergency Quota Act and the National Origins Act limited the annual number of _____.
6. Many blacks _____ to the North in the 1920's.
7. The 1920's were an age of _____, when the nation went on a buying spree.
8. Black writers of the _____ expressed pride in their race and their African heritage.
9. _____ refers to the outlawing of the manufacturing, sale, and transportation of intoxicating beverages.
10. Members of Harding's Cabinet were involved in scandals over the oil lands of _____, Wyoming.

Skills Check
1. Are any of the illustrations in this chapter *not* primary sources? Give reasons for your answers.
2. Choose one of the illustrations from this chapter and write a paragraph explaining how it shows a change in American life.

Time Check
On a separate sheet of paper, put the following events in the order in which they occurred.

1. Charles Lindbergh flies alone, nonstop across the Atlantic Ocean.
2. Police in Boston, Massachusetts, strike.
3. Henry Ford sets up the first assembly line.
4. The Eighteenth Amendment is ratified.
5. Herbert Hoover is elected President.

Think and Write
1. How did the automobile change American life?
2. In what way did the heroes and heroines of the 1920's differ from those of earlier times? Use examples in your answer.
3. Why did Prohibition fail to halt the sale of intoxicating liquors?
4. Explain how the followers of Marcus Garvey, members of the NAACP, and the writers of the Harlem Renaissance responded to the treatment of blacks during the 1920's.
5. Compare the kind of reforms favored by Herbert Hoover and Al Smith.

REVIEWING UNIT 8

Reviewing the Facts I.

On a separate sheet of paper, write the name of the person described in each of the phrases below. Some names may be used more than once.

1. This progressive governor of Wisconsin began a series of reforms in that state that spread to other parts of the country.
2. This black leader, who used experts and research to further his cause, helped start the NAACP.
3. He was the first progressive President.
4. This President urged Congress to pass the Federal Reserve Act.
5. This President secured the Canal Zone for the United States.
6. He was the President who led the nation during World War I.
7. He was the first person to fly alone, non-stop across the Atlantic Ocean.
8. This attorney general called for the arrest of subversives.
9. This President's administration was marred by serious scandals.
10. This Irish Catholic candidate from New York City was defeated in the presidential election of 1928.

Reviewing the Facts II.

On a separate sheet of paper, fill in the word or words that best completes each of the following sentences.

1. Reformers of the early 1900's who believed government should take an active role in shaping the nation's progress are called ____.
2. ____ was the name Roosevelt gave to writers who wrote popular articles about public problems.
3. The ____ Amendment says that women cannot be denied the right to vote because of their sex.
4. The ____ Amendment provides for the direct election of senators.
5. The ____ Amendment prohibited the manufacture, sale, or transport of intoxicating beverages.
6. President Wilson believed that the United States should practice ____ diplomacy in its dealings with other nations.
7. The ____, in which the German foreign minister promised to help Mexico win back its lost territory from the United States, caused anti-German feeling in the United States.
8. The United States refused to join the ____ formed by the Treaty of Versailles.
9. ____ took control of Russia after World War I and formed the Comintern to spread revolution throughout the world.
10. Writers of the ____ expressed pride in their race and their African heritage.

Reviewing Ideas

1. (a) In what ways did progressive reforms expand democracy? (b) What groups in the United States were ignored by many progressive reformers?
2. Describe the policies of Presidents Roosevelt, Taft, and Wilson in Central and South America.
3. Describe the work of the war boards during World War I.
4. (a) What were President Wilson's hopes for the world at the end of World War I? (b) Which were achieved?
5. Describe at least two different moods of the 1920's in the United States.

UNIT NINE

Depression and War

The happy days of the 1920's came to an abrupt end in the 1930's when the nation found itself in the worst depression it had ever faced. A decade later, Americans became involved in a second world war. Jasper Johns's painting captures the patriotic spirit that Americans showed during the war. When the war ended, another sort of war, a cold war, began.

Chapter 27

Fighting the Depression

Edward Hopper captured the gloom many Americans felt during the Great Depression in his painting "Room in New York."

During the presidential campaign of 1928, Herbert Hoover promised that poverty would be banished from the United States after a few more years of Republican rule. Soon after his inauguration, however, the stock market crashed and a depression began that was much worse than any the country had known before. In that Great Depression of the 1930's, poverty became commonplace.

If voters had known that such hard times were coming, they probably would have voted for Hoover anyway. He was "the great engineer," a man who knew how to make things work. In fact, Hoover did more than any President before him to repair the economy, but it was not enough. As a result, the voters elected a Democrat, Franklin Delano Roosevelt, to the presidency in 1932. They hoped that he would find a way to end their distress.

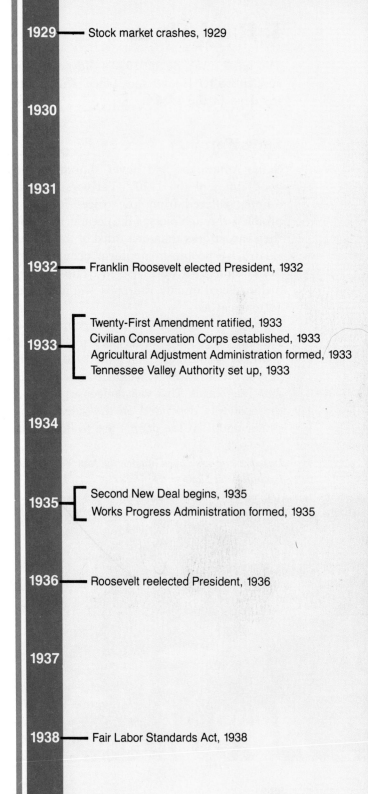

1929 — Stock market crashes, 1929

1930

1931

1932 — Franklin Roosevelt elected President, 1932

1933 — Twenty-First Amendment ratified, 1933
Civilian Conservation Corps established, 1933
Agricultural Adjustment Administration formed, 1933
Tennessee Valley Authority set up, 1933

1934

1935 — Second New Deal begins, 1935
Works Progress Administration formed, 1935

1936 — Roosevelt reelected President, 1936

1937

1938 — Fair Labor Standards Act, 1938

I. Hard Times

The hard times of the 1930's did not begin suddenly after Hoover took office. Their roots lay deep in the 1920's.

Early Warnings

Some Americans had never shared in the good times of the 1920's. Farmers, for example, suffered from low prices for farm products through most of the decade. By 1929, they earned less than one third of the wages earned by people in nonfarm occupations. Some industries were also in trouble. They included coal mining, railroads, shipping, and cotton textiles.

The real wages of employed people—the amount of goods and services their wages could buy—went up during the 1920's. Business profits, however, went up much faster than real wages. That was dangerous because the economy depended on the sale of consumer goods. If the people are to buy what

Dazed spectators crowd outside the New York Stock Exchange on October 24, 1929.

industries make, they must be well paid. Henry Ford understood that. As a result, he paid his workers a good wage for the time, five dollars a day. Other employers did not follow Ford's example.

By 1926 and 1927, there were signs of trouble in the automobile and construction industries. Americans, it seemed, had bought all the cars and new homes they could afford. By the summer of 1929, other consumer industries also had large **inventories,** or supplies of unsold goods. Since there was no sense in producing more goods, factories began to cut back. Many factory workers lost their jobs. The economy was clearly in trouble.

Secretary of the Treasury Andrew Mellon thought that companies would use their profits to build new plants or to help in some other way to make new jobs and increase production. In the early 1920's, some companies did just that, but there was not much use in building new plants if the old ones could not sell what they made.

▶**1.** What signs of trouble had appeared in the economy by 1929?

The Stock Market Crashes

Many people with money in the mid-1920's used it to speculate on the stock market. Stocks are certificates showing that the purchaser owns a small share of a corporation. People bought them in the hope that their stocks would rise in price so they could sell them for more than the purchase price. As more and more people bought stocks, stock prices rose by leaps and bounds. That made even more people decide to buy stock in hope of becoming rich. Stock market rules allowed buyers to purchase stock with 10 percent of the price in cash. Investors then borrowed the rest, sure that they could easily pay back the loans as prices rose still more.

The bonanza could not last. If stock prices started to fall, borrowers would be in trouble. They would have to sell their shares quickly to help pay off their loans. With many investors trying to sell stock at the same time, prices would fall even more.

Stock prices began to drop in September 1929. In October they crashed. On Thursday, October 24, almost 13 million shares of stock were sold at a loss of billions of dollars. By November 13, known as Black Friday, some $50 billion was lost as people scrambled to sell. Stock prices continued to drop for several years. A share of United States Steel, for example, sold for $262 on September 3, 1929, but for $22 on July 8, 1932. A share in American Telephone and Telegraph went from $304 to $72 in that same period. Many investors lost everything they owned.

▶2. When did the stock market crash?

The Great Depression Begins

After the stock market crash, industrial production declined even more. The crash destroyed people's confidence in the economy. They no longer invested money as before, and they bought fewer goods. Because the supply of goods was greater than the demand, prices began to fall. That made it difficult for businesses to pay their employees' salaries and still break even. Many companies closed their doors. Between 1929 and 1933, more than 100,000 companies went out of business. The number of unemployed people rose sharply. By 1933, a quarter of all American workers had lost their jobs. Such mass unemployment lasted deep into the 1930's. With so many Americans out of work, the demand for cars, houses, clothes, and other goods and services dropped even further. The United States had entered the **Great Depression.**

▶3. What happened after the stock market crashed?

Breadlines were a common sight during the Depression. These poor, jobless Americans stand in line, waiting to receive free food.

Depression in the Cities The cities were especially hard hit by the Depression. For example, eight out of ten people in Toledo, Ohio, were out of work by 1932. In Cleveland, Ohio, one of every two had no job.

City governments could not help so many needy people. Private charities such as the Red Cross and the Salvation Army gave out what food they could. Hungry people waited for hours in the so-called breadlines that stretched out for blocks. The desperate dug through garbage for scraps or begged for handouts from restaurants and the homes of the well-off.

▶**4.** How did the Depression affect the cities?

Depression on the Farms Conditions on the farms, which were never very good during the 1920's, became even worse during the Depression. The prices of farm products dropped 60 percent between 1929 and 1932.

William C. Palmer's painting shows the destruction caused by the dust storms of the 1930's.

Whitney Museum of American Art, New York

Many families could not meet their mortgage payments and therefore lost their farms.

The situation worsened when a severe drought hit the Great Plains starting in 1930. Lack of rain and unusually hot summers made farming there a losing battle. Great black clouds of dust that had once been fertile soil now rose up to block out the sun. The area became known as the **Dust Bowl.** Swarms of grasshoppers swept down to eat what pitiful crops some farmers managed to grow.

Many farmers decided to leave their land and look for work elsewhere. In old, broken-down cars or trucks, they headed west, hoping to find work in California. Those farmers were called "Okies" and "Arkies" because many of them came from Oklahoma and Arkansas. For them, however, California offered only hardships of a different kind. Many "Okies" and "Arkies" became **migrant workers** who moved constantly from place to place picking other people's crops. Migrants were paid miserable wages for that hard work.

▶**5.** Where was the Dust Bowl?

Hoover's Response to the Depression

Hoover saw no reason why the stock market crash should lead to a depression. The economy of the United States, he insisted in 1929, was basically sound. He believed the problem was only a lack of confidence. So he called conferences of business and labor leaders at the White House. There he gave them pep talks. Hoover got the business people to agree to maintain wages, jobs, and production. He persuaded labor leaders to stop demanding better wages and hours. Those measures should at least have kept things from getting worse.

For the economy to improve, however, Americans had to begin spending again.

Hoover urged business people to sponsor new building projects. He also asked families to fix up or add to their homes. That would help make jobs. Hoover wanted Congress to cut taxes so Americans could better afford such projects. He also asked Congress for millions of dollars in emergency funds for federal construction projects.

▶**6.** What did Hoover think was the cause of the Depression?

Hoover's Farm Program Farmers had their own ideas about what government could do for them. In the 1920's, they supported a bill that said the government would buy farm products to keep prices up. President Coolidge vetoed that bill on Hoover's advice. Self-help was the American way of solving problems, Hoover said.

In 1929, Hoover continued to urge farmers to help themselves by forming cooperative associations. He wanted them to produce less so prices would rise. The Hoover administration also tried to protect farmers from foreign competition with the **Hawley-Smoot Tariff** of 1930, which raised tariff levels to a record-breaking high.

▶**7.** How did Hoover try to help farmers?

Hoover's Program Fails For a brief time in early 1930, it looked as though Hoover's policies were working. Production, employment, and even stock prices began to turn upward, but they soon fell again. What might have been just one of the nation's periodic downturns became the severest and longest depression in our history. Why was the Depression so severe? One reason was that international trade collapsed. The Hawley-Smoot Tariff contributed to the disaster. Because Europeans could not sell their products in the United States, they stopped buying American products.

In late October 1931, the Federal Reserve Bank added to the trouble by raising interest rates. That meant businesses had to pay more to borrow money they needed. More businesses failed, and more people lost their jobs.

★★★★★★★★★★★★★★★ The United States and the World ★★
The World Economic Crisis

The collapse of the American economy affected other parts of the world, especially Europe. Germany was the country most hard hit by the Depression.

American banks and investors had lent large amounts of money to German businesses, public utilities, and even city governments. When the Depression hit the United States, those loans were called back or not renewed. That was a terrible blow to the German economy.

In the summer of 1931, a major banking crisis hit Austria and Germany, and banks were forced to close. Soon the crisis spread to Britain. The number of jobless rose in Europe as in the United States. Growing despair led many Germans to turn toward a dictator, Adolf Hitler. He came to power in 1933, the same year Franklin Roosevelt became President of the United States.

Throughout Europe, countries tried to protect themselves by increasing tariffs. That made imports, including farm products, more expensive. Agricultural countries such as the small nations of the Balkans suffered badly. Millions of peasants faced terrible misery. These developments in the 1930's moved the world toward a terrible conflict, World War II.

Bonus Marchers carried their protest through the streets of the nation's capital.

Then Hoover called for one of the biggest peacetime tax increases in American history. He did so because his spending on public projects had caused a **deficit** in the federal budget, meaning that the government had spent more money than it took in. In fact, the government overspent by $3 billion in 1931. Hoover thought he had to raise taxes to balance the budget. That, too, left people with less money to spend.

Hoover did not give up. He helped begin a program of government loans to banks that held mortgages. In that way he hoped to help people keep their homes. He supported the creation of the **Reconstruction Finance Corporation** (RFC) in 1932, which lent money to troubled businesses and to insurance companies. That program went far beyond anything the federal government had ever done before to stop a depression. However, the RFC actually lent out only part of the money

entrusted to it. Most of that money went to a few large banks.

Hoover was willing to loan government money, but he refused to give it away. Above all, he opposed direct federal payments to needy people. He insisted that local governments and private charities had to take care of such people. Even when it became clear that there were too many people for local agencies to handle, Hoover refused to change. That made him very unpopular.

▶**8.** Why did Hoover raise taxes in 1931?

The Bonus March Hoover's already sinking popularity fell even further because of his handling of an event called the **Bonus March.** In 1924, Congress had approved a bonus payment for World War I veterans. It was not to be paid, however, until 1945. Once the Depression began, veterans wanted their bonus money right away. Congress passed a bill allowing veterans to borrow up to 50 percent of their bonuses from the government, but Hoover vetoed it. To pay out the bonus money, he said, would make it even harder to balance the federal budget.

The veterans would not be put off. Some 20,000 Bonus Marchers went to Washington, D.C., in the spring of 1932. There they lived in empty government buildings or in shacks on some marshy lands across the Anacostia River. They pressed Congress for *all* of their bonuses. The House of Representatives passed a bill to pay the bonus, but on June 17 the Senate defeated it.

Most of the veterans left the capital after the defeat of the Bonus Bill. But thousands remained with their wives and children. They had no jobs to return to, and they created a kind of community in the armylike camp they had built. Their presence upset Hoover. In July, he ordered the Washington police and the army to close the camp.

The closing was carried out with far more force than Hoover had intended. The army's chief of staff, General Douglas MacArthur, used cavalry and infantry units and six tanks against the tattered veterans. The soldiers moved into the camp with bayonets drawn, throwing gas bombs, and burning the shacks so their owners could not return. More than 100 marchers were hurt.

▶**9.** Who were the Bonus Marchers?

The Decline of Herbert Hoover Increasingly, Americans began to blame Hoover for their suffering during the Depression. In fact, Hoover could not recognize how bad the Depression was. "Nobody is starving," he insisted in 1932, when millions were going hungry. What about the unemployed people selling apples on city streets? They had left their old jobs, Hoover said, because apple selling paid so well. He was not joking. He was just badly out of touch. Still, the Republicans dutifully nominated Hoover for a second term as President in 1932, but very few of them thought he would win.

▶**10.** Who was the Republican candidate for President in 1932?

FDR Defeats Hoover

The Democratic presidential candidate in 1932 was a very different kind of man. Franklin Delano Roosevelt, or FDR as the newspapers called him, was born on January 30, 1882, to an old and wealthy New York family. He suffered none of the hardships of Hoover's early life. He spent his childhood on his father's estate at Hyde Park, near the Hudson River. The schools he attended were among the nation's best—Groton, Harvard, the Columbia Law School. In 1905, he married Eleanor Roosevelt, the niece of his cousin, President Theodore Roosevelt. FDR began his own political career in 1911 by winning a seat in the New York state legislature.

Young Roosevelt rose quickly in public life. He became assistant secretary of the navy during World War I. In 1920, the Democrats nominated him for Vice President. The party lost that year's election. Still, Roosevelt seemed headed for a brilliant future. Then, in the summer of 1921, he was suddenly struck with polio, a crippling disease. Roosevelt never regained the use of his legs. For the rest of his life he walked only with help, his legs enclosed in heavy braces.

▶**11.** What tragedy struck FDR in 1921?

Governor of New York Always handsome, always charming, FDR had great courage. He also had the support of his wife, who overcame her natural shyness to do a lot of political work for him. With Eleanor's help, FDR resumed his place in public life. In 1928, he was elected governor of New York State.

When the Depression hit, FDR tried to help the people of his state. In August 1931, he became the first governor in the nation to support state aid for the unemployed. He helped set up New York's Temporary Emergency Relief Administration, which had some $20 million to help hard-pressed New Yorkers make it through the terribly hard winter of 1931 and 1932.

Obviously, Roosevelt had faced up to the needs of the hungry. The emergency, he said, was like that of a war. He was willing to break with tradition if necessary. In his presidential campaign, Roosevelt promised to give the American people a **New Deal.** He never explained just what that meant. However, the theme song of his campaign, "Happy Days Are Here Again," showed what he hoped his New Deal would accomplish.

▶**12.** As governor, how did FDR handle the Depression?

The Election of 1932 Roosevelt won the election of 1932 with 57.4 percent of the popular vote. Hoover received almost 40 percent. The Democrats also won a majority of seats in both houses of Congress. That would help FDR put his New Deal into effect.

▶ **13.** Which party won the election of 1932?

Reviewing Section I

Identify inventories, Black Friday, Great Depression, Dust Bowl, migrant workers, Hawley-Smoot Tariff, deficit, Reconstruction Finance Corporation, Bonus March, Franklin Roosevelt, Eleanor Roosevelt, New Deal

Questions to Answer
1. Why did the stock market crash in 1929?
2. How did Hoover try to end the Depression?

A Question to Think About Why did Roosevelt say the Depression was like a war?

II. The "Hundred Days"

On March 4, 1933, millions of Americans sat close to their radios, listening to the new President's inaugural address. "This great Nation," Roosevelt promised, "will endure as it has endured, will revive and will prosper." He said that, "The only thing we have to fear is fear itself—nameless, unreasoning, unjustified terror which paralyzes needed efforts to convert retreat into advance." He promised to use his office forcefully to give the nation the advance it needed.

Unlike Hoover, Roosevelt had no set theory about how government should affect the economy. He wanted to find out what worked and thought it was time to experiment.

Immediately after his inauguration, FDR called a special session of Congress. It met for 100 days between March 9 and June 16. In that time, FDR presented, and the Congress approved, an almost bewildering set of new laws. Those **"Hundred Days"** changed the nation forever.

Ending Prohibition

Even before Roosevelt took office, Congress had approved the **Twenty-First Amendment,** which ended Prohibition. By the end of the year, enough states had approved the new amendment to put it into effect. In the meantime, Congress, urged on by FDR, made the sale of beer and wine legal. Roosevelt hoped that some Americans would find jobs in the liquor industry. Congress imposed a new tax on those drinks to reduce the federal deficit.

▶ **1.** What was the purpose of the Twenty-First Amendment?

The Bank Holiday

At the time of FDR's inauguration, the United States was in the midst of a banking crisis. Some banks had failed early in the Depression. People who had money in those banks lost their savings. The bank failures made other people fearful for their savings, so thousands tried to withdraw their money from the banks. No bank, no matter how sound, ever has enough money on hand to pay out all of its accounts. That is because banks invest much of the money deposited with them by making loans to individuals and businesses. Now hundreds of banks found they could not meet their customers' demands for withdrawals, so those banks also went out of business. That made even more people

Eleanor Roosevelt was born into the well-known Roosevelt family in 1884. Her father, the brother of President Theodore Roosevelt, adored her, but Eleanor and her mother were not close.

When Eleanor was eight, she lost her mother as a result of diphtheria. Two years later her father died. Orphaned at young ages, Eleanor and her younger brother went to live with their stern grandmother in her New York mansion. There they had few carefree moments.

When Eleanor was 15, her grandmother sent her to a private school outside London. It was in London that Eleanor gained the self-confidence she had always lacked.

When Eleanor returned to New York, she was a sophisticated young woman with a strong social conscience. Her seriousness impressed a distant cousin whom Eleanor happened to meet. Three years later she married the cousin. His name was Franklin Delano Roosevelt.

From the beginning, Sara Roosevelt, Franklin's mother, tried to control her son's marriage. At Sara's insistence, Eleanor gave up her work in a New York settlement house. Instead, she devoted herself to her growing family.

In 1910, Franklin was elected to the New York State Senate. Two years later he was appointed Assistant Secretary of the Navy. During these years, the strain between Eleanor and her mother-in-law increased. Then, in 1922, a tragic incident occurred. Franklin Roosevelt was stricken with polio.

Sara wanted her son to live the life of an invalid. Eleanor insisted he fight his illness by going for physical therapy. She also made sure voters did not forget the Roosevelt name by becoming active in politics herself.

In 1928, New Yorkers elected Franklin Roosevelt governor. During his term, Eleanor crisscrossed the state, inspecting hospitals as well as prisons. When Roosevelt became President

four years later, Eleanor simply extended the range of her travels. During the Depression, she traveled from coast to coast visiting soup kitchens, miners' homes, and rural schools.

Wherever Eleanor went, she observed prejudice firsthand. At a time when many Americans cared little for minority rights, Eleanor took a strong stand against racial discrimination. To make her point, she resigned from the Daughters of the American Revolution because it would not let black singer Marion Anderson perform at Constitution Hall.

Unlike many Presidents' wives, Eleanor's career did not end after her husband's death. Instead, she worked for other Presidents. When she died at 78, thousands mourned the death of a woman who was not afraid to speak out for those who had no voice.

run to withdraw their savings. It looked as though the entire banking system might collapse.

Two days after taking office, the President declared a **Bank Holiday.** That is, he closed all the country's banks until he could get some new laws passed. He sent an emergency banking bill to Congress on the first day it met. There was only one copy of the bill available, and not many members of Congress understood it entirely. Nonetheless, Congress passed the bill, and FDR signed it that night.

The law set up new ways for the federal government to funnel money to troubled banks. It also said the Treasury Department had to inspect banks before they could reopen.

On March 12, FDR made a radio broadcast. In that first of his **fireside chats,** as he called

When FDR ordered a four-day bank holiday, many banks were in danger of closing because frightened depositors were withdrawing so much money.

The New York Times.

LATE CITY EDITION

VOL. LXXXII No. 27,488.   NEW YORK, MONDAY, MARCH 6, 1933   TWO CENTS

ROOSEVELT ORDERS 4-DAY BANK HOLIDAY, PUTS EMBARGO ON GOLD, CALLS CONGRESS

his radio talks, Roosevelt told the people he wanted to speak to them about banking. "I can assure you," he said, "that it is safer to keep your money in a reopened bank than under the mattress." When the banks opened again over the next few days, people deposited more money than they took out. The banking crisis was over.

Later, Congress made sure no similar crisis would happen again. In June 1933, it set up the **Federal Deposit Insurance Corporation** (FDIC), which insured bank deposits up to $2,500. Even if a bank failed, most depositors could get their money back, so they would have no reason to panic in the future.

▶**2.** How did FDR handle the bank crisis?

The NRA

The problems of American industry were more complicated than the problems of the nation's banks. As sales fell during the Depression, many industries tried to cut their prices to win customers. Then they had to cut costs, including wages. If they could not cut costs enough, businesses had to close, leaving workers without jobs.

To try to break that cycle, Congress set up a program of government-business cooperation. A new federal agency, the **National Recovery Administration** (NRA), encouraged the nation's industries to draw up codes for production. By defining minimum prices, wages, and workers' hours, the codes were supposed to end excess competition and the economic decline it caused.

In several ways, the program was like Hoover's. He, too, tried to get businesses to cooperate. Now, however, the NRA could enforce the codes it approved. The NRA also protected the rights of labor. The NRA's charter said workers could legally join unions to bargain for better wages and hours.

The NRA used advertising techniques to win support from the people. It organized torchlight processions and big rallies for the new program. Businesses that agreed to honor NRA codes hung signs in their windows with the program's symbol, a blue eagle, and the motto "We do our part." Before long the blue eagle seemed to be everywhere.

▶3. What was the NRA?

The Farmers' New Deal

The New Deal's program for the farmers was decidedly different from Hoover's. A new **Agricultural Adjustment Administration** (AAA) took charge of farmers' welfare. The basic problem, the government said, was that farmers were producing more than they could sell. That caused prices to fall. Therefore, the AAA paid farmers to leave acres unplanted. In that way, it hoped to reduce crops and raise prices.

By the time the AAA was begun, the 1933 cotton crop had already been planted. The United States still had more unsold cotton on hand than the world would buy that year. Consequently, the government ordered that millions of acres of cotton fields be plowed up. The government also had six million baby pigs destroyed to keep pork prices up. The killing of those little pigs caused great dismay in a nation where so many of the people were hungry.

▶4. Why did the AAA pay farmers not to grow crops?

The Tennessee Valley Authority

Nowhere did the federal government take more control than in the valley of the great Tennessee River. That river sweeps from the southwest corner of Virginia through much of Tennessee, northern Alabama, the northeast

This 1930's song sheet shows the popular symbol of the NRA.

corner of Mississippi to northern Kentucky where it empties into the Ohio River.

In the Tennessee River Valley lived some of the poorest people in the nation. That was so, in part, because the valley suffered almost yearly from severe floods. So much of the valley's soil had been washed away that crops did not grow well. To add to the problem, over the years nearby forests had been cut down. As a result, the soil eroded even more.

During World War I, the government started to build a dam at Muscle Shoals on the Tennessee River in Alabama. Since the dam would be used to generate electricity as well as to prevent floods, private power companies fought hard to keep the government from finishing it.

In 1933, FDR and his advisers decided not only to complete the Muscle Shoals Dam but also to build other dams. They would use

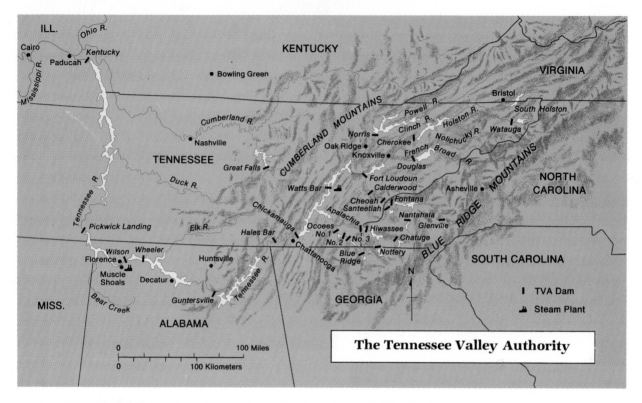

Map Study *Along what river are both the Hales Bar and Wheeler dams? What two mountain ranges are shown on the map?*

The Tennessee Valley Authority

the government's control of water resources to build up the area along the Tennessee River. In the process, they would give jobs to many people.

To complete that task, Congress created the **Tennessee Valley Authority** (TVA) in May 1933. The TVA was to end the flooding problems and start other conservation projects. It was to use its dams to produce cheap electricity, which it would then sell to homeowners, farmers and new industries.

In general, the TVA was a success. It brought new life to a poverty-stricken region. Again, not everyone benefited equally. The TVA did little for blacks. It would not even employ them on most of its projects.

▶**5.** What did the TVA try to accomplish?

Relief

TVA and other government programs were intended to help the people by helping banks and industry to recover and resume normal operations. However, many Americans needed aid more speedily. They needed immediate **relief,** money for food and shelter.

Congress approved several relief programs. By the end of March 1933, it had set up a **Civilian Conservation Corps** (CCC). The CCC hired young men between the ages of 18 and 25 years to plant trees or work on other government conservation projects. The young men lived in camps and were required to send part of their pay home to their families.

In May, Congress approved the **Federal Emergency Relief Association** (FERA). It gave

CCC workers in Washington State replant a section of trees in the Columbia National Forest. ▶

more than $500 million to state and local governments to help pay people for working on various sorts of construction and education projects.

The New Deal planners tried to create more jobs for people through the **Public Works Administration** (PWA), which began major new construction projects, such as the Triboro Bridge in New York. Because such projects took time to plan, the PWA was slow in getting going.

Roosevelt's relief projects provided work relief—that is, jobs—not handouts. FDR and his major adviser, an Iowa-born social worker

IMPROVE YOUR SKILLS
Interviews

When historians study events in recent history, they can interview people who experienced those events first-hand. Franklin Delano Roosevelt took office in 1933. People who were in their twenties then are now in their seventies. Interviewing people who remember the New Deal or reading interviews with such people can show how large-scale events such as the Depression and New Deal affected individuals.

Follow these steps in conducting an interview.

- Make an appointment with the person you wish to interview.
- Be prepared with a list of questions you want to ask. Your primary role as an interviewer is that of listener. However, you may wish to ask questions that will spark a response in the person you are interviewing. The more questions you are prepared to ask, and the

more kinds of questions, the more information you are likely to obtain.

Some of your questions should be very general, for example: "What do you remember about the New Deal?" Some of your questions should be very specific, for example: "What did you think about Roosevelt's attempt to create more jobs for people through the Public Works Administration?"

- Take careful notes, or if you have permission from the person you are interviewing, use a tape recorder.

On a separate sheet of paper, write five questions that you could use in an interview with someone who remembers the New Deal. Focus your questions on the effect of New Deal legislation on the person being interviewed and his or her attitude toward Roosevelt.

named Harry Hopkins, thought work relief was better for people's spirits. It let them use their skills and gave them a chance, Hopkins said, "to do something useful."

The list of new federal programs—FDIC, NRA, AAA, TVA, CCC, FERA, PWA—was bewildering. Some people called them "alphabet soup." However, one thing was undeniable. The government was taking responsibility for the economic welfare of the people.

▶6. Name three relief programs started in FDR's first hundred days.

Reviewing Section II

Identify "Hundred Days," Twenty-First Amendment, Bank Holiday, fireside chats, Federal Deposit Insurance Corporation, National Recovery Administration, Agricultural Adjustment Administration, Tennessee Valley Authority, relief, Civilian Conservation Corps, Federal Emergency Relief Association, Public Works Administration, Harry Hopkins

Questions to Answer
1. How did the "Hundred Days'" legislation try to help farmers, banks, and other businesses recover from the Depression?
2. What was the purpose of the TVA?

A Question to Think About What might have happened if FDR had not stopped the bank panic?

III. New Problems at Home

Under the New Deal, the American economy began to recover. The number of people out of work fell from about 13 million in 1933 to 9 million by 1936. Most Americans were very grateful to FDR. However, he had critics and opponents. Some Americans thought that his programs had not done enough to help the people. Others argued that FDR had made the government too large and given it too much power.

Roosevelt's Critics

One of Roosevelt's critics was a California doctor named Francis E. Townsend. He said the New Deal did not do enough for old people. He wanted every American older than 60 years to receive $200 per month from the government, provided the recipients promised to retire and spend all that money before the next check came.

Father Charles Coughlin, a Catholic priest from the town of Royal Oak, Michigan, was another popular critic of the New Deal. Every Sunday millions of listeners tuned in to his radio program. Like the Populists of times past, Coughlin wanted the government to put out more paper money and silver dollars. He also wanted the government to take over the banking system. Coughlin made bitter attacks on FDR and also on bankers and Jews.

▶1. What were Francis Townsend's and Father Charles Coughlin's proposals to help the needy?

Huey Long Huey Long of Louisiana also criticized FDR. Long became governor of Louisiana in 1928. He was so powerful that people called him a dictator. By 1930, Long was serving in the Senate. At first, he supported Roosevelt. But soon he decided FDR was too timid. Long wanted to take money from the richest people in the country and distribute it among more needy people. His "Share-Our-Wealth Plan" attracted many new followers. Then, in September 1935, an assassin shot and killed Long on the steps of the Louisiana capitol in Baton Rouge.

▶**2.** What was Long's plan to help the needy?

A Call for Less While people like Townsend and Long called for more government action, others thought the government had already done too much. Many business people resented the new government rules and restrictions that the New Deal had begun. Banks, for example, were now regulated by the federal government. The stock market also had to follow new rules. Some business people were angered, too, by the NRA's protection of labor unions. The great growth in the federal government, such critics said, undermined the American tradition of local power. They called Roosevelt a dictator.

▶**3.** Why were some business people critical of the New Deal?

The cartoon shows Uncle Sam being tied down by FDR's many alphabet agencies.

The Second New Deal

In 1935, the President sponsored a series of new programs known as the **Second New Deal.** They were meant to win support from the champions of the underprivileged such as Townsend, Long, and Coughlin, and to help the nation recover further from the Depression. FDR was also forced to propose new measures because the Supreme Court had declared some of his other programs unconstitutional.

▶**4.** Why did FDR propose his Second New Deal legislation?

Labor In 1935, the Supreme Court ruled that the NRA was unconstitutional. In some ways, that was a help to the President. The NRA had become unpopular, in part because it helped businesses keep prices too high.

The Supreme Court's decision ended not just the NRA's support for business but also its protection of unions. So Senator Robert Wagner of New York proposed a new law. It was passed in 1935 and became known as the **Wagner Act.** That law protected the right of workers to join unions and defined "unfair practices" used by employers against labor unions. The law also set up a **National Labor Relations Board** (NLRB) to protect workers against such unfair practices. The NLRB, for example, supervised union elections so workers could decide freely whether or not they wanted to join a union.

With those new protections, millions of workers did decide to join unions. The organization of unskilled workers was especially strong. Many of them joined the new **Congress of Industrial Organizations** (CIO), which had about 3.7 million workers by 1938. It organized all the workers in a particular industry into one union. That was different from the American Federation of Labor (AFL), which preferred to bring together workers in a craft—plumbers, for example, or steamfitters. From its beginning, the CIO, led by John L. Lewis of the United Mine Workers, competed for members with the AFL, which was led by William Green.

▶5. What were some of the major provisions of the Wagner Act?

Social Security A **Social Security Act**, passed by Congress in 1935, was a particular favorite of Frances Perkins. She was Roosevelt's secretary of labor and the first woman to hold a cabinet position. The Social Security Act set up the first federal system of old age pensions and unemployment insurance. The program was financed partly by the workers who participated in the social security system and partly by their employers. Not all workers were covered, but the law of 1935 gave the federal government new responsibility for the welfare of the old and unemployed.

▶6. What new responsibility did the Social Security Act give the federal government?

The Works Progress Administration A new program of work relief was another part of the Second New Deal. The **Works Progress Administration** (WPA) went far beyond any earlier federal relief program. It put more than 8.5 million people to work between 1935 and 1941 at a cost of approximately $11 billion. Some of those people helped build schools, post offices, civic centers, bridges, and roads. Others were employed as artists and writers, even as historians. For example, the WPA hired artists to paint murals in post offices and other public buildings.

▶7. What was the WPA?

The Wealth Tax All of the Second New Deal measures brought help to people who were relatively poor. At the same time, the President tried to shift the cost of government toward those who were more able to pay. A new tax law passed in 1935 raised the taxes on inheritances and on high personal and business incomes.

The law did not actually do much to redistribute wealth from the rich to the poor. Still, it made FDR more unpopular than ever among wealthy people. Congress angered those people further by placing new restrictions on banks and on interstate power companies. Soon a new anti-Roosevelt campaign was in full swing.

▶8. Why did the new tax law anger the rich?

The Election of 1936

By 1936, criticism of the New Deal was so strong that it seemed the Republicans might recapture the presidency. The Republicans chose as their candidate Governor Alfred M. Landon of Kansas. Landon and his party promised to keep most New Deal programs. They also vowed to keep government from going further into debt and to encourage competition and economic freedom, or **free enterprise,** in business.

The Democrats renominated FDR, who promised voters more of what he had already done. They gave him an astounding 61 percent of the popular vote and 523 of the 531 electoral votes. Once again the Democrats won majorities in both houses of Congress.

The election of 1936 showed that the Democrats had put together a new coalition of voters. Their supporters included farmers in the South and West, industrial workers, and city people, including the children of immigrants. Those people often benefited directly from New Deal programs. Roosevelt also carried the votes of American blacks, which was surprising in some respects.

▶9. What did their victory in 1936 show about the Democratic Party?

Blacks and the New Deal

Since the Civil War, blacks had supported the Republicans—the "Party of Lincoln." The New Deal did not do much before 1936 to win black support for the Democrats. In some ways, in fact, the New Deal hurt them.

In the South, AAA payments for not planting cotton went to landowners, not tenant farmers or sharecroppers. As a result, many people, especially blacks, were forced off the land. Blacks who worked for projects like the CCC often had to work in segregated camps.

Nonetheless, black voters turned out for Roosevelt in 1936. He was their best hope. Even a segregated job in the CCC seemed to them better than no job at all.

Blacks had a powerful supporter in Eleanor Roosevelt. The President's wife had dedicated herself to the cause of the underprivileged, including blacks. She invited black leaders to talk with her at the White House, and then saw to it that they met FDR as well.

Others among FDR's advisers, such as Clark Foreman, fought discrimination in the federal government and tried to find government jobs for able blacks. Foreman's assistant was a young Harvard-trained black economist named Robert Weaver, who went on to a distinguished career in public service.

Among the most important of Roosevelt's black appointees was a woman, Mary McLeod Bethune. She was born in 1875, the seventeenth child of a South Carolina family only recently freed from slavery. Her early life was spent on her parents' small farm in Maysville, South Carolina, but by her own determination, she managed to get an education. She became a teacher and eventually founded a school for blacks in Daytona, Florida. By 1935, she was a founder and first president of the National Council of Negro Women, and was also an active member of the NAACP. Roosevelt made her director of

Mary McLeod Bethune, a well-known educator, was appointed to various government posts by four Presidents—Coolidge, Hoover, Roosevelt, and Truman.

Minority Affairs in the National Youth Administration, which was part of the WPA. She became a very strong voice for black interests within the government.

▶10. What roles did Weaver and Bethune play in the Roosevelt administration?

Mexican Americans and the New Deal

During the 1920's, more than 150,000 Mexicans legally entered the United States. Probably at least as many or more entered illegally, that is, without the proper papers. Almost all of the Mexican Americans suffered severely during the Depression.

Many of these newcomers worked as farm laborers or migrant workers. In the 1930's, most of those jobs were taken by people from the Dust Bowl. The AAA offered no help to migrant workers. Many Mexican immigrants who were not yet citizens were deported. In 1932 alone, Los Angeles County deported about 200,000 Mexicans.

▶ **11.** How did the Depression affect Mexican Americans?

Indians and the New Deal

The New Deal did significantly improve life for Indians. The **Indian Reorganization Act** of 1934 ended the Dawes Severalty Act (see page 467). The new law forbade the division of Indian lands into small plots and restored group lands. It also provided for loans to Indian groups so they could develop economically, and it encouraged the preservation of Indian culture and religion.

▶ **12.** How did the Indian Reorganization Act help Indians?

The Court-Packing Scheme

After his solid victory in 1936, Roosevelt felt strong enough to fight the Supreme Court. The Court had declared unconstitutional one part of Roosevelt's program after another. The Court said Congress was giving too much power to the President. It also questioned whether Congress's power to regulate interstate commerce included power to regulate all businesses that operated in different states.

Often the Court struck down popular New Deal legislation by a vote of 5 to 4. Roosevelt believed that if he could appoint more members to the Court, then the Court would more often rule in favor of his programs.

In 1937, the President sent Congress the Judiciary Reorganization Bill. He asked for authority to appoint a new Supreme Court justice for every member older than 70 years. He also wanted to appoint 50 new federal judges, including 6 to the Supreme Court.

The proposal caused quite an uproar. The President was violating the independence of the judiciary, people argued. Throughout the country, Americans rallied to defend the Constitution and separation of powers. As a result, Congress refused to approve Roosevelt's new bill, which they referred to as his **court-packing** proposal. But soon the Supreme Court started approving New Deal measures. So the Court became less of a problem for FDR.

▶ **13.** What was FDR's court-packing plan?

The Recession of 1937–1939

By 1937, unemployment had fallen to 7.7 million people. The worst of the Depression was over, FDR decided. Maybe, finally, he could get the government back to normal. For him that meant getting the federal budget back in balance. To do that, he cut government spending drastically. The WPA reduced its job rolls by half, for example. Private business was not yet ready to absorb so many workers. By the next year, 10.4 million people were unemployed.

The nation had slipped into a severe **recession,** which is a decline in overall business activity. Congress quickly poured more money back into the WPA, the CCC, and other programs. It also passed a Fair Labor Standards Act in 1938. That law is sometimes called the last New Deal measure. It set minimum wages and maximum hours for many workers. The economy did not recover quickly. Not until late 1939 was employment back to the 1937 level.

▶ **14.** What did Congress do to stop the recession of 1937–1939?

The Meaning of the New Deal

There was a lesson to be learned by the recession of 1937–1939. Obviously, government spending had become important to the American economy. New Deal programs put to work people who then had wages to spend, which created a demand for more goods and services. If the government spent more money than it raised, the federal budget would be unbalanced. Most New Dealers believed that an unbalanced budget was better than having millions out of work.

A British economist, John Maynard Keynes (kānz), even argued that **deficit spending**—spending money beyond that raised by taxes—was an especially powerful way of getting a sick economy going again. Keynes explained his ideas in an important book, *The General Theory of Employment, Interest and Money*, which was published in 1936.

President Roosevelt once met Keynes, but he never really understood his theories. FDR was unwilling to spend on the scale Keynes recommended. Only when the government started massive spending in preparation for war in the early 1940's did the American economy recover completely from the Great Depression. That seemed to show that Keynes's ideas were right.

Before long, Keynesian economics became popular in the United States. Keynes suggested that the government could defend the welfare of its people without taking over businesses and industries. In other words, Keynesian theories and free enterprise were compatible, which was why Keynes's arguments seemed so well suited to the economic needs of the United States.

Later Americans questioned Keynes's ideas of how the government should act. After the 1930's, however, few Americans denied that the national government was responsible for the people's economic welfare. The New Deal

This cartoon shows the reaction many Democrats had to Roosevelt's court-packing proposal.

had added that responsibility to the federal government. In that way, and through its many programs, the New Deal moved power from the local level, where it had been since the days of Jamestown, to the national government in Washington, D.C.

Besides increasing the role of the federal government, the New Deal changed the role of the President. No previous President brought his office so closely into people's lives as did FDR. His fireside chats allowed him to talk to the American people in their own homes, like a friend. Millions of ordinary people believed FDR had helped them save their homes or find them work when all else had failed.

It is difficult to be a great President in times of prosperity and peace. Roosevelt won the respect and affection of Americans by leading them through the Depression. Later, he added to his accomplishments by becoming, like Lincoln, a great war leader.

▶**15.** What did John Maynard Keynes believe about government deficit spending?

Reviewing Section III

Identify Francis E. Townsend, Father Charles Coughlin, Huey Long, Second New Deal, Wagner Act, National Labor Relations Board, Congress of Industrial Organizations, John L. Lewis, William Green, Social Security Act, Frances Perkins, Works Progress Administration, Alfred M. Landon, free enterprise, Robert Weaver, Mary McLeod Bethune, Indian Reorganization Act, court-packing, recession, John Maynard Keynes, deficit spending

Questions to Answer
1. Why did Roosevelt's court-packing scheme create such an outcry?
2. How did Keynesian economics fit New Deal methods of fighting the Depression?

A Question to Think About In what ways did FDR's court-packing plans violate the spirit of the Constitution?

IMPROVE YOUR READING
Sequence and Cause/Effect

You have learned that historical events can be linked in a *sequential* relationship or in a *causal* relationship. You have also learned that certain "signal" words give you clues to the type of relationship an author is describing. For example, words like "before" and "after" signal a sequential relationship. Words like "because" and "as a result" signal a causal relationship.

The following exercise consists of five pairs of sentences based on events discussed in this chapter. Anaylze each pair and decide if the two sentences are linked by a sequential relationship or a causal relationship. Then for each pair of sentences, write on your paper either "sequential" or "causal."

1. Ford believed that if people are to buy factory-made products, they must be paid well. As a result, he paid his workers well.
2. The supply of goods was greater than the demand. So manufacturers lowered their prices.
3. The Hawley-Smoot Tariff raised tariffs to record-breaking levels. Consequently, Europeans could not sell their products in the United States.
4. Franklin Delano Roosevelt was inaugurated President in January. Soon afterwards he called a special session of Congress.
5. The United States still had more unsold cotton on hand than the world could buy that year. So the government ordered that millions of cotton fields be plowed up.

CHAPTER 27 REVIEW

Vocabulary Check
Write a short definition for each of the following words.

1. Inventories
2. Deficit
3. Relief
4. Free enterprise
5. Recession

Fact Check
On a separate sheet of paper, write the name of the person or program described in each of the sentences below.

1. He was President when the Depression began.
2. Once the governor of New York State, this Democrat was elected President in 1932.
3. This New Deal program of government-business cooperation was authorized to enforce business production codes.
4. This New Deal program promoted the welfare of farmers.
5. This New Deal program built dams, produced electricity, and also encouraged industry in a large region.
6. This program hired young men to work in conservation programs.
7. He was the head of the CIO.
8. This secretary of labor was the first woman appointed to a cabinet position.
9. First president of the National Council of Negro Women, she was a strong voice for black interests in the Roosevelt administration.
10. This British economist argued for government deficit spending.

Skills Check
1. What can be gained from interviewing people about historical events that they remember?
2. Write four interview questions about the Great Depression.

Time Check
On a separate sheet of paper, put the following events in chronological order.

1. FDR is elected for a second term.
2. FDR declares a Bank Holiday.
3. The Supreme Court rules that the NRA is unconstitutional.
4. Congress passes the Hawley-Smoot Tariff.
5. Bonus Marchers go to Washington, D.C.

Think and Write
1. Why did the stock market crash in 1929?
2. Why did Hoover's efforts fail to restore economic health to the nation?
3. How did the TVA and the AAA extend government power?
4. How did the New Deal affect blacks, Mexican Americans, and Indians?
5. Why did FDR's court-packing scheme create such an uproar among Americans?

Chapter 28

The Second World War

Flames engulf the American fleet anchored at Pearl Harbor shortly after the Japanese attack on December 7, 1941.

After the First World War, many Americans called for a policy of **isolation.** The United States, they said, should avoid alliances with other countries that might draw it into another foreign war. American isolation was never complete, however. The nation was involved in several international agreements in the 1920's. In 1928, for example, the United States helped to negotiate the **Kellogg-Briand Pact,** by which 62 nations agreed to outlaw war as a way of settling disputes. The Kellogg-Briand Pact contributed to a widespread hope that the world had finally left war behind. Yet peace did not last. Once the world began sinking into war, it soon became clear that the United States could not just stand aside.

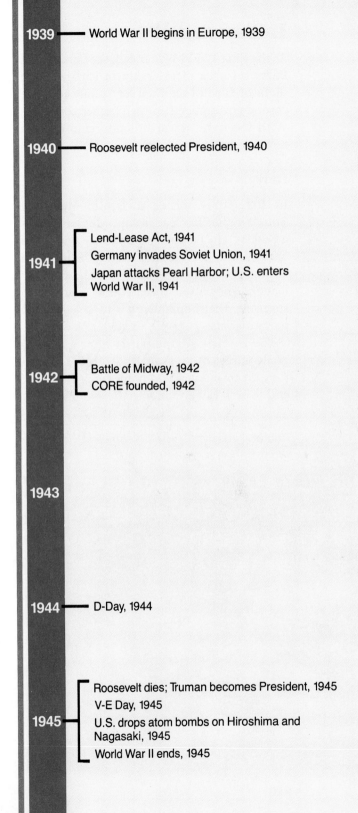

1939 — World War II begins in Europe, 1939

1940 — Roosevelt reelected President, 1940

1941 — Lend-Lease Act, 1941
Germany invades Soviet Union, 1941
Japan attacks Pearl Harbor; U.S. enters World War II, 1941

1942 — Battle of Midway, 1942
CORE founded, 1942

1943

1944 — D-Day, 1944

1945 — Roosevelt dies; Truman becomes President, 1945
V-E Day, 1945
U.S. drops atom bombs on Hiroshima and Nagasaki, 1945
World War II ends, 1945

I. Toward War

As the First World War ended, the Communist Party set up a dictatorship in Russia. Soon dictatorships of another sort replaced democratic governments in many other countries. With the trend toward dictatorship came a new threat to world peace.

Italy

In 1922, Italy turned to Benito Mussolini (mus'ə le'nē) for leadership. Mussolini was a **Fascist.** The Fascists were at once a political party and a private army. They believed in strong government under an authoritarian leader. They used threats and violence to suppress their opponents and reach their party's goals.

The Fascists rose to power after a time of great unrest in postwar Italy. To the fearful they promised peace at home by bringing an end to strikes and unions. Mussolini and his

Crowds gather as Mussolini (left) and Hitler ride through the streets of Berlin in 1943.

followers also reduced the power of the Italian Parliament, ended other political parties, and controlled the press. By the 1930's, they glorified the Italian state and called for an expansion of its power abroad.

▶**1.** What sort of government did the Italian Fascists favor?

Germany

In Germany, democracy collapsed in the early 1930's. After the First World War, Germany became a republic. However, many Germans, including some military leaders, said their nation was betrayed by its democratic rulers. The Germans resented the humiliating terms imposed on them after the First World War. As the world depression hit Germany and unemployment rose, desperate German voters chose an extreme solution to their problems. They gave their support to Adolf Hitler's National Socialist, or Nazi Party.

The **Nazis** were much like Mussolini's followers in Italy. Both groups called for authoritarian rule and used force against their opponents. Both called for national expansion, even at the cost of war. But the German Nazis were even more violent than the Italian Facists.

▶**2.** What were conditions like in Germany after World War I?

The Führer In early 1933, the German president named Hitler as chancellor, or prime minister. Within months, Hitler began a dictatorship more extreme than even that of Mussolini. Only a dictatorship, Hitler thought, could bring back German strength and prosperity. He arrested his political opponents, violated civil liberties, took power from the legislature, and suppressed other parties and labor unions. A year later, Hitler took over the office of president and named himself **Führer** (fy'rər), or leader.

Many Germans supported the new government because Hitler managed to cut back unemployment with government spending projects. Those who opposed the Nazis either kept quiet or were forced into silence.

▶**3.** Why did many Germans support Hitler's government?

Hitler and the Jews Hitler looked for people to blame for Germany's troubles. He placed special blame on the Jews. Nazism included a hatred of Jews among its major beliefs.

Soon after they took power, the Nazis forced German Jews out of government jobs and the universities. Later, they said Jews could not attend German schools or marry non-Jewish Germans. In 1938, the Nazis destroyed many of the synagogues where Jews worshiped. The Nazis also made Jews wear yellow stars to set them apart from other Germans.

Many of Germany's half million Jews managed to leave the country, but often it was difficult for the immigrants to get permission to enter other countries. Even the United States was slow to admit those Jews who did not have relatives there already.

Later, when German armies controlled most of Europe, the Nazis rounded up the remaining Jews in Germany, as well as Jews in the Netherlands, France, Belgium, Poland, the Soviet Union, and Hungary. Between 1941 and 1945, they forced whole families into special extermination camps. There, about six million Jews were worked to death or killed with an awful efficiency in gas chambers. That mass killing is remembered as the **Holocaust.**

The Nazis did not limit their killings to Jews. They also murdered five million Christians in the extermination camps.

▶**4.** What was the Holocaust?

The Nazis rounded up millions of Jews and sent them to extermination camps during the war.

Japan

In Asia, too, people were turning against their neighbors. In 1931, aggressive young Japanese army officers pressed their government into seizing the northern provinces of China, known as Manchuria. During the next few years, military leaders won complete control of the Japanese government. Like the Fascists and Nazis, they silenced their opponents and insisted that Japan should dominate Asia. They glorified the emperor, who was ruler of Japan in name but who actually had very little involvement in the government or the military affairs of the nation.

▶**5.** What leaders won control of Japan in the 1930's?

Steps toward War

In 1935, Mussolini invaded Ethiopia, a nation in east Africa. At about that time, Hitler began building a strong army and air force. Under the Treaty of Versailles, Germany promised to keep troops out of the German Rhineland, which lay along its border with France. But

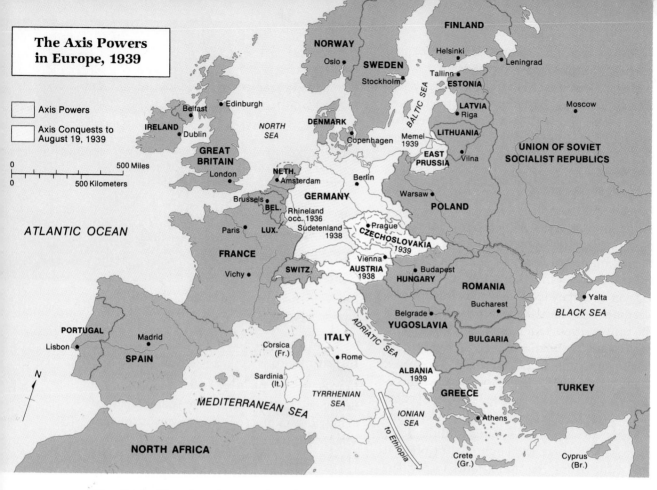

The Axis Powers in Europe, 1939

□ Axis Powers

■ Axis Conquests to August 19, 1939

0 ——— 500 Miles
0 ——— 500 Kilometers

ATLANTIC OCEAN

NORTH SEA

BALTIC SEA

FINLAND
Helsinki
• Leningrad
NORWAY
Oslo •
SWEDEN
Stockholm •
Tallinn •
ESTONIA
LATVIA
• Riga
Moscow •
Belfast
• Edinburgh
IRELAND
• Dublin
DENMARK
Copenhagen •
Memel 1939
LITHUANIA
• Vilna
UNION OF SOVIET SOCIALIST REPUBLICS
GREAT BRITAIN
London •
NETH.
• Amsterdam
Berlin •
EAST PRUSSIA
Brussels •
BEL.
Rhineland occ. 1936
Warsaw •
POLAND
Paris •
LUX.
Sudetenland 1938
• Prague
CZECHOSLOVAKIA 1939
GERMANY
FRANCE
Vichy •
SWITZ.
Vienna •
AUSTRIA 1938
• Budapest
HUNGARY
ROMANIA
Bucharest •
• Yalta
BLACK SEA
PORTUGAL
Lisbon •
Madrid •
SPAIN
Corsica (Fr.)
ITALY
• Rome
Sardinia (It.)
ADRIATIC SEA
Belgrade •
YUGOSLAVIA
BULGARIA
ALBANIA 1939
N
MEDITERRANEAN SEA
TYRRHENIAN SEA
IONIAN SEA
to Ethiopia
GREECE
• Athens
TURKEY
NORTH AFRICA
Crete (Gr.)
Cyprus (Br.)

Map Study *How does the map show that Ethiopia had been taken over by Italy? In what year was Albania taken over?*

in 1936, Hitler violated the treaty by moving his army into the Rhineland.

Hitler seized Austria in the spring of 1938. Then he began eyeing the nearby Sudetenland, where many German-speaking people lived, even though the Sudetenland was part of Czechoslovakia.

The most powerful countries of Western Europe wanted to stay out of war almost as much as the United States did. Many people in those countries believed Germany had legitimate complaints as a result of the Treaty of Versailles. They thought that if Germany could only regain some of its power and standing in the world, Hitler would be satisfied and all threats to peace would end. That policy of allowing Hitler to seize territory without opposition from other countries became known as **appeasement.** Its greatest spokesman was Neville Chamberlain, prime minister of Britain in the late 1930's.

Appeasement reached its peak in a series of meetings at Munich, Germany, in September 1938. There, British and French officials agreed to let Hitler take over the Sudetenland without a fight. In return, Hitler assured them that he would take no more territory. He also moved toward an alliance with Italy. A formal

618

pact between Italy and Germany was signed in 1939. Mussolini called the line between Rome and Berlin the **Axis,** as if the world revolved around those two capitals.

▶**6.** What was appeasement?

War

Then suddenly, in the spring of 1939, German troops took over the rest of Czechoslovakia. Next, after negotiating a treaty with the Soviets to make sure they would not interfere, Hitler invaded Poland on September 1, 1939. Finally the Western democracies understood that only force could stop the Nazis. Determined to support the Poles, France and Great Britain declared war against Germany on September 3, 1939. The Second World War had begun in Europe. Asia was already at war, since in 1937, the Japanese had expanded beyond Manchuria and begun a full-scale invasion of China.

▶**7.** Why did France and Great Britain declare war on Germany?

Reviewing Section I

Identify isolation, Kellogg-Briand Pact, Benito Mussolini, Fascist, Nazis, Adolf Hitler, Führer, Holocaust, German Rhineland, appeasement, Axis

Questions to Answer
1. How did Fascist and Nazi governments differ from democratic governments?
2. What happened to the Jews of Europe during the Holocaust?

A Question to Think About What might have happened if European leaders such as Chamberlain opposed appeasement?

★★★★★★★★★★★★★★★★ The United States and the World ★★
India Looks for Freedom

The fight for freedom in India began in 1858, as soon as India became a colony of Great Britain. In 1885, a group of Indians set up the Indian National Congress. The Congress had no power to make laws, but it did bring together leaders from all parts of India and from many groups and religions. However, the Congress lost British approval when it started working for independence.

Because the National Congress was dominated by Hindus, who were also a majority in the nation, the Muslims pulled out of the National Congress in 1906. They started the Muslim League.

India declared war on Germany on September 3, 1939, the same day Great Britain did. Many Indian leaders refused to give Britain their full support, however, until Britain gave India its independence.

During the war, the British tried to make plans for independence. However, Indian leaders were very divided. Muslim leaders insisted that a separate nation, Pakistan, had to be created for the Muslims of India.

In August 1946, terrible riots broke out between Hindus and Muslims throughout the country. The violence continued until 1947, when British and Indian leaders agreed to partition India.

India became an independent dominion in the British Commonwealth of Nations on August 15, 1947. Pakistan had joined the day before. A kind of war began at once between Hindus and Muslims. Whole villages were wiped out. India and Pakistan continued fighting until 1949.

II. Toward American Involvement

Most Americans reacted to developments abroad by vowing to keep their country out of the wars in Asia and Europe. Those Americans determined to keep the United States from becoming involved in the affairs of other countries were called **isolationists.**

Not all isolationists were the same. There were isolationists in both political parties and in all parts of the country. Many isolationists were progressive reformers who feared that involvement abroad would take attention away from the need for reform at home. Many German Americans and Italian Americans were also isolationists. Even if they disliked Hitler and Mussolini, those Americans did not want war with their old homelands.

The Neutrality Acts

As conditions in Europe worsened between 1935 and 1937, the isolationists succeeded in passing a series of laws that were known

Students from the University of Chicago take part in a demonstration for peace that was part of a nationwide antiwar movement.

as the **neutrality acts.** Those laws made it illegal to sell arms to nations at war. They also made it illegal for Americans to lend money or to sell on credit to such nations. Finally, the neutrality acts said the United States government would not protect Americans who traveled on the ships of warring nations.

▶**1.** What were the major provisions of the neutrality acts?

Roosevelt's Position

President Roosevelt recognized that the isolationists were very strong. He knew, however, that the United States could not remain at peace in a world ruled by dictators.

Many of FDR's advisers also opposed isolationism. They included Roosevelt's secretary of state, Cordell Hull of Tennessee. Such men, like FDR himself, thought the neutrality acts were a mistake.

In a famous speech on October 5, 1937, the President said that no nation could isolate itself from the spreading troubles abroad. As a result, the free nations should join to quarantine, or set apart, nations that threatened the peace. Public reaction to that speech was negative. If FDR fought the isolationists more openly, he might lose votes in Congress for his programs. With the nation still in the middle of the Depression, the President could not take such a risk.

▶**2.** What stopped FDR from opposing the isolationists more vigorously?

The War in Europe, 1939–1940

It took only a few weeks in September 1939 for the Germans to defeat Poland. Then, between November 1939 and March 1940, the Soviets attacked Finland. The next month

World War II in Europe, 1939-1945

Legend:
- Allied or Allied Controlled Territory, Dec. 1941
- Major Axis Powers
- Greatest Extent of Axis Powers, Dec. 1941
- Neutral Nations
- → Allied Forces

(Map labels include:) FINLAND, NORWAY, SWEDEN, DENMARK, NORTH SEA, IRELAND, GREAT BRITAIN, London, Dunkirk, NETH., BELG., LUX., NORMANDY, Reims, Paris, FRANCE, Vichy, VICHY FRANCE, ATLANTIC OCEAN, PORTUGAL, Lisbon, Madrid, SPAIN, Gibraltar, SP. MOROCCO, Casablanca, FR. MOROCCO, ALGERIA (Fr.), TUNISIA (Fr.), LIBYA (It.), ESTONIA, LATVIA, LITHUANIA, EAST PRUSSIA, Leningrad, Moscow, UNION OF SOVIET SOCIALIST REPUBLICS, Berlin, Warsaw, GERMANY, POLAND, UKRAINE, Stalingrad, Prague, CZECHOSLOVAKIA, Munich, Vienna, AUSTRIA, SWITZ., Budapest, HUNGARY, ROMANIA, Yalta, CASPIAN SEA, BLACK SEA, ITALY, Corsica, Rome, Naples, Salerno, ALBANIA, Sardinia, Palermo, Sicily, YUGOSLAVIA, BULGARIA, GREECE 1941, Crete (Gr.), MEDITERRANEAN SEA, TURKEY, IRAN, Cyprus (Br.), SYRIA, LEBANON, IRAQ, PALESTINE, TRANS-JORDAN, SAUDI ARABIA, El Alamein, EGYPT, Cairo

Scale: 0 250 500 Miles / 0 250 500 Kilometers

Map Study *What two countries were not taken over by the Axis Powers even though they were surrounded by Axis-controlled countries?*

the Germans invaded Denmark and Norway. In May they overran Belgium and the Netherlands. Finally, in June 1940, France also fell to Hitler's armies.

Hitler began preparing for an invasion of Britain. The first step of the invasion was conducted from the air. By the fall of 1940, German bombers were making massive attacks on London and other English cities.

The **Battle of Britain,** as the German air attack was called, deeply moved Americans.

Winston Churchill and his wife, Clementine, sadly survey the wreckage caused by German bombers during the Battle of Britain. ▶

621

They followed its progress closely over the radio. Every night from London the broadcaster Edward R. Murrow described the heroism of Londoners in the face of war's terrible destruction. The British were, in fact, better prepared than the French for war. Britain had used the last years of the peace to build fighting planes for their defense. A new invention, radar, helped locate the attacking bombers for Britain's Royal Air Force (RAF).

Hitler lost the Battle of Britain. He caused great destruction and loss of life, but he did not break the spirit of the British. He was never able to launch a land attack against Great Britain. By his efforts against Britain, however, Hitler helped to undermine isolationism in the United States.

▶3. What was the Battle of Britain?

Roosevelt and Churchill

Roosevelt did what he could to help the British and their leader, Prime Minister Winston Churchill. First, in 1939, FDR persuaded Congress to allow the United States to sell arms and other goods to fighting nations by a **cash-and-carry policy.** That is, countries at war could buy such goods so long as they paid for them right away and took them away on their own ships. That policy worked to Britain's advantage, since Britain had the ships to carry supplies across the Atlantic.

Then, in September 1940, when Churchill appealed for more help, the President gave Britain 50 destroyers in return for 99-year leases on bases in Newfoundland, Bermuda, and Jamaica. The **destroyers-for-bases deal** ended American neutrality. From that time on, the United States was actively trying to keep Hitler from taking over the British Isles.

In September 1940, while the Battle of Britain raged, Roosevelt even approved a Selective Service Act. It provided for the drafting of 80,000 men into the United States Army. Never before had there been an American draft law during a time when the United States was formally at peace.

▶4. How did FDR help the British in 1940?

The Election of 1940

FDR's policy involved great risks for the United States and for himself as well. In 1940, Roosevelt was in the midst of a presidential election campaign. His Republican opponent, Wendell Willkie, accused FDR of "warmongering." Willkie said that if Roosevelt was given a third term in office, the United States would be at war within six months.

FDR tried hard to defend himself. He promised American parents that their "boys were not going to be sent into any foreign wars." All he was doing, he argued, was helping the British defend themselves. Roosevelt said that the United States could serve as the "arsenal of democracy," supplying arms to other free countries without itself going to war.

Opinion polls showed that the American people wanted to help the British but did not want to enter the war directly. Apparently, then, they approved of Roosevelt's policy. They gave him 54.8 percent of their votes in the election of 1940—less than in 1936, but still enough to ensure a solid victory.

▶5. How did FDR defend himself against the charge of warmongering?

The Battle of the Atlantic

Soon after the election, Churchill told Roosevelt that the British needed still more help. They were running out of money to pay for all the supplies they were buying in the United States. Also, the Germans had destroyed so many British transport ships that the British were having trouble carrying supplies from the United States to Britain.

Roosevelt responded by abandoning the cash-and-carry policy. He did that with two steps. First, he asked Congress to approve a **Lend-Lease Act,** which allowed the President to send war supplies to any country whose defense he considered vital to the United States. Such countries could pay for those supplies after the war. Some isolationists complained bitterly about the Lend-Lease Act, but Congress approved the measure and the President signed it in March 1941. Then, when Hitler broke his treaty with the Soviets by attacking the Soviet Union in June 1941, the United States sent aid to the Soviets too.

The President also committed American sea power to protect British transport ships against the Germans. Thus, American ships began taking an active part in the **Battle of the Atlantic.** In September, after a German submarine fired on an American ship, the President ordered the navy to "shoot on sight" any German submarines. Although the United States Navy was battling against Germany on the Atlantic, the war was still undeclared.

▶**6.** In what two ways did FDR help Britain after the election of 1940?

Pearl Harbor

Relations between the United States and Japan were also moving toward a crisis in 1940. In September of that year, Japan joined Germany and Italy as one of the Axis Powers.

Roosevelt was determined to keep Japan from taking over China. Japanese aggression also threatened the American-controlled Philippine Islands, the British colonies at Singapore and Malaya, and the oil-rich Dutch colonies in Indonesia. To bring pressure on the Japanese, Roosevelt cut off shipments of scrap metal and fuel to Japan. The loss of fuel was especially important. The Japanese desperately needed oil. When talks failed to reopen trade, the Japanese decided they would have to go to war and conquer the Dutch East Indies. There the Japanese could get the oil they needed.

American officials knew that. They knew, too, that a large Japanese fleet, including 6 big aircraft carriers loaded with more than 400 planes, had gone to sea in late November. It seemed unlikely that the Japanese would attack the Hawaiian Islands, which are 3,000 miles from Japan. American sailors were still sleeping at the naval base at **Pearl Harbor**

On December 8, 1941, FDR asked Congress for a declaration of war against Japan.

when the Japanese opened fire on the base shortly after 7 A.M. on December 7, 1941.

By the end of the day, 6 huge battleships and many other American vessels were sunk and 200 planes had been destroyed. More than 2,400 Americans had been killed. Within hours, Japanese bombers had also attacked the island of Guam and the United States Army base at Manila in the Philippines. The Japanese landed troops on Malaya too.

Many Americans heard the horrible news while eating their Sunday dinners. There was

no doubt about what the United States had to do. The next day, an angry Congress declared war on Japan. Then, on December 11, Japan's allies, Germany and Italy, declared war on the United States. In return, Congress declared war on them. Like it or not, the American people had entered the Second World War.

▶**7.** What event made the United States enter the Second World War?

Reviewing Section II

Identify isolationists, neutrality acts, Cordell Hull, Battle of Britain, Winston Churchill, cash-and-carry policy, destroyers-for-bases deal, Wendell Willkie, Lend-Lease Act, Battle of the Atlantic, Pearl Harbor

Questions to Answer
1. What measures did the United States take to help Great Britain before the attack on Pearl Harbor?
2. What prompted the Japanese attack on Pearl Harbor?

A Question to Think About If the Japanese had not attacked Pearl Harbor, do you think the United States would have entered the war? Explain your answer.

III. Fighting the War

Well before the attack on Pearl Harbor, the United States had begun to plan for war. In March 1941, American and British military leaders met and came to some important decisions. If the United States entered the war, they agreed, its main efforts would be in Europe. Only when Hitler was defeated would the United States turn its full power against Japan.

North Africa

The United States joined Great Britain, the Soviet Union, and other nations as one of the **Allies,** the nations fighting the Axis. The Soviet Union had become one of the Allies after it was invaded by Germany in 1941. Stalin, leader of the Soviets, urged the Allies to open a "Second Front" by attacking Hitler in Europe. That would force Hitler to pull troops out of the Soviet Union where the fighting was very heavy. However, Winston Churchill successfully opposed Stalin's plan. He thought the Allies should attack the Axis on the fringes of its power, such as along the Mediterranean Sea. There the Axis was much weaker than it was farther north.

In October 1942, British and American forces began their first major campaign not in Europe but in North Africa. Led by the American General Dwight D. Eisenhower, the Allied army quickly overcame the Nazis in Morocco and Algeria. Both those countries were governed by the pro-Nazi French government set up at the town of Vichy (vē′ shē) in southern France.

Then, as Eisenhower moved eastward across North Africa, the British General Bernard Montgomery led troops westward from Egypt. They met in Tunisia, where the Allies faced fierce resistance led by German Field Marshall Erwin Rommel, known as the "Desert Fox." However, on May 12, 1943, Rommel and a quarter million German and Italian troops surrendered. The Allies now controlled all of North Africa. For the first time since the war had begun, Churchill allowed the church bells of London to ring in celebration.
▶**1.** How did the Allies take North Africa?

Italy

"Where do we go from here?" Roosevelt asked. On to northern France to open the "Second Front," Stalin urged. But Churchill disagreed. He said the Allies should simply cross the Mediterranean from Tunisia to Sicily and then take Italy. That would give the Allies control of the Mediterranean. It would also weaken the Axis. Once again, Churchill had his way.

The Allies invaded Sicily in July 1943, and then landed south of Naples in Italy during September. The Italian people were weary of Mussolini and his Fascist dictatorship. After they deposed him, the new government quickly surrendered. But the Germans had moved large numbers of troops into Italy through the summer, and they waged a bitter battle. So the fighting continued.

Because the Allies had to fight their way through Italy, their progress was discouragingly slow. Allied troops did not take Naples until October 1943. They did not reach Rome until eight months later, in June 1944. Most of Italy's northern industrial region still remained in German hands.
▶**2.** Why did the Allies have to fight their way through Italy?

The Pacific

The Japanese surprise attacks of December 1941 temporarily destroyed American power in Asia. Then, as the Allies concentrated their efforts on the war in Europe, Japan seemed to overrun the Pacific. It quickly took Guam, Wake Island, and Hong Kong. Next it seized Singapore and Java. Then, in January 1942, Japan took the Philippines. The Americans on the islands had to retreat. As the American commander in Asia, General Douglas MacArthur, evacuated the Philippines, he promised, "I shall return." At that time, though, it seemed unlikely he would keep his promise.
▶**3.** What territory had the Japanese seized in the Pacific by January 1942?

Stopping the Japanese The Allies realized that the Japanese had to be stopped or they would take over Australia and India. The Allies were successful in the **Battle of the Coral Sea** in the South Pacific during May 1942. That battle was fought from aircraft carriers that never fired at one another. The

IMPROVE YOUR SKILLS
Reading Maps: Using Longitude

In Chapter 17, you learned about parallels of latitude, the imaginary lines that circle Earth. There is a second set of imaginary lines that run from the North Pole to the South Pole. Those lines are called meridians of longitude. The starting point for meridians of longitude is a 0° line called the prime meridian, or first meridian. The line numbered 180° is the end point for measuring lines of longitude. It is exactly halfway around Earth from the prime meridian. All lines east of the prime meridian to the 180° meridian are east longitude. All lines west of the prime meridian to the 180° meridian are west longitude. Longitude is expressed in degrees and minutes in the same manner as latitude. Using latitude and longitude lines, you can locate any place on Earth.

Use the map below to answer the following questions.

1. At what interval are meridians of longitude shown on the map?
2. At approximately what longitude is Midway Island?
3. What Japanese city is located at approximately 130° E longitude?
4. Which important event of the war occurred at 157°53′W longitude?
5. At approximately what degree of longitude is Toyko?

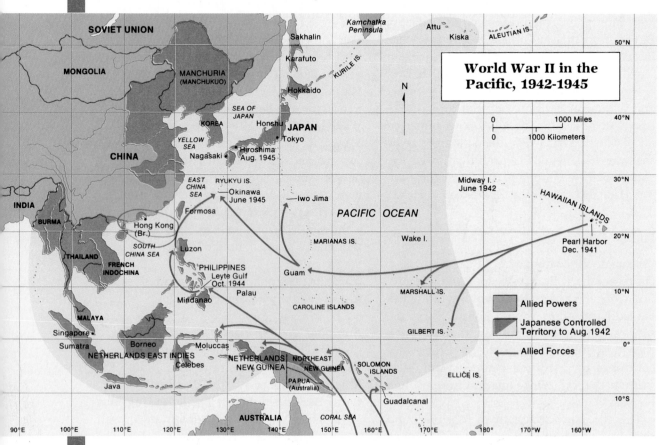

World War II in the Pacific, 1942-1945

Fighting was bitter as Japanese planes attacked American battleships in the Pacific during the Battle of Midway.

fighting was done by airplanes that took off from those carriers. The Americans did so much damage that the Japanese had to give up their drive toward Australia.

▶**4.** What did the Allies accomplish in the Battle of the Coral Sea?

The Battle of Midway The Japanese found new targets, however. In June 1942, they sent a powerful fleet toward Midway Island, which is west of Hawaii. But the Japanese ships never got there. The Americans intercepted the Japanese orders. Although the orders were in code, the Americans had broken the Japanese code and were able to read the message. After locating the Japanese ships on radar, American bombers attacked from June 3 to June 6. They destroyed four Japanese aircraft carriers and many other vessels. In that **Battle of Midway**, the Americans stopped Japanese expansion in the Central Pacific.

▶**5.** How did the Allies stop the Japanese attack on Midway Island?

Pushing Back the Invader The victory at Midway was the turning point of the war in the Pacific. Soon afterwards, the Allies began to retake territory from the Japanese. They did that by "island hopping"—moving from one Pacific island to another, toward Japan.

The first Allied offensive was at the **Battle of Guadalcanal** in the Solomon Islands, where American marines landed in August 1942. After months of intense jungle fighting, Japanese resistance collapsed. Then the Allies moved on to take the Gilbert Islands, the Marshall Islands, the Marianas, and Guam. Finally, in 1944, General MacArthur was able to keep his promise to return to the Philippines. After the great naval **Battle of Leyte Gulf** in October 1944, the Americans had control of the waters around the Philippines. Soon they would control the islands themselves. Farther north, Americans and Canadians had won back the Aleutian Islands.

The Battle of Midway was a turning point for another reason as well. From that time on, the Japanese had a hard time replacing lost ships and planes. American war production, on the other hand, was moving into high gear to replace lost equipment. Success in the war, in short, depended upon developments on the homefront.

▶**6.** Why was the Battle of Midway the turning point of the war in the Pacific?

Reviewing Section III

Identify Allies, Dwight Eisenhower, Erwin Rommel, Douglas MacArthur, Battle of the Coral Sea, Battle of Midway, Battle of Guadalcanal, Battle of Leyte Gulf

Questions to Answer
1. What was the strategy behind the Allied invasions of North Africa and Italy?
2. Why was the Battle of Midway an important battle in the Pacific?

A Question to Think About Why do you think the United States agreed to try to win the war in Europe before turning its full power against Japan?

IV. The Home Front

Even before the United States declared war, it had begun to build its defenses. It increased production of airplanes, tanks, and other military supplies. That eliminated all lingering unemployment, finally bringing the Great Depression to an end. In addition, war production changed the patterns of American life. Some of those changes lasted long after the war was over.

War Production

Soon after the attack at Pearl Harbor, Roosevelt set up the **War Production Board** (WPB) to help the American economy shift into full-scale wartime production. Under WPB direction, the United States greatly increased its production of war supplies in a very short time. In 1940, for example, the country produced about 6,000 military planes. Three years later, it was producing 85,000 a year.

Many factories that had made consumer goods in peacetime were now refitted for war production. Some entirely new industries grew up as well. For example, because Japan had seized almost all of the world's supply of rubber, a substitute for rubber was badly needed. With the help of massive government funds, Americans developed synthetic rubber and were able to manufacture it in great quantities.

▶**1.** How did the WPB affect the production of war supplies?

Women Workers Quite suddenly, American workers found there were plenty of jobs to be had. In fact, with so many men going off to fight, there were more jobs than there were white male workers. Employers had to find new workers. They turned to women.

Since the early nineteenth century, the number of women working for wages had been growing. The Depression, however, hit working women especially hard. Married women were expected to give up their jobs so that men, presumably the heads of households, could have more jobs. Even Secretary of Labor Frances Perkins advised women to give up their jobs. But once the war began, more women than ever went to work outside the home. Some 57 percent of adult women were wage earners.

Of the six million women who took jobs during the war, almost half worked in manufacturing. They filled positions traditionally saved for men. Women worked, for example, as welders or as steelmakers. "Rosie the Riveter" was a popular song about a female worker. Even more striking, most of the new female workers were older than 35 years, and about 75 percent of them were married. Some even had children.

▶ **2.** What percentage of women worked outside the home during the war?

Jobs for Blacks Black workers were also available for war work. At first, however, the opportunities for good wartime jobs were denied to them. Then, in 1941, A. Philip Randolph, head of the sleeping car porters' union, began to organize a great march on Washington. By July 1, 1941, he said, there would be as many as 150,000 blacks marching to demand jobs in the defense industries as well as to end segregation in the armed forces.

President Roosevelt quickly saw that such a march would be a great embarrassment to the government. To satisfy Randolph, he issued an executive order that said jobs in defense industries had to be assigned "without discrimination because of race, creed, color, or national origin."

The President's policy did not have much effect in ending segregation in industry. However, the policy did open up some jobs

Women workers replaced men in defense industries during the Second World War.

for blacks, including those who still lived in poverty in the South. During the war, some 1.2 million southern blacks moved to industrial cities in the North or West to take advantage of new employment opportunities. The war also let black women, who had worked as servants or in other low-paying positions, find more rewarding jobs in industry.

▶ **3.** How did A. Philip Randolph convince the President to stop discrimination in defense industries?

The Economy

As war production put people back to work, Americans suddenly found they had money to spend again. There were, however, fewer consumer products available for purchase. Much factory production was earmarked for the war. Even foods had to be shipped overseas to feed the army. With demand increasing and supplies dropping, prices seemed likely to shoot upwards.

The government tried to ward off inflation by setting limits on some prices and starting a rationing system. Families were given coupons that allowed them to purchase limited amounts of products that were in short supply, such as sugar, meat, coffee, and gasoline. The government also raised taxes and urged people to use their money to buy war bonds. Nonetheless, prices rose nearly 137 percent during the war years.

▶**4.** How did the government try to prevent inflation during the war?

The Family

Wartime prosperity affected the American family. During the hard times of the 1930's, people hesitated to get married and start families. However, as soon as war production gave the economy a boost, the marriage rate began to rise. It shot up dramatically during the war years, as did the birthrate.

Prosperity also let unhappily married couples afford divorces. There were 264,000 divorces in the United States in 1940. But in 1945, the number had grown to 485,000.

▶**5.** What effect did wartime prosperity have on the birthrate?

The Armed Forces

The biggest employer during the war was the armed forces. More than 12 million Americans volunteered for or were drafted into the armed services during the Second World War.

Nearly one million blacks served in the armed forces, mostly in the army. Some became officers. In 1940, for example, Benjamin O. Davis became the country's first black brigadier general. However, blacks generally served in all-black units.

The end of the war was near before the navy and coast guard allowed blacks into combat service jobs. The air force and marines refused to accept any black recruits at all until protests by black leaders were successful.

Although the task of actually fighting battles was reserved for men, the armed forces recruited women for office work and messenger service. Some women served as noncombat pilots. They piloted planes across the Atlantic to bases in Europe. About 100,000 women served in the Women's Army Auxiliary Corps (WAACS). In the WAACs, blacks were trained as officers because the director of the WAACs, Oveta Culp Hobby of Texas, insisted upon it. In the navy, women served in the WAVES. Women could also join the air force WAFS, the coast guard SPARS, or the marine corps' Women's Reserve.

▶**6.** What roles did blacks and women play in the armed forces?

Navy mess attendant Dorie Miller won the Navy Cross for shooting down four Japanese planes during the attack on Pearl Harbor.

"above and beyond the call of duty"

DORIE MILLER
Received the Navy Cross
at Pearl Harbor, May 27, 1942

Racial Conflict

Racial conflict scarred the home front during the war. Black soldiers from the North experienced more intense segregation at army bases in the South than they had known at home. At the same time, many southern blacks moved into northern cities, where they competed with white workers for scarce housing.

In such situations, violence frequently broke out. White soldiers attacked blacks at several army camps, including Fort Dix in New Jersey. In some northern cities, there were terrible riots. One of the worst happened in Detroit on June 20 and 21, 1943, when 34 people were killed.

Also in June, violence broke out between whites and Mexican Americans in Los Angeles. For several nights, mobs of whites attacked Mexican Americans there.

The violence of the 1940's made many blacks decide that it was time to fight for their rights. The NAACP had about 50,000 members in 1940. That number grew to 450,000 members by 1946. Other activists, black and white, joined the new **Congress of Racial Equality** (CORE), started in 1942. It vowed to fight segregation without violence but to fight it to the end. That fight was to last for many years.

▶**7.** What sort of racial violence occurred during the war?

Japanese Internment

As soon as Americans heard the news of Pearl Harbor, many became suspicious of Japanese Americans, especially those living on the West Coast. Although there was no evidence of disloyalty by Japanese Americans, more than 110,000 of them were interned, or kept confined, during the war. Under the **internment policy,** whole families were taken to out-of-the-way camps where they lived in cramped

Japanese Americans had to register at reception centers like this one at Santa Anita, California, before being sent to internment camps.

quarters surrounded by barbed wire. They were never charged with any crime, much less convicted of treason. Still, they lost their homes, their farms, and other businesses having a total value of nearly $500 million. Around 1,200 Japanese men from the internment camps volunteered for the armed forces. Other Japanese Americans from Hawaii also fought in the war.

▶**8.** What happened to interned Japanese Americans?

Reviewing Section IV

Identify War Production Board, A. Philip Randolph, Benjamin O. Davis, Oveta Culp Hobby, Congress of Racial Equality, internment policy

Questions to Answer
1. What progress did blacks make toward job equality during the war?
2. How did women help to win the war?

A Question to Think About What constitutional rights did the internment of Japanese Americans violate?

V. Winning the War

By 1944, the United States and its Allies could see victory ahead. American war production was in high gear. The Nazis were being pushed back in Europe, and the Japanese were being pushed back in Asia. The time had come for a dramatic attack on the enemy. In keeping with the prewar plans, that attack came first in Europe.

In December 1943, Roosevelt, Churchill, and Stalin met at Teheran, the capital of Iran. Again Churchill argued for delay in opening a "Second Front," but Roosevelt and Stalin were tired of delay. Finally the Allies agreed to land troops in northern France with the hope of moving from there into Germany itself. That attack was known as **Operation OVERLORD.**

Air Strikes

Long before troops went to northern Europe, Allied bombers tried to weaken German resistance by bomb attacks. The British began bombing Germany in 1941. In August 1942, the first American planes began to bombard Germany.

At first, Allied planes dropped their bombs on factories, dams, or other targets essential to German war production. But it was hard to pinpoint such targets, and the Germans rebuilt them quickly. So bombers were sent against Germany's big cities to disrupt them and, it was hoped, disorganize the country. Hundreds, even thousands of planes went on raids that destroyed the cities of Hamburg, Cologne, Berlin, and Dresden. Hospitals, art museums, and ancient castles—all were lost. Thousands of people were killed.

In earlier wars, attempts were made at least to draw a distinction between soldiers and civilians. The bombings of World War II erased that line. In Europe—as earlier in the final days of the American Civil War—war had become total, a threat to soldier and civilian alike.

▶**1.** Why did Allied bombers attack German cities?

D-Day

While the bombings went on, more than one million American, British, and Canadian soldiers gathered in Britain for Operation OVERLORD. Landing ships, floating docks, airplanes, and other supplies also arrived.

Finally **D-Day**—the day the attack began—arrived on June 6, 1944. Throughout the night before, Allied ships traveled across the English Channel. Then, in the dark early hours of the morning, soldiers under the command of General Dwight D. Eisenhower made their way onto the beaches of Normandy in northern France. They dug in at places they called Omaha Beach and Utah Beach and fought off German attacks with tanks until reinforcements came.

The Germans expected the attack to be made farther east, where the Channel was much narrower. Consequently, the Allies soon broke through the German lines, moving inland.

▶**2.** When and what was D-Day?

Toward Victory in Europe

The first few weeks after the landing at Normandy were very difficult. The Germans managed to hold the Allies within Normandy. Then in July, the Allied forces pushed forward and the Germans fell back. Several units of Free French and Free Poles, Europeans who had kept up the fight against the Nazis, joined

On June 6, 1944, D-Day, thousands of American, British, and Canadian soldiers landed on the beaches of Normandy.

the Allies in the race toward Paris. Finally, on August 24, the Allies entered that city in triumph.

By late August 1944, the Allies had retaken most of France. The Soviets, who had cleared German soldiers out of their homeland, had moved westward, deep into Poland. Germany was threatened from two sides. Many believed, mistakenly, that the Nazi regime would collapse within a few weeks.

Then, however, the Allied drive slowed. The Soviets became bogged down in Poland. The Allies were advancing only slowly in Italy. They still had not reached the important northern cities of Milan, Genoa, and Turin when cold weather set in.

That December, the Allied troops were stretched in a line across Europe from the Netherlands to Switzerland, ready to push

into Germany. Then, on December 16, 1944, the Germans counterattacked through the Ardennes Forest in the north. They pushed back the Allied lines in the **Battle of the Bulge.**

The fighting was hardest near Bastogne in Belgium. However, when the Germans invited American General Tony McAuliffe, to surrender, McAuliffe replied "nuts" and kept fighting. Within weeks, the Allies had resumed their advance. In early March, they crossed the Rhine River into Germany over the only bridge the Germans had not destroyed.

In the east, the Soviets had moved through Poland and reached Berlin in April 1945. American and Soviet troops met at the Elbe River on April 25.

At about the same time, German resistance in Italy collapsed. As the Soviets advanced toward his underground hideout in Berlin, Hitler committed suicide on April 30. So did his close associates, Joseph Goebbels and Heinrich Himmler. German leadership passed to an admiral, Karl Doenitz, who announced his readiness to surrender.

On May 7, 1945, German forces in Western Europe surrendered. Germans in Eastern Europe surrendered on May 8, which is known as **V-E Day**—Victory in Europe.

▶**3.** What was the Battle of the Bulge?

The Death of Roosevelt

Franklin Roosevelt was not there for the moment of triumph. His long, difficult years in office had left him worn and tired. He wanted to see the country through the war. So he ran for a fourth presidential term in 1944 and easily defeated his Republican opponent, Thomas E. Dewey of New York.

The strains of office did not go away after the election. Roosevelt met with Churchill and Stalin at the town of Yalta on the Black Sea to discuss the peace settlement at the end of the war. He left that conference exhausted. To recover, he went to his favorite vacation spot at Warm Springs, Georgia. Two weeks later, on April 12, 1945, FDR was sitting at his desk when suddenly he put his hand to his forehead and said, "I have a terrific headache." Then he slumped over, dead from a cerebral hemorrhage.

Americans were stunned. It was hard to imagine the country without Roosevelt's leadership.

▶**4.** When did FDR die?

President Truman

The new President was a little-known senator from Missouri, Harry S Truman. Roosevelt had chosen Truman as his vice presidential candidate in 1944 because he was a middle-of-the-roader with few enemies. When he became President, Truman was not prepared for the international issues he would have to help settle. Roosevelt had not kept his Vice President well informed.

As time would show, Truman was intelligent and had a strength of spirit that served him well. He needed all those resources because he would be called upon to make some of the hardest decisions any President has had to make. Above all, he had to decide how to bring the war with Japan to an end.

▶**5.** Who succeeded President Roosevelt?

Toward Victory in the Pacific

In early 1945, as the Allies moved toward Germany in Europe, they were also moving toward Japan in the Pacific. In February, American marines landed on Iwo Jima, an island 750 miles from Tokyo. The marines took the island after suffering heavy casualties in a month of bitter fighting. Then they moved on to the Kurile Islands to the south of Japan. They captured the island of Okinawa there on April 1, but at great cost—45,000 Americans were killed or wounded.

The rulers of Japan were growing desperate. Because American submarines had destroyed so many Japanese ships, the country could not import more needed goods. Neither could it bring home its large armies in Manchuria and China. As Americans moved onto islands within striking range of Japan, American planes began to bomb Japanese cities. Those cities were filled with light wooden buildings that burned easily, and the Americans dropped thousands of firebombs. Raids on Tokyo in April 1945 probably cost 100,000 civilian lives.

▶**6.** Why were the rulers of Japan becoming desperate in early 1945?

Harry S Truman, the thirty-third President of the United States, was born in Lamar, Missouri, on May 8, 1884. At six, he moved with his parents to Independence, Missouri, where he spent his childhood. Thick eyeglasses prevented the young boy from playing sports with his classmates. Instead, he spent his days reading books in the Independence Public Library.

After high school, Harry applied to West Point but was rejected because of poor eyesight. Instead, he worked at a variety of jobs, including bank clerk and bookkeeper. When he was 22, he took over the family farm and spent the next 12 years as a prosperous Missouri farmer.

World War I ended Harry's days as a farmer. Instead, he went to fight on the Western Front in France. In 1919, he returned home and married his childhood sweetheart, Bess Wallace. He also teamed up with a wartime buddy to open a clothing store in Kansas City.

Truman worked hard to make his store a success. Despite his efforts, a farm depression in 1921 doomed the store to failure. Rather than declare bankruptcy, Truman spent the next 15 years paying off his debts.

The failure of his store discouraged Truman. When his friendly manner and farm background impressed the political boss of Kansas City, Truman decided to end his career in business and go into politics. With the boss's help, Harry won the position of county judge.

As county judge, Truman supervised building projects that were paid for with tax money. He carried out his duties honestly and efficiently. By the time he left the position in 1934, he had earned a reputation as a man to be trusted.

In 1934, Truman's reputation helped him win a seat in the United States Senate. At age 50, Harry moved his family to the nation's capital, never dreaming that one day he would live in the White House.

Truman served two terms as senator. During his second term, he helped set up a committee to investigate defense spending. Truman's efforts saved the nation over $1 billion.

In 1944, Franklin Delano Roosevelt ran for his fourth term as President, and the Democratic Party chose Truman to be Roosevelt's running mate. Roosevelt and Truman easily defeated their Republican opponents. Then, tragically, less than three months into his fourth term, the President died.

When Vice President Harry Truman heard the news that the President had died, he told reporters that he felt "like the moon, the stars, and all the planets have fallen on me." In a sense, all that and more had happened. Upon Truman's shoulders rested the enormous task of ending the most devastating war the world had ever known. Truman proved to be worthy of the job.

The atom bomb left the city of Hiroshima in ruins. A watch, found among the rubble, marks the time of the explosion.

Kamikaze Still the Japanese did not surrender. Instead, they enlisted volunteer suicide pilots, called **kamikaze** (kä'mē kä'zē). Those pilots would crash explosive-filled planes into American ships, killing themselves in the process.

The main effect of the kamikaze was to convince the Americans that if they invaded Japan itself, they would face fierce resistance. Victory would be won only at the cost of thousands of American lives. The high death tolls at Iwo Jima and Okinawa also made that clear. Obviously, the United States should avoid a land war in Japan if that was at all possible.

▶**7.** What was the major effect of the kamikaze?

The A-Bomb There was a way to avoid an invasion of Japan. It was called the **atom bomb,** or A-bomb. By the late 1930's, nuclear physicists had known that the splitting of uranium atoms could let loose tremendous energy. During the war, American scientists, including a Jewish refugee from Nazi Germany named Albert Einstein and a refugee from Fascist Italy, Enrico Fermi, urged President Roosevelt to develop a bomb using the energy of atom splitting before the Germans did so. The bomb was first tested successfully in New Mexico on July 16, 1945.

News of this success reached President Truman at Potsdam, Germany, where he was meeting with other Allied leaders. There, on July 26, the Americans and British offered the Japanese terms of surrender. The Japanese would have to surrender completely, give up their conquests, and allow Allied troops to occupy their country. Otherwise, the Americans and British said, Japan would suffer "prompt and utter destruction." The Japanese refused to surrender.

The United States shipped two atom bombs to the Pacific. One bomb was loaded onto a bomber called the *Enola Gay,* commanded by Colonel Paul W. Tibbets. On Truman's orders, the bomb was dropped on the morning of August 6 over Hiroshima (hir'ō shē'mə), a city that had not been bombed before. After a blinding flash, a great mushroom cloud rose up into the sky, leaving the city a rubble and killing 70,000 or more people. Three days later, only hours after the Soviets had finally declared war on Japan, the second bomb was dropped on the port city of Nagasaki (nä'gə sä'kē).

Even then some of Japan's military leaders wanted to continue the fight, but the emperor knew better. On August 14, Japan accepted the terms offered at Potsdam. Finally on September 2, aboard the United States battleship *Missouri* in Tokyo Bay, the Japanese signed a formal document of surrender. The Second World War was over.

▶**8.** Where did the United States use its atom bombs?

An Agonizing Question Destruction by the atom bombs did not end in 1945. The bombs caused many people to die slowly of radiation poisoning. The radiation caused deformities in children who were born many years after the bombings.

Many times since August 1945 thoughtful people have asked whether it was necessary to drop the atom bomb. At the time, it seemed to be a way to end the war. President Truman wanted above all to avoid the terrible cost in American lives that a land invasion would probably have entailed.

▶**9.** Why did Truman use the A-bomb?

The Toll of the War

The deaths at Hiroshima and Nagasaki were added to an already huge toll. Perhaps 30 to 50 million people, nearly half of them civilians, died during World War II. That number includes those who died in Nazi concentration camps and the Chinese peasants who starved in a terrible famine that hit their country in 1945. Almost 6 million Poles were killed, and 4.5 million Germans died. In Europe, the Soviets were the hardest hit. They lost 15 to 20 million people. The Americans were more fortunate. The United States lost around 300,000 lives. That was three times the number of Americans killed in World War I, and about half as many as died in the Civil War.

Almost every American knew someone who had lost a family member, but the Americans did not feel bitter about their losses. Most thought that they had to fight the war to stop Japanese aggression and bring an end to a monstrous German regime. They had succeeded, and now American soldiers looked forward to returning home. Through their years away, they had dreamed of being with their families and of building homes.

By 1945, the United States had inherited leadership of much of the world. It would be hard to keep its soldiers at home if fighting broke out in the world again.

▶**10.** How many Americans were killed during World War II?

Reviewing Section V

Identify Operation OVERLORD, D-Day, Battle of the Bulge, V-E Day, Thomas E. Dewey, Harry S Truman, kamikaze, atom bomb

Questions to Answer

1. What happened at the Battle of the Bulge?
2. How did the Allies force the Japanese to surrender?

A Question to Think About What might the end of the war have been like if Truman had not ordered the use of the atom bomb?

IMPROVE YOUR READING
Using Context Clues

In earlier reading skill activities, you learned how context clues can help you figure out the meaning of new or unusual terms. Sometimes the author provides you with a direct definition of a new word. Sometimes the author does not give a direct definition, but through indirect hints you may make an educated guess at the meaning of a word.

Read this sentence: "The Selective Service Act allowed the *drafting* of 80,000 men into the army." The word *drafting* is not directly defined. However, the sentence contains clues to the word's meaning such as the phrase "80,000 men into the army." You can infer that *drafting* means requiring enrollment in the army.

The following exercise gives you more practice in using context clues. After reading each sentence, select the correct meaning of the italicized word from the choices given. Write your answer on a separate sheet of paper.

1. The United States, *isolationists* said, should stand alone in the world and avoid entangling alliances with other countries.
   (a) people who did not wish the United States to become involved in world affairs
   (b) people who wished the United States to play an active role in world affairs
   (c) people who wished to reform the economic policies of the United States

2. Hitler and the Nazis sent millions of Jews to *extermination* camps where they were worked to death or killed with an awful efficiency in gas chambers.
   (a) hospital
   (b) death
   (c) immigrant

3. It seemed that Japan was determined to seize China, and Japanese *aggression* also threatened the Philippine Islands, British colonies at Singapore and Malaya, and the Dutch colonies in Indonesia.
   (a) diplomacy
   (b) pollution
   (c) unprovoked attacks

4. American scientists, including a *refugee* from Nazi Germany named Albert Einstein and a *refugee* from Fascist Italy named Enrico Fermi, urged President Roosevelt to develop an atom bomb.
   (a) person who flees from his or her homeland
   (b) patriotic person
   (c) person who is interested in science

5. In 1928, the United States helped *negotiate* the Kellogg-Briand Pact, by which 62 nations agreed to outlaw war as a way of settling disputes.
   (a) discuss so as to reach an agreement
   (b) force upon another
   (c) write about

CHAPTER 28 REVIEW

Vocabulary Check
Write a short definition for each of the following terms.

1. Isolation
2. Fascist
3. Nazi
4. Appeasement
5. Internment policy

Fact Check
On a separate sheet of paper, fill in the word or words that best complete each of the following sentences.

1. Fascists believed in strong government under an _____ leader.
2. In 1934, Hitler made himself president of Germany and took the title _____.
3. The mass killing of European Jews during World War II is called the _____.
4. The alliance between Italy, Germany, and Japan was called the _____.
5. The United States entered World War II after the bombing of _____.
6. The Battle of _____ was the turning point of the war in the Pacific.
7. The Allied attack in northern France was called Operation _____.
8. The German counterattack through the Ardennes in 1944 is called the Battle of the _____.
9. Japanese volunteer suicide pilots were called _____.
10. The atom bomb was dropped on the cities of _____ and _____.

Skills Check
Use the map on page 618 to answer the following questions.

1. What is the subject of this map?
2. Name two countries that had been conquered by the Axis by August 1939.
3. Name the territory between France and Germany that the Germans had taken in 1936.
4. Approximately how far is it from Berlin, Germany, to London, England?
5. What Axis country conquered Ethiopia?

Time Check
On a separate sheet of paper, place the following events in chronological order.

1. Japan signs terms of surrender.
2. Japanese planes bomb Pearl Harbor.
3. France and Great Britain declare war on Germany.
4. D-Day invasion is launched.
5. The Battle of Britain begins.

Think and Write
1. Explain the ways the United States became more involved with the Allies up to Pearl Harbor.
2. How did World War II affect the economy of the United States?
3. What advances in the job market and in the armed forces were made by women and blacks during the war?
4. How did the Soviet Union come to be an ally of the United States?
5. How was the United States different after World War II?

Chapter 29

The Cold War, 1945–1960

The sky is lit by flames, and a mushroom-shaped cloud rises as an atom bomb is tested on Enewetak Island in the South Pacific on October 31, 1952.

When American soldiers met their Soviet allies in Germany at the Elbe River in May 1945, they greeted each other as friends. But once Germany and Japan were defeated, a great conflict developed between the United States and the Soviet Union. Because in most places the two sides fought without exchanging gunfire, their conflict was known as the **Cold War.**

The Americans and Soviets fought at first over the future of war-torn Europe. Before long, the struggle spread to other parts of the world. The conflict also affected the internal affairs of the United States, where crusaders fought the "Communist menace" at home just as they opposed the spread of Communist governments abroad.

I. The Beginnings of the Cold War
Postwar Aims
The Yalta Conference
The Postdam Conference
The Conflict Widens
Containment
The Election of 1948
NATO
The Cold War Deepens

II. Anticommunism at Home
HUAC
The Loyalty Issue
McCarthy

III. A World Divided
The Korean War
The Elections of 1952 and 1956
Peace in Korea
Brinkmanship
Summit at Geneva
New Alliances
Avoiding War

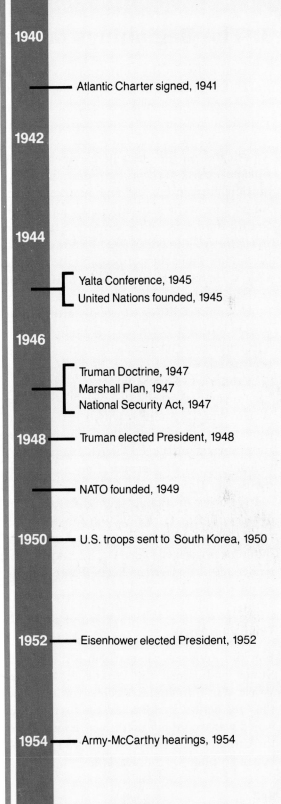

1940

Atlantic Charter signed, 1941

1942

1944

Yalta Conference, 1945
United Nations founded, 1945

1946

Truman Doctrine, 1947
Marshall Plan, 1947
National Security Act, 1947

1948 — Truman elected President, 1948

NATO founded, 1949

1950 — U.S. troops sent to South Korea, 1950

1952 — Eisenhower elected President, 1952

1954 — Army-McCarthy hearings, 1954

I. The Beginnings of the Cold War

Tension between the United States and the Soviet Union began at the time of the Russian Revolution. The Soviets resented the fact that President Wilson had sent troops into their country in 1918 and 1919 (see page 570). Americans, on the other hand, resented the Soviets' efforts to encourage Communist revolutions in nations throughout the world. Americans were also suspicious of Joseph Stalin, the leader of the Soviets. Stalin had strengthened his control over the Soviet Union by having thousands of people killed in the 1930's. He had also been an ally of Hitler for a time. Hitler and Stalin divided Poland. Stalin supported the Allies only after Hitler invaded the Soviet Union in June 1941. Such a leader, many Americans thought, could not be trusted.

In some ways, the Americans and Soviets became more suspicious of each other during World War II. Stalin resented the Western Allies' delay in attacking the Germans in Europe. Such an attack, he thought, would draw at least part of the German army away from the Soviet Union.

The Allies overcame their differences in order to defeat Germany. But when it was time to work out a peace agreement, their differences surfaced again. The major contenders, it turned out, had very different ideas about the postwar world.

Postwar Aims

Franklin Roosevelt thought that if the United States had joined the League of Nations, World War II might have been avoided. Now the President wanted to be sure that a third world war would not take place. Even before the United States entered World War II, FDR began to plan for the peace.

In August 1941, FDR secretly met with Prime Minister Winston Churchill of Great Britain at Argentia Bay near Newfoundland. There they agreed on the **Atlantic Charter,** a statement of "certain common principles" that might lead to "a better future for the world." Those principles included freedom of the seas, freedom of trade, freedom from want, and freedom from fear. The charter said people should have the right "to choose the form of government under which they will live." The charter also described a new international organization to settle disputes and protect the peace. Soon other nations, including the Soviet Union, endorsed the Atlantic Charter. One result was the founding of the **United Nations** (UN) by some 50 countries, including the United States, in 1945.

Stalin endorsed the Atlantic Charter. Still, his ideas of the postwar world differed from those of Roosevelt and Churchill. He wanted the Soviet Union to control the countries of Eastern Europe. Stalin decided that control of Eastern Europe required setting up Communist governments there like that of the Soviet Union. Then friendly nations would lie between the Soviet Union and Germany. The Soviets had suffered terribly after the Germans attacked them in 1941 and wanted to prevent such attacks in the future. But Stalin's ambitions violated the principles of the Atlantic Charter in ways that neither Roosevelt nor Churchill could approve.

▶ **1.** What was the Atlantic Charter?

The Yalta Conference

Differences between the Allies over the shape of the postwar world were a source of trouble even during the war. They came up each time the Allies met.

The most important meeting between FDR, Churchill, and Stalin was held at Yalta, in the Soviet Union, in February 1945. There, the Allies discussed the future of Poland. In the early days of fighting, the Soviet Union had taken over the eastern third of Poland. Roosevelt and Churchill agreed that the Soviets could keep some of that land. In exchange, postwar Poland would be given a part of eastern Germany.

By the time of the Yalta Conference, however, Stalin had placed Communists loyal to the Soviet Union in charge of the Polish government. Leaders of the **Big Three,** as the United States, Great Britain, and the Soviet Union were called, agreed at Yalta to set up a more broadly based government for that country. At some time in the future, the Poles would hold elections to decide how they would be governed.

Also at Yalta, the Big Three agreed to divide Germany into four "zones" of occupation,

The Big Three—Churchill (left), FDR (center), and Stalin—meet at Yalta to discuss ending the war and to make plans for the postwar world.

★★★★★★★★★★★★★★★ The United States and the World ★★
The United Nations

On April 29, 1945, representatives from 50 nations met in San Francisco to adopt a charter for a new organization, the United Nations. The purpose of the UN is to prevent war.

The charter agreed on in San Francisco created two major bodies. The General Assembly is the legislative body of the UN to which all member nations send delegates. Its powers are limited to discussion and recommendation, although its recommendations can carry much weight. The General Assembly now has more than 150 members.

The Security Council is the UN's action agency. It consists of five permanent members—the United States, Great Britain, France, the Soviet Union, and China. Ten more members are elected by the General Assembly.

The council has power to investigate disputes and suggest ways to settle them peacefully. It can ask all UN member nations to break economic and political ties with a nation that has broken the peace. The Security Council can also authorize the use of armed forces supplied by UN members. Each permanent member has the power of veto on important measures. That sometimes prevents the UN from acting.

There are numerous specialized agencies that operate under the UN's general supervision. They include, for example, the International Labor Organization and the International Court of Justice.

one each for the Americans, the British, the Soviets, and the French. The capital, Berlin, lay completely within the Soviet zone, but that city was itself divided into four "sectors," each to be controlled by one of the Allies. In time, the Allies assumed, all the zones and sectors would be brought together in a re-united Germany.

▶ **2.** What decisions were reached at Yalta?

The Postdam Conference

The Big Three met again at Potsdam near Berlin in July 1945. Stalin still represented the Soviet Union. Midway through the conference, Churchill's party lost a general election. As a result, a new prime minister, Clement Atlee, took Churchill's place. And a new President, Harry S Truman, represented the United States. He had a blunt manner, and was in general a less skilled diplomat than FDR.

Truman was already concerned that Stalin was not keeping his agreements, so he decided to "get tough" with the Soviets. At Yalta, the Americans had agreed to let the Soviets take reparations, or payments in money and goods, from Germany to help make up for their wartime losses. Now Truman objected to that. After hard bargaining, it was agreed at Potsdam that the Soviets, British, Americans, and French would take reparations mainly from their own occupation zones. The Soviets tightened their hold on East Germany, from which they soon drew reparations worth billions of dollars a year.

▶ **3.** Who represented each of the "Big Three" nations at Potsdam?

The Conflict Widens

The Polish elections agreed upon at Yalta were postponed. In the meantime, Poland's Communist rulers arrested the leaders of the opposition and broke up meetings of other political groups. When the elections were finally held, the Communists were already in complete control of the government and the elections were meaningless. Since Soviet troops still occupied Poland, there was little that could be done to change the situation.

What had happened in Poland was repeated throughout much of Eastern Europe. The Soviets set up Communist governments in Bulgaria and Rumania. After allowing brief democratic experiments, they also established a Soviet-controlled **satellite government** in Hungary in 1947 and in Czechoslovakia in 1948. A satellite government is one that is dependent upon a more powerful country. Yugoslavia had a Communist government too. That country was, however, more independent of the Soviet Union than were the other Communist nations of Eastern Europe.

Churchill, though out of office, watched the spread of Soviet power with alarm. In a speech at Fulton, Missouri, on March 5, 1946, he warned that an **"iron curtain"** was falling across Europe, cutting the Communist East from the democratic West.

The Soviet Union, it seemed, wanted to spread its influence even farther. In the Middle East, Iran was a cause of concern. The Allies had placed troops there during the war because it was a vital supply route to the Soviet Union. In early 1946, Soviet soldiers were still there. Those troops were withdrawn only because of harsh threats from the West. The Soviets also put pressure on Turkey for rights along the passage from the Black Sea to the Mediterranean. An armed Communist movement also threatened Greece's weak pro-Western government. Even in France and Italy, the Communist Party was becoming stronger.

▶ **4.** What did Churchill mean by the term *iron curtain?*

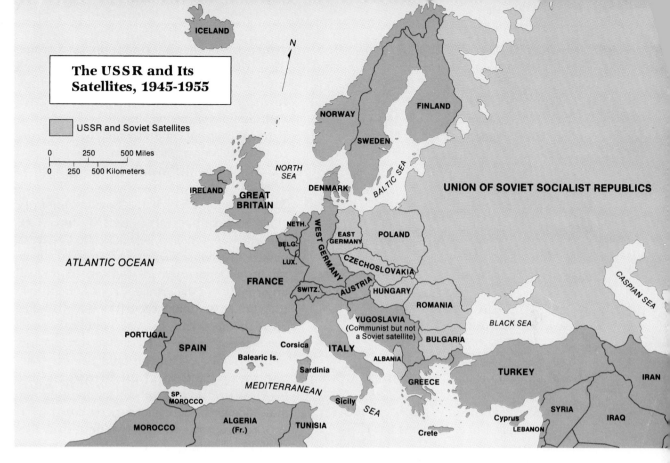

The USSR and Its Satellites, 1945-1955

USSR and Soviet Satellites

| 0 | 250 | 500 Miles |
| 0 | 250 | 500 Kilometers |

ICELAND

NORWAY

FINLAND

SWEDEN

NORTH SEA

BALTIC SEA

IRELAND

GREAT BRITAIN

DENMARK

UNION OF SOVIET SOCIALIST REPUBLICS

NETH.

WEST GERMANY

EAST GERMANY

POLAND

BELG.

ATLANTIC OCEAN

LUX.

CZECHOSLOVAKIA

FRANCE

SWITZ.

AUSTRIA

HUNGARY

ROMANIA

YUGOSLAVIA (Communist but not a Soviet satellite)

BLACK SEA

CASPIAN SEA

PORTUGAL

SPAIN

Corsica

ITALY

BULGARIA

Balearic Is.

ALBANIA

Sardinia

TURKEY

IRAN

MEDITERRANEAN

GREECE

SP. MOROCCO

Sicily

SEA

Cyprus

SYRIA

IRAQ

MOROCCO

ALGERIA (Fr.)

TUNISIA

Crete

LEBANON

Map Study *Name two Soviet satellite nations that border the Soviet Union. How many Communist satellite nations are shown on the map?*

Containment

To many leaders in the West, it seemed that the spread of Soviet power had to be stopped. The effort to stop the Soviets was called the **containment policy.**

President Truman was among those who supported containment. On March 12, 1947, when it looked as though the Communists were about to take over Greece, he went before Congress and announced a new policy. That policy, which became known as the **Truman Doctrine,** stated that the United States would help free peoples who were trying to resist being taken over by outsiders or armed minority groups such as Communists. Congress granted $400 million for economic aid to Greece. It also agreed to strengthen the armed forces of Greece and of Turkey.

▶**5.** What was the Truman Doctrine?

The Marshall Plan The next step in halting the spread of communism was developed by Truman's secretary of state, George Marshall. At Harvard University in June 1947, he announced what became known as the **Marshall Plan.** The United States, he said, was ready to give massive "friendly aid" to help European countries recover from the war. Countries under the plan would decide how to use the funds. Later, other programs were

A parade celebrating the one-millionth ton of Marshall Plan goods sent to Greece moves up one of Athens's main streets.

set up to give economic and military aid to countries outside Europe.

The Soviet Union and its satellite countries could have received funds under the Marshall Plan. They refused to ask for it. The plan, they said, was just an attempt to shape Europe in ways that suited the United States. In contrast, 16 countries of Western Europe were happy to participate. They received more than $13 billion by 1952, which they used to rebuild their economies.

Why was the United States willing to give so much? In part, it offered such aid out of sympathy for the suffering people of Europe. Also, the United States realized that once Europe recovered, it could again begin buying American goods. Even more important, communism would be less attractive to prosperous European countries than to those sunk in poverty.

▶**6.** What was the Marshall Plan?

Preparing for War If the Soviet Union decided to take over new lands by force, the United States had to be ready. So Congress passed a National Security Act in 1947, which set up a **Department of Defense** to control all branches of the armed forces. In addition, it created a **National Security Council,** made up of the President, the Cabinet officers, and some other advisers, to decide foreign and military policy. The National Security Act also set up the **Central Intelligence Agency (CIA).** The CIA was to collect information and engage in secret activities abroad.

Of course, any new major war could involve the use of atomic, or **nuclear weapons.** To avoid that tragedy, some effort was made to ban their further development and to turn those bombs that already existed over to the United Nations. That effort came to nothing. The Soviet Union wanted the United States first to give up its weapons, which it refused to do. The United States wanted controls to keep the Soviets from developing atomic weapons, which the Soviets refused to accept. Consequently, the United States increased its research, making nuclear weapons an important part of its defense.

Bombs were not enough, however. Millions of soldiers were released from military service at the end of the war. When it looked as though they might be needed again, Congress passed a new Selective Service Act in 1948.

▶**7.** What institutions were created by the National Security Act?

Berlin The Soviet threat also changed American attitudes toward Germany. That country was now the first line of defense against the Soviets. So the United States, Britain, and France agreed to merge their three western occupation zones into a new German republic. Stalin reacted quickly to stop that plan.

The western part of Berlin, which had been occupied by the British, French, and Americans, was surrounded by Soviet-occupied territory. On June 24, 1948, the Soviets suddenly cut off all highway and railroad traffic to West Berlin. West Berlin, Stalin seemed to say, could not become part of any new West German republic. All of Berlin would have to become part of the Soviet-dominated eastern section.

Truman would not give in to Stalin. He ordered food, fuel, and other supplies to be brought to West Berlin by air. Beginning in the summer of 1948, British and American planes sent millions of tons of food and supplies to West Berlin. Cargo planes flew in every few minutes at the height of the Berlin airlift, which lasted ten months. It became a symbol of the West's determination to resist Communist expansion. Finally, in May 1949, the Soviets once again let the city be supplied over land.

That very same month, the western part of Germany officially became a new nation, the **Federal Republic of Germany,** better known as West Germany. It included West Berlin. Then the Soviet Union created the **German Democratic Republic,** called East Germany, out of its occupation zone. It included East Berlin. The Soviets had not been able to defeat Truman, but Germany was divided into two new countries. Berlin also remained a divided city.

▶**8.** Why did the Soviets try to isolate West Berlin?

West Berliners watch as an American plane carrying needed supplies flies to its drop-off point during the Berlin airlift.

The Election of 1948

While the Berlin airlift was still going on, the United States held a presidential election. President Truman was the Democratic Party's candidate, but his chances of winning seemed slim. He did not even have the full support of the Democrats.

The Republican candidate was Governor Thomas Dewey of New York. He ran a very quiet campaign, trying hard to avoid making enemies. Truman, however, refused to accept defeat sitting down. He traveled 32,000 miles, making 356 speeches.

The experts were so sure that Dewey would win that they hardly noticed when voters started to swing toward their battling President. One newspaper, the *Chicago Daily Tribune*, went to press early on election night. "Dewey Defeats Truman," its headline said. But Truman got the last laugh. He won 49.5

An early edition of the Chicago Daily Tribune *mistakenly proclaimed Dewey victorious in the 1948 election. Truman, however, had the last laugh.*

percent of the popular votes to Dewey's 45 percent. Third party candidates won the other popular votes. Truman took the electoral vote by 303 to 189.

▶**9.** Who won the election of 1948?

NATO

After his reelection, Truman continued to work for containment. In April 1949, the United States, Canada, and many countries of Western Europe founded the **North Atlantic Treaty Organization** (NATO). NATO allies promised to defend one another against outside attacks. Never before had the United States joined a military alliance with a European country during peacetime. Now an alliance seemed necessary to protect Europe from the Soviet threat. An American, Dwight D. Eisenhower, became supreme commander of the NATO forces in Europe.

▶**10.** What was the purpose of NATO?

The Cold War Deepens

By the spring of 1949, there was reason to believe that the threat of communism had been contained. That illusion was quickly laid to rest.

First, in September 1949, the Soviet Union announced that it had successfully exploded an atom bomb. No one had expected them to succeed at that so quickly. Suddenly, the Soviet threat became much more serious.

In the fall of 1949, China fell to Communist revolutionaries led by Mao Zedong (māu′ dzā′ dong′) and Zhou Enlai (zhō′ en′ lī′). The pro-western government of Chiang Kai-shek (chyäng′ kī′ shek′) fled to the island of Taiwan. The United States refused to recognize the Communist **People's Republic of China,** even though that government ruled millions of people. Instead, the United States supported Chiang Kai-shek's government in Taiwan. American opposition drove the Chinese Communists closer to the Soviet Union.

▶**11.** Who led the People's Republic of China?

Mao Zedong (right) and Chiang Kai-shek were together in Chungking, China, in 1945, four years before the Communist takeover.

Identify Cold War, Atlantic Charter, United Nations, Big Three, satellite government, iron curtain, containment policy, Truman Doctrine, Marshall Plan, Department of Defense, National Security Council, Central Intelligence Agency, nuclear weapons, Federal Republic of Germany, German Democratic Republic, North Atlantic Treaty Organization, Mao Zedong, Zhou Enlai, Chiang Kai-shek, People's Republic of China

Questions to Answer
1. How did Germany become divided into two nations?
2. In what ways did Truman attempt to contain communism?

A Question to Think About Why did the United States not declare war on the Soviet Union after World War II?

II. Anticommunism at Home

Events abroad made the danger of communism very real to many Americans. They worried that some people in the United States might help the Soviet Union. During the 1930's and the early 1940's, the Communist Party recruited Americans who sympathized with the Soviets. By 1944, it had around 80,000 members. Some Americans believed that those men and women were a threat to the security of the United States. Soon the nation found itself in a Red Scare much like that after World War I. The anti-Communists were determined to protect the American way of life. But too often, they themselves threatened the liberty and freedom of their fellow Americans. Many innocent people suffered from their attacks before the wave of fear finally declined.

HUAC

The House of Representatives first set up a committee to investigate subversives, the **House Un-American Activities Committee** (HUAC) in 1938. By 1947, when the Cold War was well under way, HUAC began a major campaign against Communist subversion within the United States.

HUAC was mainly concerned with Communists in government. In 1948, a former Communist spy named Whittaker Chambers testified before the committee. He told its members that Alger Hiss, who once worked

Alger Hiss is shown testifying before the House Un-American Activities Committee in 1948.

649

for the State Department, had given him secret documents to send to the Soviets in 1937 and 1938. Hiss insisted he was innocent, but he was tried and convicted of lying under oath, and sent to prison.

By 1948, most of the members of HUAC were Republicans. Many Republicans hoped to use the issue of subversives in government against the Democrats.

▶**1.** What was HUAC?

The Loyalty Issue

President Truman was not about to let the Republicans get away with accusing him and his fellow Democrats of being "soft" on communism. In 1947, he set up a loyalty program for federal employees. All federal employees would have to pass a loyalty examination. They could lose their jobs if there were "reasonable grounds" to think that they were disloyal to the government of the United States. Later that standard was changed so it became easier to take people's jobs away without firm proof that they were disloyal.

Thousands of people either resigned or were fired because of the investigations. The evidence against them was often very weak. The employees found it hard to defend themselves because they were not allowed to confront those who accused them.

▶**2.** Why was it difficult for federal employees to defend themselves against accusations under Truman's loyalty plan?

Spies Concern with internal security became more intense as the Cold War continued. Many people thought the Soviets were able to develop atomic weapons so quickly because spies in the West gave them information. In 1950, in fact, a British scientist admitted that he had passed crucial data to the Soviets. In 1953, two New Yorkers, Edith and Julius Rosenberg, were executed as spies for passing information about nuclear weapons to the Soviet Union.

▶**3.** Who were the Rosenbergs?

The McCarran Act In 1950, Congress passed the **McCarran Internal Security Act.** It said that all Communist groups had to register with the government and show their records. American Communists could not have passports. Members of foreign "subversive organizations" were not allowed to enter the United States. Persons guilty of working for revolution could be put in prison. Truman vetoed the act, but Congress passed it over his veto.

▶**4.** What were the major provisions of the McCarran Act?

McCarthy

The most famous of the anti-Communists did the least to protect the country from subversion. Senator Joseph McCarthy of Wisconsin took up the cause of anticommunism in 1950 when he needed an issue to help him win reelection. In a speech at Wheeling, West Virginia, in February 1950, McCarthy made a startling announcement. He claimed to have a list of 205 known Communists still working in the State Department. Later, he said he had 81 names, and, still another time, that he had 51. Just how many names were on the list, or even if he had a list, is still unclear. McCarthy seems to have made up a lot of what he said as he went along. If people dared to oppose him, however, McCarthy was sure to brand them as Communists or "Communist sympathizers." He used that method of discrediting people without proof so often that it became known as **McCarthyism.**

▶**5.** What did McCarthy claim he knew about the State Department?

In 1950, when Senator Joseph McCarthy was falsely accusing many Americans of being Communists, one senator was not afraid to speak out against him. The senator's name was Margaret Chase Smith.

In a 15-minute speech, Smith boldly announced that the American people were "sick and tired of being afraid to speak their minds lest they be . . . smeared as Communists . . ." It was the first time a senator had spoken out against McCarthy on the Senate floor. McCarthy retaliated by having Smith removed from a powerful Senate committee. But the courageous senator from Maine never regretted her actions.

The oldest of six children, Margaret Chase Smith was born in 1897 in the small town of Skowhegan, Maine. As a little girl, Margaret watched her father in his barber shop, and before long she was able to cut hair almost as well as he. Margaret also helped out by working Saturday evenings at a local dime store.

After graduating from high school in 1916, Margaret wanted to go to college but could not afford to do so. Instead, she taught for a short time in a one-room school and then went on to take a job with the local telephone company. Starting out as an operator, she soon moved up to become an executive.

In 1919, Margaret changed jobs once again. This time she became circulation manager of a local newspaper, the *Independent Reporter*. In 1930, she married Clyde Harold Smith, one of the newspaper's owners.

Six years later when Clyde Smith won a seat in the House of Representatives, Margaret went with him to Washington. There she served as his secretary.

In 1940, just before the filing date for the primary, Clyde Smith suffered a heart attack and died shortly afterward. Before his death, he

urged the voters of Maine to let his wife complete his term. In a special election held in May, Margaret was chosen to occupy his seat. She was reelected in 1942, in 1944, and again in 1946.

In 1947, after Maine's Republican Senator Wallace White decided not to seek reelection, Margaret Chase Smith chose to run for his seat. Her subsequent election made her the first woman elected to both houses of Congress.

Margaret Chase Smith remained in the Senate for the next 24 years, where she built a reputation for honesty and independent thinking. In 1964, members of the Republican Party placed her name in nomination for President. Although the party selected another candidate, Smith polled the second highest number of votes.

In 1972, Smith's 33-year career in Congress finally came to an end when the voters of Maine turned down her bid for another term. She was 75 years old when she left office.

Chief Counsel Joseph Welch holds his head in disgust as he listens to the accusations of Joe McCarthy during the Army-McCarthy Hearings.

McCarthy's Power Grows McCarthy ruined the lives of many people. Most of those labeled unjustly as pro-Communist lost their jobs and found it difficult to secure new ones. McCarthy even helped to defeat a fellow senator, Millard Tydings of Maryland, after Tydings denounced McCarthy as a fraud and a hoax. Tydings's defeat frightened many politicians, and strengthened McCarthy.

From then on, McCarthy felt free to attack some of the most respectable Americans, including General Marshall and Governor Adlai Stevenson of Illinois. Almost no one was brave enough to criticize McCarthy for fear of being branded a Communist.

▶**6.** What happened to Senator Tydings after he denounced McCarthy?

The Army-McCarthy Hearings McCarthy finally went too far. In January 1954, he attacked the secretary of the army, Robert Stevens. That was the beginning of the end.

The Senate held a series of special meetings to study McCarthy's accusations. Those Army-McCarthy Hearings were televised. At times, 20 million Americans watched the hearings. Day after day, they saw McCarthy bully witnesses. Yet he avoided answering questions himself and made one new accusation after another. When he attacked a young lawyer who had nothing to do with the hearings, the Army's chief counsel, Joseph Welch, had had enough. "Have you no sense of decency, sir?" he asked. The audience burst into applause.

In December 1954, the Senate voted 67 to 22 to condemn McCarthy for "conduct unbecoming a senator." He remained in the Senate until his death three years later. However, his power and influence as a leading public figure were greatly weakened. The American people simply no longer believed in him.

▶**7.** Why did McCarthy lose power after the Army hearings?

Reviewing Section II

Identify House Un-American Activities Committee, ~~Whittaker Chambers~~, Alger Hiss, ~~McCarran Internal Security Act~~, Joseph McCarthy, McCarthyism, ~~Millard Tydings~~, Army-McCarthy Hearings

Questions to Answer
1. What did party politics have to do with the investigations by HUAC and Truman's loyalty program?
2. How did television contribute to the downfall of McCarthy?

A Question to Think About What events helped make people believe McCarthy's charges?

III. A World Divided

The McCarthy era reached its peak at the time of an actual war in Korea. By the time McCarthy fell from power, that "hot" war was over. In the years that followed, however, the United States continued to oppose the Soviet Union and the spread of communism in other faraway parts of the world.

The Korean War

Korea, which occupies a peninsula east of China, had been taken over by Japan in 1910. At the end of World War II, Korea was divided. The Soviets occupied the northern part of the country, where they set up a Communist government. The United States held the southern part. In 1948, most of the American troops left South Korea, and a pro-Western government led by Syngman Rhee took control.

On June 25, 1950, Communist soldiers from North Korea swept across their southern border, the 38th parallel, into South Korea. Three days later, President Truman ordered American air and naval forces to aid the South Koreans. The United Nations also called for international troops to stop the North Korean invasion. The Soviet Union could have vetoed that action, but the Soviet delegate was boycotting the UN at the time.

General Douglas MacArthur became commander of the UN forces, which consisted mainly of Americans and South Koreans. They faced a difficult task. By September 1950, the North Koreans had taken all of South Korea except for a small area of land in its southeastern corner.

Then, on September 15, General MacArthur made a brilliant move. He landed troops at Inchon, a South Korean port on the Yellow Sea, way behind the line of battle. The UN forces quickly gained ground. By October 1,

they had recaptured almost all the land south of the 38th parallel.

▶1. When and how did the Korean War begin?

Crossing the Border The UN forces then moved northward across the 38th parallel and into North Korea. They wanted to defeat the Communists in their own territory.

Map Study *What sea lies to the east of North and South Korea? Approximately how far is Pyongyang, North Korea, from Seoul, South Korea?*

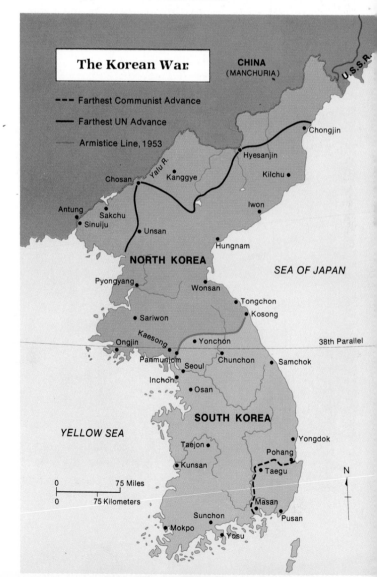

According to instructions from the UN General Assembly, the UN soldiers were also to establish by military force "a unified, independent, and democratic Korea."

At first, the fighting went well. The North Korean capital, Pyongyang (pyong' yäng'), fell to MacArthur's armies on October 19. By November, the UN forces were near the Yalu River, Korea's border with China. Then, suddenly, large Chinese armies joined in the fight. Again, the course of the war changed. Through the winter, the Communist armies pushed the UN forces back into South Korea. By spring, UN troops had recovered some land. The line of battle settled near the prewar

In 1951, cheering New Yorkers gave General MacArthur a tickertape parade up Broadway to welcome him back from Korea.

dividing line, the 38th parallel. It remained there for the next two years.

▶**2.** What happened in the Korean War when the Chinese came to the aid of North Korea?

MacArthur versus Truman The war's slow progress was hard for MacArthur to take. He wanted to win, and winning, he thought, would require bombing China. President Truman thought bombing China might start another world war.

Truman was commander in chief of the army and MacArthur's superior. He told MacArthur to keep his views to himself, but MacArthur disobeyed. "There is no substitute for victory," he said in a letter to a Republican member of the House of Representatives. By then, Truman had had enough. On April 11, 1951, he removed General MacArthur from his command.

That proved to be unpopular. According to one poll, almost seven of ten Americans took MacArthur's side in the controversy. When the general came back to the United States, cheering crowds welcomed him everywhere he went. The Americans were a people who wanted to win. However, Truman understood that the United States had to fight a **limited war** in Korea. That is, it had to fight without using all the force it could muster in order to win. The United States would not use nuclear weapons in Korea. Otherwise, Americans might face a still bigger war, one in which victory would cost more than they were willing or able to pay.

▶**3.** Why did Truman remove MacArthur from command in Korea?

The Elections of 1952 and 1956

In 1952, President Truman, still brave but still unpopular, decided not to run again in the presidential election. Instead, he gave his support to Governor Adlai Stevenson of Illinois. Stevenson won the Democratic nomination for President. A thoughtful man with a fine sense of humor, Stevenson attracted a strong following among many educated people.

The Republicans chose as their candidate Dwight D. Eisenhower, the president of Columbia University in New York. Eisenhower was a World War II hero and the former commander of NATO. Who was better qualified to lead the nation during a time of war? Eisenhower even promised that, if elected, he would personally go to Korea to end that conflict. Eisenhower was well known but because he had not been in politics before, he had no political enemies.

Eisenhower's running mate was a senator from California, Richard M. Nixon. Nixon had been a member of HUAC during the Hiss case, and made a name for himself there as a crusader against communism. Nixon was ready to call the years of Democratic rule "twenty years of treason." No Republican had been elected president since 1928. That was so long ago that the two-party system seemed to be in danger. Many voters agreed with the Republicans that it was "time for a change."

The major factor in the election, however, was Eisenhower's genial personality. "I like Ike" campaign buttons appeared everywhere. Ike won 6 million more popular votes than Stevenson and a 442 to 89 victory in the electoral college. When the same two candidates faced each other again four years later, the voters liked Ike even more. In the election of 1956, Eisenhower won 35.5 million popular votes to Stevenson's 26 million and swept the electoral college by a vote of 457 to 74.

▶4. What was the major factor in the election of 1952?

National committee-women from 11 states meet with Eisenhower during his 1952 campaign.

Peace in Korea

Eisenhower kept his campaign promise by going to Korea in December 1952. The next July, an armistice was signed. Under its terms, a demilitarized zone, or buffer zone where neither side was allowed to send troops or weapons, separated the Communists and the Allies. To create the demilitarized zone, each side pulled its troops back approximately a mile and a quarter from the line of battle, which was roughly at the old border between North and South Korea.

Another conference at Geneva, Switzerland, would decide how to reunite the nation. That conference met in 1954 but could reach no agreement. As a result, the 38th parallel remains the border between the two Koreas. No permanent peace treaty has ever been signed.

▶5. What is the border between North and South Korea?

"Don't Be Afraid—I Can Always Pull You Back"

Secretary of State Dulles tells Uncle Sam not to be afraid that his brinkmanship policy will lead the country into another war.

Brinkmanship

The end of the Korean War was not the end of the policy of containment. Eisenhower and his secretary of state, John Foster Dulles, continued Truman's anti-Soviet policies, but with some new twists. Dulles was an all-out cold warrior. He was determined to contain Soviet expansion and hoped to roll back the power of the Communists. Dulles also talked about liberating peoples who had fallen under Soviet control. He argued that the United States should be prepared to go to the very brink of all-out war to get its way in the world. That policy became known as **brinkmanship.**

Dulles and others in Eisenhower's Cabinet also favored the threat of **massive retaliation** against the nation's enemies. That is, they threatened to use atomic weapons against the homeland of any military aggressor. In that way, they hoped to deter the Soviets or Chinese from trying to take over new territory. Reliance on atomic **deterrence,** or the threat of the use of nuclear weapons to prevent war, also promised to cut military costs because the government would need fewer guns, tanks, and other such equipment.

▶**6.** What is massive retaliation?

Summit at Geneva

Within a few years, it became clear that Dulles's ideas were dangerous. By 1954, both the United States and the Soviet Union were close to having hydrogen bombs, or H-bombs, which were much more powerful than the weapons that destroyed Hiroshima and Nagasaki. To begin full-scale war using such weapons would be suicidal. Fortunately, both sides saw that. After the death of Stalin in March 1953, the new leaders of the Soviet Union were ready to reduce tensions between the East and West. President Eisenhower welcomed the opportunity.

One result of the relaxing of tensions was a **summit conference,** a meeting of the leaders of Great Britain, France, the Soviet Union, and the United States at Geneva in July 1955. Nothing important was settled there, but the fact that a meeting had taken place seemed to promise a thawing of the Cold War.

In 1959, Soviet leader Nikita Khrushchev (krüsh chôf') visited the United States at the President's invitation. The next year, Eisenhower was supposed to visit the Soviet Union and attend yet another summit meeting in Paris. However, before that could happen, the Soviets shot down an American spy plane, known as a "U-2," over Soviet territory. At first, the United States denied that its planes made such flights to gather military information. But the Soviets had proof. They had captured the pilot, Francis Gary Powers. They also had the pictures he had been taking from the air. Khrushchev demanded that the United States end such flights and apologize for the incident. When the United States refused, Khrushchev cancelled plans for his meetings with President Eisenhower.

▶**7.** What prevented Eisenhower from visiting the Soviet Union?

New Alliances

Secretary of State Dulles did not rely on nuclear weapons alone to stop the spread of communism. He worked hard, for example, to set up military alliances in different parts of the world. In that way, he hoped to keep the Soviet Union from seizing more territory by force.

In 1955, the United States, Britain, France, Australia, New Zealand, Pakistan, Thailand, and the Philippines formed the **Southeast Asia Treaty Organization,** (SEATO). In the Middle East, the United States and Great Britain joined Turkey, Iraq, Iran, and Pakistan in the Baghdad Pact, later called the **Central Treaty Organization** (CENTO). In Europe, West Germany was brought into the NATO alliance in 1955. At the same time, West Germany was allowed to create an army. The Soviet Union was distressed to see West Germany rearm. As a result, the Soviets brought their Eastern European satellites together in the **Warsaw Pact,** an alliance similar to NATO, in 1955. Those organizing efforts made it clear just how divided the world had become.

▶**8.** What alliances did the United States join in the 1950's?

Hungarian freedom fighters take down a picture of Lenin from the city hall in Gyor, Hungary.

Avoiding War

Though the United States remained ready to fight Communist expansion throughout the world, it tried to do that without risking war. In some cases, it found other ways of opposing its enemies.

Dulles talked about liberating people from Communist rule. But when the East Germans rose against their Communist government in June 1953, the United States did not come to their aid. Neither did it help the Poles and Hungarians when they rebelled against the Soviets in the fall of 1956. To do so might have meant war with the Soviet Union. By doing nothing, the United States in effect recognized the permanent division of Europe.

▶**9.** What European peoples tried to revolt against Communist rule in the 1950's?

IMPROVE YOUR SKILLS
Using Maps: Projections

Mapmakers translate a curved and three-dimensional Earth onto a flat, two dimensional piece of paper. No map can be drawn that does not in some way distort the shapes of landforms, bodies of water, and the distances between them. Depending on the area of the world to be shown and the purpose of the map, a mapmaker chooses a *projection*, a systematic way of locating the points of Earth on a map. In all projections, mapmakers draw their maps as if the viewer were looking down at all points.

In the map below, the area nearest the North Pole is the least distorted in size and shape. Look at the map and answer the questions.

1. What is the purpose of this map?
2. What is the central point of this map?
3. Look at the map of the world in the atlas. In that map the distortion is greatest near the poles, while the area nearest the equator is the least distorted. (a) In which map does Greenland appear to be larger? (b) Describe the size and shape of Alaska on each map.
4. Which nations might be most concerned with exploration of the North Pole?
5. The United States and Canada have linked their air defenses. Can you tell from this map why that would be helpful?

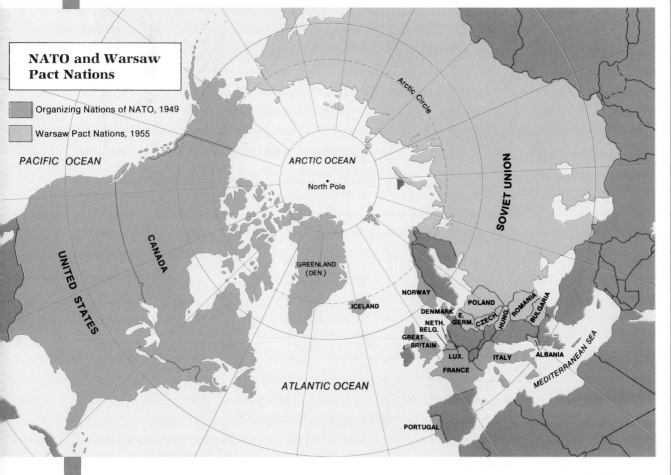

NATO and Warsaw Pact Nations

Organizing Nations of NATO, 1949

Warsaw Pact Nations, 1955

Iran In the Middle East, the United States used means other than warfare to keep out the Communists. In 1953, the CIA helped military leaders in Iran overthrow the government of Mohammed Mossadegh. He had seized oil companies from British developers and, American observers charged, had become friendly with the Soviet Union. The United States then helped the young shah of Iran, Mohammed Reza Pahlevi (ri zä′ pä′lə vē′), take power. The shah was anti-Communist. He was also willing to make important concessions to American oil companies.

▶**10.** Why did the United States help the shah of Iran?

Egypt From the State Department's view, Egypt was also a problem. Its leader, Gamal Abdel Nasser, was too willing to work with the Soviet Union. Dulles tried to use economic pressure against Nasser. In 1956, the United States took back an earlier promise to help Egypt build a great dam across the Nile River. As a result, Nasser seized control of the Suez Canal, which was still owned by British and French investors. He would use income from the canal to build his dam, he said.

With the help of Israel, the Jewish state founded in Palestine with American support in 1948, France and Britain invaded Egypt to retake the canal. The United States refused to support them because it was afraid the affair would provoke a new world war. Instead, the United States told the invaders to withdraw and then helped arrange a cease-fire between the invaders and Israel.

▶**11.** Why did Nasser seize the Suez Canal?

Vietnam The United States also avoided a major military intervention in Southeast Asia in the 1950's. Since 1945, the French had fought to reestablish control over their former colony of Vietnam. France was opposed by

Ngo Dinh Diem became the leader of South Vietnam after the country was divided in 1954.

followers of Ho Chi Minh (hō′ chē′ min′), who had fought the Japanese in Vietnam. Now Ho and his followers wanted independence for their country. Ho asked for American aid but was refused, so he turned to Communist China and the Soviet Union. The United States helped pay for the French effort to regain control of Vietnam.

By 1954, it was clear that the French were losing. President Eisenhower refused to send troops or use atomic weapons to help them. On May 7, 1954, the French military post of

Dien Bien Phu (dyen' byen' fü') was overrun by Ho's soldiers, and the French gave up.

The peace terms were set up in the Geneva Accords of 1954, which divided Vietnam into two parts separated by the 17th parallel. The North was governed by Ho Chi Minh. South Vietnam set up a pro-Western government headed by Ngo Dinh Diem (nō din zē' em). In 1956, elections were supposed to be held to unite North and South Vietnam under one government.

The United States did not sign the Geneva Accords because an election would probably have given power to Ho Chi Minh. Instead, the United States promised military aid to Diem. That promise would cause trouble later, when Diem's refusal to hold elections led to civil war. For the moment, however, Eisenhower had kept American involvement in Southeast Asia at a very low level.

▶ **12.** What were the peace terms of the Geneva Accords of 1954?

Cuba   A revolution in Cuba brought trouble closer to the United States. The United States had helped Fulgencio Batista, a military dictator, take power in Cuba in 1952. As his rule became more oppressive, his opponents joined a revolutionary movement led by Fidel Castro. Finally, the revolutionaries became strong enough to seize control. Batista fled. On January 1, 1959, Castro marched into Havana, the capital, and there set up a new government.

Although the United States offered aid, Castro was wary of it. He took over foreign companies, including many owned by Americans, in Cuba. And in 1960, he accepted aid from the Soviet Union. The United States responded by cutting back its purchases of Cuban sugar. In 1961, before Eisenhower left office, the CIA even began training Cubans who had fled from Castro. When ready, the exiles would invade the island and then force Castro from power.

▶ **13.** Why did the United States fear Castro?

Questions and Doubts   The United States entered the Cold War with the highest ideals. It meant to support the cause of freedom against Soviet communism. That was what it tried to do in the case of Poland. But in other places—Cuba, for example, or Vietnam—the situation was less clear. Could it be that the United States was opposing not so much Communists as nationalists, people who wanted to rule themselves?

Chiang Kai-shek of China, Syngman Rhee in South Korea, Ngo Dinh Diem in South Vietnam, Fulgencio Batista in Cuba, the shah of Iran—all were supported by the United States because they were anti-Communist. But they were also dictators who violated their people's liberties. Could it be that, in fighting against communism, the United States had forgotten the Atlantic Charter with its emphasis on democracy and the right of self-government?

In 1960, only a handful of people asked those questions or shared those doubts about the role of the United States in the world. Such questions and doubts would become very important in the next few years, as the nation became deeply involved in one Asian country—Vietnam.

▶ **14.** Why did the United States support dictators in various parts of the world?

Reviewing Section III

Identify   Korea, Douglas MacArthur, limited war, Adlai Stevenson, Dwight D. Eisenhower, John Foster Dulles, brinkmanship, massive retaliation, deterrence, summit conference, Nikita Khrushchev, Southeast Asia Treaty Organization, Central Treaty Organization,

Warsaw Pact, ~~Mohammed Reza Pahlevi~~, ~~Gamal Abdel Nasser~~, Ho Chi Minh, ~~Ngo Dinh Diem~~, Fidel Castro

Questions to Answer

1. How did John Foster Dulles think the United States should deal with the Soviet Union?

2. What major crises took place during the 1950's in Iran, Egypt, Vietnam, and Cuba?

A Question to Think About

Why was control of the Suez Canal an important issue to many countries of the world?

IMPROVE YOUR READING
Problems and Solutions

In an earlier reading skill activity, you practiced identifying problems and their solutions as presented by an author. The following exercise is designed to help you distinguish between some of the problems and the attempted solutions discussed in this chapter.

In each of the following pairs of sentences, one sentence states a problem, and one sentence describes an attempted solution to the problem. On a separate sheet of paper, write "problem" or "solution" for each sentence.

1. (a) The Marshall Plan gave war-torn countries in Europe funds to restore their economies.
   (b) The Soviet Union took control of several nations in Eastern Europe and gave signs of wishing to spread its power even farther.
2. (a) The McCarran Internal Security Act was passed in 1950.
   (b) Concern grew in the United States that spies in the West were passing information to the Soviets.
3. (a) The United States had to be ready if the Soviet Union decided to take over new lands by force.
   (b) Congress set up a Department of Defense to control all branches of the armed forces.
4. (a) By 1954, both the United States and the Soviet Union were close to having hydrogen bombs, or H-bombs.
   (b) The leaders of the United States, the Soviet Union, France, and Great Britain met in a summit conference in July 1955.
5. (a) Secretary of State Dulles set up military alliances in different parts of the world.
   (b) Communist aggression occurred in several parts of the world.

CHAPTER 29 REVIEW

Vocabulary Check
On a separate sheet of paper, write a short definition for the following terms.

1. Satellite government
2. Iron curtain
3. Containment policy
4. Nuclear weapons
5. McCarthyism

Fact Check
On a separate sheet of paper, fill in the word or words that best complete each of the following sentences.

1. After World War II, the Soviets and the Western democracies fought what is called the _____ War.
2. The international organization formed in 1945 to protect the peace was called the _____.
3. The _____ gave aid to war-torn countries in Europe.
4. In 1947, Congress set up a Department of _____ to control all branches of the armed forces.
5. The United States airlifted food and other supplies into _____ when the Soviets cut off access to that city.
6. Under _____, the United States, Canada, and many countries of Western Europe promised to defend one another against outside attack.
7. Joseph McCarthy claimed that many people working for the State Department were _____.
8. The _____ is the border between North and South Korea.
9. In 1955, the leaders of Great Britain, France, the Soviet Union, and the United States met in a _____ at Geneva, Switzerland.
10. The Soviets brought the Eastern European satellites into the _____ in 1955.

Skills Check
Use the map on page 653 to answer the following questions.

1. What is the subject of this map?
2. Through what cities does the line for the farthest advance of UN forces pass?
3. On what line is Pammunjom located?
4. What river divides North Korea from China?
5. In what direction is Pusan from Seoul?

Time Check
Place the following events in chronological order.

1. North Korea attacks South Korea.
2. France, Britain, and Israel invade Egypt.
3. Fidel Castro sets up a new government in Cuba.
4. A new nation, the Federal Republic of Germany, is formed.
5. Eisenhower is elected President for the first time.

Think and Write
1. What were the post-war aims of the Atlantic Charter?
2. Trace the spread of Communist control in Eastern Europe from 1945 to 1955.
3. Explain the alternative to limited war in Korea.
4. How did Senator McCarthy become such a power in the United States?
5. Describe Secretary of State Dulles's theories of foreign affairs.

REVIEWING UNIT 9

Reviewing the Facts I.

The sentences below are not correct. On a separate sheet of paper, rewrite each sentence changing what is needed to make it correct.

1. The Great Depression affected only the poorest Americans.
2. Herbert Hoover understood the severity of the Depression and was able to design programs to restore the economy.
3. Franklin Roosevelt's program was called the Square Deal.
4. The Eighteenth Amendment to the Constitution ended Prohibition.
5. The Dawes Severalty Act of 1934 encouraged the preservation of Indian culture and religion.
6. FDR was succeeded in office by Alfred Landon.
7. When the United States joined World War II, it put its main effort into defeating Japan.
8. The Soviet Union became an Axis nation after Hitler invaded that country.
9. After World War II, relations between the United States and the Soviet Union were friendly until the Korean War.
10. Eisenhower was a popular candidate with much political experience in 1952.

Reviewing the Facts II.

On a separate sheet of paper, write the name of the person described in the phrases below.

1. FDR's secretary of labor
2. President who wished to change the number of justices of the Supreme Court
3. Prime Minister of Great Britain during World War II
4. The Führer
5. Fascist dictator of Italy during World War II
6. Leader of the Soviet Union during World War II
7. President who ordered the use of the atom bomb
8. American general fired by Truman during the Korean War
9. Eisenhower's Vice President
10. The Vietnamese leader who defeated the French

Reviewing Ideas

1. (a) Why did opponents of big government criticize the New Deal? (b) Why did some people criticize the New Deal for not doing enough for the poor?
2. Describe the role of the United States in World War II before Pearl Harbor.
3. How did World War II affect women and blacks?
4. Describe three major conflicts of the Cold War.
5. What were the foreign policies of John Foster Dulles?

UNIT TEN

Times of Challenge

Over the last 200 years, the United States has developed into one of the most powerful nations in the world. That was possible because of the talents and energy of the American people. Americans must be ready to meet new challenges in the twenty-first century. The lift-off of the space shuttle *Discovery* in the fall of 1984 may be symbolic of the nation's readiness to do so.

Chapter 30

The Post-War Nation

Levittown in Philadelphia, Pennsylvania, was one of the first housing developments built after the Second World War.

Each crisis in the Cold War caused fears that a third world war might soon begin. In other ways, however, the years after World War II brought good times to the United States. Americans became more prosperous, or "affluent," than they had ever been before.

Not everyone shared equally in that prosperity. Before long, those who were left behind began to demand a fairer share of the good things their country had to offer.

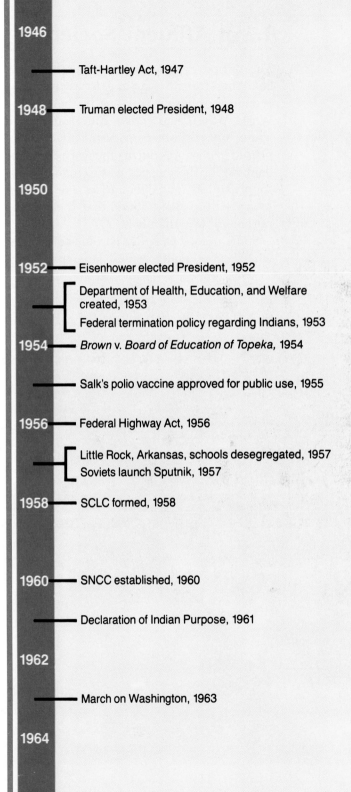

1946

Taft-Hartley Act, 1947

1948 — Truman elected President, 1948

1950

1952 — Eisenhower elected President, 1952

Department of Health, Education, and Welfare created, 1953

Federal termination policy regarding Indians, 1953

1954 — *Brown* v. *Board of Education of Topeka*, 1954

Salk's polio vaccine approved for public use, 1955

1956 — Federal Highway Act, 1956

Little Rock, Arkansas, schools desegregated, 1957

Soviets launch Sputnik, 1957

1958 — SCLC formed, 1958

1960 — SNCC established, 1960

Declaration of Indian Purpose, 1961

1962

March on Washington, 1963

1964

I. An Affluent Society

The nation experienced some problems in changing from a wartime to a peacetime economy. Inflation was one of them. Once World War II had ended, Americans could again buy consumer goods that had disappeared from stores during the war years. The demand for those goods was so high and the supply still so limited that prices shot upward. As a result, workers found that their wages purchased less than before.

Some unions called strikes for better pay, which occasionally caused other problems.

As a result of the baby boom, many new businesses, such as diaper services, also boomed.

When the United Mine Workers went on strike in 1946, it looked as though many other industries would have to close for lack of coal. So President Truman took control of the mines to keep them producing. He also got striking railroad workers back to work by threatening to use the army to run the nation's trains.

Despite such difficulties, the gross national product (GNP)—the total value of goods and services produced for sale—began to grow. After 1949, that growth was spectacular. The GNP went from $200 billion in 1945 to $500 billion in 1960. By 1970, it was $1 trillion! Almost everyone who wanted a job could find one. And inflation, which was about 15 percent in the first years after the war, stayed at 3 percent or less through the 1950's and early 1960's. In short, for at least two decades after World War II, Americans enjoyed some very good times.

The Causes of Growth

Why did the American economy grow so rapidly? For one thing, the government continued to spend huge sums of money on defense as a result of the Cold War. Between 1949 and 1953 the defense budget increased from $13 billion to more than $50 billion. In 1957, the Soviet Union fired the first intercontinental ballistic missile (ICBM). In response, the United States stepped up its development of missiles, and defense spending rose even higher.

The post-war boom was also caused by consumer spending. Soldiers returning home from the war married and started families as soon as they could. So many children were born in the late 1940's and early 1950's that people began calling it the **baby boom**. The baby boom meant prosperity for dozens of industries. Parents had to buy all kinds of goods, including diapers, cribs, high chairs, clothing, and baby food.

More important, new families bought houses. In the late 1940's and 1950's, **housing starts**—the number of new houses on which construction had begun—reached a new high. The government helped create that boom in housing by giving mortgages at low rates of interest to those who had served in the armed forces. Growth in the construction business meant growth throughout the economy as people bought paint, plumbing supplies, light fixtures, and all the other things needed for new houses.

Americans often paid for their new purchases on credit, promising to pay later. Credit cards made it easier than ever to buy clothes or gasoline on time. The amount of credit purchases in the United States went from $8 billion in 1946 to an astounding $127 billion by 1970. Americans were willing to buy on credit because they were confident that they would keep their jobs and so would be able to pay their bills.

▶**1.** Give two reasons the economy grew rapidly after World War II.

Mastering the Economy

Many Americans thought the good times of the 1950's would go on forever because economists had figured out how the economy worked. Roosevelt had groped his way through the Depression, learning by his mistakes. By the 1950's, however, policymakers could learn the "rules" of economics from textbooks, and the rules they studied were first taught by the British economist John Maynard Keynes. Those who believed in Keynes's ideas thought the economy could be kept on a steady upward trend through government spending programs and by regulating credit. In 1946, Congress created the **Council of Economic Advisers** to help keep the economy in a healthy state.

▶**2.** What rules of economics did policy makers follow after World World II?

Post-War Life

A healthy economy made it seem to many Americans, especially middle-class white Americans, that the American dream had been realized. That dream centered around a home in the suburbs with a green lawn and trees, with good schools and a church or temple nearby. Builders were happy to meet that dream. They built long streets of mass-produced houses in the late 1940's and 1950's. By 1970, more Americans lived in suburbs than lived in cities.

▶**3.** Where did many white middle-class Americans wish to live after World War II?

The Car Most suburbanites depended on their cars to get to work. They also needed their cars to shop. They drove to huge shopping centers, complete with huge parking lots, that sprang up across the landscape almost overnight. The two-car family became commonplace in the suburbs as automobile ownership more than tripled between 1940 and 1970. By 1970, about 90 million cars were registered in the United States. By then, Americans were driving an average of 10,000 miles per year.

The automobile brought with it some problems, however. More and more people died in automobile accidents. Cars also polluted, or dirtied, the air with their exhaust.

▶**4.** Why did suburbanites need cars?

Medical Breakthroughs Scientists and technologists made many medical breakthroughs

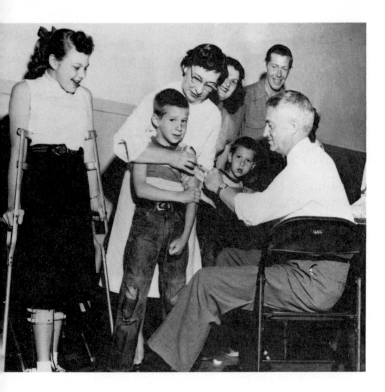

Dr. William S. Burgoyne administered the Salk vaccine to Michael Urnezis in 1955 while his sister Joanne, a victim of the disease, watched.

Many new "wonder drugs" were also coming on the market. Sulfa drugs and then antibiotics such as penicillin allowed doctors to cure many diseases that used to kill people. Another wonder drug, the anti-histamines, brought relief to many people who suffered from allergies.

▶**5.** Who invented a vaccine for polio?

Television Dozens of new inventions also changed American life after World War II. Some, like jet airplanes and plastic, were developed during the war. Others were invented much earlier. Television, for example, was invented in the late 1920's, but the first commercial television station did not begin broadcasting until 1941. In 1945, there were

I Love Lucy starring Lucille Ball and Desi Arnaz was a popular television show in the 1950's.

in the 1940's and 1950's. Those discoveries changed the lives of all Americans and people in other countries as well.

Medical researchers discovered startling new ways to fight diseases. In the 1940's, polio—the disease that had crippled Franklin Roosevelt—was still a great threat, especially to the nation's children. About 60,000 people came down with that illness in 1952 alone. Then Dr. Jonas Salk developed a polio vaccine, a serum that made those who received it immune to the disease. Salk's vaccine was approved for public use in 1955. Through public programs, it was administered to millions of Americans. By 1962, the number of reported cases of polio had been reduced by 97 percent.

only about 6,000 sets built. Within just one generation, almost every American home had a television set. By 1970, the number had jumped to seven million.

Television had a far-reaching impact on American life. Because Americans stayed home to watch television, many movie theaters closed. Because Americans watched news programs on television, newspapers became less important.

Perhaps the most popular television programs in the 1950's were comedies. American families watched weekly situation comedies about other American families. The families shown on television in the 1950's were usually white and middle class, with a father who went to work and a mother who stayed home.

▶ **6.** What effect did television have on movie theaters and newspapers?

The Computer Another invention to have a great effect on American life, the digital **computer,** was first developed during World War II. Computers are electronic machines that can be programmed, or instructed, to perform calculations and solve problems far faster than human beings. Although several inventors and mathematicians developed computers during the 1940's, Harvard professor John Aiken is regarded as the builder

IMPROVE YOUR SKILLS
Using a Pictograph

A pictograph can be used to illustrate statistical information. Each figure represents a number. Therefore, it is important to study the key.

Pictographs rarely provide exact numbers. Therefore, they are used to show a trend rather than exact statistics. A pictograph is useful in helping people recognize a trend. Pictographs are often used in oral presentations.

Look at the pictograph and answer the questions that follow.

1. What is the subject of the pictograph?
2. What does each television set represent?
3. What do the incomplete television sets represent?
4. Write a sentence describing the change in the number of households with television sets between 1950 and 1960.

U.S. Households with Television Sets, 1950-1970

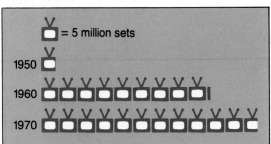

Sources: Statistical Abstract, 1982-1983
Historical Statistics of the United States

5. Draw a pictograph illustrating the following data: numbers of workers that are employed in the manufacture of office and computing machines.
1967—594,000
1977—610,000
1980—381,000

671

◀UNIVAC I (Universal Automatic Computer) was the first computer available for commercial use.

of the first electronic digital computer. Aiken built his machine, called Mark I, in 1944. In 1951, a team of scientists at the University of Pennsylvania developed a more advanced computer called UNIVAC. UNIVAC became the first computer available for sale.

The computer industry grew quickly. In the 1970's and 1980's, computers became faster and smaller, and they were able to store more information. The price of computers also dropped so that many small businesses and families could afford to buy their own computers. By the 1980's, over 500,000 workers were employed by the computer companies.

Computers changed the way Americans do business. Managers can plan company operations on computers. Word processors allow

★★ The United States and the World ★★★★★★★★★★★★★★★ Post-War Changes in Japan

After World War II, Japan made changes in its economy. Japanese business leaders invested heavily in factories and equipment and used the latest technology, which they often imported from the West. Japanese business leaders also concentrated on making items for which there was world-wide demand.

By the mid-1980's, Japan's major industry was the manufacturing of transportation equipment. Japan led the nations of the world in ship-building and automobile manufacturing. Japan was also an important producer of electronics products and precision instruments such as cameras. Japanese business methods were so successful that by the 1980's, Western business leaders were looking to the Japanese for new ideas and methods.

The growth of industry brought other changes as well. Today over 78 percent of the Japanese people live in cities that look much like Western cities with concrete and steel buildings.

Many new Japanese apartments have one or two rooms furnished with Western-style furniture instead of the traditional Japanese mats, cushions, and low tables. Since the end of the war, Japanese family life has become less formal. Children have more freedom, and most children now select their own spouses, rather than enter arranged marriages as in the past. However, traditional customs continue to be important.

letters, reports, and other kinds of manuscripts to be edited, printed, and stored.

▶7. When was the first computer made available for sale?

Truman's Fair Deal

In the good times of the 1950's, the nation's voters saw no need for the massive government programs of the New Deal. Since the late 1930's, in fact, a growing number of conservative members of Congress had been working to cut back or stop many federal programs. In 1945, that group had enough power to reject most of President Harry S Truman's reform program, which Truman called the **Fair Deal.** The Fair Deal included proposals to help the poor and underprivileged who did not share in the overall affluence of the nation. For example, Truman wanted to raise the legal minimum wage from forty to sixty-five cents an hour, to expand benefits under the Social Security program, to give more federal funds to schools, to clean up slums, and to build more public housing for the poor.

Republicans, however, took control of both the House and the Senate after the election of 1946. Truman's chances of getting his legislation passed all but disappeared.

▶8. What was the Fair Deal?

The Taft-Hartley Act Many members of the new Congress wanted to reduce the power of the unions. They did that by passing the **Taft-Hartley Act** in 1947. That act gave the President power to halt any strike that endangered the nation's safety or health for a "cooling off" period. During that period, both sides would have time to reconsider their positions. The law also made the **closed shop** illegal. In a closed shop, only union members can be hired. **Union shops,** which required

new employees to join a union after they were hired, were still legal, but they, too, could be outlawed by state "right-to-work" laws. That upset the unions. Why, they asked, should workers be allowed to enjoy the benefits unions won without paying union dues?

▶9. What provision did the Taft-Hartley Act make about closed shops?

Civil Rights Truman was able to accomplish some of his program without Congress. In 1946, he appointed a President's Committee on Civil Rights to study and report on racial justice in the United States. The next year the committee issued a report calling for an end to segregation. Truman agreed. He urged Congress to protect the rights of black voters, make lynching a federal crime, and permanently prohibit racial discrimination in the hiring of government workers. Congress did not do as he asked. Truman was able to

Blacks in New York's Harlem show their support for President Truman as he addresses the crowd.

eliminate segregation in the armed forces and discrimination in the hiring of federal employees anyway. He also encouraged the Justice Department to support court cases attempting to have laws that violated civil rights declared unconstitutional.

▶10. In what ways did Truman support civil rights?

After the Election Truman's attempts to provide a Fair Deal helped him win the election of 1948. After the election, Truman was able to get part of his program through Congress. For example, the National Housing Act of 1949 provided federal support for more than 800,000 units of housing for low-income families. However, Truman did not get a civil rights law passed. Southern Democrats in Congress killed that bill by a **filibuster**—that is, they kept speaking for days and nights without stopping so a vote could not be taken.

▶11. What technique did southern Democrats use to kill Truman's civil rights legislation?

Eisenhower's Social Program

When Dwight Eisenhower became President in 1953, he called for **dynamic conservatism.** That meant he wanted the government to be active in helping people, but not to spend more money than was necessary.

In 1953, however, Congress approved a new **Department of Health, Education, and Welfare** to administer the federal government's many social programs. Eisenhower appointed Oveta Culp Hobby, who had headed the WAACS during World War II, as the department head.

During Eisenhower's terms in office, a few other federal social programs were extended. That was partly due to the Democrats who took control of Congress in 1954. The President signed bills to expand Social Security

so that it covered more people. He also approved an increase in the minimum wage to $1 per hour.

As a result of an event in the Soviet Union, the President also expanded the federal government's role in education. In 1957, the Soviets launched *Sputnik*, the first space **satellite,** an object that revolves on a planned course around the earth. Americans were shocked. They expected the United States to be first in the race to explore outer space. If the United States was going to catch up with the Soviets, its children would have to be well trained. As a result, in 1957 Eisenhower signed a

Oveta Culp Hobby was the second woman to be appointed to a Cabinet position.

National Defense Education Act. It provided money for loans to college students and for school programs in science and foreign languages. The next year Congress authorized $4 billion for rocket and missile research. A new organization, the **National Aeronautics and Space Administration** (NASA) would head that research.

The most important legislation of the Eisenhower presidency was perhaps the **Federal Highway Act** of 1956. That law authorized the government to spend billions of dollars to build a new interstate **highway** system. Highways are roads that are designed for long-distance driving at higher speeds than on local roads.

By building new highways, the government helped to make jobs and keep the economy growing. It also made travel by truck or car much faster and easier. The final portions of the federal highway system are scheduled to be finished in the 1990's.

12. How did Eisenhower and Congress respond to *Sputnik*?

Reviewing Section I

Identify baby boom; housing starts; Council of Economic Advisers; Jonas Salk; computer; Fair Deal; Taft-Hartley Act; closed shop; union shops; filibuster; dynamic conservatism; Department of Health, Education, and Welfare; Oveta Culp Hobby; *Sputnik;* satellite; National Defense Education Act; National Aeronautics and Space Administration; Federal Highway Act; highway

Questions to Answer
1. How did the post-war baby boom affect the economy?
2. What parts of his Fair Deal did Truman get through Congress?

A Question to Think About How did a post-war suburban neighborhood differ from an immigrant city neighborhood of the 1890's?

II. Toward Greater Equality

Not all Americans participated equally in the affluent society of the 1950's. For example, black Americans were often deprived of the economic and political advantages available to other Americans.

The fight of black Americans for equality began early in the 1900's with W.E.B. DuBois's Niagara Movement. In the 1950's and 1960's, the **civil rights movement**—the effort to win racial justice—won more widespread support than ever before. First blacks fought against segregation. Then they demanded voting rights in the South. Finally, by the mid-1960's, they were demanding access to better jobs and housing throughout the nation.

By then, other minority groups and women began to realize that they, too, were subject to discrimination. The demand for equal rights and equal opportunities spread.

The Situation of Blacks after the War

In many ways, black Americans in the years after World War II were better off than ever before. The armed forces were integrated. So were the many departments of the federal government. Professional sports were becoming integrated too. In 1947, Jackie Robinson became the first black in the major leagues. He played for the Brooklyn Dodgers.

Jackie Robinson's success in the major leagues is a source of pride for black Americans.

Those advances also showed how far blacks remained from full equality. Even Jackie Robinson had to stay in segregated hotels, apart from his teammates, when the Dodgers were on the road. In the South, three out of every four eligible black voters still were not allowed to vote. As landowners there began to use more machines in farming, sharecroppers—most of whom were black—were forced off the land. Millions moved to northern cities just as the white middle class was rushing to the suburbs. Soon, the population in many city neighborhoods was almost totally black. Conditions in some of those neighborhoods were awful.

Most of the newcomers were unskilled and found it hard to get jobs. Assembly-line jobs

were disappearing. **Automation**—the use of machines to run other machines—had eliminated many such positions. Even blacks who had skills were excluded from many kinds of work.

▶**1.** Why did many blacks move north after World War II?

Brown v. Board of Education of Topeka

The NAACP led the fight for equality during the 1940's and 1950's in the nation's courts. Under the direction of Thurgood Marshall, a black lawyer, the NAACP won a number of cases. Each victory was a small step toward ending segregation. Then, in 1954, Marshall and the NAACP lawyers won the biggest case of all. It destroyed the legal foundations of segregation.

The case was brought in the name of black schoolchildren in several different communities. It took its name from the first name on the list—Oliver Brown of Topeka, Kansas. He wanted his eight-year-old daughter, Linda, to be able to attend a nearby all-white public school.

The Supreme Court heard arguments on the case in 1952. Then the Chief Justice, Fred Vinson, died. In his place, President Eisenhower appointed the governor of California, Earl Warren. Warren delayed the court's decision on the case until all nine justices were in agreement. On May 17, 1954, Warren announced the Court's unanimous ruling on the historic case, *Brown* v. *Board of Education of Topeka*.

Education, the Court said, had to be available to all American children on equal terms. Was it all right to send white and black children to separate schools so long as those schools were equal in other ways? In *Plessy* v. *Ferguson* (1896), the Court said yes. Now it overruled that earlier decision. Segregation, the Court said, gave black children a sense that they were not as good as whites. That was wrong. Segregated schools put black children at a disadvantage in life.

The Court's decision in *Brown* v. *Board of Education of Topeka* opened a whole new phase in the black struggle for equality. Many more cases were brought to court in an effort to end segregation in other parts of American life. Once those cases were won, blacks fought to make sure their legal rights were honored.

▶**2.** What was the issue and the decision in *Brown* v. *Board of Education of Topeka*?

Opposition In the first year after the *Brown* decision, many communities quietly integrated their schools. How soon did the others have to comply? In 1955, the Supreme Court ruled that school authorities had only to make a "prompt and reasonable start" and that desegregation should go forward "with all deliberate speed." The ruling allowed a lot of foot-dragging.

Throughout the South, the opponents of **desegregation,** or the end of segregation, began to organize. In 1956, 101 members of Congress from states in the South signed a declaration asking their states to disobey the *Brown* decision. Many states passed laws to impede desegregation.

▶**3.** What is desegregation?

Little Rock Opposition to desegregation became violent in 1957 after a federal court ruled that nine black students had to be admitted to Central High School in Little Rock, Arkansas. The state's governor, Orval Faubus, ordered the National Guard to keep the blacks from entering the school. When the courts told Faubus to stop, an angry crowd threatened the black students. No local officials stepped in to protect the students.

NAACP officials—Thurgood Marshall (center) and Mrs. C. Bates (left center)—asked the Supreme Court to take action to allow these black students to attend Central High School in Arkansas.

In September 1957, paratroopers guarded black students as they entered Little Rock, Arkansas's Central High School for the first time.

Rosa Parks and E. D. Nixon, former president of the Alabama NAACP, arrive at the Montgomery County Court House for the start of her trial.

That put President Eisenhower in a difficult position. He did not agree with the *Brown* decision. But Eisenhower believed that he had to defend the authority of the federal government. He sent in federal troops to see to it that black students could attend classes.

Still, progress was very slow. By 1964, only 123 of Little Rock's 7,000 school children were in desegregated schools. Other communities made even less progress.

▶**4.** Why did Eisenhower send federal troops to Little Rock?

Higher Education Segregation was not limited to elementary and high schools. Colleges were also segregated in many southern states. Then, in 1962, federal courts ordered the University of Mississippi to admit a young black man, James Meredith, as a student.

Governor Ross Barnet objected. An angry mob supported the governor. Again, federal troops were necessary to defend Meredith's rights.

The next year, Alabama's governor George Wallace promised to "stand in the schoolhouse door" rather than let blacks attend the University of Alabama. Once again, federal troops protected black students and prevented an outbreak of violence.

▶**5.** Why were federal troops used at the universities of Mississippi and Alabama?

Boycotts and Sit-ins

The struggle against segregation was not confined to education. Blacks also fought to end segregation on public transportation after December 1, 1955. That was the day Rosa Parks, a black seamstress, refused to give a white man her seat on a bus in Montgomery, Alabama.

Parks, a quiet woman, was secretary of the Alabama NAACP and a believer in equal rights for black Americans. Still, she did not mean to start a movement on that December day. She was simply tired after a hard day's work. "If you don't stand up," the bus driver said, "I'm going to have you arrested." The law was on his side. Still she refused, even when he called the police. "I felt it was just something I had to do," Parks later explained.

The president of the Alabama NAACP helped organize a boycott by blacks of the city buses until their rights were respected. For a year, the blacks of Montgomery walked or formed car pools rather than ride the city buses. Then, in November 1956, the Supreme Court declared unconstitutional Alabama's laws requiring that buses be segregated. On December 21, the 381-day struggle ended. That day leaders of the boycott boarded a Montgomery bus and sat in the front, where in the past only whites could sit.

▶**6.** How did Montgomery blacks win the right to integrated seating on public buses?

Martin Luther King, Jr. One of the leaders of the bus boycott was the Reverend Martin Luther King, Jr. From then on, King became a central figure in the growing civil rights movement. He urged blacks to insist on their rights but to avoid all forms of violence, even if their enemies used violence against them. Blacks should answer hate with Christian love, King said. That would give them strength in the face of danger. King pointed to the Montgomery bus boycott as an example of a peaceful movement that triumphed.

King was a moving speaker and was able to draw many to his point of view. In 1958, he and his followers formed the **Southern Christian Leadership Conference** (SCLC). SCLC fought for equal rights for blacks in the way King taught.

▶**7.** How did Martin Luther King, Jr., think blacks should fight for their civil rights?

The Sit-ins As the civil rights movement continued, four black college students in Greensboro, North Carolina, began a **sit-in** at a segregated lunch counter. On February 1, 1960, they took seats and sat and waited all day for service. The waitress would not serve them. Still, the students refused to leave. The next day, more blacks came and sat at the counter. The sit-in spread to other lunch counters. Six months after the movement began, Greensboro's white leaders gave in. At last, blacks could be served at any lunch counter in the city.

Sit-ins spread to other cities in the South. Students tried to integrate restaurants and lunch counters. They also wanted to end segregation in movie theaters and other public facilities. So they held not just sit-ins but "sleep-ins" in hotels, "read-ins" at libraries, "watch-ins" at movie theaters, and "swim-ins" at pools and beaches. They made some headway. But resistance to change was strong, especially in the states farthest south.

▶**8.** What were sit-ins?

New Challenges

Young black students, like those who began the sit-in movement, were impatient. They wanted equality right away, not in the faraway future. In 1960, they formed their own organization, the **Student Nonviolent Coordinating Committee** (SNCC). Members of SNCC were determined to end segregation by **civil disobedience,** by disobeying laws they considered unjust. Many whites were ready to join in their fight.

▶**9.** Why did students form SNCC?

Rides for Freedom Other blacks agreed with the founders of SNCC. In 1961, James Farmer became the head of the Congress of Racial Equality (CORE), which was begun in 1942. Farmer wanted an immediate end to segregation, and he had a plan. The Supreme Court had recently declared segregation illegal not only on trains and buses but also at all stations and terminals. Farmer organized groups of people, many from CORE and SNCC, to travel through the South on **freedom rides** to demand that their rights be honored.

The first such "freedom riders" climbed aboard two buses on May 4, 1961. Within two weeks, their trip was over. In one place after another, passengers were beaten, and the police refused to help them. Finally, the Justice Department flew the last freedom riders from Birmingham, Alabama, to New Orleans.

SNCC volunteers, however, continued the project. By the end of the summer, more

Highlighting People
Martin Luther King, Jr.

In April 1968, the Reverend Martin Luther King, Jr., delivered his Sunday sermon at the Ebenezer Baptist Church in Atlanta, Georgia. On this particular morning, the Reverend King described how he would like to be remembered after his death. He said, "I'd like somebody to mention . . . that Martin Luther King, Jr., tried to give his life serving others."

Today Martin Luther King, Jr., is remembered for this and more. During the 1950's and 1960's, his courage inspired thousands of others to take a stand against racial discrimination. Through it all, his message was peace and love.

Martin Luther King, Jr., was born in Atlanta, Georgia, in 1929, the second of three children. From an early age, King's family expected him to become a Baptist minister as his father and grandfather had been before him. So at the age of 17, King entered Crozer Theological Seminary in Pennsylvania.

At Crozer, King first learned about the work of Mohandas K. Gandhi, a man who used nonviolence to help free the people of India from British rule. Under Gandhi's leadership, the people of India did not fight the British. Instead, they refused to obey British laws. The idea of using nonviolence in this way appealed to King. He saw it as a way to break down the barriers that black Americans faced in the 1950's.

After graduating from Crozer, King continued his studies at Boston University, where he earned a doctorate in religion. It was there too that he met and married Coretta Scott.

In 1953, at the age of 25, King arrived in Montgomery, Alabama, to begin his work as a minister. Two years later he tried out nonviolent resistance during the boycott of Montgomery buses. The success of the boycott convinced King that his method would work.

For the next ten years, King crusaded for civil rights. His crusade reached a high point on August 28, 1963. On that day, more than 200,000 people, many of them white, came to Washington, D.C., to show their support for civil rights. Their efforts helped win rights for blacks in every part of the country.

As King continued his work, he began to see the need to help all poor people. He was in the middle of planning a poor people's march on Washington when black leaders in Memphis, Tennessee, asked him to come to their city. As King stood on the balcony of his motel room, a hidden gunman shot and killed him. Martin Luther King, Jr., was dead at the age of 39.

King's senseless death marked the outbreak of rioting in black slums throughout the country. In more quiet ways, millions of other Americans—both black and white—mourned the loss of this extraordinary man.

than 1,000 people had taken part in the freedom rides. The rides were a great success. In September 1961, the Interstate Commerce Commission demanded that all interstate carriers, including bus lines, railroads, and air lines, post signs in their terminals stating that seating was "without regard to race, color, creed, or national origin." A year later, CORE announced that the battle for integrated travel had been won.

▶**10.** What was the goal of the freedom rides?

Registering Black Voters In 1962, SNCC began trying to register black voters in the South. They opened "freedom schools" to teach blacks how to register. Then they led new voters to city halls and other local voter registration centers. However, whites blocked such efforts in many southern communities, often with violence. Blacks who tried to register were sometimes evicted from their rented farms or fired from their jobs. At the end of 1962, not many blacks were added to the voting lists.

▶**11.** Why were SNCC volunteers unable to register many black voters in 1962?

Birmingham

Martin Luther King wanted to keep the civil rights struggle alive. He also wanted to show that nonviolence was still the best way to win justice. In 1963, King led a campaign against segregation in Birmingham, Alabama. Blacks there still had to use separate schools, restaurants, and even water fountains. The city's white leaders had closed its parks rather than integrate them. Only one black adult in eight could vote, although blacks made up 40 percent of the city's population. Job opportunities for blacks were also limited.

Under King's leadership, blacks boycotted businesses that were segregated. They held

Police in Birmingham, Alabama, use attack dogs against peaceful black demonstrators.

peaceful marches and demonstrations. Thousands of black children joined the marches. Their call for equal rights was answered with violence. During demonstrations in April 1963, the local police used high-powered fire hoses, vicious dogs, and clubs to break up the marches. Television cameras brought those scenes into living rooms across the country. Millions of Americans, both black and white, were outraged by what they saw. They now began to understand what the fight for equal rights was all about—some for the first time.

On May 10, the city leaders finally gave in. Reverend King announced that the SCLC had won "the most magnificent victory for justice we've ever seen in the Deep South." A committee of whites and blacks was established to oversee the gradual desegregation of the city, and to see that more jobs would be opened to blacks.

▶12. How did King and his followers work for desegregation in Birmingham?

"Freedom Now"

One group of blacks, the **Black Muslims,** who followed the teachings of the religion of Islam, rejected King's program of integration and nonviolence. Black Muslims such as Malcolm X called on blacks to separate from whites and to conquer poverty by their own efforts. The day of nonviolence, Malcolm X said in 1963, "is over."

Even the older civil rights groups like the NAACP became more aggressive after the Birmingham incidents. Hundreds of marches, sit-ins, and boycotts throughout the South won success by mid-1963. Groups such as CORE now carried their fight against discrimination to many northern cities. Blacks throughout the nation began to demand "Freedom now."

▶13. What did Malcolm X ask blacks to do?

The March on Washington

On August 28, 1963, hundreds of thousands of blacks converged on the nation's capital for a great **March on Washington.** Some 75,000 whites joined that march. They came to demand that the federal government help in the fight for "Freedom now."

The high point of the day came when the Reverend King addressed marchers from the

Hundreds of thousands of Americans, black and white, gather at the Lincoln Memorial to hear Martin Luther King, Jr., tell of his dream for the nation.

Lincoln Memorial. He told of his dream "that my four little children will one day live in a nation where they will not be judged by the color of their skin but by the content of their character." Someday, he predicted, "All God's children" would be "free at last." The crowd responded with a roar of approval.

▶14. What was the purpose of the March on Washington?

Reviewing Section II

Identify civil rights movement; Jackie Robinson; automation; Earl Warren; *Brown* v. *Board of Education of Topeka*; desegregation; James Meredith; Rosa Parks; Martin Luther King, Jr.; Southern Christian Leadership Conference; sit-in; Student Nonviolent Coordinating Committee; civil disobedience; freedom rides; Black Muslims; Malcolm X; March on Washington

Questions to Answer
1. What was the significance of the *Brown* v. *Board of Education of Topeka* decision?
2. What methods did Martin Luther King use to win civil rights victories?

A Question to Think About What might have happened if Eisenhower refused to send troops to Little Rock?

III. The Rights Movement Spreads

By 1960, the demand for justice and civil rights had spread from the black population to other minority groups. American Indians and Spanish-speaking Americans began to use some of the techniques of black activists. Some American women, although not a minority in the nation's population, also began to work for equal treatment on the job, in school, and in society.

The American Indian Movement

In 1953, the federal government had changed its Indian policy once again. Under its new policy, which was called the **termination policy,** the federal government planned to turn over all responsibility for Indian life to the states. The reservations would be abolished. Indians were to be given help in relocating to cities where they could find work. However, at that time, many Indians had no desire to live in large cities. They wanted to live in more traditional ways.

Indians used sit-ins and demonstrations to press their demands. A National Indian Youth Council, begun in 1961, worked for the return of Indian lands. Also in 1961, more than 400 American Indians gathered in Chicago and adopted a "Declaration of Indian Purpose." It demanded that Indians be given more control over their own lives and be under less government control. Before long, Indians, like blacks, fought for their rights in the courts and through direct action. As a result, the termination policy failed and in 1963 it was abolished.

▶1. What was the termination policy?

Spanish-Speaking Americans

Spanish-speaking Americans were the fastest-growing minority group in the United States. They numbered approximately three million in 1960. By 1970, their numbers had tripled.

Some Spanish-speaking Americans had lived in the Southwest since long before that

683

area became part of the United States. Other Spanish-speaking people in the continental United States are from Puerto Rico. They are not immigrants either, since Puerto Rico is part of the United States.

Many other Spanish-speaking Americans had recently moved north from Mexico. Among them were many illegal immigrants, who made their way into the country without legal immigration papers. Still other Spanish-speaking Americans came from Cuba and other islands in the Caribbean, from the various nations of Central and South America, and from the Philippines.

Cesar Chavez organized the National Farm Workers Association in 1962 to help farm workers. Many Americans have supported his union boycotts.

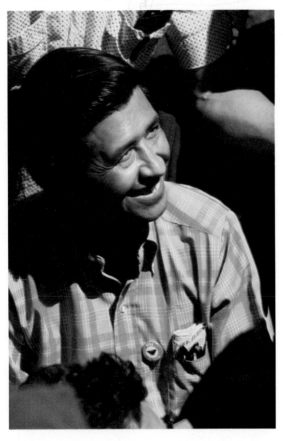

Regardless of their homeland, Spanish-speaking Americans often were the victims of discrimination. Many Mexican Americans in California and other western and southwestern states were migrant farm workers. Their wages were low and working conditions poor. Those who were illegal immigrants could not complain about their pay or working conditions for fear of being sent back to their homelands.

An Arizona-born American of Mexican descent, Cesar Chavez, started a union, the National Farm Workers Association, to help those farm workers. That union later merged with another to become the **United Farm Workers.** Chavez organized successful national boycotts of grapes and lettuce to force growers to recognize his union and accept the demands of its members. His effort was supported by CORE and SNCC.

▶**2.** Why did Cesar Chavez organize boycotts of lettuce and grapes?

The Women's Movement in the 1960's

Women, too, began to see a need for equal rights and better economic opportunities in the 1960's. After the war, millions of educated women chose to be full-time homemakers instead of pursuing careers. Two decades later, many of them were having second thoughts. Betty Friedan's book, *The Feminine Mystique* (1963), explained their discontent. Women were able to do more than be wives and mothers. Even their families would be better off, Friedan suggested, if women took jobs that let them use more of their talents.

Many women were, in fact, going to work whether or not they agreed with Friedan's reasoning. Often married women worked because their families needed the money their jobs brought in. But job opportunities were limited. Even those women who managed to get a good education and hold down responsible jobs were often paid less than men doing the same work. Many universities also discriminated against women by requiring them to have higher grades than male students to enter medical or law school.

In 1966, feminists formed the **National Organization for Women** (NOW) to work for equal rights and to change American notions about the proper roles for men and women. Not all women supported the movement. In the years ahead, the feminists would score some victories but they also would suffer some strong defeats.

▶**3.** Why was NOW formed?

The Warren Court

During the 1950's and 1960's, the Supreme Court seemed to be on the side of those seeking equal rights and equal opportunities. For example, the Court's *Brown* decision of 1954 dealt a stunning blow to segregation. By so doing, the Court helped to extend equal rights to black Americans.

In the 1960's, the Court turned also to the cause of criminal rights. It ruled that people accused of crimes had a right to have lawyers, even at government expense. In the famous case of *Miranda* v. *Arizona* in 1966, the Court said the police have to warn suspects that any statements they make can be used against them in a court of law. The Court also said that suspects had a right to talk with a lawyer before speaking with the police.

A friendly Supreme Court was not, however, enough for those who wanted "Freedom now." By the mid-1960's, it became clear that freedom also required help from Congress and, even more, from the White House.

▶**4.** What was the Supreme Court's ruling in the case of *Miranda* v. *Arizona*?

Betty Friedan was one of the leaders in the movement for equal rights for women in the 1960's.

Reviewing Section III

Identify termination policy, Cesar Chavez, United Farm Workers, Betty Friedan, National Organization for Women, *Miranda* v. *Arizona*

Questions to Answer
1. From what countries have Spanish-speaking Americans emigrated?
2. How did the case of *Miranda* v. *Arizona* change a police officer's job?

A Question to Think About How might the growth of the civil rights movement have been related to economic prosperity?

685

IMPROVE YOUR READING
Problem/Solution

Chapter 30 describes some problems faced by Americans in the 1950's and 1960's. The task that follows will help you review some of the problems and the solutions that were discussed in this chapter.

The column below lists problems and the column at the upper right lists solutions. Match the appropriate solutions to each of the problems. Number your paper from 1 to 5. Next to each number, write the letter of the statement that represents the solution to the problem. You will not use all the solutions.

Problems

1. A strike by coal miners made it seem that other industries would have to close for lack of coal.
2. After the Soviets launched *Sputnik,* some Americans thought that their nation's schools needed improvement.
3. Many black American children attended segregated schools.
4. Governor Faubus of Arkansas vowed to block the integration of Central High School in Little Rock.
5. By law in Montgomery, Alabama, blacks had to give up seats on public buses to white riders.

Solutions

a. Southern Democrats in Congress killed Truman's proposed civil rights bill by a filibuster.
b. Congress passed the National Defense Education Act.
c. Congress approved a new Department of Health, Education, and Welfare.
d. President Truman took control of the mines to keep coal in production.
e. The NAACP brought the case of *Brown* v. *Board of Education of Topeka* to the Supreme Court.
f. President Eisenhower sent in federal troops to see that black students could attend class.
g. Blacks boycotted public buses until their rights were respected.
h. Volunteers traveled through the South on freedom rides.
i. Martin Luther King, Jr., led the March on Washington in 1963.
j. Cesar Chavez started a union for migrant farm workers.

CHAPTER 30 REVIEW

Vocabulary Check
Write a short explanation for each of the following terms.

1. Filibuster
2. Union shops
3. Satellite
4. Civil rights movement
5. Freedom rides

Fact Check
On a separate sheet of paper, write the name of the person or group described in each of the following sentences.

1. President who took control of the nation's coal mines.
2. Group formed to keep the nation's economy healthy.
3. Scientist who developed a polio vaccine.
4. President who called for dynamic conservatism in government.
5. Cabinet position established to administer the government's social programs.
6. First black major league baseball player.
7. Woman who helped start the civil rights movement by refusing to give her bus seat to a white man.
8. Leader of the civil rights movement who taught non-violence.
9. Mexican American who started a union for farm workers.
10. Organization formed in the 1960's to work for equal rights for women.

Skills Check
The following data gives the number of blacks, 25 years or over, who had completed at least 4 years of college in 1960, 1970, and 1980. Numbers are in the thousands. Illustrate the data on a pictograph.

1. 1960 males: 119
   females: 159
2. 1970 males: 212
   females: 241
3. 1980 males: 440
   females: 584
4. In which decade was the number of black male college graduates closest to the number of black female graduates?
5. What general trend is shown by the pictograph?

Time Check
On a separate sheet of paper, write the following events in the order in which they occurred.

1. Supreme Court rules in *Miranda* v. *Arizona*.
2. King leads March on Washington.
3. Supreme Court rules in *Brown* v. *Board of Education of Topeka*.
4. Truman is elected President.
5. Eisenhower becomes President.

Think and Write
1. How did the baby boom of the 1940's and 1950's affect the nation's economy?
2. In what way was Eisenhower's dynamic conservatism similar to Truman's Fair Deal?
3. What methods did people use to oppose desegregation?
4. What influence did the civil rights movement have on the American Indian movement?
5. What kinds of discrimination did women face in the 1960's?

Chapter 31

A Time of Crisis, 1960–1972

Chief Justice Earl Warren administers the oath of office to John F. Kennedy. Millions of Americans watched the event on television.

When President Dwight Eisenhower retired from office, the American voters chose a much younger man to take his place. The new President, John Fitzgerald Kennedy, wanted "to get the country going again." But he was unable to do much to improve life within the United States. Instead, he spent his few years in the White House fighting communism in other parts of the world. That same problem dominated the presidencies of Kennedy's two successors in office, Lyndon B. Johnson and Richard M. Nixon.

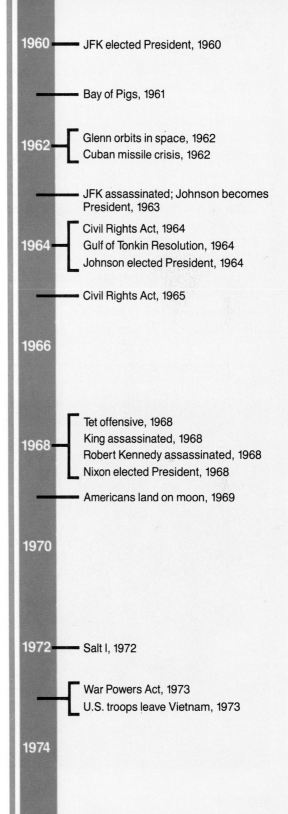

1960 — JFK elected President, 1960

— Bay of Pigs, 1961

1962 — Glenn orbits in space, 1962
Cuban missile crisis, 1962

— JFK assassinated; Johnson becomes President, 1963

1964 — Civil Rights Act, 1964
Gulf of Tonkin Resolution, 1964
Johnson elected President, 1964

— Civil Rights Act, 1965

1966

1968 — Tet offensive, 1968
King assassinated, 1968
Robert Kennedy assassinated, 1968
Nixon elected President, 1968

— Americans land on moon, 1969

1970

1972 — Salt I, 1972

— War Powers Act, 1973
U.S. troops leave Vietnam, 1973

1974

I. The Kennedy Years

Senator John F. Kennedy of Massachusetts, the Democratic candidate for President in 1960, was a Harvard graduate and a World War II hero. His family was of Irish descent. One of Kennedy's grandfathers had been a popular mayor of Boston. Kennedy's father was a wealthy businessman. Kennedy was young—only 43 years old—and handsome, and he had a winning smile, a quick wit, and great skill as a speaker.

When Kennedy first entered the presidential race, some people considered him less qualified than the Republican candidate, Richard Nixon. Nixon had been Vice President under Eisenhower and had represented California in the House and Senate before that.

Kennedy was a Roman Catholic. From the time that Al Smith lost the election of 1928, many Americans said a Catholic could never be President. So at first, Nixon had the lead in the race. Then came four nationally televised debates between the two candidates. Unlike Nixon, Kennedy knew how to use television. During the debates he seemed confident and bright, whereas Nixon appeared tired and slow.

When the votes were counted, Kennedy won a clear victory in the electoral college. But out of the 68.8 million votes cast, he received only about 112,350 more votes than Nixon. That made the election of 1960 one of the closest in American history.

In 1960, Americans were able to watch the presidential candidates debate on television. Nixon and Kennedy are shown here during the second debate.

The New Frontier

Kennedy, or JFK as he was called, wanted to be a President in the tradition of Franklin Roosevelt. He wanted a tax cut so people would have more money to spend to boost the economy. He wanted to provide a national health insurance plan for the elderly, aid to education, and help for the nation's cities. Kennedy called his domestic program the **New Frontier.** It did not get very far. Both Republicans and southern Democrats in Congress voted down one Kennedy proposal after another.

▶**1.** What was the New Frontier?

Civil Rights

Defeats in Congress made Kennedy cautious on the issue of civil rights. If he came out strongly against segregation, he would lose all hope of support from southern Democrats. Therefore, at first he did not propose civil rights legislation.

Kennedy did appoint several blacks to important government positions. He selected Robert Weaver as head of the Housing and Home Finance Agency, and Kennedy also made Thurgood Marshall, an NAACP lawyer, a federal judge.

Kennedy supported the civil rights movement in other ways as well. For example, he ordered the use of federal troops to help integrate the universities of Mississippi and Alabama. JFK's attorney general, his brother Robert Kennedy, fought for the integration of airports and for black voting rights. Finally, in 1963, JFK called for a new, wide-ranging Civil Rights Act that would have made segregation illegal in all public facilities. But Congress refused to approve it.

▶**2.** How did President Kennedy support the civil rights movement?

Space

Kennedy was more effective in launching the space program. In April 1961, the Soviets sent the first person into space. Yuri Gagarin (gə gär′ən) orbited Earth in a spaceship. Once again, Americans worried that the Soviets had a large edge in the space race.

In May 1961, JFK asked Congress to approve a major space program. It would seek

Highlighting People
The Kennedys

John Fitzgerald Kennedy, the nation's thirty-fifth President, and his brother Robert Francis Kennedy, attorney general of the United States, were both born in Brookline, Massachusetts. The second oldest of nine children, John was known to his family and friends as Jack. His brother Robert, nine years younger, was called Bobby.

Jack and Bobby grew up in a close, competitive family that was proud of its Irish ancestry. Their father, Joseph Kennedy, was a self-made millionaire who had served as ambassador to Great Britain. Their mother, Rose Fitzgerald Kennedy, was the daughter of a Boston politician known familiarly as Honey Fitz. Both parents encouraged their children to be the best they could possibly be. To Joseph Kennedy, the best meant nothing less than perfect.

Jack Kennedy was born on May 29, 1917. When he was 18, he entered Harvard University, where he majored in government. Soon after graduation, he enlisted in the navy. At the age of 25, he found himself in command of a torpedo boat whose mission was to fight the Japanese in the South Pacific during World War II.

Jack won a Purple Heart when he rescued crew members from their sinking boat in the South Pacific. His courage almost cost him his life. The very same year his older brother Joseph was not as fortunate. He was killed in a military mission over Belgium.

When Jack returned home, his father urged him to enter politics as he had hoped his oldest son Joseph would do. In true Kennedy spirit, Jack responded by running for and winning a seat in the House of Representatives. Six years later, in 1952, he ran for the Senate and won.

Jack's whole family helped him campaign for the Senate. None did more, however, than his younger brother Bobby. A promising young attorney, Bobby left his job in the Department of Justice to manage his brother's campaign. The campaign marked the start of a political partnership based on love, trust, and mutual admiration.

In 1960, when Jack ran for President, Bobby once again managed his brother's campaign. When Jack won, he chose Bobby to serve as attorney general. As attorney general, Bobby advised his brother on all legal issues, including civil rights. At the time, it was said of Bobby Kennedy that he did more to help blacks and other minorities than all other attorneys general combined.

Jack Kennedy's sudden death by an assassin's bullet in 1963 shocked the nation. Several months later, his grieving brother resigned his post as attorney general and moved to New York. From there, he ran for a seat in the United States Senate and won.

The 42-year-old senator seemed close to winning the Democratic Party's nomination for President when he suffered the same fate as his brother. An assassin's bullet shot and killed Bobby Kennedy in 1968. Once again the country mourned the death of a Kennedy.

to send an American to the moon before 1970. Congress agreed.

The National Aeronautics and Space Administration (NASA) moved quickly. In February 1962, an American astronaut, John Glenn, made a trip much like Gagarin's. In the years that followed, other American astronauts made longer voyages into space. Then, in July 1969, when Richard Nixon was President, Neil Armstrong and Edwin Aldrin became the first human beings to set foot on the moon.

▶3. What was JFK's goal for the space program?

The Cold War under Kennedy

In his inaugural address, Kennedy supported the Cold War. He said the United States would "pay any price, bear any burden, meet any hardship . . . in order to assure the survival and the success of liberty." Kennedy, however, understood that times had changed since the Cold War began. By 1961, the Soviet Union had atomic bombs and other weapons as powerful as those of the United States. The **arms race,** the effort of each side to surpass the other in military strength, had become more dangerous and expensive than ever before. As a result, JFK thought it made good sense to try to come to terms with the Soviets. "Let us never fear to negotiate," he said upon becoming President. "But let us never negotiate out of fear."

Unlike many leaders before him, Kennedy also understood that not all struggles in the world were between Communists and anti-Communists. Some nations simply wanted to be free of all outside control. He supported their right to do that. If such nations were to develop as they chose, however, Kennedy believed that they would have to remain free of Soviet control.

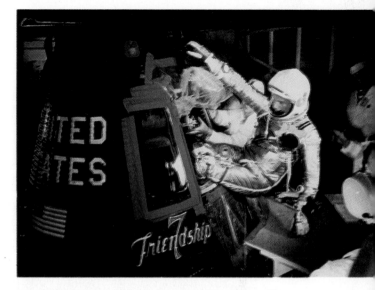

John Glenn enters Friendship 7 *in preparation for his historic space flight.*

JFK thought, too, that the struggle between communism and freedom would be fought in the future not so much in Europe as in the newer countries of Asia, Africa, and Latin America. Those countries were sometimes called **developing nations** because they were only starting to build industries. They were also described as the **Third World** because they did not choose to ally themselves with either the United States or the Soviet Union.

JFK wanted to help Third World nations become strong enough to protect themselves against outside threats. For that reason, he helped found the **Peace Corps,** an organization that recruited and trained Americans willing to help the people in developing nations improve their lives.

Under Kennedy, the United States also sent economic aid to many countries. For example, through the **Alliance for Progress,** which was started in March 1961, the United States sent billions of dollars to Latin American countries to improve living standards there. JFK hoped by reducing poverty to make communism

693

Peace Corps workers in Niger help farmers there produce stronger crops.

less appealing to people in Central and South America.

▶**4.** Where did Kennedy think the struggle between communism and freedom would take place in the future?

The Bay of Pigs On several occasions, the Kennedy administration fought communism with arms. One such conflict was in Cuba. Under President Eisenhower, the CIA had begun training Cuban exiles to overthrow Fidel Castro, the pro-Soviet leader of Cuba. By 1961, the exiles were ready for their mission and Kennedy gave it his approval.

On April 17, 1961, a force of 1,200 trained men landed at the **Bay of Pigs** in western Cuba. They expected help from Cubans eager to overthrow Castro, but that help never came. Instead, Castro's army quickly put down the invasion, killing or taking prisoner all the invaders.

The defeat was a terrible disgrace for the United States and its new President. It also increased tension between the United States and the Soviet Union, which was allied to Castro.

▶**5.** Why did the Bay of Pigs invasion fail?

The Berlin Wall After the Bay of Pigs incident, Kennedy met with the Soviet leader, Nikita Khrushchev, in Vienna, Austria. Their talks did not ease tensions between the two nations. Soon after, another crisis arose over Berlin. By 1961, West Berlin was a prosperous "showcase of democracy," an island of freedom surrounded by Communist-ruled territory. Despite guards and mines to prevent escapes, many East Germans were fleeing to West Berlin in search of jobs and freedom.

On August 13, 1961, the East Germans closed the border between East and West Berlin and began to build a concrete and barbed-wire barricade between the two sectors. It was called the **Berlin Wall.** The United States protested the building of the Berlin Wall because prior agreements said there would be free access between East and West Berlin. It was not ready, however, to risk war by destroying the new wall.

▶**6.** Why did many East Germans flee to West Berlin?

The Missile Crisis The tension between the United States and the Soviet Union was also felt in the Americas. That tension almost led to war in the fall of 1962. Again, the crisis involved Cuba. The Soviets began to build missile bases on Cuba, only 90 miles from the coast of Florida. The missiles were a serious threat to American security.

On October 22, 1962, JFK announced a blockade of Cuba to prevent the Soviets from completing the bases. Then the United States military was placed on alert. Americans nervously watched Soviet ships approach the blockade. Only when the Soviet ships turned back did the nation breathe a sigh of relief.

Then Khrushchev sent Kennedy a message. The Soviet Union would remove its missile bases if the United States would promise not to invade Cuba. Kennedy agreed. The **Cuban missile crisis** was over.

▶**7.** How did the Cuban missile crisis end?

Vietnam As the Cuban missile crisis was ending, still another crisis deepened thousands of miles away in Vietnam. There the United States supported the forces that opposed Vietnamese nationalists led by Ho Chi Minh (hō'chē'min'). After World War II, the United States had helped the French try to regain control over their old colony. When the French were defeated in 1954, the United States promised to help the anti-Communist regime of Ngo Dinh Diem (dyem) in South

The USS Barry *(foreground) stands by as a Soviet freighter leaves Cuba with a load of objects that appear to be Soviet missiles.*

Vietnam (see page 660). Diem, however, did not have the support of his own people.

In 1958, civil war broke out in South Vietnam. Diem's opponents were known as the **Viet Cong.** They received help from Ho Chi Minh, who headed a Communist government in North Vietnam. When Diem seemed to be

★★★★★★★★★★★★★★★★★★★★★ United States and the World ★★
Kennedy Abroad

John Kennedy, like all modern Presidents, made trips abroad during his months in office. Presidents travel to other nations to earn goodwill for the United States, to meet with other heads of state, and not incidentally, to make favorable headlines back home.

Kennedy and his wife, Jacqueline, were very popular in the nations they visited. "Jackie" was an attraction on her own because of her wit, charm, and sense of style. Once in Paris, France, JFK said at a luncheon, "I am the man who accompanied Jacqueline Kennedy to Paris."

In 1961, Kennedy met with Khrushchev in Vienna. The talks did not go well. However,

Kennedy and his wife were welcomed with wild enthusiasm elsewhere in Europe. Kennedy profited from the newspaper and television coverage showing the warm greetings.

In the summer of 1963, Kennedy made a 10-day tour of Europe. He and his wife visited Italy, Ireland, and Great Britain. They also visited West Germany and West Berlin. There JFK electrified the beleagured city by declaring "Ich bin ein Berliner," or "I am a Berliner."

The President's role is complex. The task of representing the United States to the people of other nations has become an increasingly important part of the President's responsibilities.

losing to the Viet Cong, the United States increased its aid. Under President Eisenhower, the United States had sent arms and other supplies along with about 650 military advisers. Now JFK increased the number of American military advisers in Vietnam to more than 15,000.

In early November 1963, South Vietnamese military leaders took over the government and murdered Diem. The United States had helped plan that take-over, but not the murder. Before Kennedy decided what to do next, he himself became a victim of violence.

▶8. Who were the Viet Cong?

Dallas

On November 22, 1963, the President and his wife, Jacqueline, visited Dallas, Texas. As they rode in an open car through streets lined with cheering crowds, shots rang out. The President slumped over. The car rushed off to a hospital, where John Kennedy was pronounced dead.

Americans sadly watched the funeral procession of John F. Kennedy in Washington, D.C.

Later that day, police arrested a man named Lee Harvey Oswald for the crime. Oswald was himself shot and killed two days later by a Dallas nightclub owner named Jack Ruby. For years, Americans wondered whether Oswald and Ruby had each acted alone or whether others had been involved in the assassination. A presidential investigation commission reported that no conspiracy had been involved in JFK's death. Many Americans were still not convinced.

For days after the assassination, the nation seemed to stand still. Families huddled before their television sets to watch the long, sad funeral in Washington, D.C. No one had expected the youngest elected President in the nation's history to die in office. The nation was now in the hands of Kennedy's Vice President, Lyndon Johnson of Texas.

▶9. Who assassinated John Kennedy?

Reviewing Section I

Identify John F. Kennedy, Richard Nixon, New Frontier, Robert Weaver, Thurgood Marshall, Robert Kennedy, Yuri Gagarin, John Glenn, Neil Armstrong, Edwin Aldrin, arms race, developing nations, Third World, Peace Corps, Alliance for Progress, Bay of Pigs, Berlin Wall, Cuban missile crisis, Ngo Dinh Diem, Viet Cong

Questions to Answer
1. How successful was Kennedy in getting his New Frontier legislation approved by Congress?
2. Why did Kennedy think the future of the Third World countries was important?

A Question to Think About Which of his goals might Kennedy have accomplished if he had served a second term as President? Explain your answer.

Civil rights leaders, members of Congress, and members of Johnson's Cabinet watch as the President signs the Civil Rights Act of 1964.

II. President Johnson

Lyndon Baines Johnson was a very different person from John Kennedy. LBJ, as the newspapers called him, grew up in a poor family in the ranch country of west Texas. By his own efforts, he managed to get an education. He then became a teacher and later made a career in politics. By 1960, LBJ had held the powerful post of Senate majority leader for five years. Many people were surprised when he agreed to run for Vice President with Kennedy, since that job was less powerful than the one he already had. With Kennedy's death, however, LBJ held the nation's most important office.

The President and Congress

As Senate majority leader, LBJ had perfected the art of convincing (or, as some claimed, bullying) members of Congress into voting his way. That skill would be a big help to him as President.

Johnson had another advantage when he moved into the White House. The nation was still mourning Kennedy. Johnson used that sorrow to get a number of important bills through Congress. How better to honor Kennedy, he asked, than by approving his New Frontier legislation?

At Johnson's urging, Congress passed the **Civil Rights Act of 1964,** an even stronger law than the act Kennedy had proposed. It outlawed discrimination in all projects receiving federal funds and in public facilities such as theaters and hotels.

Then Johnson went beyond Kennedy's New Frontier. He called on Congress to begin a **War on Poverty** as a step toward building what Johnson called the **Great Society.** It would be a nation in which no one suffered from hunger or want and where everyone had the same opportunities for education and jobs.

Congress passed some of LBJ's antipoverty legislation. In 1964, it set up the **Office of Economic Opportunity** (OEO). The OEO attacked poverty at every level. It set up a **Head Start** program to prepare children from poor families for school and a **Job Corps** to train young unemployed people in the cities. The OEO also set up **VISTA,** or Volunteers in Service to America, which was similar to the Peace Corps except that its volunteers worked in the United States.

▶ **1.** Why was LBJ successful in getting Kennedy's civil rights bill passed by Congress?

The Election of 1964

In 1964, the Democrats chose Johnson as their presidential nominee. Against him the Republicans ran Senator Barry Goldwater of

Trained VISTA workers use their skills to help people throughout the nation.

Arizona. It made sense for the Republicans to run a candidate from the Southwest. Since the Second World War, the population of the United States had shifted toward the warmer states of the so-called **sunbelt.** That population increase made those states more politically important than before.

Goldwater was, however, more **conservative** than most Americans. That is, he opposed many of the changes that were altering American life and he wanted the government to interfere less in the lives of its citizens. Goldwater, like many other conservatives, opposed civil rights laws. He questioned the Social Security system. And he wanted an even greater commitment by the United States military to defeat the Communists in Vietnam.

Johnson won the election with 43 million votes to Goldwater's 27 million. The Democrats also won big majorities in both houses of Congress. That allowed Johnson to push forward his Great Society legislation.

▶ **2.** Who opposed Johnson in the election of 1964?

The Great Society

The new Congress passed more far-reaching new laws in 1965 and 1966 than at any time since Roosevelt's Second New Deal. It set up **Medicare,** an extension of the Social Security program, to provide health care for the elderly. Congress provided funds to improve schools, to house the poor, and to rebuild cities. Congress also created the **Department of Housing and Urban Development** (HUD). Robert Weaver became its first head and the first American black to hold a Cabinet office. Soon blacks pushed Congress to do more for them.

▶ **3.** Who was the first head of the Department of Housing and Urban Development?

Blacks Struggle for the Vote

In the summer of 1964, approximately 1,000 black and white college students traveled to the state of Mississippi to take part in the Mississippi Freedom Summer, a massive effort to register black voters. They encountered violence from the start. In June, three students were killed. Bombings and burnings continued through the entire summer.

Next, Martin Luther King, Jr., opened yet another drive for the ballot in Selma, Alabama. The county sheriff and his men attacked groups of peaceful demonstrators with tear gas, chains, and clubs. Later, two white demonstrators were killed.

In the wave of outrage that followed, Congress passed the **Voting Rights Act of 1965,** which sent federal examiners to register voters in the South. That caused a revolution in southern politics. In Mississippi, for example, only 7 percent of the voters were black in 1964. By 1968, 59 percent of the voters were black. The number of black voters throughout the South tripled in just four years.

By 1968, workers in the civil rights movement had begun to disagree among themselves. Many blacks were unhappy with the role whites played during Freedom Summer. They wanted to control their own struggle for equality. Also, once the battles against southern segregation and for voting rights for blacks were largely won, attention turned toward the North. That made the split between whites and blacks even worse.

▶4. What effect did the Voting Rights Act of 1965 have on southern politics?

Black Power

Blacks found much to criticize in the North. Millions of blacks there lived in poor, all-black neighborhoods. The schools in those

American artist James Wilson captured the proud heritage of the black experience in many of his works of art.

neighborhoods had mostly black students because few whites lived nearby. Such schools were segregated not *de jure,* or by law, but *de facto. De facto* means "in fact." They were segregated by the fact of where people lived.

Many northern blacks wanted to end *de facto* school segregation, even if it meant busing children to schools farther from their homes. Northern blacks also wanted opportunities for better jobs and better pay.

Northern whites were less willing to fight for such changes in their own towns than they had been to fight segregation in the South. In addition, many northern blacks wanted **black power,** which meant that blacks should control their own struggle for equality. Black power also meant taking pride in being black and in their African heritage.

Some northern blacks were attracted to the teachings of the Black Muslims. A few supported the **Black Panther Party.** That was a military-like group organized in 1966 to fight for black power. Such people considered whites their enemies, and they had few qualms about using violence in their cause.

▶**5.** What was meant by the term "black power"?

The Cities Explode

The anger and impatience of urban blacks led to great outbreaks of violence in northern cities. The first great urban riot of the 1960's took place in Harlem, an almost completely black section of New York City, in 1964. The next year another riot broke out in the Watts section of Los Angeles. It began after a white policeman hit a black. That set off a week of violence in which blacks attacked whites and burned or looted local stores, especially if their owners were white. In the summers of 1966 and 1967, more cities exploded. Thousands of people—mostly black—were hurt or killed during the riots, and millions of dollars worth of property was destroyed.

President Johnson proposed another civil rights law, but he could not get it through Congress. He did appoint Thurgood Marshall to the Supreme Court in 1967. Marshall became the first black to sit on the Court. Johnson also appointed a special Commission on Civil Disorders to see what could be done about the riots. In the spring of 1968, the commission recommended massive federal spending to improve conditions for blacks in the nation's cities. That proposal did not get much support from white Americans. Black power and violence had caused a backlash among whites, a feeling that blacks deserved no more help from them. Also the government did not have money to pour into the cities.

It already was spending massive amounts to fight the Communists in Vietnam.

▶**6.** How did LBJ respond to the riots of the 1960's?

Vietnam

In August 1964, President Johnson announced that a North Vietnamese gunboat had attacked an American destroyer in the Gulf of Tonkin off the coast of Vietnam. Congress responded by passing the **Gulf of Tonkin Resolution.** It gave the President power "to repel attacks on American forces and help the government of South Vietnam."

Johnson used the Gulf of Tonkin Resolution to begin bombing North Vietnam, although the United States never declared war on that country. He also sent combat forces to South Vietnam. The United States was continuing to **escalate,** or increase, its involvement in Vietnam. By 1968, there were about a half million American soldiers fighting there.

▶**7.** What was the Gulf of Tonkin Resolution?

The Domino Theory President Johnson sent troops to Vietnam because he feared a Communist takeover there. Like Eisenhower and Kennedy, LBJ believed in the **domino theory.** According to that theory, the nations of Asia were like dominoes lined up in a row. If the first of the dominoes tipped over—that is, if South Vietnam fell to the Communists—all its neighbors were likely to fall too. But the South Vietnamese seemed increasingly unable to hold off their enemies. As a result, the Americans increasingly took over their war.

▶**8.** What was the domino theory?

The War Grows The task of the Americans in Vietnam was very difficult. The Viet Cong fought using **guerrilla warfare.** That meant that they were not organized into a regular

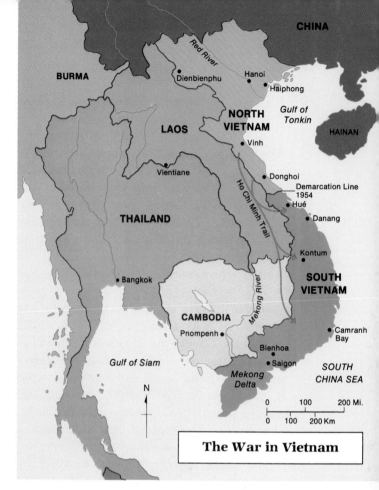

The War in Vietnam

army with headquarters and supply bases. Instead, they lived off the land so they could be anywhere, at anytime. They used ambushes, booby traps, and mines against the South Vietnamese and their American allies.

The Americans tried to destroy Viet Cong hiding places. They bombed huge areas, bulldozed villages, and sprayed chemicals on trees to make their leaves drop. American planes hit targets in North Vietnam also, since the North Vietnamese were sending supplies to the Viet Cong. To cut off that aid, the Americans bombed the main Viet Cong route, the **Ho Chi Minh Trail,** that passed through neighboring Laos.

In 1967, the American commander in Vietnam, General William Westmoreland, said victory was near. Then, on January 31, 1968, the first day of the Vietnamese New Year, called Tet, the Viet Cong began a massive attack throughout South Vietnam. Even in Saigon, the capital of South Vietnam, the Viet Cong showed amazing strength.

The Americans and South Vietnamese eventually won back the territory lost. Still, the **Tet Offensive** showed that a South Vietnamese victory was far away. That was a shock to many Americans who thought they were winning the war in Vietnam.

▶**9.** What did the Tet Offensive show about the Vietnam War?

The Antiwar Movement

The war was was very expensive. It cost the United States over $20 billion in 1967. And as the number of American troops in Vietnam

American soldiers in Vietnam used new methods to fight an enemy that was always on the move.▶

went up, the number of American deaths rose too. In 1967, almost 7,500 Americans died in battles fought in Vietnam. The next year, that number jumped to more than 12,500.

Was the war worth such a price? Even before 1968, many Americans said it was not. The Tet Offensive caused more Americans to question their country's involvement in the war. Some experts said the United States was not really fighting communism in Vietnam. Instead it was fighting people who, like the American patriots of 1776, wanted to rule themselves.

▶10. What was one result of the Tet Offensive?

Antiwar Efforts on Campus The antiwar movement was strongest on the nation's campuses. College professors and others opposed to the war led "teach-ins" in colleges and universities to spread information on Vietnam. On October 21, 1967, nearly 200,000 people joined a peace march to the Pentagon, the headquarters of the United States armed forces, located in Washington, D.C.

The peace movement became especially strong among college students as changes in the draft system made it harder for them to avoid military service. Many young men said they were conscientious objectors, people who could not fight for reasons of conscience. Some men went to jail rather than become soldiers. Others fled the country to avoid the draft. By the end of 1972, more than 40,000 draft resisters were living in Canada and abroad. There they were joined by American soldiers who deserted the army so they would not have to serve in Vietnam.

▶11. Where was the antiwar movement especially strong?

Democratic Peace Candidates By the spring of 1968, the peace movement had its own candidate for President—Senator Eugene McCarthy, a Democrat from Minnesota. McCarthy said he was running for President to end the war. With the support of many student volunteers, he managed to win a surprising 42 percent of the vote in the New Hampshire primary on March 12.

Four days later, Robert Kennedy, then a senator from New York, announced that he, too, would run for the presidency as a peace candidate. Kennedy was very popular, especially among blacks and the poor. With two other Democrats in the race, it looked as though President Johnson might have difficulty winning the nomination of his party.

▶12. Why did it appear that LBJ might have difficulty winning renomination as the Democratic presidential candidate in 1968?

Johnson Withdraws

On March 31, 1968, President Johnson appeared on national television to make an important announcement. In an effort toward peace, he was ordering an end to bombings in North Vietnam except for those in a small area near the South Vietnamese border. He also said he would not seek and would not accept the Democratic nomination for another term as President.

LBJ's announcement did not end the war. Even though a few weeks later, peace negotiations opened in Paris, the talks quickly became stalled.

Johnson's announcement did, however, mark a change in the way the Vietnam War was fought. The President decided not to increase the number of Americans fighting in Vietnam, as General Westmoreland requested. At the same time, the bombings in the South increased dramatically. American planes pounded away at supply routes and what they suspected to be enemy base camps. LBJ also tried to get the South Vietnamese to take over more of the fighting. That policy was known as **Vietnamization.** Still, at the year's end, the United States continued to do most of the fighting and pay most of the bills for the war.

▶**13.** How did LBJ change the nature of American involvement in the war after his announcement that he would not run for re-election?

Two Deaths

By 1968, Martin Luther King, Jr., who won the Nobel Peace Prize in 1964 for his work in civil rights, had become a strong supporter of the peace movement. The war in Vietnam was wrong in itself, he said, and it also distracted attention from the needs of American blacks at home.

In April 1968, King went to Memphis, Tennessee, to support a strike by black sanitation workers. There, as he stood on the balcony of his motel room, King was shot and killed by a white man named James Earl Ray. Ray's reasons are still not known.

King's death led to new outbreaks of racial violence. In more than 60 American cities, angry blacks took to the streets, setting fires and looting stores. More than 40 people were killed and about 3,000 were injured before the riots finally ended.

Just two months later, there was yet another tragic assassination. On June 6, 1968, Robert Kennedy won the California Democratic presidential primary. After talking to some of his supporters in a Los Angeles hotel that night, he was shot by Sirhan Sirhan (sir'han), a Jordanian. The next morning, Robert Kennedy was dead. One by one, it seemed, the nation's young leaders were being assassinated.

▶**14.** Which two American leaders were assassinated in April and June of 1968?

Coretta King is a picture of grace and dignity during the funeral of her husband.

The Election of 1968

In August 1968, when the Democrats met in Chicago, it was clear that they would nominate Vice President Hubert Humphrey of Minnesota for President. An old New Dealer, Humphrey, like Johnson, favored using the national government to improve the social welfare of its people. But that seemed unimportant to many voters. They saw Vietnam as a more pressing issue. And Humphrey, as President Johnson's favored candidate, was hopelessly associated with Johnson's Vietnam policy.

Before the convention began, there were rumors that the protesters intended to disrupt the convention. Chicago Mayor Richard Daley—a Humphrey supporter—was determined to keep order. On the third day of the convention, police attacked demonstrators outside one of the hotels where delegates were staying. Television cameras recorded the bloody scene. Humphrey won the nomination of the Democrats. However, his candidacy had been badly marred by the violence in Chicago.

The Republicans again nominated Richard Nixon for the presidency. There was also a third party candidate in the 1968 election. Governor George Wallace of Alabama, who had tried to keep blacks out of the University of Alabama in 1963, ran as an independent. He appealed especially to white voters who were tired of black demands and frightened by the nation's violence and disorder.

Nixon won the election, but by a mere 43.4 percent of the popular vote compared to Humphrey's 42.7 percent. Wallace won a surprising 13.5 percent of the votes. The appeal of Nixon and Wallace showed that the American people were tired of change, violence, and disorder. They wanted peace and stability again.

▶ **15.** Who won the election of 1968?

III. Nixon and Vietnam

Those who voted for Nixon in 1968 had reason to believe that they were also voting for peace in Vietnam. In his campaign, Nixon promised to end the war and even suggested that he had a plan for winning "peace with honor." Those who wanted peace at home and peace in Vietnam did not, however, get their wishes quickly.

Nixon's chief adviser on foreign affairs was Henry Kissinger, whom Nixon made his special assistant for national security affairs. Kissinger was born to a Jewish family in Germany and came to the United States in 1938. He was a professor of government at

Reviewing Section II

Identify Lyndon Baines Johnson, Civil Rights Act of 1964, War on Poverty, Great Society, Office of Economic Opportunity, Head Start, Job Corps, VISTA, Barry Goldwater, sunbelt, conservative, Medicare, Department of Housing and Urban Development, Freedom Summer, Voting Rights Act of 1965, *de jure* segregation, *de facto* segregation, black power, Black Panther Party, Gulf of Tonkin Resolution, escalate, domino theory, guerrilla warfare, Ho Chi Minh Trail, Tet Offensive, Eugene McCarthy, Robert Kennedy, Vietnamization, Hubert Humphrey, Richard Nixon, George Wallace

Questions to Answer
1. What major social legislation was passed under Johnson?
2. Why did President Johnson support the Vietnam War?

A Question to Think About For what reasons did Americans support the antiwar movement?

Harvard University and a respected scholar of international politics. He was different from Nixon, who came from a middle-class Quaker family in California and sometimes resented the world of intellect and learning. But the two men could help each other. They made a very effective team.

"Peace with Honor"

"Peace with honor," the peace Nixon promised in Vietnam, was not peace on just any terms. The United States could not simply pull out of Vietnam without a loss of influence throughout the world. For an honorable peace, the United States insisted that the Communist forces must leave South Vietnam and that South Vietnam must remain an independent country. The North Vietnamese refused those conditions. They wanted all of Vietnam to be under one government.

Nixon and Kissinger decided to force the North Vietnamese to give in. American planes began bombing the North again. Nixon also ordered massive bombings of Viet Cong hiding places in Cambodia, a country west of South Vietnam. The bombings in Cambodia were, however, kept secret even from Congress.

▶ **1.** What did Nixon mean by "peace with honor"?

Bringing the Troops Home Even as the bombings increased, Nixon began withdrawing United States forces from Vietnam. In early 1969, there were about 540,000 Americans in South Vietnam. By the fall of 1972, there were only 60,000 or so Americans left in that country.

Nixon, like LBJ, tried to build up the South Vietnamese military forces so they could not only fight the war themselves but also protect their country when peace came. The United States sent to South Vietnam weapons, ships, airplanes, helicopters, and other supplies. In addition, it helped reform the South Vietnamese armed forces and set up schools to train thousands of South Vietnamese soldiers each year.

▶ **2.** How did Nixon try to build up the South Vietnamese military?

Cambodia In the spring of 1970, military leaders in Cambodia overthrew the government of Prince Norodom Sihanouk (sē'ə nük), who had refused to support either side in the Vietnam War. The new leader quickly gave the Americans permission to enter his country

Nixon and Kissinger talk as they walk through the grounds of the White House.

to fight the North Vietnamese and the Viet Cong. On April 30, President Nixon publicly announced that he was sending American ground troops into Cambodia to "clean out" enemy bases there.

▶ **3.** Why did Nixon send ground troops to Cambodia?

The War at Home

Many Americans were outraged. They had thought President Nixon was ending the war; now he was expanding it into still another country. Antiwar protesters held demonstrations throughout the country, especially on college campuses. Hundreds of thousands of people participated. Opposition to the war was stronger than it had ever been. That opposition grew even angrier after May 4, when National Guardsmen opened fire on protesters at Kent State University in Ohio, killing four students and injuring nine.

Even Congress—which was controlled by the Democrats after the election of 1968—reacted angrily to Nixon's announcement on Cambodia. It repealed the Gulf of Tonkin Resolution of 1964, which had given a legal basis for the use of American troops in Vietnam. Some senators proposed cutting off all funds for military operations in Cambodia. Others wanted to require that the President bring all American troops home by 1971. Neither proposal was passed by Congress.

▶4. How did Congress react to Nixon's announcement on Cambodia?

Nixon under Siege

Stubbornly, Nixon held to his policies in Vietnam. He ordered more troops brought home, but he also increased the bombings in North Vietnam and along enemy supply routes in Laos and Cambodia. In February 1971, he even provided American air support for another ground operation against enemy bases in Laos. The ground troops were, however, not American but Vietnamese. Yet this time the North Vietnamese decided to counterattack.

After six weeks of bitter fighting, the South Vietnamese retreated. About half of their men had been hurt or killed. Vietnamization did not seem to be successful. Despite all the American efforts, the South Vietnamese were not ready to take over their own war.

▶5. What happened when South Vietnamese ground forces attacked Laos?

The *Pentagon Papers*

The Vietnam War caused a major change in American attitudes toward their government. Many Americans stopped believing what the President and other officials told them about the war. Such distrust became serious after the Tet Offensive of January 1968. It grew under Nixon.

In 1971, a former official in the Defense Department named Daniel Ellsberg handed the press a secret study of the war. That summer *The New York Times* and other newspapers published parts of the study, which was known as the *Pentagon Papers*. The study showed that as far back as the Kennedy administration, the government had misled the public about the war. The papers revealed, for example, that Congress did not have complete information about the 1964 incident that led to the Gulf of Tonkin Resolution. When President Johnson announced that the North Vietnamese had fired on American ships in the Gulf of Tonkin, he did not reveal that the American ships were supporting a South Vietnamese raiding party.

By mid-1971, public opinion polls indicated that only 31 percent of the American people approved of Nixon's handling of the war in Vietnam. An astounding 71 percent said the United States had made a mistake in sending troops there.

▶6. What did the *Pentagon Papers* reveal?

Détente

Without peace in Vietnam, Nixon faced a very tough battle for reelection in 1972. However, Nixon and Kissinger did have some points to help them win votes. Above all, they had achieved a **détente** (dā′tänt), or relaxation of tensions between the United States and both China and the Soviet Union.

▶7. What does *détente* mean?

China The United States had refused to recognize the Communist government of China ever since it took power in 1949. Instead, the United States government supported the government of Chiang Kai-shek, now in exile on the island of Taiwan. By 1971, the Communist People's Republic of China had been in power for more than twenty years. There was reason to believe that the Chinese Communists were ready to improve their relationship with the United States, since their friendship with the Soviet Union had gone sour. Soviet and Chinese troops, in fact, were massed on each side of their common border.

Nixon and Kissinger decided to take advantage of this rift. In July 1971, Kissinger made a secret trip to Beijing, the capital of China. Then, in February 1972, Nixon himself visited China. He stayed there one week, attending banquets and visiting historical sites. He and China's top officials agreed to reopen trade between the two countries and to allow various cultural and scientific exchanges. That fall the United Nations, with the approval of the United States, admitted the People's Republic of China to membership in place of the government of Taiwan. Those events marked a major change in American foreign policy.

▶**8.** What happened as a result of Nixon's trip to China?

The Soviet Union Relations with the Soviet Union also improved dramatically during Nixon's presidency. The Soviets wanted to buy grain from the United States. They also hoped to cut back on the huge costs of the arms race.

In 1968, when Lyndon Johnson was President, the United States and the Soviet Union agreed to work together to stop the spread of nuclear weapons. The next year diplomats from the United States and the Soviet Union began arms control talks in Helsinki, Finland. In May 1972, Nixon went to Moscow to sign the first **Strategic Arms Limitation Treaty** (SALT I). That treaty limited each side's

Leader of the People's Republic of China Zhou Enlai (left) welcomes President and Mrs. Nixon to his country at a formal Chinese banquet.

holding of certain missiles and missile systems, but it did not end the arms race. Instead, each side developed new weapons not covered by the agreement. However, friendly meetings between Nixon and top Soviet officials in Moscow did increase trade and other exchanges between the two countries.

▶**9.** What was SALT I?

Toward Peace in Vietnam

Despite those successes, Vietnam remained a problem. In March 1972, North Vietnam began a massive invasion into South Vietnam and Cambodia. The United States supported South Vietnam by bombing the North Vietnamese capital of Hanoi and the port city of Haiphong. It also mined several North Vietnamese harbors, including Haiphong. Those efforts were meant to keep supplies from reaching the North Vietnamese. Once again the war had been intensified.

707

By September, both sides were at last ready for serious peace talks. Kissinger and the North Vietnamese representative, Le Duc Tho (lā' duk' tō'), came to an agreement on several basic points. By October 31, just before the American presidential election, Kissinger announced that "Peace is at hand." He was not entirely correct.

▶ **10.** What was the aim of the bombings and mining of ports in North Vietnam in 1972?

The Election of 1972

By the time of Kissinger's announcement, it seemed that Nixon would win the election as the candidate who could best end the war. The Democratic candidate, Senator George McGovern of South Dakota, was a peace candidate, but the breakthrough at the negotiating table ensured a Nixon victory. Nixon won 60.8 percent of the popular vote—46 million votes compared to 28.5 million for McGovern, who carried only Massachusetts and the District of Columbia.

▶ **11.** Who won the election of 1972?

A Troubled Peace

Peace in Vietnam was farther away than Kissinger had indicated. The South Vietnamese insisted on changes in the peace agreement. When the North Vietnamese refused to accept them, Nixon ordered 12 days of massive bombings of North Vietnam in December 1972. Factories, airports, bus and train stations, hospitals, and homes were turned into heaps of rubble.

The bombing accomplished very little. The North Vietnamese had already agreed to most points in the agreement that was finally signed on January 27, 1973, by representatives of the United States, North Vietnam, South Vietnam, and the Viet Cong. The head of the South Vietnamese government, Nguyen Van Thieu, signed because Kissinger promised him that if the North Vietnamese broke the agreement, the United States would support him "with full force." Besides, Thieu feared that the United States would abandon him unless he signed.

The peace agreement called for a cease-fire and for the return of American prisoners held by the North Vietnamese. The United States would remove all of its troops from Vietnam, but the North Vietnamese could keep soldiers already stationed in the South. The South Vietnamese government of President Thieu would remain in place, but few people thought it would last for long.

Indeed, American military personnel had just left the country when fighting broke out again. By March 1975, the North Vietnamese had begun another major attack on the South. Thieu turned to the United States for help. Nixon was willing to give help, but his hands were tied. Congress had forbidden him to undertake any military action in that part of the world after August 15, 1973.

Congress had also limited the President's power by passing a **War Powers Act** in 1973. That act said that in the future the President would have to give Congress a full explanation within 48 hours of sending American troops abroad. Unless Congress gave its approval, those troops would have to return home within 60 days.

By March, South Vietnam had lost almost two thirds of the country. On April 21, President Thieu resigned. Those Americans still in the embassy in Saigon and their South Vietnamese supporters fled the country just before the Communists took over Saigon in late April. On April 30, the South Vietnamese surrendered to the Communists. Vietnam was reunited again, but under Communist rule.

▶ **12.** What was the War Powers Act?

Results of the War

Before South Vietnam fell, the pro-American regime in Cambodia fell to local Communist forces known as the **Khmer Rouge** (kmer rüzh). Communist forces also took over the nearby country of Laos.

Soon the Communist governments in Southeast Asia started fighting with one another. The new government of Vietnam, which was an ally of the Soviet Union, invaded Cambodia and drove the pro-Chinese Khmer Rouge from power. However, no other country in Southeast Asia became Communist once the South Vietnamese surrendered to North Vietnam.

By 1975, most Americans agreed that American participation in the Vietnam War had been a very expensive mistake. It had

IMPROVE YOUR SKILLS
Evaluating Data

Sometimes tables and graphs do not give you all of the information needed in order to answer a question. It is important to look at the title and the column headings carefully. You may also need to look for more information in order to understand the data and be able to answer a question. Study the table below. Then answer the following questions. On a separate sheet of paper, write "true," "false," or "cannot tell from the data" for each item. If you answer "cannot tell from the data," write what information you would need to decide if the statement is true or false.

1. More lives were lost in the Civil War than in any other war in the nation's history.
2. More lives were lost in each month of the Vietnam War than in each year of the Revolutionary War.
3. The Spanish-American War resulted in fewer American deaths than any other war in the nation's history.
4. More lives were lost to disease and other causes during World War I than were lost in battle.
5. About 4,000 Americans died in each year of the Vietnam War.

American Deaths in War		
War	Number Serving	Total Deaths
Revolutionary War	184,000–250,000	4,435
War of 1812	286,730	2,260
Mexican War	78,718	13,283
Civil War	2,900,000	620,000
Spanish-American War	306,760	2,446
World War I	4,734,991	116,516
World War II	16,112,566	322,000
Korean War	5,720,000	54,246
Vietnam War (1961–May 1975)	3,300,000	57,462

Data prior to World War I are based on incomplete information.

taken the lives of approximately 58,000 Americans. It also cost taxpayers some $150 billion—more than all American wars except World War II. Furthermore, the war undermined the trust and respect of many Americans for their President and their national government.

The veterans who returned from Vietnam were victims of the war. To many Americans, the veterans were a reminder of a war that was better forgotten. It took years before veterans were accepted for what they were—Americans who chose, at great cost, to obey the call of their country. In most times, for law-abiding people, that is worthy of the greatest respect and honor.

▶13. What were some of the major effects of the Vietnam War?

Reviewing Section III

Identify Henry Kissinger, Daniel Ellsberg, *Pentagon Papers*, détente, Strategic Arms Limitation Treaty, Hanoi, Le Duc Tho, George McGovern, Nguyen Van Thieu, War Powers Act, Khmer Rouge

Questions to Answer
1. Why did Nixon increase the bombing of North Vietnam while withdrawing American troops from South Vietnam?
2. Why did the Vietnam War reduce the respect of some Americans for their President and national government?

A Question to Think About   What effect did peace demonstrations have on the course of the Vietnam War?

IMPROVE YOUR READING
Supporting Opinions

It is normal to express opinions every day in conversations. Often we are asked to support our opinions. If you say, "The new movie is terrific," someone may ask why you thought that. You might cite the movie's interesting story, the good acting, and the special effects to support your opinion.

People also hold opinions regarding the history of our country. For example, some believe that Richard Nixon lost the election of 1960 because he lacked charisma, or personal appeal. They could support that opinion by noting his poor showing in the televised debates with John Kennedy.

The following list gives some statements of opinion related to the events discussed in this chapter. For each opinion, find at least one statement of fact to support it. Write that statement on a separate sheet of paper. Then decide whether you personally agree or disagree with the statement, and write "agree" or "disagree" next to the fact you have written. If you write "disagree," find a fact in the text that supports your opinion and write it on your paper.

1. President Kennedy accomplished very little during his administration.
2. Kennedy was a strong supporter of civil rights.
3. Johnson had good reason to escalate the war in Vietnam.
4. Americans had good reason to question their country's involvement in Vietnam.
5. Nixon was wise to visit China in 1972.

CHAPTER 31 REVIEW

Vocabulary Check
Write a short definition for each of the following terms.

1. Arms race
2. Developing nations
3. Sunbelt
4. Conservative
5. Escalate

Fact Check
On a separate piece of paper write the name of the person, place, or thing that completes each of the sentences below.

1. John Kennedy ran against _____ for President.
2. The first American astronaut to orbit Earth was _____.
3. The _____ was an attempt to overthrow Castro that failed.
4. The United States and the Soviet Union came close to war in 1962 during the _____.
5. _____ succeeded JFK as President.
6. Johnson wanted to eliminate poverty as one step in building the _____.
7. President Johnson used the _____ to justify sending American combat forces to South Vietnam.
8. The _____ in 1968 showed that the War in Vietnam was far from over.
9. In 1968, _____ ran for President in the New Hampshire primary as a peace candidate.
10. Nixon's chief advisor on foreign affairs was _____, formerly a professor at Harvard University.

Skills Check
Use the map on page 701 to answer the following questions.

1. What countries border South Vietnam on the west?
2. Where is Laos in relation to Cambodia?
3. The Ho Chi Minh Trail passes through what countries?
4. Describe the location of the Gulf of Tonkin.
5. Where does the Mekong River flow into the South China Sea?

Time Check
On a separate sheet of paper, place the following events in chronological order.

1. Martin Luther King, Jr., is asssassinated.
2. Tet Offensive begins.
3. South Vietnam finally surrenders to the Communists.
4. JFK is assassinated.
5. LBJ declares he will not run for reelection.

Think and Write
1. What hampered John Kennedy in achieving his New Frontier?
2. How did American involvement in Vietnam begin?
3. How did the civil rights movement change in the 1960's?
4. In what ways did LBJ increase American involvement in Vietnam?
5. How did American involvement in Vietnam end?

Chapter 32

The United States Today

Ronald Reagan takes the presidential oath of office on January 20, 1985. It was one of the coldest inauguration days in the history of the nation.

Americans were, in the nation's earliest years, a people suspicious of central power. The Constitution created a federal government that had to share power with the states. The Constitution also divided power among the legislative, the executive, and the judicial branches, so that no one of them could become all-powerful.

In the twentieth century, though, the federal government became much more powerful than the states. That happened because it assumed responsibility for the welfare of the American people and because of the increasing importance of foreign affairs. The branches of the federal government also became less balanced. The executive branch grew larger and more powerful than ever before.

In the early 1970's, the nation faced a crisis that tested the strength and wisdom of its Constitution. Then, through the 1970's and 1980's, Americans continued to question the growing power of the federal government.

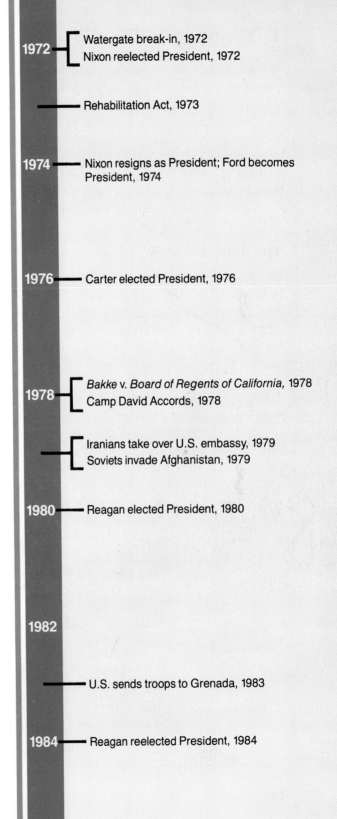

1972 — Watergate break-in, 1972
Nixon reelected President, 1972

Rehabilitation Act, 1973

1974 — Nixon resigns as President; Ford becomes President, 1974

1976 — Carter elected President, 1976

1978 — Bakke v. Board of Regents of California, 1978
Camp David Accords, 1978

Iranians take over U.S. embassy, 1979
Soviets invade Afghanistan, 1979

1980 — Reagan elected President, 1980

1982

U.S. sends troops to Grenada, 1983

1984 — Reagan reelected President, 1984

I. Watergate

On June 17, 1972, police arrested five men for breaking into the Democratic National Committee's headquarters in Washington's elegant Watergate office building. Few people paid much attention to the incident at the time. But in the years that followed, the investigation of the Watergate break-in revealed a much larger story of crime and corruption, one that centered in the White House.

The Story Unravels

The five men arrested in the Democratic headquarters in June 1972 carried cameras and "bugging" devices. Those devices could allow outsiders to hear Democratic party leaders discussing their plans for winning the November presidential election against President Nixon.

Former Attorney General John Mitchell, who was in charge of Nixon's campaign, denied that the Republican Committee to Re-Elect the President had anything to do with the break-in. However, two reporters for the

Bob Woodward (left) and Carl Bernstein are shown working at the Washington Post.

Washington Post, Carl Bernstein and Bob Woodward, were suspicious. They discovered that some of the people involved in the break-in had worked for the Committee to Re-Elect the President and received money from a mysterious fund controlled by people close to the President. The scandal they uncovered became known as **Watergate.**

▶**1.** What was the first Watergate incident?

The White House Investigates In August, President Nixon announced that White House lawyer John Dean had completed a special investigation and found that no one on the President's staff was involved in the Watergate incident. The voters believed Nixon and gave him a big victory in the 1972 election.

Then, in January 1973, the Watergate "burglars" went on trial before Judge John J. Sirica. The accused men were found guilty, but Sirica called for further investigation, saying he did not think the full story had been told.

▶**2.** What was the conclusion of John Dean's investigation of the Watergate incident?

The First Cracks in the Story One of the defendants, James W. McCord, Jr., claimed that lies had been told in the trial and pressure put on the defendants to remain silent. Then others confessed in the courts and before a Senate committee that was set up on February 7 to investigate charges of corruption in the 1972 presidential election. The committee was headed by Senator Sam Ervin of North Carolina.

It soon became clear that Nixon's closest advisers were involved in illegal efforts to hurt his political opponents. But was the President himself involved and did he try to cover up the criminal acts of those near him?

It is a crime to interfere with the investigation of criminal acts.

▶3. What was the purpose of the Senate committee headed by Sam Ervin?

The Nixon White House

The Watergate break-in was a small thing in itself, but it led to other, more serious revelations about activities in the White House. During his first term, upset by antiwar demonstrations, Nixon had stopped using his cabinet for help and advice. He still consulted Henry Kissinger, who became secretary of state in 1973, and John Mitchell. But Nixon relied mainly on H.R. Haldeman, John Ehrlichman, and other members of the White House staff.

Those men believed they were answerable only to the President. They acted as if laws did not bind them. They put wiretaps on the phones of people they thought were Nixon's enemies and read their mail. They asked for and accepted large illegal contributions from business people, and then used that money to undermine the campaigns of Democratic presidential candidates in underhanded, secret ways. They also helped the President use his office to build up his personal wealth.

▶4. Who were the major advisers to President Nixon?

The Cover-Up

One by one, Nixon's advisers became implicated in the Watergate scandal and were forced out of office. Finally, on April 29, Haldeman and Ehrlichman had to resign. By then, the Department of Justice had clear evidence against both men and John Mitchell.

Then, in July 1973, Senate investigators learned that conversations in the White House had been tape recorded since February 1971. Both the Ervin committee and Archibald Cox,

Judge Sirica was convinced after the Watergate trial that the full story was still untold.

a Harvard Law School professor whom Nixon had appointed as special Watergate prosecutor, asked for the tapes. Nixon refused to release them, citing "executive privilege." He said the President had the right to keep the records of the executive branch private, if

Senator Sam Ervin (center) was the head of the Senate committee investigating Watergate.

he so chose. He also said it was in the interests of national security that they not be released.

In October, Cox asked the courts to force Nixon to release the White House tapes. The President responded by demanding that his attorney general, Elliot Richardson, fire Cox. Instead, Richardson resigned. So did his top assistant. Nixon had to go to the third-ranking person in the Justice Department before he found someone willing to fire Cox.

Nixon's actions only made his situation worse. The House of Representatives opened hearings to consider impeachment. The pressure became so great that Nixon released transcripts (a typewritten version) of some of the tapes in April 1974. He said the transcripts proved him innocent. Many readers disagreed. The transcripts also showed clearly that the President and his advisers were petty and shabby in their treatment of others. Their language shocked many Americans.

President Gerald Ford and his wife (left) escort former President Nixon and his wife to a waiting helicopter after Nixon's resignation.

The transcripts included many gaps, where the President said the tapes were impossible to hear. But he was unwilling to let other people try. A new special prosecutor, Texas lawyer Leon Jaworski, did not give up the fight for the actual tapes. Finally, on July 24, the Supreme Court ordered the President to release the tapes.

▶**5.** What happened when investigators learned that Nixon had taped White House conversations?

Impeachment

At the end of July, the Judiciary Committee of the House of Representatives approved three articles of impeachment. They accused President Nixon of obstructing justice in the Watergate case, misusing his presidential power, and refusing to honor court orders that demanded the release of the White House tapes. Before the President could actually be impeached, the full House of Representatives would have to approve the Judiciary Committee's report. Then the President would be tried by the Senate, where a two-thirds vote is necessary for conviction. The nation anxiously waited to see what would happen next.

In early August, the President finally surrendered the White House tapes. They showed that within days of the Watergate break-in, Nixon had ordered the Federal Bureau of Investigation (FBI) to stop any investigation of the affair. Clearly, he had been involved in the cover-up from the beginning. It seemed certain that Nixon would be impeached and convicted. To avoid that disgrace, Richard Milhous Nixon became, on August 8, 1974, the first President of the United States to resign his office.

▶**6.** What grounds did the Judiciary Committee of the House give for impeaching Nixon?

The New President

Who would take Nixon's place? Not Spiro Agnew, the Vice President elected in 1972. Late in 1973, Agnew had resigned after being charged with accepting bribes while he was governor of Maryland.

The procedures for replacing a President or Vice President were set by the **Twenty-Fifth Amendment** to the Constitution, which was ratified in 1967. According to that amendment, the President could name a new Vice President, who then had to be approved by a majority of both houses of Congress. Nixon nominated the minority leader of the House of Representatives, Gerald Ford of Michigan. Congress quickly approved the appointment.

As Nixon and his wife, Patricia, flew home to California, Ford took the oath of office and became President of the United States. He chose as his Vice President Nelson Rockefeller, a descendant of John D. Rockefeller and a former governor of New York. For the first time, the nation had both a President and a Vice President who had not been elected by the people.

Ford had served in Congress for 25 years without great distinction. But he was what the country needed badly in 1974: an honest man. He was even honest about his own skills. "I am a Ford, not a Lincoln," he said.

Only a month after taking office, he made what most Americans thought was a big mistake. He gave Richard Nixon a "full, free, and absolute pardon" for any crimes he had committed while President. He did that, Ford said, because it was time to "heal the wounds" of Watergate.

It was strange to pardon a man for crimes of which he had not been convicted and which he still claimed he had not committed. The pardon made it impossible to try Nixon for his crimes, though many of his supporters were already in jail. That did not seem fair. Ford's pardon was very unpopular.

▶**7.** Who became President after Nixon resigned? Who became Vice President?

The Meaning of Watergate

The Watergate affair showed that the Constitution was still effective. President Nixon had come to think that he was above the law, but he was proved wrong. Congress and the judiciary stood up to him. So did some members of the executive branch. The power of the press also proved to be a powerful check on those who misused governmental power. Watergate showed, in short, that the government set up by the Constitution of 1787 still worked. It remained an effective protector of the basic rights and freedom of Americans.

▶**8.** What did Watergate demonstrate about the Constitution?

Reviewing Section 1

Identify John Mitchell, Carl Bernstein, Bob Woodward, Watergate, John Dean, John Sirica, H.R. Haldeman, John Ehrlichman, Archibald Cox, Elliot Richardson, Leon Jaworski, Spiro Agnew, Twenty-Fifth Amendment, Gerald Ford, Nelson Rockefeller

Questions to Answer

1. What was President Nixon's role in the Watergate affair?
2. How did the American people learn the full story of Watergate?

A Question to Think About Describe the Watergate affair and its conclusion in terms of checks and balances among the executive, legislative, and judicial branches of the federal government.

✳ II. Limiting Government ✳

After the crises of the 1960's and early 1970's, many Americans became tired of crusades. President Ford and the Presidents who followed him tried to appeal to "middle Americans," those who were neither rich nor poor but who wanted an end to high taxes, overgrown welfare programs, crime, and disorder. As a result, many social welfare programs of the 1960's came to an end. However, the Presidents of the late 1970's and 1980's found it hard to cut back on the size and power of the federal government in other areas.

The Ford Administration

President Ford vetoed one new spending program after another that Congress, with its Democratic majority, passed. Like Nixon, Ford wanted to reduce government regulation of business. Nonetheless, Americans had learned to look to the federal government for help when the economy was in trouble, and by 1974, the economy was in serious trouble.

In the late 1960's, prices had begun to rise sharply in the United States. That inflation of prices occurred in part because government spending for the Vietnam War increased the demand for a limited supply of goods and services.

▶ **1.** What effect did government spending for the Vietnam War have on the economy in the late 1960's?

OPEC Then, in 1973, inflation grew worse. That year many oil-producing countries raised the price of the oil they sold to the United States. In 1960, many oil-producing countries had formed the **Organization of Petroleum Exporting Countries** (OPEC). OPEC countries agreed to charge the same price for oil. Early in 1973, OPEC countries sold oil for $3 per barrel. Then, suddenly, they raised the price to more than $11 per barrel. Later the price rose to more than $20 per barrel. About 40 percent of the oil consumed in the United States in 1974 came from OPEC countries. As the price of gasoline and other petroleum products went up, so did the cost of the many goods and services dependent on oil.

▶ **2.** What is OPEC?

Trade and Controls As prices rose, it became harder for foreigners to buy goods made in the United States. In 1971, Americans imported more than they exported for the first time since 1893. As the cost of oil pushed prices up even further, the balance of trade became worse. American businesses could

Graph Study *How much had the price per barrel of crude oil increased from 1970 to 1975?*

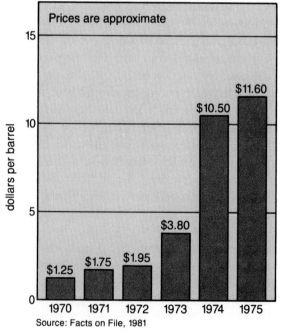

Crude Oil Prices, 1970-1975

Prices are approximate

Year	Price
1970	$1.25
1971	$1.75
1972	$1.95
1973	$3.80
1974	$10.50
1975	$11.60

dollars per barrel

Source: Facts on File, 1981

not sell goods they had manufactured for sale abroad. Workers lost their jobs.

Both Nixon and Ford tried to improve the situation by encouraging Americans to conserve energy and by cutting down American dependence on OPEC oil. They urged the development of other sources of energy, including solar and atomic energy. It would take time, however, before such efforts were effective.

Nixon tried to stop inflation by imposing strict limits on wage and price increases. That slowed down inflation, but it also led to a rise in unemployment.

Ford tried to control inflation in a different way. He raised interest rates, which caused a bad recession. Approximately 9 percent of the work force was unemployed in early 1975. A tax cut helped end the recession in 1976. Still, Americans were not impressed with Ford's handling of the economy. Economic issues, plus his pardon of Nixon, hurt Ford in the election of 1976.

▶**3.** What effect did inflation have on the balance of trade?

The Democrats Return

The Democratic Party's presidential candidate in 1976 was Jimmy Carter, a little-known peanut farmer and businessman from Plains, Georgia. He had served in the state legislature and as governor of his home state. Carter campaigned as an "outsider," as someone who had never been corrupted by power in Washington. "I will never lie to you," he promised the people.

With careful organization and hard work, Carter won the nomination, and then, in November, the presidency. The election was very close. The electoral vote was 297 to 240 in Carter's favor. But only about half of the eligible voters bothered to cast ballots. Even

During his presidency, Carter brought a relaxed, friendly style to the oval office.

many young people between the ages of 18 and 20, who had just won the right to vote when the **Twenty-Sixth Amendment** was ratified in 1971, did not bother to go to the polls.

Like Nixon and Ford, Carter promised to cut back the size of the federal government. He did manage to reform the bureaucracy so it worked more efficiently, but economic problems continued to haunt him.

Carter tried to control inflation through high interest rates. By 1980, interest rates were higher than ever before in American history, but inflation continued. So did high unemployment. Carter tried to reduce unemployment through federal work projects and a tax cut. Those efforts got people jobs, but they pushed prices up even further.

The rate of inflation in the last year of Ford's administration was about 5 percent. By 1978, it had doubled. In 1980, it reached 18 percent. **Double-digit inflation,** or an inflation rate of more than 9 percent, especially hurt retired people and others whose incomes did not go up as rapidly as the inflation rate.

Keynesian economics were not much help. By its rules, government spending should not have caused inflation while people were unemployed. Carter tried one thing after another to boost the economy, but each met with only limited success. The President vetoed federal projects and delayed tax cuts. He also began voluntary wage and price restraints.

IMPROVE YOUR SKILLS
Reading an Election Map

The election map below shows the electoral votes cast by each state and the District of Columbia in the election of 1976. Study the map and answer the questions that follow.

1. A total of 538 electoral votes were cast in 1976. (One elector voted for Ronald Reagan.) A simple majority (one more than half) is needed to win. How many votes were needed to win the 1976 presidential election?

2. (a) List the five states with the largest number of electoral votes. Total their electoral votes. (b) How many more votes are needed to win?

3. In what region of the country was Carter the strongest?

4. (a) How many states did Ford carry? (b) How many states did Carter carry?

5. How many more electoral votes did Ford need to win?

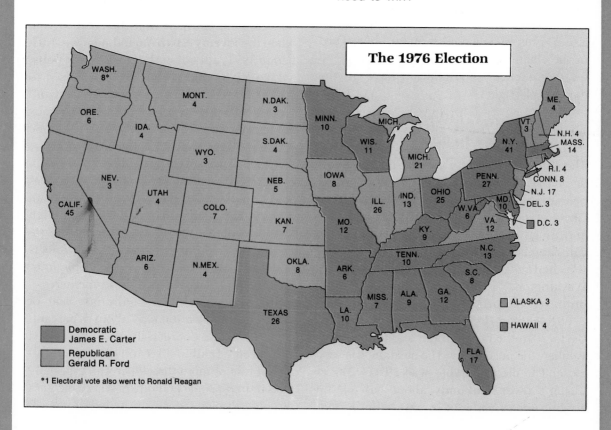

The 1976 Election

WASH. 8*
ORE. 6
MONT. 4
N.DAK. 3
IDA. 4
S.DAK. 4
WYO. 3
NEV. 3
UTAH 4
COLO. 7
NEB. 5
KAN. 7
CALIF. 45
ARIZ. 6
N.MEX. 4
OKLA. 8
TEXAS 26
MINN. 10
IOWA 8
MO. 12
ARK. 6
LA. 10
WIS. 11
ILL. 26
MICH. 21
IND. 13
KY. 9
TENN. 10
MISS. 7
ALA. 9
GA. 12
OHIO 25
W.VA. 6
VA. 12
N.C. 13
S.C. 8
FLA. 17
PENN. 27
N.Y. 41
MD. 10
D.C. 3
ME. 4
VT. 3
N.H. 4
MASS. 14
R.I. 4
CONN. 8
N.J. 17
DEL. 3
ALASKA 3
HAWAII 4

Democratic
James E. Carter

Republican
Gerald R. Ford

*1 Electoral vote also went to Ronald Reagan

That is, Carter asked businesses and industries not to raise prices or wages. Carter also went farther than Ford in encouraging Americans to conserve energy. And he successfully urged Congress to add a **Department of Energy** to the government.

▶**4.** What was Carter's political experience before becoming President?

Pollution and Conservation

Americans did not agree on the ways to cut their use of oil. Some people recommended an increased use of coal and of nuclear power as energy sources. Other Americans said that burning coal contributed to air pollution and that nuclear power plants were dangerous. Arguments against the use of nuclear power became stronger in 1979 after the Three-Mile Island nuclear plant near Harrisburg, Pennsylvania, began to leak contaminated steam into the surrounding area. Although the leak was quickly stopped, many Americans remained concerned about the possibility of accidents at such plants.

The energy debates were part of Americans' increased awareness of **ecology,** the relationship of living things with their environment. Interest in ecology and **pollution,** the spoiling of the environment by human-made waste, really began in 1962 when a marine biologist named Rachel Carson published *The Silent Spring.* In that book, Carson told how the continued use of chemicals to kill insects had harmful results on plants, animals, and humans.

As Americans began to study the environment in the 1960's, they discovered many serious problems. Most of the nation's rivers were so polluted that they were unfit for drinking and many were unfit for swimming. Air pollution was a major problem in many cities. In 1970, thousands of Americans joined in demonstrations to call attention to environmental problems.

In response to such needs, Congress passed the **National Environmental Protection Act.** That law said that before any federally-funded project could be approved by Congress, its impact on the environment had to be studied. Congress also created the **Environmental Protection Agency** to enforce a series of new antipollution laws.

By the 1980's, the effect of those new laws was being felt. The rivers were significantly improved. The air in some cities had become much cleaner. Greater attention was being paid to the disposal of hazardous wastes. However, many problems still remained.

▶**5.** What was the pollution problem?

Carter's Foreign Policy

The nation's dependence on foreign oil especially worried Carter and other Americans. They feared a war in the troubled Middle East could stop shipments of oil to the United States. Peace in the Middle East was therefore very much an American interest.

▶**6.** Why was peace in the Middle East important to the United States?

The Camp David Accords In hopes of restoring peace between the warring nations of Egypt and Israel, President Carter invited President Anwar Sadat (sà dat') of Egypt and Prime Minister Menachem Begin (be gin') of Israel to a conference at Camp David, a presidential vacation home in Maryland, in September 1978. For two weeks, Carter and other members of his administration worked with the two Middle Eastern leaders. Together they hammered out the **Camp David Accords,** which provided the framework for a peace treaty Israel and Egypt signed the next year. The treaty did not bring peace in the Middle

Anwar Sadat of Egypt (left) and Menachem Begin of Israel (right) watch as President Carter signs the Camp David Accords.

East. It was, however, an important step in that direction and an important accomplishment for the President.

▶**7.** What were the Camp David Accords?

The Panama Canal Carter's record in other areas of foreign policy was not so strong. He helped negotiate treaties by which the Panama Canal would be turned over to the Panamanians. He did that to avoid future conflicts with the people of Central America. To many Americans, however, the treaties seemed a giveaway.

▶**8.** Why did Carter return the Panama Canal to Panama?

Afghanistan In 1979, negotiations with the Soviets led to a new strategic arms limitation treaty, **Salt II.** The agreement limited the number of nuclear weapons each side could have and also limited the production of new weapons.

The Senate had to approve the new SALT treaty, and it seemed unlikely that Carter had enough votes for ratification. Then, in December 1979, the Soviets invaded Afghanistan, the small country on their southern border. In response, Carter withdrew the treaty from consideration, stopped shipments of grain and some other products to the Soviets, and tried to gain support from other nations for a boycott of the 1980 summer Olympic games. Despite Carter's efforts, the Soviets remained in Afghanistan.

▶**9.** What blocked ratification of Salt II?

Crisis in Iran

For 30 years, the United States had supported the government of Mohammed Reza Pahlevi, the shah of Iran. By the 1970's, the shah was increasingly unpopular in his own country. Many resented the methods he used, including the torture of enemies, to stay in power. Some also resented his efforts to make Iran more like nations of the West. In January 1979, the shah's opponents forced him into exile.

The new leader of Iran was an Islamic religious leader called the Ayatollah Ruhollah Khomeini (ä′ə tō′lə ru ha′ləh hō mā′nē). For many years, he had lived in exile in France. Now he returned home to restore Islamic traditions to his country.

At first, the shah made his home in Mexico, but in October 1979 President Carter allowed him to come to New York to be treated for cancer. Many Iranians were outraged. On November 4, within days of the shah's arrival in the United States, a mob invaded the American embassy in Teheran, the capital of Iran. They held the Americans there as hostages. Only when Carter sent them the shah, the Iranians said, would they release the hostages.

"The U.S. can do nothing," the Iranians claimed. As months went by, that seemed to be true. A military attempt to rescue the hostages failed when three helicopters broke

Americans cheered with delight when the hostages were finally freed.

down and several marines were killed. The United States and its President seemed weak.

▶11. What sparked the Iranians to seize the American embassy and take hostages?

The Election of 1980

By election day in November 1980, the Iranians had held the Americans in the embassy hostage for a full year. The hostages' plight and the continuing inflation at home cut deeply into President Carter's popularity. He won only 41 percent of the popular vote. His Republican opponent, Ronald Reagan, an actor who became governor of California, received 51 percent of the popular vote. Another candidate, John Anderson, who ran as an independent after failing to win the Republican

nomination, held 7 percent. The vote in the electoral college was even more lopsided, with Jimmy Carter winning only 49 votes to Ronald Reagan's 489.

In his last days in office, Carter finally negotiated the release of the hostages in Iran. Soon after Reagan took office in January 1981, the nation celebrated their return.

▶11. Who were the three candidates in the election of 1980?

The Reagan Revolution

Reagan promised the voters that he would solve the two problems that seemed most important in 1980. He would make the nation strong again, and he would restore prosperity.

President Reagan holds a dollar bill as he addresses the nation on the economy.

Reagan's economic theories were like those of many earlier Republican Presidents. He thought the government should interfere with private economic decision-making as little as possible. The economy was in trouble, he said, because the government left too little money in the hands of the people who would invest it in new and growing businesses. Therefore, he proposed tax cuts to free funds for investments in new factories and service industries that would create more jobs for Americans.

Since tax cuts would reduce federal income at first, Reagan proposed to cut federal expenses. He did not intend to continue the huge federal deficits that occurred under Carter. He promised, in fact, that the federal budget would be balanced within four years.

In 1980, voters gave the Republicans a majority in the Senate. The House was still controlled by Democrats, but many of them were conservatives, likely to vote with the Republicans. So Reagan had a good chance of getting his program through Congress.

▶**12.** How did Reagan propose to boost the economy?

Reaganomics

Reagan's first term began with one triumph after another in Congress. He and his advisers, including his young budget director, David Stockman, made major revisions in the budget for 1982. They cut many social programs in an effort to reduce costs, and they convinced Congress to pass Reagan's proposed reduction in individual and corporate income taxes.

By 1982, however, the nation was in the middle of a recession, with approximately 10 percent of American workers unemployed. Some industries were in so much trouble

★★The United States and the World ★★★★★★★★★★★★★★★★
Multinational Corporations

Since World War II the growth of multinational corporations has changed the way the world does business. A multinational corporation is a business organization that operates in two or more countries. In the early 1980's, there were over 7,000 multinational corporations. Multinational corporations account for about 15 percent of the goods and services of the world.

In the early 1900's, United States multinational corporations tended to take natural resources from other nations without trying to sell products there. Such corporations were involved in mining or growing crops such as fruit and tea. However, a few of the manufacturing companies such as Eastman-Kodak, known primarily for cameras and film, and Coca-Cola were selling their goods abroad at that time.

Many new multinational corporations, such as IBM and the Ford Motor Company, are primarily manufacturers. They set up factories in other countries to avoid import duties and taxes. There the basic products are modified to suit customers in various parts of the world. Multinational corporations must decide how to divide their resources between the parent company and smaller companies in other countries. Some observers say such companies are good, serving to tie together the world's economies. Critics, on the other hand, say they reduce an individual nation's control over its own affairs.

that large parts of the Midwest seemed like an industrial disaster area. One steel mill after another closed its doors. Only federal loans seemed to keep parts of the automobile industry going.

The state of the economy led many to question Reagan's theories—**Reaganomics**—as they were called. Yet by 1984, the economy had made a remarkable recovery. Inflation rates were lower than 5 percent. Unemployment was also down, though it remained a serious problem in some parts of the country. The American automobile industry enjoyed a record year, and the United States was not as dependent on OPEC oil as it had been ten years earlier.

Balancing the federal budget, however, remained a problem. Because Reagan refused to cut back defense spending, the United States was still spending much more money than it took in. To end the big deficits, President Reagan would have to make some major changes in his economic policies. But he refused to do that until the 1984 presidential election was over.

▶**13.** What were some of the signs of a healthier economy in 1984?

Trouble Abroad ⑬

Like earlier administrations, the Reagan administration faced problems in many parts of the world. In the Americas, Reagan charged, Cuban Communists were helping to set up governments that threatened the security of the United States. In the fall of 1983, he sent United States marines to the island of Grenada in the Caribbean to overthrow a Marxist government there.

There were long standing problems in Central America as well. The United States tried to help the government of El Salvador hold out against rebels. At the same time,

American troops in Grenada help anti-Communists there overthrow a Marxist government.

the Central Intelligence Agency (CIA) was training and supplying rebels who were attempting to bring down the leftist government of Nicaragua.

Many critics questioned the wisdom of Reagan's policies, especially in El Salvador and Nicaragua. Those policies, they argued, were wrong, and would cause resentment of the United States among the people of Central America.

▶**14.** What role did the United States play in Grenada, El Salvador, and Nicaragua in the early 1980's?

The Election of 1984

Reagan had no trouble winning votes in 1984. He promised that prosperous times would continue in his second term. He also promised to work for laws that would permit prayer in public schools and gave tax benefits to parents whose children attended private schools. His critics claimed that such measures could violate the separation of church and state set up by the Constitution.

The major surprise of the election was that the Democratic nominee for President, Walter Mondale of Minnesota, Vice President under Carter, chose a woman to run as his own Vice President. Geraldine Ferraro, an Italian American Congresswoman from Queens, New York, waged a strong campaign, although she was troubled by questions about her husband's financial affairs.

The voters were apparently delighted with the nation's economic recovery. If the situation in El Salvador and Nicaragua was disturbing, Central America seemed far away. In the end, Reagan won a bigger majority of the nation's vote than he had in 1980. He took approximately 59 percent of the popular vote and carried every state except Mondale's home state of Minnesota. The District of

Walter Mondale surprised many people when he chose Geraldine Ferraro as his running mate.

Columbia also cast its electoral votes for Mondale.

Reagan's victory ended hope for any revival of the spending programs of the 1960's such as the War on Poverty. If the President had his way, the future of the American people would be plotted more by private persons or businesses and state officials than by bureaucrats in Washington. That was what the "Reagan Revolution" was about—giving power back to those who had held it in the nation's early years.

▶**15.** What role did Geraldine Ferrarro play in the 1984 election?

The Supreme Court

The judiciary also changed dramatically between the 1960's and the 1980's. The changes began in 1969, when Chief Justice Earl Warren resigned. In his place, President Nixon appointed a conservative lawyer from Minnesota, Warren Burger. Nixon appointed four more conservative justices to the Supreme Court. Then President Reagan increased the conservative majority in 1981. His conservative appointee, Sandra Day O'Connor, was the first woman to serve as a Supreme Court justice.

The Court's decision in the important case of *Bakke* v. *Board of Regents of California* in 1978 showed the conservative trend of the Court. Since the 1960's, the government had encouraged businesses and other institutions to establish **affirmative action plans** to increase opportunities for women and minorities. In the *Bakke* decision, the Court said universities could not reject qualified white applicants in order to accept a set number of minority applicants. Then, in June 1984, the Court said employers could lay off blacks recently hired under an affirmative action plan while keeping white workers who had

On July 19, 1984, Geraldine Ferraro made history. On that day, the Democratic Party nominated her to serve as running mate to presidential candidate Walter Mondale. When Ferraro accepted the nomination, she became the first woman ever to run for Vice President on a major party ticket.

Geraldine Ferraro was born about 60 miles north of New York City on August 26, 1935. Her father, Dominick, was an Italian immigrant who owned a restaurant. Dominick showered Geraldine with affection. His sudden death when Geraldine was only eight hurt her deeply.

Soon after her husband's death, Antonetta Ferraro moved her family to the Bronx. There she earned money by crocheting beads on wedding dresses and evening gowns. By working hard and saving, she was able to send Gerry to a private Catholic school for girls. From there, Gerry went on scholarship to Marymount Manhattan College where she majored in English.

After graduating from college, Geraldine took a job teaching second grade in New York City. For the next four years, she taught in the daytime and attended Fordham Law School at night.

Gerry graduated from law school in 1960. That same year she passed the New York state bar and married real estate developer John Zaccaro. Geraldine chose to keep her maiden name.

For the next 14 years, Ferraro devoted herself to her growing family and to a part-time law practice. Then, in 1974, at the age of 39, she went to work full time as assistant district attorney for Queens County. There she handled cases involving violent crimes against children and the elderly.

Ferraro worked in the district attorney's office for four years before running for Congress. She fought a hard campaign and won. Her victory amazed many Queens Democrats, who did not

believe that a woman with liberal ideas could win in a working class neighborhood.

Ferraro's victory made her one of 22 women in the 435-member House of Representatives. During her three terms in office, she gained a reputation as a skillful, shrewd politician. Her reputation helped get her chosen to serve as chairperson of the Platform Committee for the 1984 Democratic Convention. Her skill in handling conflicting views helped convince Walter Mondale to name her as his running mate.

Ferraro worked hard to make the Mondale-Ferraro ticket a winner, standing up to intense questioning about her political views and her family's finances. Although on election day voters chose Ronald Reagan for President, Ferraro's candidacy resulted in another kind of victory. Her candidacy paved the way for other women to run for the nation's highest political offices.

more seniority—that is, who had held their jobs for a longer time. Both of those decisions were criticized by civil rights supporters. But they were welcomed by whites who feared that their rights were threatened by the effort to help less privileged Americans.

In June 1984, the Court also modified the Warren Court's defense of accused criminals' rights in the landmark case of 1966, *Miranda* v. *Arizona*. Now the Court said the police did not have to inform accused persons of their rights before questioning them if the "public safety" was at stake.

▶ **16.** What was the Supreme Court's ruling in the *Bakke* case?

Reviewing Section II

Identify Organization of Petroleum Exporting Countries, Jimmy Carter, Twenty-

Sixth Amendment, double-digit inflation, Department of Energy, ecology, pollution, Rachel Carson, National Environmental Protection Act, Environmental Protection Agency, Anwar Sadat, Menachem Begin, Camp David Accords, Salt II, Ronald Reagan, Reaganomics, Walter Mondale, Geraldine Ferraro, Warren Burger, Sandra Day O'Connor, *Bakke* v. *Board of Regents of California*, affirmative action plans, *Miranda* v. *Arizona*

Questions to Answer
1. What crises in foreign affairs troubled the Carter administration?
2. Describe Reagan's economic theories.

A Question to Think About What options did Carter have to free the American hostages in Iran?

III. A Changing People

The American people were different in the 1980's from what they had been at the end of World War II. New immigrants had arrived, and other Americans had won new power and respect during the post-war years.

New Faces

In 1965, the United States finally ended the old system of admitting immigrants to the United States according to their national origin. Instead, the new **Immigration and Nationality Act** said immigrants would be admitted to reunite families or to provide skills needed in the United States. Suddenly, immigration again became an important factor in American life.

▶ **1.** What was the Immigration and Nationality Act?

Asian Immigrants Many of the new immigrants came from Asia, especially from Korea, the Philippine Islands, South Vietnam, and Cambodia. Some were trained people who came seeking new opportunities to use their skills. Many also came to escape oppressive governments in their homelands.

The Vietnamese and Cambodians in particular came to escape Communist rule. So eager were they to escape that many of them went to sea in overloaded small boats that sometimes sunk. When those **boat people** made it to the United States, they often owned nothing. Like the poor immigrants of the nineteenth century, they were resented at first. But their determined efforts to build a new life in the United States won the respect of many Americans.

▶ **2.** Who were the boat people?

Thousands of Cambodian and Vietnamese refugees risk their lives to escape Communist rule.

Spanish-Speaking Americans Far more newcomers were from Mexico than from any other country. As their numbers increased, Mexican Americans, some immigrants and some native-born Americans whose families had lived in the United States for generations, became a force in American politics. They even had their own political party, La Raza Unida, founded by José Angel Guttierrez. Their interests were also defended by people like Representative Henry B. Gonzalez of Texas who, in 1984, headed the Hispanic Caucus in the United States House of Representatives. **Hispanic** is a term often used for Spanish-speaking Americans.

Cubans made up a large portion of the Spanish-speaking population in the United States. About 750,000 Cubans arrived at the time of the Cuban Revolution in 1959. They created entire communities of their own, especially in Florida. Then, in 1980, Castro allowed another 120,000 Cubans to emigrate.

The United States admitted the Cubans in spite of the remaining restrictions on immigration.

Americans from Puerto Rico continued to come to the continental United States in large numbers. Puerto Ricans often settled in crowded areas of cities like New York, making Spanish a language of the streets. In time, they, too, became a political force. Hispanic voters, for example, helped make Herman Badillo president of the Bronx and, later, a member of Congress. Badillo came to the continental United States from Puerto Rico.

Not all Spanish-speaking Americans came to the United States legally. Officials estimated that more than seven million illegal aliens were in the country by the mid-1970's.

In the mid-1980's, some Americans wanted to stop illegal entry and to deport the illegal

Herman Badillo, former Deputy Mayor of New York City and former member of Congress, came to the United States mainland from Puerto Rico.

729

aliens already living in the United States. Illegal aliens, they argued, took jobs from American citizens. Efforts to do something about illegal aliens faced stiff opposition from Hispanic leaders. They feared that such programs would cause harrassment and indignity for the large numbers of Spanish-speaking Americans who are citizens or legal aliens.

▶ **3.** Why did some Americans wish to stop entry by illegal aliens and to deport those already living in the United States?

Indians

The oldest Americans, the Indians, also became more self-conscious of their dignity and more demanding of their rights in the 1970's. They organized schools to teach young Indians about their past and began to fight through the courts for the return of ancestral lands wrongfully taken from them.

In 1971, Indians founded the **American Indian Movement.** It favored direct action in the Indians' cause. For example, protesters took over the Bureau of Indian Affairs in

Indians from the Southwest, joined by other Indian groups along their route, walk to the nation's capital to protest treaty violations.

Washington for six days in November 1972. The next February, they seized the town of Wounded Knee, South Dakota, where federal troops had killed many Sioux Indians in 1890. They demanded that Indian rights be more fully respected on the nearby Sioux reservation. Before the 1973 seige had ended, one Indian had died as a result of a clash with federal soldiers.

▶ **4.** Why did members of the American Indian Movement seize the town of Wounded Knee?

Women's Rights

The 1964 Civil Rights Act outlawed discrimination on the basis of sex as well as race. Southerners had added that clause to weaken the act. The bill passed anyway, and it gave a big boost to the women's rights movement. Soon many women wanted another law.

In 1972, Congress passed the **Equal Rights Amendment** (ERA) to the Constitution. The amendment said that "equality of rights under the law shall not be denied or abridged by the United States or by any state on account of sex." To become law, the ERA had to be ratified in seven years. However, Congress extended the deadline to June 1982.

Such an amendment was first proposed in 1923. It failed then, in part because some women insisted it would undermine women's special roles as wives and mothers. Similar arguments were raised in the 1970's by ERA opponents such as Phyllis Schafly of Illinois. The ERA also had many strong supporters, including Betty Ford, wife of President Gerald Ford. But it did not win the support of enough states by the 1982 deadline. Once again, the ERA failed to become law.

Even without the ERA, women entered professions such as law, medicine, and even engineering in record numbers in the 1970's. Women, including married women with children, became an increasingly large part of the American work force.

Women had also become an important political force. Many of them served in Congress. Even Ronald Reagan, whose party refused to endorse the ERA in 1980, appointed several women to responsible jobs in government. Elizabeth Dole became head of the Department of Transportation. Margaret Heckler was appointed head of Health and Human Resources (formerly the Department of Health, Education, and Welfare). Jean Kirkpatrick represented her country in the United Nations, and Sandra Day O'Connor became a Supreme Court justice.

▶**5.** What was the ERA?

Black Power

The pride and political power of blacks also increased in the 1970's. One sign of the times was the popularity of Alex Haley's book, *Roots*. Haley, a black writer, traced his family back to an African ancestor, Kunta Kinte (kün′tə kin′tā). Millions of Americans watched the television version of Haley's proud tale of his family's struggles.

A still more important change was evident in the rising number of black voters in the South and in the cities. The 1980 census showed that blacks were rapidly outnumbering whites in many American cities. There blacks began to use their numbers to win political power. City after city—including Washington, D.C.; Atlanta; Detroit; Philadelphia; and Chicago—elected black mayors. And in the Democratic primary elections of 1984, The Reverend Jesse Jackson, a black minister, politician, and educator, brought out black voters in record numbers. The black power movement of the 1960's may have come and gone, but black political power was a reality in the 1980's.

In 1983, Sally Ride, one of the first American woman astronauts, became part of the crew of the space shuttle Challenger.

▶**6.** What did the elections of black mayors in large cities and Jesse Jackson's campaign show about black power in the 1980's?

Older Americans

Other groups with special interests and special needs also worked through the political system. Approximately 1 of every 9 Americans was older than 65 years in 1980, and their

Jesse Jackson's campaign for the presidency in 1984 sparked the interest of many Americans.

numbers were rising. Older Americans had their own spokespeople in Congress and their own causes.

They were strong supporters of Medicare, of course, and they wanted no cutting back on Social Security benefits, which were becoming an increasingly heavy burden on those Americans who had to pay for them. Older Americans also wanted to strike down rules that forced people to retire at a certain age. Such rules, they said, caused discrimination on the basis of age.

▶7. What were some of the issues that concerned the older Americans?

The Handicapped

Americans with physical handicaps organized politically to draw attention to their needs. In 1973, as a result of their work, Congress passed the **Rehabilitation Act.** It forbade discrimination against the handicapped in jobs, housing, or educational opportunities.

Other laws passed in the 1970's required public buildings to be accessible to and have

Students in Rural Hall, North Carolina, help a fellow classmate on her way to class.

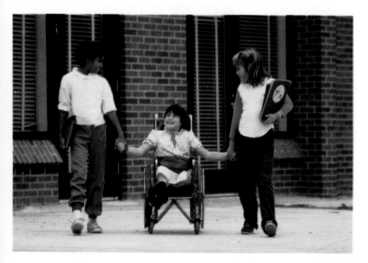

facilities for the handicapped. All public buildings had to have raised signs for the blind, and public meetings had to be interpreted for the deaf.

In 1975, Congress passed a law requiring public schools to provide free education for children with physical and mental handicaps. Wherever possible, schools began to bring handicapped students into regular school classes and activities. Educators referred to that as **mainstreaming.**

▶8. What is mainstreaming?

A Proud Past

At first, there were no people in the Americas. By 1985, more than 237 million people lived in the United States alone. Together those people had gone through a period of doubt about themselves and their country at the time of the Vietnam War. But as they looked back over their history, they could find cause for pride and for hope.

All Americans, beginning with the first hunters from Asia, have been immigrants or the descendants of immigrants. The United States, founded in 1776 by people whose ancestors had come mostly from Britain, has become a home for people from all parts of the world. And the United States has gone far toward fulfilling the promise made more than 200 years ago in the Declaration of Independence of equality for all.

Progress was not always smooth. At times, it was slowed or blocked by violence. There was still much room for improvement in the United States of the 1980's. But by then, more than ever before, Americans who differed in race, in gender, and in age were working side-by-side to defend their rights and interests through the American political system. That system had survived periods of astounding social and economic change. In spite of the fears of the nation's founders, the American Republic had lasted over 200 years, and continued to serve its people well.

▶**9.** How have Americans been able to make changes without revolutions?

Reviewing Section III

Identify Immigration and Nationality Act, boat people, La Raza Unida, José Angel Guttierrez, Hispanic, American Indian Movement, Wounded Knee, Equal Rights Amendment, Phyllis Schafly, Elizabeth Dole, Margaret Heckler, Jean Kirkpatrick, Alex Haley, Jesse Jackson, Rehabilitation Act, mainstreaming

Questions to Answer
1. How did the system of admitting immigrants to the United States change in 1965?
2. In what ways had black Americans won increased political power in the 1970's and early 1980's?

A Question to Think About As the number of elderly people in the United States grows, in what ways might the country change?

IMPROVE YOUR READING
Cause/Effect

One of the most important reading comprehension skills you have studied is understanding cause/effect relationships. In the future when you study history and read about current events, try to determine what caused an event to happen and what were the results or effects of the event.

To help you analyze and remember the causes and the effects of events, make notes on a "T-bar" diagram, such as the one shown below. The diagram looks like the letter "T." The major event is written on the first, horizontal line; its causes are written to the left of the vertical line; and its effects are written to the right of the vertical line.

Below the "T-bar" is a list of events discussed in this chapter. Make a "T-bar" for each event. You may also want to start your own cause/effect "T-bar" notebook for current events.

House Judiciary Committee Approves Impeaching Nixon (Event)	
Cause	*Effect*
The committee finds that Nixon obstructed justice, misused his power, and refused to honor court orders to release White House papers.	Nixon chooses to resign.

Events
1. Nixon asks Elliot Richardson to fire Archibald Cox.
2. The price of goods and services is dependent on imported oil use in the 1970's.
3. Camp David Accords is signed.
4. Carter allows the shah of Iran to enter the United States.
5. Reagan proposes tax cuts for corporations and private individuals.

CHAPTER 32 REVIEW

Vocabulary Check
Write a short definition for each of the following terms.

1. OPEC
2. Double-digit inflation
3. Reaganomics
4. Affirmative action plans
5. Mainstreaming

Fact Check
On a separate piece of paper, fill in the name, word, or words that best completes each of the following sentences.

1. Richard Nixon resigned as President because of the scandal that is called the ____.
2. The judge who heard the case of the men who burgled the Democratic National Headquarters was ____.
3. Nixon's first Vice President was ____.
4. ____ replaced Nixon as President.
5. ____ became President in 1976, after campaigning as a Washington outsider.
6. ____ of Israel and ____ of Egypt signed the Camp David Accords.
7. The Soviets invaded ____ in 1979, stalling any further SALT negotiations.
8. The leader of Iran when American embassy employees were held hostage was ____.
9. ____ was elected President in 1980 and reelected in 1984.
10. ____ was the first woman to run for Vice President.

Skills Check
Study the graph on page 718 and answer the following questions.

1. What is the subject of this graph?
2. What was the cost of a barrel of oil in 1970?
3. What was the cost of a barrel of oil in 1975?
4. In what year did the cost of oil make the greatest leap?
5. Write a one-sentence generalization based on this graph.

Time Check
On a separate sheet of paper, write these events in the order in which they occurred.

1. Elliot Richardson resigns and Nixon fires Archibald Cox.
2. Burglars are captured in Democratic National Headquarters in Washington, D.C.
3. The Supreme Court orders Nixon to release the White House tapes.
4. Nixon releases transcripts of the tapes of White House conversations.
5. John Dean completes a special investigation of possible White House involvement in the burglary.

Think and Write
1. What was the meaning of Watergate for the American people?
2. Why did many people oppose Ford's pardon of Nixon?
3. Why did the price of oil have such a dramatic effect on the American economy?
4. Describe Ronald Reagan's 1980 economic proposals.
5. (a) What was the ERA amendment? (b) Describe its ratification failure.

REVIEWING UNIT 10

Reviewing the Facts I.

On a separate sheet of paper, write the name of the President described in each of the sentences below. You will use some names more than once.

1. He proposed a package of legislation he called the Fair Deal.
2. This President called for a New Frontier.
3. He wanted to declare War on Poverty.
4. He was the only President to resign from office.
5. While he was President, Congress passed the Federal Highway Act.
6. He was the first President to visit the People's Republic of China.
7. He was the first President who had not been elected by the people.
8. During his administration, Americans were held hostage in Iran.
9. He appointed Sandra Day O'Connor to the Supreme Court.
10. Challengers to this President's reelection included Jesse Jackson, a black minister.

Reviewing the Facts II.

On a separate sheet of paper, fill in the word or words that best complete each of the following sentences.

1. Two inventions that greatly changed American life after World War II were _____ and _____.
2. The birth of so many children in the late 1940's and early 1950's is known as the _____.
3. In 1953, Congress approved a new Cabinet department, the _____, to administer the federal social programs.
4. In 1961, the East Germans sealed off East Berlin by building the _____.
5. LBJ urged Congress to pass the _____ which outlawed discrimination in all projects receiving federal funds and in public facilities.
6. LBJ used Congress's _____ to justify sending combat troops to Vietnam.
7. The _____ affair caused the resignation of Richard Nixon.
8. President Reagan sent United States marines to _____ to put down a Marxist government there.
9. In the case of _____, the Supreme Court ruled that universities could not reject qualified white applicants in order to accept a set number of minority applicants.
10. American Indians seized the town of _____ to publicize their demands for Indian rights.

Reviewing Ideas

1. How did American life change in the 1950's?
2. (a) Trace the involvement of the United States in the Vietnam War. (b) How did the war end?
3. How did the Watergate scandals and the Vietnam War change many Americans' attitudes toward their President?
4. Describe the advances made by the black civil rights movement from the 1950's to the present.
5. (a) What other groups of Americans started to work for increased opportunities in the 1960's, 1970's, and 1980's? (b) What progress have they made?

The Declaration of Independence

IN CONGRESS, JULY 4, 1776

The Unanimous Declaration of the Thirteen United States of America

When in the course of human events, it becomes necessary for one people to dissolve the political bands which have connected them with another, and to assume among the powers of the earth, the separate and equal station to which the laws of Nature and of Nature's God entitle them, a decent respect to the opinions of mankind requires that they should declare the causes which impel them to the separation.

We hold these truths to be self-evident, that all men are created equal, that they are endowed by their Creator with certain unalienable rights, that among these are life, liberty and the pursuit of happiness. That to secure these rights, governments are instituted among men, deriving their just powers from the consent of the governed,—That whenever any form of government becomes destructive of these ends, it is the right of the people to alter or to abolish it, and to institute new government, laying its foundation on such principles and organizing its powers in such form, as to them shall seem most likely to effect their safety and happiness. Prudence, indeed, will dictate that governments long established should not be changed for light and transient causes; and accordingly all experience hath shown, that mankind are more disposed to suffer, while evils are sufferable, than to right themselves by abolishing the forms to which they are accustomed. But when a long train of abuses and usurpations, pursuing invariably the same object evinces a design to reduce them under absolute despotism, it is their right, it is their duty, to throw off such government, and to provide new guards for their future security.—Such has been the patient sufferance of these Colonies; and such is now the necessity which constrains them to alter their former systems of government. The history of the present King of Great Britain is a history of repeated injuries and usurpations, all having in direct object the establishment of an absolute tyranny over these States: To prove this, let facts be submitted to a candid world.

He has refused his assent to laws, the most wholesome and necessary for the public good.

He has forbidden his Governors to pass laws of immediate and pressing importance, unless suspended in their operation till his assent should be obtained; and when so suspended, he has utterly neglected to attend to them.

He has refused to pass other laws for the accomodation of large districts of people, unless those people would relinquish the right of representation in the legislature, a right inestimable to them and formidable to tyrants only.

He has called together legislative bodies at places unusual, uncomfortable, and distant from the depository of their public records, for the sole purpose of fatiguing them into compliance with his measures.

He has dissolved Representative Houses repeatedly, for opposing with manly firmness his invasions on the rights of the people.

He has refused for a long time, after such dissolutions, to cause others to be elected; whereby the legislative powers, incapable of annihilation, have returned to the people at large for their exercise; the State remaining in the mean time exposed to all the dangers of invasion from without, and convulsions within.

He has endeavoured to prevent the population of these States; for that purpose obstructing the laws for naturalization of foreigners; refusing to pass others to encourage their migrations hither, and raising the conditions of new appropriations of lands.

He has obstructed the administration of justice, by refusing his assent to laws for establishing judiciary powers.

He has made judges dependent on his will alone, for the tenure of their offices, and the amount and payment of their salaries.

He has erected a multitude of new offices, and sent hither swarms of officers to harass our people, and eat out their substance.

He has kept among us, in times of peace, standing armies without the consent of our legislatures.

He has affected to render the military independent of and superior to the civil power.

He has combined with others to subject us to a jurisdiction foreign to our constitution, and unacknowledged by our laws; giving his assent to their acts of pretended legislation:

For quartering large bodies of armed troops among us:

For protecting them, by a mock trial, from punishment for any murders which they should commit on the inhabitants of these States:

For cutting off our trade with all parts of the world:

For imposing taxes on us without our consent:

For depriving us in many cases, of the benefits of trial by jury:

For transporting us beyond seas to be tried for pretended offenses:

For abolishing the free system of English laws in a neighbouring province, establishing therein an arbitrary government, and enlarging its boundaries so as to render it at once an example and fit instrument for introducing the same absolute rule into these colonies:

For taking away our charters, abolishing our most valuable laws, and altering fundamentally the forms of our governments:

For suspending our own legislatures, and declaring themselves invested with power to legislate for us in all cases whatsoever.

He has abdicated government here, by declaring us out of his protection and waging war against us.

He has plundered our seas, ravaged our coasts, burnt our towns, and destroyed the lives of our people.

He is at this time transporting large armies of foreign mercenaries to complete the works of death, desolation and tyranny, already begun with circumstances of cruelty and perfidy scarcely paralleled in the most barbarous ages, and totally unworthy the head of a civilized nation.

He has constrained our fellow citizens taken captive on the high seas to bear arms against their country, to become the executioners of their friends and brethren, or to fall themselves by their hands.

He has excited domestic insurrections amongst us, and has endeavoured to bring on the inhabitants of our frontiers, the merciless Indian savages, whose known rule of warfare is an undistinguished destruction of all ages, sexes and conditions.

In every stage of these oppressions we have petitioned for redress in the most humble terms: Our repeated petitions have been answered only by repeated injury. A prince, whose character is thus marked by every act which may define a tyrant, is unfit to be the ruler of a free people.

Nor have we been wanting in attentions to our British brethren. We have warned them from time to time of attempts by their legislature to extend an unwarrantable jurisdiction over us. We have reminded them of the circumstances of our emigration and settlement here. We have appealed to their native justice and magnanimity, and we have conjured them by the ties of our common kindred to disavow these usurpations, which, would inevitably interrupt our connections and correspondence. They too have been deaf to the voice of justice and of consanguinity. We must, therefore, acquiesce in the necessity which denounces our separation, and hold them, as we hold the rest of mankind, enemies in war, in peace friends.

WE, THEREFORE, the Representatives of the United States of America, in General Congress, Assembled, appealing to the Supreme Judge of the world for the rectitude of our intentions, do, in the name, and by authority of the good people of these Colonies, solemnly publish and declare, That these United Colonies are, and of right ought to be FREE AND INDEPENDENT STATES; that they are absolved from all allegiance to the British Crown, and that all political connection between them and the State of Great Britain, is and ought to be totally dissolved; and that as free and independent States, they have full power to levy war, conclude peace, contract alliances, establish commerce, and to do all other acts and things which independent States may of right do. And for the support of this Declaration, with a firm reliance on the protection of Divine Providence, we mutually pledge to each other our lives, our fortunes and our sacred honor.

John Hancock.

Button Gwinnett
Lyman Hall
Geo Walton.
Wm. Hooper
Joseph Hewes,
John Penn
Edward Rutledge.
Thos. Heyward Junr.
Thomas Lynch Junr.
Arthur Middleton
Samuel Chase
Wm. Paca
Thos. Stone
Charles Carroll of Carrollton
George Wythe
Richard Henry Lee
Th: Jefferson
Benja. Harrison
Thos. Nelson jr.
Francis Lightfoot Lee
Carter Braxton
Robt. Morris
John Adams
Robt. Treat Paine
Elbridge Gerry
Step. Hopkins
William Ellery
Benjamin Rush

Benja. Franklin
John Morton
Geo Clymer
Jas. Smith.
Geo. Taylor
James Wilson
Geo. Ross
Caesar Rodney
Geo Read
Tho M:Kean
Wm. Floyd
Phil. Livingston
Frans. Lewis
Lewis Morris
Richd. Stockton
Jno Witherspoon
Fras. Hopkinson
John Hart
Abra Clark
Josiah Bartlett
Wm: Whipple
Saml. Adams
Roger Sherman
Saml. Huntington
Wm. Williams
Oliver Wolcott
Matthew Thornton

Constitution of the
United States of America

The Constitution is printed below in black. The parts of the Constitution that are no longer in effect are printed in *italic* type. These parts have been changed by amendments, or additions, to the Constitution. To help in studying the Constitution, headings and explanations have been added. These are printed in color.

PREAMBLE

WE THE PEOPLE of the United States, in order to form a more perfect Union, establish justice, insure domestic tranquility, provide for the common defense, promote the general welfare, and secure the blessings of liberty to ourselves and our posterity, do ordain and establish this Constitution for the United States of America.

We, the citizens of the United States, adopt this Constitution in order to bind the states together more closely than they were under the Articles of Confederation; see that everyone receives fair treatment from the nation's laws and in the nation's courts; keep peace within the country; defend the nation against foreign enemies; work for the good of all the people; and ensure the freedom of not only our generation of Americans but also generations to come.

ARTICLE I • THE LEGISLATIVE BRANCH

The Power to Make Laws

SECTION 1. All legislative powers herein granted shall be vested in a Congress of the United States, which shall consist of a Senate and House of Representatives.

The Senate and the House of Representatives, working together as the Congress of the United States, make all national laws permitted by the Constitution.

How Representatives Are Elected

SECTION 2. The House of Representatives shall be composed of members chosen every second year by the people of the several States, and the electors in each State shall have the qualifications requisite for electors of the most numerous branch of the State Legislature.

Members of the House of Representatives are elected every two years. If a state allows a citizen to vote for members of the state legislature, it must also allow that citizen to vote for a representative to the House of Representatives.

Who May Be a Representative

No person shall be a representative who shall not have attained to the age of twenty-five years, and been seven years a citizen of the United States, and who shall not, when elected, be an inhabitant of that State in which he shall be chosen.

A representative must be at least 25 years of age, a United States citizen for seven years, and live in the state he or she represents.

Representation Is Based on Population

Representatives *and direct taxes* shall be apportioned among the several States which may be included within this Union, according to their respective numbers, *which shall be determined by adding to the whole number of free persons, including those bound to service for a term of years, and excluding Indians not taxed, three-fifths of all other persons.* The actual enumeration shall be made within three years after the first meeting of the Congress of the United States, and within every subsequent term of ten years, in such manner as they shall by law direct. The number of representatives shall not exceed one for every thirty thousand, but each State shall have at least one representative; and until such enumeration shall be made, the State of New Hampshire shall be entitled to choose three, Massachusetts eight, Rhode Island and Providence Plantations one, Connecticut five, New York six, New Jersey four, Pennsylvania eight, Delaware one, Maryland six, Virginia ten, North Carolina five, South Carolina five, and Georgia three.

The number of representatives that each state is entitled to is based on its population. A state with many people will have more representatives than one with a small population. At the time the Constitution was written, all taxes collected by state governments and paid directly to the national government were also based on the state's population. The 16th Amendment changed this rule as far as income tax is concerned. The method of counting a state's population has also changed. Today the entire population of each state is counted. Slavery is against the law (13th Amendment). So slaves are no longer counted as three fifths of a person.

Congress must count the population of the states every ten years. The first census was to take place within three years after the first meeting of Congress. The House of Representatives was to have no more than one representative for every 30,000 people in the nation, but every state was entitled to at least one representative. If there were still one representative for every 30,000 people, the House of Representatives would have over 7,000 members. To keep this from happening, Congress decided in 1929 that the House would have no more than 435 members. How many of those representatives each state has is based on its population. Every state, no matter how few people it has, is still entitled to one representative.

Filling Vacancies

When vacancies happen in the representation from any State, the Executive authority thereof shall issue writs of election to fill such vacancies.

If a representative dies or resigns before his or her term is completed, the state's governor must call for a special election to replace that representative.

Selection of Officers; Impeachment

The House of Representatives shall choose their Speaker and other officers; and shall have the sole power of impeachment.

The House of Representatives elects its own officers, including a Speaker, or chairperson. Only the House of Representatives has the right to impeach or formally accuse an official of the United States of serious misbehavior. The official is then tried by the Senate and, if found guilty, removed from office.

How Senators Are Elected

SECTION 3. The Senate of the United States shall be composed of two senators from each State, *chosen by the legislature thereof,* for six years and each senator shall have one vote.

Each state has two senators. Each senator serves a six-year term and has one vote. Before the 17th Amendment was passed, state legislatures chose all senators. Since then, senators have been elected by the voters of the state.

Continuity in the State

Immediately after they shall be assembled in consequence of the first election, they shall be divided as equally as may be into three classes. The seats of the senators of the first class shall be vacated at the expiration of the second year, of the second class at the expiration of the fourth year, and of the third class at the expiration of the sixth year, so that one-third may be chosen every second year; and if vacancies happen by resignation, or otherwise, during the recess of the legislature of any State, the executive thereof may make temporary appointments until the next meeting of the legislature, which shall then fill such vacancies.

This part of the Constitution is designed to avoid a complete turnover in the Senate every six years. During the first four years under the Constitution, senators were divided into three groups. One group served for six years, a second group for four years, and the other for two years. As a result, no more than one-third of the Senate is up for election at any one time.

Who May Be Senator

No person shall be a senator who shall not have attained to the age of thirty years, and been nine years a citizen of the United States, and who shall not, when elected, be an inhabitant of that State for which he shall be chosen.

A senator must be at least 30 years of age, a United States citizen for nine years, and live in the state he or she represents.

Officers of the Senate

The Vice President of the United States shall be President of the Senate, but shall have no vote, unless they be equally divided.

The Senate shall choose their other officers, and also a President pro tempore, in the absence of the Vice President, or when he shall exercise the office of President of the United States.

The Vice President of the United States is President, or chairperson, of the Senate. The Vice President, however, can vote only to break a tie.

The Senate chooses all of its other officers, including someone to act as President pro tempore—president for the time being. That person acts as chairperson in the absence of the Vice President.

Impeachments

The Senate shall have the sole power to try all impeachments. When sitting for that purpose, they shall be on oath or affirmation. When the President of the United States is tried, the Chief Justice shall preside: And no person shall be convicted without the concurrence of two thirds of the members present.

Judgment in cases of impeachment shall not extend further than to removal from office, and disqualification to hold and enjoy any office or honor, trust or profit under the United States: but the party convicted shall nevertheless be liable and subject to indictment, trial, judgment and punishment, according to law.

Only the Senate has the power to try officials after the House of Representatives has impeached them. In an impeachment, the official on trial is found guilty only if at least two-thirds of the senators present vote guilty. Ordinarily the President of the Senate—the Vice President of the United States—presides at impeachment trials. But when the President of the United States is on trial, the Chief Justice of the United States presides.

If the Senate finds an official guilty, it can punish that official with the loss of his or her position and of the right to hold any other office in the national government. After being put out of office, the official can be tried in a regular court for the crimes that led to removal from office.

Elections and Meetings of Congress

SECTION 4. The times, places and manner of holding elections for senators and representatives, shall be prescribed in each State by the legislature thereof; but the Congress may at any time by law make or alter such regulations, *except as to the places of choosing senators.*

The Congress shall assemble at least once in every year, *and such meeting shall be on the first Monday in December, unless they shall by law appoint a different day.*

The states may make rules about elections to Congress. But Congress may change state election laws. As a result of the 17th Amendment, both senators and representatives are chosen by the same methods.

Congress must meet at least once each year. The 20th Amendment changed the beginning of each session from the first Monday in December to January 3.

Rules of Congress

SECTION 5. Each house shall be the judge of the elections, returns and qualifications of its own members, and a majority of each shall constitute a quorum to do business; but a smaller number may adjourn from day to day, and may be authorized to compel the attendance of absent members, in such manner, and under such penalties as each house may provide.

Each house may determine the rules of its proceedings, punish its members for disorderly behaviour, and, with the concurrence of two-thirds, expel a member.

Each house shall keep a journal of its proceedings, and from time to time publish the same, excepting such parts as may in their judgment require secrecy; and the yeas and the nays of the members of either house on any question shall, at the desire of one-fifth of those present, be entered on the journal.

Neither house, during the session of Congress, shall, without the consent of the other, adjourn for more than three days, nor to any other place than that in which the two houses shall be sitting.

Both the House of Representatives and the Senate can set requirements for membership. Each can keep out any newly elected member who does not meet those requirements.

Neither the House nor the Senate can carry out official business unless there is a quorum—that is, unless more than half the members are present. If there is no quorum, members adjourn until the next day. Both houses may use penalties to force absent members to attend.

Each house of Congress may make its own rules for conducting business. Each may punish members for not obeying those rules. In both houses, two-thirds of those present must agree before a member can be expelled.

Each house must keep a record of what goes on at its meetings, and from time to time those records must be published. But members may decide to keep some things secret. How members vote on a question is published only if one-fifth of those present agree to do so.

Neither house may adjourn for more than three days or move to another city unless the other house agrees.

Privileges of and Restrictions on Members of Congress

SECTION 6. The senators and representatives shall receive a compensation for their services, to be ascertained by law, and paid out of the Treasury of the United States. They shall in all cases, except treason, felony and breach of the peace, be privileged from arrest during their attendance at the session of their respective houses, and in going to and returning from the same; and for any speech or debate in either house, they shall not be questioned in any other place.

No senator or representative shall, during the time for which he was elected, be appointed to any civil office under the authority of the United States, which shall have been created, or the emoluments whereof shall have been increased during such time; and no person holding any office under the United States, shall be a member of either house during his continuance in office.

Members of both houses are paid out of the United States Treasury. The amount they are paid is determined by law. Members cannot be arrested at meetings of Congress or on their way to and from such meetings unless they are suspected of treason, serious crimes, or disturbing the peace. They cannot be held responsible for anything they say in their meetings except by other members of their house.

No one can become a member of Congress without giving up other national positions. During his or her term in office, no member can take a position in the national government if that position was created or the pay for that position was increased while the member served in Congress.

Tax Bills

SECTION 7. All bills for raising revenue shall originate in the House of Representatives; but the Senate may propose or concur with amendments as on other bills.

Only the House of Representatives may propose a bill for raising money. But the Senate has the right to make changes in such bills.

How a Bill Becomes a Law

Every bill which shall have passed the House of Representatives and the Senate, shall, before it become a law, be presented to the President of the United States; if he approves he shall sign it, but if not he shall return it, with his objections to that house in which it shall have originated, who shall enter the objections at large on their journal, and proceed to reconsider it. If after such reconsideration two thirds of that House shall agree to pass the bill, it shall be sent, together with the objections, to the other House, by which it shall likewise be reconsidered, and if approved by two thirds of that House, it shall become a law. But in all such cases the votes of both Houses shall be determined by yeas and nays, and the names of the persons voting for and against the bill shall be entered on the journal of each House respectively. If any bill shall not be returned by the President within ten days (Sundays excepted) after it shall have been presented to him, the same shall be a law, in like manner as if he had signed it, unless the Congress by their adjournment prevent its return, in which case it shall not be a law.

After a bill has passed both houses of Congress, it must be sent to the President. If the President signs the bill, it becomes law. If the President does not approve of the bill, he or she may veto it—that is, refuse to sign it. The President then sends the bill with a list of reasons for not approving it to the house that passed it first. The members of that house vote on the bill again. If two-thirds pass it a second time, it is sent to the other house along with the President's reasons for not wanting it to be law. If two-thirds of that house also favor the bill, it becomes law. The President's reasons for not wanting the law must be published. The records of Congress must also show how each member voted.

The President has ten days (not counting Sundays) to consider a bill. If the President takes longer, it becomes law without his or her signature as long as Congress has not adjourned in the meantime. If Congress has adjourned, the unsigned bill does not become law. This is known as the "pocket veto."

Actions Requiring the President's Approval

Every order, resolution, or vote to which the concurrence of the Senate and House of Representatives may be necessary (except on a question of adjournment) shall be presented to the President of the United States; and before the same shall take effect, shall be approved by him, or being disapproved by him, shall be repassed by two thirds of the Senate and House of Representatives, according to the rules and limitations prescribed in the case of a bill.

Any action that requires the approval of both the House and the Senate must also be sent to the President for approval just as bills are. The only exceptions are votes to adjourn Congress.

Powers of Congress

SECTION 8. The Congress shall have power to lay and collect taxes, duties, imposts and excises, to pay the debts and provide for the common defense and general welfare of the United States; but all duties, imposts and excises shall be uniform throughout the United States;

Congress may collect taxes in order to pay the nation's debts, defend the nation, and provide for the good of all the people. Those taxes must be the same throughout the United States.

To borrow money on the credit of the United States;

Congress may borrow money for the use of the national government.

To regulate commerce with foreign nations, and among the several States, and with the Indian tribes;

Congress may control trade, transportation, communication, and related matters with other countries, among the states, and with Indian groups.

To establish a uniform rule of naturalization, and uniform laws on the subject of bankruptcies throughout the United States;

Congress may decide how citizens of foreign countries can become citizens of the United States. Congress may make laws for the whole country concerning the treatment of those who cannot pay their debts.

To coin money, regulate the value thereof, and of foreign coin, and fix the standard of weights and measures;

Congress may coin money and say how much it is worth. It may also put a value on foreign money. Congress also has the power to define weights and measures so they will be the same everywhere.

To provide for the punishment of counterfeiting the securities and current coin of the United States;

Congress may pass laws to punish those who make false bonds, stamps, or money.

To establish post offices and post roads;

Congress may set up post offices and build the roads over which the mail travels.

To promote the progress of science and useful arts, by securing for limited times to authors and inventors the exclusive right to their respective writings and discoveries;

Congress may help science, industry, and the arts by making laws that protect the works of authors, composers, artists, and inventors from those who would copy their works without permission.

To constitute tribunals inferior to the Supreme Court;

Congress may establish national courts that have less authority than the Supreme Court of the United States.

To define and punish piracies and felonies committed on the high seas, and offenses against the law of nations;

Congress may decide what acts committed at sea are a crime and how they are to be punished. It may also make laws about crimes in which foreign countries and foreign citizens are involved.

To declare war, grant letters of marque and reprisal, and make rules concerning captures on land and water;

Congress, and only Congress, may declare war. Until 1856, it could also set rules about warfare carried on by private citizens. Such warfare is no longer allowed.

To raise and support armies, but no appropriation of money to that use shall be for a longer term than two years;

To provide and maintain a Navy;

To make rules for the government and regulation of the land and naval forces;

Congress may raise and support armed forces. It cannot, however, provide money for the army for more than two years at a time. Congress may also make rules for the organization and control of the armed forces.

To provide for calling forth the militia to execute the laws of the Union, suppress insurrections and repel invasions;

To provide for organizing, arming, and disciplining the militia, and for governing such part of them as may be employed in the service of the United States, reserving to the States respectively, the appointment of the officers, and the authority of training the militia according to the discipline prescribed by Congress;

Congress may call out militias—citizen-soldiers of the various states—to enforce national laws, put down rebellions, and drive out invaders. Congress may organize the militias, furnish weapons to them, and make rules for them while they are in the service of the United States. Each state may appoint officers of its militia, but it must train the militia as Congress directs.

To exercise exclusive legislation in all cases whatsoever, over such district (not exceeding ten miles square) as may, by cession of particular States, and the acceptance of Congress, become the seat of the Government of the United States, and to exercise like authority over all places purchased by the consent of the legislature of the State in which the same shall be, for the erection of forts, magazines, arsenals, dock-yards, and other needful buildings;—And

Congress may make all the laws for governing the District of Columbia, which includes the national capital. Congress shall govern all places bought from the states for use as forts, arsenals, navy yards, and public buildings.

To make all laws which shall be necessary and proper for carrying into execution the foregoing powers, and all other powers vested by this Constitution in the Government of the United States, or in any department or officer thereof.

Congress may make any laws needed to carry out the powers given to the government of the United States by the Constitution. This part of the Constitution is known as the "elastic clause," because it can be stretched to fit the changing needs of the nation.

Powers Denied Congress

SECTION 9. The migration or importation of such persons as any of the States now existing shall think proper to admit, shall not be prohibited by the Congress prior to the year one thousand eight hundred and eight, but a tax or duty may be imposed on such importation, not exceeding ten dollars for each person.

Before 1808, Congress could not outlaw the slave trade. But it could tax the importer of each slave brought into the country. The tax could not be more than ten dollars for each slave.

The privilege of the writ of habeas corpus shall not be suspended, unless when in cases of rebellion or invasion the public safety may require it.

No bill of attainder or ex post facto law shall be passed.

Only when the country is in danger from a rebellion or invasion can Congress keep courts from issuing writs of habeas corpus. A writ of habeas corpus forces a jailor to bring a prisoner to court so that a judge can decide whether that person is being held lawfully.

Congress can never pass a law punishing a particular person. Nor can it pass a law punishing people for doing something that was lawful at the time they did it.

No capitation, or other direct, tax shall be laid, unless in proportion to the census or enumeration herein before directed to be taken.

Congress cannot pass any direct tax except in proportion to population as determined by the census. The only exception is the income tax. See the 16th Amendment.

No tax or duty shall be laid on articles exported from any State.

Congress may not tax goods sent from one state to another.

No preference shall be given by any regulation of commerce or revenue to the ports of one State over those of another: nor shall vessels bound to, or from, one State, be obliged to enter, clear, or pay duties in another.

Congress may not favor one state or city over the others in matters of trade. Ships from any state may enter the ports of any other state without paying charges.

No money shall be drawn from the Treasury; but in consequence of appropriations made by law; and a regular statement and account of the receipts and expenditures of all public money shall be published from time to time.

Congress cannot spend government money without passing a bill for that purpose. An account of all money taken in and spent must be made public.

No title of nobility shall be granted by the United States: And no person holding any office of profit or trust under them, shall, without the consent of the Congress, accept of any present, emolument, office, or title, of any kind whatever, from any King, Prince, or foreign State.

Congress may not create titles like that of lord, duchess, or count. No national official can accept a title, gift, or position from another country without permission of Congress.

Powers Denied the States

SECTION 10. No State shall enter into any treaty, alliance, or confederation; grant letters of marque and reprisal; coin money; emit bills of credit; make any thing but gold and silver coin a tender in payment of debts; pass any bill of attainder, ex post facto law, or law impairing the obligation of contracts, or grant any title of nobility.

No state can make treaties with foreign countries. No state can give private citizens permission to wage a war or can coin money. These powers belong to the national government. Like the national government, state governments may not pass laws that punish people without a trial, that punish people for things that were not against the law when they did them, or that grant titles of nobility.

No State shall, without the consent of the Congress, lay any imposts or duties on imports or exports, except what may be absolutely necessary for executing its inspection laws: and the net produce of all duties and imposts, laid by any State on imports or exports, shall be for the use of the Treasury of the United States; and all such laws shall be subject to the revision and control of the Congress.

States cannot tax goods entering or leaving the state without Congress's permission. But states may charge an inspection fee. Any profit from that fee must go to the United States Treasury. Congress has the power to change state inspection laws.

No State shall, without the consent of Congress, lay any duty of tonnage, keep troops, or ships of war in time of peace, enter into any agreement or compact with another State, or with a foreign power, or engage in war, unless actually invaded, or in such imminent danger as will not admit of delay.

Unless Congress gives permission, no state may tax ships, keep troops other than a militia, or keep warships in peacetime. States cannot ally with other states or with foreign countries unless Congress agrees. States cannot go to war without the permission of Congress unless invaded or in such danger that delay is impossible.

ARTICLE II ● THE EXECUTIVE BRANCH

Terms of the President and Vice President

SECTION 1. The executive power shall be vested in a President of the United States of America. He shall hold his office during the term of four years, and, together with the Vice President, chosen for the same term, be elected, as follows:

The President of the United States enforces the nation's laws. The President serves a four-year term. The Vice President also serves for four years.

The Selection of Electors

Each State, shall appoint, in such manner as the legislature thereof may direct, a number of electors, equal to the whole number of senators and representatives to which the State may be entitled in the Congress; but no senator or representative, or person holding an office of trust or profit under the United States, shall be appointed an elector.

The President and Vice President are to be chosen by electors in each state. These electors are selected according to rules set by state legislatures.

The electors from all the states form the electoral college. The number of electors in each state is equal to the number of representatives and senators the state has in Congress. No person who has a position in the national government may be an elector.

Duties of the Electors

The electors shall meet in their respective States, and vote by ballot for two persons, of whom one at least shall not be an inhabitant of the same State with themselves. And they shall make a list of all the persons voted for, and of the number of votes for each; which list they shall sign and certify, and transmit sealed to the seat of the Government of the United States, directed to the President of the Senate. The President of the Senate shall, in the presence of the Senate and House of Representatives, open all the certificates, and the votes shall then be counted. The person having the greatest number of votes shall be the President, if such number be a majority of the whole number of electors appointed; and if there be more than one who have such majority, and have an equal number of votes, then the House of Representatives shall immediately choose by ballot one of them for President; and if no person have a majority, then from the five highest on the list the said House shall in like manner choose the President. But in choosing the President, the votes shall be taken by States, the representation from each State having one vote; a quorum for this purpose shall consist of a member or members from two thirds of the States, and a majority of all the States shall be necessary to a choice. In every case, after the choice of the President, the person having the greatest number of votes of the electors shall be the Vice President. But if there should remain two or more who have equal votes, the Senate shall choose from them by ballot the Vice President.

The electors, meeting in their respective states, vote for President and Vice President on one ballot. Their votes are recorded and then sent to the President of the Senate, who counts them before both houses of Congress. The candidate with the highest number of electoral votes becomes President, and the one with the second highest total becomes Vice President. If there is a tie, or no candidate has a majority, the House of Representatives shall choose the President from the five candidates with the highest totals. In the balloting, each state has one vote. At least two-thirds of the states must be present. The candidate who wins a majority of all states becomes President. The person who comes in second will be the Vice President. This section of the Constitution was changed by the 12th Amendment. See that amendment for the way the President and Vice President are chosen today.

Election Day

The Congress may determine the time of choosing the electors, and the day on which they shall give their votes; which day shall be the same throughout the United States.

Congress can decide on what day electors are to be chosen and on what day they are to cast their ballots. Each day is to be the same throughout the United States. (The day set for choosing electors is the first Tuesday after the first Monday in November. The electors cast their ballots on the first Monday after the second Wednesday in December.)

Qualifications for President

No person except a natural born citizen, or a citizen of the United States, at the time of the adoption of this Constitution, shall be eligible to the office of President; neither shall any person be eligible to that office who shall not have attained to the age of thirty-five years, and been fourteen years a resident within the United States.

A President must be a citizen of the United States by birth or have been a citizen at the time the Constitution was adopted, be at least 35 years old, and have lived in the United States for 14 or more years.

Succession to the Presidency

In case of the removal of the President from office, or of his death, resignation, or inability to discharge the powers and duties of the said office, the same shall devolve on the Vice President, *and the Congress may by law provide for the case of removal, death, resignation, or inability, both of the President and Vice President, declaring what officer shall then act as President, and such officer shall act accordingly, until the disability be removed, or a President shall be elected.*

If the President dies, resigns, or is unable to carry out the duties of the office, the Vice President becomes President. Congress can decide by law who becomes President when neither the President nor the Vice President can serve. This part of the Constitution was changed by the 25th Amendment.

The President's Salary

The President shall, at stated times, receive for his services, a compensation, which shall neither be increased nor diminished during the period for which he shall have been elected, and he shall not receive within that period any other emolument from the United States, or any of them.

The salary of a President cannot be raised or lowered during his or her term of office. The President cannot receive any other salary from national or state governments.

The President's Oath of Office

Before he enter on the execution of his office, he shall take the following oath or affirmation:— "I do solemnly swear (or affirm) that I will faithfully execute the office of President of the United States, and will to the best of my ability, preserve, protect and defend the Constitution of the United States."

Before starting a term of office, the President is to make a solemn promise to faithfully carry out the duties of President and protect the government set up by the Constitution.

Military and Civil Powers

SECTION 2. The President shall be Commander in Chief of the Army and Navy of the United States, and of the militia of the several States, when called into the actual service of the United States; he may require the opinion, in writing, of the principal officer in each of the Executive Departments, upon any subject relating to the duties of their respective offices, and he shall have power to grant reprieves and pardons for offenses against the United States, except in cases of impeachment.

The President is Commander in Chief of the armed forces of the United States and of the state militias when they are called to national service. The President may order written reports from Cabinet officers about the work of their departments. The President may pardon people accused of crimes against the national government or delay their punishment. The President cannot, however, pardon or delay the punishment of an impeached government official.

Making Treaties and Appointing Officers

He shall have power, by and with the advice and consent of the Senate, to make treaties, provided two thirds of the Senators present concur; and he shall nominate, and by and with the advice and consent of the Senate, shall appoint ambassadors, other public ministers and consuls, Judges of the Supreme Court, and all other officers of the United States, whose appointments are not herein otherwise provided for, and which shall be established by law: but the Congress may by law vest the appointment of such inferior officers, as they think proper, in the President alone, in the courts of law, or in the heads of departments.

The President shall have power to fill up all vacancies that may happen during the recess of the Senate, by granting commissions which shall expire at the end of their next session.

The President can make treaties with foreign countries. At least two-thirds of the Senators present must approve each treaty before it becomes binding. The President can appoint people to represent the United States in other countries, judges of the Supreme Court, and other government officials unless the Constitution says differently. In each case, a majority of the Senate must approve the President's choice. Congress may pass laws giving the President, the courts, or heads of government departments the right to select people for less important government positions. The President may appoint individuals to fill vacancies that occur when the Senate is not meeting. These temporary appointments come to an end at the close of the next session of the Senate.

Other Presidential Powers

SECTION 3. He shall from time to time give to the Congress information of the state of the Union, and recommend to their consideration such measures as he shall judge necessary and expedient; he may, on extraordinary occasions, convene both houses, or either of them, and in case of disagreement between them, with respect to the time of adjournment, he may adjourn them to such time as he shall think proper; he shall receive ambassadors and other public ministers; he shall take care that the laws be faithfully executed, and shall commission all the officers of the United States.

The President is to inform Congress from time to time about the condition of the country. Traditionally the President does so at the beginning of each session of Congress. The speech is called the State of the Union message. In it the President recommends changes or improvements in government.

In emergencies the President may call meetings of the House of Representatives or the Senate or both. If the two houses of Congress disagree about the ending of a session, the President may end it. The President deals with representatives of other countries. It is the President's duty to see that the laws of the country are obeyed. The President signs official papers appointing individuals to jobs in the national government.

Impeachments

SECTION 4. The President, Vice President and all civil officers of the United States, shall be removed from office on impeachment for, and conviction of, treason, bribery, or other high crimes and misdemeanors.

The President, Vice President, and other officials of the national government (except members of Congress and military officers) can be removed from office after being accused of wrongdoing by the House of Representatives and found guilty by the Senate.

ARTICLE III ● THE JUDICIAL BRANCH

Judicial Power

SECTION 1. The judicial power of the United States, shall be vested in one Supreme Court, and in such inferior courts as the Congress may from time to time ordain and establish. The judges, both of the supreme and inferior courts, shall hold their offices during good behaviour, and shall, at stated times, receive for their services, a compensation, which shall not be diminished during their continuance in office.

The Supreme Court of the United States is the final authority in matters of law. Congress may set up other national courts with less power than the Supreme Court. Judges of all national courts hold office for life or until they are proved guilty of wrongful acts. They are to be paid a salary that cannot be lowered while they are in office.

Cases Heard in United States Courts

SECTION 2. The judicial power shall extend to all cases, in law and equity, arising under this Constitution, the laws of the United States, and treaties made, or which shall be made, under their authority;—to all cases affecting ambassadors, other public ministers and consuls;—to all cases of admiralty and maritime jurisdiction;—to controversies to which the United States shall be a party;—to controversies between two or more States;—*between a State and citizens of another State;*—between citizens of different States,—between citizens of the same State claiming lands under grants of different States, and between a State, or the citizens thereof, and foreign States, citizens or subjects.

The national courts settle disputes that have to do with the Constitution, laws of the United States, treaties, and laws about ships and shipping. These courts also settle disputes between people of different states, disputes in which people of the same state claim land in other states, and disputes between a state or citizen of a state and a foreign country. Until the 11th Amendment was passed, the national courts also settled disputes between a state and a citizen of another state.

Jurisdiction of the Courts

In all cases affecting ambassadors, other public ministers and consuls, and those in which a State shall be a party, the Supreme Court shall have original jurisdiction. In all the other cases before mentioned, the Supreme Court shall have appellate jurisdiction, both as to law and fact, with such exceptions, and under such regulations as the Congress shall make.

If a representative of a foreign country or a state is involved in a dispute, the trial may go directly to the Supreme Court. All other disputes described above are tried in a lower national court first. These cases are brought to the Supreme Court only if one of the parties in the case objects to the decision of the lower court and appeals to the Supreme Court. After a case has been tried before the Supreme Court, there is no higher court to which either side in a dispute may appeal.

Trial by Jury for Criminal Cases

The trial of all crimes, except in cases of impeachment, shall be by jury; and such trial shall be held in the State where the said crimes shall have been committed; but when not committed within any State, the trial shall be at such place or places as the Congress may by law have directed.

Except for an impeached official, anyone accused of a crime by the national government has a right to a trial by jury. The trial must be held in the state where the crime was committed. If the crime took place outside of any state—at sea, for example—the trial is to be held in a place Congress has chosen by law.

Treason

SECTION 3. Treason against the United States, shall consist only in levying war against them, or in adhering to their enemies, giving them aid and comfort. No person shall be convicted of treason unless on the testimony of two witnesses to the same overt act, or on confession in open court.

The Congress shall have power to declare the punishment of treason, but no attainder of treason shall work corruption of blood, or forfeiture except during the life of the person attainted.

Treason is carrying on war against the United States or helping the enemies of the United States. No one can be punished for treason unless two or more witnesses swear they saw the same act of treason or unless the accused confesses in court.

Congress can pass laws fixing the punishment for treason. However, the family of a person found guilty of treason cannot be punished in any way.

ARTICLE IV ● THE STATES AND THE NATION

Official Acts of the States

SECTION 1. Full faith and credit shall be given in each State to the public acts, records, and judicial proceedings of every other State. And the Congress may by general laws prescribe the manner in which such acts, records and proceedings shall be proved, and the effect thereof.

Congress can force each state to respect the laws, records, and court decisions of all other states.

Rights of Citizens of Other States

SECTION 2. The citizens of each State shall be entitled to all privileges and immunities of citizens in the several States.

A person charged in any State with treason, felony, or other crime, who shall flee from justice, and be found in another State, shall on demand of the executive authority of the State from which he fled, be delivered up, to be removed to the State having jurisdiction of the crime.

No person held to service or labour in one State, under the laws thereof, escaping into another, shall, in consequence of any law or regulation therein, be discharged from such service or labour, but shall be delivered up on claim of the party to whom such service or labour may be due.

Citizens of one state who move to or do business in another state have the same rights as citizens who live in that state.

A person accused of a crime in one state and found in another is to be returned for trial to the state in which the crime was committed. The request for the accused's return must come from the governor of that state.

Slaves do not become free by escaping to a state that does not allow slavery. Instead they must be returned to their owners. As a result of the 13th Amendment, this part of the Constitution is no longer in effect.

New States

SECTION 3. New States may be admitted by the Congress into this Union; but no new State shall be formed or erected within the jurisdiction of any other State; nor any State be formed by the junction of two or more States, or parts of States, without the consent of the legislatures of the States concerned as well as of the Congress.

The Congress shall have power to dispose of and make all needful rules and regulations respecting the Territory or other property belonging to the United States; and nothing in this Constitution shall be so construed as to prejudice any claims of the United States, or of any particular State.

Congress has the right to add new states to the United States. No state can be divided to make a new state without the consent of Congress and the original state. No new state can be formed from parts of two or more states without the agreement of the legislatures of all the states involved and of Congress.

Congress has the power to make rules about all government lands and property. Congress also may set up a government for any territory before it becomes a state.

Protecting the States

SECTION 4. The United States shall guarantee to every State in this Union a republican form of Government, and shall protect each of them against invasion; and on application of the legislature, or of the executive (when the legislature cannot be convened) against domestic violence.

It is the duty of the national government to see that every state has a government in which the people rule and that each state is protected against invasion. If a state asks the national government for help in putting down a riot or other disturbance, the United States must provide that help.

ARTICLE V ● AMENDING THE CONSTITUTION

The Congress, whenever two thirds of both Houses shall deem it necessary, shall propose amendments to this Constitution, or on the application of the legislatures of two thirds of the several States, shall call a convention for proposing amendments, which, in either case, shall be valid to all intents and purposes, as part of this Constitution, when ratified by the legislatures of three fourths of the several States, or by conventions in three fourths thereof, as the one or the other mode of ratification may be proposed by the Congress; provided that no amendment which may be made prior to the year one thousand eight hundred and eight shall in any manner affect the first and fourth clauses in the Ninth Section of the First Article; and that no State, without its consent, shall be deprived of its equal suffrage in the Senate.

The Constitution can be changed by amendment. An amendment can be proposed (1) by the vote of two-thirds of the Senate and two-thirds of the House of Representatives or (2) by a special convention called together by Congress at the request of two-thirds of all state legislatures. The amendment becomes part of the Constitution when it is approved (1) by the legislatures of at least three-fourths of the states or (2) by special conventions in at least three-fourths of the states.

Before 1808, no amendment could stop the bringing in of slaves to the United States or allow direct taxes without distributing the burden according to the population of the various states. No amendment may take away a state's right to have the same number of senators as other states unless the state affected agrees.

ARTICLE VI ● THE SUPREME LAW OF THE LAND

All debts contracted and engagements entered into, before the adoption of this Constitution, shall be as valid against the United States under this Constitution, as under the Confederation.

This Constitution, and the laws of the United States which shall be made in pursuance thereof; and all treaties made, or which shall be made, under the authority of the United States, shall be the supreme law of the land; and the judges in every State shall be bound thereby, any thing in the Constitution or laws of any State to the contrary notwithstanding.

The senators and representatives before mentioned, and the members of the several State legislatures, and all executive and judicial officers, both of the United States and of the several States, shall be bound by oath or affirmation, to support this Constitution; but no religious test shall ever be required as a qualification to any office or public trust under the United States.

Promises to repay loans made by Congress before the Constitution was adopted are still binding on the United States.

This Constitution, the laws made by Congress as permitted by the Constitution, and treaties made by the United States are the highest laws of the United States. Judges must follow these laws even if state laws contradict them.

All national government and state government officials must promise to uphold the Constitution.

No one who can meet other requirements for holding a position in the United States government can be kept out of the position because of religion.

ARTICLE VII ● RATIFICATION

The ratification of the conventions of nine States shall be sufficient for the establishment of this Constitution between the States so ratifying the same.

Done in convention by the unanimous consent of the States present the seventeenth day of September in the year of our Lord one thousand seven hundred and eighty seven and of the Independence of the United States of American the twelfth. In witness whereof we have here unto subscribed our names.

When nine states have held conventions and agreed to this Constitution, the government set up by this Constitution shall begin in those states.

The states represented in the Constitutional Convention on September 17, 1787, agreed to the Constitution as a plan of government to be proposed to the states. (Only Rhode Island refused to take part in the Constitutional Convention. The other 12 states chose 65 delegates to the convention; 55 attended most of the meetings. The day the Constitution was signed, 43 delegates were present, but only 39 actually put their signatures on the document.)

Go. Washington—*Presid't.*
and deputy from Virginia

Attest William Jackson *Secretary*

New Hampshire
John Langdon
Nicholas Gilman

Massachusetts
Nathaniel Gorham
Rufus King

Connecticut
Wm. Saml. Johnson
Roger Sherman

New York
Alexander Hamilton

New Jersey
Wil: Livingston
David Brearley.
Wm. Paterson.
Jona: Dayton

Pennsylvania
B Franklin
Thomas Mifflin
Robt Morris
Geo. Clymer
Thos. FitzSimons
Jared Ingersoll
James Wilson
Gouv Morris

Delaware
Geo: Read
Gunning Bedford jun
John Dickinson
Richard Bassett
Jaco: Broom

Maryland
James McHenry
Dan of St Thos. Jenifer
Danl. Carroll

Virginia
John Blair–
James Madison Jr.

North Carolina
Wm. Blount
Richd. Dobbs Spaight
Hu Williamson

South Carolina
J. Rutledge
Charles Cotesworth Pinckney
Charles Pinckney
Pierce Butler

Georgia
William Few
Abr Baldwin

Amendments

THE FIRST TEN AMENDMENTS: THE BILL OF RIGHTS

1st Amendment: Religious and Political Freedom (1791)

Congress shall make no law respecting an establishment of religion, or prohibiting the free exercise thereof; or abridging the freedom of speech, or of the press; or the right of the people peaceably to assemble, and to petition the Government for a redress of grievances.

Congress cannot pass the following kinds of laws: laws that would establish an official religion or that would keep people from following any religion (or none at all); laws that prevent people from speaking freely or publishing their ideas and beliefs; laws that stop people from meeting peaceably or formally asking the government to right a wrong.

2nd Amendment: Right to Bear Arms (1791)

A well regulated militia, being necessary to the security of a free State, the right of the people to keep and bear arms, shall not be infringed.

Because the people have a right to protect themselves with a militia, Congress cannot stop people from keeping and carrying firearms for military purposes.

3rd Amendment: Quartering of Soldiers (1791)

No soldier shall, in time of peace be quartered in any house, without the consent of the owner, nor in time of war, but in a manner to be prescribed by law.

In peacetime, citizens cannot be forced to give either room or board to soldiers. In wartime, however, Congress may pass such a law.

4th Amendment: Searches and Seizures (1791)

The right of the people to be secure in their persons, houses, papers, and effects, against unreasonable searches and seizures, shall not be violated, and no warrants shall issue, but upon probable cause, supported by oath or affirmation, and particularly describing the place to be searched, and the persons or things to be seized.

A person's house or belongings cannot be searched or seized unless a warrant—an official order from a judge—gives permission to do so. A judge cannot issue a warrant unless there is sufficient evidence to indicate that doing so will aid in capturing a criminal. The warrant must describe the place that will be searched and identify the persons or things that will be seized.

5th Amendment: Rights of Those Accused of Crimes (1791)

No person shall be held to answer for a capital, or otherwise infamous crime, unless on a presentment or indictment of a Grand Jury, except in cases arising in the land of naval forces, or in the militia, when in actual service in time of war or public danger; nor shall any person be subject for the same offense to be twice put in jeopardy of life or limb; nor shall be compelled in any criminal case to be a witness against himself, nor be deprived of life, liberty, or property, without due process of law; nor shall private property be taken for public use, without just compensation.

No person may be tried in a national court for a serious crime unless a grand jury has decided there is enough evidence against that individual to warrant a trial. The only individuals not covered by this rule are those serving in the armed forces in time of war or public danger.

If a person has been tried and found innocent of a crime, he or she cannot be tried a second time for the same offense. However, if the offense is a crime under state law, the person can be tried again in a state court. Also, if the offense injures another party, the person accused can be made to pay damages even though innocent of a crime.

No person can be forced to say anything in a national court that would help to prove his or her guilt.

No person can be executed, imprisoned, or fined except as a punishment after a fair trial.

The government cannot take a person's property for public use without paying a fair price for it.

6th Amendment: Protection in Criminal Courts (1791)

In all criminal prosecutions, the accused shall enjoy the right to a speedy and public trial, by an impartial jury of the State and district wherein the crime shall have been committed, which district shall have been previously ascertained by law, and to be informed of the nature and cause of the accusation; to be confronted with the witnesses against him; to have compulsory process for obtaining witnesses in his favor, and to have the assistance of counsel for his defense.

A person accused of a crime must be tried promptly and in public. That person's guilt or innocence must be decided by a jury chosen from the state and district where the crime was committed. The accused must be told what he or she is being tried for. The accused must be present when witnesses speak against him or her in court. The accused is entitled to call witnesses in his or her behalf and to have the assistance of a lawyer.

7th Amendment: Civil Suits (1791)

In suits at common law, where the value in controversy shall exceed twenty dollars, the right of trial by jury shall be preserved, and no fact tried by a jury, shall be otherwise reexamined in any court of the United States, than according to the rules of the common law.

In disputes over property worth more than 20 dollars, either party can insist on a jury trial or both can agree not to have a jury.

8th Amendment: Bails, Fines, Punishments (1791)

Excessive bail shall not be required, nor excessive fines imposed, nor cruel and unusual punishments inflicted.

A person accused of a crime can get out of jail until the trial by handing over a sum of money to the court. This money, called bail, is returned when the accused appears at the trial. If the accused fails to appear, the bail is lost. National courts cannot force the accused to pay unreasonably large amounts of bail. A person tried in a national court and found guilty cannot be punished with an unreasonably large fine or unreasonably long prison sentence. That person also cannot be punished in cruel or unusual ways—such as torture or branding.

9th Amendment: Other Rights of the People (1791)

The enumeration in the Constitution, of certain rights, shall not be construed to deny or disparage others retained by the people.

The mention of certain rights in the Constitution does not mean that these are the only rights that people have. It also does not make rights not identified in the document less important than those listed in the Constitution.

10th Amendment: Powers Kept by the States or the People (1791)

The powers not delegated to the United States by the Constitution, nor prohibited by it to the States, are reserved to the States respectively, or to the people.

All powers not given by the Constitution to the national government and not denied to the states belong to the states or to the people of the states.

THE 11TH–26TH AMENDMENTS

11th Amendment: Suits against a State (1798)

The judicial power of the United States shall not be construed to extend to any suit in law or equity, commenced or prosecuted against one of the United States by citizens of another State, or by citizens or subjects of any foreign State.

Citizens of other states or foreign countries cannot sue a state in national courts.

12th Amendment: Election of President and Vice President (1804)

The electors shall meet in their respective States, and vote by ballot for President and Vice President, one of whom, at least, shall not be an inhabitant of the same State with themselves; they shall name in their ballots the person voted for as President, and in distinct ballots the person voted for as Vice President, and they shall make distinct lists

753

of all persons voted for as President, and of all persons voted for as Vice President, and of the number of votes for each, which lists they shall sign and certify, and transmit sealed to the seat of the government of the United States, directed to the President of the Senate;—The President of the Senate shall, in the presence of the Senate and House of Representatives, open all the certificates and the votes shall then be counted;—The person having the greatest number of votes for President, shall be the President, if such number be a majority of the whole number of electors appointed; and if no person have such majority, then from the persons having the highest numbers not exceeding three on the list of those voted for as President, the House of Representatives shall choose immediately, by ballot, the President. But in choosing the President, the votes shall be taken by States, the representation from each State having one vote; a quorum for this purpose shall consist of a member or members from two-thirds of the States, and a majority of all the States shall be necessary to a choice. And if the House of Representatives shall not choose a President whenever the right of choice shall devolve upon them, before the fourth day of March next following, then the Vice President shall act as President, as in the case of the death or other constitutional disability of the President.—The person having the greatest number of votes as Vice President, shall be the Vice President, if such number be a majority of the whole number of electors appointed, and if no person have a majority, then from the two highest numbers on the list, the Senate shall choose the Vice President; a quorum for the purpose shall consist of two-thirds of the whole number of Senators, and a majority of the whole number shall be necessary to a choice. But no person constitutionally ineligible to the office of President shall be eligible to that of Vice President of the United States.

The electors meet in their own states and cast separate ballots for President and Vice President. At least one of the candidates must live outside the electors' own state. The ballots are recorded on two separate lists—one for President and one for Vice President. The lists are sent to the United States Senate, where the votes are counted in the presence of senators and representatives. The presidential candidate with the most electoral votes becomes President if he or she has a majority of the votes cast. If no candidate has a majority, the House of Representatives selects the President from the three candidates with the highest total. Each state has one vote. Two-thirds of the states must be represented when the votes are cast. The candidate who receives a majority becomes President.

If the House of Representatives does not select a President before the date set to take office, the Vice President is to act as President.

The candidate who receives the majority of the electoral votes for Vice President becomes Vice President. If no candidate has a majority, the Senate chooses between the two candidates with the largest number of electoral votes. Two-thirds of all senators must be present for the voting. The winning candidate must receive the votes of more than half of all senators.

A person who does not have the qualifications to be President cannot be Vice President.

13th Amendment: Slavery Outlawed (1865)

SECTION 1. Neither slavery nor involuntary servitude, except as a punishment for crime whereof the party shall have been duly convicted, shall exist within the United States, or any place subject to their jurisdiction.

SECTION 2. Congress shall have power to enforce this article by appropriate legislation.

No person in the United States or its territories may be held in slavery. No person can be forced to work against his or her will except as a punishment for a crime. Congress has the power to make laws that will put this amendment into effect.

14th Amendment: Civil Rights in the States (1868)

SECTION 1. All persons born or naturalized in the United States, and subject to the jurisdiction thereof, are citizens of the United States and of the State wherein they reside. No State shall make or enforce any law which shall abridge the privileges or immunities of citizens of the United States; nor shall any State deprive any person of life, liberty, or property, without due process of law; nor deny to any person within its jurisdiction the equal protection of the laws.

SECTION 2. Representatives shall be apportioned among the several States according to their respective numbers, counting the whole number of persons in each State, excluding Indians not taxed. But when the right to vote at any election for the choice of electors for President and Vice President of the United States, Representatives in Congress, the executive and judicial officers of a State, or the members of the legislature thereof, *is denied to any of the male inhabitants of such State, being twenty-one years of age, and citizens of the United States, or in any way abridged, except for participation in rebellion, or other crime, the basis of representation therein shall be reduced in the proportion which the number of such male citizens shall bear to the whole number of male citizens twenty-one years of age in such State.*

SECTION 3. No person shall be a Senator or Representative in Congress, or elector of President and Vice President, or hold any office, civil or military, under the United States, or under any State, who, having previously taken an oath, as a member of Congress, or as an officer of the United States, or as a member of any State legislature, or as an executive or judicial officer of any State, to support the Constitution of the United States, shall have engaged in insurrection or rebellion against the same, or given aid or comfort to the enemies thereof. But Congress may by a vote of two-thirds of each house, remove such disability.

SECTION 4. The validity of the public debt of the United States, authorized by law, including debts incurred for payment of pensions and bounties for services in suppressing insurrection or rebellion, shall not be questioned. But neither the United States nor any State shall assume or pay any debt or obligation incurred in aid of insurrection or rebellion against the United States, or any claim for the loss or emancipation of any slave; but all such debts, obligations and claims shall be held illegal and void.

SECTION 5. The Congress shall have power to enforce, by appropriate legislation, the provisions of this article.

Any person born in the United States and living under United States laws or who has become naturalized is a citizen of the United States. That person is also a citizen of the state in which he or she lives. No state can take away the rights of a United States citizen. No state can take away a person's life, freedom, or property except according to law. All state laws must affect everyone in the same way.

All people, except Indians who do not pay taxes, are to be counted in order to determine how many representatives a state is to have in Congress. If male citizens over the age of 21 are not allowed to vote in national or state elections, the number of representatives that state has in the House of Representatives may be reduced according to the number of people deprived of their vote. The only exception is male citizens who fought against the United States during the Civil War.

The 19th and 26th Amendments have affected this section. The 19th Amendment gave voting rights to women. The 26th Amendment states that all citizens 18 years of age and older have the right to vote.

15th Amendment: The Right of Black Americans to Vote (1870)

SECTION 1. The right of citizens of the United States to vote shall not be denied or abridged by the United States or by any State on account of race, color, or previous condition of servitude.

SECTION 2. The Congress shall have power to enforce this article by appropriate legislation.

Neither the United States nor any state may keep a citizen from voting because of race or color or because that person was once a slave.

16th Amendment: The National Income Tax (1913)

The Congress shall have power to lay and collect taxes on incomes, from whatever source derived, without apportionment among the several States, and without regard to any census or enumeration.

Congress has the right to tax income. The amount of money citizens of a state pay to the national government as income tax does not have to be in proportion to the state's population.

17th Amendment: Direct Election of Senators (1913)

SECTION 1. The Senate of the United States shall be composed of two senators from each State, elected by the people thereof, for six years; and each senator shall have one vote. The electors in each State shall have the qualifications requisite for electors of the most numerous branch of the State legislatures.

SECTION 2. When vacancies happen in the representation of any State in the senate, the executive authority of such State shall issue writs of election to fill such vacancies: *Provided,* That the legislature of any State may empower the executive thereof to make temporary appointments until the people fill the vacancies by election as the legislature may direct.

SECTION 3. This amendment shall not be so construed as to affect the election or term of any senator chosen before it becomes valid as part of the Constitution.

The Senate shall be made up of two senators from each state, elected by the people of the state for six-year terms. Each senator has one vote. Citizens entitled to vote for representatives to their state legislature may vote for senators.

The governor of a state may call an election to fill a vacancy among that state's senators. But the state legislature may allow the governor to appoint someone to fill the vacancy until an election is held.

This amendment does not affect any election already held or the term of any senator in the Senate at the time the amendment was adopted.

18th Amendment: National Prohibition (1919)

SECTION 1. *After one year from the ratification of this article the manufacture, sale, or transportation of intoxicating liquors within, the importation thereof into, or the exportation thereof from the United States and all territory subject to the jurisdiction thereof for beverage purposes is hereby prohibited.*

SECTION 2. *The Congress and the several States shall have concurrent power to enforce this article by appropriate legislation.*

SECTION 3. *This article shall be inoperative unless it shall have been ratified as an amendment to the Constitution by the legislatures of the several States, as provided in the Constitution, within seven years from the date of the submission hereof to the States by the Congress.*

One year after this amendment is ratified, it will become illegal to make, sell, or carry in the United States or its territories intoxicating drinks. It will also be illegal to import or export such beverages.

Congress and the states have the power to pass any laws needed to carry out this amendment. This amendment will not become part of the Constitution until it is ratified by state legislatures within seven years.

In 1933 this amendment was repealed by the 21st Amendment.

19th Amendment: Women's Voting Rights (1920)

SECTION 1. The right of citizens of the United States to vote shall not be denied or abridged by the United States or by any State on account of sex.

SECTION 2. Congress shall have power to enforce this article by appropriate legislation.

Neither the national government nor any state government has the right to keep a citizen from voting because she is a woman.

Congress has the power to pass any laws needed to carry out this amendment.

20th Amendment: Terms of Office (1933)

SECTION 1. The terms of the President and Vice President shall end at noon on the 20th day of January, and the terms of Senators and Representatives at noon on the 3d day of January, of the years in which such terms would have ended if this article had not been ratified; and the terms of their successors shall then begin.

SECTION 2. The Congress shall assemble at least once in every year, and such meeting shall begin at noon on the 3d day of January, unless they shall by law appoint a different day.

SECTION 3. If, at the time fixed for the beginning of the term of the President, the President elect shall have died, the Vice President elect shall become President. If a President shall not have been chosen before the time fixed for the beginning of his term, or if the President elect shall have failed to qualify, then the Vice President elect shall act as President until a President shall have qualified; and the Congress may by law provide for the case wherein neither a President elect nor a Vice President elect shall have qualified, declaring who shall then act as President, or the manner in which one who is to act shall be selected, and such person shall act accordingly until a President or Vice President shall have qualified.

SECTION 4. The Congress may by law provide for the case of the death of any of the persons from whom the House of Representatives may choose a President whenever the right of choice shall have devolved upon them, and for the case of the death of any of the persons from whom the Senate may choose a Vice President whenever the right of choice shall have devolved upon them.

SECTION 5. Sections 1 and 2 shall take effect on the 15th day of October following the ratification of this article.

SECTION 6. This article shall be inoperative unless it shall have been ratified as an amendment to the Constitution by the legislatures of three-fourths of the several States within seven years from the date of its submission.

The terms of office of the President and Vice President of the United States end at noon, January 20, and the terms of office of senators and representatives end at noon, January 3, of the same years they would have ended had this amendment not been adopted. The new terms for all these offices begin as soon as the old terms end.

Congress must meet at least once a year, beginning its meetings at noon on January 3 unless a law passed by Congress orders a different day.

If the person elected President dies before January 20, when his or her term was to begin, then the person elected Vice President becomes President. If the newly elected President does not meet the Constitution's requirements for President, then the newly elected Vice President acts as President until a President who meets those requirements can be chosen. Congress may pass a law deciding what to do if neither the newly elected President nor the Vice President meets the requirements for the office. Congress also has the power to pass a law deciding what to do if the Senate must select a Vice President and one of the candidates has died.

Sections 1 and 2 become law on October 15 following the ratification of this amendment. The amendment will not become part of the Constitution unless three-fourths of the states agree to it within seven years.

21st Amendment: The End of Prohibition (1933)

SECTION 1. The eighteenth article of amendment to the Constitution of the United States is hereby repealed.

SECTION 2. The transportation or importation into any State, Territory, or possession of the United States for delivery or use therein of intoxicating liquors, in violation of the laws thereof, is hereby prohibited.

SECTION 3. This article shall be inoperative unless it shall have been ratified as an amendment to the Constitution by conventions in the several States, as provided in the Constitution, within seven years from the date of the submission hereof to the States by the Congress.

The 18th Amendment is no longer in effect. Therefore, the national government may no longer outlaw the making, selling, or transporting of intoxicating drinks. However, any state, territory, or possession of the United States may outlaw alcoholic beverages if it wishes to do so.

This amendment must be ratified by a special convention held in each state. The amendment becomes part of the Constitution only if three-fourths of those conventions agree to it within seven years.

22nd Amendment: Terms of Office of the President (1951)

SECTION 1. No person shall be elected to the office of the President more than twice, and no person who has held the office of President, or acted as President, for more than 2 years of a term to which some other person was elected President shall be elected to the office of the President more than once. But this Article shall not apply to any person holding the office of President when this Article was proposed by the Congress, and shall not prevent any person who may be holding the office of President, or acting as President during the term within which this Article becomes operative from holding the office of President or acting as President during the remainder of such term.

SECTION 2. This Article shall be inoperative unless it shall have been ratified as an amendment to the Constitution by the legislatures of three-fourths of the several States within 7 years from the date of its submission to the States by the Congress.

No person can have more than two terms as President. If any person serves for more than two years in place of an elected President, that person may be elected President only once.

This amendment becomes part of the Constitution if three-fourths of all state legislatures agree to it within seven years.

23rd Amendment: Presidential Voting in the District of Columbia (1961)

SECTION 1. The District constituting the seat of Government of the United States shall appoint in such manner as the Congress may direct:

A number of electors of President and Vice President equal to the whole number of Senators and Representatives in Congress to which the District would be entitled if it were a State, but in no event more than the least populous State; they shall be in addition to those appointed by the

States, but they shall be considered, for the purposes of the election of President and Vice President, to be electors appointed by a State; and they shall meet in the District and perform such duties as provided by the twelfth article of amendment.

SECTION 2. The Congress shall have power to enforce this article by appropriate legislation.

Citizens living in the District of Columbia have the right to take part in the election of President and Vice President of the United States. The District of Columbia may have as many votes in the electoral college as the state with the smallest population. Members of the electoral college from the District vote in accordance with the 12th Amendment. Congress may pass any laws needed to carry out this amendment.

24th Amendment: Tax Requirements for Voting Outlawed (1964)

SECTION 1. The right of citizens of the United States to vote in any primary or other election for President or Vice President, for electors for President or Vice President, or for Senator or Representative in Congress, shall not be denied or abridged by the United States or any State by reason of failure to pay any poll tax or other tax.

SECTION 2. The Congress shall have power to enforce this article by appropriate legislation.

No government—local, state, or national—may keep a citizen from voting in national elections because of failure to pay a tax of any kind. Congress may pass whatever laws are needed to enforce this amendment.

25th Amendment: Presidential Continuity (1967)

SECTION 1. In case of the removal of the President from office or of his death or resignation, the Vice President shall become President.

SECTION 2. Whenever there is a vacancy in the office of the Vice President, the President shall nominate a Vice President who shall take office upon confirmation by a majority vote of both Houses of Congress.

SECTION 3. Whenever the President transmits to the President pro tempore of the Senate and the Speaker of the House of Representatives his written declaration that he is unable to discharge the powers and duties of his office, and until he transmits to them a written declaration to the contrary, such powers and duties shall be discharged by the Vice President as Acting President.

SECTION 4. Whenever the Vice President and a majority of either the principal officers of the executive departments or of such other body as Congress may by law provide, transmit to the President pro tempore of the Senate and the Speaker of the House of Representatives their written declaration that the President is unable to discharge the powers and duties of his office, the Vice President shall immediately assume the powers and duties of the office as Acting President.

Thereafter, when the President transmits to the President pro tempore of the Senate and the Speaker of the House of Representatives his written declaration that no inability exists, he shall resume the powers and duties of his office unless the Vice President and a majority of either the principal officers of the executive department or of such other body as Congress may by law provide, transmit within four days to the President pro tempore of the Senate and the Speaker of the House of Representatives their written declaration that the President is unable to discharge the powers and duties of his office. Thereupon Congress shall decide the issue, assembling within forty-eight hours for that purpose if not in session. If the Congress, within twenty-one days after receipt of the latter written declaration, or, if Congress is not in session, within twenty-one days after Congress is required to assemble, determines by two-thirds vote of both Houses that the President is unable to discharge the powers and duties of his office, the Vice President shall continue to discharge the same as Acting President; otherwise, the President shall resume the powers and duties of his office.

If the President is removed from office, dies, or resigns, the Vice President becomes President.

If the office of Vice President is vacant, the President may name a Vice President. If a majority of both houses of Congress approve the choice, the person so named becomes Vice President.

If the President is or expects to be disabled, he or she must make a written statement to that effect and send it to the President pro tempore of the Senate and the speaker of the House. If the President refuses to or is unable to give up his or her powers, the Vice President becomes acting

President with the approval of a majority of the Cabinet or another body named by Congress.

The President may reclaim the powers of the office when the disability ends by sending a written statement to Congress. If the Vice President and a majority of the Cabinet or other body named by Congress do not believe the disability has ended, they must state this in writing to Congress within four days of the President's announcement. Congress must decide the issue within 48 hours of receiving the second statement.

26th Amendment: Right to Vote—Citizens over the Age of Eighteen (1971)

SECTION 1. The right of citizens of the United States, who are 18 years of age or older, to vote shall not be denied or abridged by the United States or by any State on account of age.

SECTION 2. The Congress shall have power to enforce this article by appropriate legislation.

Neither the United States nor any state can keep citizens 18 years of age or older from voting because of age.

Presidential Facts

Term	President	Party	State Born/Home
1789–1797	George Washington	(no parties)	Virginia
1797–1801	John Adams	Federalist	Massachusetts
1801–1809	Thomas Jefferson	Democratic-Republican	Virginia
1809–1817	James Madison	Democratic-Republican	Virginia
1817–1825	James Monroe	Democratic-Republican	Virginia
1825–1829	John Quincy Adams	National Republican	Massachusetts
1829–1837	Andrew Jackson	Democratic	South Carolina/Tennessee
1837–1841	Martin Van Buren	Democratic	New York
1841	William H. Harrison (d. March 1841)	Whig	Virginia/Ohio
1841–1845	John Tyler	Whig	Virginia
1845–1849	James K. Polk	Democratic	N. Carolina/Tennessee
1849–1850	Zachary Taylor (d. 1850)	Whig	Virginia/Louisiana
1850–1853	Millard Fillmore	Whig	New York
1853–1857	Franklin Pierce	Democratic	New Hampshire
1857–1861	James Buchanan	Democratic	Pennsylvania
1861–1865	Abraham Lincoln (d. April 1865)	Republican	Kentucky/Illinois
1865–1869	Andrew Johnson	Republican	North Carolina/Tennessee
1869–1877	Ulysses S. Grant	Republican	Ohio/Illinois
1877–1881	Rutherford B. Hayes	Republican	Ohio
1881	James A. Garfield (d. September 1881)	Republican	Ohio
1881–1885	Chester A. Arthur	Republican	Vermont/New York
1885–1889	Grover Cleveland	Democratic	New Jersey/New York
1889–1893	Benjamin Harrison	Republican	Ohio/Indiana
1893–1897	Grover Cleveland	Democratic	New Jersey/New York
1897–1901	William McKinley (d. September 1901)	Republican	Ohio
1901–1909	Theodore Roosevelt	Republican	New York
1909–1913	William H. Taft	Republican	Ohio
1913–1921	Woodrow Wilson	Democratic	Virginia/New Jersey
1921–1923	Warren G. Harding (d. August 1923)	Republican	Ohio
1923–1929	Calvin Coolidge	Republican	Vermont/Massachusetts
1929–1933	Herbert Hoover	Republican	Iowa/California
1933–1945	Franklin D. Roosevelt (d. April 1945)	Democratic	New York
1945–1953	Harry S Truman	Democratic	Missouri
1953–1961	Dwight D. Eisenhower	Republican	Texas/New York, Penn.
1961–1963	John F. Kennedy (d. November 1963)	Democratic	Massachusetts
1963–1969	Lyndon B. Johnson	Democratic	Texas
1969–1973	Richard M. Nixon (r. August 1974)	Republican	California/New York, Calif.
1974–1977	Gerald R. Ford	Republican	Nebraska/Michigan
1977–1981	Jimmy (James Earl) Carter	Democratic	Georgia
1981–	Ronald Reagan	Republican	Illinois/California

State Facts

State	Date of Admission	Capital	Area in square miles[1] and Rank	Population (1983 est.)[2]	Representatives in Congress
Alabama	1819	Montgomery	51,609(29)	3,959,000	7
Alaska	1959	Juneau	586,412(1)	479,000	1
Arizona	1912	Phoenix	113,909(6)	2,963,000	5
Arkansas	1836	Little Rock	53,104(27)	2,328,000	4
California	1850	Sacramento	158,693(3)	25,174,000	45
Colorado	1876	Denver	104,247(8)	3,139,000	6
Connecticut	1788	Hartford	5,009(48)	3,138,000	6
Delaware	1787	Dover	2,057(49)	606,000	1
Florida	1845	Tallahassee	58,560(22)	10,680,000	19
Georgia	1788	Atlanta	58,876(21)	5,732,000	10
Hawaii	1959	Honolulu	6,450(47)	1,023,000	2
Idaho	1890	Boise	83,557(13)	989,000	2
Illinois	1818	Springfield	56,400(24)	11,486,000	22
Indiana	1816	Indianapolis	36,291(38)	5,479,000	10
Iowa	1846	Des Moines	56,290(25)	2,905,000	6
Kansas	1861	Topeka	82,264(14)	2,425,000	5
Kentucky	1792	Frankfort	40,395(37)	3,714,000	7
Louisiana	1812	Baton Rouge	48,523(31)	4,438,000	8
Maine	1820	Augusta	33,215(39)	1,146,000	2
Maryland	1788	Annapolis	10,577(42)	4,304,000	8
Massachusetts	1788	Boston	8,257(45)	5,767,000	11
Michigan	1837	Lansing	58,216(23)	9,069,000	18
Minnesota	1858	St. Paul	84,068(12)	4,144,000	8
Mississippi	1817	Jackson	47,716(32)	2,587,000	5
Missouri	1821	Jefferson City	69,686(19)	4,970,000	9
Montana	1889	Helena	147,138(4)	819,000	2
Nebraska	1867	Lincoln	77,227(15)	1,597,000	3
Nevada	1864	Carson City	110,540(7)	891,000	2
New Hampshire	1788	Concord	9,304(44)	959,000	2
New Jersey	1787	Trenton	7,836(46)	7,468,000	14
New Mexico	1912	Santa Fe	121,666(5)	1,399,000	3
New York	1788	Albany	49,576(30)	17,667,000	34
North Carolina	1789	Raleigh	52,586(28)	6,082,000	11
North Dakota	1889	Bismarck	70,665(17)	680,000	1
Ohio	1803	Columbus	41,222(35)	10,746,000	21
Oklahoma	1907	Oklahoma City	69,919(18)	3,298,000	6
Oregon	1859	Salem	96,981(10)	2,662,000	5
Pennsylvania	1787	Harrisburg	45,333(33)	11,895,000	23
Rhode Island	1790	Providence	1,214(50)	955,000	2
South Carolina	1788	Columbia	31,055(40)	3,264,000	6
South Dakota	1889	Pierre	77,047(16)	700,000	1
Tennessee	1796	Nashville	42,244(34)	4,685,000	9
Texas	1845	Austin	267,338(2)	15,724,000	27
Utah	1896	Salt Lake City	84,916(11)	1,619,000	3
Vermont	1791	Montpelier	9,609(43)	525,000	1
Virginia	1788	Richmond	40,817(36)	5,550,000	10
Washington	1889	Olympia	68,192(20)	4,300,000	8
West Virginia	1863	Charleston	24,181(41)	1,965,000	4
Wisconsin	1848	Madison	56,154(26)	4,751,000	9
Wyoming	1890	Cheyenne	97,914(9)	514,000	1

[1] Includes inland water area but not area of the Great Lakes.
[2] Source: U.S. Bureau of the Census.

MESABI RANGE

Lake Superior

St. Paul
Minneapolis

WISCONSIN

Milwaukee
Madison

Green Bay

Straits of Mackinac

Lake Huron

Lake Michigan

MICHIGAN

Lansing

St. Clair

Detroit

Lake Erie

Chicago

ILLINOIS INDIANA

CENTRAL PLAINS

Springfield

Cleveland

OHIO

Columbus

Indianapolis

Pittsburgh

Cincinnati

MISSOURI

St. Louis

Jefferson City

OZARK PLATEAU

Frankfort

KENTUCKY

Charleston

WEST VIRGINIA

ALLEGHENY PLATEAU

PENNSYLVANIA

Harrisburg

Lake Ontario

Finger Lakes

NEW YORK

Albany

Buffalo

ADIRONDACK MOUNTAINS

Lake Champlain

VT.

N.H.

Augusta

Montpelier

Concord

MAINE

Penobscot Bay

Boston

Cape Cod

MASS.

Providence

R.I.

Nantucket

Hartford

CONN.

Martha's Vineyard

Long Island Sound

New York

Long Island

NEW JERSEY

Trenton

Philadelphia

Baltimore

Dover

Cape May

Delaware Bay

MD.

D.C.

Annapolis

Washington

DELAWARE

ATLANTIC OCEAN

BLUE RIDGE

Richmond

VIRGINIA

Chesapeake Bay

CUMBERLAND PLATEAU

Nashville

ARKANSAS

Little Rock

TENNESSEE

APPALACHIAN MOUNTAINS

BLUE RIDGE

Charlotte

Raleigh

Hatteras
Cape Hatteras

NORTH CAROLINA

COASTAL PLAIN

Columbia

SOUTH CAROLINA

Atlanta

ALABAMA

MISSISSIPPI

Jackson

Montgomery

GEORGIA

PLAIN

COASTAL

LOUISIANA

Baton Rouge

New Orleans

Mobile Bay

Pensacola Bay

Lake Pontchartrain

Mississippi Delta

Tallahassee

FLORIDA

Cape Canaveral

Gulf of Mexico

Tampa Bay
Lake Okeechobee

Everglades

Cape Sable

Miami

FLORIDA KEYS

Straits of Florida

Tropic of Cancer

The United States, Physical and Political

Elevation key

Feet		Meters
14,000		4,000
7,000		2,000
1,500		500
700		200
0		0
Below sea level		Below sea level

★ Capital city
◉ State capital city
• Other city

| 0 | 100 | 200 | 300 | 400 | 500 Miles |
| 0 | 100 | 200 | 300 | 400 | 500 Kilometers |

ATLANTIC OCEAN

| 0 | 100 Miles | 20°N |
| 0 | 100 Kilometers |

PUERTO RICO
(U.S. COMM.) San Juan

CARIBBEAN SEA

90°W 85°W 80°W 75°W 70°W 65°W 60°W

45°N 40°N 35°N 30°N 25°N

The World, Political

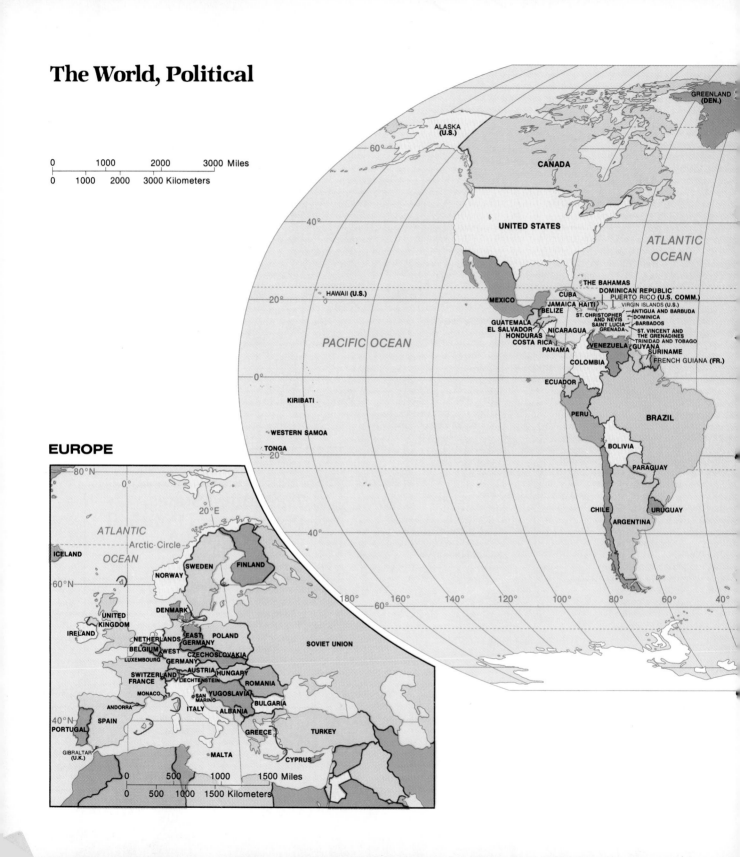

0   1000   2000   3000 Miles
0 1000 2000 3000 Kilometers

GREENLAND
(DEN.)

ALASKA
(U.S.)

60°

CANADA

40°

UNITED STATES

ATLANTIC
OCEAN

THE BAHAMAS
DOMINICAN REPUBLIC
PUERTO RICO (U.S. COMM.)
VIRGIN ISLANDS (U.S.)
ANTIGUA AND BARBUDA
DOMINICA
BARBADOS

20°

HAWAII (U.S.)

MEXICO

CUBA
JAMAICA HAITI
BELIZE

ST. CHRISTOPHER
AND NEVIS
SAINT LUCIA
GRENADA
ST. VINCENT AND
THE GRENADINES
TRINIDAD AND TOBAGO

GUATEMALA
EL SALVADOR
HONDURAS
COSTA RICA
PANAMA

NICARAGUA

PACIFIC OCEAN

VENEZUELA GUYANA
SURINAME
FRENCH GUIANA (FR.)

COLOMBIA

0°

ECUADOR

KIRIBATI

PERU

BRAZIL

WESTERN SAMOA

TONGA

20°

BOLIVIA

PARAGUAY

40°

CHILE

URUGUAY

ARGENTINA

180°   160°   140°   120°   100°   80°   60°   40°

60°

SOVIET UNION

EUROPE

80°N

0°

20°E

ATLANTIC
OCEAN

Arctic Circle

ICELAND

SWEDEN

FINLAND

NORWAY

60°N

DENMARK

UNITED
KINGDOM

IRELAND

NETHERLANDS
BELGIUM
LUXEMBOURG

EAST
GERMANY
WEST
GERMANY

POLAND

CZECHOSLOVAKIA

SOVIET UNION

SWITZERLAND
FRANCE

AUSTRIA
LIECHTENSTEIN

HUNGARY

ROMANIA

MONACO

SAN
MARINO

YUGOSLAVIA

BULGARIA

ANDORRA

ITALY

ALBANIA

40°N

SPAIN

PORTUGAL

GREECE

TURKEY

GIBRALTAR
(U.K.)

MALTA

CYPRUS

0   500   1000   1500 Miles
0 500 1000 1500 Kilometers

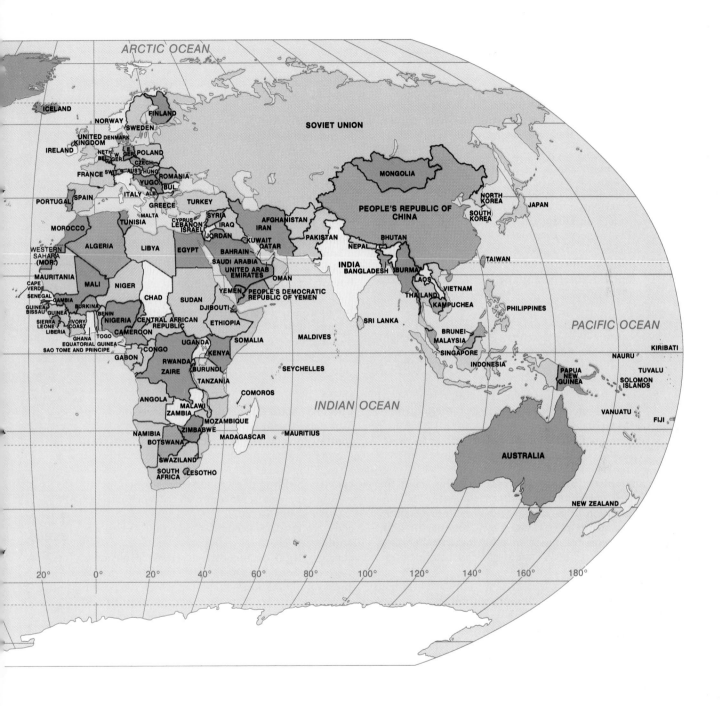

ARCTIC OCEAN

ICELAND

NORWAY
FINLAND
SWEDEN
DENMARK
UNITED
KINGDOM
IRELAND
NETH.
BEL. W. E. POLAND
GER. GER.
CZECH.
FRANCE SWITZ. AUST. HUNG.
YUGO. ROMANIA
ITALY BUL.
PORTUGAL SPAIN
GREECE TURKEY
MALTA
ALB.
CYPRUS SYRIA
LEBANON IRAQ
ISRAEL
MOROCCO
TUNISIA
JORDAN
AFGHANISTAN
IRAN
KUWAIT
QATAR
BAHRAIN
WESTERN
SAHARA
(MOR.)
ALGERIA
LIBYA
EGYPT
SAUDI ARABIA
UNITED ARAB
EMIRATES
OMAN
MAURITANIA
CAPE
VERDE
MALI
NIGER
SENEGAL
GAMBIA
CHAD
SUDAN
YEMEN
PEOPLE'S DEMOCRATIC
REPUBLIC OF YEMEN
GUINEA
BISSAU GUINEA
BURKINA
BENIN
SIERRA
LEONE IVORY
COAST
LIBERIA
GHANA
TOGO
NIGERIA
CENTRAL AFRICAN
REPUBLIC
ETHIOPIA
DJIBOUTI
EQUATORIAL GUINEA
SAO TOME AND PRINCIPE
CAMEROON
GABON
CONGO
UGANDA
KENYA
SOMALIA
RWANDA
ZAIRE
BURUNDI
TANZANIA
ANGOLA
MALAWI
ZAMBIA
MOZAMBIQUE
ZIMBABWE
NAMIBIA
BOTSWANA
MADAGASCAR
SWAZILAND
SOUTH
AFRICA
LESOTHO

SOVIET UNION

MONGOLIA

PEOPLE'S REPUBLIC OF
CHINA

NORTH
KOREA
SOUTH
KOREA
JAPAN

PAKISTAN
NEPAL
BHUTAN

TAIWAN

INDIA
BANGLADESH
BURMA
LAOS
VIETNAM
THAILAND
KAMPUCHEA
PHILIPPINES
SRI LANKA
MALDIVES

BRUNEI
MALAYSIA
SINGAPORE
INDONESIA

SEYCHELLES

COMOROS

INDIAN OCEAN

MAURITIUS

PACIFIC OCEAN

KIRIBATI
NAURU
TUVALU
PAPUA
NEW
GUINEA
SOLOMON
ISLANDS
VANUATU
FIJI

AUSTRALIA

NEW ZEALAND

20° 0° 20° 40° 60° 80° 100° 120° 140° 160° 180°

Glossary

Pronunciation Key

hat, āge, fär; let, ēqual, term; it, īce; hot, ōpen, ôrder; oil, out; cup, půt, rüle; ch, child; ng, long; sh, she; th, thin; ŦH, then; zh, measure

ə represents *a* in *about*, *e* in *taken*, *i* in *pencil*, *o* in *lemon*, *u* in *circus*; Y in French *ami*

- The glossary contains terms, concepts, organizations, and events important to the study of American History.
- The page reference tells where the term first appears in the text.
- Pronunciation of difficult terms is written next to the term where it appears in the text for the first time.

A

abolitionists antislavery reformers who thought slaves should be set free immediately (p. 336)

administration period of time during which a President is in office (p. 233)

Agricultural Adjustment Administration (AAA) federal agency set up in 1933 to help farmers (p. 603)

American Federation of Labor (AFL) loose alliance of national craft unions founded in 1886 (p. 481)

anarchists people who seek to bring about the destruction of law and government (p. 573)

annexation the taking of territory from a country to make it part of one's own country (p. 350)

appeasement policy of allowing a leader of a country to seize territory without opposition (p. 618)

archaeologists scientists who study artifacts and other evidence of human life from past cultures (p. 5)

armistice cease-fire (p. 562)

Articles of Confederation first plan of government for the thirteen states formed during the Revolution (p. 195)

artifacts objects made by human skill or labor, such as tools or weapons (p. 5)

assembly line system in which a moving belt brings parts of a product to workers who each perform one operation until the product is assembled (p. 578)

automation use of mechanical devices to do tasks formerly performed by people (p. 676)

B

bicameral legislature legislature that includes two separate parts, or houses (p. 73)

black codes laws passed by Southern states during reconstruction to control former slaves (p. 422)

Boston Massacre conflict between British troops and Bostonians in 1770 (p. 154)

Boston Tea Party incident in Boston in 1773 when patriots threw British tea into Boston Harbor (p. 155)

boycott refusal to have dealings with a merchant or a business in order to force a change (p. 150)

broad construction loose interpretation of the Constitution (p. 237)

bureaucracy complex network of people necessary to run a large corporation or organization (p. 479)

C

Cabinet team of presidential advisers made up of department heads (p. 233)

capitalist economy in which private citizens own and operate farms, stores, and factories for profit (p. 570)

caucus meeting of members of a political party to select a candidate for an election or to decide party policy (p. 307)

cede to give up, surrender, or hand over to another (p. 196)

charter legal document that allows a business to operate and sets rules for its operation (p. 236)

checks and balances system in which the power of each branch of the national government is limited by the powers of the other branches (p. 225)

civil rights movement movement to fight for equal rights and equal opportunities for all Americans (p. 675)

Civil Service Commission commission set up to conduct examinations and assign government jobs to the best candidates (p. 500)

commerce large-scale trade (p. 78)

Communist person who believes in an economic and political system in which the government owns land, factories, and other means of production and who supports the overthrow of social systems by revolution (p. 570)

confederation association or league (p. 56)

Congress of Industrial Organizations (CIO) union started in the 1930's open to all workers in a particular industry (p. 607)

Congress of Racial Equality (CORE) organization formed in 1942 to fight segregation (p. 631)

conquistadores Spanish conquerors of the Americas in the 1500's (p. 30)

conservation protection or preservation of natural resources (p. 535)

Constitutional Convention meeting in Philadelphia in 1787 to revise the Articles of Confederation (p. 193); also, a special meeting at which representatives write a constitution for a state (p. 203)

constitutions documents containing a set of basic laws that both create governments and set limits on them (p. 192)

Continental Army American army led by George Washington during the Revolution (p. 158)

corporate colonies colonies with charters granted to the colonists themselves who are bound together in a corporation (p. 119)

corporations companies that sell stock to the public (p. 473)

corruption misuse of government offices or government funds to enrich individuals (p. 427)

covenant agreement by which the Puritans promised to help one another fulfill God's will (p. 64)

craft unions unions open only to skilled workers such as machinists or plumbers (p. 481)

credit good standing among those who lend money (p. 235)

creditors people to whom money is owed (p. 306)

culture areas term scientists use to identify groups of people who share a similar way of life (p. 7)

D

debtors people who owe money (p. 306)

demand the desire and ability to buy goods or services (p. 285)

democracy government in which the people rule (p. 214)

deport to force out of a country an alien whose presence is found to be unlawful or harmful (p. 247)

depression period of low business activity when many businesses fail and many people lose their jobs (p. 201)

détente relaxing of tensions between nations (p. 706)

dictatorship government in which one person or a group of people rule a country without regard for individual liberties (p. 570)

direct primary special election in which members of a political party choose their party's candidates (p. 526)

direct representation system by which representatives elected to an assembly speak directly for the people who voted for them (p. 149)

disenfranchise to take away the right to vote (p. 304)

diversified economy economy in which people earn a living in many different ways (p. 58)

duty tax on goods brought into a country (p. 110)

E

electoral college group of people authorized by the Constitution to elect the President of the United States (p. 207)

emancipation freeing of slaves (p. 194)

empire nation and the territories and peoples it rules (p. 16)

encomienda Spanish colonial system in which land and the labor of Indian families living on the land were given to certain Spanish settlers (p. 31)

executive orders orders issued by the President that have the effect of law (p. 220)

export to sell products abroad (p. 78)

F

Fascist political party and private army that came to power in Italy under the leadership of Benito Mussolini in 1922 (p. 616)

federalism division of power between state governments and the national government (p. 215)

Federalists supporters of the Constitution (p. 208); also, those who supported Hamilton's belief in a strong national government (p. 238)

feminists defenders of the rights of women (p. 341)

filibuster to hinder deliberately, by making long speeches, the passage of a bill in a legislature (p. 674)

First Continental Congress meeting held in Philadelphia in 1774 to discuss grievances against Britain (p. 156)

foreign policy plan of action a country uses in its relations with other countries (p. 239)

franchise the right to vote (p. 304)

free enterprise economic system that allows private businesses to operate for profit in competition with other businesses (p. 608)

frontier land along the edge of a settled area (p. 79)

Fugitive Slave Law law ordering federal authorities to capture runaway slaves and return them to their owners (p. 367)

G

gold standard use of gold alone to determine the value of currency (p. 498)

Great Compromise plan reached at the Constitutional Convention that created two houses of Congress: the Senate, in which each state has two votes; and the House of Representatives, in which representation is based on a state's population (p. 205)

Great Depression period during the 1930's when many Americans lost their jobs, businesses failed, and the demand for goods and services dropped (p. 595)

gross national product total value of goods and services produced in a nation during a year (p. 577)

H

Harlem Renaissance period in the 1920's during which black writers and artists living in the Harlem section of New York City expressed in their work pride in their race and their African heritage (p. 581)

headright system agreement by which people received 50 acres for every person, or "head," they brought to Virginia in the early 1600's (p. 55)

Hessians German soldiers hired by King George III to fight the patriots during the Revolution (p. 160)

Hispanic term often used to refer to Spanish-speaking Americans (p. 729)

Holocaust the mass extermination of European Jews by the Nazis during World War II (p. 617)

Homestead Act of 1862 law that gave 160 acres of public land to settlers who agreed to live on it for five years (p. 456)

House of Burgesses the part of the General Assembly of Virginia whose members were elected by the colonists; the first elected lawmaking body in the English colonies (p. 55)

Huguenots French Protestants (p. 92)

I

impeach to formally bring charges of wrongdoing against a high public official (p. 217)

imperialists people who favor the extension of their nation's influence abroad, especially by the acquisition of colonies (p. 507)

import to buy products from abroad (p. 78)

indentured servants people who agreed to work for a set number of years in return for passage to the colonies (p. 57)

Indian Territory area of land in the western part of present-day Oklahoma set aside for Indians who were moved there from other parts of the country (p. 463)

inflation period when prices rise because the amount of money and credit is increased but fewer goods are available for purchase (p. 572)

initiative method by which voters can propose new laws and force their state legislature to vote on them (p. 526)

interchangeable parts parts that are so alike in size and shape they can be substituted for one another in the manufacture of a product (p. 293)

interest charge for the use of borrowed money (p. 431)

internment policy policy of forcing Japanese Americans on the West Coast to move to camps during World War II (p. 631)

inventories supplies of unsold goods (p. 594)

isolation policy of avoiding alliances with other countries (p. 614)

J

joint-stock common fund of a company raised by selling stocks (p. 47)

K

Knights of Labor founded in 1869, one of the first large unions made up of many smaller unions (p. 480)

Ku Klux Klan group formed after the Civil War that tried to control blacks through violence and threats of violence; later it attacked Catholics, Jews, and immigrants as well (p. 428)

L

laissez-faire doctrine that opposes government interference in business or industry (p. 496)

league association and alliance for a common purpose (p. 12)

League of Nations organization formed after World War I to work for world peace (p. 562)

long drive method used to bring huge herds of cattle from Texas to the Midwest from the 1860's to the 1880's (p. 451)

Louisiana Purchase United States purchase from France in 1803 of all the lands drained by the Mississippi River (p. 258)

Loyalists Americans who opposed independence during the Revolution (p. 170)

M

Manifest Destiny popular belief in the 1840's that the United States was fated to expand from the Atlantic to the Pacific Coast (p. 357)

manufacturing making finished products from raw materials such as trees or iron ore (p. 78)

Massachusetts Bay Company company formed by the Pilgrims in the 1620's to start a colony in North America (p. 68)

Mayflower Compact covenant drawn up in 1620 by the Pilgrims that set up a government for their colony (p. 66)

Middle Passage forced voyage of slaves from Africa to the West Indies (p. 134)

migrant workers farm workers who move from place to place working on other people's crops (p. 596)

militia citizens who are called to military duty during emergencies (p. 98)

minutemen members of colonial militias ready to fight the British "at a minute's notice" during the Revolution (p. 158)

monopoly large company that controls an entire industry (p. 477)

N

National Association for the Advancement of Colored People (NAACP) organization founded in 1909 to fight segregation and racism (p. 529)

National Organization for Women (NOW) organization founded in 1966 to work for equal rights for women (p. 685)

National Recovery Administration (NRA) federal agency created in 1933 to encourage industries to set up codes of production (p. 602)

nativism anti-immigrant movement that began in the 1830's (p. 343)

navigation science of finding position, course, and distance traveled by sea; later extended to include travel by air (p. 22)

Navigation Acts trade laws passed by Parliament in 1660 and 1663 to regulate colonial trade (p. 110)

Nazis members of the National Socialist party in Germany who supported Adolf Hitler (p. 616)

neutrality policy of not supporting either side in a conflict or a war (p. 240)

New Deal name given by FDR to his domestic policies (p. 599)

Niagara Movement group organized by W.E.B. Du Bois in 1905 to work against discrimination and segregation (p. 437)

nonimportation associations groups of colonial merchants who promised not to buy certain British goods (p. 153)

North Atlantic Treaty Organization (NATO) military alliance founded in 1949 by the United States, Canada, and Western European countries (p. 648)

nullify to cancel a law (p. 235)

O

ordinances laws (p. 197)

Oregon Trail 2,000-mile-long route from Missouri through the Rocky Mountains to the Oregon Country (p. 353)

P

Papal Line of Demarcation line drawn by Pope Alexander VI in 1493 dividing newly discovered lands between Spain and Portugal (p. 28)

pasture farming method of farming in which animals are turned loose on a plot of land to graze for food (p. 59)

patronage practice of giving out government jobs in return for political support (p. 500)

patroonships land grants given by the Dutch West India Company to people who brought 50 settlers to New Netherland (p. 92)

per capita per each unit of population; by or for each man, woman, and child (p. 335)

petitions formal written pleas to someone in authority for privileges or rights (p. 148)

Piedmont area of land between the Tidewater and the Appalachian Mountains (p. 108)

Pilgrims Puritans who founded Plymouth Colony (p. 65)

platform statement of policies or goals of a political party (p. 358)

poll taxes taxes charged to voters as a requirement for voting (p. 433)

Pontiac's Rebellion war that began in 1763 between the British and several Indian groups under the Ottawa leader Pontiac (p. 141)

pools companies that join together to eliminate competition among themselves (p. 476)

popular sovereignty pre-Civil War policy of allowing people in new territories to decide by vote whether they wanted slavery in their territory (p. 378)

popular vote votes cast by citizens in each state to decide which party's electors will vote for President and Vice President (p. 223)

presidio Spanish fort (p. 125)

privateers privately owned merchant ships armed to attack enemy ships (p. 136)

Proclamation of 1763 order issued by the British king that prohibited colonists from settling west of the Appalachian Mountains (p. 142)

Progressive Party political party formed by Theodore Roosevelt in 1912; also called the Bull Moose Party (p. 537)

progressives Americans who supported reform in the early 1900's (p. 524)

propaganda measures designed to shape people's opinions (p. 559)

proprietary colony colony granted to a person or group of people by the British Crown and governed by a proprietor or proprietors (p. 84)

protected market market in which domestic products do not have to compete with similar products from other countries (p. 289)

protective tariff tax placed on goods coming into a country so that imported goods will cost more than domestic goods (p. 282)

pueblos Spanish word for *town* or *village* (p. 9)

Puritans a group of people who wanted to simplify forms of worship in the Church of England in the 1600's (p. 64)

R

Radical Republicans members of the Republican Party who thought Lincoln was too sympathetic toward the Confederacy (p. 414)

ratify to approve (p. 193)

recession period of decline in overall business activity (p. 610)

reconstruction name given to the period of rebuilding and reunion after the Civil War (p. 419)

referendum process by which citizens can vote directly to pass or reject a proposed law (p. 526)

reparations payments made by a defeated country for damages caused by war (p. 563)

representative democracy a democratic government in which the people rule through representatives chosen by them (p. 214)

republic government in which power comes from the people; voters choose the people who represent them in government (p. 161)

right of deposit permission to unload and store goods at a foreign port (p. 242)

royal charter written permission by a royal ruler that gave people the right to settle or trade in a specific area (p. 46)

S

sagas stories of legendary people and historic events told by the Norse (p. 17)

satellite object that revolves on a planned course in outer space (p. 674)

satellite government government that is allied to and dependent on a more powerful country (p. 644)

secession withdrawal from a country or organization (p. 299)

Second Continental Congress delegates from the thirteen colonies who governed during the Revolutionary War (p. 158)

Second New Deal series of domestic programs proposed by FDR beginning in 1935 (p. 607)

segregation the separation or setting apart of people because of race (p. 432)

separation of powers division of power among the executive, legislative, and judicial branches of government (p. 224)

Separatists Puritans who broke from the Church of England and founded their own churches (p. 65)

settlement houses neighborhood centers established in the early 1900's that provided needed services to immigrants (p. 491)

sharecropping system in which people farm land for a landowner in return for a share of the crop (p. 430)

slave code set of laws that regulated slave life and stated the rights of slaver owners (p. 382)

small reservation policy policy adopted in 1867 to move Indians onto small reservations in the West (p. 463)

sod chunks of prairie grass and its roots (p. 457)

Southern Christian Leadership Conference (SCLC) organization formed in 1958 to fight for equal rights for blacks (p. 679)

sovereign supreme in power or authority (p. 193)

specie gold or silver coins used as money (p. 312)

speculators people who buy things at a low price in the hope of later selling them at a much higher price (p. 235)

spoils system practice of rewarding supporters with political offices (p. 310)

Square Deal name given by Theodore Roosevelt to his programs that were intended to ensure fair treatment for all people (p. 535)

Stamp Act Congress group of representatives from nine colonies who sent a petition to Parliament in 1765 in defense of the colonists' rights (p. 148)

states' rights policy of preserving the powers of the states from interference by the national government (p. 399)

strict construction strict interpretation of the Constitution (p. 236)

strikes job stoppages by workers in an effort to get employers to agree to employees' demands (p. 480)

subversives people who secretly try to undermine a government (p. 571)

suffragists women who worked to win the right to vote (p. 489)

summit conference meeting of the leaders of the major powers (p. 656)

suspend to stop temporarily (p. 151)

T

temperance name given to the reform movement started in the United States in the 1830's, the goal of which was to convince people not to drink alcohol (p. 334)

tepees portable houses made of buffalo skins used by the Plains Indians (p. 10)

textile cloth (p. 284)

Third World developing nations not allied with either the United States or the Soviet Union (p. 693)

Tidewater lowland along the Atlantic Coast (p. 56)

transcontinental extending across a continent (p. 453)

Treaty of Paris document signed by British and American officials in 1783 that ended the Revolutionary War (p. 184)

Truman Doctrine policy begun in 1947 that stated the United States would aid free people in resisting a takeover by Communists (p. 645)

trust a company formed by placing several competing companies under the control of a single governing board (p. 477)

U

U-boats term meaning "undersea boats," or submarines, used by the Germans during World War I (p. 553)

unicameral one-house legislature (p. 99)

unions organizations of workers formed to bargain with employers for higher wages and better working conditions (p. 480)

United Nations (UN) organization founded in 1945 to work for world peace (p. 642)

urbanization development of towns and cities (p. 288)

V

veto power of an executive such as a governor or the President to reject a bill passed by the legislature (p. 55)

viceroyalties governments set up in Spain's colonies in the Americas in the 1500's (p. 33)

Virginia Resolves resolutions against the Stamp Act proposed by Patrick Henry in the House of Burgesses in 1765 (p. 148)

virtual representation system in which members of Parliament defended not only the interests of those who elected them but the interests of all British subjects (p. 148)

W

war hawks members of Congress who supported the War of 1812 (p. 266)

Warsaw Pact alliance formed in 1955 between the Soviet Union and its Eastern European satellites (p. 657)

Works Progress Administration (WPA) program of work relief that was part of the Second New Deal (p. 608)

X

XYZ Affair incident involving French demands for bribes from the United States in 1798 (p. 246)

Y

yellow press name given to newspapers in the late 1800's that featured sensational stories to catch readers' attention (p. 485)

Z

Zimmermann note secret German message to Mexico that was intercepted by the British, was published in American newspapers, and aroused anti-German sentiment in the United States (p. 556)

Index

Black codes, 422
Blackfoot Indians, 461
Black Hawk War of 1832, 320
Black Kettle, 463
Black Muslims, 682, 700
Black Panther Party, 700
Black power, 699–700, 731
Blackwell, Elizabeth, 410
Blaine, James G., 496
Bland-Allison Act of 1878, 498
Bolívar, Simón, 273
Boll weevil, 439–440, 574
Bolsheviks, 571
Bonaparte, Napoleon, 239, 257–258, 263, 266, 268, 554
Bonus March, 598–599
Booth, John Wilkes, 419
Boston, MA: early settlement of, 70, 72, 104; before Revolution in, 116, 149, 150, 153–156, 158, 160; growth, 135, 289, 484; strikes in, 572, 582
Boston Massacre, 152, 153–154
Boston Port Act, 156
Boston Tea Party, 155, 156
Boxer Rebellion, 515–516, 585
Braddock, Edward, 137
Bradford, William, 66, 67
Bradstreet, Ann, 71
Bragg, Braxton, 407, 412
Brandeis, Louis, 541
Brant, Joseph, 176, 177
Breckinridge, John C., 389, 390
Brinkmanship, 656
Britain. See Great Britain
Britain, Battle of, 621–622
British colonies, 42–101; in Africa, 538; coastal, 82–100, conflict with, 113–118, 135–142; expansion of, 122–142; New England, 62–79; proprietary, 84, 119; royal, 119–120; rule of, 94–95, 102, 105, 108–120, 145, 146; struggle for control of, 122–142; trade with, 109–113, 118, 263; in West Indies, 89, 241. See also names of colonies
Brook Farm, 330
Brooklyn Heights, Battle of, 173
Brooks, Preston, 385–386, 394
Brown, John, 384, 386–389, 390
Brown, Moses, 290
Brown v. Board of Education of Topeka, 676–677, 678, 685
Bryan, William Jennings, 503, 505, 514, 516, 536, 537
Buchanan, James, 380, 385, 392
Buena Vista, Battle of, 361
Buffalo, 5, 9, 10, 451, 457, 461–462
Bulge, Battle of the, 633
Bull Moose Party. See Progressive Party
Bull Run, Battles of, 404, 405–406
Bunau-Varilla, Philippe, 547
Bunker Hill, Battle of, 159–160, 166, 168, 172, 174
Burger, Warren, 726

Burgoyne, John, 176–177
Burnett, Peter H., 353
Burnside, Ambrose, 410
Burr, Aaron, 234, 244, 249, 260–262
Business: competition in, 476–477; free enterprise in, 608; government regulation of, 477–478, 499, 534, 718; and Great Depression, 595; inventions and, 474–476. See also Commerce; Trade
Butler, Andrew, 385, 394

Cabinet, President's, 227, 233. See also administrations by name
Cabot, John, 37
Cabot, Sebastian, 37
Cabral, Pedro Alvarez, 34
Calhoun, John C., 266, 307, 315–317, 364, 365, 367
California: Chinese immigrants in, 455, 488; gold in, 366, 448, 455; Mexican rule over, 356, 358; and Mexican War, 361, 362; migration to, 596; settlement of, 355–356; Spanish claims in, 124, 125; statehood, 366–367, 368, 378, 380
Calvert, Cecilius. See Baltimore, Lord (second)
Calvert, George. See Baltimore, Lord (first)
Cambodia, 705–706, 707, 709
Camp David Accords, 721–722
Canada, 17, 177, 268, 273, 466, 648; boundaries of, 270; British in, 146, 266; French in, 126–129
Canals, 278, 296, 473
Canal Zone, 547, 566
Cape of Good Hope, 23–24
Capitalism, 570
Caribbean, 89, 257, 552. See also West Indies
Carnegie, Andrew, 473–474, 476, 477, 496, 514
Carnegie Steel Company, 473, 481
Carolinas, 87–90, 95, 109, 131, 282. See also North Carolina; South Carolina
Carpetbaggers, 428
Carranza, Venustiano, 551–552
Carson, Rachel, 721
Carter, Jimmy, 726; domestic policy, 719–721, 724; foreign policy, 721–723
Carteret, Sir George, 95
Cartier, Jacques, 34, 35
Cass, Lewis, 365
Castro, Fidel, 660, 694, 729
Cather, Willa, 458
Catholics, 26, 46, 166; in Canada, 126; in colonies, 86, 115, 119, 140; in England, 37, 64, 84, 115; immigrants, 380, 486; and reform, 334, 343; in Texas, 348, 349
Catt, Carrie Chapman, 528
Cattle, 89, 451–452
Cayuga Indians, 11
Cayuse Indians, 366

Central America: early civilizations in, 14–16; U.S. policy in, 725, 726
Central Intelligence Agency (CIA), 646, 694, 725
Champlain, Lake, 36, 168, 176
Champlain, Samuel de, 36
Chancellorsville, Battle of, 411
Charles I of England, 54, 68, 84, 86, 87
Charles II of England, 87, 93, 94, 96, 97, 108, 109, 113, 117
Charleston, SC, 88, 125, 155; and Civil War, 396, 397; growth of, 135, 288; and Revolution, 180, 183
Chase, Salmon P., 402
Chattanooga, Battle of, 412
Chavez, Cesar, 684
Checks and balances, 225–226
Cherokee Indians, 126, 319, 351, 463; and Trail of Tears, 317–320
Cherokee Nation v. Georgia, 318
Cheyenne Indians, 461, 463
Chiang Kai-shek, 648, 660, 706
Chicago, IL, 298, 299; fire in, 484; riots in, 480–481, 575, 703–704; trade and transport center, 379, 404, 483, 484
Chickamunga, Battle of, 412
Chickasaw Indians, 320, 463
Child labor, 290, 528, 541
China, 23, 24, 643, 659; becomes Communist, 648; Boxer Rebellion, 515, 516; and Japan, 617, 619, 623, 634; and Korean War, 654; trade with, 509, 514–515; U.S. relations with, 706–707
Chinese Exclusion Act of 1882, 488
Chinese immigrants, 453, 455, 488
Chippewa Indians, 141
Choctaw Indians, 318, 463
Chou En-lai. See Zhou Enlai
Cigar Makers' International Union, 481
Cincinnati, OH, 298
Cities: colonial, 134–135, 596; growth of, 134–135, 289, 298, 499; of late 1800's, 483–491, 499; life in, 484–485; racial violence in, 700, 703–704; reform in, 530–532; Southern, 438–439
City government, 530–531
Civilian Conservation Corps (CCC), 604, 606, 609, 610
Civil rights, basic, 339, 559–560
Civil Rights Acts: of 1866, 423–424; of 1964, 697, 730
Civil rights movement, 691; by American Indians, 683; black groups in, 676, 678, 679, 682, 684; and black power, 699–700; boycotts and sit-ins, 678–679; freedom rides, 679–681; March on Washington, 682–683; Niagara Movement, 437, 529, 675; by Spanish-speaking Americans, 683–684; the Supreme Court and, 676–678, 679, 685; violence in, 681, 700; after World War II, 673–674
Civil Service Commission, 500

Monopolies, 477, 533–534

Monroe, James, 253, 257, 258, 271, 273–275, 307, 311, 316

Monroe Doctrine, 273–275, 548–549

Montana, 260, 448, 450, 451, 466, 498

Montcalm, Marquis de, 140

Monterey, CA, 361

Monterrey, Mexico, 360

Montezuma, 31

Montgomery, AL, 678–679

Montreal, Quebec, 34, 36, 136, 140

Moral diplomacy, 550–551

Morgan, J. Pierpont, 478, 572

Morgan's Rifles, 177

Mormons, 330–331, 356–357, 362, 448

Morrill Act, 491

Morris, Gouverneur, 205

Morristown, NJ, 175

Morse, Samuel F. B., 474

Mott, Lucretia, 340, 341

Movies, 578–579

Muckrakers, 524–525, 533

Multinational corporations, 724

Murray, William Vans, 248, 249

Muslims, 30

Mussolini, Benito, 616, 617, 619, 620, 625

Nagasaki, Japan, 637, 656

Napoleon. *See* Bonaparte, Napoleon

Narragansett Indians, 106

Nashville, TN, 407

Nasser, Gamal Abdel, 659

Nast, Thomas, 222, 499

National Aeronautics and Space Administration (NASA), 675, 693

National American Woman Suffrage Association, 489, 528

National Association for the Advancement of Colored People (NAACP), 529, 575, 609, 631, 676, 678, 682

National Bank, 236–237. *See also* Bank of the United States

National Council of Negro Women, 609

National Defense Education Act, 675

National Environmental Protection Act, 721

National Greenback Party, 497, 502

National Labor Relations Board (NLRB), 607

National Organization for Women (NOW), 685

National Origins Act, 573–574

National Recovery Administration (NRA), 602–603, 606, 607

National Road, 283, 294

National Security Council, 646

National Union Party, 414

Nativism, 343, 486

NATO, 648, 657

Navigation Acts, 109–112, 117–118

Nazis, 616–617

Nebraska: farming in, 501; migration

to, 448, 456, 457, 458; slavery issue in, 378–379

Necessity, Fort, 136, 137

Netherlands, the, 51; England and, 112; Puritans in, 64, 65, 66. *See also* Dutch

Nevada, 448

New Amsterdam, 92, 93

New Deal, 599–612, 673

New England, 66; colonies of, 76, 106; Dominion of, 113–115; economy of, 282, 288–297, 356; frontier of, 132; governments of, 79, 109, 114–115; Indian wars in, 106, 125; life in, 76–77; manufacturing and trade in, 76–78, 264; population growth, 78–79, 93; religion in, 114; secession threats, 299; settlement of, 51, 62–81; towns in, 70–73, 114–115; and War of 1812, 266, 270; whaling in, 353. *See also* names of states

New England Anti-Slavery Society, 336

Newfoundland, 17, 18, 35, 37, 84

New France, 34, 35, 36, 156

New Freedom, 538

New Frontier, 691, 697

New Hampshire, 70, 113, 114, 117, 132, 194, 208

New Haven, CT, 293; early colony of, 63, 75–76, 109, 118

New Jersey, 194, 208; land claims in, 95–96; and Revolution, 150, 174, 175, 180; settlement of, 92, 93, 95, 114

New Jersey Plan, 205

Newlands Act, 536

New Mexico: and Mexican War, 358, 361, 362; settlement of, 354–355; Spanish in, 31, 124; statehood, 366–367; territory, 378

New Nationalism, 537

New Netherland, 92, 93, 94

New Orleans, Battle of, 269, 270, 306

New Orleans, LA, 128, 129, 140, 286, 407; growth of, 258, 288, 418; trade center, 202, 242, 257

Newport, RI, 75, 130, 135, 150

New Sweden, 93

New York City, 34, 92, 115, 409, 700; in 1890's, 444, 499; growth of, 130, 133–135, 283, 289; political corruption in, 499–500, 530

New York State, 11, 148, 196, 208, 209, 299, 304; antislavery movement in, 337, 338; British rule of, 114, 115, 116; Dutch in, 92, 93, 95; early colony in, 92, 93, 95, 102, 113, 151; immigrants to, 130, 343; politics in, 208, 532, 584, 599; population growth, 130–132; Revolution in, 168, 173–174, 176–178

New York State Anti-Slavery Society, 337

New York Stock Exchange, 473

New York Times, 706

Nez Perce Indians, 461, 465–466

Niagara Movement, 437, 529, 675

Nicaragua, 547, 550, 552, 725, 726

Nineteenth Amendment, 528

Nipmuck Indians, 106

Nixon, Richard M., 655, 690, 693, 716; and détente, 706–707; pardoned, 717, 719; President, 689, 704, 719, 726; resigns, 716–717, 733; and Vietnam, 704–710; and Watergate, 714–717

Nonimportation associations, 153

Nonintercourse Act of 1809, 266

Normandy, France, 632–633

Norse, 17, 18, 20

North: economy in, 282, 288–297; slavery and, 133, 194, 286, 363–368, 376. *See also* Civil War

North Africa, 549, 624–625

North America: discovery of, 4, 29; early peoples of, 2–3, 4–5, 7–12; explorations of, 34, 38

North Atlantic Treaty Organization (NATO), 648, 657

North Carolina, 130, 209, 398; early settlement in, 46, 87, 88, 95; and Revolution, 181–182

North Dakota, 259, 498, 501

North Vietnam, 708. *See also* Vietnam War

Northwest Ordinance, 197

Northwest Territory: growth of cities in, 298; Indians in, 241; land claims in, 201; slavery issue in, 365; states in, 197–198

Norway, 17, 621

Nova Scotia, 37, 146, 168

Nuclear power, 721

Nuclear weapons, 646

Nullification, 235, 248; crisis, 314–317, 321, 367

Ocala Demands, 502

O'Connor, Sandra Day, 224, 726, 731

Office of Economic Opportunity (OEO), 698

Oglethorpe, James, 129

Ohio, 197, 330, 377; statehood, 272, 298

Ohio Company, 136

Ohio Country, 131, 136, 140–141

Ohio River, 128, 136, 179, 262, 377, 406, 603

Oil: and industry, 476–477, 524; and OPEC, 718–719, 721, 725

Okinawa, 634, 636

Oklahoma, 31, 463, 467, 596

Old Northwest, 197, 242, 298, 365; Indians of, 199–201, 242, 264, 266

Old Southwest, 201–202

Oneida Indians, 11

Onis, Luis de, 271

Onondaga Indians, 11

Opechancanough, 57

Open door policy, 514–515

Operation OVERLORD, 632

Sea dogs, 38
Seattle, WA, 572
Secession, 316, 339; crisis of 1860, 389, 391–392
Second Great Awakening, 326, 328–329
Second Seminole War, 320
Secretary of state, 233
Secretary of the treasury, 235
Sedition Acts, 248, 559
Segregation: after Civil War, 432–437; *de facto* and *de jure*, 699; in industry, 629; in Progressive era, 529; in schools, 676–678. *See also* Racial discrimination
Selective Service Acts: of 1940, 622; of 1948, 646
Selma, AL, 438, 699
Seminary Ridge, 411–412
Seminole Indians, 271, 320, 463
Senate, U.S., 205, 221, 223; advice and consent, 86, 218; committees, 218–220; members and election to, 207, 216–218. *See also* Congress, U.S.
Seneca Falls Convention, 340, 341, 342
Seneca Indians, 11, 141
Separation of powers. *See* Constitution, U.S.
Separatists, 64–65, 68
Settlement houses, 490, 491, 531
Seven Days' Battles, 405
Seventeenth Amendment, 217, 526
Seward, William, 402, 507
Shakers, 330
Sharecropping, 430–431, 461
Shaw, Anna Howard, 528
Shawnee Indians, 264, 265
Shays's Rebellion, 202–203, 243
Sherman, William Tecumseh, 412, 414–415, 464
Sherman Antitrust Act, 478, 534, 541
Sherman Silver Purchase Act, 498, 503
Shiloh, battle at, 407
Shipping industry, 109–110, 289
Shoshone Indians, 259, 260
Silver, 16, 448, 498, 503
Sinclair, Upton, 535
Sioux Indians, 461, 462; wars of, 463, 464–465, 466, 730
Sirhan Sirhan, 703
Sirica, John, 714
Sit-ins, 678–679
Sitting Bull, 464, 465
Sixteenth Amendment, 225, 540
Skraelings, 17
Skyscrapers, 484
Slater, Samuel, 290
Slave codes, 382
Slave revolts, 287–288, 389
Slavery, 129, 130, 131, 288, 378; in the Caribbean, 88, 133, 257; in the Carolinas, 88, 89, 90, 133, 134; Civil War and, 408–409, 415; in colonies, 33, 57, 88; and cotton, 286–288; of 1840's,

363–368; of 1850's, 374, 376–389; Emancipation Proclamation, 408–409, 420; establishment of, 133–134; of Indians, 32, 106, 133; in the North, 93, 133, 194, 286; and politics, 343, 362–368; after the Revolution, 193–194; in the territories, 199, 354, 365, 366, 378, 380–382, 389, 392; in Virginia, 57, 108, 133, 194, 287–288
Slaves: counting, for representation, 205, 424; lives of, 134, 286–287, 338, 436; population growth of, 335–336; in Revolution, 169, 170, 172–173. *See also* Fugitive slaves
Slave states, 272, 350, 363, 384, 386, 398
Slave trade, 78, 133–134; abolished, 156, 194, 286, 367
Slidell, John, 358, 359
Smallpox, 32
Small reservation policy, 463–464
Smith, Alfred E., 532, 584–586, 690
Smith, Jedediah, 347, 352
Smith, John, 48–50, 51, 52, 66
Smith, Joseph, 330
Smith, Margaret Chase, 651
Social Security Act, 608
Social Security programs, 673, 674, 698, 732
Social work, 490
Sod houses, 457, 459
Sons of Liberty, 150, 152, 173–174
South: economy in, 282, 283–288, 429–431, 439; segregation in, 432–437; slavery and, 133–134, 194, 286–288, 363–368. *See also* Civil War; Reconstruction
South America: earliest people in, 2–3, 4–5; early civilizations in, 14–16; explorations of, 29; revolutions of, 273. *See also names of countries*
South Carolina, 208; blacks in, 428; and Civil War, 396, 397; early settlement of, 87, 88, 95; economy in, 134, 282, 283, 284, 285; and Indians, 136; and nullification, 314–317, 321; and Revolution, 172, 180, 181–182; secession, 316, 391–392, 422; slaves in, 89–90, 133, 172
South Dakota, 450, 459, 498, 501
Southeast Asia Treaty Organization (SEATO), 657
Southern backcountry, 131–132
Southern Christian Leadership Conference (SCLC), 679, 682
South Vietnam, fall of, 708–709. *See also* Vietnam War
Southwest: economy of, 298; Spain and, 124, 125, 201–202; War of 1812 in, 269–270
Soviet Union. *See* Union of Soviet Socialist Republics (USSR)
Space programs, 664, 674–675, 691–693
Spain, 26, 511; and California, 124–125;

and Caribbean, 89, 112; colonies of, 27–34, 42, 113, 122, 124, 140; and Cuba, 140, 508–514; explorations by, 21, 24–29, 32–34, 37, 124; and Florida, 42, 88, 124–126, 129, 258, 271; and the Indians, 127, 136; and Louisiana, 242, 257; and Mexico, 30–33, 37, 124, 130, 140; rule of colonies, 30–34; and South America, 124, 273; and Southwest, 124, 259; and Spanish-American War, 508–514; and Texas, 125, 348; war with England, 38, 46
Spanish-American War, 508–514, 533, 546, 557
Spanish borderlands, 124–125
Spanish-speaking Americans, 683–684, 729–730
Speese, Moses, 457
Spinning machines, 285
Spoils system, 310–311
Sputnik, 674
Squanto, 67
Square Deal, 535
Stalin, Joseph: and Cold War, 642, 647, 656; purges of, 571, 642; and World War II, 623, 624–625, 632, 634, 642, 643, 644
Stamp Act, 147–148, 149–150, 152, 174
Stamp Act Congress, 148
Standard Oil Company, 476–477, 478, 524–525
Stanton, Edwin M., 403, 425, 436
Stanton, Elizabeth Cady, 340, 341
Stanton, Henry, 340
Stark, John, 177
Starr, Ellen, 490
"Star Spangled Banner, The," 269
State constitutions. *See* Constitutions, state
State conventions, 208–209
State courts, 224
State Department, 232
State governments, 191–193; after Civil War, 421–422; powers denied to, 207, 235; powers of, 192, 193, 202, 207, 215; reform of, 525–527, 530. *See also* Constitution, U.S. *and names of states*
States' rights, 316, 399
Statue of Liberty, 424
Steamboats, 294–296
Steam engine, 285, 294, 297, 483
Steel industry, 470, 473–474
Steffens, Lincoln, 525
Stephens, Alexander, 392, 422
Stevens, Thaddeus, 423
Stevenson, Adlai, 652, 655
Stockman, David, 724
Stock market crash, 592, 594–595
Stowe, Harriet Beecher, 376–377, 378, 390
Strategic Arms Limitation Treaty (SALT), 707, 722
Strikes, 480–483, 535, 572

Student Nonviolent Coordinating Committee (SNCC), 679–681, 684
Stuyvesant, Peter, 94–95
Suburbs, 578, 669
Suez Canal, 659
Suffolk Resolves, 156
Suffrage, 194. *See also* Voting rights
Suffragist movement, 489
Sugar, 31, 78, 89, 146, 285, 507
Sugar Act, 146–147, 148
Sumner, Charles, 383–386, 394, 423
Sumter, Fort, 396, 397, 398, 402, 413
Sunbelt, 698
Supreme Court, U.S., 223, 534; under Burger, 726–728; and civil rights, 434–435, 676–677; under Constitution, 207, 215, 223–224; creation of, 207, 233; Jefferson and, 255–256; under Marshall, 256–257; members and duties, 223–226, 233–235, 256; Roosevelt and, 607, 610; under Warren, 676, 678, 685, 726, 728; and Watergate, 716
Supreme Court cases: *Bakke,* 726; *Brown,* 676–677, 678, 685; *Cherokee Nation,* 318; *Dred Scott,* 380–382; *Knight,* 478; *McCullock,* 257, 312; *Marbury,* 256–257; *Miranda,* 685, 728; *Plessy,* 434–435, 676–677; *Worcester,* 318
Susquehanna Indians, 107
Sussex Pledge, 554
Sutter, John A., 356, 361, 366

Taft, William H., 536–537, 538, 539, 550
Taft-Hartley Act, 673
Tammany Hall, 532, 584–586
Taney, Roger, 314, 381–382
Tarbell, Ida, 524, 525
Tariffs: protective, 271, 282, 290, 314–315, 497; reform, 538–540. *See also* Duty
Taxation without representation, 114, 146, 148
Taxes, 16, 145–151. *See also* Duty; Income tax
Taylor, Zachary, 359, 360, 365, 366, 367, 368
Teapot Dome scandal, 582
Tecumseh, 264–266, 268, 269, 270, 317, 322
Telegraph, 474–475
Telephone, 475
Television, 670–671
Teller Amendment, 509
Temperance movement, 334–335, 342, 489
Tenant farming, 460
Tenements, 485
Tennessee, 351, 398; and Civil War, 404, 407, 412; and reconstruction, 420, 424; revivalists in, 328–329; settlement in, 202, 298, 306; statehood, 242, 306
Tennessee Valley Authority (TVA), 603–606

Tenochtitlán, 16, 30–31, 32
Tenskwatawa, 264–266
Tenure of Office Act, 425
Tet Offensive, 701, 702, 706
Termination policy, 683
Texas, 128, 351, 391, 451, 501; annexation issue, 350–351, 358; and Civil War, 351, 404; economy in, 285, 501; independence of, 349–350, 358; and Mexican War, 358–359, 362; under Mexico, 348–349, 354; ranching in, 450, 451–452; revolution in, 349–352; slavery in, 349, 350; Spanish in, 125, 348; statehood, 351, 358
Textiles, 284, 290–293
Thames, Battle of the, 268
Thanksgiving, first, 67
Thieu, Nguyen Van, 708
Third World, 693
Thirteenth Amendment, 421
Three-Fifths Compromise, 205
Three-Mile Island incident, 721
Ticonderoga, Fort, 168
Tilden, Samuel J., 429
Time zones, 473
Tippecanoe, Battle of, 265, 266, 323
Tobacco, 28, 31, 53, 89; export of, 110, 111, 283, 285; in the South, 54–59, 86, 88
Toledo, OH, 530, 596
Topeka Constitution, 384, 385
Town covenants, 72
Town meetings, 73
Towns: government in, 72, 73, 75, 114–115; in New England, 70–73, 75–76, 114–115
Townsend, Charles, 151, 153
Townsend, Francis E., 606, 607
Townsend Act, 151
Trade, 78, 402; carrying, 289–290; colonial, 76–77, 109, 111, 147; European, 23, 110; and imperialism, 506–516; with Indians, 107, 108, 241–242; regulation of, 205, 263–264, 266; after Revolution, 242, 283, 289. *See also* Slave trade
Trade routes, 77–78
Trail of Tears, 317–320
Transcendentalists, 329, 330
Transcontinental railroad, 453–456
Transportation, 294–297, 484. *See also* Aviation; Canals; Railroads; Roads
Treasury Department, 232
Trench warfare, 560
Trenton, Battle of, 175, 176
Tripolitan War, 254–255
Truman, Harry S, 221, 634, 635, 650; and Cold War, 644, 645, 647, 656, 693; domestic policy, 668, 673–674; elected President, 647–648; and Korean War, 653–654; and World War II, 636–637
Truman Doctrine, 645
Truth, Sojourner, 338

Tubman, Harriet, 336, 337
Turner, Nat, 288
Tuskegee Institute, 435, 436
Tweed Ring, 499–500
Twelfth Amendment, 249
Twenty-Fifth Amendment, 717
Twenty-First Amendment, 600
Twenty-Second Amendment, 222
Twenty-Sixth Amendment, 719
Tydings, Millard, 652
Tyler, John, 323, 358

U-boats, 553, 555, 557
Uncle Tom's Cabin (Stowe), 376–377
Underwood Tariff, 540
Unemployment, 595, 608, 719
Union of Soviet Socialist Republics (USSR), 653, 659, 707; and arms race, 648, 668, 693, 707, 722; and Cold War, 641, 642, 644–649, 656–657, 693–695; communism in, 570–571, 616; and Cuba, 660, 694; and détente, 706, 707; expansion of, 656–660; and Middle East, 644, 659; and Space race, 674, 691–693; in World War II, 571, 619, 620, 623–625, 632–634, 637, 640, 642–644. *See also* Russia
Unions, 607; early, 479–481, 535, 608; and World War I, 557–559, 572
United Farm Workers, 684
United Mine Workers, 608, 668
United Nations, 642, 643, 646, 653–654
United States Steel Company, 474
United States v. *E. C. Knight,* 478
Universal Negro Improvement Association, 575
Urbanization, 288. *See also* Cities
Utah, 378, 489; Mormons in, 330–331, 356–357
Ute Indians, 461
U-2 incident, 657

Valley Forge, PA, 176, 178
Van Buren, Martin, 310, 313, 322–323, 352
Vermont, 132, 177, 242, 378
Verrazano, Giovanni da, 34
Versailles, Treaty of, 563, 617
Vespucci, Amerigo, 29
Vice President, office of, 223
Vicksburg, MS, 407, 412
Viet Cong, 695–696, 701, 705, 708
Vietnam, 659–660
Vietnam War: and antiwar movement, 701–702, 705–706; bombing of Cambodia, 705, 706; bombing of Hanoi, 707; Communist takeover, 708–709; Congress and, 700, 706, 708; Eisenhower and, 660, 696; escalation of, 700–701, 702; Johnson and, 700–703, 706; Kennedy and, 695–696, 706; Nixon and, 704–710; toward peace in, 707–710; results of, 709–710, 718, 732;

Collection. **90:1** Indigo Wool Quilt, c.1790 by Esther Wheat. Division of Textiles, Smithsonian Institution Photo No. 73-5252. **r** "Description de l'Universe" by Mallet. William L. Clements Library. **91:** Courtesy South Carolina Department of Parks, Recreation & Tourism. **93:** Museum of the City of New York. **96:** "William Penn" by Francis Place. The Historical Society of Pennsylvania.

Unit Three: 102-103: "Pulling Down the Statue of George III" by William Walcutt. Private Collection. **104:** "A View of Boston" by John Smibert, 1738. Courtesy of Childs Gallery, Boston. Photo by Leslie Iredell. **107:** Courtesy, The Henry Francis Du Pont Winterthur Museum **112:** *New York Magazine* III: 452, Aug. 1792. **113:** Old Sturbridge Village. **114:** "Portrait of Sir Edmund Andros" Photo #502-½ Archives of the Commonwealth, Boston, Massachusetts. **116:** "Jacob Leisler's House on Whitehall Street" 1690. Eno Collection #14, Prints Division, New York Public Library. Astor, Lenox and Tilden Foundations. **119:** Courtesy, The Henry Francis Du Pont Winterthur Museum. **122:** "Surrender of Quebec, Sept. 13, 1759" P.S. Winkworth Collection, London. **125:** "Fort of St. Augustine, Florida, 1595." Archivo General de Indias de Sevilla. **133:** "Slave Deck" by Meynell. National Maritime Museum, London. **134:** "Westover" by Lucy Harrison, 1825. Private Collection. **135:** Rare Books and Manuscript Division, New York Public Library. Astor, Lenox and Tilden Foundations. **137:** Library Company of Philadelphia. **138:** "Benjamin Franklin" by David Martin. The White House Historical Association. **140:** "Portrait of General James Wolfe" by George Townshend. McCord Museum, McGill University, Montreal, Canada. **144:** Concord Antiquarian Society. **147:** The Metropolitan Museum of Art, Bequest of Charles Allen Munn, 1924. **148:** Shelburne Museum, Shelburne, Vt. **150:** Colonial Williamsburg Photo. **151:** "Mrs. James Warren (Mercy Otis)" by John Singleton Copley, 1763. Bequest of Winslow Warren.) Courtesy, Museum of Fine Arts, Boston. **152:** "Samuel Adams" by John Singleton Copley. (Deposited by the City of Boston.) Courtesy, Museum of Fine Arts, Boston. **153:** "Boston . . . and Ships of War" by Paul Revere, 1768. I.N. Phelps Stokes Collection, Prints Division, New York Public Library. Astor, Lenox, and Tilden Foundations. **154:** "The Boston Massacre, 1770" by Paul Revere. Courtesy, Museum of Fine Arts, Boston. Centennial Gift of Watson Grant Cutter. **155:** Library of Congress. **159:** "A View of the South Part of Lexington, 1775" by Amos Doolittle. I.N. Phelps Stokes Collection, Print Division, New York Public Library. Astor, Lenox and Tilden Foundations. **163:** "The Declaration of Independence" (detail) by John Trumbull. Yale University Art Gallery. **166:** "Battle of Princeton" by James Peale. Princeton University Library. **168:** "George Washington" by Charles Wilson Peale. Washington/Custis/Lee Collection, Washington and Lee University, VA. **170:** Emmet Collection # 4730, Print Division, New York Public Library. Astor, Lenox and Tilden Foundations. **171:** "Abigal Adams" attributed to Ralph Earl c.1785. New York State Historical Association, Cooperstown. **172:** The Rhode Island Historical Society. **173:** Stockbridge Library, Stockbridge, MA. **175:** "Washington Crossing the Delaware" by Emanuel Leutze. Metropolitan Museum of Art; gift of John Steward Kennedy. **177:** "Joseph Brant" New York State Historical Association, Cooperstown. **182:** "The Surrender of Lord Cornwallis at Yorktown" by John Trumbull. Yale University Art Gallery. **184:** Courtesy, The Henry Francis du Pont Winterthur Museum.

Unit Four: 188-189: "Salute to General Washington in New York Harbor" by L.M. Cooke. National Gallery of Art, Washington, gift of Edgar William and Bernice Chrysler Garbisch. **190:** Independence National Historic Park Collection. **192:** National Portrait Gallery, Smithsonian Institution, on loan from the National Gallery of Art; gift of Marion B. Maurice. **194:** "Elizabeth Freeman by Susan Sedgwick, 1811. Massachusetts Historical Society. **199:** "Treaty of Greenville" 1795. Chicago Historical Society. **203:** National Portrait Gallery, Smithsonian Institution, Washington, D.C. **204:** Historical Society of Pennsylvania. **205:** "Gouverneur Morris" by James Sharpless. Private Collection. **206:** "James Madison" by T.C. Lubbers. The New-York Historical Society. **209:** The New-York Historical Society. **212:** Kenneth Garrett (Woodfin Camp & Associates). **215 & 217:** David Marie (Folio, Inc.) **220:** U.S. State Department. **221:** John F. Kennedy Presidential Library. **222:1** *Harper's Weekly*, Jan. 15, 1870; **r** *Harper's Weekly*, Nov. 7, 1874. **224:** Supreme Court of the United States. **230:** "The Republican Court" by Daniel Huntington. The Brooklyn Museum, Gift of the Crescent-Hamilton Athletic Association. **233:** The New-York Historical Society. **234:** *"Alexander Hamilton" by Charles Wilson Peale. Independence

National Historic Park Collection. **237:** Historical Society of Pennsylvania. **238:** University of Hartford: J. Doyle DeWitt Collection. **241:** "John Jay" 1801 by Caleb Boyle. Kirby Collection of American Painting, Lafayette College. **243:** Courtesy, The Henry Francis Du Pont Winterthur Museum. **245:1** "John Adams" by John Trumbull. Harvard University Portrait Collection. **r** "Thomas Jefferson" by Charles Wilson Peale. Independence National Historic Park Collection. **246:** The Huntington Library, San Marino, CA. **247:** Franklin D. Roosevelt Library. **249:** "Aaron Burr" by John Vanderlyn. Bequest of Oliver Burr Jennings. Yale University Art Gallery. **252:** Library of Congress. **254:** "Thomas Jefferson at Natural Bridge" 1801 by Caleb Boyle. Kirby Collection of American Painting, Lafayette College. **256:** "John Marshall" 1830 by Chester Harding. Courtesy of the Boston Athenaeum. **258:** Chicago Historical Society. **259:** *"Flora Americae Septentrionalis"* 1814 by Frederick Pursh. Print Division, The New York Public Library, Astor, Lenox and Tilden Foundations. **262:** New-York Historical Society. **265:** Courtesy, Field Museum of Natural History, Chicago. **268:** New-York Historical Society. **269:** "Battle of New Orleans" by Hyacinthe Laclotte. Collection of Edgar William and Bernice Chrysler Garbisch.

Unit Five: 278-279: "View of Harper's Ferry" Abby Aldrich Rockefeller Folk Art Center, Williamsburg, Virginia. **280:** Museum of American Textile History. **283:** Museum of the City of New York. **284:** From THE NATIONAL ARCHIVES OF THE UNITED STATES, illustrations © 1984 Harry N. Abrams, Inc., N.Y. Jonathen Wallen, photographer. **287: r** Abby Aldrich Rockefeller Folk Art Center, Williamsburg, Virginia; **l** Collection Adele Earnest. **289:** "Broadway, New York" by Thomas Horner. M. and M. Karolik Collection. Courtesy, Museum of Fine Arts, Boston. **209:** Mabel Brady Garvan Collection, Yale University Art Gallery. **292:** University of Lowell. **294:** "Steamboats on the Mississippi Below the Falls of St. Anthony" by Ferdinand Reichardt. Minnesota Historical Society. **297:** "The Lemon House" by George Storm. State Museum of Pennsylvania, William Penn Memorial. **299:** "St. Paul in 1855" by S. Holmes Andrews. Minnesota Historical Society. **302:** The Anne S.K. Brown Military Collection, Brown University Library. **305:** Memphis Brooks Museum of Art, Memphis Park Commission Purchase 46.2. **306:** Library of Congress. **308:** National Portrait Gallery, Smithsonian Institution, Washington, D.C. **309:** Library of Congress. **312:** "Highways and Byeways of the Forest" by George Tattersall. M. and M. Karolik Collection. Courtesy, Museum of Fine Arts, Boston. **313:** National Portrait Gallery, Smithsonian Institution, Washington, D.C. **315,317:** Library of Congress. **318:** "Trail of Tears" by Robert Lindneaux. Woolaroc Museum, Bartlesville, OK. **319:** The Thomas Gilcrease Institute of American History and Art, Tulsa, OK. **323:** The Mattatuck Historical Society. **326:** "Sing-Sing Camp Meeting" by Joseph B. Smith. M. and M. Karolik Collection. Courtesy, Museum of Fine Arts, Boston. **328:** The Bettmann Archive. **330:** Henry E. Huntington Library, San Marino, CA. **331: t** "Mormon Panorama Twenty-one/Winter Quarters" by C.C.A. Christensen. Brigham Young University Art Museum Collection. **b** Courtesy of the Boston Athenaeum. **333:** New-York Historical Society. **335,336,338:** The Sophia Smith Collection (Woman's History Archive Smith College. **337:** Library of Congress. **340:** National Portrait Gallery, Smithsonian Institution, Washington, D.C. **341:** Culver Pictures. **346:** "Covered Wagons Crossing Medicine Bow Creek" by Samuel Coleman. *Private Collection.* **348:** "George Allen's Plantation Home" by Frederik Jocab Rothhaas, Acc#839. Courtesy of the Texas Memorial Museum. **350:** Shostal Associates. **351:** "Sam Houston" by Seymour Thomas. The San Jacinto Museum of History Association, Houston, Texas. **354:** Scott's Bluff National Monument. **356:** "The Vaquero" by James Walker. Private Collection. **361:** California State Library. **362:** "General Scott's Entry Into Mexico" lithograph after painting by Carl Nebel (detail). Chicago Historical Society. **364:** National Portrait Gallery, Smithsonian Institution, Washington, D.C.; Transfer from the National Gallery of Art; gift of Andrew W. Mellon, 1942. **366:** California State Library. **367:** Library of Congress.

Unit Six: 372-373: "Army of the Potomac" by James Hope. M. and M. Karolik Collection. Courtesy, Museum of Fine Arts, Boston. **374:** "Cotton Plantation" M. and M. Karolik Collection. Courtesy, Museum of Fine Arts, Boston. **376: l** The Schlesinger Library, Radcliffe College. **r** The Bettmann Archives. **381:** Library of Congress. **383:1** National Portrait Gallery, Smithsonian Institution, Washington, D.C.; **r** Library of Congress. **385:** Kansas Historical Society. **386:** Library of Congress. **388:** Courtesy of the

Boston Athenaeum. **390:** New-York Historical Society. **392:** Library of Congress. **393:** Meigs Collection, U.S. National Museum. **396:** Anne S.K. Brown Military Collection, Brown University Library. **400:** Confederate Museum, Richmond, VA. **403:** Anne S.K. Brown Military Collection, Brown University Library. **406:** "Robert E. Lee" by Theodore Pine, Washington and Lee University, VA. **409:** Chicago Historical Society. **410:** t American Red Cross, b Culver Pictures. **411:** "Attack at Seminary Ridge, Gettysburg" M. and M. Karolik Collection. Courtesy, Museum of Fine Arts, Boston. **413:** National Portrait Gallery, Smithsonian Institution, Washington, D.C. **418, 420:** Library of Congress. **422:** American Antiquarian Society. **423:** The Granger Collection. **425:** *Harper's Weekly*, March 28, 1868. **427:** Library of Congress. **429:** Dukes County Historical Society, Edgartown, MA. **430:** Library of Congress. **433:** Schomburg Collection for Research in Black Culture, New York Public Library. **435,436:** Library of Congress. **437:** NAACP. **438:** The Granger Collection.

Unit Seven: 444–445: "The Bowery at Night" by W. Louis Sonntag, Jr. Museum of the City of New York. **446:** "The Sierra Nevada in California" 1868 by Albert Bierstadt. National Museum of American Art, Smithsonian Institution, Bequest of Helen Huntington Hull. **448:** California State Library. **450:** Erwin E. Smith Collection of Range Life, Library of Congress. **454:** The Oakland Museum. **455:** "Snow Sheds on the Central Pacific Railroad in the Sierra Nevada Mountains" by Joseph Becker. Thomas Gilcrease Institute of American History and Art. **456:** Smithsonian Institution Neg # 65333. **457,458:** Nebraska State Historical Society. **460:** Colorado Historical Society. **462:** "Buffalo Chase, Mouth of the Yellowstone" by George Catlin. National Museum of American Art, Smithsonian Institution, gift of Mrs. Joseph Harrison, Jr. **465:** t,bl Denver Public Library, Western History Collection; br Library of Congress. **467:** Oklahoma Historical Society. **470:** "The Gun Foundry" by John Ferguson Weir. Putnam County Historical Society. Foundry School Museum, Cold Spring, NY. **473:** *Harper's Weekly*, June 1886. **474:** National Portrait Gallery, Smithsonian Institution, Washington, D.C., gift of Mrs. Margaret Carnegie Miller. **475:** t Reproduced with permission of AT&T Corporate Archive; b Edison National Historic Site. **477:** *Literary Digest*, 1905. **479,480:** Library of Congress. **481:** George Meany Memorial Archives, AFL/CIO. **482:** Library of Congress. **483:** Chicago Historical Society. **485:** t New-York Historical Society; b Chicago Historical Society. **488:** Library of Congress. **489,490:** The Sophia Smith Collection (Woman's History Archive) Smith College. **492:** Brown Brothers. **494:** "The Naval Parade" by Fred Pansing. Museum of the City of New York. **496:** University of Hartford: J. Doyle DeWitt Collection. **498:** The Granger Collection. **499:** *Harper's Weekly*, Aug. 19, 1871. **501:** Library of Congress. **502:** Kansas State Historical Society. **503,504:** Library of Congress. **506:** "Commodore Matthew C. Perry's First Landing in Japan at Kurihama" 1853 by Gessan Ogata. Courtesy United States Naval Academy Museum. **508:** t Original in Liliuokalani Trust. Photo courtesy of the Bishop Museum, Honolulu, HI; b The Bettmann Archive. **511:** l Library of Congress; r The National Archives **513:** The Theodore Roosevelt Association. **516:** Library of Congress.

Unit Eight: 520–521: "American Landscape" by Charles Sheeler, Collection, The Museum of Modern Art, New York. Gift of Abby Aldrich Rockefeller. **522:** "The Green Car" by William Glackens, 1910. The Metropolitan Museum of Art. **525:** The Ida M. Tarbell Collection, Pelletier Library, Allegheny College, Meadville, Pa. **526, 527:** State Historical Society of Wisconsin. **528:** Brown Brothers. **529:** Library of Congress. **531:** Missouri Historical Society. **532:** Keystone-Mast Collection. California Museum of Photography. University of California, Riverside. **533:** The White House Historical Association. **534:** *Harper's Weekly*, Oct. 15, 1904. **536:** "The Grand Canyon of the Yellowstone" by Thomas Moran. National Museum of American Art, Smithsonian Institution. Lent by the U.S. Department of the Interior, National Park Service. **537:** The White House Historical Association. **540:** National Portrait Gallery, Smithsonian Institution, Washington, D.C., Transfer from the National Museum of American Art; Gift of the city of New York through the National Art Committee, 1923. **541:** Harvard Law Art Collection. **544:** "Americans Arriving in Paris" 1918. U.S. Military Academy, West Point Museum. Photo by Henry Groskinsky. **546:** The Mariner's Museum. **548:** "Building the Panama Canal" by Jonas Lie. The Detroit Institute of Arts, City of Detroit Purchase. **549,551:** Brown Brothers. **552:** UPI/Bettmann Newsphotos. **553:** Brown Brothers. **555:** UPI/Bettmann Newsphotos. **557:** Herbert Hoover Presidential Library. **558:** National Portrait Gallery, Smithsonian Institution,

Washington, D.C., Gift of the IBM Corporation. **559:** Gallery 9. **560:** Imperial War Museum. **562:** National Archives. **563:** Imperial War Museum. **564:** tr,bl Historical Pictures Service; br Library of Congress. **568:** "Travelling Carnival, Santa Fe" by John Sloan, 1924. National Museum of American Art, Smithsonian Institution. Gift of Mrs. Cyrus McCormick. **570:** UPI/Bettmann Newsphotos. **573:** "Bartolomeo Vanzetti and Nicola Sacco" From the Sacco-Vanzetti series of twenty-three paintings (1931-32). Collection, The Museum of Modern Art, New York. Gift of Aby Aldrich Rockefeller. **574:** Office of the Archive of the Capitol. **575:** "The migrants arrived in great numbers" Plate 40 from The Migration Of The Negro. (1940-41). Collection, The Museum of Modern Art, New York. Gift of Mrs. David M. Levy. **577:** Ford Motor Company. **578:** Museum of Modern Art Film Still Archive. **579:** UPI/Bettmann Newsphotos. **580:** The Schomburg Center for Research in Black Culture, New York Public Library. **581:** National Portrait Gallery, Smithsonian Institution, Washington, D.C. Gift of W. Tjark Reiss, in memory of his father, Winold Reiss. **583:** Library of Congress. **584:** The Bancroft Library, University of California, Berkeley. **585:** New-York Historical Society. **586:** University of Hartford: J. Doyle DeWitt Collection.

Unit Nine: 590–591: "Three Flags" by Jasper Johns, 1958. Collection of Whitney Museum of American Art. 50th Anniversary Gift of the Gilman Foundation, Inc., The Lauder Foundation, A. Alfred Taubman, an anonymous donor (and purchase). **592:** "Room in New York" by Edward Hopper, 1932. F. M. Hall Collection, Sheldon Memorial Art Gallery, University of Nebraska-Lincoln. **594:** Brown Brothers. **595:** UPI/Bettmann Newsphotos. **596:** "Dust, Drought and Destruction" by William Palmer, 1934. Collection of the Whitney Museum of American Art. **598:** UPI/Bettmann Newsphotos. **601:** Karsh/Ottawa (Woodfin Camp & Associates). **602:** t Copyright © 1933 by The New York Times Company. Reprinted by Permission; b Brown Brothers. **603:** New-York Historical Society. **605:** UPI/Bettmann Newsphotos. **607:** Copyright © 1935, 1963 by the Conde Nast Publications, Inc. **609:** National Portrait Gallery, Smithsonian Institution, Washington, D.C. Gift of Lawrence A. Fleischman and Howard Garfinkle with a matching grant from the National Endowment for the Arts. **611:** Brown Brothers. **614:** "Attack on Pearl Harbor" by Norman Wilkinson. National Maritime Museum, London. **616:** National Archives. **617:** Yivo Institute for Jewish Research. **620:** UPI/Bettmann Newsphotos. **621:** Brown Brothers. **624:** UPI/Bettmann Newsphotos. **627:** Smithsonian Institution. **629,630,631:** Library of Congress. **633:** Robert Capa (Magnum). **635:** Harry S. Truman Library. **636:** UPI/Bettmann Newsphotos; inset John Launois (Black Star). **640:** U.S. Department of Energy. **643:** Franklin D. Roosevelt Library. **646:** UPI/Bettmann Newsphotos. **647:** Walter Sanders, LIFE Magazine © 1948, 1972 Time Inc. **648:** t UPI/Bettmann Newsphotos; b Jack Wilkes, LIFE Magazine © 1957 Time Inc. **649,651:** UPI/Bettmann Newsphotos. **652:** Robert Phillips, LIFE Magazine © 1954 Time Inc. **654,655:** UPI/Bettmann Newsphotos. **656:** HERBLOCK © 1956 The Washington Post Company. **657:** Erich Lessing (Magnum). **659:** Howard Sochurek. LIFE Magazine © 1955 Time Inc.

Unit Ten: 664–665: NASA. **666:** Van Bucher (Photo Researchers, Inc.) **668:** Ralph Crane, LIFE Magazine © 1958 Time Inc. **670:** tl UPI/Bettmann Newsphotos; br Howard Frank. **672:** Courtesy Sperry Corporation. **673:** Cornell Capa, LIFE Magazine © Time Inc. **674,676:** UPI/Bettmann Newsphotos. **677:** t UPI/Bettmann Newsphotos; b Burt Glinn (Magnum). **678:** Wide World Photos. **680:** Ernst Haas (Magnum). **681:** Charles Moore (Black Star). **682:** Robert Kelley, LIFE Magazine © 1970 Time Inc. **684:** Bob Fitch (Black Star). **685:** Michal Ginsburg (Magnum). **688:** Black Star. **690:** UPI/Bettmann Newsphotos. **692:** Hank Walker, LIFE Magazine © 1960 Time Inc. **693:** NASA. **694:** Carolyn Redenius (ACTION). **695:** UPI/Bettmann Newsphotos. **696:** Fred Ward (Black Star). **697:** Lyndon Baines Johnson Library, photo by Cecil Stoughton. **698:** Paul Conklin. **699:** "Father and Child Reading", 1966 by John Wilson. **701:** Bruno Barbey (Magnum). **703:** Flip Schulke (Black Star). **705:** Dennis Brack (Black Star). **707:** Magnum. **712:** John Ficara (Newsweek/Woodfin Camp & Associates). **714,715:** UPI/Bettmann Newsphotos. **716:** Dennis Brack (Black Star). **719:** Arthur Grace (Sygma). **722:** D.B. Owen (Black Star). **723:** t Peter Marlow (Magnum); b Dennis Brack (Black Star). **725:** Jean Louis Atlan (Sygma). **726:** Phil Huber (Black Star). **727:** Bill Pierce (Sygma). **729:** J. Pavlovsky (Sygma); b UPI/Bettmann Newsphotos. **730:** Leif Skoofors (Woodfin Camp & Associates). **731:** t NASA; b Levenson (Liaison). **732:** Will McIntyre (Photo Researchers, Inc.)